ENGLAND EXPECTS

ENGLAND
EXPECTS

DUDLEY
POPE

WEIDENFELD AND NICOLSON
7 CORK STREET LONDON W1

SET IN 11-POINT ON 12-POINT IMPRINT TYPE
AND MADE AND PRINTED IN GREAT BRITAIN BY
COX AND WYMAN LIMITED, LONDON, READING AND FAKENHAM

R.6410

CONTENTS

CONTENTS

ILLUSTRATIONS

ILLUSTRATIONS

ACKNOWLEDGMENTS

The author would like to thank the following for kind
permission to reproduce the illustrations in this book:
The Admiralty for numbers 1, 9 and 11; Lt-Col
Harold Wyllie, OBE, 12, 13, 14 and 22; Viscount
Digby, 16 and 17; the Misses Duff, 10; the Gresham
Committee, 4; Mr Christopher Marsden, 7; Mr Colin
Mudie, AMINA, for the drawing of the *Victory*
facing page 356; the Musée de la Marine, 5 and 6;
the Museo Naval, Madrid, 15; the National Maritime
Museum, Greenwich, 3; the National Maritime
Museum, Greenwich Hospital Collection, 8 and 21;
and the National Portrait Gallery, 2.

To

Lt-Col and Mrs Harold Wyllie,

whose knowledge and artistry have contributed so much to our understanding of the great days of sail

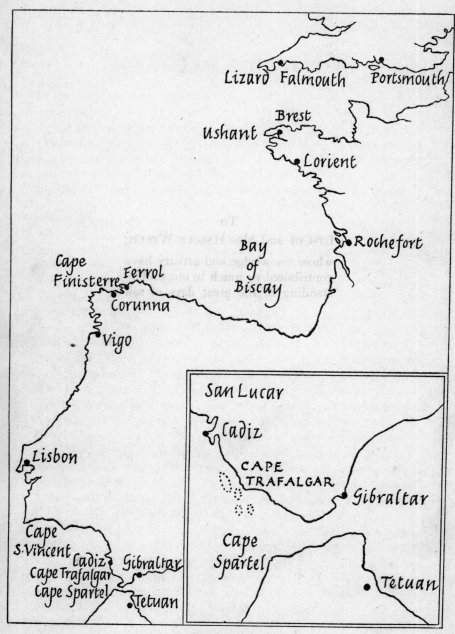

CHART No. 1:
South Western Europe

AUTHOR'S PREFACE

MY REASON for writing this account of the year of Trafalgar is that it seemed a curious omission that no book has hitherto set out to describe the most famous naval campaign and battle in history from all practicable points of view. One of the aims of my account, therefore, is to tell the story of the actual battle as it was seen through the eyes of the contending British, French and Spanish admirals, captains, lieutenants and ratings, frequently using their own words.

Since it is difficult to understand the significance of a battle unless all the many and varied circumstances surrounding it are known, I have also tried to present a picture of life and events in Britain and France during 1805: of Napoleon and Pitt, and the ordinary British folk who faced the threat of invasion and drilled with pike and pitchfork on the village greens when the French Emperor's 'Army of England' was poised on the cliffs above Boulogne and his harbours were full of landing craft.

Yet the men who actually fought the battle and helped to preserve freedom for Britain served on board the ships of the Royal Navy in conditions little removed from slavery. They lived on salt meat said to be often so hard that it could be carved and would take a polish like a fine-grained wood; they were flogged for the slightest misdemeanour; and they were frequently cheated out of what miserable wage they were paid. Yet it was these men, many of them press-ganged jailbirds, who fought the enemy like demons—and yet broke down and wept when Nelson died. Nelson made these men believe they were each worth three Frenchmen or four Spaniards; such was the magnetism of his leadership that in battle these odds were often achieved. So this account also tries to give the reader a glimpse into the Admiralty and the massive wooden ships that carried out its bidding, and to portray life afloat in the year 1805.

The victory off Cape Trafalgar was unique in many ways. Nelson, its victor and victim, was the first and last man to use gun and sail in a perfect combination on such a scale. But more important, it gave the world a standard by which daring and bravery would henceforth be measured, and established a tradition for Britain and the Royal Navy which was to prove powerful and enduring. Many of the facts surrounding this great sea battle have been or are still in dispute. Rather than go into arid detail and relate how learned men have argued through succeeding generations, I have usually given my own interpretation, but I have noted where this varies from certain hitherto accepted accounts.

In dispute at some time or another have been Nelson's actual method of attack; his intentions during the battle—whether or not he began the attack according to the pre-arranged plan; the circumstances surrounding his memorable 'England expects . . .' signal; the design of the signal flags, and what several ships did, and in particular the rear ships.

There were many reasons for the spectacular victory, when twenty-seven British ships attacked the thirty-three of the Combined Fleet of France and Spain, capturing seventeen and blowing up the eighteenth, and capturing several more a few days later; yet, as related in these pages, Napoleon himself played a significant part in the defeat of his own fleet.

While Britain waited for the Combined Fleet to sail from Cadiz, Napoleon was calling his Commander-in-Chief a traitor, and an hour or so before the battle began one of the ablest Spanish captains commented: 'The fleet is doomed. The French admiral does not understand his business.' Muttering 'perdidos', he turned up his men to prayers. Against this picture we have Nelson, dramatic, warm-hearted, cool-brained, and his sailors—men longing to see their wives, yet excited at serving once again under Nelson, painting their ships in the same yellow and black style of the Victory, and honoured to pay for the paint out of their own pockets. On the eve of the battle, a British captain complained of his indigestion, while French and Spanish captains complained that their ships were rotten. Most of the British captains were fulfilling a lifetime's ambition in fighting under Nelson, while the French and Spanish captains held a Council of War where many argued that the Fleet should not sail.

Yet the Britain these men made safe presented in 1805 a curious and often contradictory pattern: a man could be hanged for stealing a handkerchief, and MPs represented villages which had been washed away by the sea, while great new towns had no Member. Yet France was equally contradictory. Despite the Revolution, which sent the King to the guillotine, Napoleon's court was, in the year 1805, more splendid than ever before.

These are some of the reasons why the Battle of Trafalgar gave a crushing victory to the British, and why it was the final and calculated act in a campaign, and not an isolated action fought by chance off a Spanish cape.

I have had a great deal of help and encouragement in carrying out the research for this book, particularly from two acknowledged experts of this period. The first is Rear-Admiral A. H. Taylor, CB, OBE, DL, JP, an authority on Trafalgar, who placed valuable material, particularly a time-table of the battle, at my disposal and has given me many hours of his time, and read the MS.

The second is Lt-Col Harold Wyllie, OBE, perhaps best known as the brilliant marine artist, but who is also one of our greatest authorities on the construction and rigging of the 'wooden walls'. He has given me much advice on many aspects of life afloat in 1805, and read the MS. I am also greatly indebted to him for allowing me to reproduce some of his paintings and also one by his father, the late W. L. Wyllie.

I am very grateful to Professor Michael Lewis, CBE, MA, FSA, FRHistS, who read the MS and made some valuable suggestions which have been incorporated.

The rôle of the Earl of Northesk, the third-in-command at Trafalgar, has tended to be overshadowed by Nelson and Collingwood; but I have been fortunate in being allowed by the present Earl to make use of interesting material, including letters, which came to light only recently and has never previously been published. The papers are at present in the custody of his cousin, Mr John Carnegie, for whose help I am also grateful.

The Misses Duff, of Bolton Gardens, South Kensington, descendants of Captain George Duff, of the *Mars*, one of the two British captains killed in the battle, have allowed me to use hitherto unpublished documents concerning the four members of the Duff family at Trafalgar, and I am also grateful to Lt-Col T. Gordon-Duff of Drummuir Castle, Banffshire.

I am indebted to Lord Digby, concerning the captain of the *Africa*; to the Earl of Radnor for permission to use certain correspondence; to Lord Cottesloe, for material concerning Captain Thomas Fremantle, and also the Hon Mrs Christopher Fremantle for permission to quote from *The Wynne Diaries*, which she edited; to Mr Christopher Marsden, for letters written to and by his forebear, William Marsden, Secretary to the Board of

Admiralty at the time of the battle; and Sir William Codrington, Bt, for permission to use material concerning Captain Codrington of the *Orion*. I have also to thank the descendants of Captains Tyler and Blackwood for their efforts on my behalf.

My thanks are due to Lt-Cdr P. K. Kemp, RN (Retd), FRHistS, Head of Historical Section, Admiralty; to the staff of the Admiralty Library, and in particular Mr G. Young; to Miss Lindsay-Mac-Dougall, National Maritime Museum; to the staffs of the Public Records Office and British Museum, for their ready and expert help; and to Mr E. Smith, Head of AMS, Admiralty.

Many of my friends have given me encouragement and advice, but I must particularly thank Mervyn Ellis, of the Department of the Chief of Naval Information, Admiralty; Cdr T. Marchant, DSC, RN (Retd); and David Wainwright, all of whom have also read the MS; Count Henry Bentinck and Basil Bowman. Patrick Satow, DSC and H. W. Bailey read the galley-proofs and made many valuable suggestions.

Once again it is an understatement to say that without help, encouragement and constructive criticism from my wife—who has typed more than a quarter of a million words in connection with the narrative—this book would not have been attempted or completed.

To avoid having too many footnotes, various comments and additional facts are given in Notes and Bibliography, between pages 347–55.

1

PICKLE COMES HOME

*'Yet when we achieved and the new world dawned, the
old men came out again and took our victory to remake
in the likeness of the former world they knew . . .'*
—T. E. Lawrence.

TWO HOISTS of flags quivered in the moaning wind as they
streamed out from the signal halyards at the yardarm and mizen-
mast-head of the 38-gun frigate *Euryalus* which was, on this stormy
October day in 1805, serving as the flagship of Cuthbert Collingwood, Vice-Admiral of the Blue.

For the past five days—since Lord Nelson died at the close of the
battle—Collingwood had been in command of the victorious but
battered British fleet now fighting for its very life in heavy seas
only a few miles to windward of Cape Trafalgar. He had seen
many of his prizes, vast French and Spanish three-deckers which
had been the pride of the Emperor and of His Catholic Majesty,
smashed by the great waves; he had even been forced to give
orders for prize-crews and prisoners to be taken off and ships
scuttled or set on fire.

Nature, in the shape of winds raging at more than sixty knots
across the wide Atlantic, with nothing to break their fury or
quieten the great singing waves they drove before them, was
blunting the sharp edge of victory; yet despite the gales Collingwood could no longer delay the task of informing the Admiralty
in London of the best news—that the Combined Fleet of France
and Spain had been defeated, with eighteen of its ships captured
or destroyed—and the worst, that Nelson had perished, though
not before learning that the toll of the enemy had been only two
short of the twenty for which he had bargained.

Downwind from the *Euryalus* and often almost completely
hidden as sheets of spray sluiced over her flush deck, was the tiny
topsail-schooner *Pickle*. Her mainsail was furled on its long boom
and the foresail brailed up, while the three headsails were lashed
in untidy bundles at the foot of their respective stays. For the
previous five days she had been under way, sails well reefed,

hatches battened down, tidying up after the battle. More than 120 French and Spanish prisoners had been saved from the sea or brought aboard from prizes about to be scuttled, and herded down below where, under four feet three inches of headroom, the stench of bilge-water, rotting food, wet clothes and vomit did little to comfort them.

Now, after a few hours lying hove-to while some of her thirty-three crew tried to snatch some rest in between standing a watch and keeping a guard on the prisoners, the flagship was signalling. Bloodshot and salt-rimmed eyes stared up to windward, trying to focus through unsteady and spray-soaked telescopes to identify the flags. The *Pickle*'s pennants flew from one yardarm of the *Euryalus*, indicating the signal was to her. The other hoist consisted of two flags, the upper one white and the lower one quartered in red and white—eight and four. And in the signal book, number eighty-four meant 'Pass within hail'.

Wearily Lt John Richards Lapenotiere, the thirty-five year old Devonian who was commanding the schooner, gave the order to get under way. Each man in the crew moved cautiously, using one hand for his task and the other to hold on, for the ship was rolling and pitching like a log launched into a mountain torrent. Some of the seamen went to the brails to loose the foresail, others to the halyards ready to haul up the big mainsail as soon as the gaskets lashing the stiff, sodden canvas and gaff to the boom were let go. More men stood by at the sheets, ready to trim the sails the minute they were hoisted.

Above the noise of the wind in the masts and rigging—which tore at already frayed nerves like the shrill voice of a shrewish woman—came orders shouted by George Almy, the Second Master, whose accent betrayed his American origins.

The constant soaking and the cold made the skin of the men's hands white and dead-looking, and the ropes they seized were stiff and swollen, intractable and unwilling to run through the blocks. And as is the way with ropes in bad weather, they looped themselves in tiresome bights round any and every projection on deck and masts, exasperating the tired seamen and slowing up their tasks.

'Ease away vangs, downhauls and tack tricing lines . . . ease away boom sheets!' With the help of a speaking trumpet Almy's voice won its fight against the wind. 'Man the main halyards . . . haul taut!' The men, having taken the strain on the halyards, prepared to haul up the big mainsail now that everything was clear.

'Hoist away!'

With maddening slowness the sail crawled up the mast, the canvas beginning to flog as the wind got into it. Eventually it was hoisted and sheeted in. The middle jib followed, and a few minutes later the foresail was sheeted in and drawing. Slowly the *Pickle* began to move through the water, her bluff bows shouldering through the waves and bursting the crests into showers of spray. Right aft, unprotected from wind and sea, the quartermaster watched the leech of the jib as he moved the tiller inch by inch to bring the schooner hard on the wind to start the wearisome beat up to the *Euryalus*.

As soon as the leech began to quiver—showing the ship was sailing as close to the wind as she could without losing speed—he eased the tiller a fraction. With his legs straddled to keep his balance on the heaving deck, his eyes were busy watching the leech of the *Pickle*'s jib and the relative position of the *Euryalus*, while his ears listened for any orders which might be shouted at him. He became part of the quivering, plunging ship, sensitive to her every yaw and anticipating the way an extra heavy sea would try to barge her bows off course. He knew, by a mixture of instinct and experience, just how a sudden stronger squall could run her head up into the wind, with every resulting vicious flap and slat of the sail liable to slit the canvas from top to bottom. Slowly the *Pickle* worked her way across the desolate and heavily-furrowed grey waste separating her from the *Euryalus*, and when Lapenotiere sailed her close down the frigate's lee side, someone bellowed from the quarter-deck through a speaking-trumpet, and ordered him on board. The *Pickle* was hove-to, the set of her sails so balanced that the pressure of the wind on one neutralized the other. The jolly-boat was lowered, and as it rose and fell several feet on the restless water, Lapenotiere scrambled in.

On board the *Euryalus* Vice-Admiral Collingwood was waiting. His despatch, addressed to William Marsden, the Secretary to the Board of Admiralty and dated '*Euryalus*, off Cape Trafalgar, October 22nd, 1805', was ready in his cabin, together with copies of a general order to the Fleet issued on the day after the battle, paying his tribute to the fallen Nelson and thanking every man in the Fleet for his 'highly meritorious conduct'. He had also written, with a heavy and anxious heart, a second letter to Mr

Marsden describing the damage the gale had since wrought to the prizes. He had been forced to order the scuttling of the huge 130-gun *Santissima Trinidad*, the greatest warship ever built and flagship of Rear-Admiral don Baltazar Hidalgo Cisneros; the 112-gun *Santa Ana*, flagship of Vice-Admiral don Ignatio Maria de Alava, had no doubt also sunk. Of the remaining prizes, he had written, 'Unless the weather moderates, I doubt whether I shall be able to carry a ship of them into port'.

Captain Henry Blackwood, commanding the *Euryalus*, had been writing regularly to his wife and was waiting to send the letters home by the first ship—which he hoped would be his own frigate, so that he should have the honour of carrying back the first news of the battle, and also Captain Hardy with Nelson's body. To his wife at 1 a.m. on the night after the battle he had begun his letter with: 'The first hour since yesterday morning that I could call my own is now before me, to be devoted to my dearest wife, who, thank God, is not a husband out of pocket. My heart is, however, sad, my Harriet, and penetrated with the deepest sorrow. A victory, and such a one was never before achieved, took place yesterday in the course of five hours; but at such an expense, in the loss of the most gallant of men—the best and kindest of friends, as renders it to be a victory I could hardly have ever wished to witness on such terms. . . .'

But Blackwood was disappointed: by the 26th, five days after the battle, Collingwood had decided to send his despatches home in the second smallest ship in the Fleet, the *Pickle*. According to descendants of her commanding officer, the reason why Colling-wood chose Lapenotiere and his little schooner was that several years earlier the Admiral had been travelling in a ship with the young Lieutenant. An order had been given to the man at the wheel and Lapenotiere, although only a passenger, had realized that if it was obeyed the ship would go on the rocks. He promptly gave another order and saved the ship. A grateful Collingwood had said: 'If ever I have the opportunity, I will do you a service.' Now that opportunity had come and Lapenotiere—whose family came to England in the revolution of 1688 with 'Dutch William', and whose father and grandfather had served in the Navy—had been chosen to take the despatches home. When Lapenotiere finally scrambled on board the *Euryalus* from his jolly-boat he was taken to the Admiral's cabin. According to the same source Collingwood reminded the young Lieutenant of his promise and said: 'Now take these despatches to England; you will receive £500 and your Commander's commission. Now I have kept my word.' After collecting various other letters—including Blackwood's—to deliver in England, and receiving orders to transfer the rest of the prisoners he still had on board to the *Revenge*, Lapenotiere went back on board the *Pickle*. By noon the jollyboat had returned from its task of moving the prisoners, and once again Lapenotiere had a full crew to work the ship, instead of having to use some of them as guards. 'In boat and made sail for England,' Almy's spidery handwriting noted in his log.

With more than a thousand miles to go from Trafalgar—which is only a few score miles along the Spanish coast from Gibraltar— the *Pickle* had a long, tedious and dangerous voyage ahead of her. The four enemy battleships[1] under the French Rear-Admiral Dumanoir, which had fled from the battle, might fall upon her; French or Spanish ships could swoop out from Vigo, Corunna, Ferrol or Brest. In addition, another French admiral, Allemand, was at sea with at least five more battleships. But despite the threat of enemy ships lying across his track, Lapenotiere knew that the weather would probably turn out to be his worst enemy. The *Pickle* had already endured a heavy pounding in gigantic seas— Blackwood had written on the 23rd, 'It has blown a hurricane'— and the wrenching strain on her frames and timbers was probably squeezing the caulking oakum out from between the planks of her hull.

Now, on Saturday, October 26, from off Cadiz (where three years later she was to be wrecked while entering the harbour) the quartermaster steered the *Pickle* west-north-west to round Cape St Vincent. The gale slowly eased down until there was only a fresh breeze blowing under a cloudy sky, but the strong winds on the previous days had left a heavy swell which made the ship's timbers creak and groan, as if she resented every wave which alternately lifted her on its crest and then tumbled her into the trough. Soon she could carry more sail. The main-topmast, which had been sent down and lashed at the beginning of the gale, was sent up again; reefs were shaken out of the mainsail and the topsail was set. But the topsail stood for less than an hour, because the wind quickly piped up again and backed just before midnight, forcing Lapenotiere to sail the *Pickle* in almost exactly

---

[1] The more conventional phrase 'line-of-battle ship' will be rendered as 'battleship' in this narrative.

the opposite direction to the course for England. His great danger now was that the *Pickle* would be trapped in the great bay formed by the rocky outcrop of Cape St Vincent. Wise seamen feared a lee shore in a gale more than the most heavily-armed enemy.

By dawn on Sunday the wind had veered, and at noon the *Pickle* was back on course some twelve to fifteen miles off Cape St Mary, with Cape St Vincent yet to be weathered. On Monday, with the wind lighter and more canvas set, Lapenotiere decided to muster the crew. The *Regulations and Instructions Relating to His Majesty's Service at Sea* laid down that a commanding officer 'is himself to muster the Ship's Company at least once a week at sea', and in addition to checking them against the ship's books, form number fifteen had to be filled in.

This had several columns with different headings—the date the man joined the ship, whether 'prest' (press-ganged) or a volunteer, name, rating, age, stature, complexion, leave allowed, etc. There was one column headed ominously 'D, DD, or R'—discharged, discharged dead, or 'run' (deserted). Of the ship's complement of forty there were now only thirty-two men on board; the rest had 'run' or been discharged. And even though the *Pickle* had been at sea continuously for several weeks, there were no sick men wanting the attentions of Mr Britton, the surgeon from Bristol.

The muster list gave a good indication of the cosmopolitan crowd of men who, volunteers or prest, manned His Majesty's ships at this time. Of the thirty-two men whose names appeared on form fifteen, seventeen were English, nine Irish, two American, one Norwegian, one Scots, one Welsh and one a Channel Islander. But compared with battleships this was nothing—the *Victory*, as we shall see later, numbered Americans, Swiss, Germans, Maltese, Russians, Swedes, Italians, Norwegians and even Frenchmen among her crew as well as men from Salvador and Guadeloupe.

With the *Pickle*'s crew mustered on deck, the first man's name was called and his details noted down—James Rowden, bosun's mate, joined the ship on December 1, 1804, volunteer, born at Saltash, Cornwall and aged thirty. One after another the men were checked. The ninth and tenth names on the ship's books were of Irishmen, one from Cork and the other from Dublin, who were marked 'run'; the eighteenth and nineteenth names were of Norwegians, John Ellingson, who was rated a carpenter's mate, and Wildred Andrus, able seaman. Both were volunteers, joining the ship on December 1, 1804, and both were marked down as having 'run' at Plymouth. One prest American, Thomas Bascombe of New York, rated able seaman and twenty-six years old when he suddenly found himself in His Majesty's Service, was noted down as having been discharged at Bermuda in time to have missed Trafalgar. Farther down the list was another Norwegian, I. Ellingson, the brother of John. He had joined as a carpenter's mate five weeks before his brother—and deserted in September, just before the *Pickle* sailed from Plymouth for Cadiz. Immediately below, Wildred Andrus's name appeared once again—he had rejoined the ship after having 'run' on the same day that his countryman deserted, and he was marked down 'returned after run'. The name of Almy, the Second Master,[1] with a note that he came from Newport, Rhode Island, was next to that of John Oxford, a twenty-four-year-old able seaman from the same town.

The *Pickle*'s crew had just been dismissed after the muster when a look-out hailed the quarter-deck: 'Sail in sight to the west-north-west standing towards us.'

A few minutes later, as the *Pickle*'s bluff-bowed hull was lifted up on the crest of an extra high wave, thus helping the eyes of the anxious men on the quarter-deck to see a little farther over the curvature of the earth, they identified her as a ship-rigged sloop. From her course she was obviously steering to intercept the *Pickle*, so Lapenotiere decided to keep sailing as fast as possible, to be on the safe side until he was sure of her identity. He ordered the fore-topsail to be set. However, the sloop slowly closed on the *Pickle* and Lapenotiere had the private signal hoisted. As soon as the flags were streaming from their halyards the sloop answered and ran up the numbers which identified her—451.

She was the 26-gun *Nautilus*—a new ship built eighteen months earlier at Milford Haven and now commanded by Captain Sykes. Soon the two ships were hove-to near each other, and the *Nautilus* lowered a boat for Captain Sykes to go aboard the *Pickle*. As soon as a weary Lapenotiere had told him the news of the victory and of the tragedy Sykes, realizing its importance, decided to go at once to Lisbon to warn the British Ambassador. The *Nautilus* headed for the Tagus, but darkness brought a fresh gale and both ships had to reef down hurriedly. The *Nautilus* finally reached the mouth of the Tagus early on Tuesday, firing several guns to bring out a pilot boat. None came, and after waiting two hours the sloop hove-to while a Portuguese fishing boat was

[1] The *Pickle* did not at this time have a Master. See Notes, p. 347

boarded and her master paid to take a despatch into Lisbon and have it delivered to Mr Gambier, the British Consul. By 9.30 a.m. the *Nautilus* was under way again—this time heading for England, because Captain Sykes had decided that the task of carrying the news of the victory off Cape Trafalgar was too important, in case she was captured, to leave entirely to the *Pickle*.

By Wednesday, October 30, the *Pickle*'s log noted that they were off the Burlings, the rocks to the north-west of Lisbon, and they 'saw the *Notlas*' (Almy's spelling of the *Nautilus*). Despite her long detour to the Tagus she had caught up. She was, of course, a larger ship and she was still in sight next day when yet another gale blew up from the south-west.

Once again the crew of the *Pickle* went through the back-breaking task of shortening sail, starting by sending the topgallant-yard, with its heavy weight and windage, down to the deck and lashing it. Mainsail and middle jib were reefed, but still the *Pickle* plunged and pounded, as if she was trying to run amok in the screaming wind. Finally, with topsail furled and the yard sent down, and the foresail brailed up, she seemed to ride a little easier. But it gave the crew only a short respite—at 9 a.m. on Thursday, as they were rounding Finisterre before entering the Bay of Biscay, a heavy sea swept the ship, wrenching away the jib-boom and spritsail-yard. Within a few minutes Copeland, the carpenter's mate, was reporting that the limber holes in the frames which drained the forepeak were blocked up, preventing the water running aft to the pump. As a result the forepeak was flooding. Lapenotiere sent men down to start baling with buckets.

By 11 p.m. the little *Pickle*'s position was rapidly becoming critical. Somewhere forward below the waterline there was a leak, and the more the ship laboured the worse it would get. The wind increased in the darkness, whipping up vicious seas which were superimposed in complicated patterns on the heavy swell already rolling in without interruption from another great storm-centre in the heart of the Atlantic. As each crest passed under the bows, the ship reared up and then plunged into the next trough, sending a great shudder through her timbers. In the forepeak, barely able to keep a foothold on a deck which seemed more like a see-saw, men scrambled and cursed, filling buckets and passing them up to be emptied. But however fast they baled, the level of the water swilling and sucking round their legs seemed to remain the same. Farther aft men manned the pump which gushed and gurgled but, however hard they worked, never sucked dry. Midnight came unnoticed, bringing in its train Friday, November 1.

In the small hours, in the darkness of a night which brought a chill to men's spirits, the wind increased its frenetic screaming in the rigging and masts. Extra men at the tiller struggled to keep the *Pickle* on something approaching a safe course. By 5 a.m. the gale was worse. The wind, exerting a pressure of many pounds on each square foot of the weather side of the hull and the masts and rigging, was now so strong that as the ship rolled to leeward she hung there sluggishly for minutes on end, seemingly reluctant to steady herself and roll back to windward. She began to feel dead in the water and Lapenotiere, weary and worried, anxious both for his ship and the despatches entrusted to him, decided he would have to clear some of the top-weight off the ship. The easiest way of doing it was to get rid of some of the 12-pounder carronades on deck. Each weighed six hundredweight on its wooden slide, and since they were fitted high up and well out against the ship's side, where they exerted a great leverage, they were from the point of view of stability in almost the worst possible position. Lapenotiere therefore ordered four of them, with their slides, to be heaved over the side. Lightened by more than a ton, the *Pickle* then seemed to ride a little easier, but still she plunged and pounded, her apple-cheeked bow lifting and then smashing down in a welter of solid water and spray, straining the whole ship.

Dawn came cold, grey and disheartening, and it brought no improvement in the weather. By 10 a.m. this miserable Friday, the time had come to reduce sail even more. Men scrambled to halyards, sheets and vangs, while others had to cling precariously to the boom to stifle the flogging canvas as the halyards were slackened away and the sail brought down. The wind whipped and tore it like a petulant giant until gaskets could be passed and secured. But the crew still had work to do: the fore-topmast had to be sent down in an attempt to reduce the windage, and lashed securely to the deck. At noon Almy recorded in the log that a strong gale was still blowing, but under the low scudding clouds it seemed to be getting a little lighter, and the more hopeful among the crew hazarded a tentative guess that the wind was easing slightly. And indeed it was, though to men who had not had a decent sleep for eleven days and whose clothes had been wringing wet for most of that time it seemed to do so with tantalizing tardiness. More sail was set as gradually the wind veered and dropped to a fresh breeze. The fore-topmast was sent up once again, and at 5 p.m. the fore-topsail-yard was swayed up. By the time it was dark the *Pickle* had all her working canvas set and drawing. The leak had stopped and although the swell kept the *Pickle* pitching and rolling violently, the watch below thankfully wriggled into their sodden hammocks and slept.

The next day was Saturday, November 2, and the *Pickle* reached the entrance of the Channel, west of Ushant. The Lizard was 151 miles away to the north-north-east according to Almy's calculations, though much of them had to be guesswork and dead reckoning because of the gales. The quartermaster at the helm was steering the ship on a north-easterly course, and a following wind kept her sailing fast. On deck and down below the crew were hard at work tidying up, sorting out the sodden tangle of gear and clothing. By now the *Pickle* was no longer alone: on the horizon all round were sails, sails of merchant ships converging on or leaving English ports, bringing in much-needed cargoes and outward-bound with others, and sails of warships—battleships going out on patrol or returning frigates bearing despatches to far-flung commanders-in-chief or bringing some back—and tiny sloops and cutters of all descriptions on a variety of missions.

Yet even now, within a day's sailing of the Lizard, given a decent wind, Nature had not finished with the *Pickle*: the wind dropped right away so that the once arched and over-strained sails flattened like limp curtains, and as the way came off the schooner they slatted and flapped while she rolled in the slight swell, the trucks of her masts scribing invisible circles in the sky. And slowly the ships on the horizon faded from sight, blurred and then hidden by banks of sea-mist forming as the warm air rolled in across the cold sea, to be chilled and its invisible water vapour condensed into myriads of dank and visible droplets. Lapenotiere, knowing how urgent was his task of delivering Collingwood's despatches, set the crew to work with sweeps. These large oars, with three or four men thrusting at each of them, soon had the *Pickle* heading the right direction with a knot or two of way on her.

The oars had been groaning rhythmically for more than four hours when the perspiring men—and Lapenotiere on the quarter-deck—saw a ruffle on the water ahead: a breeze was coming up from the eastward. A light head-wind was certainly better than rowing; but would they never get a reasonable beam wind to

give them a fast reach, which was the schooner's fastest point of
sailing? Thankfully the men hauled the sweeps inboard and
stowed them while others hurried to sheet in jibs, foresail and
mainsail, to catch every miserable catspaw of wind and enable
them to creep nearer to the Lizard. The breeze pewtering the sea
soon became steady and then it increased to fresh and later strong,
so that the *Pickle*, from heeling gently and steering through calm
seas with almost feline grace, was soon lumbering along like an
overloaded farm cart, with more wind and sea than she wanted.
At 5 p.m. Lapenotiere ordered the fore-topsail to be taken in, and
a few minutes later he ordered the yard to be struck down on deck.

Late this Sunday afternoon a powerful 74-gun ship, the black
and yellow hull identifying her as one of Nelson's fleet, came
down on them fast, ploughing her way south-westward out of
the Channel. After the private signal was run up on each ship they
exchanged numbers. Three flags from the seventy-four identified
her as the *Superb*, commanded by Captain Richard Gardiner
Keats. The signal flags 351—'I have some intelligence to com-
municate'—hoisted from the *Pickle*'s yardarm soon brought a
scurry of activity aboard *Superb*: her jibs and staysails came
tumbling down, the courses—the lowest of the big sails on the
fore and mainmasts—were clewed up, and her topgallants lowered.
Her helm was put a'lee to bring her up to the wind and then
backed her main-topsail, so that the wind filling the fore-topsail
tried to move the ship ahead but was counter-balanced by that on
the backed sail trying to push her astern. She was now hove-to
and in the meantime the *Pickle* had lowered a jolly-boat which was
bringing Lapenotiere across.

For Keats, the news that Lapenotiere took only a few moments
to relate was one of the greatest shocks of his life. His reactions
can easily be imagined, for he was Nelson's special favourite, and
up to this moment he had been hurrying to Cadiz, hoping desperately that he would be in time for the battle. Now, on this drab
November Sunday, with the battle fought and his friend and
patron dead, perhaps Keats's mind went back to a morning some
seven weeks earlier in the grounds of Nelson's home, Merton
Place, in Surrey. There he had walked with the Admiral, who in
an excited voice had described his plans for fighting the Combined
Fleet of France and Spain. When Lapenotiere left to return to
the *Pickle* he left behind men who were openly shedding tears.
As the *Superb* got under way again for Cadiz, every man aboard

was conscious that he had missed a rendezvous with history and, in Nelson's death, suffered a personal loss.

The *Pickle* was less than sixty miles from the Lizard and with night falling the wind eased and veered, and Almy noted in the log that the ship had 'all sail set to advantage' as she made her way up to the north-east. Here, as the broad Atlantic funnelled into the narrow Channel between England and France, the tidal stream was getting stronger every mile made to the eastward, adding to the problem of dead-reckoning navigation. At midnight the deep-sea lead was got out and a cast gave fifty-two fathoms under the *Pickle*'s keel. Two hours later a sharp-eyed look-out spotted the Lizard Light perched some two hundred feet up atop Lizard Head and bearing east by north, an estimated nine miles away.

Sailing ships had made this very landfall for centuries, returning from the four corners of the earth laden with rare cargoes which had made England rich, or bearing the scars of sea battles which had created—and maintained—her greatness. And the Lizard was often the last sight of land for ships making their departure, bound for remote ports and unexplored coasts to trade or blockade, survey, barter or battle. Even as the Lizard was the first sight of England for the Duke of Medina Sidonia and the Spanish Armada, so it was the last for the Pilgrim Fathers sailing for America. Drake's last glimpse of England before he died on board his own ship off Portobello in 1596 had been this very headland, and Nelson, too, had seen it for the last time a bare few weeks before the *Pickle* nosed her way past.

In the darkness she sailed past the sleeping villages along the Cornish coast: past Landewednack, hidden under the lee of the Lizard, whose parish church was the most southerly in England, past Cadgwith Cove, and the hump of Black Head. Beyond was Coverack, a small fishing village with its own stone quay, a favourite landing place for smugglers. These men still managed to bring in brandy from across the Channel after successful deals with equally unscrupulous enemy traders who, like themselves, placed cash above conscience to satisfy customers who put palate above patriotism.

By the time dawn diluted the black night to a chilly grey, the *Pickle* was abeam of the Manacles, that most dreaded group of rocks lying near the track of ships off this coast. Many seamen, washed ashore lifeless from ships which came in too close under the cliffs through faulty navigation or were driven ashore by gales, were buried in St Keverne's churchyard a mile or so inland. Lapenotiere could see Falmouth Bay and the whole of the Cornish coast up to Rame Head opening out as he brought the schooner round to the north, following the shore-line and broad-reaching —at long last—the last few miles to Falmouth, whose entrance was guarded by the twin castles of Pendennis and St Mawes, constructed by a thoughtful Henry VIII. As the *Pickle* reached Falmouth Bay with the wind light and the tide foul, Lapenotiere gave his orders to Kingdom, his second-in-command, who was taking the ship on to Plymouth. Lapenotiere then went below to his tiny cabin and struggled into his best uniform, mildewed and creased as it was. He then took a pouch containing Admiral Collingwood's despatches, Blackwood's letters and various other papers from the desk in which he had kept it under lock and key, buckled on his sword and went back on deck.

It was at 9.45 a.m. on Monday, November 4, that he gave the order first to shorten sail, and then heave-to. The jolly-boat was swung over the side once again and he stepped into it. The menacing bulk of Pendennis Castle was more than half a mile away, and it was some time before the tall, quietly-spoken lieutenant stepped ashore from the boat and began to arrange for a postchaise to take him and his precious despatches the 266 miles to the Admiralty in London.[1]

Lieutenant Lapenotiere and his coachman were not, however, the only carriers of the news. Captain Sykes and the *Nautilus* had been following close astern of the *Pickle*, but on the previous Saturday had narrowly escaped being captured a hundred miles south-west of Ushant. Steering north-eastwards in a light breeze, the horizon fading in the haze so that it was impossible to see where sea ended and sky began, the *Nautilus*'s look-outs had sighted the sails of four ships to the eastwards. Through telescopes her officers saw they were steering to the westward and would pass across the sloop's bows from starboard to larboard. The private signal was hoisted at one of the *Nautilus*' yardarms and two guns were fired to draw attention to it. But the four ships made no reply.

[1] The semaphore telegraph stations between London and Plymouth were being built at this time but were not yet completed; the nearest was at Portsmouth. For a painting of the *Pickle*'s arrival, see p. 32

Sykes, uncertain what was going on, kept a respectable distance and his wariness was rewarded. After identifying the vessels as a battleship, two frigates and a brig, he saw another brig come into sight and pass near the battleship, which hoisted French colours to it. He was just digesting this fact when the battleship hoisted a French pennant over two strange flags at the mizen peak. That was more than enough for Sykes. He gave the order to beat to quarters, and the staccato rattle of the drum beating to the tune of 'Hearts of Oak' sent the *Nautilus*'s crew of a hundred and twenty-one to their stations. Bulkheads were hinged up or taken down; decks were wetted and sanded against fire and slipping feet; the galley fire was doused. Fighting lanterns, with candle-ends in them, were put ready; the gunner went to the magazine, and the carpenters stood by with their sounding irons and shot plugs. The gun captains had their powder horns and priming irons ready; slow matches—long twists of cotton or worsted impregnated with a composition which made them burn slowly—were lit and hung over tubs half-filled with water; powder boys brought up cartridges; fire screens—mostly wet blankets—were rigged.

The little sloop had eighteen 9-pounders on the upper-deck, with six 12-pounders on the quarter-deck and two more 12-pounders in the fo'c'sle. At the first roll of the drum the crews had swarmed to their guns, cast off the lashings and tackles securing them, and run them in ready to load. While this was going on the ship's fore-topsail and fore-topgallant were being set. All sails were sheeted in hard as Sykes turned the *Nautilus* away to make her escape to the south-east. But the French ships did not follow him and by 5 p.m. had gone out of sight over the horizon to the north-west.

At 10 a.m. on Sunday, after an uneventful night, Sykes came on deck and ordered the lieutenant to send the hands aft to witness punishment: two seamen were to be flogged for 'insolence and neglect of duty'. A midshipman passed the order on to the bosun's mates, and to the accompaniment of their shrill pipes it was shouted throughout the ship. Marines in white breeches and red tail-coats, their white cross-belts newly pipeclayed, hats high and round, the brims looped up at the side like a bishop's, fell in on the poop with muskets and side-arms; the captain and lieu-tenants waited on the weather side of the quarter-deck, with the junior officers gathered respectfully to leeward. The rest of the crew fell in anywhere—on the boats, on the booms—wherever they could get a view.

Sykes ordered: 'Rig the gratings.' Two of the gratings covering a hatch were brought aft, and while one was put flat on the deck, the other was lashed vertically above it, against a bulkhead. Then Sykes called for Alexander Petrie, sentenced to thirty-six lashes. Had he anything to say in extenuation? That formality over, the next order was 'Strip', and Petrie took off his jacket and shirt. At 'Seize him up' he leaned against the vertical grating and the quartermaster lashed him to it. Sykes then read out the particular Article of War which Petrie had infringed, and while he was doing so one of the burliest of the bosun's mates took the red-handled cat-o'-nine tails from a red baize bag. The cat was a brutal weapon, symptomatic of a brutal age. It consisted of nine long and thin lines which hung like poisonous tentacles from a short rigid handle. One lash stripped the skin from the man's back whereever the tails fell, the knots biting deeper and drawing blood. Six lashes—for each was skilfully placed by the bosun's mate in a different place—made all the skin completely raw, while twelve mangled the flesh so that it looked like butcher's meat. A man who frequently witnessed flogging said that after two dozen lashes—which left the bosun's mate exhausted, so that another man took over—'The lacerated back looks inhuman; it resembles roasted meat burnt nearly black before a scorching fire'. Yet seventy-two lashes were regarded as common, and even five hundred were sometimes given.

The punishment for striking an officer was invariably flogging through the fleet. For this a man was lashed to a grating in a boat and, to the accompaniment of half-minute bells and a drummer beating the 'Rogue's March', he was rowed to each ship in turn and flogged. If he became unconscious half-way through he was often brought back, nursed to health, and weeks later the flogging resumed. Even if he died on the grating—and many men did from shock—the punishment often was completed, It was rare but not unknown for a corpse to be brought alongside a ship and the remaining lashes administered before it was rowed ashore and buried, without religious rites, below the tide-line.

Yet some captains used the cat rarely, if at all. Collingwood, a stern disciplinarian, had his men working cheerfully and efficiently and yet he used the cat less than once a month. When bad sailors were brought before Nelson he had often said 'Send them to

Collingwood: he will tame them if no one else can.' He could deal with the worst of them, making good seamen of those whom others might have flogged to death or hanged from the yardarm.

A few captains in Nelson's time were complete tyrants; bolstered up by the Articles of War, they were able to use the cat indiscriminately to work off deep-rooted grudges against life in general. At least one captain flogged the last man down on deck after setting sail aloft—which often meant the best man got the cat, since it depended how far out on the yard he was working. One man who served in nine battleships said only two had humane commanders. It is a sad fact that a tyrant—in defiance of Admiralty regulations—could so harry and haze a seaman he disliked (and men served for upwards of two years in the same ship without setting foot on shore) that the wretched fellow was goaded into an offence for which the only punishment was death; a comparatively quick end if hoisted in a hangman's noose from a yardarm, or the slow, agonizing death resulting from being flogged round the fleet.

So Alexander Petrie paid the price for 'Insolence and neglect of duty', and at the end of his thirty-six lashes he was cut down from the grating and taken away to the sick bay, where the surgeon tried to patch him up. The second offender, William Donaldson, was then tied up to receive two dozen lashes. And in the *Nautilus*'s log it was noted down briefly: 'At 10 punished Alexr Petrie and Wm Donaldson seamen with 36 lashes and 24 lashes for insolence and neglect of duty. . . .'

Late on Monday night, nearly twelve hours after Lapenotiere left Falmouth in his postchaise, the *Nautilus* hove-to off Plymouth and Captain Sykes went ashore by boat, reported, and took a postchaise for London.

Lying-to in heavy weather with a mizen (left), a close-reefed main-topsail (centre) and main-staysail (right)

2

PRICE OF VICTORY

'The death of Nelson was felt in England as something more than a public calamity; men started at the intelligence, and turned pale, as if they had heard of the loss of a dear friend.'

—Southey

LIEUTENANT LAPENOTIERE was already well on his way. By noon on Monday his postchaise was clattering out of Falmouth up the road to Penryn, where it took the right-hand fork for Truro. Lapenotiere was glad the roads were dry—it had not rained for five days—and his coachmen kept up a good speed, unaware that he was bearing momentous news.

The coach clattered into Truro, Cornwall's only city and placid with good breeding, where the county gentry had their town houses and paced over cobblestones along walks lined with palm trees. At the Royal Hotel the ostlers were ready with four fresh horses, and as soon as they were changed the coach drove on to Liskeard, the old market town which had been the Royalist head-quarters when England was torn between Cavalier and Roundhead.

Changing horses once again—they, and sometimes the post-chaise as well, were to be changed nineteen times before he reached London—Lapenotiere approached the Devon border. He left behind him a Cornwall full of colour and contradictions. Wesley's influence was strong and there were books of his hymns in nearly every house, while each village had its thatched chapel. Men played kayle, or skittle-alley, while they drank ale or cider; they held competitions among the tin mines to catch greased pigs, and watched cockfighting and bull-baiting, or a lunatic in a cage. From Cornwall a lumbering stage wagon took three weeks to get to London, and many a man made his will before embarking on such a journey.

The young Lieutenant was soon at Tavistock, passing within a mile of where Sir Francis Drake was born. Then on the post-chaise thundered, to Dartmoor bleak and foreboding, passing close to Princetown, soon to have a huge prison built there to house French prisoners of war, but now just a village with quarries and a few farms.

The road swept slowly down among gaunt tors on its way to Postbridge, with its ancient clapper bridge across the West Dart. On and on the horses galloped, with Lapenotiere sitting in uncomfortable silence grasping his despatches. From Exeter the 'chaise turned on to the post road for the lace-making town of Honiton, with its 14th-century leper hospital. Once clear of its wide streets he was soon heading on to Axminster, past rich meadows whose sturdy-framed and red-coated South Devon cattle yielded milk of just the right type for the country's famous scald cream, past orchards whose apples, under the farmers' presses, gave up a fine and potent cider.

This was the land that Nelson's victory had made safe for another century, although few men working in the fields bothered to glance up to see the messenger who was bringing the news. It was a land where poverty rubbed shoulders with richness, but which bred a sturdy race of people. Veal and pork cost about threepence a pound and rhubarb was the main medicine.

A woman was paid sixpence a day for weeding a field, plus a penny-ha'penny for beer. A maid received £5 a year and a farm-hand £10 if he lived in. They ate their food from wooden plates, and their homes were lit by candles and cruses fed with fish or animal oil. Schoolteachers were paid a pound a month, and burying a pauper cost the parish twenty-seven shillings for a coffin and half a crown for the minister. If the local people went far afield they would travel by wagon. Those with first-class tickets stayed in when they reached a hill while the second-class got out and walked, and those with third-class tickets had to push.

It was a jaded and weary Lapenotiere who sat back as the fresh horses galloped through finely wooded country alongside the Test at Laverstoke and Overton, and then on to Basingstoke, where seven roads met at what was once one of the manors held by King Harold before the Conquest. There remained some fifty miles to London. Many miles farther back along the road—which, coming from Plymouth, he had joined at Two Bridges—was Captain Sykes, of the *Nautilus*, also bound for the Admiralty as fast as postchaise would bear him.

Lapenotiere left Basingstoke in the late afternoon of November 5 and the weather gave a warning of fog to come. Smoke from the chimneys of the cottages along the side of the road rose in

The schooner *Pickle* arrives off Falmouth with Collingwood's despatches announcing the victory at Trafalgar.

From the painting by W. McDowell

Nelson. *From the portrait by Abbott*

Sir Henry Black-wood, the 'Prince of frigate captains'. *From the portrait by Hoppner*

vertical threads or mingled with hints of mist, and the smell of
burning logs introduced a new and welcome odour into the musty
'chaise. Sure enough, as he approached the outskirts of the great
capital, the stratified sheets of mist lying in the hollows gradually
thickened into banks of fog, white in the glow from the lamps at
first, but yellowing with the throat-catching tang of sulphur as
bunches of cottages merged into terraces of houses. The cursing
coachman slowed from a gallop to a trot, from a trot to a walk, and
from a walk to a crawl. Gales and calms, head-winds and leaks
had conspired to slow the *Pickle*, and now one of London's
famous November fogs was marking down the bearer of Collingwood's despatches for its special attention.

The fog which hampered Lapenotiere also caught, among
hundreds of others, the vivacious Lady Bessborough, who wrote:
'I drove to town intending to go . . . to Queen Street and Dun-
cannon's house, where I had appointed people to meet me. The
fog, which was bad when I set out, grew thicker and thicker, but
when I got into the Park was so complete it was impossible to
find the way out.' But the woman who was four years later, when a
grandmother, to suffer the attentions of the corpulent and dissi-
pated Prince Regent, was not put out. 'My footman got down to
feel for the road, and the holloing of the drivers and the screams
of people on foot were dreadful. I was one hour driving through
the Park; Queen Street was impossible to find . . . I set out with
two men walking before the horses with flambeaux, of which we
could with difficulty perceive the flame—the men not at all.
Every ten or twenty yards they felt for the door of a house to ask
where we were—it was frightful beyond measure. . . . I find Lady
Villiers, who rode to see me, was overtaken by it on her return,
and nearly drown'd by riding into the Thames. How many
accidents she has!'

Her Ladyship had safely negotiated the worst fog the capital
had seen for many years by the time the fretting Lapenotiere
approached Westminster Bridge and Whitehall, stiff and weary
from nearly thirty-seven hours' hard driving from Falmouth.
Midnight had struck and November 6 had been ushered in.

A fog-bound Whitehall was deserted and in the Admiralty the
silver-haired and sharp-eyed Lord Barham, now seventy-nine
and First Lord, had retired to bed. England owed much to Lord
Barham, a tough man and a brilliant administrator, whose life was

devoted to the good of the Service he loved. He had been Comptroller of the Navy from 1778 to 1790 and thus was responsible for its material. As we shall see later, he had set the stage for Nelson to fight the Combined Fleet in the same competent, clear and concise way that he had, within a few days of taking over as First Lord, set out the duties of the Board of Admiralty. His own rôle occupied a sentence—'The First Lord will take upon himself the general superintendence of the whole.' The duties of the 'Senior or First Professional Lord,'[1] the Second and Third Lords, and Civil Lords took only a few lines. Then he outlined the tasks of the Secretary, Second Secretary, clerks ('To be in their desks by 10 o'clock'), confidential clerks, nine principal clerks 'and an extra clerk to be under the First Lord's Secretary'.

The Secretary to the Board probably had the hardest task of all. With the help of the Second Secretary he had to open all incoming correspondence, examine and sign outgoing letters, countersign orders, commissions and warrants signed by the Board, and run the whole office through the First Clerk.

It was the weight of all this work that kept the Secretary working late in the Board Room on this foggy November night. He was an Irishman, William Marsden, son of an Irish banker with shipping interests. Originally intended for the Church he had, via the East India Company, become Secretary to the Board of Admiralty, thanks to the influence of Earl Spencer (such appointments were held almost entirely by influence in those days). The Board Room where Marsden worked had been the centre of Britain's dominion of the seas since Ripley constructed the building in 1725. From here orders had gone out which sent Anson on his great voyage of exploration in 1740; Byng to Minorca—and his death before a firing squad after a court-martial in England; Cook on three voyages which opened up the entire Pacific; Howe to his great battle in 1794 on 'The Glorious First of June'; Admiral Sir John Jervis to the St Valentine's Day victory off Cape St Vincent in 1797, and Nelson himself to the great victories of the Nile, Copenhagen and now against the Combined Fleet of France and Spain.

The ebb and flow of British naval history—and land history, for the two were interdependent—had been planned in this room, and somehow it had absorbed this atmosphere. It was rectangular, with three windows on one long side overlooking some stables.

[1] Now termed the First Sea Lord.

The high white ceiling was decorated with gilt emblematic roses
and heavy 17th-century oak panelling covered the walls. A log
fire burnt in the grate which still bore the arms of Charles II, and
on the wall over the fireplace were several charts, wound round
rollers so that they looked like white sun-blinds. A long, heavy
mahogany table occupying the middle of the room had its legs
inset so that people sitting round it were not inconvenienced as
they discussed, argued and decided policies which could send
fleets to victory or to their doom, break an admiral or promote the
humblest lieutenant. On the north wall, flanked by bookcases, was
what at first glance appeared to be a huge clock face, but closer
inspection showed that it was a circular map depicting Europe
from the Baltic to the north of Spain. In its centre was fixed a
gilded pointer, and round the edge were marked the points of the
compass. The pointer was geared to a wind-vane on top of the
Admiralty building. Sitting round the Board Room table, the
members could see which way the wind was blowing and thus
have an idea whether or not the Fleet could sail. The dial had
worked continually since 1695, having previously been in Walling-
ford House, on the site of which Ripley built the present building.
The North Sea bore the name 'The British Ocean'; the Scillies
were labelled 'Silly I.'; Calais was 'Calice', and Dieppe was
spelled 'Diep'. The arms of the royal houses of Europe were
painted in their once appropriate geographical locations.

The most striking features of the whole room were the magnificent Grinling Gibbons carvings in pear wood. Among them were
intricate working models of dividers and cross-jacks, a pelorus,
astrolabes and a shot-gauge. Almost hidden was a tiny open pod of
peas, Grinling Gibbons's own trade-mark. And tucked away,
where it was to remain undiscovered for 263 years, was carved a
date, 1695. In a corner of the room a tall and stately grandfather
clock told both time and date, as it had been doing for the past
hundred and five years, ever since it was made by Langley Bradley, the man who constructed the great clock of St Paul's Cathedral.
The mirror on the door of the clock had reflected the Board's
deliberations since 1700.[1] The fire glowed and Bradley's clock
ticked away the passing minutes as Marsden sat working in the
light of a few candles set in silver candlesticks on the huge table.

[1] The Board Room has been changed only slightly since Nelson's day.
The wind dial is over the fireplace, but the table, clock, carvings, panelling,
fireplace and most of the chairs still remain. The date on Gibbons's carving
was discovered by Mr E. Smith, of the Admiralty, in September, 1958.

Out in Whitehall Lapenotiere's postchaise carried him the last few
yards of his long journey, turning through the narrow arch of the
Admiralty and into the cobbled courtyard. It rumbled to a stop
in front of the four columns guarding the main door, and in the
fog two lanterns guttered fitfully as the young Lieutenant climbed
stiffly from the carriage and walked up the shallow steps. The
clatter of the horses' hooves had roused the night-porter from
the comfort of his hooded chair and he opened the door. Lapenotiere quickly told him that he bore urgent despatches for Mr
Marsden. His mission was too urgent for him to be left in the
little waiting-room on the left of the glowing fire, so he followed
the porter out of the hall and past another room where Nelson's
body was soon to lie in state. Climbing up two flights of narrow
stairs, he came to the door of the Board Room.

Inside the room a tired Marsden had just finished his work. 'It
was', he wrote, 'about one o'clock a.m. of the 6th November,
when I was in the act of withdrawing from the Board Room to my
private apartments, after having opened the common letters
received in the course of the evening.' The night porter knocked
and went in, announcing an officer bearing despatches. Lapenotiere, unshaven, uniform crumpled, his face lined with tiredness,
but still alert in his unaccustomed surroundings, strode into the
candlelit room and stopped before Marsden. Without any preamble he said: 'Sir, we have gained a great victory; but we have
lost Lord Nelson.'

Lapenotiere then handed over the despatches, addressed simply
to 'W. Marsden Esq.' The secretary broke the seal and started
reading. The despatches said:

'*Euryalus*, off Cape Trafalgar, Oct. 22, 1805.

'The ever-to-be lamented death of Vice-Admiral Lord
Nelson, who, in the late conflict with the enemy, fell in the
hour of Victory, leaves me the duty of informing my Lords
Commissioners of the Admiralty, that on the 19th instant it
was communicated to the Commander-in-Chief, from the
ships watching the motions of the enemy in Cadiz, that the
Combined Fleet had put to sea. . . . On Monday, the 21st
instant, at daylight, when Cape Trafalgar bore E. by S. about
seven leagues, the enemy was discovered six or seven miles
to the eastward, the wind about west, and very light.

'The Commander-in-Chief immediately made the signal

for the Fleet to bear up in two columns, as they are formed in order of sailing; a mode of attack his Lordship had previously directed, to avoid the inconvenience and delay in forming a line of battle in the usual manner. . . . The Commander-in-Chief, in the *Victory*, led the weather column, and the *Royal Sovereign*, which bore my flag, the lee. The action began at Twelve o'clock by the leading ships of the columns breaking through the enemy's line. . . . The enemy's ships were fought with a gallantry highly honourable to their officers; but the attack on them was irresistible, and it pleased the Almighty Disposer of all events to grant His Majesty's arms a complete and glorious victory. . . .

'His Lordship received a musket ball in his left breast, about the middle of the action. . . . I have also to lament the loss of those excellent officers, Captains Duff, of the *Mars*, and Cooke of the *Bellerophon*. . . .'

Shocked as he was by this double-edged news, Marsden remembered he was the Secretary to the Board. 'The effect this [news] produced, it is not my purpose to describe,' he wrote later, 'nor had I the time to indulge in reflections, who was at that moment the only person informed of one of the greatest events recorded in our history, and which it was my duty to make known with the utmost promptitude.

'The First Lord [Barham] had retired to rest, as had his domestics, and it was not till after some research that I could discover the room in which he slept. Drawing aside his curtains, with a candle in my hand, I awoke the old peer from a sound slumber; and to the credit of his nerves be it mentioned that he showed no symptoms of alarm or surprise, but calmly asked: "What news, Mr M.?" [*sic*]'.

There were many people to inform—among them the King at Windsor, the Prince of Wales, the Duke of York, Mr Pitt in Downing Street, other Ministers and the Lord Mayor, 'who communicated the intelligence to the shipping interest at Lloyd's Coffee House'. A notice for the royal salutes was also necessary and preparations had to be made for a *Gazette Extraordinary* that would, as Marsden noted, 'be eagerly read with mixed feelings of exultation and grief'.[1] The night porter was sent round the

---

[1] The people of Britain were not, however, the first to hear the news: the *Gibraltar Chronicle* printed on October 24 a letter from Collingwood to Lt-General Fox, the Commander-in-Chief of the fortress.

Admiralty building to rouse anyone who could help—even if they were only useful for sending out into the fog to fetch in regular clerks.

The first task was to make several copies of Collingwood's despatch. One of the first completed was sent round by a messenger at 3 a.m. to the Prime Minister, who had just gone to sleep after writing a long letter to Nelson. 'I shall never forget', wrote Lord Malmesbury, 'the eloquent manner in which he described his conflicting feelings when roused in the night to read Collingwood's despatches. Pitt observed that he had been called up at various hours in his eventful life by the arrival of news of various hues; but that whether good or bad he could always lay his head on his pillow and sink into a sound sleep again. On *this occasion*, however, the great event announced brought with it so much to weep over, as well as to rejoice at, that he could not calm his thoughts, but at length got up, though it was three in the morning'.

An Admiralty messenger arrived at Windsor Castle at 6.30 a.m. with the news for the King, who on hearing of Nelson's death 'was so deeply affected that a profound silence of nearly five minutes ensued before he could give utterance to his feelings'. The Queen called the weeping princesses round her and read Collingwood's despatch to them. 'The whole Royal group shed tears to the memory of Lord Nelson.'

The Duke of York arrived at the Castle 'to congratulate Their Majesties on the victory and to condole with them on the heavy and great loss by which it had been purchased'. The Royal Family then went to St George's Chapel, 'to return thanks to Almighty God to the success of His Majesty's arms', and at one o'clock the Staffordshire Militia marched to the Little Park, where 'they fired three volleys in honour of the great event'.

Back in London a great deal of work had already been done by the time the Second Secretary to the Board, Sir John Barrow, arrived at the Admiralty. 'Never can I forget the shock I received, on opening the Board Room door . . . when Marsden called out—"Glorious news! The most glorious victory our brave Navy ever achieved—but Nelson is dead!"' he wrote.

Despite the fog—which had also delayed Captain Sykes, of the *Nautilus*, who arrived later in the day—rumours of Nelson's great victory and of his death spread across London like wildfire. The Park and Tower guns boomed out at ten o'clock, while the *London Gazette*'s compositors worked hurriedly to set up Collingwood's despatch in type and rush out the *Gazette Extraordinary*. As soon as it was printed, three thousand copies were sped to Yarmouth by coach and loaded aboard a fast cutter, which immediately set sail with a fair wind to take the news to the Continent. The Government were well aware of the propaganda value of the victory.

'Good heavens! What news!' wrote Lady Bessborough to Lord Granville Leveson-Gower. 'How glorious if it was not so cruelly damp'd by Nelson's death. How truly he has accomplish'd his prediction that when they meet it must be to extermination. To a man like him he could not have pick'd a finer close to such a life. But what an irreparable loss to England! . . . Do you know, G., it makes me feel almost as much envy as compassion; I think I should like to die so. Think of being mourned by a whole nation, and having my name carried down with gratitude and praise to the latest generations.'

Crowds besieged the newspaper offices, clamouring for news: not news of the victory, but to discover whether it was true that Nelson, the man they had huzza'd so recently, was dead. 'The scene at the Admiralty,' reported Lady Bessborough, 'was quite affecting—crowds of people, chiefly women, enquiring for husbands, brothers, children. . . .'

The *Gazette Extraordinary* was not on sale until late afternoon, but by then shop windows had been draped with hurriedly purchased purple cloth. Within a few hours, 'almost everybody wears a black crape [*sic*] scarf or cockade with "Nelson" written on it—this is almost general high and low.'

That evening 'the Metropolis was very generally and brilliantly illuminated on the occasion; yet there was a damp upon the public spirit, which it was impossible to overcome. Even many of the devices and transparencies indicated that the loss of Lord Nelson was more lamented than the victory was rejoiced at', reported the *Naval Chronicle*. And Lady Elizabeth Harvey, writing to her son in America, said that illuminations were begun but discontinued, 'the people being unable to rejoice'. Later she wrote: 'As we came away [from the Admiralty] there was a vast rush of people, but all silent, or a murmur of respect and sorrow; some of the common people saying, "It is bad news if Nelson is killed", yet they knew twenty ships had been taken.'

The theatres quickly added their tribute. That same evening at Drury Lane, after the performance of *The Siege of Belgrade*,

the actors sang 'Rule Britannia', and were followed by Mr
Wroughton, the acting manager, who recited:

'Is there a man who this great triumph hears
And with his transports does not mingle tears?
For, whilst Britannia's Flag victorious flies,
Who can repress his grief when *Nelson* dies?'

Those lines, and several more, had been written that afternoon
by Mr Cumberland, 'a veteran favourite of the Muses', and, said
the *Naval Chronicle*, 'this simple yet elegant address, which spoke
the genuine language of the heart, was delivered by Mr Wroughton
with that propriety, pathos and energy, which can never fail of
making a powerful impression'.

At Covent Garden the stage manager had worked even harder.
After the nightly performance of the comedy *She Wou'd and She
Wou'd Not* the curtain went up to show the British Fleet riding
triumphantly, with a group of naval officers and seamen at the
front of the stage in attitude of admiration. 'Suddenly a medallion
descended, representing a half-length of the Hero of the Nile,
surrounded by rays of glory, and with these words at the bottom—
"Horatio Nelson". The effect was electrical and the house resounded with the loudest plaudits and acclamations.' The audience
was soon on its feet singing 'Rule Britannia', and the orchestra
then played the Dead March.

At Chester, when the city heard the news, the cathedral's bells
rang out first with joyful peals for the victory, and then alternated
with solemn tolling for Nelson; at Christ's Hospital the schoolboys
'lit the fireworks for the victory and then drank a little glass of
sherry for Lord Nelson in solemn silence'. Countess Brownlow,
then a child at school, fainted in horror, although she had never
seen Nelson. Army officers went on parade in full mourning and
with their colours and brightly polished band instruments 'draped
in crape ribbon'.

Off Elsinore, north of Copenhagen, all the ships anchored under
Kronborg Castle, Hamlet's legendary home, 'fired three dis-
charges in celebration of the victory off Cadiz. Immediately afterwards their flags were lowered and three-minute guns fired, on
account of the death of Lord Nelson'. At Kingston, in Jamaica, a
funeral pyre forty-seven feet high and forty-seven feet in breadth—
representing Nelson's age—was lit in forty-seven places at once by
the militia, and as it blazed a funeral oration was delivered by the

Governor, followed by the firing of forty-seven minute-guns and forty-seven rockets. In many ships of the Royal Navy hardened seamen broke down and wept openly when they heard the news.

At the Admiralty a messenger soon arrived from Windsor Castle with a letter for Marsden from the old King's private secretary, Colonel Taylor. 'However His Majesty rejoices at the signal success of his gallant fleet, he has not heard without expressions of deep regret the death of its valuable and distinguished commander; although he added that a life so replete with glory and marked by a rapid succession of such meritorious services and exertions, could not have ended more gloriously.' And Colonel Taylor added: 'I have not upon any occasion seen His Majesty more affected.' Four days later Taylor wrote again to Marsden, and a postscript said: 'The King is of opinion [*sic*] that the battle should be styled that of Trafalgar.' (See picture facing page 65.)

The women who did not know whether the great victory had also taken their loved ones behaved bravely. Lady Arden was worried about her son serving in the *Orion* in the battle, but her husband wrote she was 'full of hope that the *Orion* had not had less than her share in this glorious conflict! This was worthy of a Roman matron in Rome's best days'.

The wife of Captain Edward Codrington, who commanded the *Orion*, was startled by her maid coming into her room at Brighton and saying suddenly 'There has been a great action and Lord Nelson is dead.' A friend with her tried to get more news from Colonel Savery, then in waiting on the Prince Regent at Brighton. 'After *to me* ages of misery,' she later wrote to her husband, 'he returned with a very kind note with all the particulars the Prince had had: and all the officers names who had been wounded. Never did Heaven pour such balm into a distracted mind as this communication. For your glorious leader I grieve most sincerely; but for the safety and honour of my husband how can I picture to you my ecstasy and gratitude!!'

As an English refugee Betsey Fremantle had been evacuated from Italy by a British warship, the *Inconstant*, a few hours before Napoleon's troops arrived. She had fallen in love with the warship's captain, Thomas Fremantle, and married him. Now she wrote in her diary on November 7: 'I was much alarmed at *Nelly's ghastly* appearance immediately after breakfast, who came in to say Dudley had brought from Winslow the account that a most dreadful action had been fought off Cadiz, Nelson and several captains killed, and twenty ships were taken, I really felt undescribable misery until the arrival of the post, but was relieved from such a wretched state of anxious suspense by a letter from Lord Garlies, who congratulated me on Fremantle's safety and the conspicuous share he had in the victory. . . . In the midst of my delight to hear Fremantle had been preserved in this severe action, I could not help feeling greatly distressed for the fate of poor Nelson. . . . Regret at his death is more severely felt than joy at the destruction of the Combined Fleets.'

Betsey's sorrow at the Admiral's death was deep and genuine, for when she and the *Inconstant*'s captain had fallen in love on the way from Leghorn, Nelson and Lady Hamilton had been two of the witnesses at the wedding which soon followed in Naples.

Fanny, the wife from whom Nelson finally parted in 1801, had the news of her husband's death direct from Lord Barham. Although the First Lord was more than busy the day Collingwood's despatches arrived he found a few minutes to write to Lady Nelson. 'Madam,' his letter began, 'It is with the utmost concern that in the midst of victory I have to inform Your Ladyship of the death of your illustrious partner, Lord Viscount Nelson . . . it is the death he wished for and less to be regretted on his own account. . . .'

At Merton, the home Nelson had left for the Battle, his beloved Emma was grief-stricken, sending messages to her friends that she was very ill. Her lover and protector was dead. England would now turn its back on her.

Honours were soon awarded: three days after his despatches arrived, Collingwood was made a baron and promoted, while Nelson's brother, the Reverend William Nelson, within three days of hearing that he had inherited Nelson's barony, received an earldom.

[Later there was a Parliamentary grant of £120,000 to the Nelson family. Of this the new Earl received £90,000 to buy an estate to go with the title (another £9,000 was added later by Parliament) and Nelson's two sisters received £15,000 each. An income of £5,000 a year was granted to those who succeeded the title, and Nelson's widow received £2,000 a year.]

But Nelson's last wishes were ignored. In a codicil to his will he had detailed Emma's 'eminent services' to her King and country, and said 'could I have rewarded these services, I would not now call upon my Country, but as that has not been in my power, I leave Emma Hamilton therefore a legacy to my King and Country, that they will give her an ample provision to maintain her rank in life.'

There remained one other dearly loved person to be cared for —his daughter Horatia. 'I also leave to the beneficence of my Country my adopted daughter Horatia Nelson Thompson, and I desire she will use in future the name of Nelson only. These are the favours I ask of my King and Country at this moment when I am going to fight their Battle. . . .' But to the majority of the ruling class in England, Nelson and Lady Hamilton had committed almost the greatest sin of all—they had sinned openly; and Emma and Horatia were left to their own devices.[1]

[1] Lady Hamilton received private assistance, but was so badly in debt in 1807 that she had to sell Merton. Harried by creditors and twice arrested for debt, she fled to France where she drank excessively and died in misery, poverty and squalor in 1814. In 1822 Horatia married a parson, the Reverend Philip Ward, and had eight children.

3

JUMPING 'THE DITCH'

*'Now tell us all about the war,
And what they fought each other for.'*
—Southey

VERY FEW sea battles are merely haphazard clashes of opposing ships and seamen: the actual fighting is usually the final climax, the ultimate test of plans made and matured amid rapidly changing circumstances, with luck and weather intervening capriciously, favouring one side and then the other. For this reason the Battle of Trafalgar was not only the greatest sea victory ever won by British arms but the climax of the greatest campaign fought up to then in the whole of British history.

After a long and bitter struggle against France which had started in 1793, the Treaty of Amiens in 1802 brought a brief fourteen months of peace. During that time Napoleon swiftly tidied up after the war and the Revolution and started to get France's economic life running smoothly once again. He had every reason to be pleased with himself: victorious in his land battles against the best troops that Europe had up to then put in the field, he had also won in the diplomatic field, for under the terms of the Treaty his African, Indian and West Indian colonies were returned to him. But he made one big mistake, and this was to think that Britain's urgent and honest desire for peace was the subservient cringing of a defeated people. While Napoleon put all his efforts into filling his arsenals, forging more guns, building new and more powerful warships and restocking a France whose storehouses had been emptied by the British blockade, most of Britain sighed with relief and sat back to enjoy the peace.

True to form, the British Premier, Addington, halved the size of the Army, demobilized the Volunteers, and paid off more than sixty of the Royal Navy's hundred battleships. Worse than that, more than forty thousand trained seamen were discharged— veterans of Camperdown and Cape St Vincent, the Glorious First of June, the Nile, Copenhagen and the never-ceasing blockade through high summer and winter storms alike. Surplus war stores were sold to the highest bidders—and they were often French agents, who gleefully shipped them across the Channel, where Napoleon watched, waited and planned.

While the wealthier Britons flocked to France to sample once again its geographical, artistic and culinary delights, their coaches rattled and clattered through a land which was, without question, then the most powerful nation the world had ever seen—whose Navy and Army were still mobilized, biding their time and gathering their strength.

However, not every Briton was taken in by Napoleon's outwardly peaceful intentions. There was Richard Brinsley Sheridan, for instance, the Irish playwright who had exchanged pen for politics and brought his brilliant eloquence to bear as Member of Parliament for Stafford: he told the House that Napoleon's great ambition was to rule England. 'This is the first vision that breaks on the First Consul through the gleam of the morning,' he declared, 'this is his last prayer at night, to whatever deity he might address, whether to Jupiter or Mahomet, to the Goddess of Battles or to the Goddess of Reason.'

But Britain wanted peace so blindly and passionately that few heeded the warnings; even the great Earl St Vincent, at that time one of Britain's finest sailors, plunged headlong into the task of pruning the Royal Navy—although at the same time he succeeded in stopping many nefarious practices, particularly in the dockyards.

So peace there was throughout the length and the breadth of the British Isles. Betsey Fremantle stoically bore more children and wrote in her diary. 'Fremantle went with my three sisters to the Buckingham Ball, I stayed at home with my four brats . . . He has ordered a new carriage and a new gig prices £160 and £80 . . . Fremantle offered himself for election . . . Fremantle dined at Lord Nelson's, and met us in the evening at Sir Lionel Darrell's at Richmond where there is a very pleasant ball every Friday . . . Poor little Harry's humour is breaking out again violently. Mr Nagle calls it an inveterate species of the tetters, and will try something to cure them, he don't approve of bathing him in salt and water, which would throw the child in agonies. He really suffers very much and is a miserable little creature . . .'

Across the Channel, Napoleon reviewed his veteran troops in the Place du Carrousel while newly-arrived British tourists watched open-eyed before going to gaze in awe and admiration at the priceless paintings and statues in the Louvre; much of it, however, was plunder transported from pillaged palaces and castles, stately châteaux and galleries all over Europe. But as the First Consul, plainly dressed in a simple blue uniform, strode through his magnificent apartments in the Palais des Tuileries, past bowing footmen decked out in green and gold, he thought and planned and plotted new conquests; he was living, waking and praying even as Sheridan had said. He had conquered Europe, and it had seemed easy.

From being an insignificant but rebellious Corsican boy knowing scarcely a word of the French language, taciturn, shy and small in stature, born in an island where an insult could be answered only with a dagger and where overnight neighbours' quarrels became vendettas, he had gone to the Paris Cadets' School. After graduating and becoming an artillery subaltern he had then but a single dream—of freeing Corsica from the bondage of France. Now, amid the splendour of his home in the Tuileries, he had another dream—of conquering a world whose sun would rise and set over Paris.

Only one country apparently stood in his way—that damnable nation of shopkeepers across the Channel and their thrice-damned Navy. However much he might overrun Europe, defeating or double-crossing kings and princes, making promises and treaties he never intended to honour, wheedling where necessary or threatening with cold fury when wheedling failed—his great enemy was Britain. Placed by a geographical quirk so that she was the main gateway on the sea highway to Europe, Britain had stood firm behind her moat, safe up to now from his Grand Army. Her Navy was a net cast round his great continental conquests, preventing him from breaking out to sail down the trade routes of the world and conquer the lands at the end of them.

He cast greedy eyes towards the riches of the East: to India whose very name conjured up visions of wealth and splendour and to the great continents of America and Australia. Despite the beating which the French Fleet had taken from Nelson at the Nile, Napoleon's spies were once again hard at work in Egypt. The world, Napoleon thought, was a ripe fruit waiting for him to pluck. Indeed, this was true; but between him and the trees that bore it was a fence—the ships of the Royal Navy. They had to be destroyed before Napoleon could regain and extend France's colonial greatness to make Paris the centre of the world, a city to which kings and princes, queens and envoys, premiers and pashas would come to pay him court, beg his favour and plead their cause.

Being a land animal, unable to understand sea power and its uses, he could visualize only one sure way in which France, the greatest of land powers, could challenge, fight and defeat the greatest of the maritime powers—by invasion. If the Royal Navy was a thousand-headed hydra (and he began to think it was) then its heart was London. Destroy that heart, he decided, and the heads would wither and die of their own accord.

However, because of the unpredictable British, war broke out again before Napoleon was ready, but he was quick to recover his stride. 'They want us to jump the ditch,' he declared, 'and we *will* jump it.' Napoleon, with all the zest, dynamism and fire in his belly that lifted him from an artillery subaltern to be the First Consul and the only contender for the title of Emperor of the World, set his nation to work: she was to produce the craft which would bridge the Channel and set the Grand Army ashore on the Kent coast for its triumphal march through the Garden of England to London.

Surrounded by sycophants who hardly dared to disagree on even the slightest tactical question, let alone the broad strategic concept, Napoleon received the reports of his naval officers. With few exceptions they thought the best type of craft to carry the Grand Army would be flat-bottomed and propelled by simple sails and oars (we can call them by the more modern term of landing craft). There would be four types—barges, sloops, pinnaces and gunboats.

Napoleon reckoned that his Grand Army—by now camped 150,000-strong on the cliffs above Boulogne and rechristened the 'Army of England'—need take only 6,000 horses with it. The rest of the cavalrymen would go over carrying their saddles and capture or commandeer horses in England. Within a few days of the war beginning once again, Napoleon had ordered several hundred landing craft to be built at Dunkirk and Cherbourg, while Boulogne was chosen as the point where they would be assembled. His plans changed frequently, but to begin with he calculated that he would need about 2,500 craft. As the invasion planning got under way, more craft were ordered to be built in twenty other Channel ports. The Minister of Marine, Admiral Denis Decrès, who at the age of forty-two had a great reputation for hard work, bore the brunt of Napoleon's broadside of orders and determined prodding: instructions arrived almost daily from the First Consul concerning the invasion flotillas.

France's pulse quickened under the influence of Napoleon's tremendous drive. In all the Channel ports, both large and small, the shipyards echoed to the rhythmic thud of shipwrights' adzes, the clatter of hammers and the hoarse cough of long rip-saws as they shaped great baulks of oak, spruce and pine into planks and frames, beams and masts, keels and yards. In the forests tall trees tumbled under the violent assaults of foresters' axes, and in the clearings large ovens glowed and turned wood into charcoal. In the arsenals skilled men mixed the charcoal with the appropriate portions of saltpetre and sulphur to make gunpowder, and in the foundries perspiring men worked day and night, fired with Napoleon's enthusiasm, casting cannon and round-shot, musket balls and grape-shot.

This massive plan for the invasion needed a great deal of money to put it into execution. The bankers of France, realizing that the defeat of England was a good proposition in which to invest, readily lent the First Consul twenty million francs. But this was by no means enough, and the wily Napoleon ordered his ministers to tackle all the wealthy people whose vanity and patriotism could be played on to produce the money to build warships which would be named after them. To Napoleon's surprise and disgust, the majority of the wealthy citizens of the Republic apparently saw little to appeal to their vanity or patriotism, and only a few paid up for the pleasure of having their names carved across the transoms of invasion craft.

Since the people appeared to be keen enough to defeat England as long as it did not affect their personal pockets, the Minister of the Interior was instructed to attempt to broach the coffers of cities and departments. He wrote to the chief magistrates the length and breadth of France, enclosing a price list, and adding that the craft would be distinguished by the names of the authorities paying for them. 'If each department by a rapid movement puts the vessels on the stocks,' he wrote, 'the French Army will soon go and dictate laws to the British Government.'

This time Napoleon was to be pleasantly surprised by the response: offers came flooding in—and they were handsome offers, too, as if the towns and departments had at last caught his hitherto uninfectious enthusiasm. Lyons offered a 100-gun battleship, and

Bordeaux an eighty-four. The department of Loiret paid for a 30-gun frigate and Seine-Inferieure put up a seventy-four, while Seine-et-Marne, not to be outdone, came along with a similar offer. Various battalions of the Army of England gave a day's pay; Paris, the city from which Napoleon proposed to rule the world, dipped deep into its coffers to buy a 120-gun battleship, while the Senate followed suit. Small towns bought barges or pinnaces to carry their names to victory.[1]

Napoleon and his wife Josephine went on a grand tour of the invasion ports in the summer of 1803. *The Times* reported that at Calais the First Consul arrived 'On a small, iron-grey horse of great beauty. He was preceded by about 300 infantry, and about 30 mamelukes formed a kind of semi-circle round him'.

He was not at all pleased with what he saw at Boulogne; and as if to display how the Royal Navy ruled the Channel, one of its frigates came close in to attack seven landing craft which were sailing into the port. The guns of Boulogne opened fire but their shot fell short, infuriating the First Consul, who had all the pride of an old artilleryman. According to a Briton living at Boulogne at the time, he 'became fidgety, uttered a few *sacrés*'—and then discovered the guns were accidentally being loaded with saluting charges. He promptly flew into a fury, tearing the epaulettes from the shoulder of the officer responsible and telling him he was no longer in the French Army.

By July 1803 Napoleon's plans allowed for this: the Dutch division, with its headquarters at Flushing, would consist of three hundred landing craft; the Right division, based on Ostend and Nieuport, would also have three hundred. The Centre division, at Dunkirk, Gravelines and Calais, would handle three hundred while the Left division, based on Wissant, Ambleteuse, Boulogne and Etaples, would have about 1,650 landing craft of various types and a thousand transports. That, at least, was Napoleon's great plan on paper, but when one came to examine the actual craft on moorings in the Channel ports the position was vastly different. The man who had to discover the sobering difference between the fleet of fantasy represented by the piles of orders and the fleet of reality represented by craft on the stocks, afloat or hauled out, was

[1] The three main types of landing craft were:

Type	Length	No. of crew	Armament	Troops
Barge	100 ft	38	24-pounders (12)	120
Sloop	70–80 ft	30	24-pounders (3)	120
Pinnace	60 ft	5	- -	55

Forfait, the Inspector-General of Flotillas. With the date that
Napoleon decreed the whole invasion force must be ready to sail
only six weeks away, Forfait had to report a deficit of a thousand
craft.

Apparently ignoring these unpalatable figures, Napoleon's blood
stayed hot with fever heat engendered by his desire to become
Emperor of the World, but the summer of 1803 gave way to
autumn. Although the adze hacked and sliced trunk and bough
into frames and timbers, the furnaces ran hot metal into the moulds
of great guns, and patriots gave francs and sous for the war chest

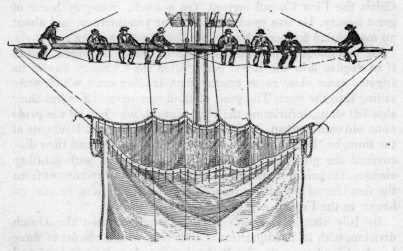

Hoisting up the foresail to bend it to the yard. The men in the centre are
standing on the footropes, or horses, with their arms over the yard

according to their means, September brought the vicious equi-
noctial gales in the Channel, and still Napoleon waited.

The Royal Navy continued to harry the landing craft as they
sailed from the shipyards to the assembly ports, and in desperation
Napoleon ordered batteries to be set up along the coast. Two stone
forts and a wooden one were built to cover Boulogne harbour from
the forays of the British, and soon 60,000 men were guarding the
beaches and giving covering fire to the landing craft as they
hugged the shore.

Slowly but reluctantly Napoleon began to see some of the snags
in his invasion plan. Originally he had reckoned on rowing his
heavily-laden invasion fleet across to the Kent beaches on one of

those summer days when the sea was calm and the Channel thick with fog. Then, he had reasoned, the British Fleet would be becalmed and unable to interfere, and he would not have to risk using his own Fleet as a covering force. But, probably under the influence of Decrès, he slowly changed his mind. As he stood in the little wooden hut which he had built on the cliffs overlooking the Channel at Boulogne, he realized that the ideal weather conditions he sought rarely occurred. His Fleet would have to be used to wrest control of the Channel from the Royal Navy—by battle or stratagem—for several hours. Yet off the French Atlantic ports, come sun or rain, gentle breeze or raging storm, the Royal Navy under Cornwallis was waiting. At the Texel, Admiral Keith kept guard, and off Toulon, in the Mediterranean, Nelson waited fretfully.

As Admiral Mahan wrote, 'Those far-distant, storm-beaten ships upon which the Grand Army never looked stood between it and the dominion of the world.'

4

MARTIAL MUDDLE

*'Their force is wonderful, great and strong, yet we
pluck their feathers by little and little. . .'*
—Lord Howard of Effingham, on the Armada, 1588

WHILE NAPOLEON drove the French nation even harder, England,
whose government had cut the Navy and Army so drastically that
its very freedom stood in mortal danger, viewed his invasion plans
with mixed feelings. Some people became alarmed and excited;
some refused to believe he would be so foolhardy. Others affected
not to worry whatever the Corsican proposed doing. At his home
at Dropmore Lord Granville wrote: 'You will find me here, very
peaceable, rolling my walks and watering my rhododendrons,
without any thought of the new possessor to whom Napoleon
might dispose them'.

Captain Fremantle managed to get a ship, and poor Betsey wrote:
'He really goes to sea quite *à contre cœur* as he was now so comfortably settled here, and I feel not a little anxiety at being left alone
with five such young children'. Later she added, 'I begin to be
half alarmed at the attempt to invade which is now daily expected
to take place, and these horrid French are such desperate wretches
that I quite dread their attack, tho' I trust it will prove unsuccessful.' Already that autumn she had been badly scared when she
went to visit her husband at Portsmouth. They had gone for a walk
on the walls of the town 'where we were not a little surprised at
seeing a great concourse of people on the beach, the yeomanry out,
guns frequently fired, signals made, the tellegraphes at work and
many sails in sight. On enquiring I was told it was supposed the
French were affecting a landing as numbers of the flat-bottom
boats were seen making towards the shore'. 'This created a very
great alarm,' wrote Betsey, but next day she was happy to hear
'that a fleet of coasters who had been becalmed at the back of the
Isle of Wight had occasioned our alarm.'

In the face of Napoleon's massive threat, Britain quickly roused
—and frightened—itself. To the uneducated but sturdy masses of
the people, rapidly arming themselves with whatever weapons they

could lay their hands on, from musket to pike and pitchfork, Napoleon appeared an ogre whose size, villainy and cruelty grew in the telling: he poisoned the sick to save food, he gloated over corpses scattered on the battlefields. Now he was variously building a massive bridge from Calais to Dover, across which his Army of England would march to the sound of fifes and drums and directed by the equivalent of military policemen stationed in balloons overhead; serving as a seaman in an English fishing smack off the South coast, tending his lines at night and searching the shore with his spy-glass by day; and digging a tunnel under the Channel, out of which he was to pop to stride across the Kentish meadows at the head of his huge army.

The Government under Addington tried to arm Britain overnight. Producing arms was the most difficult task, while there were three ways of finding the men to handle them—offering bounties to lure them into the regular Army, appealing to their patriotism to join the Volunteers, and balloting to raise a Militia. But one method tended to cancel the other out. For instance, any man picked by the ballot for the Militia—which was a home defence force—could pay someone else to take his place, and the price for substitutes soon went up to £30 a head. But the harassed and brass-lunged recruiting sergeant trying to drum up recruits for the regular Army could offer a bounty of only £7 12s. 6d. Most men preferred to take the £30 and serve only in Britain with the Militia rather than accept the recruiting sergeant's meagre bounty and risk being sent overseas in the regular Army. As a result, the Government soon discovered that, instead of raising a large regular Army which could defend Britain and then strike back at Napoleon on his own soil, they had landed themselves with a completely untrained 'Home Guard'.[1]

After a series of confused, overlapping and frequently contradictory orders, the Government finally decreed that 40,000 men were to be raised by ballot in Britain and 10,000 in Ireland. This was followed by a levy en masse which gave the old King powers to make each parish in the country provide (at their own expense) 'the necessary implements of warfare for the male inhabitants'. These unspecified implements would be kept locked up in the

---

[1] The regulations for Volunteers laid down that 'two shirts, a pair of shoes and stockings, combs, brushes (and a horseman what is necessary for the care of his horse) is all a soldier ought to carry'. He would have bread for four days and sixty rounds for his musket.

parish church under the watchful eye of the churchwarden. The men were to be trained for at least two hours every Sunday 'either before or after Divine Service'. The local constable was to attend—and be paid £5 a year out of the poor rate for doing so. The Volunteer who dodged a drill would be fined five shillings, and dodging it three times would land him in jail. If Army pensioners put the Volunteers through their paces on the village green they would get a wage 'not exceeding 2s. 6d. a day'—also out of the poor rate.

The Volunteers went to work with a will: armed with ancient fowling pieces, home-made pikes, pitchforks and muskets if they could be obtained, they drilled on the greens, marched along country lanes, drew up plans for the defence of their villages over pints of home-brewed ale, and waited hopefully for Boney's Army of England to appear so that they could give it a drubbing. Meadows were used as firing ranges and resounded to the rattle of musket and fowling pieces; local pensioners assumed a new importance in their villages and strutted and yelled at squire and yokel alike, marching and wheeling them in some semblance of martial formation.

Local tailors worked to make uniforms to the specifications of individual commanding officers, for each company could design its own. Men vied with each other to become the most efficient on parade. In the secrecy of their kitchens they practised musket drill with broomsticks and gave their wives the benefit of their new-found military knowledge by describing where Napoleon would land and how he would be beaten—by the Volunteers, of course. Naturally all this martial fervour affected women's fashions: one of the dresses which soon became the vogue was 'a short round dress of white muslin, with a rifle dress of dark-green velvet and a rifle hat to correspond'.

From the time the war began again in May 1803 until the Battle of Trafalgar was fought in October, 1805 the 'Corsican Ogre' dominated the lives of the people of Britain. When invasion failed to materialize in the summer or autumn of 1803 it was assumed that Napoleon would arrive in the summer of 1804. Having been made Lord Warden of the Cinque Ports in 1791, William Pitt—now out of office—was living at Walmer Castle on the Kentish shore opposite Calais. He stayed away from Parliament and, as Colonel of the Cinque Ports Volunteers, drilled his troops on the foreshore and kept an eye open for a sight of the enemy's invasion barges. Even Charles James Fox, previously so violently against the war and forever finding excuses for the French, joined the Chertsey Volunteers as a private soldier.

The Church became militant. Dr Watson, the Bishop of Llandaff, told the clergy of his diocese: 'You will not, I think, be guilty of a breach of Christian charity in the use of even harsh language when you explain to your congregations the cruelties which the French have used in every country they have invaded . . . they everywhere strip the poorest of everything they possess; they plunder their cottages, and they set them on fire when the plunder is exhausted; they torture the owners to discover their wealth, and they put them to death when they have none to discover; they violate females of all ages. . . . Can there be men in Great Britain of so base a temper, so maddened by malignity, so cankered by envy, so besotted by folly, so stupefied as to their own safety, as to abet the designs of such an enemy?'

And so from the pulpits the length and breadth of the country hitherto timorous parsons girded their loins, took deep breaths, and called the nation to arms. The Reverend Cornelius Miles took the thirty-sixth verse of the twenty-second chapter of St Luke— 'And he that hath no sword, let him sell his garment, and buy one'—for his stirring sermon, while at Colchester a prayer offered up for preservation from the invasion of Napoleon ended with: 'O Lord God, be pleased to change his wicked heart or stop his wicked breath.'

George Cruickshank, the famous cartoonist of the period, wrote: 'Every town was, in fact, a sort of garrison—in one place you might hear the tattoo of some youths learning to beat the drum, at another some march or national air being practised upon the fife, and every morning at five o'clock the bugle horn was sounded through the streets, to call the Volunteers to a two-hour drill, and the same again in the evening.'

But martial glory was not only the aim of every man in the country: the boys wanted it too. They banded themselves into juvenile regiments. Cruickshank's brother formed one and appointed himself its Colonel. 'We had our fife and drum', he wrote, 'our "colours" presented by our mammas and sisters who also assisted in making our accoutrements. We procured gun-stocks into which we fitted mop-sticks for barrels.' These sticks were polished with boot-black by the maids of the house to make them look like real metal. The boys held their parades and manœuvres in the no-man's-land between Bloomsbury Church and where Russell Square and Tavistock Square now stand.

In South-east England the invasion scares were frequent. Eastbourne, for instance, nestling under the lee of Beachy Head, was almost deserted in the autumn of 1803 after rumour selected it for Napoleon's landing place. A barracks for 10,000 men was hurriedly built on the beach, and another was built at Pevensey Bay nearby. Farmers had orders that if the French came they were to burn the crops and houses. In Wales, Mr James Nield was innocently enjoying a tour of the countryside round Radnor when some people thought they recognized him as Napoleon, and without waiting to see if his Army of England was at his heels they wanted to throw him into prison.

The Press loved the situation and spread itself in a rash of adjectives and adverbs. The *Bath Herald* declared: 'If you have qualities for a soldier you are imperiously called upon, by everything valuable to man, to be a soldier.' Later it was able to report: 'Sixteen honest sons of St Crispin have been taken down by their employer, Mr James Phipps [a bootmaker] of St Margaret's Buildings and entered as Volunteers—each man determined to sacrifice his all.'

As the months slipped by, so the nation's plans to beat an invasion became more effective. The Government stored enough flour in London to last the capital a fortnight, while the millers had enough for another three weeks. Beacons made of at least eight wagon-loads of faggots, brush and cordwood and several barrels of tar were set up all round the coasts, ready to be lit at night as a warning visible for at least three miles. By day wet hay was to be burned to make smoke signals. Inevitably some of the beacons were lit by accident or because of a false alarm. The poet Crabbe was staying at Aldeburgh, in Suffolk, when his son ran into the room and woke him with, 'Do not be alarmed, but the French are landing and the drum on the quay is beating to arms.' His father replied, 'Well, you and I can do no good, or we would be among them; we must wait upon the event.' With that he went back to sleep.

The way in which the Mortella Tower in Corsica held out in 1794 against British troops had created a great impression. The Tower had but three guns and only thirty-three soldiers manned it. Its effectiveness led the British Government to build seventy-four such towers round the south-eastern coast of England. Looking like inverted flower-pots, they were eighty feet high and cost more than £7,000 each to build. The forts, which were named Martello Towers (the English rendering of the original name), had two storeys, the lower acting as a magazine and the upper as accommodation. On the seaward side the brickwork was nine feet thick. Each mounted a swivel-gun or howitzer.[1]

The great flat area of Romney Marsh, stretching inland from Hythe, in Kent, to Rye, in Sussex, with its long and flat beaches, was reckoned to be an ideal place for Napoleon to land. A plan for flooding it by damming up the sluices was abandoned, so it was cut off by digging a deep canal along its inland edge. It would probably have been of no practical use had the French landed, but more than a century and a half later it still served as an excellent fishing ground for small boys.

Under Addington's vacillating leadership Britain stayed on the defensive, and through his Government's muddle and indecision the people lost what little trust they had in him. They wanted to fight back, and they felt that William Pitt was the only man who could give them the leadership they wanted. So, by circumstances we need not go into here, Pitt became Prime Minister on May 18, 1804—on the same day that Napoleon was declared the Emperor of France. Britain's leaders—or was it the Channel?—had so far saved the island from capture, yet to establish a lasting peace they had to rid themselves, and Europe, of Napoleon. Drained by a long and expensive war in which many mistakes had cost them dearly, they could only wait until the few remaining free states in Europe could be rallied into a Third Coalition; they could then be led united against Napoleon. Pitt was a sick man when he went to Downing Street—indeed death had already given him a warning tap on the shoulder—but he knew only too well that the sole hope for Britain lay in gaining allies on the Continent. He therefore began negotiations with young Alexander, the Czar of All the Russias, to begin the Third Coalition.

Meanwhile Napoleon had frequent and tantalizing glimpses of his objective. He liked to ride along the beaches round Calais and Boulogne, when the waters of the Channel lapped or raged as if mocking him. 'I have passed these three days amidst the camp

[1] Many of the Martello Towers still exist along the coasts of Kent and Sussex.

and the port,' he wrote, 'from the heights of Ambleteuse I have
seen the coast of England as one sees the Calvary from the
Tuileries. One could distinguish the houses and the bustle. It is
a ditch that shall be leaped when one is daring enough to try.'

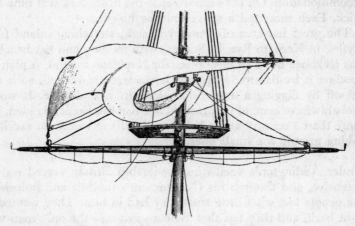

Clewing up a topsail to take in a third reef

5

THE NAVIES

'If they are kept off the sea by our superior strength, their want of practice will make them unskilful and their want of skill, timid.'

—Pericles

IN SPITE of Atlantic storm, the Royal Navy had blockaded Brest and Rochefort, and despite Mediterranean mistral it had blockaded Toulon.[1] While its ships tacked and wore in every sort of weather, beating up close to the entrance of the harbours when the wind was off-shore and the enemy could sail, and clawing off-shore when the wind came from seaward, the sweepings of the jails were transformed into hardened seamen.

But the French Navy, its ships bottled up in harbours, sailed only in men's memories, across the wine-soaked tables in the *bistros*. In the previous chapters we have had a glimpse of how Napoleon prepared for the last great thrust that would make him Emperor of All the World, and how he hesitated before 'The Ditch'. We have seen how the people of England, blundering yet brave, slow to anger but terrible when their wrath was roused, had left their mansions and cottages, farmhouses and crofts, to drill furiously on town squares and village greens, determined to sell their lives dearly when Napoleon arrived.[2] Now we can turn to the opposing navies and see the human and material problems facing each of them before the great battle on October 21, 1805.

The greatest defeat suffered by the French Navy up to the eve of Trafalgar had been at the hands of its own people. While a King sat on the throne of France, service as an officer in the French Navy had been one of the most aristocratic of professions, but during the Revolution which dragged Louis XVI from the throne to the guillotine, Paris had rung to Danton's impassioned

[1] It is worth noting that 'blockade' is not the correct word to use: Nelson waited off Toulon, for instance, in the hope that the enemy would come out and fight, giving him an opportunity of destroying it.

[2] More than a century and a quarter later Winston Churchill, the Premier of the day, had an appropriate slogan ready should Hitler's invasion have taken place—'You can always take one with you'.

cries in the Champs de Mars. It had also rung to the screams of hundreds of aristocrats—or any person that looked like one—being marched off to jail or to meet the hooded executioner. And while a young Corsican artillery captain named Bonaparte watched the mob in Paris worship the red cap of liberty as the symbol of its new-found freedom, the Revolutionaries had started to democratize the French Navy, after their own crude and short-sighted fashion. Almost every officer, from admiral to the most junior *ensign de vaisseau* who had the taint of blue blood in his veins, was arrested and flung into jail or forced to flee. Despite the invaluable experience and skill they had, many of them were later dragged from their dark cells into the blinding sunlight and carried to town squares, where hastily erected guillotines rewarded their services with a mercifully quick death.

On board the ships the revolutionary cry of *Liberté*, *Fraternité et Egalité* had put the heaviest emphasis on *Egalité*, and the Revolutionary with the shrill voice and glib tongue held sway. When the *Patriote* and *Entreprenante* (the latter shortly to be captured by the British and later used at Trafalgar) sailed into Brest from Toulon, all their officers had been arrested in the name of the Committee for Public Safety and flung into jail. The officers of the *Apollon* were less fortunate when they brought their ship into Rochefort: Citizen Hugues, 'an excellent Jacobin, whose *civisme* and activity were of the desirable degree', denounced them and they were led from the quarter-deck to the town square, and once again the guillotine's sharp blade flashed in its sudden downward drop as it did its swift work of purifying the post-Revolution Navy.

In the place of the 'aristos' had come men whose single-minded devotion to the Revolution far outweighed their professional abilities as seamen: surviving junior lieutenants with the correct political outlook had become captains almost overnight; captains of small merchantmen were given great ships of the line to command; ratings were made into officers on the strength of their Jacobinism. And quite inevitably discipline had vanished: any attempts by newly-appointed officers to enforce it put them in peril of being denounced by Citizen Hugues and his numerous colleagues. The seamen and the revolutionary committees ashore found their new freedom more heady than the strongest draught of cognac, but it certainly gave them no stomach for going to sea.

When Napoleon had lifted himself by his boot-straps to power he saw the reason for the Navy's weakness and restored some of the surviving 'aristos' to high commands, but those he chose were, for the most part, of an inferior breed when compared to their equivalents in the Royal Navy, which sent its would-be officers to sea at the age of twelve or thirteen and kept them there. Much of the fighting spirit was thus driven out of the French Navy by its own people. The names of ships—names proudly borne for centuries—were changed; old emblems of the Fleet were destroyed, and in place of discipline, tradition and experience, the red cap of liberty was unceremoniously placed on the quarter-deck.

The French Navy's position had only slightly improved when nineteen of its ships, manned by more than 11,000 men, were attacked while at anchor in Aboukir Bay in 1798 by a British Fleet of fourteen ships, manned by just over 8,000 men. By midnight, when the Battle of the Nile had ended, nine of the French ships had been captured, two more destroyed, and 9,830 men killed, wounded or taken prisoner. Napoleon's Army in Egypt was thus isolated and doomed to failure, and the French Navy suffered a blow to its self-confidence from which, under Napoleon, it was not to recover.

Many years later when sadder, defeated, and perhaps wiser, Napoleon, while he was in exile at St Helena, said that he had been unable to find a man sufficiently strong to raise the character of the French Navy. 'There is in the Navy a peculiarity,' he declared, 'a technicality that impeded all my conceptions. If I proposed a new idea, immediately Ganteaume [who commanded the blockaded squadron at Brest] and the whole Marine Department, were against me. "Sire, that cannot be." "Why not?" "Sire, the winds do not admit of it." Then objections were started respecting calms and currents, and I was obliged to stop short.' Hitler, just a century and a quarter later, also blamed the Navy for not performing the miracles that his own orders precluded.[1]

Yet it was not only the leadership problem at all levels which bedevilled Napoleon's efforts. The dockyards were centres of inefficiency, short of everything needed to make them function. There were not enough shipwrights, carpenters, seamen and soldiers for the ships or the forts and dockyards. The mountings

[1] After an abortive action on New Year's Eve, 1942, Hitler flew into a fury and paid off every ship larger than a destroyer. Yet the defeat had been due to his own cautionary orders and a complete lack of understanding of naval strategy. See the author's *73 North* (Weidenfeld & Nicolson, 1958).

of the guns in the forts protecting the dockyards and harbours were rotten and the guns themselves were unfit to be used. Soldiers had to be drafted in to man the ships, and the seamen were deserting. As will be seen later, Nelson was well aware of the quality of the enemy ships and seamen he had to fight, for the Spanish Fleet was in no better shape than the French.

Nevertheless it would be very wrong to assume that the Royal Navy at the time of Trafalgar was faultless, although it is a common assumption that because the victory was so overwhelming the Navy must have been in almost perfect shape. There was considerable corruption in the dockyards (a former First Lord of the Admiralty was charged the year after Trafalgar with malversation) and our warships were, for the most part, not nearly as well designed as all their French and Spanish counterparts. They were generally slower, could not sail as close to the wind, and were not so weatherly. The seamen manning the ships were seldom paid the wages due to them and the press-gangs which combed the countryside were little better than kidnappers covered by laxly interpreted laws.

The Navy Estimates[1] for 1805 proposed 'that 120,000 men be employed for the sea service, including 30,000 Royal Marines'. Of actual battleships, the Royal Navy had a total on paper of 181 —this being made up from twenty-six building or ordered, thirty-nine on harbour service, thirty-three 'in ordinary' (i.e. officially ready for fitting out, but usually in need of repairs costing nearly as much as rebuilding them) and eighty-three in commission. Among the eighty-three were included ships such as Nelson described in a letter to the Prime Minister only three months after the war had started again. Of his fleet, only four could keep the sea in winter, he said. Of seven others 'it is not a storeship a week which could keep them in repair.'

That autumn of 1803 he wrote, 'I bear up for every gale. I must not, in our present state, quarrel with the north-westers—with crazy masts and no port or spars near us. Indeed, on the whole Mediterranean station there is not a topmast for a seventy-four.'

At the beginning of December he was writing to Sir Evan Nepean, then Secretary to the Board, about the *Excellent*, enclosing

[1] The Estimate was for just over £15 million and included £2,886,000 for wages, £2,964,000 for victualling, and £582,000 for the upkeep of prisoners-of-war confined in hulks.

a survey report on the main and mizenmast rigging. 'It is to be lamented that a ship so recently from England, and coming direct abroad from a King's Yard, should have sailed in such a state; the Master-Attendant at Portsmouth must either have been blind to the situation of the rigging, or not have given himself trouble to discover its miserable state.'

Since the ships of the Royal Navy had to stay at sea almost continuously to contain Napoleon's fleet, much of the damage to the ships was 'fair wear and tear', but much of it was not. There was corruption everywhere in every service. When a firm of London copper merchants was condemned for having naval stores—copper nails marked with broad arrows—the Attorney-General said the jury 'would hear with astonishment, but it was a fact capable of the strictest proof, that the depredations upon the King's naval stores did not annually amount to less than £500,000.'[1] The *Naval Chronicle* estimated that the losses in the war up to 1802 'in consequence of the peculation or negligence of its servants in the naval departments' amounted to £20 millions.

At Portsmouth it was discovered that John Freeborne, the foreman of the labourers, and two other men, kept hogs in the warehouses and fed them with 'the King's serviceable biscuits'. The same trio also stole planks, spars, staves and barrels, which were sold at a shop which Freeborne kept in Portsmouth. When a commission checked the accounts some time before Freeborne was discovered, it was found that the dockyard was short of 278,042 pounds of bread, 11,162 pieces of beef, 4,649 pieces of pork, 3,746 pounds of flour and 2,798 pounds of suet, 'besides considerable deficiencies in other species of victualling stores'. A report by the same commission twenty years later showed no improvement.

This type of corruption was partly due to the natural dishonesty which spread through every branch of what would now be called the Civil Service; but perhaps most of the blame must be put on the men in authority—up to and including Ministers of the Crown—who, as rewards for votes in Parliament or the exercise of some favours or 'interest', gave unqualified and unscrupulous men jobs in various departments. The pay was poor, but there were plenty of opportunities for fraud which were exploited to the full.[2] The net effect of this was that many of the

[1] Equal to more than a sixth of the Navy's wage bill in 1805.

[2] Lord Melville was impeached for alleged misappropriation of public money during his term as Treasurer of the Navy.

ships which went out to fight the enemy and keep England free from invasion sailed from the dockyards incompletely repaired or equipped so that the dishonest could flourish. Twelve days after Nelson wrote home from the Mediterranean about the dreadful condition of the *Excellent*, Collingwood wrote from the Channel saying that the *Venerable*'s condition was so bad that 'we have been sailing for the last six months with only a sheet of copper between us and eternity.' However, much of the rot so frequently discovered in the ships was due to the methods of building and the types and condition of wood used.

Most of the King's ships were built at Deptford and Woolwich on the Thames, at Chatham on the Medway, and at Plymouth. But there were other yards, often privately owned. One was at Buckler's Hard, a small and picturesque village three miles from Beaulieu on the west branch of the Beaulieu River, which flows into the Solent. Three of the British ships fighting at Trafalgar were built there. As the second Lord Montagu of Beaulieu wrote, the yard 'helped in no small degree to lay the foundations of our Empire.'

In the 1740s John, the second Duke of Montagu (not to be confused with the second Lord Montagu) was looking for a suitable place to create and encourage local industries, and Buckler's Hard (originally called Buckle's Hard, probably after the local family of Buckle, who lived there for generations) was, with its hard gravel foreshore (The Hard) an ideal place. The Duke's manor at Beaulieu had a great number of oak trees growing on it, and there was an ironworks—where the great forge hammer was worked by a water-wheel—at Sowley Pond only four miles away. And thanks to a legacy from the Abbots of Beaulieu, the Manor enjoyed all the privileges of the Cinque Ports as a free harbour.

The small shipbuilding firm of Wyatt & Company, then at Bursledon, accepted the Duke's offer and moved their business to Buckler's Hard in 1743, bringing with them their overseer, Henry Adams. While houses were built for employees, 'ways'— strongly built ramps leading down into the water—were constructed, and a kiln for boiling wood erected. Very soon great oaks on the Beaulieu estate toppled under the woodmen's axes, startling the herons and swans abounding along the muddy edge of the river. The branches were lopped and teams of horses dragged the trunks to the Hard. Here they were cut into planks and left to season in great stacks between the two rows of houses

Nelson leaves England for the last time, boarding his barge at Southsea to join the *Victory. From the painting by Gow*

Captain Lucas, commanding the French *Redoutable*

Rear-Admiral Magon

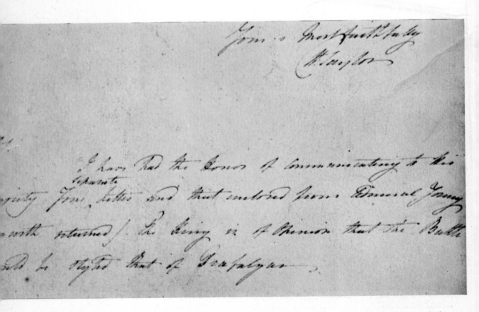

Part of a letter written by the King's secretary to William Marsden, Secretary of the Admiralty. The last few words read: 'The King is of opinion that the Battle should be styled that of Trafalgar'. (The original letter is in the possession of C. Marsden, Esq.)

which were then being built.[1] Wyatt's soon had their first order, and over the years the orders were for larger vessels, until they were commissioned to build a 64-gun ship. A cradle on which the hull would rest was constructed; then long sections of elm were put down to form the keel, or backbone, of the new vessel. On this backbone were built the ribs—each made up of several pieces of wood called futtocks. Because these were curved, like ribs of a skeleton, trees of the right shape had to be found. For the smaller and thinner pieces, the wood could be put into the kiln and boiled until it became pliable enough to be bent to shape.

So the fast-growing little village nestling among the trees, beside the quietly ebbing and flowing water of the river, rang to the sound of the saw and the adze—a tool used for shaping wood and looking like a heavy, short-handled hoe with a very sharp edge. Quickly the ship took shape on the slipway. The hull planks were clenched to the frames and timbers by copper nails and bolts or wooden treenails, and then the caulkers got to work hammering twists of cotton into the gaps between the planks. Finally, on April 10, 1781, the *Salisbury and Winchester Journal* reported, 'There was launched at Buckler's Hard the *Agamemnon*, a fine 64-gun ship, built by Mr Adams of that place.' After the launching she was towed round to Portsmouth and entered a dry dock to have her hull copper-sheathed. A ship's great enemy—particularly in a warm climate—were the tiny little teredo worms which bored into the hull and then, making thousands of tunnels up and down the lengths of the planks, reduced them to mere honeycombs. But the teredo was powerless against the thin sheets of copper.

Twelve years after the *Agamemnon* was commissioned a young Captain Nelson, after spending five years unemployed 'on the beach', was appointed to her. There was no prouder man in the Navy. He wrote to his parson brother, 'My ship is, without exception, the finest sixty-four in the Service, and has the character of sailing most remarkably well.'

The years slipped by, and although the map of Europe changed at the hands of Napoleon, Buckler's Hard remained much the same: Henry Adams lived in the master-builder's house; timber was stacked high in the street and the village kept busy. Nineteen years after the *Agamemnon* was built Adams supervised the laying down of the keel of a frigate for the Royal Navy. She was the

[1] This is the reason why the street is so wide today. The houses are still inhabited.

c

Euryalus, due to become, as a result of Trafalgar, perhaps the most famous frigate of all time. It took fifteen months to build her. Most of the oak came from the Forest of Dean, in Gloucestershire, and the New Forest, and she cost £15,568. But before she was completed Henry Adams had another order—the biggest yet. It was for a 74-gun ship, to be called the *Swiftsure*, third of the Buckler's Hard ships which was to be at Trafalgar. By the time she was completed two thousand great oaks had been used in her construction, along with a hundred tons of wrought ironwork from Sowley Pond, and thirty tons of copper nails and bolts. When he finished his task of building the *Swiftsure*, which took thirty months, Henry Adams was ninety-one; he had only one year more to live.

Yet for all the romance in the building of the ships which made the Royal Navy the greatest maritime force the world had known, there were many bad constructional practices which meant that the wood started to rot even before the ships had been launched. At least one great three-decker was condemned within a year of being launched. The timber used to build the ships in the yards of England should have been seasoned for a year or more, but all too often it was used green, making it more prone to rot quickly. To make matters worse, the ships were built in the open air and it was the custom to let the vessel stand exposed 'for a twelvemonth or a little more' before the deck and hull planking was put in place. It was not unusual to have the whole frame green with the growing spores of rot before planking-up started.

At this time the French and Spanish warships were far better designed than the British. Some of the fastest ships in service with the Royal Navy were, ironically enough, those captured from the enemy. The *Tonnant*, which kept her name although she had her Tricolour changed for the British ensign, was 'the finest two-decker ever seen in the Royal Navy', and the *Egyptienne*, captured in 1800, 'the finest ship on one deck we ever had'. The reason for this state of affairs is not hard to find: the French were imaginative in their approach to ship designing. Some of the country's finest brains drew up the lines for them, or shaped them in model form, striving for three main and often (from the naval architect's point of view) opposing characteristics. They aimed at producing a fast ship which must have fine lines and a long and narrow-beamed hull. It must carry a large number of guns, requiring a hull with plenty of beam and rising high out of the water. Finally the ship must point high (i.e. sail close to the wind); this called for a long and low hull but with plenty of beam and sufficient stability to carry a lot of sail.

In Spain an Irishman named Mullins, who as a master-shipwright was a genius, improved the Spanish Navy's warships considerably. Only in Britain did conservative methods mean that the shipyards continued to build badly designed ships which were frequently slow, difficult to manœuvre and not particularly good in heavy weather. It was a common saying that our ships were built by the mile and cut off as required. Naval officers were usually very free in their praise of the French ships, but the constructors failed to learn anything from the prizes.

In view of this, it should seem strange that the Royal Navy was so successful in battle. The answer is that—apart from the quality and experience of the officers and men compared with the French and Spanish—the British gunnery was superb, and in addition they had plenty of carronades—short-barrelled guns, rather like a mortar, which had a very big bore. They received their name from the Carron Company, who made them. They were easily handled and very destructive at short range. 'In this war,' wrote Napoleon, 'the English have been the first to use carronades, and everywhere they have done us great harm.' Later he wrote to Decrès: 'For God's sake ship me some more carronades.'

Battles were fought at close quarters: ranges varied from a few hundred yards to a few feet, ships sometimes being lashed together or locked by their rigging. This reduced warfare, once the opposing fleets had closed with each other, to a battle of broadsides, and the ships which could fire the fastest generally won. Because of their training this was usually achieved by the British.

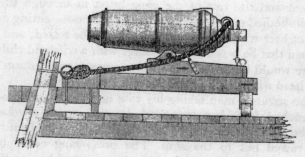

A carronade, showing the slide and a section of the deck and bulwark

6

SALT-PORK DAYS

*'The man who wants to be fully employed should procure a
ship, or a woman, for no two things produce more trouble.'*
—Plautus

MANNING the great ships of the Royal Navy (a three-decker
needed some 850 officers and men) was always a great problem,
especially in wartime when there were rival claims from the
mercantile marine—in which discipline was much less harsh and
the pay higher—and the Army. Some of the seamen had joined
as boys and stayed in the Navy because they knew no other life
or were too closely watched to escape, but many of the men were
pressed. The impressment of seamen is believed to date back to
King John—long before the days when England had a regular
royal fleet.

By law the whole of the seafaring population of Britain was
liable to serve the King at sea, and if a man was given an imprest
or advance payment by a King's agent—'taking the King's
shilling'—he had to serve. In practice this meant that a captain
short of crew—and captains were always in this unhappy state—
would send out a dozen or so strong and reliable seamen under a
lieutenant as a press-gang. Rowing ashore, usually after dark, and
armed with clubs and cutlasses, they would probably make their
way to an inn. Some men would guard the back door while the
lieutenant and the rest of the gang burst in through the front.
Any able-bodied man—whether a seafarer or not—sitting drinking
a glass of beer with his friends was liable to be seized; and even if
he argued that he was a farm-labourer with a wife and children to
keep, he would be carried off. Any argument could mean a bang
on the head with a club or the flat of a cutlass blade.

In the streets a man taking his wife or sweetheart home could
be wrenched from her arms and dragged away; a yokel tired
from the harvest field might be seized and bundled into a boat
to be rowed out to the ship. The press-gang could board a
merchantman and take off the best men; it could go to the local
assizes, and the prisoners in the jail would be turned over to it.

All debtors, before being sent to the Marshalsea or some other debtors' prison, were given the option of going to sea. An unrepealed law dating from the time of Queen Elizabeth decreed that 'rogues, vagabonds and sturdy beggars shall be, and are hereby directed to be taken up, conducted, and conveyed unto HM Service at sea'. Magistrates in courts near the seaports would send miscreants on board a warship with the request to the captain that they should not be allowed on shore again.[1]

Yet because jail-birds were pressed into the Royal Navy it must not be thought that the majority of these men were criminals in the modern sense of the word. In Nelson's day men were given extremely heavy sentences by judges and magistrates for even the most trivial offences—among them were the poacher, the petty pickpocket, the smuggler, the man who stole a few pence because he was hungry and could not get work, and the debtor. The laws of George III's reign allowed a man to be hanged for stealing a handkerchief from another's pocket, and death, jail or transportation followed automatically for offences which today would often result only in a small fine or probation.

So the fact that the jails were emptied to help man the King's ships does not mean that a constant stream of hardened criminals left dank stone cells to infect the men already serving in the Navy: instead, there was a stream of young men who, for the most part, had committed very minor offences against society. The agile young poacher—who usually had plenty of initiative and a light tread—frequently made a good topman; the deft pickpocket soon learned to turn a neat splice.

To many men serving long jail sentences for trivial offences the prospect of being pressed into the Navy was the prospect of being given comparative freedom, for the prisons were a disgrace to society, even by the standards of Nelson's day. At that time it was usual for twenty prisoners at Newgate to be kept for twenty-four hours a day in a cell measuring twenty feet by fifteen; nearly twenty years later the Inspectors of Prisons condemned Newgate as 'a monstrous place'. Certainly no seaman lived on board His Majesty's ships in such conditions.

The hard core of the Navy consisted of men who had served as seamen all their lives in warships, merchantmen or fishing craft. They were tough, skilled, rough and honest men, and at a time

[1] The pressing of allegedly British seamen from American ships was one of the main causes of the War of 1812 between Britain and America.

when the Royal Navy was desperate for recruits it would be wrong to think that even the hardened criminal brought on board in any way lowered the standards of the regular seamen: on the contrary, the seamen very quickly raised the standards of the criminal. The fact that a raw recruit had come on board thin and white-faced, verminous and hungry from one of His Majesty's jails, whence he had been sent for taking one of his squire's prime pheasants, mattered not at all to captain, bosun or seamen. What did matter was whether or not he would make a good seaman. The pickpocket who failed to break himself of his lightfingered habits quickly found that the seamen's own rough and ready justice helped him out and made him once again an honest man.

In addition, one must bear in mind that life in England in 1805 was, for the bulk of the population, hard and full of injustice. It is necessary to avoid falling into the trap of judging the conditions in the Navy, described in these pages, by the liberal standards of the welfare state. The seamen often found life hard, unpleasant and sometimes unjust; but hardness, unpleasantness and injustice were the common lot of seamen and landsmen alike. A captain might flog a seaman for a trifling offence; yet ashore a magistrate might condemn a man to death, jail for life or transportation for a comparable misdeed.

It should be mentioned that a man pressed into the Navy could, legally, appeal. The people and the courts were very much against impressment, and the naval officer knew that the courts would nearly always find against him should a pressed man have the knowledge and the time to appeal. As the naval officer could be prosecuted for wrongful impressment—and would get his knuckles rapped by the Admiralty as well—he nearly always gave up the man rather than face a court at all. However, a landsman pressed into a ship on the eve of sailing often had no time to exercise his constitutional right!

Once on board, the pressed men were required by regulations to be examined to see if they 'have any hurts or diseases which may render them unfit to serve in His Majesty's Navy'. Since there was always a desperate shortage of men, this regulation was not enforced very strictly, and certainly not more than the rule that only seafarers could be pressed. Having passed his perfunctory medical examination, the new recruit was then taken into the Navy.

On March 22, 1804, an Italian—one of many foreigners to serve on board the *Victory*—was sworn in as a member of the crew of Nelson's flagship. First of all he had to make and sign an attestation:

> I Gaetan Loyagalo, do make an oath that I am by trade a bricklayer, and to the best of my information and belief was born in Milan, and am entirely free from all engagements, and that I have no rupture nor was ever troubled with fits and that I am in no wise disabled by lameness or otherwise but have the perfect use of my limbs and that I have voluntarily enlisted myself to serve his Britannic Majesty King George the Third in his Royal Marine Forces during the present war under an agreement that I shall be discharged at the end of it and a passage free of expense to the Mediterranean.
>
> Witness present *C. W. Adair*, Captain, Inspecting Officer of Recruits for the Royal Marines
> As witness my hand this 22nd day of March 1804
> His
> *Gaetan* X *Loyagalo*
> Mark

That done, the new recruit then took the oath of allegiance to 'his Sovereign Lord King George the Third', promising to serve him faithfully 'in defence of his person, Crown and dignity against all his enemies and oppressors whatsoever'. Finally a certificate was drawn up, signed 'Sworn before me on board HMS *Victory* this twenty-second day of March 1804, *Nelson and Bronte*', which said:

> These are to certify that Gaetan Loyagalo aforesaid aged 27 years 5 feet 10 inches high sandy hair grey eyes freckeled complexion came before me and declared he had voluntarilly enlisted himself to serve his B. Majesty King George the Third in his Royal Marine Forces, he is therefore duly enlisted and the second and third Articles of War against mutiny and sedition are likewise read to him and he has taken the oath of fidelity mentioned in the said Articles of War . . .

So now Marine Loyagalo, handed his five guineas' bounty by Captain Adair, was taken to the purser, who issued him with the regulation suit of bedding, two checquered [*sic*] shirts and 'a red cloth coat, white cloth waistcoat and breeches, one shirt with one black stock, one pair of shoes, a hat'. The former bricklayer from Milan was now to be paid eightpence a day. For that he could be flogged to death or promoted, hanged or rewarded in the name of the King he had sworn to serve.

Once a man was on board a warship he never knew when he would again get ashore: it might be five or ten years before he was paid off, and all that time his pay would be accumulating—with deductions for clothes and tobacco—at the rate of 22s. 6d. a month if he was rated a landsman or 25s. 6d. for an ordinary seaman. But he would be lucky if he was paid off in cash—all too often he would be given tickets instead, and they were very difficult to cash. He would probably end up cashing them with some sharp rogue who would give him anything from a half to three-quarters of its face value.

With the crew on board at the beginning of a commission, the first lieutenant (the senior of the lieutenants and second-in-command) would sort them out and, with the captain, allocate the scores of jobs that had to be done continually, whether the ship was under way, in port or in action. The experienced seamen who were getting on in years were stationed on the fo'c'sle, to work at the anchors, bowsprit and fore-yards. Called fo'c'sle or sheet-anchor men, they were, after the bosun's mates and gunner's mates, among the most reliable in the ship. Then the topmen would be chosen. These were usually young and active, because they had the most dangerous job of all—working the sails above the lower yards, where one slip could mean a plunge to death scores of feet below. The topmen were divided into three divisions, one for each mast. Since a ship's smartness was reputedly shown by how quickly her topmen could set, furl or reef the sails and scramble down on deck again, every captain's eye was on them, and they were usually hurried along by blows from a bosun's mate's starter or colt—a length of knotted rope. Some captains arbitrarily flogged the last man down.

The third group selected by the first lieutenant was the after-guard—usually sneered at by the fo'c'sle and topmen. Their job was working the braces (the ropes which hauled the yards round to trim the sails), the spanker, mainsail and lower staysails. They kept the after part of the ship clean and when in action they worked at the guns or trimmed the sails.

The fourth and largest group were the waisters, so called because they were stationed in the waist, the midship section between the fo'c'sle and the quarter-deck. They handled the fore and main-sheets and kept the waist spotless. But because the waisters were generally a collection of landsmen and doltish seamen, they had plenty of other unskilled tasks such as looking after the pigs and sheep, pumping out the ship, and anything else the first lieutenant could devise.

The idlers formed the fifth group. They worked during the day but did not stand a watch at night, and included the butchers who slaughtered the livestock (and made sure there was plenty of swill on which to fatten them); the barbers who dressed the men's pigtails and tidied up the officers' wigs; the painters, the coopers who made and repaired the casks, the captain of the head, who looked after the crude lavatories, and the loblolly boys who helped the surgeon, and various others. Each man was issued with two hammocks, one being a spare. The hammocks were slung from the beams and each man was allowed a width of only fourteen inches. Slung side by side across the width of the ship, each slightly overlapped those forward and aft of it, like sardines in a tin. However, with the normal watch and watch system, every alternate hammock would be empty.

For meals the whole crew was divided up into messes consisting of up to eight men. Each mess sat at its own table slung from the deckhead between two guns. The table itself was normally kept hooked up between the beams overhead when not in use. Each mess would elect a cook whose job it was to collect the mess's provisions from the purser and take them along to the ship's cook in the galley, where they would be cooked—in water which was usually so bad that it was stagnant and stinking, its contents as interesting and lively as a village pond. Few people had stomachs strong enough to drink it, and while there was enough, men drank beer. This was, as Masefield describes it, 'small beer, of poor quality, not at all the sort of stuff to put the soul of three butchers into one weaver.' Every man was entitled to a gallon of beer a day, but when it ran out—as it usually did after a month at sea—the regulations laid down that instead he was to be issued with a pint of wine or half a pint of rum or brandy. If it had to be wine, then the sailors preferred white. Red was known as 'Black Strap', while the favourite white, the Spanish Mistela, was known affectionately as 'Miss Taylor'. When the wine had gone, the sailors had rum or brandy.

If there was a shortage of any particular item on board, something else was substituted according to a set scale. In addition to the alternatives to beer already mentioned, four pounds of flour, for instance, were rated equal to four pounds of beef.

On paper the food ration issued was generous—but much of it was bad. It was laid down that everyone serving in one of His Majesty's ships should get a daily ration according to a specified table which was in fact a weekly menu as well. Thus Tuesday and Saturday were salt-beef days, while Sunday and Thursday were for pork.[1] The meat would probably have been in salt for several years before it was eaten, by which time, says Masefield, 'it needed rather a magician than a cook to make it eatable. It was of a stony hardness, fibrous, shrunken, dark, gristly, and glistening with salt crystals . . . the salt pork was generally rather better than the beef, but the sailors could carve fancy articles, such as boxes, out of either meat. The flesh is said to have taken a good polish, like some close-grained wood.'

Usually at least half a seaman's meat ration was fat, bone or gristle. The oatmeal issued as a corrective to 'acid and costive humours' was called burgoo, or skillagolee, but under either name it was usually so rotten as to be almost uneatable and, after being cooked in ship's water, unbearable. Pea soup, issued on salt-pork days, was always a favourite meal; and another favourite among the men was Scotch coffee, which consisted of ship's biscuits burnt in the oven (thus killing and cooking the weevils) and then boiled in water until transformed into a thick liquid and finally sweetened with sugar. On Monday, Wednesday and Friday no meat was issued. The biscuits given to the men were invariably full of weevils—so much so, according to one source, that 'the most common custom was to leave the creatures to their quiet and to eat the biscuits at night, when the eye saw not and the tender heart was spared'. Altogether, it is not surprising that the men liked to chew tobacco. . . .

Every man in the crew had a series of jobs to do, depending on whether the ship was at anchor, under way or in action. He would be given a number when the ship commissioned—between one

---

[1] The total weekly ration for a seaman was: biscuits, 7 lbs; beer, 7 gallons; beef, 4 lbs; pork, 2 lbs; pease, 2 pints; oatmeal, 1½ pints; sugar, 6 ozs; butter, 6 ozs; cheese, 12 ozs, 'together with an allowance of vinegar not to exceed half a pint to each man'.

and five hundred and seventy if there were that many men in the crew. By looking at his number on the ship's 'General Quarters, Watch and Station Bill' he could see the tasks allocated to him. We can arbitrarily choose number eighty-eight in an 80-gun ship with five hundred and seventy in the crew (the Bill would vary from ship to ship, depending on the captain, but this particular one was used frequently). Our seaman would be a fore-topman and in the first part of the larboard watch (each of the two watches was divided into two parts) and the Bill would also tell him that at general quarters[1] he was a sponger at number two gun on the main-deck. When boarders were called for he would be in the second division and would be issued with a cutlass and pistol, but not a pike, tomahawk or musket. He was not a fireman or pumper. For furling and loosing sails he worked on the fore-topsail-yard. When the ship weighed anchor he would be down at the capstan. There were a dozen or more other jobs for him, and if he wanted to avoid having his ribs bruised by a bosun's mate's starter, he had to learn by heart what they were, so that he could go to his correct station in any eventuality.

Now for the day's routine—a Sunday. Once again it varied from ship to ship, but we will follow the one laid down to go with this particular watch bill. The starboard watch would have gone on deck at 8 p.m. the night before, and at midnight the bosun's mates would have gone to the hatchways and bellowed 'Larboard watch ahoy! Rouse out there, you sleepers!' To avoid the starters the men would roll smartly out of their hammocks, waking up on the way. Snatching up their clothes—if, in fact, they had undressed—they would head for the upper-deck, leaving the fetid atmosphere of the lower-deck to the starboard watch for the next four hours. At 4 a.m. the ungentle cries of the bosun's mates would rouse out the starboard watch after their brief respite, and they would rush on deck, instinctively side-stepping the starters, take off their shoes and roll up their trousers ready to holystone the deck. While some men rigged the pump, others would get out buckets and scrubbers and the more unfortunate would take up pieces of holystone—known as 'prayer books'. With the deck wetted and sand sprinkled over it, the men with holystones would go down on their knees and start scouring the sand into the deck, gradually getting it clean. Following behind them would be

[1] Known in the Royal Navy today as 'action stations'. The original phrase is still retained in the United States Navy.

scrubbers, washing and brushing the sand into the scuppers and over the side. Finally came the swabbers, drying the decks with their swabs.

While the decks were being cleaned, other men would be polishing up the brightwork with brick dust and rags, taking care to keep ahead of the scrubbers who would wash away the dust. As dark gave way to daylight, the look-outs on deck would be sent up aloft to the masthead; then at 6.45 a.m. the bosun's mates would cry 'All hands, up hammocks!' and each man would run down to the lower-deck to lash his hammock into the shape of a long sausage—with the straw mattress, familiarly known as a 'donkey's breakfast', and a couple of blankets inside—with the seven regulation turns of a lanyard.

'Muster and stow hammocks' came at 7 a.m., with all hands shouldering their hammocks and dashing up on deck to their respective divisions. There they would stow their hammocks in the nettings which formed a bulwark round the upper part of the ship, still under the watchful eyes of the bosun's mates, reinforced by quartermasters and midshipmen. Apart from keeping the lower-deck clear during the day, the hammock stowage served as a protection when in action, the solid banks of canvas helping to stop grapeshot and musket balls sweeping the decks. To protect the hammocks from the weather, long strips of canvas were placed over them and tucked well in. At 7.30 a.m. the upper-deck would be spotless, the brightwork gleaming, hammocks stowed, and the log hove over the side to determine the ship's speed and the result noted down on a slate. The idlers, who had also been called at 4 a.m., would be busy. The cook would have lit the fire in the galley and the abominable burgoo would be bubbling with all the smell and steam of a witch's brew, the gruel cooking alongside the maggots for whom it had previously provided such a nourishing home. In other pots the Scotch coffee would be coming to the boil, the stagnant water rousing itself to blend with the burnt biscuits and charred weevils and to provide a hot, if not exactly nourishing, drink for the seamen. The Marines would have been busy cleaning muskets, polishing cutlasses (three feet long and curved, with a basket handle), tomahawks, which were small axes with spikes sticking out from the back of the blade, and half-pikes—ash handles with steel tips.

At 8 a.m. came the welcome pipe of 'Hands to breakfast', and the men would troop down to their messes and rig the tables between the guns; when the mess cooks returned from the galley with the day's offering, they would spend the next half hour eating and reviling the cook.

At a few minutes before 10 a.m. the sweepers would make a last sally across the decks with their brooms; then at 10 a.m. precisely (9.30 on weekdays) all hands were called for divisions. The men would be newly shaved, their pigtails tidied, and smart in clean shirts; the Marines would be resplendent in their black, narrow-brimmed hats and red and white cockades, red tail-coats, spotless white breeches, buttoned-up gaiters and brown shoes and with their cross-belts newly pipeclayed.

The captain would inspect the men and then go round the whole ship, looking for a spot of grease on the deck, a trace of rust on a cannon, a speck of dirt on the cook's pots and pans. Some captains wore white gloves, so that an exploratory finger could always find if there was some dust at the back of a rack of half-pikes or behind a carronade slide. With the inspection over, the men were herded aft to the quarter-deck for Divine Service. There would be prayers, perhaps a couple of hymns helped along by the energetic sawings of a fiddler, and a short address. A good captain could learn a lot about the happiness or otherwise of his crew from the way they sang the hymns.

After church came the order to clear the decks and 'Up spirits'. A fifer would play some cheery tune like 'Nancy Dawson' and the master's mate would stand by at the tub to issue the Royal Navy's liquid happiness. Mess cooks would grab their tin flagons to collect the share for their mess. The issue at noon would be a gill of pure rum mixed with three gills of water. With this inside him —plus any more he could scrounge or which was due to him as a gambling debt—the sailor 'thought foul scorn of the boatswain's mate, and looked upon the world with charity'. If too many of his mates repaid their debts he might, before Sunday afternoon was very old, find it hard to lie on the deck between the guns without holding on.

After dinner, as the midday meal was called, the watch on deck again swept up, but the watch below was free to sleep—on the deck, for the hammocks were still in the nettings, but beer, 'Black Strap', 'Miss Taylor' or rum softened the planks. They could also play chequers or—if they found a quiet enough spot out of the way of authority—throw dice or play cards, both of which were forbidden, and hazard their tots of rum against the mathematical laws of chance and the watchful eyes of the bosun's mates.

At 5 p.m. (the exact time varied with the ship's latitude and was usually an hour before dusk) the hands would be piped to supper, the third and last meal of the day, when the tough ship's biscuits and lively cheese would be washed down with a second ration of beer, wine or grog. Half an hour later a drum would beat to quarters and the men would run to their stations for battle. Guns would be cast loose and the ship's officers would carry out a detailed inspection.

Evening quarters were a dangerous time for those who had hoarded their noon issue of liquor so that they could add it to the supper issue: the master-at-arms would cast an experienced eye over the assembled men, and any that swayed more than the ship's pitch and roll warranted, would provide material to be hauled, thick-headed and repentant, before the captain in the morning. On a weekday the men would exercise at the guns for half an hour after quarters, but on Sundays they were excused. As dusk fell the look-outs would be brought down from the mast-head and placed on deck, and at 8 p.m. 'Down hammocks' would be piped. The men would collect their hammocks from the nettings and get down to the lower-deck as fast as possible to sling them before 'Ship's company's fire and lights out' was piped ten minutes later.

The day had ended: it was, as far as the Navy was concerned, a day of rest. The watches would change in monotonous regularity. From 5 p.m. in the evening[1] the men would have nothing to eat until 8 a.m. the next morning. If there was rain or a heavy sea the water would probably drip through on to their hammocks. The great hawse-pipes, through which the anchor cables led, were at the forward end of their deck; in anything of a sea no plugs or oakum could stop the water getting in and sloshing back and forth along the deck, stirring up the livestock in the manger. The odours assaulting the nose on the lower-deck of a ship-of-the-line were an invisible maelstrom: to the reek from the manger, which in hot, rough weather, was like a farmyard midden, was added the stench of the bilges, of unwashed and perspiring humanity in unventilated quarters, and the pungent smell from wet clothing. It was in these conditions that men lived for years on end— spending a whole winter of Atlantic gales off Brest, or two years

---

[1] Times varied considerably with the ship's position.

at sea in the Mediterranean and Atlantic, as Nelson had just done, without setting foot on shore. (A three-page drawing of the *Victory* is given facing page 356.)

This was the prize paid by the seamen to ensure that, ashore at least, 'Britons never will be slaves'. Yet the life was not without its advantages: under the harsh discipline, leading an extremely active life, the criminal was usually turned into a good seaman. And if the seaman of England was harshly treated afloat, the plebeian of England fared little better ashore: he could be hanged for more than two hundred offences, ranging from murder to sheep-stealing. The farm hand 'living in' was paid about £10 a year; his brother serving at sea as an ordinary seaman received £5 a year more, for which he hazarded his life as regularly as the farm labourer had meals. Against that there was a life of excitement, some chance of prize money, comradeship—and the comforts of beer, rum or 'Miss Taylor'.

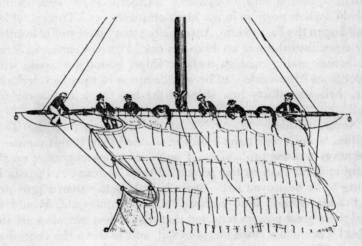

Reefing a topsail

7

NAPOLEON SNUBBED

'What fates impose, that men must needs abide;
It boots not to resist both wind and tide.'

—Shakespeare

AS CHURCH BELLS boomed out the twelfth stroke of midnight and men raised their glasses to toast the New Year of 1805, the future for Britain seemed like a long dark tunnel with no hint of its length and no sign of light at its end. Napoleon with his invasion fleet was apparently poised on the eastern flank of the Channel. Holland, Switzerland and North Italy were mere subject nations of France whilst Napoleon was threatening southern Italy—endangering Britain's whole position in the Mediterranean—and Turkey, which would open the East to him. Anticipating that Spain would eventually come into the war on France's side, Pitt had earlier ordered the home-coming Spanish treasure ships, bound for Spain with silver from Montevideo, to be seized. Spain in turn had declared war, bringing thirty-two ships-of-the-line to join Napoleon's fleet.

'Never, perhaps,' wrote Nelson to the Queen of the Two Sicilies, 'was Europe more critically situated than at this moment, and never was the probability of universal monarchy more nearly being realized than in the person of the Corsican . . . Prussia is trying to be destroyed last—Spain is little better than a province of France—Russia does nothing on the grand scale. Would to God these great powers reflected that the boldest measures are the safest! They allow small states to fall, and to serve the enormous power of France, without appearing to reflect that every Kingdom which is annexed to France makes their existence, as independent states, more precarious . . .'[1] Nelson was writing from his great strategic knowledge and insight, not because of a passing mood of depression, and in 1805, as in previous years, Britain's very existence depended on her control of the sea.

The great blockade of France's ports had begun in May 1803

[1] These sentiments were equally as true for the periods before and after the Second World War.

and had gone on ever since. Twenty-one battleships under Ganteaume were held in Brest by the ceaselessly watching ships of Admiral Cornwallis; five more battleships and five other warships under Missiessy were kept in Rochefort; fifteen Spanish battleships under Gravina were fitting out at Ferrol and Cadiz, and eleven more battleships and eight frigates, under Latouche Tréville and later Villeneuve, were penned in at Toulon by Nelson. Not that Nelson wanted them penned in: his great hope was that they would come out and fight. In the previous June he had written, 'Do not think I am tired of watching Mr Latouche Tréville. I have now taken up a method of making him angry. I have left Sir Richard Bickerton, with part of the fleet, twenty leagues from hence, and, with five of the line, am preventing him cutting capers, which he had done for some time past, off Cape Sicie . . . Some happy day I expect to see his eight [sic] sail which are in the Outer Road, come out . . .'.

Exactly a week after Nelson wrote that, the French admiral did in fact sail out of Toulon with eight battleships and six frigates. As Nelson said, they 'cut a caper off Sepet, and went in again. I was off, with five sail of the line, and brought to for his attack, although I did not believe that anything was meant serious, merely a gasconade'. That ended it as far as Nelson was concerned —until he saw Latouche Tréville's official report on the incident. Nelson, had, according to the French admiral, 'recalled his ship and his two frigates, which were among the islands, and bore away. I pursued him until night; he ran to the south-east.' Nelson was furious at this barefaced lie. To a friend he wrote: 'If any Englishman has believed for one moment the story, I may, to my friend, say without fear of being thought arrogant, that they do not deserve to have me serve them; but I have kept Monsieur Latouche's letter; if I take him, I shall either never see him, or, if I do, *make him eat* his letter.'

But, he was destined never to have the chance, for nine days later Latouche Tréville died. 'He is gone, and all his lies with him', reported Nelson, 'the French papers say he died in consequence of walking so often up to the signal post, upon Sepet, to watch us: I always pronounced that would be his death.'

Napoleon's moves and counter-moves towards the end of 1804 and at the beginning of 1805 are an essential part of the campaign and battle of Trafalgar. On December 2, 1804, Napoleon and

Josephine were crowned in the beautiful cathedral of Notre Dame—or rather, Napoleon lifted the golden laurel wreath before the Pope could reach it, and placed it on his own head. Napoleon was now at the height of his power. Professor Fournier, the Austrian historian and one of the most acute of Napoleon's biographers, wrote that 'Instead of the enthusiasm for Liberty which had inspired the armies of the Revolution, the soldiers were now possessed by the love of glory and a desire for distinguishing themselves and receiving distinctions. And the Emperor . . . began to talk to them of the Empire of Europe.' Fournier adds: 'In these schemes they seconded him willingly, and so the Republican army became Imperialist, and such it loyally remained as long as the *petit caporal* had even a gleam of victory.'

Despite the cheers of his massed armies, the flattery of his generals and admirals, and the glitter of his court at the vast and beautiful Palais des Tuileries (shortly after Napoleon moved into the Palais it was noted that his court was 'a more brilliant one perhaps than that of the unfortunate Louis XVI'), he still had to face the problem of England. He appears not to have been working to any long-term plan: this was because he was one of the greatest —and at first successful—opportunists in history. His Army of England, as we have seen, had been constantly drilling with its landing craft, and France was waiting for the master-stroke. Yet Napoleon hesitated once again. He had delayed in 1803 and 1804. What had he in mind for 1805?

He had spent eighteen months and millions of francs in preparing for the great *descente* for which all France waited. But now, at the beginning of 1805, was he looking for something which would avoid the necessity of him giving the possibly fatal order for the invasion to begin? A war on the Continent, for instance? Certainly this would give him a loophole. Austria, with the backing of Russia, was becoming restive, and his spies had already warned him that England was negotiating with Russia. His situation on the Continent, he realized, could become potentially dangerous. Some authorities claim that Napoleon never intended to invade; that the whole scheme was a gigantic bluff. But as that great historian Sir Julian Corbett has pointed out, 'By the universal testimony of his relations, his most intimate friends and his most capable and best-informed enemies, he at this time believed he had escaped gracefully from having to attempt the invasion of England . . . Austria, it seemed, was about to give him a pretext for escape without loss of prestige, but he had to justify to his Council the terrible cost which his pose had involved.'

But according to Miot de Melito, who was a member, Napoleon told the Council: 'For two years past France has been making the greatest sacrifices. A general war on the Continent would entail none greater. I now possess the strongest army, a highly developed military organization, and I am at present situated exactly as I would need to be if war should break out [on the Continent]. But in order to amass such forces in time of peace—20,000 artillery horses and complete baggage trains—I required a pretext which would allow all this to be prepared and collected without arousing the suspicions of the other continental powers. The plan of the invasion of England afforded this pretext.' De Melito, who claims to have heard the speech, says Napoleon added: 'For two years I have not been able to tell you this, but that nevertheless was my sole aim. You know it now and you see the explanation of many things. But we shall not have war, and I have just opened negotiations with the King of England.'[1]

With Spain now in the war on his side he could count on another thirty-two battleships to back up his fleet, making him powerful enough to challange Britain at sea—the only way he could make a challenge. But Spain had already warned him that, because Britain caught her unawares, the first twenty-five ships would not be ready for sea before March. Thus Napoleon could not make his challenge until the spring, but in the meantime he had to do something to keep Britain occupied until he resolved the Austrian problem. He therefore decided to make a peace offer to Britain, and at the same time launch a heavy attack on her rich sugar islands in the West Indies, and also recapture those that Britain had taken. This sudden assault, he guessed, would throw the merchants of the City of London into a panic, and Pitt's ministry, which held power by only a very slender majority, would probably topple amid clamour for peace at any price. In addition, he thought, the Royal Navy's strength would be drawn away from his Atlantic coast in a hurried dash to the West Indies.

Napoleon's 'direct negotiations with the King of England' started on January 2, 1805. Proud of his month-old title of

---

[1] Although the French Staff accepted de Melito as trustworthy it is curious the biographies, memoirs and papers of people like Ney, Marmont and Davout—all of whom commanded corps—make no mention of the 'pose'; and nor does Decrès, who should have been in a position to know.

Emperor, he sent a letter not to the British Government but to the old King, addressing him as 'My dear Brother'. Since he had been called to the throne of France 'by Providence and the suffrage of the Senate, the people and the Army,' he said, his 'foremost and most earnest desire has been for peace'.

Somewhat belying his earnest declaration were two sets of orders sent off that same day. The first was to Missiessy at Rochefort, the second to Villeneuve, who had taken over command of the fleet at Toulon after Latouche Tréville's death. They were to take on troops and sail independently for the West Indies, where they

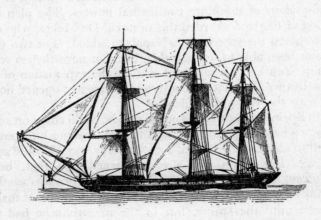

Taking soundings: the deep sea lead is being heaved by a man on the spritsail yardarm. A second man on the jib-boom end holds a bight of the line while a third in the mizen-chains has the reel

were to conduct operations against the British and then return to Rochefort. At the same time Napoleon sent a sharp note to the Austrian Emperor, Francis, demanding to know why certain troop movements were being made and warning him against any breach of the peace.

Thus the first move in the train of events that was to lead directly and inexorably to the Battle of Trafalgar began with Missiessy taking 3,500 troops on board. Rochefort was an extremely difficult port to blockade and for several reasons which we need not trouble with here, the British ships were not on their station when Missiessy sailed on January 11 in a snowstorm. His squadron was, however, spotted by a Royal Navy schooner, which was able to report his course. He had been at sea three days when, on January 14, Britain's reply to Napoleon's peace offer arrived in Paris. Addressed simply to 'The Head of the French Government' —a deliberate insult which successfully infuriated the Emperor— and signed not by the King but by Pitt, it said Britain was not prepared to negotiate without consulting the other powers, particularly with the Czar, 'who had always shown a warm interest in the integrity and independence of Europe'. Once bitten—by the Treaty of Amiens—Britain was twice shy. Far from being ready to sue for peace she realized that there could be no peace in the world while Napoleon was alive.

8

THE EMPEROR'S PLAN

*'Dost thou not know, my son, with how little wisdom
the world is governed?'*

—Count Oxenstierna

VILLENEUVE had not been able to sail from Toulon until January
18—a week after Missiessy and four days after Pitt's reply was
received in Paris. But like Missiessy, he was lucky. In a brisk
north-westerly breeze he took his squadron to sea—and found
that instead of Nelson waiting over the horizon to fall on him,
there were only two British frigates. But strong winds turned into
a gale, and in the darkness of his first night at sea Villeneuve was
soon in trouble. His crews were little more than raw landsmen and
there were 6,500 soldiers cluttering up the ships, adding their
sea-sick contribution to the chaos and rapidly-falling morale. By
the time daylight came to the turbulent Gulf of Lyons, Villeneuve's telescope showed him a miserable picture: there were only
four of the original eleven battleships still in company, struggling
along with tattered sails, torn rigging and broken spars. He had
covered only a few score of the five thousand-odd miles to the
West Indies, and already one ship had lost her mainmast, another
smashed her fore-yard and a third had had one of her topmasts
topple over the side.

Villeneuve gave up: he and the remains of his squadron were
back in Toulon by the 21st, and to Decrès he wrote: 'I declare to
you that ships of the line thus equipped, short-handed, encumbered with troops, with superannuated or bad materials, vessels
which lose their masts or sails at every puff of wind, and which in
fine weather are constantly engaged in repairing the damages
caused by the wind, or the inexperience of their sailors, are not
fit to undertake anything. I had a presentiment of this before I
sailed; I have now only too painfully experienced it.'

Meanwhile Nelson, warned by his two frigates which both left
the enemy fleet on the 19th (why they both left together is not
explained), combed the Mediterranean for Villeneuve. He thought
the French might be heading for Naples or Sicily and slowly

fought his way south in the teeth of the gale which had dealt Villeneuve such a blow. 'I have neither ate, drunk, or slept with any comfort since last Sunday,' he wrote, '. . . I consider the destruction of the enemy's fleet of so much consequence, that I would willingly have half of mine burnt to effect their destruction. I am in a fever. God send I may find them!'

Working to a strict plan of searching the areas where Villeneuve could do the most damage, Nelson eventually went as far as Egypt, but finding no trace of him, sailed back westward to Malta, where on February 19 he found that Villeneuve had been back in Toulon since January 21. 'Those gentlemen are not accustomed to a Gulf of Lyons gale,' he wrote, 'which we have buffeted for twenty-one months, and not carried away a spar. I most sincerely hope they will soon be in a state to put to sea again.' Three days at sea had been more than enough for Villeneuve, with his untrained crews and ill-conditioned ships, yet for eighty-four weeks Nelson's ships had defied those same storms in those very waters—often, as we have seen, in unseaworthy ships. Napoleon was furious at Villeneuve's failure. 'The great evil of our Navy is that the men who command it are unused to the risks of command. What is to be done with admirals who allow their spirits to sink and resolve to be beaten home at the first damage they suffer?' he asked.

Something of an answer to Napoleon's exasperated comment on the leadership of the French Fleet can be gleaned by looking at the men who led the Royal Navy at this time. Head and shoulders above them all stood Nelson, the possessor of perhaps the most contradictory personality in British history. The legend of Nelson as the fearless fighter, the master strategist and tactician, and the greatest sailor-warrior in the Navy of great sailor-warriors, has tended to obscure the Nelson known to the men who fought with him, the women who loved him, and those of both sexes who met him yet rarely in the gay, etiquette-ridden and gossip-conscious salons that were the centres of London society.

By the standards of a Welfare State, Nelson at any period in his adult life was an undersized weakling. 'What,' enquired his uncle, Captain Suckling, when asked to take the twelve-year-old boy into his ship as a midshipman, 'has poor little Horatio done, who is so weak, that, above all the rest, he should be sent to rough it at sea?' Nor did the sea strengthen that thin body; in fact the sea, tropical sickness, and the wounds of war conspired only to shatter even

further his fragile constitution. Physically and mentally Nelson is
the odd man out in the gallery of great war leaders. His face has
none of the dour sternness of purpose of 'Old Jarvie', later Earl St
Vincent, who had grimly declared on St Valentine's Day 1797,
before fighting the battle from which he took his title, that 'A
victory is very essential to England at this moment', and it had
none of the steadfastness of Wellington.

Instead of a square jaw, thin, firm lips and jutting chin, Nelson's
face was narrow and half-boyish, with sensitive lips forming a
pouting mouth. The chin belied the strong will; in fact at first
glance the head, with its careless hair and mobile, almost womanish
features lined with pain and anxiety, might be that of a restless
poet. A young midshipman who was destined to become William
IV first met Nelson when he was twenty-four years old and commanding a frigate, and noted him as 'the merest boy of a captain I
ever beheld'; many years later Sir William Hamilton, meeting
Nelson for the first time, referred to him as 'a little man and far from
handsome'. Yet the personality emerging from that frail body is a
contradiction of that associated with leadership, completely different from the calm, stern manner of St Vincent and Wellington,
who were men competent but cold, and brave but reserved, in the
usual British tradition.

Nelson, 'that cripple-gaited, one-eyed, one-armed little naval
critter', was as emotional as a young woman; constantly moody
and temperamental, he was one moment suicidally depressed and
the next almost childishly elated. Of a race that prided itself on
never revealing its feelings, he was a melodramatic and emotional
exception. We will see from his letters how depressed he could
become when Villeneuve proved so elusive, and how that depression affected him physically. From this his whole personality
appears unstable—yet he rarely made a wrong decision, whether
it was one long debated or suddenly arrived at in the heat of battle.
It seemed as if he had two distinct personalities—the hot-blooded,
hyper-sensitive and erratic one which manifested itself in his
relations with people, and the ice-cold, steely, questing and
unswerving personality which turned him into the most perfect
human fighting machine ever seen, as brave and brilliant wielding
a sword and leading a boarding party as when coolly handling a
large fleet.

His extraordinary depression before battle is almost unbelievable. Yet his elation and bravery once battle started injected him

with life: it is as if he only really lived at full capacity when his ears were deafened by the thunder of the guns, nostrils dilated with the smoke of powder and his remaining eye assaulted by the swirling panorama of massive ships pounding the enemy into bloody submission according to a plan previously conceived by his own brain. Then the pain and misery left that little body; all pettiness and melodrama dissolved.

His health greatly affected his mental outlook. Born a weakling, he was constantly ill when at sea. ('Dreadfully seasick', he wrote the year before Trafalgar, 'always tossed about, and always seasick'.) His health was ruined by fever in the West Indies, and sickness dogged him from then on. At Copenhagen the cold almost killed him; he broke down after his victory at the Nile— 'I never expect to see your face again,' he wrote to Jervis. When operating in the Channel off Boulogne his thin body was racked with spasms of perpetual coughing and seasickness and his head buzzed with toothache. Off Toulon while waiting for Villeneuve his muscles were knotted with rheumatism, he had a regular pain in the chest and 'the constant sense of the blood gushing up the left side of my head'. He appears to have had nervous dyspepsia almost without pause.

But these were not the moanings of a hypochondriac: when being given a pension in 1797 he had first to present a memorial outlining his service. 'Your memorialist has been in four actions with the fleets of the enemy, in three actions with frigates, in six engagements against batteries, in ten actions in boats employed in cutting out of harbours, in destroying vessels, and in the taking of three towns . . . He has assisted in the capture of seven sail of the line, six frigates, four corvettes, eleven privateers of different sizes, and taken and destroyed near fifty sail of merchantmen. [He] has been actually engaged against the enemy upwards of one hundred and twenty times, [and he] has lost his right eye and arm, and been severely wounded and bruised in his body . . .' When that was written Nelson had just celebrated his thirty-ninth birthday; the Nile, Copenhagen and Trafalgar were yet to be fought.

While constantly complaining of illness he also retained an ironic sense of humour. 'I have all the diseases there are,' he once wrote, 'but there is not enough in my frame for them to fasten on'. To the future William IV he wrote after losing his arm at Santa Cruz, 'I assure your Royal Highness that not a scrap of that ardour with which I served our King has been shot away!' And if one gets the impression that he made the most of his illnesses, one should remember that at Santa Cruz, shot down, with his right arm shattered and badly bleeding, Nelson was rowed back to the nearest ship, which was Thomas Fremantle's *Seahorse*, with Betsey—newly-married—waiting anxiously on board for her husband to return from the landing beaches. Nelson, half-unconscious and in urgent need of medical attention, refused to go on board and ordered that he was to be rowed to his flagship, the *Theseus*. Told his life was in danger, he said: 'Then I will die rather than alarm Mrs Fremantle by her seeing me in this state when I can give her no tidings of her husband.'

Alongside the *Theseus* he refused any help in climbing on board. 'I have got my legs left, and one arm', and he scrambled up the ship's side, face white as a sheet, uniform covered in blood, and the shattered arm roughly tied up. Once on deck he ordered the surgeon to bring the instruments. 'I know I must lose my right arm, and the sooner the better.' Yet he could write words of self-pity to his beloved Emma which must have wrenched at her heart: 'Nothing can be more miserable and unhappy than your poor Nelson,' he wrote from off Toulon. 'My heart is almost broken.'

But Nelson could be petty, and there is often a hint of the shrewishness of a woman in his temper, usually where little things were concerned. He was a great friend of Captain Ball, yet when he first met him—in France during the brief period of peace in 1783—he was annoyed because Ball wore epaulettes, which were not part of an officer's uniform in the Royal Navy until several years later. 'Two noble captains are here—Ball and Shepherd', he wrote acidly. 'They wear fine epaulettes, for which I think them great coxcombs. They have not visited me, and I shall not court their acquaintance.' Nelson met him again fifteen years later, when Ball came on board to report. 'What,' said Nelson sarcastically, 'have you come to have your bones broken?' Less than a month later Nelson's ship lost her masts in a gale and her helpless hulk was being swept ashore. Ball, in the *Alexander*, immediately took the flagship in tow, and tried to get her out to sea. But there was a grave danger that both ships would be lost on the lee shore and Nelson ordered Ball to cast off the tow. The slow-moving, phlegmatic Ball refused, whereupon Nelson became extremely angry and ordered the tow to be cut, leaving himself and the flagship to their fate. Ball, however, carried on, and many hours later the flagship was saved. Nelson immediately went aboard the *Alexander* and, embracing the embarrassed Ball, declared: 'A friend in need is a friend indeed.'

It was Nelson's essential humanity which endeared him to his officers and men; hard-bitten seamen genuinely loved him. When he was ill they nursed him with all the tenderness they might have lavished on a woman. From the Baltic in 1801, when he was ill and irritated with the Admiralty, he wrote, 'All the fleet are so truly kind to me that I should be a wretch not to cheer up. Foley has put me under a regimen of milk at four in the morning; Murray has given me lozenges; Hardy is as good as ever, and all have proved their desire to keep my mind easy.' As one writer says, 'That picture of one sea veteran administering warm milk to his admiral at four o'clock in the morning, and to another feeding him tenderly with lozenges, is amusing enough; but it shows more effectively than graver things could do the feeling Nelson inspired in his captains.'

Warm-hearted with those he liked and respected, Nelson also had a tremendous loyalty—whether to a man, a ship or a fleet. Merely because it was his, then each was of the best. We have already seen his comment on the *Agamemnon* when he was given her to command. ('She is without exception the finest sixty-four in the service.') So it was with the *Albemarle*. 'Not a man or officer in her I would wish to change.' His ships of the Mediterranean Fleet were 'the best commanded and the best manned afloat'. That warm loyalty was, of course, returned, and it was often returned in a similar, spontaneous and dramatized way. Thomas Troubridge, for instance, was a fine seaman with vast experience. He was heavily-built and handsome, frank in manner and destined to be as good an administrator as he was a fighter. Jervis, at the Battle of St Vincent, watching the way Troubridge handled the *Culloden*, exclaimed: 'Look at Troubridge! He tacks his ship into battle as if the eyes of all England were on him; and would to God they were!'

Yet this same Troubridge, upset at something Nelson had written, sat down and wrote: 'Your letter has really so unhinged me that I am quite unmanned and crying. I would sooner forfeit my life—my everything—than be deemed ungrateful to an officer and a friend I feel I owe so much. Pray, pray acquit me . . . I pray your Lordship not to harbour the smallest idea that I am not the same Troubridge you have known me.'

It is a great leader whose slightest word can make strong men weep—not because of the power he holds over their careers but because of the power he holds over their hearts. The gallant and wounded Captain Riou, reluctantly obeying Sir Hyde Parker's signal to withdraw from the action against the Trekroner Forts at Copenhagen, said bitterly, 'What will Nelson think of us?' He then gave the order to cut the anchor cable—and was almost immediately killed by a cannon ball.

If it seems strange that Nelson's dying words were 'Kiss me, Hardy', remember this was the Thomas Masterman Hardy, the massive, grave and kindly man who, when the frigate *Minerve* was being chased by several Spanish battleships, lowered a boat and rowed after a seaman who had fallen over the side. The Spaniards were coming up fast and Nelson was faced with the danger that the *Minerve* would be captured before the boat could get back. However, he did not hesitate. 'By God, I'll not lose Hardy! Back the mizen-topsail.' The *Minerve* lay-to, motionless, while the boat caught up, and the nearest Spanish battleship, apparently bewildered by the tiny frigate's unexpected action, and probably fearing a trap, backed a topsail as well. This gave Nelson enough time to get Hardy and his boat's crew on board, and the *Minerve* escaped.

Nelson, of course, played the game of favourites in an age of favouritism, but apart from a few glaring exceptions each man deserved his loyalty. Each was an outstanding seaman, and each became Nelson's friend—one of his 'band of brothers'—because he could and did fight the enemy like a demon, and because he could and did accept the kind of leadership Nelson offered, exploiting it to the full. Nelson's leadership was that of example and trust, accompanied with a warm smile—the rarest of all, the most easily abused, and yet, if followed, the most successful.

On February 1 a French ship sailed from Lorient bound for the West Indies with new orders for Missiessy, warning him that Villeneuve would not be joining him. Decrès told him that Villeneuve's squadron 'is to have another destination' and Missiessy was to reinforce St Domingo and then sail back across the Atlantic to Rochefort. What was Villeneuve's new destination? Probably Napoleon had not made up his mind, though he ordered General Lauriston to disembark the troops which had been on board Villeneuve's ships. 'You will receive an order to re-embark for elsewhere, for the season is past for your former destination,' he wrote on February 5—the day he cancelled orders for a campaign against Austria, a cancellation forced upon him by the Austrian Emperor's placatory reply. Even now it is almost impossible to know what Napoleon had in mind.

At the Palais des Tuileries in the spring of 1805 most of the outward signs of the Revolution had gone. In place of boots men wore stockings and buckled shoes; elaborately wrought ceremonial swords replaced clumsy sabres. Men addressed each other as 'monsieur' instead of 'citoyen' and the Palais d'Égalité was once again known by its old name of the Palais Royal. Italian singers sang to the accompaniment of soft music to amuse the Emperor, and often he would fall quiet, as if in a daydream, and no one dared move until he recovered. Sometimes in Josephine's salon he would have the candles shrouded in white gauze, to cast an eerie light while he told ghost stories. On Sundays he would review a few thousand troops drawn up in the courtyard of the Palais, speaking to individual soldiers and hearing their complaints. While he grew more distrustful and more withdrawn from his generals and ministers, ancient court posts were brought back into use as if Napoleon gloried in the splendours and routine that dated back to Charlemagne, and some aristocrats who had fled France at the Revolution flocked back to new posts at Court.

But if the Palais des Tuileries was a place where Napoleon lived in great splendour, it was also the place where he worked hard. Two or three secretaries were always at hand in his study, pens ready to fly across paper as their master dictated letters to kings and princes, orders to his generals and admirals, plans for new conquests. Maps hung on walls or lay unrolled on tables; the latest figures on the state of the Army, the Navy and the invasion flotillas were kept handy for instant reference. It was not unusual for Napoleon to work all night; indeed, when the English Ambassador left Paris just before war was declared again in 1803, Napoleon worked for three consecutive days and nights, keeping busy a relay of three secretaries at a time. 'On the evening of the fourth day he took a warm bath to counteract his excitement, and remained in it for six hours, during which time he dictated important despatches. Finally he went to bed, giving orders to call him at three in the morning, so that he might see four or five couriers whom he was expecting.' Each day he was up by seven in the morning, reading his own correspondence—and that of several other select people, many of them his ministers, which had been intercepted by his Postmaster-General. (He once boasted that a special department could decipher a coded letter, no matter what the language.) While he dressed, a secretary would read aloud various items from the newspapers. Breakfast, usually eaten alone and always hurriedly, followed. And then the real work of the day began.

So it was that on March 2, 1805, he made the third move in his great plan. The first move had been on February 27, when new orders were sent to Missiessy in the West Indies, cancelling the previous orders to return to France and instructing him to wait in the West Indies until the end of June for another French squadron, and if none came, to return to France. The second move, on the same day, had been to order Gourdon, at Ferrol, with four battleships (a fifth was in dock being repaired) and two frigates to be ready to join any French squadron which might arrive off the port to drive off the British ships and release him. Now, on March 2, the time had come for the third and most vital move. He had bathed, shaved and breakfasted, and he had read the correspondence. His secretaries were ready in the study, quills sharpened, ink-wells full. The Emperor then began dictating one of the most fantastic orders he had ever given.

> *Monsieur L'Admiral Ganteaume, vous appareillerez dans le plus court délai possible avec notre escadre de Brest forte de 21 vaisseaux, 6 frégates et 2 flûtes . . . vous vous dirigerez d'abord sur le Ferrol . . . vous ferez au contreamiral Gourdon . . . le signal de vous joindre.*
>
> *Ayant ainsie rallié ces escadres, vous vous rendrez par le plus court chemin dans notre île de Martinique . . .*

Ganteaume was to embark three thousand soldiers and take his twenty-one battleships, six frigates, and two transports out of Brest and sail for Ferrol. There he was to beat off the blockading British ships and fetch out Gourdon's four battleships and two frigates, and also the Spanish squadron. He was then to sail across the Atlantic to Martinique, where he would find Villeneuve with the Toulon squadron and Missiessy. . . . Once at Martinique he was to join his own twenty-one battleships with Gourdon's four, Villeneuve's eleven and Missiessy's five, making a total force of forty-one battleships and nineteen frigates, plus the Spanish squadron. He was then to return to Europe immediately. Arriving off Ushant he was to attack any British warships he found there and then sail on to Boulogne, where he was to arrive between June 10 and July 10.

That was the main plan; but Napoleon knew his admirals—especially Villeneuve—and allowed for eventualities. If Villeneuve failed to turn up in the West Indies, he told Ganteaume, he would still have more than twenty-five battleships, and after waiting thirty days for Villeneuve, he should fight his way through to Boulogne. If for any reason he had less than twenty-five, he was to sail back to Ferrol, where he would find every available French and Spanish warship waiting for him, and without going into port, he would take them under his command and sail on for Boulogne. Napoleon then drew up corresponding orders for Villeneuve. He

Ship rig

was to sail from Toulon direct to Cadiz, where he was to pick up a French seventy-four and the Spanish Admiral Gravina with as many of his fifteen battleships as were ready. Then he was to sail direct to the West Indies to join Missiessy and wait for Ganteaume, being ready to sail immediately he arrived. So this was Napoleon's great plan—for operations which, he ended his letter to Ganteaume, 'will have so much influence on the destiny of the World. . . .'

But seldom had operations been planned with so little regard for what the enemy might do. Ganteaume was blockaded in Brest and would probably have to fight his way out; so would Villeneuve and Gourdon. Ganteaume would have to raise the blockade at Ferrol and Villeneuve at Cadiz. There would be three separate groups of ships crossing the Atlantic and going to the West Indies; he also assumed that the British would not follow even one of them. And if Villeneuve was not at Martinique, Ganteaume was to wait thirty days; if Ganteaume did not arrive, Villeneuve was to wait forty days. In other words, there was to be a minimum wait at Martinique of a month during which time he assumed the Royal Navy would have done nothing towards their destruction, an assumption which hardly corresponded with his plan that the Royal Navy should be led to the West Indies in a wild-goose chase.

In addition, Napoleon ignored a basic and age-old tenet of Britain's naval strategy: in a crisis, concentrate on the point of greatest danger. As at the time of the Armada, so now with the constant threat of invasion, the Western Approaches to the Channel held this focal point. With the Royal Navy holding the Western Approaches, Napoleon's invasion force could never sail, or if they did, the British Squadrons would run up the Channel and destroy them. And for Napoleon's ships to be able to seize control of the Channel they would have first to defeat the Royal Navy in the Western Approaches. 'Against this fundamental strategy, imperturbably adhered to, all Napoleon's combinations were to be shattered,' wrote Desbrière.

9

THE GREAT CHASE

*'The advantage of time and place in all martial actions
is half a victory, which being lost is irrecoverable . . .'*
—Drake to Elizabeth I, 1588

THE EMPEROR'S brave new plan soon started to go adrift. At
Brest, Ganteaume set to work getting his ships manned to their
full strength, taking on board stores, water, powder and shot.
The only thing he could not store was experience. A fortnight
later an impatient Emperor wrote spurring him on with the news
that he had not a moment to lose. 'Do not forget the great destinies
which you hold in your hands. If you are not wanting in enterprise,
success is certain.'

By March 24, Ganteaume was ready to sail and there was only
one snag: seventeen British battleships were waiting for him
outside. It was impossible to sail without risking an engagement:
what should he do? The jerking arms of the telegraph swiftly
sped the question to Paris, but Napoleon's reply completely
ignored the situation. 'A naval victory in these circumstances
would lead to nothing. Have but one object, to fulfil your mission.
Go out without fighting.' Three days later Ganteaume made a
half-hearted attempt to 'Sortez sans combat', but the seventeen
British battleships soon persuaded him to return. By March 29
his ships were safely moored up in harbour. And the next day,
March 30, Villeneuve made his second attempt to leave Toulon
with his eleven battleships, some frigates and two brigs. The ships
had enough stores for six months, and they carried more than
three thousand soldiers under General Lauriston.

Once again Nelson was not waiting for Villeneuve outside
Toulon; instead two British frigates kept a watch. The reason for
this was that Nelson knew that with the frequent Gulf of Lyons
gales it was impossible to wait outside Toulon all the time, and in
any case he wanted to destroy Villeneuve's squadron, not frighten
it into staying in port. He knew that once the squadron sailed, it
had but two courses open to it—to sail out of the Mediterranean
into the Atlantic, or in the direction of Sicily, Sardinia and Egypt.

In planning which to cover, he had to decide which was potentially the most dangerous and that was, of course, the route which led towards Egypt.

So Nelson waited off Sardinia, but before doing that he laid a trap. He left Toulon and sailed over to the Spanish coast, rattling the bars and making sure that his fleet was seen and reported to Villeneuve, reasoning that this would prevent the French admiral from sneaking along the Spanish coast—if he intended leaving the Mediterranean—and force him on a more easterly course, where Nelson would be waiting for him. If he was bound eastwards, Nelson was still in the best position. And this plan worked—at first. Villeneuve, sailing before dawn on March 30 and having heard that Nelson had been seen off Barcelona, sailed to the south, to pass outside the Balearic Islands. He wrote to Decrès, 'May fortune fulfil the hopes which the Emperor has founded upon the destination of this squadron.' Not that he knew the ultimate destination was Boulogne—Napoleon had not mentioned it in his orders, although his instructions to General Lauriston, which were to be opened only at sea, did.

The British frigates shadowed Villeneuve for a short time, and then went off to report to Nelson that the French Fleet was sailing south. But soon after they left, Villeneuve met a merchantman whose captain reported that Nelson, far from being off the Spanish coast, was south of Sardinia. Villeneuve immediately altered course and headed direct for the Strait of Gibraltar while Nelson covered the gap between Sicily and Tunisia, confident that Villeneuve's reported southerly course meant that he was bound for Egypt. He searched for three days, without success. By April 7 he was writing from between Sicily and Tunisia. 'I am, in truth, half dead; but what man can do to find them out shall be done,' he wrote, 'but I must not make more haste than good speed,' and leave Sardinia and Sicily or Naples open to capture. Nor would he search towards Gibraltar until his frigates could bring him definite news. He was covering the point of greatest danger, and although his excited body ('I can neither eat, drink or sleep') gave him no rest, his brain was as cold and calculating as always.

But on April 9, Captain Lord Mark Kerr, at Gibraltar, was startled to see Villeneuve's eleven battleships with attendant frigates and brigs go scudding past into the Atlantic. His own frigate *Fisgard* was being refitted, so he scribbled a note to Nelson, hired a brig and, putting one of his own officers in command, sent him off to the eastward to deliver it as quickly as possible. He set his own crew to work to get the *Fisgard* ready to sail and within four hours—leaving a launch, barge, an anchor, twenty-two tons of water in casks, and a lot of other equipment behind on the quayside—the frigate was at sea. Out in the Atlantic, however, there was no sign of Villeneuve, so Kerr decided to hurry northwards with what news he had (see Notes, p. 350).

Villeneuve, however, had been spotted earlier coming through the Strait by Sir Richard Strachan in the *Renown*, who immediately went about and headed for Cadiz to warn Vice-Admiral Sir John Orde, who was blockading the Spanish Admiral Gravina's squadron of fifteen battleships (only a few of which were ready for sea) with a force of four battleships. When the *Renown* came in sight flying the flags for a superior enemy fleet and firing guns to draw attention to her signal, Orde's ships were taking on stores from supply ships. The admiral promptly cast off the transports and ordered them to head for the neutral waters off Lagos, in Portugal.

Meanwhile Villeneuve steered for Cadiz while Orde made up his mind what to do next. One thing was obvious—he was far outnumbered by Villeneuve's ships, and the French Admiral had obviously come to bring out Gravina's squadron. What was more, Orde knew Ganteaume was preparing to sail from Brest. Considering that the combined French and Spanish fleet—which he estimated at nineteen or twenty battleships—could be at sea in forty-eight hours, Orde wrote to the Admiralty: 'I think the chances are great in favour of their destination being westward where, by a sudden concentration of several detachments, Bonaparte may hope to gain a temporary superiority in the Channel, and availing himself of it to strike his enemy a mortal blow.'

So lifting his blockade of Villeneuve, he took his battleships north to reinforce the British fleet off Brest, which he regarded as the point of greatest danger. For this he was later strongly criticized and condemned.

Captain Lord Mark Kerr, in the meantime, had sped north. He warned one of the British fleet off Ushant on the way, sent a Guernsey privateer into Plymouth with a letter to the Admiralty, and sailed on to raise the alarm in Ireland.

Night was falling as Villeneuve sailed up to Cadiz, and he sent a frigate ahead to signal Gravina that the French battleship and the

Spanish ships should sail at once. By the time darkness cut off the land he could see the French battleship, the *Aigle*, and several other ships getting under way, and he anchored his squadron. The anchor of his own flagship, the *Bucentaure*, was hardly down before news came that six Spanish battleships and a frigate would be joining him before midnight, but the dreadful picture of Nelson arriving on the scene like an avenging fury kept bothering him, and he sent his flag-lieutenant ashore to warn Admiral Gravina that 'every minute was precious, that the enemy's Mediterranean squadron must be in pursuit and might effect a junction with the force that had blockaded Cadiz up till then and that it was essential to set sail for our destination'.

By 2 a.m. next morning the French ships were on their way to Martinique with the Spaniards doing their best to catch up. By daylight only the *Argonaute*, Gravina's flagship, was in company. Villeneuve slowed down during the day and the following night, but daylight showed that only one more Spanish ship, the *America*, had joined. With four other Spanish battleships and a frigate still out of sight astern, Villeneuve's nerve or patience was exhausted. He ordered his ships to cram on sail. It 'was not desirable to wait any longer', he wrote. The date was April 11. It was to be May 26 before the rest of the ships joined him—in Martinique.

On April 11 Nelson was off Palermo, in Sicily, a sad and bitter man. At 7 a.m. the day before one of his captains, Hallowell, arrived from Palermo with a report that General Craig's expedition—which, unknown to Nelson, was intended to operate with Russian forces in southern Italy—had sailed from England. This was the first news he had had of it and it completely changed the picture. The expedition would be an easy prey for Villeneuve. 'I may suppose the French fleet are bound to the westward. . . . I am very, very miserable. . . .' So he set sail to the westward, but almost immediately ran into heavy weather and strong headwinds which held him up for four days. On the 15th he was joined by a ship bringing more news of Craig's expedition—but still no word of it had come from the Admiralty. He had no idea of its whereabouts. Was it already in the Mediterranean? Had it already fallen foul of Villeneuve and been destroyed? Nelson had no means of knowing.[1] On the 16th he had just signed his name to a letter to the British Minister in Naples, complaining bitterly that the Admiralty had not warned him of Craig's expedition, when serious

[1] In fact it was still windbound in England.

news arrived that startled him. He added a postscript to the letter: 'Noon. A vessel just spoke says that on Sunday, April 7, he saw sixteen ships of war, twelve of them large ships off Cape de Gatte [Cape de Gata, on the Spanish coast south-west of Cartagena] steering to the westward, with the wind at the east. If this account is true, much mischief may be apprehended. It kills me, the very thought.'

He decided to go first to Toulon, to make sure that the enemy was not once again returning to port, 'and that is all I can tell at the present.' If the French fleet had left the Mediterranean he would go after them. He was still heading for Toulon when, on April 18, a frigate reported that a neutral ship had seen the French squadron go through the Strait of Gibraltar ten days earlier. Nelson rapidly recast his plans. He wrote, 'I am going out of the Mediterranean after the French Fleet. It may be thought I have protected too well Sardinia, Naples, Sicily, the Morea [the southern part of Greece] and Egypt from the French; but I feel I have done right, and am, therefore, easy about any fate which may await me for having missed the French Fleet.'

His main task had been to keep command of the Mediterranean, and now he decided to leave behind five valuable frigates and other ships 'to protect our commerce and to prevent the French sending troops by sea', as he wrote to the Admiralty. By April 19—eight days after Villeneuve left Cadiz for the West Indies—Nelson had made hardly any progress against strong westerly winds. 'My good fortune seems flown away,' he wrote to Ball, 'I cannot get a fair wind, or even a side wind. Dead foul!—dead foul!'

He wrote to Marsden that he was satisfied that the French Fleet were not heading for the West Indies 'but intend forming a junction with the Squadron at Ferrol, and pushing direct for Ireland or Brest, as I believe the French have troops on board'. Therefore he would bring his ships—'eleven as fine ships of war, as ably commanded, and in perfect order and in health, as ever went to sea'—up to the approaches to the Channel. But Nelson and his fleet had many more days of thrashing to windward before they were clear of the Mediterranean. They did not arrive at Tetuan, on the south side of the Strait of Gibraltar, until May 4. While he was anchored there, restocking his ships with food and water, news came from Captain Otway, the Navy Commissioner in Gibraltar, that the general feeling was that Villeneuve had gone to the West Indies.

Nelson was both surprised and puzzled; his own evaluation led him to think that the French Fleet had gone north; now. . . . To Otway he wrote grumbling that 'I believe my ill-luck is to go on for a longer time'. He could not run to the West Indies 'without something beyond mere surmise; and if I defer my departure Jamaica may be lost. Indeed, as they have a month's start of me, I see no prospect of getting out time enough [*sic*] to prevent much mischief from being done.'

As he turned over the possibility of the West Indies, the idea seemed to harden in his mind, and a possibility turned into a probability. To Dr Scott, his chaplain, Nelson commented wryly, 'If I fail, if they are not gone to the West Indies, I shall be blamed; to be burnt in effigy or Westminster Abbey is my alternative.' He knew how fickle the Press and the public could be.

When the wind came round to the east Nelson gave the order to sail, and once through the Strait he steered northwards towards Lisbon, keeping a sharp lookout for the frigate *Amazon*, which had earlier been sent to Lisbon in a last desperate attempt to get some reliable information about Villeneuve, amid the welter of rumours. Next day, May 7, Nelson was still without news. To Marsden he wrote, 'If nothing is heard of them from Lisbon or from the frigates I may find off Cape St Vincent's [*sic*], I shall probably think the rumours are true, that their destination is the West Indies, and in that case I shall think it my duty to follow them. . . .'

Early on the 9th the Fleet arrived under the cliffs of Cape St Vincent. Nelson's ships still had not all the necessary stores on board, so they sailed on to Lagos Bay, where Sir John Orde's transports were still at anchor, and while Nelson waited for the *Amazon* his sailors worked like slaves filling their ships' holds. The *Amazon* arrived later with news from the American brig *Louisa*, of Baltimore, commanded by Peter Billings, who reported that a French fleet had arrived at Cadiz on April 9 and several Spanish battleships had sailed. Billings, who had just left Cadiz, said that three thousand Spanish troops, including a great number of cavalry, had been embarked 'with great confusion'. Seamen were scarce, and 'were forced with great reluctance aboard the men-of-war'.

That night, May 10, Rear-Admiral Donald Campbell is reported to have gone on board the *Victory* while Nelson's Fleet was still at anchor.[1] Campbell, a British officer employed by the Portuguese, who were using him to help improve their own Navy, is said to have told Nelson, in confidence, that the Combined Fleet was undoubtedly heading for the West Indies.

(The effect this visit had on Campbell's career was disastrous. The French and Spanish Ambassadors in Lisbon succeeded in forcing the Portuguese Government to sack him and he returned to England, where he died in poverty, neither the Admiralty nor the Government lifting a finger to help him.)

That night Nelson, in the great cabin of the *Victory*, reviewed all the factors in his mind. There was little chance now of getting any further information, and he had to decide what to do. Finally he made a decision. 'My lot is cast,' he wrote to Ball, 'and I am going to the West Indies, where, although I am late, yet chance may have given them a bad passage and me a good one.' To another friend he wrote, 'Disappointment has worn me to a skeleton, and I am, in good truth, very, very far from well'. Next day flags run up on the *Victory*'s signal halyards turned his decision into action. His ten battleships and three frigates, provisioned for five months, laboriously weighed anchor and set sail. The chase was on, but Villeneuve had a thirty-one days start . . .

In London the Admiralty already knew, on the day Nelson sailed westwards towards the setting sun, that the Combined Fleet's destination was almost certainly the West Indies, and the news of Villeneuve's break-out from Toulon could not have arrived at a worse time. On February 13, the commission set up to inquire into the state of the Navy issued a report showing various irregularities in the Navy's finances. The blame fell on the First Lord, Melville, who was a great friend of Pitt. This was just the sort of ammunition the Opposition was waiting for, and while Napoleon in Paris dreamed up his plans for the invasion of England, the Opposition in the Mother of Parliaments planned and schemed to overthrow Pitt and his Government. News that Missiessy had sailed to the West Indies added to the uproar and the debate in the Commons was fixed for April 8.

On that day, while Villeneuve neared the Strait of Gibraltar, constantly watching over his shoulder for Nelson, the Opposition

[1] Some sources say Campbell went on board at Gibraltar, but since Nelson's mind was not then made up, this seems most improbable. The author has found no conclusive proof that Campbell gave information to Nelson.

had great sport in the Commons. Pitt fought bravely for Melville, but a vote of censure was put down. And despite all of Pitt's impassioned efforts, it was carried by one vote, that of the Speaker. Next day, as Villeneuve passed Gibraltar and Lord Mark Kerr hastened to get the *Fisgard* to sea, Melville resigned as First Lord. A jubilant Opposition forecast Pitt would soon follow, but they under-estimated the Premier's courage. His enemy was Napoleon, not the Opposition, and he was going to carry on the fight. To fill Melville's post he turned, after some Party squabbling, to the man who had been both Melville's unofficial adviser and also a kinsman, an eighty year old admiral who had never flown his flag at sea, but who was famous in the Service for his strict honesty and ability as an administrator. Admiral Sir Charles Middleton was not a Member of Parliament, so to get over that he was created Lord Barham. On April 21 he took over as First Lord against the wishes of the old King and many of Pitt's own Cabinet.

Two days earlier General Craig's expedition of 7,000 troops, embarked in more than forty ships and escorted by only two battleships, sailed from Spithead bound for Italy. Negotiations with the Czar had up to now been extremely difficult. To Pitt and his Cabinet it seemed that Russian demands were quite unrealistic. The temperament and outlook of the autocratic young Czar Alexander were far removed from those of Downing Street. But the one thing, apparently, that impressed the Czar brooding in the winter fastness of his palace at St Petersburg was that Britain was prepared to send troops to Italy to fight side by side with a Russian force. So the little army which began its 2,500 mile voyage from Spithead, and which had to pass five ports holding sizeable enemy squadrons—Brest, Ferrol, Cadiz, Cartagena and Toulon—contained Britain's hopes for the future. As it ran down the Channel and into the Bay of Biscay it passed two other ships heading north, the *Fisgard*, with the resourceful Lord Mark Kerr on board, taking the news to Ireland that Villeneuve was in the Atlantic, and the Guernsey lugger *Greyhound*, a privateer to whom Kerr had entrusted a letter to the Admiralty, and which was heading for Plymouth.

The news reached Barham at the Admiralty on April 25, four days after he took over his new office, and a fortnight after Villeneuve had left Cadiz. There was little in it to cheer him but, being a man with an immense knowledge of naval strategy, there was not much to alarm him. He already knew Villeneuve had been embarking troops at Toulon, and Pitt's spies had warned him to expect an attack on the West Indies. Barham therefore thought at first that Villeneuve would probably join Missiessy in the West Indies. A British squadron under Cochrane had already sailed to cover Missiessy. Working alone in his office near the Board Room, Barham drafted his first order. This was to Gibraltar, ordering the senior officer present to send two battleships to reinforce Cochrane in the West Indies if Nelson had not followed Villeneuve.

Two days later, on April 27, Barham had some doubts about Nelson's moves, knowing that he would most probably cast to the eastward first unless he had definite news that Villeneuve had gone westwards to the Strait. So he decided to send part of the Flying Squadron under Collingwood direct to the West Indies. This would weaken the force off Brest under Lord Gardner (who had taken over from Cornwallis), but to make up for it the dock-yards were working night and day to get more ships to sea. But before the orders to detach Collingwood reached him Gardner had received some startling news: Villeneuve's sudden arrival at Cadiz had caused Orde to fall back. Gardner therefore decided to use his discretion and not send Collingwood to the West Indies until further orders arrived from Barham.

As soon as Barham heard that Orde no longer guarded Cadiz and that Villeneuve and Gravina had linked up, he realized that Craig's expedition, on which so much depended, was sailing possibly to its destruction. The news was sent round to No 10 Downing Street on April 29 to await Pitt's return from the House of Commons. The Premier had had a terrible day: the Opposition had set up a loud clamour over the report of the Navy Commission, and in the rough-and-tumble put down a motion aimed at bringing Lord Melville to trial. Pitt, a sick man, had fought back and the motion was beaten. Melville was saved— temporarily.

When Pitt got back to Downing Street it was 2 a.m. on the morning of April 30. He read through the papers waiting for him —and realized they contained dreadful news. There was Bar-ham's report that Craig's expedition was in mortal danger, and also reports from one of his spies, who signed himself 'L'Ami', saying that Villeneuve was probably heading for Jamaica, and a later one saying that Napoleon was trying to divert the Royal Navy from his real attack. The weary Pitt sat down to write a note to Barham saying that 'We must not lose a moment in taking measure to set afloat every ship that by any species of extraordinary exertion we can find means to man . . .'

Later next day the old Admiral and the young Prime Minister (whose forty-sixth and last birthday was but twenty-eight days off) met and discussed plans. Then Barham went back to the Admiralty to turn their decisions into orders. These aimed at three main objectives—to save Craig's convoy from annihilation, to keep Ferrol blockaded, and to block the Western Approaches should Orde's guess that the Combined Fleet's destination was the Channel prove correct. The key figure in Barham's consideration was, of course, Nelson: where was he? Had he gone to Egypt? News took a long time to travel, and for this reason Barham's orders to the various commands were complex and overlapping.

The main point that concerns this narrative is that Collingwood was ordered to take Craig's convoy under his wing and escort it as far as Cape St Vincent. If he met Nelson, he was to place himself under the Admiral's command. But if he discovered that Nelson had not followed Villeneuve to the West Indies Collingwood was himself to go in pursuit.

Although Barham had the situation well in hand, the rest of the country was far from calm. The *Morning Chronicle* spoke for many people when it said: 'During the eight days which have just passed no one has slept in peace. Judge of the situation in which our Ministers have placed us when they have reduced us to hope that the French will content themselves with going to conquer our colonial possessions and ravage our settlements.'

Admiral Lord Radstock wrote on May 13 to his son, whom he thought was still in the *Victory* but who had been transferred to the *Hydra*, 'Where are you all this time? For that is a point justly agitating the whole country more than I can describe. I fear your gallant and worthy chief will have much injustice done him on this occasion, for the cry is stirring up fast against him, and the loss of Jamaica would at once sink all his past services into oblivion.'

A week later he reported that 'You may readily guess that your chief is not out of our thoughts at this critical moment. Should Providence once more favour him, he will be considered our guardian angel; but on the other hand, should he unfortunately take a wrong scent, and the Toulon Fleet attain the object, the hero of the 14th of February [the Battle of Cape St Vincent] and of Aboukir [the Battle of the Nile] will be—I will not say what, but the ingratitude of the world is but too well known on these occasions.'

Then, on June 4, the man of whom all Britain wanted news arrived at Barbados, and on the same day three letters which he had sent off a month earlier were delivered to Marsden at the Admiralty. They described his chase to Gibraltar, and said that he had now provisioned his ships for five months and was sailing for Barbados . . . Nelson had done it!

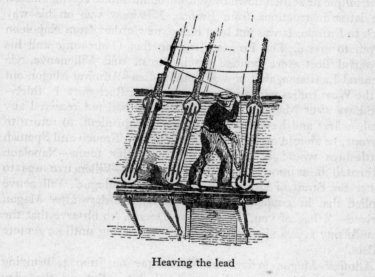

Heaving the lead

10

THE RENDEZVOUS

'Now mark me how I will undo myself . . .'
— Shakespeare (*Richard II*)

VILLENEUVE had arrived in the West Indies on May 16, and at
Martinique he settled down to wait for Ganteaume. Having missed
the latest instructions from France, Missiessy was on his way
back to Europe. It was not long before new orders from Napoleon
began to arrive. The Emperor, seeing that Ganteaume and his
powerful fleet were penned up in Brest, told Villeneuve, via
General Lauriston, that he was sending Rear-Admiral Magon out
to the West Indies with two battleships from Rochefort. If, thirty-
five days after Magon's arrival, Villeneuve had not received any
fresh orders and he deemed it 'proper and prudent' to return to
Europe, he should go to Ferrol. There fifteen French and Spanish
battleships would be waiting, and with this force—Napoleon
estimated it at more than fifty battleships—Villeneuve was to
'enter the Strait of Dover and join me off Boulogne'. Villeneuve
replied that he could not wait for thirty-five days after Magon
arrived—'I beg of you,' he wrote to Decrès, 'to observe that the
state of my stores absolutely forbids my waiting until so remote
a date.'

Admiral Magon arrived in Martinique on June 4, bringing
Villeneuve's fleet up to twenty battleships. But on that day
another fleet arrived in the West Indies. 'At daylight saw Barbados bearing west ten leagues. . . . At eleven received salutes of
Rear-Admiral Cochrane and Charles Fort . . .' wrote Nelson in
his private diary.

In the meantime Villeneuve left Martinique on June 5, the day
after Magon arrived, planning to attack some British-held islands
to the north. Instead, his fleet captured fourteen merchantmen—
not a difficult task, since they were escorted by only a 14-gun
schooner. But from prisoners Villeneuve heard some dreadful
news: Nelson had arrived in the West Indies 'with twelve or
fourteen of the line'.

The French did not know what to do next. 'In this dilemma,'

he wrote, 'I desired to confer with Admiral Gravina. I found him fully agreed as to the necessity of immediately making our way back to Ferrol, there to effect our junction [as Napoleon had ordered] . . . I therefore determined for the greatest advantage to the state, to set sail for Europe.' And on June 11, a week after Nelson's arrival in the West Indies, Villeneuve and his fleet were heading eastwards.

Nelson had, in the meantime, searched first to the southward, owing to a mistaken report, and then come north again. On the 13th, two days after Villeneuve, he 'sailed in my pursuit of the enemy', guessing they had gone back to Cadiz or Toulon. Just before he finally decided to sail for Europe Nelson wrote some letters. One, to Marsden at the Admiralty, said that when he finally returned to European waters he would 'take their Lordships' permission to go to England, to try and repair a very shattered constitution'. A postscript added fresh news which had just been received. 'The French fleet passed to leeward of Antigua on Saturday last, standing to the northward . . . [and I] hope to sail in the morning after them for the Straits mouth.' To a friend in London he wrote: 'I have only a moment to say I am going towards the Mediterranean after Gravina and Villeneuve, and hope to catch them.' And to the Duke of Clarence, he said: 'My heart is almost broke, and, with my very serious complaints I cannot expect long to go on.'

These and other letters were given to Captain G. Bettesworth, of the 18-gun brig *Curieux*, with orders that he was to sail straight to England and deliver them to the Admiralty. Nelson now knew he was close behind the Combined Fleet: the gap of thirty-one days between them had in fact been reduced to two days. On the 19th, when he was six hundred miles out into the Atlantic from Antigua, an American ship, the *Sally*, gave him the enemy's position. Nelson wrote to Marsden, 'I think we cannot be more than eighty leagues [240 miles] from them at this moment, and by carrying every sail, and using my utmost efforts, I shall hope to close with them before they get to either Cadiz or Toulon.'

Once again he was to be unlucky. He crossed Villeneuve's tracks one night and for the rest of the voyage back to Europe the Combined Fleet was to be to the north of him. But Captain Bettesworth of the *Curieux* had better luck: sailing a more northerly course because he was bound for the United Kingdom, he spotted the Combined Fleet. It was so far north that he realized it was bound for somewhere in the Bay of Biscay, and not the Strait of Gibraltar, as Nelson expected. Should he dash back to warn Nelson, or press on to warn Barham? Quite rightly he decided to sail on and warn the Admiralty. Nelson, however, was having second thoughts. He sent a frigate to warn the admiral blockading Ferrol to watch for the returning enemy; Captain Sutton, in the frigate *Amphion*, was sent ahead to Tangier to find out if the Combined Fleet had gone into the Mediterranean; later the *Amazon* was sent to search off Cape St Vincent and Cadiz.

In the meantime Napoleon was busy changing his plans. Realizing that Villeneuve would not be able to wait thirty-five days in the West Indies, he ordered him to come back to Europe as quickly as possible, free the squadrons of Gourdon, Missiessy and Ganteaume, and get to the Channel—'the principal object of the whole operation is to procure our superiority before Boulogne for some days'. However, if Villeneuve could not do all this, he was to go to Cadiz. Unfortunately for Napoleon, these orders arrived in the West Indies after Villeneuve had sailed. . . . In Rochefort, Commodore Allemand succeeded Missiessy and was told that if the British blockade lifted, he was to go to sea and wait for Villeneuve one hundred and twenty miles west of Ferrol from July 29 to August 3.

The *Curieux* arrived at Plymouth on July 7 and Captain Bettesworth immediately rushed to London with Nelson's letters and his own news of sighting the Combined Fleet. As a result of this sighting, Barham straightway changed his plans. Previously he had reinforced Collingwood's weak force off Cadiz to make 'a strong force at the very spot where they might be expected'. Now here was Bettesworth reporting that the Combined Fleet was heading farther north. He therefore sent off orders reinforcing Calder's squadron and ordering it to patrol from thirty to one hundred and fifty miles to the west of Cape Finisterre. These orders were written by the octogenarian First Lord early in the morning a few minutes after waking and before he had time to dress. They were contained in half a dozen lines scribbled on a piece of paper, and they were quite sufficient.

On July 22 Villeneuve, with his twenty French and Spanish battleships, ran into Calder's fifteen battleships off Cape Finisterre. Beginning in the late afternoon, the battle lasted four hours in bad visibility. Calder captured two of Villeneuve's battleships and Villeneuve damaged several of the British ships. 'A very decisive action,' wrote Calder, who was to be court-martialled later for not doing his utmost to renew the battle. Villeneuve naturally saw it differently. 'The enemy then made off. . . . He had had several ships crippled aloft, and the field of battle remained ours. Cries of joy and victory were heard from all our ships.' But Calder prevented Villeneuve going into Ferrol, and the next day Villeneuve decided to steer for Cadiz. Then bad weather

A barque

sprang up and he changed his mind and ran into Vigo. The Combined Fleet was back in port—and its troubles were only just starting.

Hopefully Nelson had sailed back across the Atlantic, praying that he would catch up with Villeneuve. On June 21 he wrote in his private diary: 'Midnight, nearly calm, saw three planks, which I think came from the French fleet. Very miserable, which is very foolish.' Nearly a month later, with the African shore close by, he wrote another entry: 'Cape Spartel in sight, but no French fleet, nor any information about them—how sorrowful this makes me, but I cannot help myself!' Nelson finally anchored his fleet at Gibraltar on July 19. He wrote once again in his private diary on the 20th: 'I went on shore for the first time since the 16th of

June, 1803; and from having my foot out of the *Victory*, two years wanting ten days.'

In a letter to Barham he said: 'I have yet not a word of information of the enemy's fleet; it has almost broken my heart.' But on July 25 a ship arrived with a Lisbon newspaper which told him about Bettesworth's glimpse of the Combined Fleet, and the position was so far north that Nelson guessed Villeneuve must have been making for the Bay of Biscay. He immediately sailed northwards—running into strong headwinds—to join the Brest fleet off Ushant. 'I shall only hope, after my long pursuit of *my* enemy, that I may arrive at the moment they are meeting you; for my very wretched state of health will force me to get on shore for a little while,' he wrote to Cornwallis, who was once again off Brest.

But, as we have seen, Nelson was too late: by the time he joined Cornwallis, Villeneuve was safe in Vigo. Then, worn-out and with an ever-increasing sense of failure weighing him down, Nelson left his ships under Cornwallis's command and sailed for Portsmouth in the *Victory*, taking only the battered old *Superb*, commanded by Richard Keats, with him.

11

TWENTY-FIVE DAYS

*'I was only twenty-five days, from dinner to dinner,
absent from the Victory. In our several stations, my dear
Admiral, we must all put our shoulders to the wheel, and
make the great machine of the Fleet intrusted to our charge
go on smoothly.'*

—Nelson, September 30, 1805

THE WIND was very light, and with irritating slowness the *Victory*
worked her way up Channel. Daylight on August 17 showed
Portland Bill over on the port beam, with Weymouth Bay stretching away on the bow and farther ahead the heavy indistinct
masses, dark and menacing, in the chilly early mist, of St Alban's
Head and Anvil Point.

A day earlier Nelson received the first news of how England
had reacted to Calder's action. Although worried about the
reception in England of his own failure to capture Villeneuve—
he feared the worst—he wrote to his friend Captain Thomas
Fremantle that he 'was in truth bewildered by the account of Sir
Robert Calder's victory, and the joy of the event; together with
the hearing that *John Bull* was not content, which I am sorry for.
Who can, my dear Fremantle, command all the success which
our Country may wish?

'We have fought together [at Copenhagen], and therefore well
know what it is. I have had the best disposed fleet of friends, but
who can say what will be the event of a battle? And it most
sincerely grieves me, that in any of the papers it should be in-
sinuated, that Lord Nelson could have done better. I should
have fought the enemy, so did my friend Calder; but who can say
that he will be more successful than another—I only wish to stand
upon my own merits, and not by comparison, one way or the
other, upon the conduct of a brother officer.'

The wind was still light as the day passed and it was dark by
the time the *Victory* nosed past St Catherine's Point and then,
after losing the wind altogether, anchored off Dunnose Head.
She was there for nearly six hours while Nelson waited

impatiently, anxious to be on his way to Merton Place, where his beloved Emma was waiting for him.

In addition to being tired after two years and three months at sea, he was anxious at the reception that might be waiting for him, both from the crowds probably waiting at the quay and at the Admiralty, where Lord Barham was an almost complete stranger. He had all the misgivings that bedevil a long absence. There were, however, more delays. The *Victory* got under way just before dawn and sailed round to Spithead, but Nelson was not allowed ashore because there was yellow fever in Spain and Portugal, and the *Victory* had, of course, called at Gibraltar. Despite his protestations that there was no fever there 'nor any apprehension of one' when he left, and that 'neither the *Victory* nor the *Superb* have on board even an object for the hospital', he had to stay in the ship for another day—until the evening of the 19th.

By the time his barge reached the shore a large cheering crowd had gathered. After a courtesy call on the Commander-in-Chief, Nelson went along to the George, in the High Street, to wait for a postchaise. Rain was pouring down when finally he climbed into the carriage and the horses plunged forward up the London road. It was a wearisome journey through the night with raindrops streaming down the windows of the coach, but dawn brought Nelson his first sight for many months of the lush green fields. At 6 a.m., tired, cramped, dusty and yet excited, he reached Merton.

His home was a red-brick, two-storey house. A tributary of the River Wandle—Lady Hamilton called it 'The Nile'—passed through the grounds and a previous owner had built an elaborate, Italian-style bridge across it. Many strange trees grew round the house and Virginia creeper climbed over the porch. And now his dreams had come true—he was back again, with Emma to welcome him. Soon they would be laughing with their daughter Horatia, now four and a half and learning to play the piano. His first day at Merton was spent quietly. Various members of his family were staying there, and apart from the uncertainty of his meeting with Barham, there was little to trouble him. He was a vice-admiral and viscount, and when he set foot in the streets the crowds cheered him for a popular hero. He loved a woman deeply and was deeply loved in return. The fact that the woman was not his wife did not damage that love; perhaps it made it more urgent.

At long last he had a home befitting his position—even though he still had to repay the money he had borrowed to buy it. Horatia had been born, and successfully passed off as his adopted daughter. The ruse did nothing to lessen his love for her. He knew he had the love and respect of his captains; his circle of friends was a large one.

For the next three weeks Nelson was to be busy discussing high policy with the nation's leaders, knowing his opinion was wanted and listened to with great interest. He knew, as will be seen, that his days were numbered; yet these few remaining days were perhaps the happiest of his life. He was a man consumed with zeal and ambition—ambition for his King and for his country. Now they were being recognized and fulfilled. Although he had to die, he was to die content.

Next morning, August 21, he set off early for London with Emma. Whitehall was an hour's drive from Merton, and Emma left him at the Admiralty at 9.30 a.m., going on to her little house in Clarges Street.

It is unlikely that Nelson was looking forward to his meeting with Lord Barham when his carriage clattered through the narrow Whitehall entrance of the Admiralty. There is no doubt that Barham was not unreasonably suspicious of the vain and colourful young Admiral. Had Nelson's conduct in his long and fruitless chase of Villeneuve been all that it should have been? Could he be trusted once again with command in the Mediterranean during what were obviously going to be extremely critical days?

The shrewd old First Lord was certainly determined not to let Nelson's previous victories at the Nile and Copenhagen blind him to possible faults or errors of judgment. In fact Nelson had been greeted, on arriving in England, with a request that he forward journals for the First Lord's inspection. It was at that period an unusual thing to do, but typical of Barham's sensible, down-to-earth approach. From his chilly reply Nelson apparently read into the request a possible criticism of his conduct—a point about which he was already very sensitive, as we have seen—and he replied to Marsden: 'I beg leave to acquaint you that never having been called upon (or understanding it to be customary) as Commander-in-Chief to furnish their Lordships with a journal of my proceedings, none has been kept for that purpose, except for different periods the fleet under my command was in pursuit of the enemy . . . which I herewith transmit for the information of the Lords Commissioners of the Admiralty.'

The happy result is reported by Nelson's biographers, writing only a short time after the event. Lord Barham 'perused the whole narrative with an attention which enabled that Minister to form a more complete idea of the Admiral's professional character; and Lord Barham afterwards liberally declared he had not before sufficiently appreciated such extraordinary talents. This opinion of the noble Admiral's late proceedings was immediately communicated to the Cabinet, with an assurance from Lord Barham that unbounded confidence ought to be placed in Nelson; who was above all others the officer to be employed on the station he had so ably watched, and whose political relations he had so thoroughly understood.' We have no reason to think that the biographers exaggerated, because every door in Whitehall was opened to him. He saw Mr Pitt and Lord Castlereagh almost immediately, and later reported to his friend Keats that both men 'were all full of the enemy's fleet, and as I am now set up for a *Conjuror*, and God knows they will very soon find out I am far from being one, I was asked my opinion, against my inclination, for if I make one wrong guess the charm will be broken. . . . You will see [by] my writing tackle that I am not mounted as Commander-in-Chief.'

The discussions he had with Pitt and Castlereagh during the next few days covered a wide range of subjects. Russia, after a lot of delaying, had just signed the new Treaty and should already be marching through Austria. The time was rapidly coming for Craig's attack from southern Italy, although it was not yet known whether he had reached Malta. On the other hand the Neapolitan kingdom might give way to Napoleon before Craig arrived. Nelson's knowledge of the Mediterranean in general and the Kingdom of Naples in particular was invaluable, though his suggestions for securing Sardinia as a powerful base were less well received.

Nelson had many other calls to make and people to see. One visit was to Mr Peddison in Brewer Street, off Regent Street. Mr Peddison was an upholsterer who had in his care Nelson's coffin. This was a gift from Captain Benjamin Hallowell, a burly Canadian with the build and face of a prize-fighter. A devoted friend of Nelson's—they had slept in the same trench at the siege of Calvi and fought together at Cape St Vincent—he had, at the Battle of the Nile, commanded the *Swiftsure*. After the French *L'Orient* blew up, part of her mainmast was brought on board. Hallowell (according to his brother-in-law, Rear-Admiral Inglefield), fearing the effect of all the praise and flattery being heaped on Nelson, ordered a coffin to be made from it. He gave instructions that nothing should be used which had not come from the mast. Nails and staples were made from metal fittings, and when the coffin was completed a piece of paper was pasted on the bottom saying 'I do hereby certify that every part of this coffin is made from the wood and iron of *L'Orient*, most of which was picked up by His Majesty's ship under my command, in the Bay of Aboukir. *Swiftsure*, May 23, 1797—Ben Hallowell.'

He then sent the coffin to Nelson with a covering letter: 'My Lord, Herewith I send you a coffin made of part of the *L'Orient*'s mainmast, that when you are tired of this life you may be buried in one of your own trophies—but may that period be far distant, is the sincere wish of your obedient and much obliged servant, Ben Hallowell.' Although the officers aboard the Admiral's flagship were appalled when they saw it being brought on board, Nelson was delighted. Far from being disturbed by a constant reminder of his mortality, he had it placed upright, with the lid on, against the bulkhead of his cabin, behind the chair on which he sat at dinner.[1] It was finally removed after 'the entreaties of an old servant' and ended up in Mr Peddison's care at Brewer Street until its owner was ready for it.

Now apparently having a premonition that he would shortly be making his last voyage, Nelson went to have a look at it and also give some more instructions. Made entirely of half-inch thick planks of fir, the outside was covered in fine black cloth. Mr Peddison's upholsterers had made a good job of the inside, which was padded with cotton and then lined with silk, the top being trimmed with a quilting of mitred silk. The coffin was six feet long but narrow. Nelson inspected the upholstery and then told Mr Peddison to have the wording of Hallowell's certificate of authenticity engraved on the lid, 'for,' he said, 'I think it highly probable that I may want it on my return.'

Among his many visits, both ministerial and macabre, Nelson found time to entertain a Danish author. Mr Andreas Andersen Feldborg had met Nelson accidentally in Pall Mall and this led him to pay a call on August 26, when the Admiral had been at

---

[1] Nelson, seeing his officers looking at it one day, said: 'You may look at it, gentlemen, as long as you please; but, depend on it, none of you shall have it.'

home at Merton for nearly a week. An erudite man who spoke fluent Russian, Feldborg had published a slim book on the Battle of Copenhagen, which a year earlier had been translated into English and published in London. He had sent a presentation copy to the victor, and thanks to this urge to talk with him we can get a glimpse of Nelson at the height of his power and within a few weeks of his death, for Feldborg, under the pseudonym of 'J. A. Andersen', was preparing another volume, finally published four years after Trafalgar. Called *A Dane's Excursions in Britain*, it describes his first visit to Merton.

'Merton Place is not a large, but a very elegant, structure; in the balconies I observed a great number of ladies, who I understood to be Lord Nelson's relations,' he wrote. 'Entering the house I proceeded through a lobby, which, among a variety of paintings, and other pieces of art, contained an excellent marble bust of the illustrious Admiral. . . . I was then ushered into a magnificent apartment, where Lady Hamilton sat at the window; I at first scarcely observed his Lordship, he having placed himself immediately at the entrance on the right. The Admiral wore a uniform emblazoned with different orders of knighthood; he received me with the utmost condescension.[1]

'Chairs being provided, Lord Nelson sat down between Lady Hamilton and myself, and having laid an account of the Battle of Copenhagen on his knee crosswise, a conversation ensued which I strongly imprinted on my memory the following particulars.' The conversation, according to Feldborg, was as follows, with Nelson saying:

'It seems you have written an account of the Battle of Copenhagen, sir!'

'I have, my Lord.'

'Well, sir! Since we did not fight the Danes from choice, I hope we are friends again.'

'I trust so, my Lord, since the obstinacy of their resistance has so eminently tended to exalt the character of the Danes in the opinion of the British nation.'

'I have found a passage in your account, which is not, perhaps, quite correct, sir.' Nelson paused for some time, and then continued: 'However, in the distribution of shadow, you would of

---

[1] Feldborg uses the word 'condescension' in the sense of 'kindliness'. Nelson's chaplain, writing after the Admiral's death, uses the word in the same way.

course hold the pencil in a manner different from what an English-man would have done.'

Feldborg said he was going to publish in English a book on Denmark and Norway soon, and Nelson asked: 'You intend to embellish the work with a portrait of the Crown Prince of Denmark? Come with me, and you shall see your Prince.' The two men went upstairs, where Nelson pointed out a portrait. 'Descending from the drawing-room, Lord Nelson paused on the staircase, the walls of which were adorned with prints of his Lordship's battles, and other naval engagements; he pointed out to me the Battle of Copenhagen, which was a tolerably correct engraving,' commented Feldborg.

As frequently as he was able, the Dane closely observed the man who, on the eve of Good Friday four years earlier, had sailed past Kronborg Castle to attack nineteen ships and floating batteries off Copenhagen in a battle which broke up one of Napoleon's most cherished ambitions—a Northern coalition against Britain. Mr Feldborg was impressed with what he saw: 'Lord Nelson was in his person of a middle stature, a thin body, and an apparently delicate constitution. The lines of his face were hard; but the penetration of his eye threw a kind of light on his countenance which tempered its severity, and rendered his harsh features in some measure agreeable. His luxuriant hair flowed in graceful ringlets down his temples, and his aspect commanded the utmost veneration, especially when he looked upward. Lord Nelson had not the least pride of rank; but combined with that degree of dignity, which a man of quality should have, the most engaging address in his air and manners.'

Another man whom Nelson met was Henry Addington, now Viscount Sidmouth, whose weak and vacillating premiership had been superseded by that of Pitt. 'Lord Nelson surprised me yesterday in Clifford Street,' Sidmouth recorded, 'without my coat, just as I had undergone the operation of bleeding. He looked well, and we passed an hour together very comfortably.'

The Admiral met a deputation from the committee of Merchants of London trading to the West Indies. The merchants had unanimously agreed 'That the prompt determination of Lord Nelson to quit the Mediterranean' in search of the French Fleet had been 'very instrumental to the safety of the West India islands.'

And he found time, in the evenings, for entertainment. Lady Bessborough reported the gossip from one dinner table to Lord

Leveson-Gower: 'Bess [Lady Elizabeth Foster] and Ca [Lady Exeter's son] din'd at Crawford's Tuesday to meet him. Both she and he say that so far from appearing vain and full of himself, as one has always heard, he was perfectly unassuming and natural. Talking of popular applause and his having been mobbed and huzza'd in the City, Lady Hamilton wanted him to give an account of it, but he stopped her. "Why," she said, "you like to be applauded—you cannot deny it." "I own it," he answered, "popular applause is very acceptable and grateful to me, but no man ought to be too much elated by it; it is too precarious to be depended upon, and as it may be my turn to feel the tide set as strong against me as ever it did for me."

'Everybody joined in saying they did not believe that it could happen to him, but he seemed persuaded that it might, but added: "Whilst I live I shall do what I think right and best; the country has a right to that from me, but every man is liable to err in judgment. . . ." He says nothing short of the annihilation of the enemy's fleet will do any good. "When we meet, God be with us, for we must not part again till one fleet or other is totally destroyed." He hopes to be returned by Christmas. . . .'

Later she wrote: 'Lord Holland says Lady Hamilton told the Fish [Mr James Crawford] that if she could be Lord Nelson's wife for one hour she should die contented, and that he always invokes her in his prayers before action, and during the battle cries out very often, "For Emma and England".'

Nelson's favourite, Richard Keats, who had returned to England with the *Superb* at the same time as the *Victory*, soon arrived at Merton Place. He and Nelson walked through the grounds together, talking cheerfully as they skirted 'The Nile' with its ornate bridge, and passed from the sunshine into the shade of the tall cedars of Lebanon. The two old friends were soon talking of naval battles. Nelson said: 'No day can be long enough to arrange a couple of fleets, and fight a decisive battle, according to the old system.

'When *we* meet them [Keats was expected to be with him], for meet them we shall, I'll tell you how I shall fight them. I shall form the fleet into three divisions in three lines. One division shall be composed of twelve or fourteen of the fastest two-decked ships, which I shall keep always to windward, or in a situation of advantage; and I shall put them under an officer who, I am sure, will employ them in the manner I wish, if possible.

'I consider it will always be in my power to throw them into battle in any part I may choose; but if circumstances prevent their being carried against the enemy where I desire, I shall feel certain he will employ them effectually, and, perhaps, in a more advantageous manner than if he could have followed my orders.

'With the remaining part of the fleet formed in two lines I shall go at them at once, if I can, about one-third of their line from their leading ships.'

Keats, describing the rest of the conversation, wrote: 'He then said, "What do you think of it?" Such a question, I felt, required

The wheel and tiller: the tiller ropes go from the barrel of the wheel down to the tiller—a horizontal beam on the head of the rudder. In front of the men is the binnacle, containing the compass. The wheel would normally be double—the forward one is not shown

consideration. I paused. Seeing it, he said, "But I'll tell you what I think of it. I think it will confound and surprise the enemy. They won't know what I am about. It will bring forward a pell-mell battle, and that is what I want." '

Richard Keats, although he was destined to miss the battle, appears to have been the first to have heard from Nelson his plan of attack, which he was to modify when he finally caught the Combined Fleet. The other person who heard his plan was Lord Sidmouth. Nelson went over to Richmond Park to see him several days after he knew he was to rejoin the Fleet. Sidmouth's biographer says, 'His Lordship was accustomed in after years to relate to his friends interesting particulars of this interview. Among other things, Lord Nelson explained to him with his finger, on the little study table, the manner in which, should he be so fortunate as to meet the Combined Fleet, he purposed to attack them. "Rodney," he said, "broke the line in one point; I will break it in two." '[1]

[1] A tablet which Sidmouth later had inscribed and put on the table, stated that Nelson said 'he should attack them in two lines, led by himself and Admiral Collingwood [he had not mentioned Collingwood's name to Keats]; and felt confident that he would capture either their van and centre; or centre and rear'.

12

NEWS AT LAST

'Happy thou art not;
For what thou hast not, still thou strivest to get;
And what thou hast, forgett'st.'
　　　　　　　—Shakespeare (*Measure for Measure*)

THE NOISE of a dusty postchaise drawn by four horses clattering up the drive at five o'clock in the morning on Monday, September 2, warned Nelson—who was already up, shaved and dressed—either that urgent orders were coming from the Admiralty or, judging from the time, an important and unexpected visitor was arriving. It turned out to be a visitor—a tired man whose round and ruddy, sun-burned features with an incongruous aquiline nose were more those of a rich farmer than the naval captain that his creased uniform proclaimed him. And when he was ushered in, Nelson's face lit up, for he was Henry Blackwood of the *Euryalus*, at thirty-five years of age one of the greatest frigate captains the Navy has ever had, and whom Nelson knew had been watching the French.

As Blackwood gripped Nelson's left hand in greeting, the Admiral exclaimed: 'I am sure you bring me news of the French and Spanish fleets, and I think I shall yet have to beat them!'

And that was, indeed, why Blackwood had called: searching for the enemy after the Combined Fleet left Ferrol and Corunna, he had found them off Cape St Vincent and shadowed them. He had been chased but held on until he made sure the enemy had gone into Cadiz. Then, using every trick of seamanship he knew to keep the *Euryalus*'s sails drawing in fluky winds which strained every ounce of his patience, Blackwood hurried north to raise the alarm. Sixty miles from Cape St Vincent he met Calder who, as soon as he heard Blackwood's news, sped south to join Collingwood's small force and slam the door on Cadiz.

Within ten days Blackwood had reached the jagged rocky outcrop at the western tip of the Isle of Wight so aptly named the Needles, but night was coming on—which meant the telegraph from Portsmouth to London could not be used—and the wind was falling away. The quickest way now of getting his news to London was to go himself. So he had taken the *Euryalus* into Alum Bay and anchored in the lee of the Needles. As soon as a boat was lowered he had been rowed across the Solent to Lymington Creek, as it was then called, and between the salt pans and mud flats flanking the river up to the village of Lymington, then sleeping on the edge of the New Forest. Hiring a postchaise and four—he later sent the Admiralty a £15 9s. bill for the journey—he was soon rattling northwards into the gloomy New Forest, startling the sturdy wild ponies as they grazed beside the road and bound for the Admiralty by way of Merton.

His brief message to Nelson delivered, Blackwood climbed back into his carriage and the driver started off again. Nelson, left behind in the chilly house, had to break to Emma the news which she had been dreading to hear yet knew must one day arrive. There are several apocryphal accounts of that conversation which need not be repeated here, but she described her feelings two days later in a letter to Nelson's niece. 'I am again heartbroken,' she said, 'as our dear Nelson is immediately going. It seems as though I have had a fortnight's dream, and am awoke to all the misery of this cruel separation. But what can I do? His powerful arm is of so much consequence to his country. . . . My heart is broken.'

Nelson's exclamation at whatever reply Emma had made is, however, on record: 'Brave Emma! Good Emma!' he said. 'If there were more Emmas there would be more Nelsons.' And within a short time the pair of them were in a carriage chasing up the London road after Blackwood, Nelson bound for the Admiralty and Emma, after leaving him there, for her house in Clarges Street.

Nelson knew beyond doubt that his hour had come. As he wrote later to his friend Davison, 'I hope my absence will not be long, and that I shall soon meet the Combined Fleets with a force sufficient to do the job well; for half a victory would but half content me. But I do not believe the Admiralty can give me a force within fifteen or sixteen sail of the line of the enemy . . . but I will do my best; and I hope God Almighty will go with me. I have much to lose, but little to gain; and I go because it's right, and I will serve the country faithfully.'

Lord Barham was in his little office at the Admiralty when Nelson strode into the hall, turned left past the small, bare waiting-room, where in a few weeks his body would be lying in

Ben Hallowell's coffin for a brief few hours before the funeral at St Paul's Cathedral, and up the narrow stairs. The old and white-haired First Lord and the young Admiral sat down to discuss plans upon which, quite simply, the whole safety and future of Britain depended; plans which could make history take a sharp turn; plans which could and would affect the future of the world for more than a century.[1] Fortunately, both men knew it. They were superb strategists and for once war plans were being made which paid no court to fickle chance, and which were not hurried half-measures drawn up by amateurs to placate an angry and alarmed Parliament nor desperate attempts to plug the breach after some ill-digested scheme dreamed up by ineffectual ministerial placemen had inevitably gone awry.

Both Barham and Nelson knew they had a most formidable task before them. The overall situation in Europe at this time, as far as British policy was concerned, was extremely delicate. The Czar had at last ratified the Anglo-Russian treaty—the despatch from St Petersburg revealing this had arrived on August 22, and furthermore he was sending an army to help Austria. Austria in turn had said she would adhere to the Third Coalition, but first she wanted to try to mediate. At the same time the Russians were becoming impatient for action in southern Italy: their General Lacy was waiting for Craig to arrive, and London still did not know where Craig's convoy was. While they waited anxiously, they knew that Napoleon's emissaries were trying to frighten the Neapolitan Court. . . .

But Blackwood's news that Villeneuve was in Cadiz eased their minds on one point: while at sea the Combined Fleet had been a powerful threat both to Craig and to British shipping returning from the four corners of the world. There was, for instance, the rich convoy from India, valued at £15 million, which was also bringing back a young major-general named Sir Arthur Wellesley, the future Duke of Wellington, but now thirty-six and fresh from his victories at Assye and Angaum.

The precise problem now facing Barham and Nelson was how to deal with the new situation brought about by Villeneuve's move to Cadiz. Villeneuve had a total of thirty-three battleships in that port, while Allemand was at sea with four more battleships, and

[1] If the Royal Navy lost control of the sea, then the Army could not have been transported to strike back at Napoleon; by the same token Napoleon would have been free to strike where he wished.

Ganteaume was still in Brest with twenty-one battleships. At this moment, on September 2, Calder was off Cadiz, adding his eighteen battleships to Collingwood's small force. Nelson had two bare alternatives—to force or lure Villeneuve to sail, and then fight a completely decisive action; or to blockade the Combined Fleet in Cadiz through the whole of the coming winter. How was he to get Villeneuve out of Cadiz? Ironically enough, the very weakness of the British fleet off Cadiz might do the trick by giving the French Admiral enough courage to sail: yet that very weakness could possibly prevent Nelson from delivering the decisive blow that would, once and for all, put an end to Napoleon's threats at sea. While Nelson waited off Cadiz, Barham would send out every ship he could repair or refit, man and get to sea.

The first of many orders to leave the Admiralty after the two men started their task was telegraphed to Portsmouth to stop the *Victory* sailing, for she had just been ordered to join Cornwallis off Brest.

With Nelson resuming his rôle of Commander-in-Chief in the Mediterranean, which would include the Cadiz area, there came the question of which ships and officers he was to have. Once again Barham showed his admiration for Nelson's leadership. He gave him the latest edition of the *List of the Navy* containing the names of all its officers, and told him to choose whom he wanted. Nelson handed it back. 'Choose yourself, my Lord, the same spirit actuates the whole profession; you cannot choose wrong.' Barham then told him to dictate to his secretary, Mr John Deas Thompson, the ships he wanted to join his squadron off Cadiz, and they would be ordered to follow him as soon as they were ready. 'Have no scruple, Lord Nelson, there is my secretary. I will leave the room. Give your orders to him, and rely on it that they shall be implicitly obeyed by me.' Nelson started dictating.

Later that same day an unconfirmed report reached London that Napoleon's Great Army of England was breaking camp at Boulogne. It was only a report, but it held out hope. . . . Was the great invasion threat about to end?

The seven senior clerks at the Admiralty, who were paid between £350 and £800 a year, and the seventeen junior clerks, who received between £90 and £250, had on August 29 put in a claim for higher pay. It could not have been better timed, for between September 2 and September 6 they had to work like slaves preparing orders to set in motion Barham's and Nelson's decisions, and of course this came on top of their normal routine work.

Although Nelson had refused Barham's offer to choose his own captains, undoubtedly he did name at least a few. One was Captain Sir Edward Berry, a man who, coming from a poor family, had won command and fame with a pistol in one hand and a cutlass in the other. He was a fearless, desperate fighter, never happier than when leading hand-to-hand fighting across the decks of an enemy ship. He had little or no ability as a tactician or thinker, but fortune had smiled on his bravery. He had been with Howe on the Glorious First of June; at Cape St Vincent he had been on board Nelson's *Captain* when the battered seventy-four had captured two Spanish battleships with pistols and cutlasses, and he had led the party which took one of them, the *San Nicolas*. At the Nile he had been Nelson's flag captain in the *Vanguard*, and it was into his arms that the wounded Nelson, blood streaming down his face, had reeled with the words: 'I am killed. . . .'

Now, however, Berry was being neglected by the Admiralty and could not get a ship. As soon as Nelson had arrived at Merton, Berry wrote to him complaining of the treatment he had received. 'A man's standing in the Service, and his *reputation* (and who has *not reputation* that has served with you?) all goes for nought,' he had declared, expressing a wish that he could once again be at sea with the Admiral. A few days later, thanks to the news Blackwood had brought home, Nelson could satisfy Berry. He was to command the *Agamemnon*, which was considered by the French Admiral Allemand to be 'England's fastest ship,' and, as mentioned earlier, was one of the ships built by Henry Adams at Buckler's Hard.

Orders to place themselves under Nelson's command went out to Berry; to Henry Blackwood, who commanded another of Adams's ships, the *Euryalus*; to Richard Keats and his *Superb*, which was now being hurriedly repaired at Portsmouth; to the faithful Hardy in the *Victory*; to the *Royal Sovereign*, and the *Defiance*, which was in Portsmouth repairing the damage received in Calder's action against Villeneuve. Captain Philip Durham, who commanded the *Defiance*, had gone to the Admiralty and by chance met Nelson, who said, 'I am just appointed to the command in the Mediterranean, and sail immediately. I am sorry your ship is not ready; I should have been glad to have you.' This was quite enough for Durham: 'Ask Lord Barham to place me under Your Lordship's orders and I will soon be ready,' he replied. Nelson agreed and promised to leave orders for him at Portsmouth.

The preliminary orders to the ships already mentioned (and to the *Ajax*, commanded by Captain William Brown, and the *Thunderer*, under Captain William Lechmere, both of whom had been with Durham in Calder's action and were now at Plymouth) were identical and brief and began with the time-honoured preamble.

> You are hereby required and directed to put yourself under the command of the R^t Honble Lord V^t Nelson, K.B. Vice Admiral of the White, and follow his lordship's orders for your proceedings.
>
> Given &c 5th September 1805.
>
> J. Gambier[1]
> P. Patton
> Garlies.

And among the many other orders sent out and aimed at reinforcing the fleet of Cadiz was one to Lt Lapenotiere. The little *Pickle* had been busy for the past few months operating off the French, Spanish and Portuguese coasts. Now she was at Plymouth having some repairs done. The order said:

> You are hereby directed and required to put to sea in the gun vessel you command the moment she shall be ready, and wind and weather permit, and use your best endeavours to join Vice-Admiral Lord Viscount Nelson agreeably to the accompanying rendezvous; and having so done, put yourself under his command and follow his orders for your further proceedings.

The remaining days that Nelson spent in England were busy while he prepared for his last expedition. There were more orders to draft, and more talks with ministers. On Thursday, September 5, the same day that the orders for the ships at Portsmouth and Plymouth were despatched, his steward, Henry Chevalier and valet, Gaetano Spedilo, left Merton for Portsmouth and the *Victory* with Nelson's heavy baggage. On Friday, after Nelson returned from a visit to Downing Street to see Pitt, the Duke of

---

[1] Gambier, the First Sea Lord, was Barham's nephew and held the post before Barham's appointment. Vice-Admiral Philip Patton and Lord Garlies were also members of the Board of Admiralty.

Collingwood. *From the painting by Howard*

Nelson's Hardy. *From the painting by Abbott*

Captain George Duff, who was killed in the battle while in command of the *Mars. From the painting by Raeburn in possession of the Misses Duff*

Nelson explains his plan of attack before the Battle of Trafalgar. *From a print dated January 9, 1806*

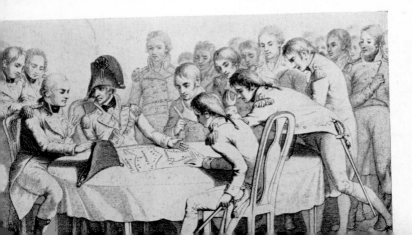

Clarence arrived at Merton for the christening of the son of Colonel Maurice Suckling, Nelson's cousin.

On Saturday a letter arrived from Marsden saying that Nelson's orders were ready and asking him to call at the Admiralty to collect them. The Admiral went straight away, to find that the First Lord had given him a free hand for all intents and purposes: he was to stop the enemy putting to sea from Cadiz, and protect the convoys in the Mediterranean. While at the Admiralty, Nelson wrote a short note to reassure Collingwood. 'My dear Coll,' he said, 'I shall be with you in a very few days, and I hope you will remain second-in-command. You will change the *Dreadnought* for *Royal Sovereign*, which I hope you will like.'

On the comparatively quiet Sunday all the Merton household headed by the Admiral (himself the son of a country parson) went off to the parish church of St Mary the Virgin where the Reverend Thomas Lancaster took the service. Mr Lancaster's feelings must have been very mixed. No doubt gratified to see the Admiral with his household and friends, he also knew that the great man was about to join the *Victory*, and he had agreed to take one of the vicar's younger sons with him as a volunteer. The subject of the sermon he preached has not been recorded.

Nelson was at the Admiralty again on Monday; on Tuesday he went over to Richmond Park to see Lord Sidmouth and, as already mentioned, to tell him his plan for fighting the Combined Fleet. In the evening he went to the dinner with Mr Crawford which Lady Bessborough has described. Wednesday was spent at the Admiralty issuing more orders, while Thursday was a day of official farewells. He also made his final visits to the Admiralty. One of the main reasons for this was his anxiety over a signal code, copies of which he wanted to take out to the Fleet with him.

Until quite recently the signals used by the Navy consisted of ten flags representing the numbers one to nine and zero, plus flags for a substitute (so that the same number could be used twice) and 'Yes' and 'No'. *The Signal Book for the Ships of War* at this time gave more than four hundred sentences, each of which were represented by two or three figures. Number thirteen, for instance, was *Prepare for battle*, and number sixteen *Engage the enemy more closely*. This was comparatively simple, but the code had to deal with every eventuality its compilers could think of— thus number 280 meant *Send for fresh beef immediately*, while 254

E

was *Fire ships are to prime and to be held in constant readiness to proceed on service*, and number sixty-three was *Anchor as soon as convenient*.

The limitations of the system, where a group of two or three figures meant a whole sentence or order, are obvious: the orders the Admiral could give to his fleet were limited entirely to the signals in the book. By 1805, when the signal book was only six years old, another eighty orders had been written into it. But the effect was to shackle the admiral, for he could not order any manœuvre unless it was 'in the book'. The system was not nearly flexible enough: it was as if a Frenchman was trying to write poetry in English using only an English tourist phrase book containing less than five hundred phrases.

To overcome this problem, Sir Home Popham had produced a system where flags meant individual words. His first volume was called *Telegraphic Signals, or Marine Vocabulary*.[1] Containing nearly a thousand specially chosen words, it was a revolution in signalling—similar to giving the French poet a small dictionary in place of the phrase book. It meant that the Admiral could signal his own words—and therefore original thoughts and ideas —to his fleet, within the limits of Home Popham's choice. To avoid confusion with the 1799 code, a Popham code signal would be indicated by a white and red preparative or telegraph flag.

Popham's code was not adopted immediately: for at least twelve years he produced the books privately and gave them away to his brother officers with the request that they try it out. He issued a second part in 1803, and this added another thousand words, while part three, a little later, added a number of sentences and phrases. Even though the system had not been fully adopted by 1805, many warships had copies.

Nelson wanted to get enough copies of Home Popham's complete code to supply all his ships; they had been ordered from the printer, Mr C. Roworth, of Bell Yard, Temple Bar, earlier, but had not yet arrived. When he got to the Admiralty the Admiral was disappointed. Sir John Barrow, the Second Secretary, wrote that in the morning Nelson had been 'anxiously inquiring and expressing his hopes about a code of signals [Home Popham's] just then improved and enlarged. I assured him they were all but ready; that he should not be disappointed, and that

---

[1] 'Telegraph' in this sense, some thirty years before the invention of the electric telegraph, was used in the literal sense of writing at a distance.

I would take care they should be at Portsmouth the following morning.'

Nelson then went off to say his official farewells to Pitt and Castlereagh, and it was while waiting to see the latter at the Colonial Office in Downing Street that he met an unusual man. He had been taken into the little waiting-room on the right of the hall. An Army officer was soon shown in—a man with a haughty air and a curt manner. The Army officer describes the meeting: 'I found, also waiting to see the Secretary of State, a gentleman who from his likeness to his pictures and the loss of an arm, I immediately recognized as Lord Nelson. He could not know who I was, but he entered at once into conversation with me, if I can call it a conversation, for it was almost all on his side and all about himself, and in, really, a style so vain and so silly as to surprise and almost disgust me.

'I suppose something that I happened to say may have made him guess that I was *somebody*, and he went out of the room for a moment, I have no doubt to ask the office-keeper who I was, for when he came back he was altogether a different man, both in manner and matter. All that I had thought a charlatan style had vanished, and he talked of the state of this country and of the aspect and probabilities of affairs on the Continent with a good sense, and a knowledge of subjects both at home and abroad that surprised me equally and more agreeably than the first part of our interview had done; in fact he talked like an officer and a statesman.'

Nelson had discovered that he was talking to none other than the victor of the Mahratta War, Major-General Sir Arthur Wellesley, who was destined to be the victor of Talavera, Salamanca and Waterloo, and better known in history as the Duke of Wellington. His recent safe arrival in England in the India convoy, mentioned earlier, was due, in part at least, to Nelson's actions in driving Villeneuve back to Europe and frightening him into inactivity.

'The Secretary of State,' recorded Wellesley, 'kept us long waiting, and certainly, for the last half or three-quarters of an hour, I don't know that I ever had a conversation that interested me more. Now if the Secretary of State had been punctual, and admitted Lord Nelson in the first quarter of an hour I should have had the same impression of a light and trivial character that other people have had, but luckily I saw enough to be satisfied that he was really a very superior man; but certainly a more sudden and complete metamorphosis I never saw.'

After seeing Castlereagh and Pitt, Nelson was long overdue at Merton, where guests were waiting for him, but he made one final call at the Admiralty, which Barrow records: 'In the evening he looked in upon me at the Admiralty, where I was stopping to see them [the signal books] off. I pledged myself not to leave the office till a messenger was dispatched with the signals, should the post have departed, and he might rely on their being at Portsmouth the following morning.

'On this he shook hands with me; I wished him all happiness and success, which I was sure he would command as he had always done; and he departed apparently more than usually cheerful.'

Back at Merton, Lord Nelson's guests waited uncomfortably: there were Lord Minto, who thoroughly disliked Lady Hamilton, and Mr James Perry, editor of the *Morning Chronicle*. They were not introduced until Lord Nelson and Emma arrived, two hours late, and Lord Minto then remembered without apparent embarrassment that the last time he had seen Perry he had jailed him for a libel on the House of Lords. Perry, in turn, bore no ill-will since Parliament was in those days easily libelled, and jail an accepted occupational hazard to those who reported and commented on the political activities and antics of their hereditary rulers and elected representatives.[1]

Lord Minto had an uneasy feeling when Lady Hamilton came into the room, eyes puffed and red from crying, that it was to be a strained and uncomfortable evening, and he was right. Sitting at the place of honour beside Lady Hamilton, he found her weeping. He reported, apparently shocked, that 'she could not eat, and hardly drink, and near swooning, and all at table.' Although it is unfortunate that his Lordship's appetite was probably affected, this was a somewhat arid judgment on Nelson's mistress. It is clear that the Admiral felt that he would die in the now nearly

---

[1] The veneer of democracy in those days of 'rotten boroughs' was spread very thinly: many boroughs with less than two thousand inhabitants regularly returned Members of Parliament while the great new industrial towns like Manchester and Birmingham with their teeming populations were not represented at all. Dunwich, which had been swallowed up by the sea, still had a Member. The rotten boroughs were often advertised for sale: indeed there were complaints that war profiteers, wanting to add a little tone to their newly-acquired wealth, were bidding against each other and forcing the prices up.

inevitable battle, and however much he tried, it is doubtful if he could hide this premonition from Emma, who almost certainly knew it instinctively. Nor did she have the comfort of being Nelson's wife, for he was being torn from her without their extremely happy union being recognized by the outward symbol of legality, and to someone of Emma's background (she came from an obscure family and was reputed to have become Sir William Hamilton's wife after being cast off as a mistress by the aged envoy's nephew) this would be of great importance. As we have seen, she had already said that if she could be married to Nelson for an hour she would die content. The dinner guests departed early.

Friday, September 13, dawned at Merton and as usual Nelson was up early, long before the sun thought of dissolving the chilly autumn mist. The house was comparatively empty. His sister Susanna and her husband Thomas Bolton had left with their children and only his sister Catherine and her husband, George Matcham, and their young son remained in the house with the Admiral, Emma and Horatia. In the soft sunshine of an English autumn, taking his last stroll round the grounds of Merton, seeing the house, the graceful cedars, the quietly flowing river, and drinking in the quietness and beauty of a September day, he heard little Horatia's cheerful chattering. Perhaps he shook off the black thoughts which were creeping into his mind like a cold evening mist rising almost imperceptibly in a quiet spinney.

But the day was soon over. The sun set and Horatia was given her supper and put to bed, perhaps wrenching Nelson's heart as she kissed him goodnight. Dinner was served and it stuck in the throats of those eating it, for they felt as helpless to alter destiny as the warders keeping vigil over a prisoner in the condemned cell. The candles in silver candlesticks flickered as people moved about restlessly in the drawing-room, and the hands of the clock moved on with geometric precision and cold, remote inexorability. They all listened for the clatter of the coach, and ten o'clock of an autumn night had long struck before it arrived. Upstairs Nelson went quietly to the bedside of his daughter, conceived aboard the *Foudroyant* in the warm Mediterranean nearly four and a half years earlier. The little man knelt. Resting his head in his hand, he said a quiet prayer, and tiptoed out of the room and out of Horatia's life for ever. Finally, having said farewell to a distraught Emma, kissed his sister Catherine goodbye, and shaken George by the hand with as much cheerfulness as he could muster, he walked to the carriage. Catherine and George were left to comfort Emma as the measured cadence of horses' hooves, overladen with the rumble of the carriage wheels, died away in the distance.

In the solitude of the long night spent on the Portsmouth road Nelson had time for reflection. While the horses were being changed at Guildford he wrote in his private diary, in the upright, jerky writing that he contrived with his left hand, a prayer which gives a clearer insight into his feelings than anything else. 'At half past ten, drove from dear, dear Merton, where I left all which I hold dear in this world, to go to serve my King and country. May the Great God whom I adore, enable me to fulfil the expectations of my country; and if it is His good pleasure that I should return, my thanks will never cease being offered up to the throne of His Mercy. If it is His good Providence to cut short my days upon earth, I bow with the greatest submission, relying that He will protect those so dear to me, that I may leave behind. His will be done. Amen. Amen. Amen.'

At six o'clock next morning the carriage arrived at the George Inn, Portsmouth. Nelson, tired and stiff, went in to find his friend George Rose and a comparative stranger, George Canning, a brilliant orator and writer, a great friend of Pitt's and now the new Treasurer of the Navy. When breakfast was over, Nelson made some official calls and went back to the George, where by now an eager crowd had gathered. While Nelson talked with Rose, Canning and Hardy, the crowd and the clamour outside in the High Street increased and soldiers arrived to try to clear a way for the Admiral and his party. In an attempt to avoid the crowds, Nelson decided to board his barge at the bathing-machines behind the Assembly Rooms on the front some half a mile away at Southsea, instead of using the sally port steps at the end of the High Street. However, as soon as he left the George by the back door for his last brief walk on English soil the people of Portsmouth gathered round him. Some cheered; others knelt before him in the dirty street and clasped their hands in prayer as he passed; many more stood unashamedly weeping. Whereas in London the crowds had cheered and jostled, joyful at being able to mob their hero, here in Portsmouth the people were more closely connected with the sea. In London the departure of a hero to join his ship and sail to meet the enemy presented the aspect of a carriage swaying off down a dusty street; here in Portsmouth it was a more urgent sight. From the Southsea beach they could see the *Victory* even now waiting at a single anchor across the Solent at St Helen's, a brave sight with her black hull relieved by the yellow strakes, and her sails neatly furled on the yards.

Finally Nelson reached the sea, where his barge waited at the bottom of the steps. He paused while Hardy, Rose and Canning walked down and boarded the barge. The swirling mob of people surged forward as Nelson paused at the top of the steps and waved before following the others. (See picture facing page 64.) The crowd reached the edge of the parapet and became mixed up with the soldiers. An excited Army officer 'who not very prudently upon such an occasion, ordered them to drive the people down with their bayonets, was compelled speedily to retreat; for the people would not be barred from gazing till the last moment upon the hero'.

Nelson seated himself in his barge, the coxswain gave the order 'shove off', and within a few moments the crew were pulling at their oars, keeping perfect time, and the crowd redoubled its cheering. Nelson raised his hat, and turning to Hardy said: 'I had their huzzas before—I have their hearts now.'

Soon his barge was alongside the *Victory*, and his flag—the White Ensign—was hoisted once again. To Marsden at the Admiralty Nelson wrote:

> You will please to acquaint the Lords Commissioners of the Admiralty that I arrived at Portsmouth this morning at six o'clock, hoisted my flag on board the *Victory* at this anchorage [St Helen's] about noon. The *Royal Sovereign*, *Defiance*, and *Agamemnon* are not yet ready for sea, so that I must leave them to follow the moment they are complete. The ships named in the margin [*Victory* and *Euryalus*] only accompany me.

Rose and Canning had dinner with Nelson while the *Victory* prepared to sail. Next morning her log reported with stark brevity the beginning of Nelson's last voyage: 'Sunday 15th. 8 a.m. weighed and made sail to the S.S.E. *Euryalus* in company.' Once again the wind was foul, and by next day the two ships had got only as far west as Portland. Nelson wrote to a friend:

'My fate is fixed, and I am gone, and beating down Channel with a foul wind'.

On September 17 he wrote to Emma, dating his letter off Plymouth, 'Nine o'clock in the morning, blowing fresh at W.S.W. dead foul wind'.

> I sent, my own dearest Emma, a letter for you, last night in a Torbay boat, and gave the man a guinea to put it in the post-office. We have a nasty blowing night, and it looks very dirty. I am now signalizing the ships at Plymouth (*Ajax* and *Thunderer*) to join me; but I rather doubt their ability to get to sea. However, I have got clear of Portland, and have Cawsand Bay and Torbay under the lee. I intreat, my dear Emma, that you will cheer up; and we will look forward to many, many happy years, and be surrounded by our children's children. God Almighty can, when he pleases, remove the impediment. My heart and soul is with you and Horatia. I got this line ready in case a boat should get alongside.

However, he was unlucky, and added to the letter next day.

> I had no opportunity of sending your letter yesterday, nor do I see any prospect at present. The *Ajax* and *Thunderer* are joining; but it is nearly calm, with a swell from the westward. Perseverance has got us thus far; and the same will, I dare say, get us on.

He remembered that the vicar of Merton would probably be worrying about his young son, now experiencing his first few days at sea.

> Thomas seems to do very well, and content. Tell Mr Lancaster that I have no doubt that his son will do very well. God bless you, my own Emma! I am giving my letters to Blackwood to put on board the first vessel he meets going to England or Ireland. Once more, heavens bless you! Ever, for ever, your Nelson and Bronte.

And to Rose he wrote a letter with a typical ring:

> I shall try hard and beat out of the Channel, and the first northerly wind will carry me to Cape St Vincent, where nothing be wanting on my part to realize the expectations of my friends. I will try to have a motto, at least it shall be my watchword, '*Touch and Take*'. I will do my best; and if I fail

at any point I hope it will be proved that it was owing to no fault of, my dear Mr Rose, your very faithful friend, Nelson & Bronte.

On Thursday the *Victory*, with the *Euryalus*, *Ajax* and *Thunderer* in company, took her departure from the Lizard, following in the wake of Drake when he went off to 'Singe the King of Spain's beard' at Cadiz in 1587; of the gallant Sir Richard Grenville who sailed in the *Revenge* to meet a brave death at 'Flores, in the Azores', and of Raleigh who went to find El Dorado. So Nelson sailed on to meet his destiny with open arms but with occasional half-ashamed backward glances. He was willing to accede to the need for his death, and would gladly exchange his life for England's safety, if his life was to be the price exacted for England's past mistakes in the war against the French. It was as if he was reconciled to the fact that his personal happiness was always to be fleeting, and as if he knew that in this last and greatest battle he would be the victor, but also the victim. Death had its sting—that Emma and Horatia would not have him to shelter them. Mercifully he would never know the depths to which Emma would be left to sink. But he was to die in good company; this was in many ways a compensation. There may be a few Judases, he was to say, but in fact there were none. No one did less than was expected of him, and most did more.

A brig

13

'IT IS TREASON!'

'When the sea was calm all boats alike
Show'd mastership in floating.'
—Shakespeare (*Coriolanus*)

BEHIND the bare report that Blackwood had brought to Merton
on September 2, that the Combined Fleet had put into Cadiz,
was a series of catastrophes for both Napoleon and Villeneuve.
As we have seen, the orders that the Emperor had sent to Villeneuve in the West Indies—that he was to return to Europe and,
with the Rochefort, Ferrol and Brest squadrons 'procure our
superiority before Boulogne for some days'—arrived after the
French admiral had sailed for Ferrol. After running into Calder
and finally putting into Vigo, Villeneuve found no new orders
waiting for him. He despatched a tale of woe to Decrès in Paris.
'Urgent, irresistible necessity has obliged me to put into Vigo,' he
wrote, 'misfortunes in an ever-increasing progression have accumulated on this squadron.' In another letter he listed those misfortunes—one ship had lost her main-topmast, another had two
hundred men on the sick list and water on board for only five days,
three others each had more than one hundred and fifty sick, and
every other ship had between sixty and a hundred and twenty
sick.[1]

Nevertheless, he worked swiftly: the ships were watered and
all the sick crammed aboard the *Atlas*, which he proposed to leave
behind with two Spanish ships 'which cannot manœuvre with the
squadron and seem made to compromise everything'. Then after
warning Gourdon at Ferrol that he was to do his utmost to join,
he sailed again. But on arriving at the entrance to Ferrol and
Corunna—with Admiral Gravina and two Spanish ships already
in the narrows leading to Ferrol—he met a boat which came
alongside with orders from Napoleon. They prohibited him from

---

[1] Compare with the conditions of Nelson's ships on their return from
the West Indies: the Admiral wrote from Gibraltar on July 20 'The
squadron is in the most perfect health, except some symptoms of scurvy,
which I hope to eradicate by bullocks and refreshments from Tetuan'.

putting into Ferrol. Instead he was, with the Rochefort and Brest squadrons, to 'make himself master of the Strait of Dover, were it only for four or five days'.

Decrès, in a covering letter, added an important point: the Emperor had anticipated that in certain circumstances 'the situation of the Fleet would not allow of our carrying out his designs which would have so great an influence on the fate of the world; and in this case alone the Emperor desires to assemble an imposing array of forces in Cadiz.'

Gravina and his two Spanish ships had not been able to anchor off Corunna in time and had gone up to Ferrol. Villeneuve followed to have a talk with Gravina, and both men decided that Napoleon's new plan was dangerous. Gravina said he was quite ready to follow Villeneuve, but in the sixty days since the Combined Fleet had left the West Indies the English had had time to receive warning. 'As we are getting out of this place they will be able to give us battle and provide us with a second fight before our approach to Brest,' he said.

And once again Villeneuve took up his pen to write to Decrès. Had he made a fast Atlantic crossing, defeated Calder, joined with Ganteaume at Brest 'and enabled the great expedition to take place', he said, 'I should be the foremost man in France. Well, all this should have happened—I do not say with a squadron of fine sailors—but even with very average vessels . . . two north-easterly gales damaged us because we have bad sails, bad rigging, bad officers and bad seamen. The enemy have been warned, they have been reinforced, they [i.e. Calder] have dared to attack us with numerically inferior forces, the weather favoured them. Unpractised in fighting and fleet manœuvres, in the fog each captain carried out but one rule, that of following his next-ahead; and behold us the laughing stock of Europe'.

On August 6, with eight English battleships reported waiting outside, Villeneuve wrote to Decrès, 'I am about to set out but I do not know what I shall do. . . .' Four days later he worked out of the bay with four French and eight Spanish battleships, but his troubles were far from over: the north-east wind dropped before the last three Spanish ships were clear, and the Fleet had to anchor. As if the element of farce was to enter into everything connected with Villeneuve, 'All the ships, French and Spanish, ran aboard each other in anchoring'. Finally, on August 13, the Combined Fleet of twenty-nine battleships (eighteen French and eleven Spanish) sailed, heading westward. It is difficult to know exactly what was in Villeneuve's mind. He may have intended to sail for Brest and the Channel, but Gravina's chief of staff, Escaño, wrote in his journal: 'We sailed for Cadiz.'

That evening, according to Villeneuve, some battleships were sighted at 6 p.m., followed next day by a report of fourteen more, then eight others. Ironically enough it is now known that the only battleships in the area were probably French—those of Commodore Allemand, to whom Villeneuve had sent the frigate *Didon* with orders to meet him off Brest.

The rest of the day was uneventful. During the night Allemand's squadron again passed close but unseen. The 15th was a busy day for Villeneuve's frigates, which searched neutral ships and sank a British merchantman. Then in the evening one of them reported sighting a ship with another in tow. Although Villeneuve did nothing about identifying them, they were in fact the British *Phoenix* towing the *Didon*, which she had captured after a bitter fight in which seventy of the French ship's crew of three hundred and seventy had been killed. Captain Baker of the *Phoenix* had thus brought to nought Napoleon's plan for Villeneuve to link up with Allemand's Rochefort squadron. Without the *Didon*'s despatches from Villeneuve, Allemand was without information or new orders. The Combined Fleet and Allemand were destined never to meet, and Allemand, like a latter-day Flying Dutchman, was left roaming the seas.

Another British ship, Captain Griffith's *Dragon*, also played her part in deciding Villeneuve's destiny. Griffith boarded a Danish merchantman and said, quite casually, that his ship was part of a fleet of twenty-five British battleships. Later on Griffith sighted a strange fleet, and then saw a French frigate boarding the Danish merchantman. Had the Danes seen any British ship? Indeed they had, the Danes told the Frenchmen, reporting Griffith's visit and the 'intelligence' that his ship was part of a fleet of twenty-five battleships.

This news was hurriedly relayed to Villeneuve, who immediately assumed that Captain Griffith's imaginary fleet was one sent out to chase him. During the rest of that night, however, he continued steering towards the first rendezvous arranged for Allemand— although he had more than a suspicion that the ship seen under tow earlier was the *Didon*.

That evening, September 15, two days after he left Corunna,

Villeneuve made his great decision, based on two factors—the eight ships sighted on the 13th[1] and the threat he thought existed from the Dane's report of Captain Griffith's 'fleet' of twenty-five British battleships. Villeneuve was well aware of the proviso in his orders allowing him to go to Cadiz; as night fell a signal from his flagship, the *Bucentaure*, turned the Combined Fleet southwards, heading for Cadiz.

Since August 2 Napoleon had been waiting at Boulogne, frequently riding up and down the beach on his famous horse Marengo. Events were moving fast. On August 5, he heard that Nelson was back in Europe, and two days later news reached him that Villeneuve had left Vigo for Ferrol. His plan was apparently beginning to mature. Along the French coast facing England his great army was waiting, led by a formidable array of warriors. Marshal Davout commanded the right wing at Ambleteuse; Soult had the centre at Boulogne; Ney had the left wing at Etaples, and the advance guard at Wimereux was under Lannes. Yet while Napoleon and his look-outs stared up and down the Channel watching for the squadrons of Villeneuve and Ganteaume to come sailing up, the alliance between England, Russia and Austria was, as we have seen, growing stronger each day. Napoleon was beginning to have to face both ways—eastwards to Austria and Russia and westwards to Britain.

Where was Villeneuve? For several days the Emperor ranted and raged; then on August 22 he heard that Villeneuve and the Combined Fleet had sailed from Ferrol on August 13. The fact that he had not yet appeared off Brest, explained Decrès, was because the wind was foul. However, Napoleon was not convinced and gave instructions in case Villeneuve had gone to Cadiz. They had a familiar ring—he was to reinforce his Combined Fleet with the six battleships in Cadiz and others in Cartagena and 'proceed up to the Channel'. But this brought an agonized wail from Decrès, who believed that if Villeneuve had gone to Cadiz the great invasion scheme should be abandoned. He wrote on August 22 [two days after Villeneuve had, unknown to the Minister, arrived in Cadiz] imploring Napoleon not to associate the Spanish ships with the French squadron's operations. 'If your squadron

---

[1] Villeneuve made no attempt to identify these as friendly or enemy; they were probably Allemand's, and in any case would have been no match for Villeneuve's twenty-nine battleships.

is at Cadiz,' he wrote, 'I implore you to look upon this occurrence as a decree of destiny, which is reserving it for other operations. I implore you on no account to order it to come round from Cadiz to the Channel, because if the attempt is made at this moment it will only be attended with misfortune.

'In truth, sire,' he declared, 'my situation is becoming too painful. I reproach myself for not knowing how to persuade your Majesty. I doubt if one man alone could. . . . And to be candid, a Minister of Marine overawed by your Majesty in those matters which concern the sea, is serving your Majesty ill and is becoming a cipher. . . .'

But Napoleon now apparently had no further patience to waste on Villeneuve. The day after Decrès made his plea, the Emperor wrote to his Foreign Minister, the lame and brilliant aristocrat Talleyrand, a man who successfully combined debauchery with diplomacy, who was as cultured as he was rakish, and who had that invaluable asset for a politician, the ability to survive when one régime crumbled and was replaced by another.

His Emperor, who had made the pilgrimage to Aix-la-Chapelle to worship in his fashion at the tomb of the great Frankish emperor Charlemagne, said that in the following April he would find 100,000 Russians—supplied with British equipment—in Poland; up to 20,000 Englishmen in Malta, and 15,000 Russians in Corfu. 'I shall then find myself in a critical situation. My decision is made.' That decision was to declare war on Austria. His Army of England, camped on the cliffs before him, was to become once again the Grand Army. Breaking camp and marching swiftly and secretly across Europe, it would deal the impertinent Austrians a crushing blow before they realized what was happening and, so Napoleon planned, before they had time to attack him.

Yet apparently Napoleon did not entirely wash his hands of Villeneuve. 'If he follows his instructions, joins the Brest squadron, and enters the Channel, there is still time; I am master of England,' he told Talleyrand. On the other hand, if his admirals hesitated he would have to 'wait for winter to cross with the flotilla'. In the meantime he would 'replace my war battalions with my third battalions, which will still give me a sufficiently formidable army at Boulogne'. Although Talleyrand was to draw up the declaration of war against Austria, it was to be kept secret for the time being. Napoleon then started drafting the first orders which would start his Grand Army marching towards Austria. On the 24th the

routes to Vienna were decided; on the 25th he dictated the
detailed orders for the whole forthcoming Austrian campaign—
with its victories of Ulm and Austerlitz. By August 29 the Grand
Army was tramping eastwards, leaving the Channel coast behind
them. And in the harbours hundreds of transports began to rot.

On September 1, as Blackwood arrived off the Isle of Wight
on his way to Merton with the news that Villeneuve had reached
Cadiz, Napoleon at Boulogne received the identical information.
The next day, when Nelson followed Blackwood to the Admiralty,
Napoleon left the seashore that now mocked him. For three days
after receiving the information—while he was on his way to Paris,
and after he arrived—the Emperor was silent on the subject of
Villeneuve. However, he soon made up for it. 'Admiral Villeneuve',
he wrote to Decrès on September 4, the day the clerks at the
Admiralty worked overtime on Nelson's orders, 'has filled the cup
to overflowing. . . . It is treason beyond all doubt. . . . Villeneuve
is a scoundrel who must be dismissed from the service in disgrace
. . . he would sacrifice everything to save his own skin. . . .'

14

RATTLING THE BARS

'The fathers have eaten sour grapes, and the
children's teeth are set on edge.'
—Ezekiel XVIII, 2

ON SEPTEMBER 14, the day that Nelson boarded the *Victory* off St Helen's to sail for Cadiz, Napoleon drew up the orders for Villeneuve which were to lead directly to the Battle of Trafalgar, the greatest victory yet won by British arms. From then on the Royal Navy would be the most powerful force afloat for more than a century and a quarter.

Twelve days earlier, Villeneuve had reported that there were eleven British battleships off Cadiz, although a further twenty-three were reported from Lisbon to be steering south. Napoleon's new orders for Villeneuve were based on the fear of what General Craig's tiny expedition might do when it linked up with the Russians in southern Italy. The Emperor saw this British and Russian move as an attack on his 'soft under-belly', and a threat to his Austrian campaign. To crush it he finally abandoned his Channel venture and ordered Villeneuve to sail the Combined Fleet into the Mediterranean. He was to go to Naples, land the troops he had on board, and then take the Fleet back to Toulon. . . . But there was one snag: although Villeneuve reported only eleven British battleships off Cadiz, the situation had changed considerably by the time Napoleon's orders were drafted. Calder had been reinforced, and now twenty-six of the Royal Navy's battleships were waiting.

Decrès forwarded the Emperor's orders to Villeneuve on September 16 with a covering letter which contained this strong hint to the man the Emperor now regarded as a coward: 'I cannot too highly recommend you, M. L'Amiral, to seize the first favourable opportunity to effect your departure; and I repeat my most earnest wishes for your success.' Yet Decrès did not tell Villeneuve the most vital news of all, that Napoleon, having on September 14 ordered Villeneuve to sail for Naples, had decided next day to sack him and place Admiral Rosily in command of the Combined Fleet.

Rosily was told of his new appointment on the 18th, and on the same day Decrès sent him Napoleon's orders, saying, 'It is the Emperor's intention that you should proceed in all haste to the port of Cadiz'. And whereas Villeneuve's orders said he was to sail for Naples immediately, the orders to Rosily gave the new Commander-in-Chief a loop-hole—if 'insuperable obstacles' were found, he was to 'cause either the whole Fleet or several divisions to leave port whenever the weather permits', to rattle the bars, keep crews active, and 'put an end to this blockade which is an insult to the flags of the two Powers'. Four days after Villeneuve's orders had been despatched a curt letter was written telling him 'His Majesty the Emperor and King has just appointed Vice-Admiral Rosily to the command of the naval forces assembled at Cadiz and has given orders that you are to proceed to Paris in order to give an account of the campaign on which you have been recently employed'. Oddly enough this letter was not immediately sent off to Cadiz: instead it was given to Rosily to deliver personally to Villeneuve, even though he was not leaving until the 24th. As we shall see later, reports that he was sacked were to reach Villeneuve through unofficial channels and drive him to such a desperate act that the letter never reached him.

In Paris the Emperor packed his bags and on September 23 left the city; by the 26th he was in Strasbourg, and his five great armies—three from Boulogne, one from Holland and one from Hanover—were marching across Europe. By October 5 it was poised within twenty miles of the Danube, ready to strike the Austrians a crippling blow. The Austrian General Mack, imagining the Grand Army still on the seashore at Boulogne, had decided not to wait for his new Russian allies, and pushed ahead with 70,000 men across the River Inn into Bavaria on September 8. By the 14th he reached Ulm, where he planned to hold the French, taking up the defensive rôle beloved of the Austrian Army which, though brave, was riddled with red-tape and unsuited to mobile warfare.

Napoleon, by transferring his Grand Army secretly from the Channel to the Danube before the Russians could get their troops to Ulm, had the chance to fling 200,000 tough, highly-trained veterans against 70,000 troops officered by elegant, highly cultured and highly inefficient amateurs. On October 7 Napoleon struck his blow. By the 17th General Mack (of whom Nelson had warned the Duke of Clarence less than two months earlier 'if

Your Royal Highness has any communication with Government, let not General Mack be employed, for I know him to be a rascal, a scoundrel, and a coward'.) was surrounded. By the 20th—the day the Russians were to have joined him on the River Inn had he stayed there—he had surrendered. It was the eve of Trafalgar. At Ulm Napoleon had scored his first victory of the Austrian campaign.

In the great Spanish port of Cadiz, conditions for Villeneuve were about as bad as they could be. The newly arrived Combined Fleet was in a poor state and he had hardly got the ships anchored before he fell ill with 'bilious colic', a stomach upset which had troubled him at sea and which was probably brought on by worry. For eleven days he waited for some word from Decrès or Napoleon, but none came. 'My Lord,' he wrote to Decrès, on September 2, 'I was awaiting the arrival of a courier from your Excellency every minute, in the supposition you could but too clearly surmise that the Fleet has put into Cadiz. The lack of funds, the poverty of the port, the great requirements of the ships, and those of the crews, increase in proportion to the time passing and to the season that is approaching.'

The 'lack of funds' which he mentioned had soon reached almost farcical proportions. Villeneuve wanted cash to provide supplies for some 17,000 men for at least fifty days, plus the normal daily rations, but as soon as he arrived in Cadiz, the French Agent General, le Roy, warned that he had no money and his credit was exhausted. The French Ambassador in Madrid tried to get money from the Spanish Government, but they were in the midst of a financial crisis and, the Ambassador reported, had not 'the flimsiest credit'. The Ambassador had himself been 'obliged to glean from all the bankers in order to get the money for the couriers that I despatch'. The Inspector of Artillery refused to supply any powder or shot unless it was paid for with cash, until direct orders came—very late—from Madrid. Apart from supplying the ships with food, powder and shot, it was a massive task to get them ready for sea again. The frigates were all short of sails; one battleship needed a new main-yard, another had lost her rudder-head, a third had a broken bowsprit, and a fourth had damaged her sternworks in a collision. Two others were leaking badly and several more needed various vital repairs.

Not only were the ships sick; the crews were decimated by

illness. On September 2 Villeneuve reported that he had 1,731 seamen in hospital, 311 more had deserted since he originally left Toulon, and altogether he was short of more than two thousand men. Later this deficit totalled 2,207, of whom 649 were in hospital in Cadiz. Fortunately for Villeneuve, the French Ambassador in Madrid finally managed to get some help from a French banker, who lent some cash and paid various bills.

The Spaniards were in no better condition regarding their ships. One of Gravina's battleships had been left behind in Ferrol, and three more at Vigo. There should have been six fresh battleships waiting for him in the roads at Cadiz, but in fact there were only four, and two of these were useless and had to be replaced. The Spanish Navy suffered from the same weakness that troubled the Royal Navy, the difficulty of getting seamen to man the ships. Recruiting, says Desbrière, 'was too often the result of sweeping in beggars, vagabonds and common-law prisoners, owing to the scarcity of enlisted seamen. In this respect the English were hardly better, but long cruises and a terrible discipline had transformed the bad material—too often recruited by force—into splendid topmen and gunners. The inferiority of the Spaniards in this respect was manifest; their guns, served by untrained sailors under the direction of artillerymen from land—but little practised themselves and altogether insufficient in number—were to exercise but poor effect.' This was 'still further lessened by the singular predilection—which, moreover, the Spanish shared with the French—for aiming at the rigging in preference to the hulls of their opponents; thus wasting their ammunition for a problematical result'. (See Notes, p. 351).

Villeneuve, reporting to Decrès on the Spanish squadron, said: 'It is very distressing to see such fine and powerful ships manned with herdsmen and beggars and having such a small number of seamen.'

Moreover, there were no extra men available in Cadiz: the press-gangs roamed the streets, looking particularly carefully for the hardy fisherman. But Cadiz, like the rest of Andalusia, had already suffered the ravages of yellow fever. Those not struck down by the disease were already serving or had managed to hide. This forced Gravina to pay off the worst and slowest of his ships and use the crews to reinforce the fifteen best ships. With the eighteen French battleships, this gave the Combined Fleet a strength of thirty-three.

But Gravina was still short of men, and the only solution was to draft soldiers on board: they could at least man some of the guns, freeing trained seamen for the more skilled tasks. The troops were drawn from some of the most famous units in Spain, among them a battalion of the Regimiento de Cordoba, which was sent aboard the *Santissima Trinidad* and *Argonauta*, and battalions from the Regimiento de Soria, Regimiento de Africa and Regimiento del Corona which joined the *San Juan Nepumuceno*, *Neptuno* and *San Francisco de Asis*. These men were to fight at Trafalgar even as their forebears fought the British from the decks of ships of the Armada in 1588: the Regimiento de Africa, for instance, then named the Tercio de Sicilia, had men on board the *Nuestra Senora del Rosario* which Sir Francis Drake himself had brought to action in Torbay, and the rest were in the Duke of Medina Sidonia's flagship *San Martin*.

It was against this background that Villeneuve worked hard to get his ships ready for sea. Equally busy was General Lauriston, who commanded the French troops aboard the ships and who had been sending reports to the Emperor which were highly critical of Villeneuve. On September 16 he wrote to Napoleon that 'Reports from Tangiers, which Admiral Gravina regards as being very reliable, state that Admiral Nelson, with six more line-of-battleships, is to arrive directly to take command.'

Meanwhile Villeneuve, still preparing the Combined Fleet to carry out Napoleon's orders to go to the Channel, was reporting regularly to Decrès. 'We have seen twenty-four or twenty-five line-of-battleships, of which seven are three-deckers, appear off this bay. . . . I await the Emperor's [latest] orders with the great anxiety, and I count the minutes and hours until they arrive,' he said. When the last two Spanish ships were ready 'and I have a fair wind to put to sea with both squadrons, we shall set sail to carry out the Emperor's orders'. These orders were that he should take the initiative against the enemy whenever possible. The second set of instructions, ordering him to Naples, were still on their way from Paris, taking many days to cross the rugged countryside.

The courier bearing them finally arrived in Cadiz on September 27. The watchword for the Naples expedition, Napoleon said, was '*L'audace et la plus grande activité*'. This stirring phrase did little to bolster up Villeneuve's morale, and the orders were a good example of Napoleon's lack of understanding of the best way of using his fleet. Bearing in mind that at this time it was only at sea that he could bring Britain to battle, he now proposed using the major part of his available fleet to carry out a comparatively unimportant landing. He was cheerfully hazarding some thirty-three battleships—there would have been more if crews had been available—to land four thousand troops.

Thus Pitt's plan for sending Craig and his tiny expedition of six thousand men to Naples was beginning to have an importance out of all proportion to its size or power. Its mere existence posed so real a threat in the Emperor's eyes that he was apparently willing to sacrifice his fleet to defeat it.

There is no doubt that he let the Combined Fleet sail knowing that it might well be annihilated. His orders of September 14 were admittedly based on the report that there were only eleven British ships off Cadiz, but by the 20th—three days before he left Paris for Strasbourg—he knew that there were by then some twenty-seven battleships waiting off Cadiz. Orders took under a fortnight to pass between Paris and Cadiz, so from September 20 he had more than a fortnight to cancel or delay the order to sail for Naples, since Villeneuve did not sail until twenty-nine days after Napoleon had found out the British strength. Yet the Emperor did nothing.

In Cadiz itself the French and Spanish admirals received the order without fuss. Gravina read his copy on board the *Principe de Asturias* and straightaway had himself rowed across to see Villeneuve in the *Bucentaure*, where he told him that the fourteen battleships under his command were 'absolutely ready to set sail, and to accompany the Imperial Fleet anywhere'. Villeneuve in turn reported to Decrès—in four letters written on the same day, September 28—that 'the captains in command will realize from the position and strength of the enemy before this port that an engagement must take place the very same day that the Fleet puts to sea'. Then he wrote with a sudden burst of confidence: 'The Fleet will see with satisfaction the opportunity that is offered to it to display that resolution and daring which will ensure its success, revenge the insults offered to its Flag, and lay low the tyrannical domination of the English upon the seas.

'Our Allies will fight at our side, under the walls of Cadiz and in sight of their fellow citizens; the Emperor's gaze is fixed upon us.'

But the news he sent in the last of the four letters, written at midnight, must have tempered his earlier elation. 'I have just been informed that the enemy squadron has just been joined by three sail of the line—one of which is a three-decker—coming from the west. There are now thirty-one line-of-battleships well known to be in these waters.'

The three ships were the *Victory*, *Ajax* and *Thunderer*.

Tacking: with the wind coming from the right, the left-hand ship is on the starboard tack. She turns (centre sketches) head to wind and then pays off on the larboard tack. The word 'port' (left) is used today instead of 'larboard'

15

THE NELSON TOUCH

'The golden rule is that there are no golden rules.'

—Shaw

NELSON had passed Lisbon on September 25 while Napoleon's orders to the sick and harassed Villeneuve and to Gravina were still being carried over the hot and dusty roads of France and Spain. Thinking that he could lure the Combined Fleet out of Cadiz only by letting them think that there was but a small British force blockading them, he also tried to ensure that his own name would not scare the enemy into staying in port. He therefore wrote to Collingwood, giving the letter to Henry Blackwood to take on ahead in the *Euryalus*, with the request that 'if you are in sight of Cadiz, that not only no salute may take place, but also that no Colours may be hoisted, for it is as well not to proclaim to the enemy every ship which may join the Fleet'. Perhaps realizing that neutral ships with prying eyes might be in the vicinity, he added a postscript, 'I would not have any salute even if you are out of sight of land.' And in his private diary that night he recorded: 'At sunset the captain of the *Constance* came on board. . . . The enemy's fleet had not left Cadiz the 18th of this month, therefore I yet hope they will await my arrival.'

Saturday, September 28, brought a fresh north-westerly breeze in the morning and the *Victory*, with the *Ajax* and *Thunderer* in company, ran before it across Cadiz Bay. The breeze almost fell away during the late afternoon, and once again Nelson wrote in his private diary: 'In the evening joined the Fleet under Vice Ad^l Collingwood, saw the enemy's fleet in Cadiz amounting to thirty-five or thirty-six sail of the line.'

The effect on the Fleet of his arrival was instantaneous. Captain Edward Codrington of the *Orion* wrote to his wife Jane: 'Lord Nelson is arrived. A sort of general joy has been the consequence, and many good effects will shortly arise from our change of system.' One of these, Codrington hoped, would be a little more social life in the Fleet: he found Collingwood a dull fellow. The next day was Sunday, September 29, and Nelson's birthday: he had been born forty-seven years earlier, the sixth child and fifth son of the Rector of Burnham Thorpe, in Norfolk. It was an appropriate day to take over command of the Fleet from Collingwood. And one of Nelson's first visitors was in fact Collingwood, whose barge brought him over from the *Dreadnought* to the *Victory* at 7 a.m.

It is almost impossible to imagine two more different men. Cuthbert Collingwood was now fifty-five, of medium height, thin, with a small head and a round face. In a crowd he would pass without notice except for his penetrating blue eyes, and his thin lips, which betrayed a firm and unruffled character. His hair was powdered and worn in a pigtail; his square-cut coat had a stiff, stand-up collar and what were now unfashionably long skirts, over blue knee-breeches and white stockings. A weary man now, his thoughts were constantly turning to Morpeth, in his native Northumberland, where his wife Sarah had waited so long for his return. He had married her just fifteen years earlier, and they had two daughters—Sarah, now thirteen and named after her mother and grandmother, and Mary Patience, a year younger. Most of his married life had been spent at sea, yet fewer men longed more urgently for home. A week before Nelson's arrival he had written: 'How happy I should be, could I but hear from home, and know how my dear girls are going on! Bounce [his dog] is my only pet now, and he is indeed a good fellow: he sleeps by the side of my cot, whenever I lie in one, until near the time of tacking, and then marches off, to be out of the hearing of the guns, for he is not reconciled to them yet. I am fully determined, if I can get home and manage it properly, to go on shore next spring for the rest of my life; for I am very weary.'

Tragically enough, although he was not to die until five years after Trafalgar, Collingwood was doomed never to see England or his family again: succeeding to the command on Nelson's death, he was left at sea despite his protestations over the years that followed. Commenting on how he had been forgotten the year after Trafalgar, he wrote: 'Fame's trumpet makes a great noise, but the notes do not dwell long on the ear.' His thoughts turned on 'those delightful blackbirds whose morning and evening song made my heart gay'.

'Tell me,' he wrote to Sarah, 'how do the trees which I planted thrive? Is there shade under the three oaks for a comfortable summer seat? Do the poplars grow at the walk, and does the wall of the terrace stand firm?' And at the prospect of his wife moving house he regretted losing 'those beautiful views' from Morpeth, which he was in any case never to see again, 'and even the rattling of that old wagon that used to pass our door at six o'clock on a winter's morning had its charms'. He wished he was with his wife and her sister 'that we might have a good laugh. God bless me! I have scarcely laughed these three years'.

This was the heart of a man who had gone to sea at the age of eleven and led a party of seamen at Bunker's Hill at twenty-four. Strangely enough he had, for many years, followed in Nelson's footsteps: when Lt Nelson was promoted out of the *Lowestoft*, Lt Collingwood succeeded him; when Commander Nelson of the *Badger* was promoted to post captain in command of the *Hinchinbrooke*, Lt Collingwood was promoted to Commander and given the *Badger*. When Nelson left the *Hinchinbrooke*, Collingwood was promoted to post captain, and took over command. And at St Vincent, when Nelson hauled out of the line in a desperate attempt to head off the enemy, followed by Troubridge in the *Culloden*, Collingwood in the *Excellent* immediately went to his aid. A strict and stern disciplinarian, he nevertheless ruled his ships and later a fleet with a light hand: as mentioned earlier he hated flogging and rarely used the cat-o'-nine-tails. His ships were famous for the fitness of their crews, and Nelson when taking over command reported to the Admiralty that the fleet was 'in very fair condition and good humour'.

Nelson's first day in command was a busy one. After meeting Collingwood and receiving from him the various unexecuted Admiralty orders, he proposed changing the whole system of blockade. By shifting his entire fleet over the horizon he would take it out of the sight of the prying eyes of the French and Spanish look-outs whose telescopes pointed westwards from the San Sebastian Tower at Cadiz.

By staying some fifty miles to the west he could watch over the Combined Fleet whether it went north to the Channel, south to Gibraltar or west into the broad Atlantic. More important, he would be sufficiently far offshore that a westerly gale would not force him to run before it through the Strait of Gibraltar and into the Mediterranean with his unwieldy three-deckers, leaving the stable door open for the Combined Fleet to bolt before he could get back on station again. Nelson also realized that famine in Cadiz itself might well drive the Combined Fleet to sea, and he

approved of Collingwood's decision to seize the neutral coasters
—most of them Danish—which were trying to take supplies into
the blockaded port, and send them off to the prize court at
Gibraltar.

On this first day nearly all his captains, wearing their best
uniforms with swords at their sides, left their ships and were
rowed across to the *Victory* to meet their new Commander-in-
Chief. It might be thought that most of these men were simply
renewing their acquaintanceship with Nelson—that they were
already tried and trusted members of his 'Band of Brothers', who
knew from past experience that he was a leader to be loved and
trusted. But this was far from being the case. Of the twenty-seven
British battleships which were to fight at Trafalgar—and several
of them had not joined at this stage—only five belonged to Nelson's
own Mediterranean Fleet. One had joined in the West Indies,
and the other twenty-one were sent out from the Channel Fleet.
Only eight of the twenty-seven battleship captains had previously
served with Nelson. One of the two who had been with him since
1803 was Thomas Hardy, his own flag captain. Only five had
commanded their ships since 1803; only five had previously commanded a battleship in action. Thus Nelson had but twenty-two
days to get to know those nineteen captains who had never
previously served with him. In that time he had to gain their
confidence, let them see how he reasoned and what he expected
—so that they could read this thoughts—and train them as a fleet.

One by one the captains clambered up the ship's towering black
and yellow sides and went on board through the entry port
abreast of the mainmast on the middle-deck. Forward and aft of
them the great 24-pounder guns, gleaming black on carriages
painted with yellow ochre, ran in even lines down each side the
full length of the ship. (See picture facing p. 356).

Turning aft, the captains walked a few feet to the ladder leading
up through the hatchway to the upper-deck. Once there they
turned aft to Nelson's cabins. The first of these was the dining
cabin, and walking through they came to his day cabin. This ran
the width of the ship, and light streamed in through the windows
built right across the raking stern. The deck of the cabin, covered
in canvas painted with a black and white chess-board pattern, was
cambered, and the thick beams overhead followed the same curve
so that each side of the cabin seemed to sag away from the centre-
line. A large table dominated the cabin; several armchairs were

scattered about, among them a particularly deep one, leather-covered, which was Nelson's favourite. It was very narrow so that it held his slim body comfortably, and on each side there was a pocket into which he could slip papers.

Incongruous among the finely carved pieces of furniture and the paintings on the bulkheads (among them one of Horatia, a dumpy little girl in a high-waisted dress) were two 12-pounder cannon, one on each side. The solid wooden wheels of the carriages reached nearly to a man's knee; the blocks (pulleys) of the side-tackles were twice as thick as a man's fist, and above the guns, between the beams overhead, were more tackles for opening the gun-ports. Most of the cabin was painted in pale green and buff, but grey and yellow were used to pick out some of the woodwork; and the deep rich browns of the polished furniture made the yellow ochre on the gun carriages look dull and heavy, as if emphasizing how out of place they were in such surroundings. The sun sparkling on the sea surging and rippling under the *Victory*'s massively ornate stern reflected up through the windows and made dancing patterns on the white deckhead; the slow, easy movement of the ship caused the thick oak timbers which made up her huge bulk to move a fraction of an inch, so that they groaned as if in protest. The distant shouts of orders, the occasional slap of canvas and the air of controlled bustle all gave the ship life and movement.

One by one the captains were announced and strode into the cabin to grip Nelson firmly by his left hand, and also wish him a happy birthday. Among them were a handsome Scot from Banff, George Duff of the *Mars*, and John Cooke of the *Bellerophon* (both of whom, like their Admiral, had but another twenty-two days to live), and Israel Pellew of the *Conqueror*, one of the finest sailors Cornwall ever produced, and younger brother of the famous Lord Exmouth. Nelson had a special word for Edward Codrington, of the *Orion*, who had not heard from his wife Jane for some time. 'He received me in an easy, polite manner,' Jane was told by a proud husband, 'and on giving me your letter said that being entrusted with it by a lady, he made a point of delivering it himself.'

And when Fremantle of the *Neptune*, whose Betsey had been expecting another baby, came on board Nelson greeted him warmly and immediately asked: 'Would you have a girl or a boy?'

'A girl,' replied Fremantle, who already had two boys and two girls.

'Be satisfied,' said Nelson, and gave Fremantle a letter. It was from Betsey's sister Harriet and told him that he had a new daughter whom Betsey was proposing to call Christine.

Nor were there only captains present: apart from Collingwood there was also Rear-Admiral the Earl of Northesk, another Scot, who was flying his flag in the *Britannia*, and who was to be third-in-command at the Battle. The fourth admiral, Louis, was still close off Cadiz with the *Canopus*.

Very soon the cabin was echoing to the sound of their voices, and the talk was young men's talk, for few of them had reached their mid-forties. Codrington was thirty-five, Duff and Cooke were forty-two, Hardy, commanding the *Victory*, was thirty-six, while Charles Tyler of the *Tonnant* was at forty-five one of the oldest present.

Nelson was well pleased with the way he was received: indeed, the Fleet's reception, he wrote later, 'caused the sweetest sensation of my life. The officers who came on board to welcome my return forgot my rank as Commander-in-Chief in the enthusiasm with which they greeted me. As soon as these emotions were past I laid before them the plan I had previously arranged for attacking the enemy; and it was not only my pleasure to find it generally approved, but clearly perceived and understood'. And to Lady Hamilton he described it more jubilantly: 'When I came to explain to them the *Nelson Touch* it was like an electric shock. Some shed tears, all approved—"It was new—it was singular—it was simple!" and, from Admirals downwards, it was repeated—"It must succeed, if ever they will allow us to get at them! You are, my Lord, surrounded by friends, whom you inspire with confidence." Some may be Judases; but the majority are certainly much pleased with my commanding them.'

Unfortunately none of the officers present left a description of what Nelson said when he explained his plan, and this has caused a lot of misunderstanding to historians ever since. In addition to describing what he intended to do, he later issued a Memorandum to all senior officers and captains, and the way he fought the battle varies from what he laid down in the Memorandum. This led many people to suppose that in the heat of the moment, with the Combined Fleet in front of him, he completely abandoned his plan in his excitement and fought what at best could be called a free for all. However, the answer seems to be that at this meeting with the captains he so inculcated them with his own ideas that they knew what to do, and the subsequent Memorandum was simply an aide-mémoire. When other captains joined fresh from England they too were told verbally the basic plan. (The contents of the Memorandum will be dealt with later and are given fully in Appendix III.)

The discussion on strategy and tactics over, Nelson was able to play the rôle of genial host. His steward, Henry Chevalier, was hard at work taking bottles from the circular wine cooler, un-corking them and pouring drinks for the thirsty captains, who were perspiring freely in the uncomfortable tightness of high, stiff collars and cravats. When the time came for them to go back to their ships, fifteen of them received invitations to stay to lunch with Nelson and the rest were promised invitations for the following day.

Next day, Monday, presented several new and varied difficulties for the attention of the Commander-in-Chief. By now Henry Blackwood in the *Euryalus*, and the *Hydra*, were off Cadiz as the new inshore squadron, but the *Hydra* had left the Admiral with a human problem. Her lieutenant had deserted his ship and run away in Italy with a ballet dancer from Malta. He had left a series of unpaid debts behind him—his father reckoned between £200 and £300—and was 'very probably in prison'. Now Nelson sat down to try and sort out the mess. He wrote to Captain Sotheran, commanding the *Excellent*, in Naples Harbour, asking him to try, with the help of the British Embassy, to trace him. The lad's father would pay the accumulated debts, Nelson said, 'and if now a few more [pounds] are necessary to liberate the youth, I will be answerable. All we want is to save him from perdition.'

Then there was the problem of Vice-Admiral Sir Robert Calder. That officer was, this very day, writing to Marsden at the Admiralty demanding an inquiry into his conduct against Ville-neuve's Fleet on July 22. He had just 'learnt with astonishment yesterday by the ships just arrived, and by letters from friends in England, that there has been a most unjust and wicked endeavour to prejudice the public mind against me as an officer'. His decision to ask for an inquiry seems to have been based on a talk with Collingwood and Nelson—of whom he had previously been reckoned an enemy. Now he was asking that Captain William Brown of the *Ajax*, Captain William Lechmere of the *Thunderer*, and Captain Durham of the *Defiance*, who were with him in the action, should be allowed to return home with him as witnesses.

The *Defiance* had in fact not yet joined the Fleet. Nelson was touched by Calder's anguish and reported to Lord Barham, 'It will give your Lordship pleasure to find, as it has me, that an inquiry is what the Vice-Admiral wishes. . . . Sir Robert felt so much, even at the idea of being removed from his own ship which he commanded, in the face of the Fleet, that I much fear I shall incur the censure of the Board of Admiralty.' He then went on to explain why. He felt he could not insist on Calder leaving the *Prince of Wales* for a smaller ship for the voyage home, and although he could ill afford the loss of such a powerful, 98-gun ship, 'I trust that I shall be considered to have done right as a man, and to a brother officer in affliction—my heart could not stand it, and so the thing must rest.'

There were plenty of other letters to write that Monday morning, and his Secretary, Mr John Scott (not to be confused with the *Victory*'s chaplain, the Reverend Dr Alexander Scott), was kept busy. There was a gentle reproof to be sent to Rear-Admiral Knight ('I was only twenty-five days, from dinner to dinner, absent from the *Victory*. In our several stations, my dear Admiral, we must all put our shoulders to the wheel, and make the great machine of the Fleet intrusted [*sic*] to our charge go on smoothly)': to Lieutenant-General Fox at Gibraltar, saying that if the enemy 'know of our increased numbers we shall never see them out of Cadiz'; to his old friend Ball at Malta, grumbling that 'I know not a word of Sir James Craig or his troops, or what they are going about, except, as the man said of the parson, "he preached about doing good"'. And among several other letters he signed was one to his old friend Alexander Davison. 'Day by day, my dear friend, I am expecting the [enemy] Fleet to put to sea— every day, hour, and moment; and you may rely that, if it is within the power of man to get at them, that it shall be done; and I am sure that all my brethren look to that day as the finish of our laborious cruise. The event no man can say exactly; but I must think, or render great injustice to those under me, that, let the Battle be when it may, it will never have been surpassed. My shattered frame, if I survive that day, will require rest, and that is all I shall ask for.

'If I fall on such a glorious occasion,' he wrote, 'it shall be my pride to take care that my friends shall not blush for me. . . . My mind is calm, and I have only to think of destroying our inveterate foe.'

By 1.30 in the afternoon, the captains who had not lunched with Nelson the previous day came on board the *Victory*. They included Thomas Fremantle, George Duff and Edward Codrington ('What our late Chief [Collingwood] will think of this,' he wrote to Jane, 'I don't know; but I well know what the fleet think of the difference; and even you . . . will allow the superiority of Lord Nelson in all these social arrangements which bind his captains to their admiral.') It was a jovial lunch:[1] gusts of laughter frequently rattled the thin, elm-wood bulkheads, and the steward Chevalier was busy at the wine cooler, broaching bottles and filling glasses while Nelson and his captains drank bumpers, toasting victory, the King, and Emma. The *Victory*'s own band played, and soon the time came for the captains to return to their ships. Nelson, however, asked Fremantle to stay—'to see a play that was performed by the seamen on board the *Victory*', as the young captain later told Betsey. 'I assure you it was very well conducted, and the voice of the seaman, who was dressed in great form and performed the *female part* was entertaining to a degree.'

Nelson went to bed that night in his long, narrow cot, which hung from the deckhead. Its hangings had been embroidered by Emma, and he quickly fell asleep as it swung gently with the roll of the ship. But he woke at 4 a.m. with 'one of my dreadful spasms, which had enervated me'. 'However,' he wrote next day to Emma, 'it has entirely gone off, and I am only quite weak. The good people of England will not believe that rest of body and mind is necessary for me. . . . I had been writing seven hours yesterday; perhaps that had some hand in bringing it upon me.'[2]

Some of the other captains also found that waiting off Cadiz was not a very healthy occupation. Fremantle, telling Betsey that 'I shall be outrageous if you do not christen my new tittler by the name of Louisa. I have taken such an aversion to Christine that I shall be sick and melancholy,' grumbled about his rheumatism. However, at the moment the weather was so hot that he slept with the stern windows and the doors of his cabin open, and this seemed to do the rheumatism some good. He found half a pint of wine made him heavy and dozey, but fortunately the spruce beer

[1] Nelson usually breakfasted early, had 'dinner' at about 2 p.m. and supper at about 7 p.m.

[2] Beatty, the surgeon, diagnosed these spasms as indigestion. They might well have been attacks of nervous dyspepsia.

he had taken aboard the *Neptune* 'turns out famous, I drink it all day'. Indeed, since he stopped drinking wine and stuck to spruce beer, 'I have not had so much bile'.

Over in the *Mars* the big and burly Captain George Duff was a happy man. His thirteen-year-old son Norwich had joined the ship a few days earlier and it was becoming quite clear to the proud father that the boy was making good progress. 'He seems very well pleased with his choice of profession,' Duff wrote home to his wife Sophia at 30, Castle Street, Edinburgh, where a Raeburn portrait showed the fair-haired Captain looking down from the wall with clear eyes and a friendly smile. Duff was a good example of a man who lived and died for the Royal Navy. He had been born in the little port of Banff, on the north-east coast of Scotland into a family descended from the old earls of Fife. His mother had died within six weeks of his birth, and the whole of his childhood was spent, when not in his father's study with a private tutor, scampering among the sailing ships in the little harbour half a mile from the town, or playing with boats on the River Doverean which ran near his home on its way to the sea. Young George listened to the tales the sailors told—there were many sailors along this stretch of the coast—and his imagination did the rest. He dreamed of going to sea like his great-uncle Robert, who was already a commodore. His father disapproved, but the boy, at the age of nine, stowed away on board a small merchant ship which arrived at a neighbouring port before he was discovered. His father, a sensible man, then relented and the tutor was ordered to change the curriculum to one more suited to a prospective sailor. At thirteen George joined great-uncle Robert in the *Panther*. By the time he was sixteen he had fought in sixteen actions.

The arrival of young Norwich and his cousin Thomas on board the *Mars* brought the muster of Duffs up to four, because Thomas's elder brother Alexander was an acting lieutenant, being too young to take his lieutenant's examinations. Thomas and Alexander were sons of Lachlan Duff, of Park. Also in the *Mars* was a boy from Banff whom Norwich knew well, Midshipman T. Robinson. The *Mars* was something of a family ship, for another of the lieutenants, Benjamin Patey, had his fifteen-year old nephew George on board as a midshipman. Benjamin was one of ten sons of a Royal Navy gunner.[1]

[1] Nine of them joined the Royal Navy. One of the Gunner's grandsons became an admiral, another a rear-admiral and a third a captain.

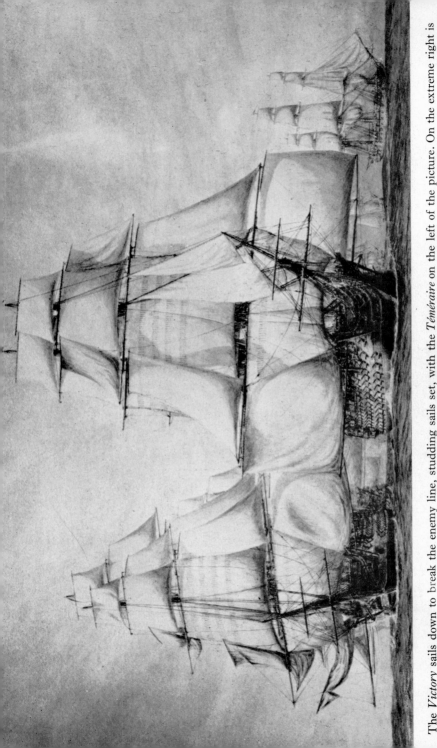

The *Victory* sails down to break the enemy line, studding sails set, with the *Téméraire* on the left of the picture. On the extreme right is Blackwood's frigate *Euryalus* and, in the distance, the schooner *Pickle*. *From the painting by Harold Wyllie*

Captain Codrington's view of the battle from the deck of the *Orion* at about 2 p.m. This painting by Harold Wyllie shows, from left to right, the *Britannia*, Spanish *S. Trinidad*, British *Neptune*, *Leviathan*, French *Bucentaure* (dismasted and heeling to starboard), *Conqueror*, *Victory* (heeling to port), French *Redoutable*, *Téméraire*, French *Fougueux*, French *Neptune* and, with just her bows showing, the Spanish *San Justo*.

Tuesday, October 1 found the crews of most of the ships in the British Fleet hard at work with scrapers, paint pots and brushes. The *Victory*'s hull was painted in the Nelson style—in black with three horizontal yellow bands or strakes. Each yellow strake was at the same level as a tier of gun ports, but the port lids were painted black on the outside so that with the lids closed they gave a chequer-board effect. This looked smart and impressive and, what was more important, it was the Nelson style. Individual captains were quick to emulate it, and although many of them probably had to foot the paint bill themselves, they did it willingly. It was a proud Fremantle who reported to Betsey from the *Neptune* (which was, he pointed out, 'only a foot shorter than the *Victory* and appears much larger upon deck') that 'we are all busy scraping our ships' sides to new paint them in the way Lord Nelson paints the *Victory*'.

Nelson himself, lying in his cot in the *Victory*, was weak and weary after the 'dreadful spasm' during the night, but he was up early as usual attending to the day's business. His valet Gaetano helped him wash, shave and dress; then Chevalier served his breakfast. After that there was the usual crop of letters. To Emma he wrote of his reception from the Fleet; to Lord Castlereagh he wrote of the enemy. Colonel Congreve's new rockets might, if they had a range of one and a half miles, do execution among the ships of the Combined Fleet, then lying abreast of the town of Cadiz, which was itself on a narrow spit of land jutting into the bay; but he thought 'we have a better chance of forcing them out by want of provisions: it is said hunger will break through stone walls—ours is only a wall of wood'.

In the afternoon the little schooner *Pickle* joined Nelson's Fleet after a fairly fast passage out from Plymouth. She had taken seven days to reach Cape St Vincent and just over a day from there to rendezvous with the Fleet.

Collingwood came over to the *Victory* to have a quiet meal with his old friend: at lunch the previous two days Nelson's dining cabin had been full of his captains; now the two admirals were able to talk freely.

Although Nelson was sure that the Combined Fleet faced a famine, he was worried about his own supply situation, which was far from good. The Fleet needed more than eight hundred bullocks (these had to come from Tetuan, on the African coast inside the Strait of Gibraltar) and a transport laden with wine

F

each month, and a lot of fresh water. He therefore decided to send small groups of his ships to Gibraltar and Tetuan, starting with Admiral Louis and the battleships *Canopus*,[1] *Queen*, *Spencer*, *Zealous* (which had just come out from England to find her mainmast sprung and rotted in several places) and the frigate *Endymion*, which had also joined the Fleet with a sprung mainmast. Louis and his flag captain, Charles Austen, who was in command of the *Canopus* and one of Jane Austen's three sailor brothers, were not very pleased at the idea of being sent away at this time. The two of them dined with Nelson in the *Victory* just before leaving, and when the time came to return to the *Canopus*, Louis said: 'You are sending us away, my Lord—the enemy will come out, and we shall have no share in the battle.'

'My dear Louis,' replied Nelson, 'I have no other means of keeping my Fleet complete in provisions and water, but by sending them in detachments to Gibraltar. The enemy will come out, and we shall fight them; but there will be time for you to get back first.' To reassure Louis, Nelson added: 'I look upon *Canopus* as my right hand; and I send you first to insure your being here to help beat them.'

With Blackwood in the *Euryalus*, and the *Hydra* watching every movement of the Combined Fleet from close in to Cadiz, Nelson needed a string of ships stretching from the look-out frigates across the fifty-odd miles to the westward where the Fleet waited, so that as soon as the *Euryalus* ran up a flag signal it could be repeated from ship to ship until it reached the *Victory* fifty miles away. To provide this link Nelson needed at least three more ships. He had no other frigates available and had already appealed to the Admiralty for more. To Castlereagh he had also written: 'I have only two frigates to watch them, and not one with the Fleet. I am most anxious for more eyes, and hope the Admiralty are hastening them to me. The last fleet was lost to me for want of frigates; God forbid this should.' The only thing he could do now was to use three battleships. He chose the *Mars*, *Defence* and *Colossus*, and a delighted Duff found he was to command this little squadron. To Sophia he wrote that he could manage only a short letter because 'since *I am Commodore* I have not much time during the day, and am ready for my nap as soon as I can in the evening.' Later, grumbling that Admiral Louis would presumably

---

[1] The *Canopus* was formerly the French 80-gun battleship *Le Franklin*, captured at the Battle of the Nile.

soon return and 'deprive me of my honours' by taking over the
command of the advance squadron, Duff said of Nelson: 'He is
so good and pleasant a man, that we all wish to do what he likes,
without any kind of orders. . . . Even this little detachment is a
kind thing to me, there being so many senior officers to me in the
Fleet.'

Blackwood was warned by Nelson of 'the importance of not
letting these rogues escape us without a fair fight, which I pant
for by day, and dream of by night.' Four more frigates were
expected soon, and two would be sent to help him. 'In fresh
breezes easterly[1] I shall work up for Cadiz, never getting to the
northward of it; and in the event of hearing they are standing out
of Cadiz, I shall carry a press of sail to the southward towards
Cape Spartel and Arrache [i.e. the North African coast]. He added,
'I am confident you will not let these gentry slip through our
fingers, and then we shall give good account of them, although
they may be very superior in numbers.'

With so much work to do, the days passed quickly. On Thursday, October 3, a sharp letter was sent to Lord Strangford, the
British Minister in Lisbon, about the churlish treatment of
British warships in Lagos by the Portuguese Government. When
a vessel went there for food and water, as provided for by treaty,
'She seems placed under the direction of the consul of one of our
enemies and very improper language is held by our enemies to
the British officers and seamen and inducements held out to them
to desert. The enemy's consul then directs that only so many
cabbages, or bullocks, or sheep shall go on board—and, at his will
and pleasure, so much water.' To this degradation, declared
Nelson, no nation can submit. He was certainly not going to allow
any French or Spanish consul to say, 'You English shall either
wear a dirty shirt, or go without water to drink.'

He wrote to the Earl of Northesk that 'It is likely to be a very
fine day, therefore will you do me the favour of dining on board
the *Victory*. Your captain [Bullen] I shall of course expect with
you.' The Earl treasured this letter and sent it home to his wife at
Rosehill, near Winchester, as an indication of Nelson's friendliness. On the back of the letter he also wrote a brief message—'*Do
not* pay the duty for the wine that comes home in the *Prince of
Wales* [Calder's flagship, due to sail for England in a few days]
till I tell you.'

[1] This was the wind with which the Combined Fleet could sail.

On Friday, October 4, the little cutter *Entreprenante*, commanded by Lt Robert Young, joined the Fleet. Next day the wind went round to the east and Nelson sent the *Pickle* to help Blackwood's two frigates off Cadiz. 'The French and Spanish ships have taken the troops on board,' he wrote to Barham, 'and it is said they mean to sail the first Levant wind.[1] The enemy ships in the Spanish port of Cartagena, inside the Mediterranean, had hoisted their topsails and, Nelson concluded, 'it looks like a junction.'

By Sunday the wind was in the east, and with the Combined Fleet embarking troops Nelson was a very anxious man. The clash seemed to be imminent. 'I verily believe,' he wrote to George Rose in London, 'the country will soon be put to some expense for my account, either a monument, or a new pension and honours; for I have not the very smallest doubt but that a very few days, almost hours, will put us in battle; the success no man can ensure, but the fighting them, if they are to be got at, I pledge myself.' He was equally anxious while he waited for more reinforcements to arrive. 'It is, as Mr Pitt knows, annihilation that the country wants, and not merely a splendid victory of twenty-three to thirty-six—honourable to the parties concerned, but absolutely useless in the extended scale to bring Bonaparte to his marrowbones: numbers can only annihilate.'

On Monday the 74-gun *Defiance*, commanded by Captain Philip Durham, arrived from England to join Nelson's Fleet. It will be remembered that he served with Calder in the action of July 22 against Villeneuve, and he held very strong views about it. After the action, Calder had thought it necessary to bring his squadron to, in order to cover the captured ships, and both the British and the enemy spent the night repairing damage. Next morning Durham in the *Defiance* had been ordered to take his station between the two fleets. He did this fully expecting the action to be renewed, his biographer wrote. He signalled to Calder, 'You can weather the enemy', but there was no reaction from the flagship. Villeneuve's fleet then started to draw away, and Durham signalled 'The enemy increase their distance.' Still there was no reply, and a desperate Durham made a final signal, 'Am I to keep sight of the enemy?' To which Calder replied by recalling him to take his station in the line. Aware of the consequences of Villeneuve's escape, Durham called his officers together and told

[1] A Levanter is a strong easterly wind blowing out of the Mediterranean.

them to 'be particular in their journals, as that was not the last they would hear of that affair'. His words were prophetic, for no sooner had he boarded the *Victory* two and a half months later to report to his Commander-in-Chief than Nelson greeted him with: 'Durham, I am glad to see you, but your stay will be very short, for Sir Robert Calder sails tomorrow, and takes with him all the captains who were in his action, to give evidence at his court martial. I am very sorry to part with you, but you will have to leave your ship under the command of your first lieutenant: but go on board the *Prince of Wales* and settle that with Sir Robert. The wind is at the north-east; the enemy will be out. . . .' Durham took the hint: he had been more than thankful for the chance meeting with Nelson at the Admiralty several weeks before which led to him being in the Fleet, and he was in no mood to be thwarted by Calder, having got so close to Cadiz and so obviously near to a battle.

Leaving the *Victory*, Durham went across to the *Prince of Wales*, where he found Captain William Brown, who had left the *Ajax* under the command of his first lieutenant, John Pilford, and Captain William Lechmere, who had left the *Thunderer* under the command of Lt John Stockham. Both captains were apparently quite willing to return home with Sir Robert Calder, but Durham asked to see the Admiralty order. When he discovered that it said the captains were to go home to England to give evidence only if willing, he told Sir Robert he was certainly not willing, and at the same time he refused to sign a public letter applying for leave to quit his ship. With that gesture he took his farewell, climbed back into his boat and returned to the *Defiance*.[1] His biographer makes it quite clear that Calder was probably better off without Durham's presence at the court martial since he would have given evidence unfavourable to the Admiral.

The *Royal Sovereign*, freshly repaired, joined the Fleet from England on Tuesday, and she brought further problems for Nelson. Secret orders from Admiralty, enclosing a letter from Lord Castlereagh, told him that in addition to dealing with the Combined Fleet off Cadiz he was to cover Craig's operations in the Mediterranean, and that in the event of hostilities on the Continent

---

[1] The *Defiance* took on board 750,000 Spanish dollars before leaving England. As soon as it appeared the Combined Fleet was preparing to sail Durham asked Nelson what should be done with the money. 'If the Spaniards come out, fire the dollars at them,' replied his lordship, 'and pay them off in their own coin!'

—which were virtually certain—Craig's men might be used on the coast of Italy. With a small convoy due to sail from Gibraltar for Malta with reinforcements for Craig, it meant Nelson's force of battleships would be even further denuded: the convoy would have to be guarded against any sally by enemy ships from Cartagena.

To a friend Nelson wrote on this same day, October 8: 'I have 36 sail of the line looking me in the face; unfortunately there is a strip of land between us, but it is believed they will come to sea in a few days. The sooner the better. I don't like to have these things upon my mind; and if I see my way through the fiery ordeal, I shall go home and rest for the winter.' And even as Nelson wrote those words, events reached a crisis aboard Villeneuve's flagship anchored in Cadiz.

Wearing: with the wind coming from the left, the left-hand ship is on the larboard tack. She turns (centre sketches) away from the wind, which crosses her stern, and comes round until she is on the starboard tack

16

COUNCIL OF WAR

'But I'll endeavour deeds to match these words.'
—Shakespeare (*Troilus and Cressida*)

WE HAVE SEEN how Napoleon's orders for Villeneuve to sail for Naples had arrived in Cadiz on Friday, September 27, two days before Nelson took over command of the British Fleet off the port, and how on Saturday, Villeneuve reported that the troops would embark within a day or two. On Monday as Villeneuve paced up and down on board the *Bucentaure*, he was a lonely man, prey to many emotions. He knew he had little or no sympathy from the Emperor; Decrès was clearly doing his best, but he had to obey Napoleon. His own flag officers, Rear-Admiral Magon and Rear-Admiral Dumanoir, were not, apparently, giving him the support he expected. The French and Spanish captains were saying openly that they stood very little chance against the British. In addition friction was growing between the French and Spanish squadrons. French sailors were being murdered in the streets; stories that the French had treacherously abandoned the two Spanish warships in the action of July 22 against Calder were spreading through Cadiz, and there were many people only too willing to believe them.

Already extremely anxious at the reported strength of the British fleet awaiting him over the horizon, he now knew that at last Nelson had arrived, and the knowledge that the almost legendary figure of that terrible fighter was poised a few leagues away to the westward almost unnerved him.

The wind had stayed in the west—foul for getting the Combined Fleet out of Cadiz; then later on Monday afternoon (the day Durham arrived in the *Defiance* and refused to go back with Calder) it went round to the north-east. At last they could leave. Villeneuve made his decision, and within a few minutes the signal for the Combined Fleet to prepare to put to sea was run up aboard the *Bucentaure*. At once there was a great deal of bustle aboard all the ships: captains were called from their cabins, first lieutenants gave orders which called all hands, and men went to the capstans to get ready to heave up the anchors. Then more flag hoists were run up from the *Bucentaure*: the order was cancelled. The Fleet would not now sail after all.

Next day Villeneuve wrote his excuses in a letter to Decrès and contradicted himself. 'In my impatience to carry out the Emperor's orders,' he said, 'heeding neither the strength of the enemy nor the condition of the greater number of the ships in the Combined Fleet, I desired yesterday to take advantage of an easterly breeze on which the Fleet could work out, and I made the signal to prepare to sail, but the wind having blown a gale from this quarter and being therefore diametrically opposed to the course that I was to shape, I was not able to carry out my design.'

That much was quite clear: the breeze had increased so much that it threatened a Levanter, so that the wind which took him out of Cadiz would prevent him getting through the Strait of Gibraltar. But then, as if that was not a good enough reason for not sailing, he added another—which contradicted his first sentence. 'Nevertheless I could not turn a deaf ear to the observations which reached me from every side, as to the inferiority of our force in comparison with that of the enemy, which is at the present time from thirty-one to thirty-three line-of-battleships, of which eight are three-deckers, and a large number of frigates; to put to sea in such circumstances has been termed an act of despair which is not consonant with the prestige of the Allied cause . . . an action on the very day of our leaving port was inevitable; that to hope for a favourable issue of an action at the mouth of the harbour with crews such as those in our ships and more especially in those of His Catholic Majesty, would be a strange self-deception.'

So Villeneuve that Tuesday morning called a council of war of all the flag officers of the Combined Fleet and the senior captains. They totalled fourteen men, of whom seven were French and seven Spanish. Those fourteen men who sat down in Villeneuve's cabin on board the *Bucentaure* were to bear the responsibility for the Combined Fleet's success or failure against the British. At their head was Villeneuve, now aged forty-one, who had fought at the Nile and was later to be described by a British officer as 'a tallish, thin man, a very tranquil, placid, English-looking Frenchman.''[1] One of his ancestors had fallen at the side of Roland in the

[1] Collingwood described him as 'a well-bred man, and I believe, a good officer: he has nothing in his manners of the offensive vapouring and boasting which we, perhaps too often, attribute to Frenchmen'.

pass of Roncesvalles; another had charged beside Richard Coeur-de-Lion in Palestine. The Admiral himself was a Knight of Malta—the ninety-first member of the family to belong to the Order—and had gone to sea while very young. He was one of the few members of the nobility who did not leave the Navy at the Revolution. Like Collingwood, Villeneuve thought longingly of his wife and his home among the pine-trees in Provence. Like Collingwood he was never again to see his village of Bargemon; he was not to hear the song of the cicada, nor feel the sun rising over the Alps to warm and ripen the peaches and the melons. Instead he was to meet his death at the hands of the Emperor he now tried to serve. Rear-Admiral Dumanoir le Pelley, Villeneuve's second-in-command, was thirty-five; his family was one of the wealthiest on the Cotentin peninsula and his background was that of the rolling green hills of the Calvados country. Like Villeneuve, he had served the King yet survived the Revolution, and he owed much of his promotion to Murat, who escaped from Egypt at the same time as Napoleon in a frigate commanded by Dumanoir.

The third-in-command of the French Fleet was an impetuous —almost reckless—Breton, Rear-Admiral Magon. His full name, de Magon Clos-Doré, showed he was of noble birth, and like his two superiors he had first served in the Navy under the King. He now had little but contempt for Villeneuve; indeed he was reported to have got into such a rage when Villeneuve did not renew the action against Calder on July 22 'that he stamped and foamed at the mouth'. While he paced furiously up and down aboard his own ship, Villeneuve's flagship passed and Magon 'gave vent to furious exclamations, and flung at him in his rage whatever happened to be at hand, including his field-glass and even his wig.'

The senior French captain at the Council of War was Cosmao-Kerjulien, round-faced, burly and grave; a Breton who was perhaps one of the finest captains in the French Navy. He had run away to sea at the age of twelve and had been in action many times. The other three Frenchmen were Captains Maistral, Lavillegris and Prigny, who was Villeneuve's Chief-of-Staff.

The Spaniards were led by Don Federico Gravina, a grandee of old Spain, with the right to put on his hat in the Presence Chamber of the King. Now forty-nine, he had been at sea since he was twelve and he was the most highly regarded officer in the Spanish Navy. His second-in-command was Vice-Admiral Ignatio Maria de Alava, fifty-one years old, grey-haired and round-faced, who had fought with Gravina at the siege of Gibraltar. The third Spanish flag officer was Rear-Admiral Don Baltazar Hidalgo Cisneros, who had commanded the *San Pablo* at the battle of Cape St Vincent. The other Spaniards present were Rear-Admiral Don Antonio de Escaño, who was Gravina's Chief-of-Staff, Commodore Don Rafael de Hore, and Commodore Enrique MacDonell.[1]

Villeneuve, dressed in a long-tailed uniform coat, green corduroy breeches with a two-inch wide stripe down each side, and half-boots with sharp toes, opened the Council of War by saying that the Emperor's instructions were that the Combined Fleet should weigh at the first favourable opportunity and that 'wherever the enemy should be encountered in inferior strength they must be attacked without hesitation in order to force them to a decisive action.' From various sources—the Spanish Ambassador in Lisbon, an agent at Tangiers, look-outs and coastal craft—it had been discovered that the British had between thirty-one and thirty-three battleships. Would everyone, Villeneuve asked, 'be so good enough as to give his opinion upon the situation in which the Combined Fleet is placed?'

In the discussion that followed the Spanish were at an advantage: unlike the French they had talked it over among themselves before they boarded the *Bucentaure*. Some of the French officers at first declared that there was no doubt about the proposal to sail: the result would be the rout of the British and 'the consequent ease' of carrying out their orders to make for Naples.

The Spanish officers replied simply that they agreed with Rear-Admiral Escaño, their Chief-of-Staff, since they had all discussed the situation. And Escaño,[2] reporting his own remarks later, wrote that he asked the French: 'Whether in the circumstances —the English having twenty-five to thirty ships at the harbour mouth—it were preferable to leave port or to receive an attack at anchor?' He made several comments on 'the difference between the skilled seamanship of those [British] who had been at sea with their squadrons without the least intermission since 1793 and

[1] Commanding the *Rayo*, he was in fact an Irishman, born in Ireland of Irish parents and christened Henry. He had joined the Spanish Regimiento de Hibernia—originally raised from Jacobite refugees in Spain—to fight against Britain during the American War, and later transferred to the Navy.

[2] See Notes, page 352.

those who had spent eight years without putting to sea, pointing out to the Spanish that they were not able to rely on their short-handed unskilled seamen'.

He concluded: 'Superior orders cannot bind us to attempt the impossible, as nothing would serve as an excuse in the event of a disaster, which I see to be inevitable if we weigh.'

The impetuous Breton, Rear-Admiral Magon, immediately leapt up, angry and red in the face, to contradict Escaño. He spoke so hotly that he very soon upset the Spaniards. The sensitive and punctilious Commodore Galiano interrupted angrily, demanding that Magon withdraw several expressions concerning the Spanish, and within a few moments there was uproar in Villeneuve's cabin as several other Spaniards joined in the demand that Magon retract. Magon, on the other hand, loudly refused. Finally Admiral Gravina stood up and, quietening them all, requested that they ought to vote—without any further arguing—on the question: should or should not the Combined Fleet put to sea considering that it had not a superiority of force to make up for its inherent inferiority. Villeneuve took a vote—and the majority verdict of the French and Spanish senior officers was that they should stay at anchor. After a brief discussion about forming a defence flotilla in case Nelson should attempt to attack the Fleet in Cadiz itself, the men present signed the minutes of the meeting and the Council of War broke up.

All present recognized, the minutes said, that the Combined Fleet was for the most part badly manned and that several of the ships had not even been able to exercise their crews at sea. 'They are by no means in a state to render the service in action of which they will be capable when they are organized.' They concluded with a paragraph which can hardly have expressed their true feelings, but which was a sop to Decrès and the Emperor: 'In all these observations, the officers of the two nations composing this assembly have borne witness to the desire that they will always feel of going out to engage the enemy, whatever his force, as soon as His Majesty desires it. . . .'

On the day the turbulent Council of War was being held aboard the *Bucentaure*, Nelson was, as we have seen earlier, writing that 'I have 36 sail of the line looking me in the face.' Later in the day he sat down at his desk in the great day cabin aboard the *Victory*, took up his pen and started to write laboriously with his left hand.

Heading it with the two words 'Secret' and 'Memorandum', and paying scant regard to punctuation, he wrote:

'Thinking it almost impossible to bring a fleet of forty sail of the line into a line of battle in variable winds thick weather and other circumstances which must occur, without such a loss of time that the opportunity would probably be lost of bringing the Enemy to battle in such a manner as to make the business decisive.

'I have therefore made up my mind to keep the fleet in that position of sailing (with the exception of the first and second in command) that the order of sailing is to be the order of battle, placing the fleet in two lines of sixteen ships each with an advanced squadron of eight of the fasting [sic] sailing two decked ships which will always make if wanted a line of twenty-four sail, on whichever line the Commander-in-Chief may direct.

'The second in command will in fact command his line and' he wrote, then crossed out the last six words, put a comma after 'will' and continued, 'after my intentions are made known to him, have the entire direction of his line to make the attack upon the enemy, and to follow up the blow until they are captured or destroyed.'

Nelson was writing his famous Memorandum, 'The Nelson Touch', which his secretary, John Scott, was to correct. Describing how Collingwood's division was to break through the enemy line about the twelfth ship from the rear and his own would break through about the centre, he emphasized that 'the whole impression of the British Fleet' must be to overpower the enemy from two or three ships ahead of their Commander-in-Chief—whom he supposed to be in the centre—to the rear. In this way the whole of the British Fleet (which he estimated at about forty ships) would be concentrated on half the Combined Fleet. The rest of the enemy ships would take some time to re-form and join in the battle.

'Something must be left to chance,' he wrote, 'nothing is sure in a sea fight beyond all others. Shot will carry away the masts and yards of friends as well as foes; but I look with confidence to a victory before the van of the enemy could succour their friends.' (He then crossed out the last word and substituted 'rear' adding that his ships would be 'ready to receive the twenty sail of the line, or to pursue them, should they endeavour to make off . . .')

He then went on to give his plan in greater detail. (The complete Memorandum is given in Appendix III.) John Scott was kept busy for the rest of the day and much of the night supervising the many copies which had to be made of the Memorandum and distributed next day to the captains throughout the Fleet.

That night Nelson wrote in his private diary: 'Fresh breezes easterly. Received an account from Blackwood, that the French ships had bent[1] their topgallant sails. Sent the *Pickle* to him, with orders to keep a good look-out. Sent Admiral Collingwood the Nelson Touch. At night wind westerly.'

Next day, Thursday, October 10, he wrote to Collingwood: 'The enemy's fleet are all but out of the harbour—perhaps, this night, with the northerly wind, they may come forth, and with the westerly sea breeze tomorrow go into the Mediterranean.' But he was disappointed: as we have already seen, the Council of War had decided otherwise. This Thursday was another busy day for John Scott: Nelson sent fourteen standing orders 'to the respective captains' in the Fleet, and they covered subjects ranging from sending in copies of their logs to vouchers for bullocks, lemons and onions, muster books, returns of killed and wounded, shortening sail at night because of sudden gales, and an order concerning the colours that ships were to wear. At this time admirals, vice-admirals and rear-admirals were designated of the blue, the white, or the red. Nelson was a vice-admiral of the white and the ships in his division would wear the White Ensign. Collingwood, however, was a vice-admiral of the blue, and his division would normally wear the Blue Ensign. Now, however, Nelson ordered, 'When in presence of an enemy, all the ships under my command are to bear White Colours, and a Union Jack is to be suspended from the fore-topgallant stay.'

A further letter went to Blackwood, keeping vigil off Cadiz: 'Keep your five frigates, *Weazle* and *Pickle*, and let me know every movement. I rely on you, that we can't miss getting hold of them, and I will give them such a shaking as they never yet experienced: at least I will lay down my life in the attempt. We are a very powerful fleet and not to be held cheap.'

On the 11th he began a letter to Emma which he continued on the 12th. He told her that a mutual friend, Captain Sutton, was being invalided back to England. 'Ah, my beloved Emma,' he wrote, 'how I envy Sutton going home; his going to Merton and seeing you and Horatia. I do really feel that the twenty-five days I was at Merton was the very happiest of my life. Would to God

[1] Sent the sails up the mast and secured them to the yards ready for use.

they were to be passed over again, but that time will, I trust, soon come, and many, many more days added to them.' He added to the letter on the 13th, 'I am working like a horse in a mill, but never the nearer finishing my task, which I find difficulty enough in getting and keeping clear from confusion, but I never allow it to accumulate. *Agamemnon* [from England] is in sight, and I hope I shall have letters from you, who I hold dearer than any other person in this world, and I shall hope to hear that all our family goes on well, at that dear, dear cottage. . . .'

More ships were coming out to reinforce his Fleet. In addition to the *Royal Sovereign*, which joined on the 8th, the *Belleisle*, commanded by Captain William Hargood, arrived on the 10th. Two frigates which arrived on the 11th were sent on to Gibraltar to help escort the convoy. When the *Agamemnon*, one of the ships built at Buckler's Hard, was signalled, Nelson rubbed his hands and exclaimed with glee, 'Here comes Berry; now we shall have a battle!'

Sir Edward Berry had indeed only just avoided a battle with Allemand, who was still at sea with his battleships, a constant threat to Nelson's communications. Berry reported that he had run into Allemand's force and had been chased, a three-decker getting within gun-shot on the weather quarter and an 80-gun ship on the lee. He had had to pump fresh water over the side and cut away a boat to lighten the ship, and had only escaped after a seventy-mile dash, after which Allemand had recalled his ships. Allemand's ships also chased the British frigate *L'Aimable*, which made an equally skilful escape. A twelve-year-old midshipman who was on board wrote an uninhibited letter to his mother saying:

I hope you are all well at home and I am sure will be very glad to hear from me, but you were very near losing me on the 10th of this month, for we were chased by the French Squadron and were very near being come up with, but we cut away two of our boats and one anchor and hove two or three hundred shot overboard. . . . We were so deep we could not sail [fast] until we staved in nine butts of water and pumped it out, and cut the boats adrift. Besides all, there was a very heavy squall came, and we had all sails set [and] were very near going down. She laid down on her beam ends for several minutes. . . . Do not fret about me, for if you cared no more for the French than I, you would care very little about them. Give my love to father, brothers and sisters. Success to William and his rabbits. Dear Mother, I remain, your ever affectionate son, Charles.

Calder left for England in the *Prince of Wales* on October 13, the same day that the *Agamemnon* arrived and next day the *Africa*, commanded by Captain Henry Digby, joined the Fleet. The little *Africa*, with sixty-four guns and a crew of only 490, was the smallest battleship on either side in the battle and was commanded by one of the most successful of captains. The third of the Dorset captains at Trafalgar (Hardy, and Bullen of the *Britannia* were the other two) he was the eldest of three sons of the Dean of Worcester. Going to sea at the age of thirteen, he was later very fortunate with prize money: he was only twenty-nine when, with three frigates, he captured two Spanish ships carrying three million dollars. Each Captain received £40,130. Digby had also captured twenty merchant ships, and by the time he was thirty he had received £57,000 in prize money, adding another £6,000 in the next six years. But he was as brave as he was successful: despite her size, the little *Africa* was to tackle the biggest ship in the world, the 130-gun *Santissima Trinidad*.

These October days were now passing quickly, with the Fleet constantly taking on stores from transport ships. Nelson's plans for the battle were made; it only remained to wait patiently for the enemy to make the first move, and to hope that they did so before the winter gales came whirling in from the Atlantic. The crews of the British ships had little trouble in keeping themselves amused. In the *Britannia*, for instance, the Earl of Northesk's flagship, there was a flourishing amateur dramatics group which had been putting on shows regularly from the time the ship first arrived off Cadiz. The producer was Second Lieutenant L. B. Halloran, of the Marines, whose father, Dr Halloran, was also on board the *Britannia* as chaplain and secretary to Lord Northesk. The Admiral always lent his fore-cabin for the performances, but they had become so popular it was impossible to get both audience and stage into the fore-cabin. Lord Northesk agreed to the forward bulkhead of the cabin being taken down, leaving the cabin open to the main-deck. Thus the audience could sit on the main-deck looking aft into the cabin, which would be the stage. The doors on either side leading aft into the Admiral's day cabin were useful as the stage exits. Previous performances—including *Lord Hastings*, *Miss in Her Teens*, *The Siege of Colchester* and *The Mock Doctor*—had whetted everyone's appetite for *Columbus, or a World Discovered*, to be performed on October 9, the day Nelson's Memorandum was delivered on board. Mr Adams, the Master's Mate, had proved an excellent artist and he had painted the scenery which the carpenter had proudly built in his spare time. A large play bill was prepared which announced: 'In the course of the performance will be two splendid processions—a view of the Interior of the Temple of the Sun with a Grand Altar burning incense, etc.—Grand Hymn of Priestesses etc.—Towards the close of the play the Destruction of the Temple by an Earthquake accompanied by Thunder, Lightning and Hail Storms! ! With the rescue of Cora from the ruins by Alonzo! !' For several days beforehand the cast had been busy, when off watch, learning their lines. Lt Wilson was to be the High Priestess of the Sun, with other parts being taken by various other officers, with the midshipmen acting as 'priestesses and ladies'. Lt Halloran was also busy putting the finishing touches to a short play he had written called *The Village* which, with *Catharine and Petruchio*, was scheduled for performance a few days later.

In the late afternoon the stage hands—there were always plenty of volunteers—took the bulkheads down, set up the scenery under the direction of Mr Adams, trimmed the lanterns which were to act as footlights and, after supper, brought up forms from the mess decks and chairs from the wardroom for the audience to sit on. The play bill had announced 'Doors to be open at 6.30. To begin at 7.' The crew were in their places promptly at 6.30, the lucky ones getting seats on the forms, the less fortunate squatting on the guns. The officers sat down in the chairs and waited while, in the Admiral's cabin, the cast donned wigs made from teased-out ropes' ends, rouged their faces with red lead, and dressed themselves in clothes skilfully adapted from their workaday rig. Finally Lord Northesk and Captain Bullen made their appearance and sat down in two chairs in the centre of the front row.

At this moment, fifty miles to the eastward, Villeneuve was waiting on board the *Bucentaure* in Cadiz; a few score miles to the north an officer was galloping *à franc étrier* for Paris, taking the Council of War's decision to Decrès, riding day and night, pausing only to change horses and, if he had time, snatch a meal, but frequently having to eat in the saddle. Nelson now could only wait. Close in to Cadiz Henry Blackwood watched with the *Euryalus*, and in company were four other frigates (*Naiad*, under Thomas Dundas, *Phoebe*, commanded by the Hon Thomas Bladen Capel, *Sirius* under William Prowse, and the *Amazon* under command of Captain William Parker), the schooner *Pickle*, and the 16-gun brig *Weazle*. Out to sea, just in sight of the *Euryalus*, and forming the first link in the chain which stretched to the Fleet waiting some fifty miles to the westwards, was Captain George Hope with the 74-gun *Defence*. To the west of him Berry waited with the 64-gun *Agamemnon* and beyond him Captain James Morris tacked and wore the *Colossus*. The last link was Captain George Duff, with the *Mars*.

'Touch and Take', Nelson said, was to be his motto; but for the time being it might well have been 'Watch and Wait'. And while he waited he wrote in his diary. The entry for Wednesday, October 16, said: 'Moderate breezes, westerly. All the forenoon employed in forming the fleet into the Order of Sailing . . . in the evening fresh gales. Enemy as before, by signal from *Weazle*.' Next day he wrote 'Moderate breezes, north-westerly. Sent the *Donegal* to Gibraltar to get a ground tier of casks . . . at midnight the wind came round to the eastward.' And on Friday: 'Fine weather, wind easterly; the Combined Fleets cannot have finer weather to put to sea.'

Early on Saturday morning the British fleet was sailing in two divisions, the one to windward led by Nelson and the other to leeward by Collingwood. Several flag signals were made by the *Victory* to the captains of certain ships asking them to lunch that day and telling them to signal their reply. At the same time Nelson wrote to Collingwood, ending his letter with: 'What a beautiful day! Will you be tempted out of your ship? If you will, hoise the "assent" and *Victory*'s pendants.' A boat took this letter across to Collingwood in the *Royal Sovereign*. While he was reading it and before he had time to send his reply, the *Victory* signalled to the *Bellerophon*, which was the fourth ship in Collingwood's division, to close. Captain Cooke had just had time to order the *Bellerophon* to make more sail before she hauled up to windward when his first lieutenant, William Cumby, spotted that the nearest look-out ship, the *Mars*, was flying a hoist of flags from her mast-head. Putting his telescope to his eye he read them—a yellow diagonal cross on a blue blackground; blue, white and blue vertical stripes, and a flag divided diagonally in white and blue. The signal 370.

'I immediately reported this to Captain Cooke,' Cumby wrote later, 'and asked his permission to repeat it. The *Mars* at that time was so far from us that her topgallant-masts alone were visible above the horizon; consequently the distance was so great for the discovery of the *colours* of the flags that Captain Cooke said he was unwilling to repeat a signal of so much importance unless he could clearly distinguish the flags himself, which on looking through his glass he declared himself unable to do.

'The very circumstances of the importance of the signal, added to my own perfect conviction of the correctness of my statement founded on long and frequent experience of the strength of my own sight, induced me again to urge Captain Cooke to repeat it, when he said if any other person of the many whose glasses were now fixed on the *Mars* would confirm my opinion he would repeat it. None of the officers or signalmen, however, were bold enough to assent positively, as I did, that the flags were number 370, and

A topsail schooner—the *Pickle* had this rig

I had the mortification to be disappointed in my anxious wish that the *Bellerophon* should be the first to repeat such delightful intelligence to the Admiral.

'Soon afterwards, the *Mars* hauled the flags down, and I said, "Now she will make the distant signal 370." '[1] The sharp-eyed and thwarted Cumby added: 'She did make the distant signal 370 as I had predicted; this could not be mistaken and we were preparing to repeat it, the *Mars*'s signal was answered from the *Victory*, and immediately afterwards the dinner signal was annulled and the signal given for a general chase.' The reason for Cumby's anxiety over signal number 370 was shown by its meaning given on page nine of the *Signal Book for Ships of War*: '*The Enemy's ships are Coming out of port, or are getting under sail*'.

[1] Distant signals were used when distances were so great that colours of flags could not be distinguished, or when the wind blew the wrong way (i.e. directly towards or away from the ship to which the signal was made). They consisted of various flags and shapes hauled up at different mastheads, the combination of shape and mast giving the meaning. Those for 370 were a flag, a ball and a pendant.

17

SIGNAL NUMBER 370

'Had I but serv'd my God with half the zeal
I serv'd my king, he would not in mine age
Have left me naked to mine enemies.'
—Shakespeare (*Henry VIII*)

VILLENEUVE was now a man for whom the future held little promise. On October 15 he heard from Bayonne, on the Franco-Spanish border, that Vice-Admiral Rosily had passed through on his way to Cadiz. At the time this report was not alarming, because although Rosily was at the top of the vice-admirals' list he had not been to sea for a dozen years or more, and was often employed by Decrès and Napoleon for various administrative missions. The unfortunate Rosily, bearing the secret orders which sacked Villeneuve and put himself in command of the Combined Fleet, was having a rough time. The journey from Paris to Bayonne presented no difficulties, but the first lap from there to Madrid started off badly. There was only one carriage in Bayonne and the owner made Rosily pay heavily for it. The coach travelled very slowly, and it took Rosily eleven days ('halting at inns where with difficulty I found a bed and leaving at one or two in the morning,' he complained to Decrès) to cover the three hundred miles across the Pyrenees to Madrid.

Even in the capital his troubles were by no means over. The French Ambassador warned him that he would not be able to travel by postchaise over the remaining four hundred and fifty miles to Cadiz because there would be no horses for the carriage. From Madrid to beyond Cordoba—more than two hundred and fifty miles—he could not be given a mounted escort. Instead, to defend him from 'a considerable gang of bandits' lurking along forty-five miles of road beyond Cordoba he would have to collect an escort of militia in the town who would march on foot beside him. He expected to reach Cadiz in ten days, he wrote to Decrès from Madrid on October 12.

Although the real reason for Rosily's journey was being kept as secret as possible, rumour travelled a good deal faster than the

Admiral, and within a few hours of learning that he had passed through Bayonne, Villeneuve heard reports that Rosily was in fact coming to take over command of the Combined Fleet. Apparently he regarded them as true, and in any case it was now quite clear to him that, whatever Rosily's mission, Decrès and the Emperor were deliberately keeping him in ignorance of it, and that in itself was significant. Swiftly, and without telling anyone, Villeneuve made his plans. His orders from the Emperor to sail at once to Naples still held good, and if he had carried them out before Rosily arrived he could not be blamed—and his honour would be satisfied. His Order of Battle, showing how the ships were divided into three squadrons with two further squadrons of observation, had been distributed on October 6, before the Council of War.

The final instructions to the Fleet—Villeneuve's equivalent of the Nelson Touch—was an extraordinary document. It showed that he had in fact correctly guessed the way Nelson would attack and, what is more, he had guessed it ten months to the day before Nelson carried it out. It might be asked why he had not, during that time, attempted to work out a method of countering it; but in fact there was no real defence. It was as if Villeneuve was being forced to behave like a mesmerized rabbit which knew it would be killed by the stoat but was rendered powerless to do anything. Villeneuve's final instructions consisted, in fact, of a re-issue of the last few paragraphs of the general directions given to his captains many months earlier (the originals were dated December 21, 1804) when preparing to leave Toulon. They dealt first with signals, and then said: 'I by no means propose to seek out the enemy; I even wish to avoid him in order to proceed to my destination. But should we encounter him, let there be no ignominious manœuvring; it would dishearten our crews and bring about our defeat.' He described what the Combined Fleet was to do if the British were to leeward, and emphasized that 'any captain who is not under fire will not be at his post; any whose next ahead or next astern is closer than he to the enemy will not be doing his duty and a signal recalling him to his post will be a reflection on his honour.' And if the British attacked from to windward, the Combined Fleet would meet them in a close-formed line of battle.

He then wrote the paragraph which showed he had penetrated Nelson's mind. 'The enemy will not confine himself to forming on a line of battle parallel with our own and with engaging us in an artillery duel, in which success lies frequently with the more skilful but always with the more fortunate; he will endeavour to envelop our rear, to break through our line and to direct his ships in groups upon such of ours as he shall have cut off, so as to surround them and defeat them.' Having got as far as this, Villeneuve offered no defensive measure to combat it. Instead he wrote: 'In this case, a captain in command must consult his own daring and love of honour far more than the signals of the Admiral, who being perhaps engaged himself and shrouded in smoke, may no longer have the power of making any. Here again it is a case of repeating that a captain who is not under fire is not at his post.'

He rounded off the instructions with some wishful thinking. 'Nothing in the sight of an English Squadron should daunt us . . . they are worn out with a two years' cruise; they are not braver than we and have infinitely less feeling of enthusiasm and patriotism. They are skilled in seamanship; in a month's time we shall be as skilful. Finally, everything unites to give us the firm hope of the most glorious victories and of a new era for the seamen of the Empire.'

With his final orders in the hands of all the French and Spanish captains, Villeneuve's first step was to plan a night attack by a squadron of seven battleships under Magon on Blackwood's five frigates waiting outside Cadiz. With Nelson's 'eyes' captured, Magon would then be able to reconnoitre to see where the British Fleet was and what was its strength. If Magon's report was favourable, the Combined Fleet would sail immediately. Once again Villeneuve had to wait for a favourable easterly wind and a moonless night. On Wednesday evening, October 16, there was a westerly gale which by Thursday morning had dropped to a moderate breeze and veered to north-west. Would it continue to veer? Villeneuve waited, and by midnight it had gone round to the east. Next morning (as Nelson wrote 'The Combined Fleet cannot have finer weather to put to sea'), Villeneuve sent orders across to Magon: he was to sail with his force that night. But by this Friday evening, before darkness fell, a message arrived in Cadiz. It came from Algeciras, the Spanish frontier town overlooking Gibraltar, and had been passed up the coast from one look-out post to another. The British convoy which had been waiting at Gibraltar had at last sailed with an escort of four battleships, while a fifth battleship was at Gibraltar with her mainmast out, and a sixth was steering up the Strait to anchor in the port.[1] Realizing that Nelson's fleet had now been weakened by six battleships, Villeneuve knew he had to seize this chance. He called on Gravina and told him he had made up his mind to sail the next day.

Back on board the *Bucentaure* a series of signal flags was soon fluttering at the masthead. The first, according to the Spanish ship *Montañes*, ordered the removal of the guns from the longboats, which had been armed so that they could patrol the entrance to Cadiz. The second hoist ordered each ship to summon its crew on board. This, according to Major-General Contamine (who had just taken over command of the troops from Lauriston) filled the men 'with the most ardent desire to give battle; our invalids, soldiers and sailors forsook the hospitals; they rushed to the quay in crowds to embark'. The next signal told every ship to send an officer on board the flagship to receive orders, and this was followed by the order to hoist in the boats and to be ready to weigh anchor. But Villeneuve did not attempt to get to sea under the welcome cover of darkness.

He had written to Decrès earlier in the day saying that he had given Magon orders to sail with his squadron next morning to drive off the frigates and carry out a reconnaissance, and that if all was well the Fleet would follow. Then he added: 'I am informed that Vice-Admiral Rosily has arrived at Madrid; the common report is that he is coming to take over the command of the Fleet; undoubtedly I should be delighted to yield him the foremost place if I am permitted to occupy the second; it is due to his seniority and his abilities, but it would be too terrible to me to lose all hopes of having an opportunity of showing that I am worthy of a better fate.'

Next day, Saturday, broke with a clear sky and the wind variable, little more than a balmy breeze. Between 5 a.m. and 6 a.m. Villeneuve hoisted the signal for the ships to sail, but the individual captains seem to have been far from clear whether this was intended only for Magon, the frigates or the whole Fleet.

[1] The convoy consisted of the forty-nine transports taking reinforcements to Craig which sailed from Gibraltar on October 17, the day before the news reached Villeneuve and the same day that Louis received orders to take his four battleships and escort it past Cartagena. The fifth battleship was the *Zealous*, whose mainmast was to be replaced, and the sixth the *Donegal*, which was going in for water.

Magon's flagship, the *Algésiras*, hove up her anchor, set sail and managed to catch a breeze which took her out of Cadiz, followed by the *Achille*. The frigate *Hermione* was less fortunate and lost the breeze altogether, so Commander Mahé ordered the boats to be put over the side to tow the ship out.

Although some of the battleships and frigates managed to sail out or use their boats for towing before the young flood tide became too strong, the majority of the Combined Fleet did not have enough breeze to warrant their weighing anchor. Gravina's flagship, the *Principe de Asturias*, Villeneuve's *Bucentaure* and the great 130-gun *Santissima Trinidad* stayed where they were. The *Montañes* spent an hour trying to work her way through the tangled mass of ships, many of which had their sails set with boats rowing ineffectually ahead at the end of anchor cables, looking like captive water-beetles. By the evening the only battleships which had managed to get out were Magon in the *Algésiras*, the French *Neptune*, *Héros*, *Argonaute*, *Achille*, *Duguay-Trouin* and the Spanish *Bahama*. With them were the frigates *Hermione*, *Themis* and *Rhin*. Once outside, Magon ordered his motley squadron (only two of them actually belonged to his division) to form line of battle, while Villeneuve was forced to order the ships left in Cadiz to anchor. By 10 p.m., to Magon's annoyance, the breeze faded away until his ships barely had steerage way. He tried to keep them together, but in the darkness they lost each other and two of them anchored for the rest of the night off Rota. Thus, as far as the Combined Fleet was concerned, Saturday, October 19 drew to a close. All this time the British ships had kept discreetly to seaward. And now Villeneuve knew the alarm had been raised. What would Nelson do?

Long before daylight that Saturday morning Henry Blackwood and his little squadron had been keeping their usual vigil, tacking back and forth watching the five miles between Cadiz and Cape San Sebastian on the south side of the anchorage and Rota on the north side. They were so close in, wrote Midshipman Hercules Robinson of the *Euryalus*, 'as to see the ripple of the beach and catch the morning fragrance which came off the land'. Day after day the routine had been the same. At 3.30 a.m. on this day the *Euryalus* reached the Rota end of the bay with the rest of the squadron in company and prepared to tack to get the wind on the other side and sail back again.

'Ready ho!' called a voice from the quarter-deck, clear and sharp in the night air. 'Put the helm down.'[1]

The wheel was eased over so that the frigate's bow began to swing across the wind, pointing directly towards Cadiz for a moment as it came round.

'The helm's a'lee!'

Up forward the men working in the darkness let go the headsail sheets so that the sails lost the wind and did not stop the ship's swing. In a few moments she had come so far round that the wind, instead of hitting the great square sails at right angles, blew along their edges, making the canvas flutter and flap instead of arching with its thrust.

'Off tacks and sheets!'

Men scrambled to new positions, throwing some ropes off their cleats, hauling on others and preparing to trim the sails. The ship's bow was now almost pointing into the wind.

'Mainsail haul!'

Quickly men hauled sheets and tacks so that the sails, now hanging loose and fluttering from the yards, would be ready to receive the wind as the bow swung across and brought it on to the other side.

'Let go and haul!'

They braced the great yards smartly round, the sails filled and the *Euryalus* heeled over slightly on the other tack, heading for San Sebastian and Cadiz, with canvas taut and bulging, the sea creaming under the bow and gurgling under the stern. The man at the wheel continually glanced at the compass, his face faintly lit by the reflection of the oil lamp in the binnacle, and then peered at the leech of the sails. Frederick Ruckert, the *Euryalus*'s Master, filled in his log. '*At* 3.30 *tacked ship. Moderate and clear. Out 2nd reef, set foresail and spanker. At 4, ditto weather. Squadron in company. At 5.30, tacked. Sebastian NE, about 4 miles. . . .*' Very slowly the sky lightened over the land, the dark grey transmuting itself to a faint pink. The sails overhead, the deck underfoot, the wind-rippled sea and the next man's face slowly began to take on their own colours albeit, with the sun still well below the horizon, pale and washed out.

---

[1] The actual wording of orders tended to vary from ship to ship: there were no standard instructions laid down by the Admiralty, and the only attempts at standardization were made by individuals who wrote and published seamanship books.

Closer inshore, Captain William Prowse in the *Sirius* was aiming his telescope at one ship of the Combined Fleet and then another as they swung, like grotesque swans, at anchor in the Roads and inside the protective peninsula on which Cadiz stood. His eye ran from mast to mast; then he gave an order which the signal midshipman and signalman went scurrying to execute. Flags were bent on to the halyards and the blocks squealed as, hand over hand, the signalman hoisted them up, each group forming a word in Sir Home Popham's telegraphic code. Over in the *Euryalus* Midshipman Bruce read them off, conscious that every ear on the quarter-deck waited on his words. '249—"Enemy"—354—"have" 864—"their"—875—"top"—756—"sails"—986—"yards"—1374—"hoisted".'

It was 6.4 a.m., and men's pulses quickened as the sun climbed higher over the land, shortening the shadows. Yet on board the frigates the shipboard routine continued as if nothing had happened. The look-outs were now at the mastheads, hammocks were lashed up and stowed in the nettings round the upper decks; in the galleys the cooks stoked up the fires while the crews kept their fingers crossed that breakfast would be prepared before the captains ordered the drummers to beat to quarters—an order which meant, among other things, that the galley fires would be doused. The minutes sped by and warmth came into the sun. From all the frigates and the *Pickle* and the *Weazle*, telescopes watched the enemy. Were there men climbing the rigging of those northernmost ships like spiders up a web?

There was a slight movement, just visible to Prowse in the *Sirius*, in the upper parts of the masts. Suddenly the topsails were let fall, and they could see the wrinkles in the canvas disappearing as the sheets were hauled. Then the masts moved slowly against the backcloth of the land as the ships got under way, coming slowly round to the north-west, towards the entrance of the anchorage and the broad Atlantic. The signal midshipman quickly went to work, and farther out to sea Midshipman Bruce in the *Euryalus* read off the next signal: '370—"Enemy's ships are coming out of port, or getting under sail" '.

Blackwood had several things to do now. He ordered Bruce to signal the *Phoebe* to go to the westward and repeat signals between the *Euryalus* and the *Defence*, the first link in the chain of ships stretching out to where Nelson waited. Peter Parker in the *Weazle* was ordered to sail immediately to warn Rear-Admiral Louis that the enemy were coming out (Blackwood assumed he would be at Gibraltar or Tetuan), and Signalman Soper hauled up one last cryptic signal to speed Parker on his way: 'Make all possible sail with safety to the masts.' By this time the *Phoebe* was heading westwards, like a blackbird squawking in the hedge, towards the *Defence*, firing three minute guns and flying the signal that the enemy were coming out of port. Blackwood then ordered Dundas in the *Naiad* to take up a position between the *Euryalus* and the *Phoebe*, ready to pass on further signals. The *Sirius* was left close in to Cadiz with the *Euryalus* farther out. The *Defence* soon repeated the long-awaited warning to the *Agamemnon*. She passed it on to the *Colossus*, who signalled it to the last link, the *Mars*. From the *Mars*, as we have already seen, it reached the *Victory* without the *Bellerophon* being able to get the credit for being the first to spot and repeat it.

Nelson had reacted quickly by making a signal to the Fleet for 'General chase south-east', his plan being to steer immediately for The Gut, as the Strait of Gibraltar was known, to cut off the Combined Fleet and prevent it sailing through into the Mediterranean. In addition Nelson hoped to meet Louis; he did not know that Louis had been delayed, and instead of being on his way back from escorting the Malta convoy, was still sailing eastwards with it.

In a faint wind the British Fleet slowly made its way to the south-east, each ship with its yards braced hard up to catch every scrap of breeze. At noon Nelson went down to his cabin and sat once again at his desk to write two letters, one to each of the people he loved and longed for so dearly.

> *Victory*, October 19th, 1805, Noon, Cadiz, E.S.E. 16 leagues
>
> My dearest beloved Emma, the dear friend of my bosom. The signal has been made that the Enemy's Combined Fleet are coming out of port. We have very little wind, so that I have no hopes of seeing them before tomorrow. May the God of Battles crown my endeavours with success; at all events, I will take care that my name shall ever be most dear to you and Horatia, both of whom I love as much as my own life. And as my last writing before the Battle will be to you, so I hope in God that I shall live to finish my letter after the Battle. May Heaven bless you prays your
>
> Nelson & Bronte.

He put the letter away in his desk. He was to make one more addition to it. He still had another letter to write, and it was to Horatia.

My dearest Angel, I was made happy by the pleasure of receiving your letter of September 19th, and I rejoice to hear that you are so very good a girl, and love my Dear Lady Hamilton who most dearly loves you. Give her a kiss for me. The Combined Fleets of the Enemy are now reported to be coming out of Cadiz; and therefore I answer your letter, my dearest Horatia, to mark to you that you are ever uppermost in my thoughts. I shall be sure of your prayers for my safety, conquest and speedy return to dear Merton, and our dearest good Lady Hamilton. Be a good girl, mind what Miss Connor says to you. Receive my dearest Horatia, the affectionate parental blessing of your Father.

Nelson & Bronte.

At 3 p.m. Captain Morris's *Colossus*, the ship beyond the *Mars* in the communication chain, came hurrying up, all sails set and firing guns to draw attention. From her mastheads flew another series of signals reporting that the enemy's fleet was at sea. Unfortunately this information, following the report that they were leaving port, was only partly accurate.

Blackwood, in the meantime, had continued watching the enemy ships as they slowly worked their way out of the Bay. By 10 a.m. the breeze had shown every sign of fading right away, and by noon had carried out its threat. The *Euryalus* and *Sirius* wallowed and drifted, sails hanging limply from the yards like so much old and much-patched laundry. In the entrance to Cadiz the enemy ships had been in the same plight.

Blackwood had taken the opportunity to go down to his cabin and wrote a letter to his wife:

What think you, my own dearest love? At this moment the enemy are coming out, and as if determined to have a fair fight; all night they have been making signals, and the morning shewed them to us getting under sail. They have thirty-four sail of the line and five frigates. Lord Nelson has but twenty-seven sail of the line with him; the rest are at Gibraltar, getting water. Not that he has not enough to bring them to close action; but I want him to have so many as to make this the most decisive battle that was ever fought, and which may bring us lasting peace and all its blessings.

Within two hours, though our fleet was sixteen leagues off, I have let Lord N. [sic] know of their coming out, and have been enabled to send a vessel to Gibraltar, which will bring Admiral Louis and the ships there.

At this moment (happy sight) we are within four miles of the enemy, and talking to Lord N. by means of Sir H. Popham's signals, though so distant, but reached along by the rest of the frigates of the Squadron.

You see dearest, I have time to write to you, and to assure you that to the latest moment of my breath, I shall be as much attached to you as man can be. It is odd how I have been dreaming all night of carrying home despatches. God send me such good luck. The day is fine, and the sight magnificently beautiful. I expect before this hour tomorrow to carry General [sic] Decrès[1] on board the *Victory* in my barge, which I have just painted nicely for him.

As evening came on Nelson formed the Advance Squadron visualized in his Memorandum by putting eight of his fastest ships under the command of that appreciative Scot, Captain George Duff in the *Mars*. They were to burn lights during the night and some of them were to keep to the eastward and maintain contact with Blackwood's frigates. The three slow ships of the British Fleet, the 100-gun *Britannia* and the two 98-gun ships *Prince* and *Dreadnought*, were ordered to 'take station as convenient'.

While Nelson was under the impression that all the enemy had sailed, the position at midnight was that most of the French and Spanish ships were still at anchor in Cadiz. Outside, the *Achille* and *Bahama* were at anchor off Rota, while Magon's other five battleships were scattered to the north-west of Cadiz, with the frigates well up to windward. Blackwood with the *Euryalus*, *Sirius* and *Phoebe* were close by to seaward. Beyond them, forming the link with the main fleet which was now some twenty-five miles west of Cadiz and steering for The Gut, were the *Defence*, then the *Colossus* and finally, nearest to Nelson, the *Mars*.

A letter Codrington of the *Orion* wrote in the evening gives a good description of the day.

[1] The British Fleet had heard as early as October 9 that Villeneuve was to be superseded, and it was assumed that Decrès would take command.

How would your heart beat for me, dearest Jane, did you but know that we are now under every stitch of sail we can set, steering for the enemy. . . . We have now a nice air, which fills our flying kites and drives us along four knots an hour [*sic*].

I trust by the morning we shall be united and in sight of the enemy. As to my coming out of the battle alive or dead, that is the affair of chance and the little cherub: but that I shall come out without dishonour is my affair; and yet I have but little apprehension about the matter, so great is my confidence in my ship, and in our excellent Admiral.

It is not, my dear Jane, that I am insensible to the value of life with such a domestic circle as I belong to: no, my heart was never more alive to the sacrifice than at this very moment. But life in such a situation as this, even with the delightful prospect of returning to pass years in the society of a wife and children whom I love with a religious reverence, is really but a secondary consideration. . . .

I feel a little tired; and as I have now nothing to do but keep the ship's head the right way, and take care that the sails are well trimmed, in readiness for the morning, I shall even make that over to the officer of the watch and go to my cot; nor do I think I shall sleep the worse for my cabin being only divided from the quarter-deck by a boat's sail. [The bulkheads had been removed because the ship was expecting to go into action.] And so, dear, I shall wish thee once more a good night, and that thy husband's conduct in the hour of battle may prove worthy of thee and thy children.

Overhead, the sky which had in the later afternoon speckled its blue dome with white feathery mares' tails, gave its silent warning of the promise of bad weather.

Dawn on Sunday, October 20 brought with it dull weather: thick cloud masked the sun, and what wind there was came up from the south. About 6 a.m. Villeneuve once again ordered the Combined Fleet to weigh anchor and make for the open sea. Shortly after 7 a.m. the *Bucentaure* hoisted a signal ordering the ships to clear for action and prepare for battle. By 8 a.m. all the ships were under sail except the Spanish *Rayo*, commanded by the Irishman, MacDonell. Lt Taillard's little brig *Argus*, which had been given the task of acting as whipper-in, set her topsails and tacked patiently back and forth. Finally Taillard had a boat lowered and sent across to ask Macdonell what was delaying him. The Irishman answered that he had a lot of anchors to raise, but he would soon be ready.

Ashore, the quays and roads overlooking the anchorage were now thronged with people—many of them in tears—to bid the Combined Fleet farewell. Mothers and fathers, wives and sweethearts of many of the Spanish crews queued outside the Iglesia del Carmen, the old sailors' church, to be admitted in relays; at the High Altar of the Oratorio de San Felipe Neri, Archbishop Utrera spent the day on his knees pleading with his God for the safety of the great ships.

By 10 a.m. the weather was rapidly worsening; the wind went round to the south-west and increased, bringing heavy seas and rain squalls. One of the first orders Villeneuve gave that morning when he got outside was for his fleet to reef. And the wind was foul for the Strait of Gibraltar, the very course he wanted to steer. . . . The *Argus*, having at last seen the *Rayo* on its way, hurried out of Cadiz to report to Villeneuve that all was well.

Villeneuve had great trouble in getting the Combined Fleet, consisting of thirty-three battleships, five frigates and two brigs, into some semblance of formation. He ordered the Fleet to sail on a course of west-north-west, which was about the closest even a well-handled battleship could steer to the wind. Raw seamen, hastily trained while the ships were at anchor, were now having to scramble aloft and lay out on yards swaying upwards of a hundred and fifty feet above sea level with strong winds tearing at them and trying to fling them off. The thick, stiff canvas flogged and thrashed as they tried to tie reef points, tearing the nails from their fingers and stripping off the skin. The result was that several of the ships sagged off to leeward of the main fleet; and in the midst of the confusion a man fell overboard from the *Bucentaure*. She immediately signalled this to her next-astern, the *Redoutable*, commanded by Lucas. He at once hove-to, had a boat lowered, picked up the man and got under way again with the minimum delay.

At about noon Villeneuve signalled his fleet to form itself into three columns—a disposition which meant that only one column could fire at the enemy without the risk of hitting their own ships. Once again there was confusion as the ships manœuvred to get into position. They still had not managed to get into position when the wind suddenly swung round to the west. If Villeneuve kept the Fleet on the same tack it would be forced up to the north —the opposite course to the one for the Strait. So he ordered the Fleet to go about, to bring the wind on to the starboard side and thus steer southwards. But ordering a half-formed fleet to tack was a dangerous business, and as he saw his ships milling around the *Bucentaure*, falling astern or sagging down to leeward, giving the appearance of a flock of startled sheep, he must have known in his heart that the dice was loaded against him.

Blackwood's frigates stayed on the edge of the horizon, watching every move, yet Villeneuve himself still had no news of the whereabouts of Nelson's Fleet until six o'clock in the evening, when the *Achille* reported sighting eighteen ships in the distance. The French Admiral, frightened of the consequences of meeting Nelson with the Combined Fleet in three columns, promptly ordered it to form line of battle. The result was something approaching chaos, because the ships still had not formed into three columns and they could not sort themselves out before night came down. The *Achille* later reported that a ship would take station as soon as she saw three or four ahead of her in the darkness. Thus it was with his ships moving southwards in a vast, unco-ordinated mass, lights showing from ports and through the tiers of windows in the stern galleries, that Villeneuve spent Sunday night. Round the fleet, hidden in the darkness, the British frigates watched in silence.

Nelson was cheerful enough at first, because he did not have to worry about ships manned by raw sailors and tardy and un-skilful captains. Steering south-east during the night, by dawn on Sunday morning the British Fleet was some dozen miles off Cape Trafalgar and thirty miles from the narrowest part of the Strait of Gibraltar. The weather had changed for the worse, as we have already seen, and with daylight coming anxious eyes searched all round the horizon for a sight of the enemy. Codrington of the *Orion* gave vent to his feelings in another letter to Jane which he wrote before breakfast:

> All our gay hopes are fled; and, instead of being under all possible sail in a very light breeze and fine weather, expecting to bring the enemy to battle, we are now under close-reefed

Into battle: the gun-deck of a line-of-battleship, from a painting by Harold Wyllie. The man with his arms outstretched is the gun captain pulling the trigger line.

The *Santa Ana* at bay: the Spanish flagship is in the centre with the *Royal Sovereign* almost hidden in the smoke on her starboard side

topsails in a very strong wind with thick rainy weather, and the dastardly French we find returned to Cadiz. . . .

Nelson's cheerfulness quickly disappeared. Strong winds, rough seas and heavy rain which cut visibility down to a few hundred yards, was just the weather—as Codrington had realized —to send the Combined Fleet scurrying back to Cadiz with broken topmasts, torn sails and seasick crews. The Admiral knew that, had Villeneuve sailed on, the Combined Fleet would now be very near, and that was quite clearly not the case. And it was equally clear that the British Fleet could not stay off Cape Trafalgar under present conditions lest a storm blew up. He was probably making up his mind to take the Fleet to the north-west, back the way they had just sailed, when the *Mars*, closely followed by the *Defiance*, *Defence* and *Phoebe*, signalled that the enemy was to the northward. So at 6.20 a.m. on Sunday morning Nelson gave the order for the Fleet to wear and sail back to the north-west.

What had happened was that the British Fleet had arrived too early: Nelson, understanding from the frigates on Saturday morning that the whole of the Combined Fleet had sailed, had promptly headed for the Strait, but as we have already seen, only a few enemy ships, led by Magon, had succeeded in getting out that day. And it was not until ten minutes after Nelson ordered the Fleet to retrace its steps this Sunday morning that Villeneuve, still in Cadiz Roads, had hoisted the signal for the Combined Fleet to sail. Collingwood was now invited to the *Victory*, and Duff, Morris and Hope were told to drop to leeward with their ships so that they could support Blackwood's frigates.

However, the bustle of organizing the Fleet did not interrupt the shipboard routine: it was Sunday, and at nine o'clock the Reverend Dr A. J. Scott, as the *Victory*'s Master noted briefly in his log, 'performed Divine Service'. It was uncomfortable for the crew, with the ship rolling and rain squalls sweeping the deck. Just after the service began the *Agamemnon* passed on a signal to the *Victory* from the *Euryalus* which began to correct the some- what distorted picture of the enemy's strength and position: thirteen of the enemy had left Cadiz, and the rest had their yards hoisted and were about to follow.

By noon the British Fleet was south-west of Cadiz, steering west-north-west, and unknown to Nelson the Combined Fleet, having now successfully emerged from port, was twenty-five miles away to the north attempting to steer a similar course. Above all else, Nelson was anxious to know whether there was a chance of Villeneuve doubling back into Cadiz. Fortunately Henry Blackwood must also have realized this: signalling to the *Sirius*, 'I am going to the Admiral, but return before night', he reached the Fleet by 3 p.m. and twenty minutes later on board the *Euryalus* Midshipman Bruce and his signalman, Soper, were busy with a new signal: 'The enemy appears determined to push to the westward: thirty ships.' 'And that,' the Admiral wrote later in his private diary, 'they shall *not* do if in the power of Nelson & Bronte to prevent them. At 5 telegraphed Captain B., that I relied upon his keeping sight of the enemy.'

That Sunday afternoon the Admiral walked up and down the weather side of the poop, watching the ships, hearing Lt Pasco reading off the signals they made, fitting the scraps of information together in his mind like a man doing a jig-saw puzzle. He had already said to both Hardy and Dr Scott that 'The 21st of October will be our day.' Now, to a group of young midshipmen standing near him, he said with a smile: 'This day or tomorrow will be a fortunate one for you young men.' It was a grim jest, but one they understood: heavy casualties in the Fleet, especially among the lieutenants, would mean promotion to acting rank for some fortunate midshipmen.

Nelson's night orders for the watch on the enemy were drawn up so that Blackwood with two frigates would keep in sight of the enemy, passing signals to two other frigates. They in turn would link with the *Defence*, which would keep in touch with the *Mars*, the last ship in the chain to the *Victory*. The signals for the night were: 'If the enemy are standing to the southward, or towards the Strait, burn two blue lights together, every hour, in order to make the greater blaze. If the enemy are standing to the westward three guns, quick, every hour.'

Yet even though Nelson was, without being able to see his opponent's moves, playing a most intricate game of chess upon which the fate of Britain—indeed, of freedom itself—depended, he still had time to remember the smaller details which contribute to victory. Midshipman Richard Roberts recorded it thus: '*Victory* tellegraphed [*sic*] to the *Africa* to paint the hoops of her mast yellow'. The signal was also made to the *Belleisle*, because she too had her masthoops painted black. Nelson knew that this was a French custom, and in the thick smoke of battle the colour of the masthoops might well be the only way of identifying a ship before pouring a broadside into her.

Earlier in the day Nelson had added a few more sentences to his letter to Emma, describing the day's events:

> In the morning we were close to the mouth of the Strait, but the wind had not come far enough to the westward to allow the Combined Fleets to weather the shoals off Trafalgar; but they were counted as far as forty sail of ships of war, which I suppose to be thirty-four of the line and six frigates. A group of them was seen off the Lighthouse of Cadiz this morning, but it blows so very fresh and thick weather, that I rather believe they will go into the Harbour before night. May God Almighty give us success over these fellows, and enable us to get a peace.

By Sunday evening, however, he was fairly sure that the enemy were not going into Cadiz for the night, and at supper he commented to those sitting at his table: 'Tomorrow I will do that which will give you young gentlemen something to talk and think about for the rest of your lives, but I shall not live to know about it myself.' He added that he expected to capture from twenty to twenty-two enemy ships.

So Sunday, October 20, drew swiftly to a close. At 5 p.m. the *Naiad* reported that the Combined Fleet was at last steering to the south. Nelson did not want to get too close, in case Villeneuve was frightened back into port. He therefore signalled that the Fleet would go on to the starboard tack at the close of the day, putting them into a commanding position, ten miles to windward and five miles ahead of the enemy, ready to counter any move Blackwood's frigates might report. At 8.30 p.m. the order for the Fleet to come on to the starboard tack and thus sail south was given. One ship missed the signal—the little *Africa*, commanded by Digby. She continued sailing north.

Everything was now ready. The fact that the enemy had stayed at sea in the heavy weather instead of turning back made Nelson certain that there would be a battle on the morrow. His Fleet was concentrated up to windward, with the frigates down to leeward watching Villeneuve's every move and lighting flares or firing guns.

Aboard the *Britannia*, Lord Northesk and Captain Bullen had supper with the officers but did not linger long over the port. As soon as they had gone back to their cabins the officers and men went to work taking down the bulkheads and stowing them in the holds, and clearing the ship for action. 'We, however, all went to rest at our usual hours,' wrote Lt Halloran, 'having only hanging screens instead of cabins.' Monday was going to have a different climax than the one he and his fellow amateur actors had planned. Lord Northesk, at forty-six a quiet, stolid and efficient officer,

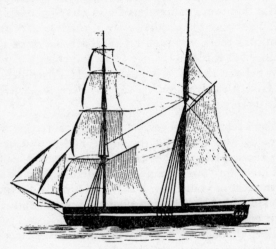

An hermaphrodite brig

went back to his cabin after supper and wrote to his wife, dating the somewhat clumsily phrased letter:

Britannia, off Cadiz at 10 o'clock p.m. Oct 20 1805.
My dearest wife,
    We have every hope of bringing the enemy to action; if I should not survive the glorious day; take care of yourself and my dear children and I beg you may have one [he then crossed out 'one' and wrote 'two' above it] thousand pounds after my death for your own use and at your own disposal beside what I left you by will—made in Scotland and at Battle—Believe me ever to have been your affectionate husband, Northesk.

He folded and interleaved the sheet, heated some black sealing-wax and dropped a blob on to the paper. Then he pressed his seal on to it and wrote on the outside simply: 'Countess of Northesk'.

In the *Neptune*, young Midshipman William Lovell, little guessing that one day he would become a vice-admiral, was excited. 'All hearts towards evening beat with joyful anxiety for the next day, which we hoped would crown our anxious blockade labours with a successful battle,' he wrote. 'When night closed in, the rockets and blue lights, with signal guns, informed us that the inshore squadron still kept sight of our foes, and, like good and watchful dogs, our ships continued to send forth occasionally a growling cannon to keep us alert, and to cheer us with a hope of a glorious day on the morrow.'

As far as the frigates were concerned, Midshipman Robinson felt that at least the *Euryalus* had done her share: 'When we had brought the two fleets fairly together we took our place between the lines of lights, as a cab might in Regent Street, the watch was called and Blackwood turned in quietly to wait for the morning.'

18

'PREPARE FOR BATTLE'

'O, that a man might know
The end of this day's business ere it come!
But it sufficeth that the day will end,
And then the end is known.'
— Shakespeare (*Julius Caesar*)

ON MONDAY, October 21, men of many nations waited with ill-concealed impatience for the dawn, but it seemed reluctant to lighten the black of night to the eastwards, as if unwilling to begin such a dreadful day. In the darkness, the British Fleet tacked and then sailed slowly northwards, more than thirty miles from Cape Trafalgar. Inshore of them, some fifteen miles away, the Combined Fleet was on an almost opposite course, heading south-east and dogged by Blackwood's frigates. They, like dark phantoms on the edge of a dozing man's consciousness, lit two blue flares from time to time which bathed their ships in an eerie light, bringing disquiet to many French and Spanish hearts.

In the *Victory* a Marine sentry, hot and sticky in short scarlet jacket and white pipeclayed crossbelts, white breeches and gaiters, shifted the weight from one foot to the other as he stood guard over Lord Nelson's cabin, and hidden away in some dark corner within earshot the Admiral's steward, Henry Chevalier, snatched some sleep, Inside the cabin Nelson's slender body was resting, lying in the narrow cot slung from the deckhead, half hidden by the hangings which Emma had embroidered. The cot swung from side to side as the *Victory* pitched and rolled in the heavy swell which was welling up in the darkness under an otherwise calm and breeze-dappled sea.

Two decks below and farther forward, the men who were off watch slept in a fetid atmosphere, their hammocks swinging in unison, their snores punctuating the creaking of the timbers. There were Richard Collins, of Philadelphia, now twenty-one years old, who had been press-ganged into the Royal Navy and transferred to the *Victory* two years earlier, and William Thompson, from the same town, who was a volunteer. Hans Yaule, a Swiss, had been twenty when his ship brought him to the Thames and he was seized by the press-gang. A Frenchman whose name was put down on the *Victory*'s muster list as John Packett—the nearest the English ear could approximate to his pronunciation—came from Le Havre (better known then as Havre-de-Grace). Now, at forty-five a press-ganged able seaman, he was about to fight his own countrymen. Samuel Lovett, born forty years earlier at Portsmouth, America, had suddenly found himself press-ganged at Portsmouth in England, and hustled aboard the *Victory*. Stromblo Milligue, a Sicilian from Messina, was a volunteer, as was another Frenchman, John Dupuis, of Nantes. The press-gang had also caught Matthew Miers, a German from Hamburg, and Dominick Dubine, from Italy. William Sweet, of New York, had been in Nelson's flagship for a year and a day—he had been brought on board on October 20, 1804.

The *Victory* was a cosmopolitan ship: of the 663 officers and men (excluding Marines and boys) mustered four days earlier, there were 441 English, sixty-four Scots, sixty-three Irish, eighteen Welshmen, three Shetlanders, two Channel Islanders and one Manxman. Of the seventy-one foreigners who volunteered or were press-ganged, twenty-two were Americans, seven Dutch, six Swedes, three Frenchmen, two Danes, three Norwegians, one Russian, three Germans, two Swiss, two Portuguese, four Italians, four Maltese and two Indians, while one man was African and nine came from the West Indian islands.

The 441 Englishmen on board came from many parts of the country. Included among them were more than a hundred from London, and twenty-seven from Kent. Twenty-four were Devonians, but only six Cornishmen; fifteen were, like Nelson, from Norfolk and twelve came from Suffolk, while Hampshire contributed twenty and Northumberland, Lancashire and Yorkshire eighteen each. Essex and Lincolnshire each sent nine, and Oxfordshire and Herefordshire a dozen, while Durham—reflecting perhaps the number of its men who went into the coasting trade from its flourishing ports and were seized by the press-gangs—sent seventeen. The youngest of the *Victory*'s crew was Johnny Doag, aged ten and rated 'boy, first class'. Four others were only twelve, and six but a year older. And also on board—although none of the crew knew it—was a woman dressed as a man. She was the wife of one of the four Maltese seamen.

Now, whether they were white or coloured, British or foreign, they had taken the oath, swearing to be true to his Sovereign

Lord King George the Third and to 'serve him honestly and faithfully in defence of his person, Crown and dignity against all his enemies and oppressors whatsoever'. Whether they heeded or even understood that oath, they were now—like their fellow seamen in the other twenty-six battleships of the British Fleet—being borne along in the great wooden ship towards a battlefield where death waited to look them over. Having long since ceased to be masters of their fate—the press-gangs, their oath and the Articles of War had seen to that—they waited, in their hammocks or on watch, to become heroes or cowards, corpses or cripples. Living a life little removed from slavery, fed with food rather more suited to swine, rarely given leave to go ashore, and having frequently been snatched up while going about their lawful occasions on land, they would meet the enemy shouting defiance, showing raw bravery and fighting like fiends, proud of their hour of glory.

Looking back on the scene from more than a century and a half away, one might be forgiven for musing that by contemporary standards the food and the system might well have produced men who were sick and sullen, mutinous and cowardly. Instead, strange material and unpromising circumstances were about to be forged by the Royal Navy into a great British tradition.

In each of the British ships as they continued steering northwards in the darkness before Monday's dawn, a faint light from the binnacle lit the compass and reflected in the helmsman's face as he stood sure-footed at the wheel easing the spokes this way and then that, using a mixture of craft and guile to keep his ship on course. Overhead the great yards creaked and groaned (the *Victory*'s main-yard was more than a hundred feet long); the massive, arching sails occasionally gave prodigious flaps as an extra large swell rolled the ship and the to-and-fro movement of the masts snatched the wind out of the canvas. The ropes of the sheets and braces grumbled to themselves as they rendered through numerous blocks before reaching their respective cleats, and the slings and trusses which held up the yards and kept them close to the masts creaked in sympathy. The slow roll tried to shift the guns; the breeching and tackles added their murmur as the carriages pulled and strained against the ropes fixed to eye-bolts in the ship's side.

Then the ships suddenly came to life. The bosun's mates with their shrill pipes—which earned them the nickname of 'Spithead

Nightingales'—soon had the men lashing up their hammocks and stowing them in the nettings on the upper-deck. And over to the eastwards, almost imperceptibly, a small band of blackness on the horizon diluted into grey and began to spread outwards and upwards. In his cabin Nelson scrambled awkwardly from his cot and began to wash, while Chevalier brought him a hot drink. The breeze was showing signs of becoming fitful, but the sea still creamed away from the cutwater at the bow in lazily folding waves and swilled under the stern, acting invisibly against the rudder as it bubbled aft to become the wake. Gradually the ship moved from its black world into the greyness of morning twilight. From the quarter-deck of each ship, the long, smoothly rounded crests of the swell waves could now be distinguished, rippling like shadows across the otherwise calm sea. As it grew lighter the waves seemed to grow bigger, but this was a common optical illusion.

In the *Victory* a small figure wearing a black patch over one eye and with an empty sleeve stepped up the weather ladder on to the poop, and everyone already there automatically moved respectfully over to the lee side. Nelson was wearing his usual threadbare frock coat, with his orders of knighthood embroidered on the left breast. They were, as always, tarnished from the salt air and spray. His sword had been taken down from the rack in his cabin but left lying on a table.

The first sight of the enemy is perhaps best described by an able seaman in the *Victory*, J. Brown, born twenty-three years earlier in Waterford and writing to 'Mr Thos Windever, at the Sign of the blue bell new Albs Street Liverpool'. With scant regard to punctuation he wrote: 'At day light the french and Spanish Fleets was like a great wood on our lee bow which cheered the hearts of every british tar in the *Victory* like lions Anxious to be at it. . . .'

Dawn had given way to what young Hercules Robinson in the *Euryalus* called 'a beautiful misty sun-shiny morning', with the sea like a mill-pond, apart from the ominous ground-swell rolling in from the Atlantic. And Midshipman Badcock in Fremantle's *Neptune* described the scene years later when he was himself an admiral: 'The sun rose, which, as it ascended from its bed of ocean, looked hazy and watery, as if it smiled in tears on many brave hearts which fate had decreed would never see it set.'

On board the *Royal Sovereign* Collingwood's servant, Smith, had gone into the Admiral's cabin at daylight and found him already up and dressing. 'Have you seen the French Fleet?' Collingwood asked. Smith replied that he had not. 'Then look out at them,' said Collingwood, 'in a very short time we will see a lot more of them.' In recalling that morning Smith wrote: 'I then observed a crowd of ships to leeward; but I could not help looking with still greater interest at the Admiral, who, during all this time, was shaving himself with a composure which quite astonished me.' After dressing with particular care Collingwood went up on deck. He saw Lt John Clavell wearing high leather boots. 'You had better put on silk stockings as I have done,' the Admiral observed, 'for if one should get a shot in the leg, they are so much more manageable for the surgeon.'

Nelson, standing on the poop of the *Victory*, surveyed the enemy ships silhouetted to leeward against the lighter eastern sky and apparently making their way towards the Strait. Although to leeward, as he intended, they were not as he had pictured, 'in the line of battle ready to attack'; instead they appeared to be in no formation at all, simply a mass of ships scurrying southwards. However, with this light wind it would be several hours before they could be brought to action. In the meantime it was now light enough for the British ships to see the *Victory*'s flag signals, and Nelson set about putting his own Fleet in order. Up to then it had been in a loose formation and at 6.10 a.m., before the sun had risen over Cape Trafalgar to the eastward, Nelson gave instructions to Lt Pasco to hoist the signal for the Fleet to form the order of sailing in two columns. Signal number seventy-two was run up, and the ships of the Fleet quickly hoisted the answering pennant and prepared to get into station astern either the *Victory* or the *Royal Sovereign*, depending upon their division.

Nelson had two main concerns, now that he had spotted his quarry. Keeping the weather gage was the first, allowing his Fleet to manœuvre much more freely and disguise until the last moment exactly where it would attack the enemy (preventing Villeneuve from reinforcing any part of it, since he would not know where the blow would fall); the second was to cut off the enemy from their bolt-hole of Cadiz which, for all the manœuvring since they sailed, was still only a bare twenty-five miles away to the northwards. If Nelson sailed to the east-north-east he would both stay up to windward *and* cut them off, and at 6.13 a.m. a second signal was run up aboard the *Victory*: to bear up and sail large on an east-north-easterly course. (Sailing large meant that the wind was free—abaft the beam.) Then, at 6.46 a.m., he made one more order to the Fleet—to come round two points to starboard and steer due east.

Now Nelson's column was heading towards the rear of the enemy's line and Collingwood's, a mile away to the south, was heading for the van. He may well have guessed that Villeneuve would eventually turn back to the north, towards Cadiz, and this order to steer east, although it was made five and a quarter hours before the first British ship fired a shot at the enemy, was the last manœuvring signal he had to give to the Fleet as a whole.[1]

The *Victory*'s signal lieutenant was having a busy time. Nelson regarded the signal lieutenant's job as a very important one, and had given it to John Pasco, who was senior lieutenant. He then appointed a junior officer to take over what should have been Pasco's job of being first lieutenant, choosing John Quilliam, who was fifth in seniority.[2] This switching round had annoyed Pasco considerably, and he had a very legitimate grievance. After a successful action it was usual to promote the first lieutenant who was, of course, normally the senior. Under Nelson's system, however, the senior might receive no recognition, but the lucky junior would. Pasco was waiting to point this out to Nelson, but had up to now been unable to find an opportunity.

More than twenty minutes before the order to steer east was given, Pasco had been ordered to hoist the signal for which the Fleet had been waiting with ill-concealed impatience for many weary months. It was number thirteen—*Prepare for battle*. 'Flagship signals "Prepare for battle"' the signal officers in various ships reported to their captains. Immediately the order 'Clear for Action!' was shouted from the quarter-decks. Bosun's mates ran to the hatchways, their pipes sounding the call like a chorus of angry birds. At once the men went to work.

In the *Victory*, Lt Quilliam detailed off parties of men to go round and finish off the already partly completed task of clearing away the bulkheads forming the cabins. If they were hinged at the top

[1] For those who are concerned that Nelson did not attack exactly according to his Memorandum, the fact that the Fleet as a whole sailed for five and a quarter hours without further manœuvring signals, shows that the captains knew all along exactly what was expected of them, and that the Memorandum was regarded only as an *aide-mémoire*. For the signal to bear up, see Notes, p. 353.

[2] Quilliam was a Manxman who had been pressed into the Navy.

they were swung up horizontally to the deckhead and secured out of the way, making a false ceiling; if they were not hinged they were knocked down section by section and carried below into the hold. In this way the decks were opened up from one end of the ship to the other: a man standing at the after end of Nelson's cabin against the stern windows could now look right through to the forward end of the fo'c'sle, past the mizenmast where it came through the deck, the elm tree pump which was hollowed from a solid tree and past the mainmast and the foremast. He could see fifteen 12-pounder guns ranged uniformly along each side of the ship, and the shot, like black beads, stowed in the racks round the hatchways.

The men took the furniture—chairs, tables, a cot and desk—from Captain Hardy's cabin under the poop and carried it carefully down four ladders to the orlop, from where it was lowered into the holds. Most of the Admiral's furniture was left for the time being until he had given his special instructions, but the few pieces of furniture and sea chests in the lieutenants' cabins were dragged below. On the mess-decks the tables now slung up on the deckhead between the guns were taken down and stowed in the hold together with the forms on which the men sat. All this was done not to protect the furniture but the men: a shot hitting a bulkhead or a piece of furniture would shatter it into scores of splinters—sharp slivers which could kill or wound a man almost as effectively as grape-shot or musket balls. All wooden ladders not needed in action were unshipped and taken below, rope ladders being fitted in their place; leather fire buckets were moved away from the ship's side and placed near the centre-line.

While Quilliam's men cleared the ship below decks, William Willmet, the *Victory*'s bosun, collected his mates and some seamen to carry out Article VII in *Regulations and Instructions* relating to the boatswain's duties—'When the ship is preparing for battle, he is to be very particular in seeing that everything necessary for repairing rigging is in its proper place, that the men stationed to that service may know where to find immediately whatever may be wanted.'

The first task for Willmet and his 'Spithead Nightingales' was to make sure that the great yards on which the sails were set would not come crashing down on to the deck, where they would do untold damage. The thick rope slings were reinforced with chains. Extra sheets and braces were rove in case those in use should be shot away, and by exercising a little cunning much of the rigging could be arranged so that if some was cut the rest would take the strain of holding up masts and yards. Grappling irons (large grapnels) were secured to ropes and hung from the lower yardarms or ranged along the bulwarks ready to be hooked to an enemy ship to clutch it in a lethal embrace. The boats stowed amidships would be left, but the quarter boats would be towed astern in action, comparatively safe from shot and where they did not get in the way of the guns. Axes were placed round the upper-deck where they could be snatched up by men to cut away wreckage. Splinter nets were slung between the masts.

The surgeon, William Beatty, went down to the cockpit amidships on the orlop-deck with the two assistant surgeons, and the loblolly men who acted as nursing orderlies. As soon as the ship was in action the purser, Mr Walter Burke, would join them to bear a hand, and the *Victory*'s chaplain, Dr Scott, would be there to help comfort the men. The cockpit was a dark and cheerless place, lit only by a few dim lanterns and now cleared of everything except for a few forms and tables which stood starkly in the middle of the open space like altars. This was, indeed, where the wounded men would be offered up to Beatty's skill: limbs would be amputated without anaesthetics—other than perhaps a stiff tot of rum—and with the loblolly men holding down the unfortunate and writhing victim. A couple of tubs would soon be rolled along and put by the table ready, as the men termed it, for the 'wings and limbs' that accumulated as Beatty went about his gruesome work.

Forward in the cable tier, on the same deck, men were wrestling with the massive rope anchor cables (each twenty-four inches in circumference) to make as level a surface as possible; awnings and spare sails would then be laid out flat on top, and here wounded men would lie awaiting their turn to be treated. To avoid favouritism it was a strict rule that the wounded were attended to in the same order that they were brought down to the cockpit or cable tier. It was a fair rule in the sense in which it was intended; in practice, however, it meant that many of the badly wounded—especially those who had lost limbs—died from loss of blood before their turn came.

The Gunner, Mr William Rivers, and his mates, went to the main and the two hanging magazines, the most carefully protected parts of the ship. Built below the water-line, where they could be quickly flooded in case of fire, their bulkheads were lined with felt and no lanterns were allowed inside. To provide light there were small light rooms with glass windows built on to the side of the magazines. Lanterns placed in the light rooms showed a dim light without any danger of fire. With the lanterns lit, Rivers and his mates put on soft leather or felt slippers—the nails in ordinary shoes or boots might kick up sparks—before unlocking the doors and going inside. Ranged on the deck in the magazines were hundreds of cartridges, which were simply flannel bags filled with gunpowder. The largest were for the thirty 32-pounders, the biggest guns in the *Victory* which, because of their weight, were kept on the lower-deck. With a distant charge[1] they could fire a 32-pound shot, which was nearly six and a half inches in diameter, more than a mile and at a range of about three hundred and fifty yards the shot would penetrate at least three feet of solid oak and six feet of fir.

In peace or war, fire was the great enemy in a wooden ship, and in action the main danger was that loose grains of gunpowder, falling along the passageways or on to the decks round the guns, would be ignited by a spark. To guard against this the planking of the gun decks and passageways would be washed down with water before the ship went into action. Now, while Rivers and his mates were checking over the charges, making sure there were also plenty ready in the two smaller hanging magazines on the orlop, other men were letting down screens of thick flannel which would be soaked with water immediately the drummer beat to quarters. There were holes in the screens through which the charges would be passed from the magazine to the powder monkeys, whose task was to carry them to the guns.

On the gun-decks fire-screens were being let down and match tubs dragged to each gun. Although the guns would generally be fired by flintlocks, slow-burning matches—lengths of loose-laid rope steeped in nitre, which burnt at the rate of about an inch an hour—had to be kept ready. Since they were a fire risk, they were kept in the match tubs, which were casks filled with water. The lid of each tub was perforated with several holes, and the burning end of the match was thrust down through one of them, hanging

---

[1] There were three types of charges—'distant' for maximum range and labelled with black paint, containing ten pounds eleven ounces of gunpowder; 'full', marked in blue and holding eight pounds of powder, and 'reduced' marked in red and with six pounds of powder.

over the water. It was thus ready for the gun captain. Should his flintlock fail to produce a spark, his second-in-command would snatch a match from the tub, blow on it to make it glow, and then press it on to the priming powder when the gun captain gave the order.

Spare casks of water with swabs beside them were placed round the decks. The water could be used to douse a small fire, or the men could snatch a quick drink and sluice their faces to refresh themselves during the action. Other casks by the guns were for soaking the sponges which would be rammed in after each firing to clean out any burning residue in the barrels.

Each gun captain—the leader of a gun team—had gone to his guns at the order to clear for action to make sure that all the items of equipment (with the exception of flintlocks and other items which the Gunner, Mr Rivers, would issue when the drummer beat to quarters) were ready and secured to the deckhead: the sponge on its stiff rope or wooden handle; the worm—a spiral of metal, like a spring, on a similar rope or wood handle, which cleared out anything the sponge missed; the rammer, used for pushing home the cartridge, wad and shot, and the handspikes used to lever the carriage round bodily to train the gun. Each captain checked the breeching, a thick rope securing the gun to the ship's side and preventing it from recoiling too far, and the gun-tackles which were used to pull the gun up to the ship's side after loading, so that the muzzle was poking out through the port, ready for firing.

Mr William Bunce, the *Victory*'s carpenter, and his mates, went down to their storerooms to get out the shot plugs, which would bung up any holes that the enemy's shot might tear in the *Victory*'s hull. The plugs were cone-shaped pieces of wood, of various sizes and covered with oakum and liberally spread with tallow. They could be pushed into the smaller shot holes and hammered home. For the bigger, more jagged holes, sheets of lead and salted hides were put ready, along with nails and hammers to secure them. The carpenter also had to make sure the ship could still be steered if the tiller or wheel were smashed by an unlucky shot. Relieving tackles and rudder tackles had to be hooked on ready for immediate use; the spare tiller was in position, waiting to be shipped on the rudder head should the standard one be shattered. (See picture of a wheel and tiller on page 121.)

While the specialists were methodically working through the pre-arranged and frequently practised drill for preparing a huge ship like the *Victory* for battle, dozens of men—rated landsmen, ordinary seamen, Marines and volunteers, many of whom had never heard a gun fired in anger—were scrambling up the ladders dripping with perspiration, cursing with what little breath they had left inside them, carrying extra shot. Rings of rope called garlands were in position behind the guns and into them the men rolled the shot, an extra ten or dozen for each gun, in addition to those nestling like innocent black eggs in the racks.

The fire engine was prepared; the Marines under Captain Charles Adair checked over their muskets; the Master-at-Arms, Mr William Elliott, who was the ship's policeman, walked along the decks keeping an eye on the hundreds of men, conscious that few gave him glances which conveyed any fondness. The lieutenants supervised the decks for which they were responsible; the excited midshipmen dashed here and there, carrying messages or supervising men old enough to be their fathers.

In every ship the men were waiting for the staccato rattle of the drum beating to quarters, a tattoo which surprised some because they found they were not frightened, and sickened others because it left them craven. It showed many men to be fearful at heart yet for all that brave, because they were more frightened of revealing their fear than they were frightened of fear itself.

In the *Euryalus*, out ahead of the Fleet, Blackwood went down to his little cabin. He was now thirty-five and had been in the Navy since he was eleven years old. He had risked death several times before while fighting the French, and now, as Nelson was about to signal for the captains of his frigates to come on board, Blackwood added to his previous letter to Harriet:

> The last 24 hours has [*sic*] been most anxious work for me; but we have kept sight of them, and at this moment bearing up to come into action. Lord N. 27 sail of the line. French 33 or 34. I wish the six we have at Gibraltar were here. My signal just made on board *Victory*; I hope, to order me into a vacant line of battleship. [*Ajax* and *Thunderer* were, since their captains went back with Calder, under the command of their first lieutenants.] My dearest Harriet, your husband will not disgrace your love or name; if he dies, his last breath will be devoted to the dearest best of wives. Take care of my boy; make him a better man than his father.

Blackwood then went down over the side of the *Euryalus* into his boat, to be rowed across to the *Victory*, but in the meantime another captain was also writing a letter to his wife. In the *Mars* George Duff wrote:

> My dear Sophia, I have just time to tell you that we are just going into action with the Combined [Fleet]. I hope and trust in God that we shall all behave as becomes us, and that I may have the happiness of taking my beloved wife and children in my arms. Norwich is quite well. I have, however, ordered him of [*sic*] the quarterdeck. Yours ever, and most truly,
>
> Geo. Duff.

He had made four blots on the paper before he folded and sealed the letter, addressing it to 'Mrs Duff, Castle Street, Edinburgh'. He then placed it in his desk where—for the hope he expressed to Sophia was never realized—it was found after the action and sent home with a poignant letter from Norwich who, at the age of thirteen, had to write to his mother and tell her she was a widow.

Blackwood arrived on board to find Nelson 'in good, but very calm, spirits'. The young frigate captain congratulated his Admiral on the approach of the moment he had so often and so long wished for, and received the reply: 'I mean today to bleed the captains of the frigates, as I shall keep you on board until the very last minute.' The four frigates were in fact his messengers: if he wished for last-minute instructions to be given to another ship which were too complicated for flag signals, he could always send it by frigate. Blackwood had not been on board the *Victory* more than a few minutes when a shout made everyone look towards the enemy. The three masts of each of the enemy ships —for the hulls still could not be seen above the horizon—appeared to be getting closer together and the sails were at the same time broadening: the enemy were turning away. Then the sails began to narrow and the masts appeared to draw apart.

Villeneuve had ordered his fleet to wear. Like a line of marching soldiers doing an about-turn, they came off their southerly course and headed up to the north. What had been the rear ship now became the leader. Instead of heading boldly southwards towards the Strait of Gibraltar, the Combined Fleet was now sailing back towards Cadiz. Although he had anticipated that they would probably do this, Nelson was far from pleased. With the Combined

Fleet in its present position or any farther to the north, the shoal-strewn and dangerous coast between Cape Trafalgar and Cadiz was close to leeward, a dreadful trap for any ships crippled in battle, particularly since the weather was obviously going to get a great deal worse and a westerly gale was brewing. Had the French and Spanish ships continued sailing southwards they would be bringing the Strait of Gibraltar under their lee, providing an escape route into the Mediterranean for damaged ships.

Nelson, still on the poop, then gave instructions for the removal of various items of furniture and personal belongings in his cabins. He warned the men to be very careful when they took down the portrait of Lady Hamilton from the bulkhead. 'Take care of my Guardian Angel,' he said. But before they cleared away all the furniture he left the poop and went down to his day cabin, where he knelt at his desk—the chairs had already been removed. Through the stern windows of the great cabin he could see his ships strung out astern, some behind the *Victory*, others astern of the *Royal Sovereign*. The weak sun sparkled off the water, reflecting through the windows on to the deckhead above him. He took a pen and started writing in his private diary.

> At daylight saw the Enemy's Combined Fleet from East to E.S.E.; bore away; made the signal for Order of Sailing, and to Prepare for Battle; the Enemy with their heads to the Southward: at seven the Enemy wearing in succession. May the Great God, whom I worship, grant to my Country, and for the benefit of Europe in general, a great and glorious Victory; and may no misconduct in any one tarnish it; and may humanity after Victory be the predominant feature in the British Fleet. For myself, individually, I commit my life to Him who made me, and may his blessing light upon my endeavours for serving my country faithfully. To Him I resign myself and the just cause which is entrusted to me to defend. Amen. Amen. Amen.

While he had been writing this prayer Lt Pasco had come down to the cabin with a message, fully intent on seizing the opportunity of telling the Admiral that he regarded himself as very unfortunate, on such an occasion, 'to be doing the duty in an inferior station, instead of that to which his seniority entitled him'. But Pasco was disappointed. 'On entering the cabin,' he wrote later, 'I discovered his Lordship on his knees writing. He was then penning that beautiful prayer. I waited until he rose and communicated what I had to report, but could not at such a moment disturb his mind with any grievances of mine.'[1] As soon as Pasco had made his report and left the cabin Nelson took a sheet of paper and started writing a codicil to his will. 'October the twenty first, one thousand eight hundred and five, then in sight of the Combined Fleets of France and Spain, distant about ten miles', he wrote, and went on to list the 'eminent services of Emma Hamilton, widow of the Right Honourable Sir William Hamilton', for which she had received no reward 'from either our King or Country'. 'Could I have rewarded these services,' he wrote, 'I would not now call upon my country; but as that has not been in my power, I leave Emma Lady Hamilton, therefore, a legacy to my King and Country, that they will give her an ample provision to maintain her rank in life. I also leave to the beneficence of my country my adopted daughter, Horatia Nelson Thompson; and I desire she will use in future the name of Nelson only. These are the only favours I ask my King and Country at this moment when I am going to fight their Battle. May God bless my King and Country, and all those I hold dear. My relations it is needless to mention: they will of course be amply provided for.' Nelson sent for Hardy and Blackwood to come down and witness his signature.

After signing, the three men went back on deck again, and a few minutes later Hardy decided the time had come for all the men in the *Victory* to go to their battle stations.

'Mr Quilliam,' he called, 'send the hands to quarters.' The acting first lieutenant glanced round for the bosun and the drummer, who was standing on the quarter-deck with his heavy drum slung over his shoulder.

'Mr Willmet! Hands to quarters! Drummer—beat to quarters!' Within a few seconds the staccato beat of the drum, to the tune of 'Hearts of Oak', reverberated across the upper-deck, through the hatchways and down to the gun decks. Up and down the drummer

---

[1] Pasco's delicacy cost him dear: Quilliam, fifth in seniority, who acted as First Lieutenant in place of Pasco, was promoted to captain after the battle; but Pasco, with his protector dead, was promoted only to commander. The three other lieutenants senior to Quilliam suffered in the same way. Pasco says he went to Nelson's cabin 'About 11 a.m.', but it might have been earlier. Nelson, likewise was mistaken in saying the enemy wore at 7 a.m.: the *Redoutable* wore then to get into position, but the Fleet was not ordered to wear until about 8 a.m.

paced, conscious that he held the stage for a brief few moments.
Doom-da-doom-da-da-doom—'Hearts of Oak are our ships . . .'
Willmet and his mates ran to the hatches to sound their shrill
pipes.

'All hands to quarters! All hands to quarters! Rouse out there
and look alive! All hands to quarters!'

The decks looked like a suddenly disturbed ant-hill, but behind
the apparent chaos of running men there was order. Fifty men
were heading for the twelve 12-pounders on the quarter-deck
(four of them in Hardy's cabin), while twenty more made for the
fo'c'sle to handle the two 68-pounder carronades. One hundred
and fifty were running to the thirty 12-pounders on the upper-deck
(four of them in Nelson's cabins) and nearly two hundred for the
twenty-eight 24-pounders on the middle-deck. The thirty 32-
pounders on the lower-deck had more than two hundred men
to load and fire them. Another fifty men and boys went to the
magazines and the passageways to fill or pass cartridges and ten
more were needed in the cockpit to help the surgeons and loblolly
men.

Those whom the watch bills ordained should also have small
arms ran to the arms stands or Gunner's store to collect their
weapons—pistols, cutlasses, pikes, tomahawks or muskets—
before going to their guns. Lieutenants, usually two to a deck, one
commanding the forward part and one aft, went to their quarters.
The captain of each gun fitted on the lock, made sure its flint was
a good one and checked the trigger-line—a lanyard which would
allow him to fire the gun while standing well back out of reach of
the recoil. His priming wire was tucked in his belt and a powder
horn was hung up on the deckhead. The powder monkeys had to
run to the magazine scuttles. They carried the cartridges in
special cases, and by now Marine sentries were guarding the fore
and after hatches. Their orders were to allow no one up or down
unless he was an officer, midshipman or powder monkey. To
prove he was a powder monkey, a man or boy had to show his
cartridge case as he reached the hatch. Any man trying to force
his way through the hatchway would be assumed to be deserting
his post and the sentries could shoot him. While the guns' crews
assembled at their stations the Marines in their scarlet jackets
were clumping to the quarter-deck and to the poop where,
under the eagle eye of their sergeants, they assembled in neat and
orderly lines, muskets at their sides, bayonets at their belts.

In the galley the cook had doused his fire as soon as he heard the first clatter of the drum. On all the decks men with buckets were flinging water over the fire-screens while others were sluicing the decks. Others sprinkled sand to give a better grip for the men's feet. Most of the seamen were now stripped to the waist. Many had narrow bands of cloth which they would bind round their heads, covering their ears, to lessen the deafening effect of the guns firing, and also to prevent the salty perspiration running into their eyes.

Every gun was short of men. The ship's complement normally allowed full crews only for the guns on one side. The 32-pounders, weighing nearly three tons, needed fourteen men to fire them, according to the drill books, but there were only seven. To make up for the shortage the men ran from side to side as each broadside was required. As the men fell in at their respective guns the loader and the sponger went to the muzzle and took out the tompion, the plug which sealed the barrel when the gun was not in use. While they were doing that, others were hauling on a tackle, raising the port lid which came up like a vertical trap-door, letting sunlight stream in. For a few moments the effect on the lower decks, previously only dimly lit by the flickering fighting lanterns, was blinding. The inside of the lids and the woodwork round the ports were painted red, but not for aesthetic reasons: in action, splashes of blood would not show. With the squeal of the port lid tackles, the movement of the men round each of the guns ceased to be an apparently aimless and disorganized fussing: instead they settled down into a rhythmic tempo.

The lieutenants, seeing the tompions out of each of the guns and the port lids up, started the stream of orders which had in past months been used so frequently in practice. Each of the lieutenants put a speaking trumpet to their mouths.

'Load!'

Each powder monkey slipped a bulky cartridge out of the carrying case and gave it to the assistant loader, who quickly took a couple of paces and handed it to the loader as if it was a hot potato. The loader, standing by the muzzle, slid the cartridge into the barrel. The sponger took up the rammer and pushed the cartridge home, giving it a couple of sharp blows to bed it in. Because the gun would not be fired for a while, a wad was rammed in before the shot, but once the ship was in action this would not be necessary. Then the shot was handed to the loader, who tipped it into the barrel. He then helped the sponger ram it home. Another wad followed and that too was rammed in. As soon as the gun was loaded the men stood back, waiting for the next order.

'Run out!'

All the crew except the captain and powder monkey grabbed the gun-tackle falls and hauled. The gun rumbled out until the forward edge of the carriage was hard up against the ship's side and the muzzle projected through the port.

'Prime!' bellowed the lieutenants.

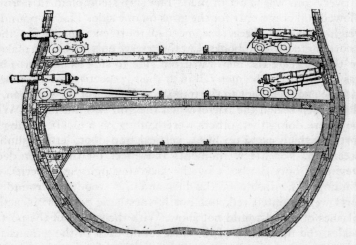

A section through a two-decker. The upper left gun is in position for firing, but breeching and tackles are not shown. The gun below has the train-tackle fitted. The upper right gun is secured against recoil; the one below is secured for sea.

The gun captain thrust the priming wire into the vent so hard that it made a small hole in the flannel covering the cartridge. He then pulled out the wire and slipped a thin tube—in effect a fuse made of a quill—into the vent, and poured some gunpowder into the pan of the lock.

The *Victory*'s guns were now prepared. Since it was unlikely that firing would start for some time, the flintlocks would not be cocked. The lieutenants reported that their decks were ready. For another hour there was little for the men to do. The midshipmen, pistols tucked in their belts, waited at the hatchways ready to run messages for the lieutenants. Mr Elliott, the Master-at-Arms, strode round deck after deck, his eyes, sharpened by many years of looking upon the weakness and shortcomings of man, casting about, watching for trouble.

From the flagship's decks Nelson could see the Union Flag flying from the fore-topgallant and maintopmast-stay of each of the British ships, as if waving defiance.

Lt Quilliam reported to Captain Hardy on the quarter-deck that the ship was ready for action. More than eight hundred men in the *Victory* were at general quarters. Midshipman Richard Francis Roberts's *Remark Book* noted the next thing that concerned the sailors and Marines waiting at the guns, in the magazines, and on deck. 'At 11—Dinner and grog.'

19

'BRITONS, STRIKE HOME!'

'Take therefore no thought for the morrow; for the morrow shall take thought for the things of itself. Sufficient unto the day is the evil thereof.'

—St Matthew VI, 34

WITH the unruffled majesty of swans the British battleships sailed down towards the Combined Fleet drawn up across their course. The four frigates and the *Pickle* and *Entreprenante* were ranged on the larboard side like attendant cygnets. Some of the slower battleships already had studding sails at the end of their yards. It seemed incredible that so much canvas could be set. Leading the straggling windward column was the *Victory*. Just astern of her was the *Téméraire*, nicknamed then the 'Saucy' *Téméraire*—the prefix 'Fighting' was not to be coined for another thirty-four years, when Turner sent his famous painting to the Royal Academy.

An Essex man, Captain Eliab Harvey, commanded the 98-gun ship, which was one of the few with an almost complete crew. She had an official complement of 738, and when the whole crew mustered the previous day they totalled 718. Of these, two hundred and twenty were Irishmen, fifty-three Scots and thirty-eight Welshmen. Of the Englishmen, nearly a third were Devonians. Like the Victory, she had a number of foreigners on board.[1]

Next astern of the *Téméraire*—although the British Fleet was far from being in precise formation—was the *Neptune*, commanded by Thomas Fremantle. One of the midshipmen serving on board was William Badcock, who regarded Betsey's husband as 'a clever, brave and smart officer'. Now aged seventeen, Badcock had been in the Navy for seven years. After several cutting-out expeditions and actions in the Mediterranean, followed by a winter of Atlantic storms while blockading Brest, he was excited

[1] There were sixty-six altogether, and among them were twenty-eight Americans, nine Germans, six Swedes, five Portuguese, three Frenchmen and three Spaniards.

at the prospect ahead of him this Monday morning. 'It was my morning watch,' he wrote, 'I was midshipman of the fo'c'sle, and at the first dawn of day a forest of strange masts was seen to leeward. I ran aft and informed the officer of the watch. The captain was on deck in a moment. . . . Our ship had previously prepared for battle, so that with the exception of stowing hammocks, slinging the lower-yards, stoppering the topsail-sheets, and other minor matters, little remained to be done. . . .

'The old *Neptune*, which was never a good sailer, took it into her head to sail better that morning than I ever remember to have seen her do before.'

Close astern of the *Neptune* were the *Leviathan* and the *Conqueror*. The latter was commanded by Captain Israel Pellew, a name already famous enough to bring Cornishmen flocking to join his ship as volunteers. Pellew was a gunnery expert, and knowing the French ships would be full of soldiers, with sharpshooters in their tops, had ordered his Marines below out of the way of musket balls until they should be needed.

Astern of the *Conqueror* came the *Britannia*. The Earl of Northesk and Captain Bullen were on her quarter-deck and the crew were at general quarters. They had had their breakfast by 8 a.m. and an hour later the rhythmic thumping of the drum had sent them to the guns. Now they were getting bored, and Lt Halloran, the amateur actor, was delighted to hear them amusing themselves by repeating scraps from a prologue he had recited at a previous performance. The favourite lines seemed to be:

'We have great guns of tragedy loaded so well,
If they do but go off they will certainly tell.'

Halloran was stationed at the after-most gun on the larboard side of the lower-deck, and he chatted with Midshipman Tompkin. Now and again they scrambled past the muzzle of a gun, looking out through the port to see how near they were to the Combined Fleet.

The commanding officer of the *Ajax*, just astern, could be forgiven any nervousness he felt over his responsibilities. He was Lt John Pilfold, whose captain had gone back to England with Calder. When Lt Ellis, of the *Ajax*'s Marines, was sent below about this time with orders he was 'much struck with the preparations being made'. Some of the men, stripped to the waist, were sharpening their cutlasses. Others were polishing the guns 'as though an inspection were about to take place, instead of a mortal combat, while three or four, as if in mere bravado, were dancing a hornpipe; but all seemed deeply anxious to come to close quarters with the enemy. Occasionally they would look out of the ports and speculate as to the various ships of the enemy, many of whom had been on former occasions engaged by our vessels'.

The impetuous Sir Edward Berry in the *Agamemnon* followed the *Ajax*, and close to him was the *Orion*. Codrington was just about to order his crew to dinner, and was himself looking forward to a leg of cold turkey which had, with commendable forethought, been prepared by his steward. 'We were,' he reported, 'all fresh, hearty and in high spirits.' The panorama stretched out before him, with eight ships of his own division preceding the *Orion* and heading for the waiting enemy with all sail set, was impressive. 'I suppose no man ever before saw such a sight as I did,' he wrote, 'or rather as we did, for I called all my lieutenants up to see it.'[1]

A considerable distance behind the *Orion* was the *Prince*, commanded by Captain Richard Grindall. She was a 98-gun ship and really belonged to the head of Collingwood's division, but she had been forced to shift a topsail and this, combined with the fact that she was a very slow ship at the best of times, made her lag behind to become involved in the rear of Nelson's division.

The men of the *Minotaur*, next astern of the *Prince*, were standing to their guns after hearing a rousing speech from Captain Mansfield. The ship had cleared for action by 8 a.m., and before beating to quarters he had every available man assembled on the quarter-deck. Standing at the break of the poop and facing forward, he could see each man's face. Behind them, in perspective beyond the bowsprit and irregularly spaced, were ten British battleships. Beyond, their hulls now visible over the rim of the horizon, were the enemy ships ranged like a sea wall protecting a flat shore.

'Men,' Mansfield said loudly, 'we are now in the sight of the enemy'—the seamen began a ragged cheer, but he held up his hand for silence—'whom there is every probability of engaging; and I trust that this day, or tomorrow, will prove the most glorious our country ever saw.

[1] The view that Codrington had later, when the battle started, is vividly portrayed by Harold Wyllie's painting, which is reproduced facing page 161.

'I shall say nothing to you of courage: our country never produced a coward. For my own part I pledge myself to the officers
and ship's company not to quit the ship I may get alongside of
till either she strikes or sinks—or I sink.

'I have only to recommend silence and strict attention to the
orders of your officers. Be careful to take good aim, for it is to
no purpose to throw shot away. You will now, every man, repair
to your respective stations, and depend, I will bring the ship into
action as soon as possible.' He paused a moment, and then cried:
'God save the King!'

The men promptly cheered him: blunt words, a short speech
and a rousing finish appealed to them. Mansfield watched them
dismiss, and perhaps he wondered how many of the grinning,
eager faces would answer at the next muster. The cheers carried
across the water to the next ship astern, the *Spartiate*, commanded
by Captain Sir Francis Laforey. She was the last in Nelson's
division and there was one ship missing, the *Africa*, which had
lost sight of the Fleet the previous night.

Blackwood's *Euryalus* was up on the larboard side of Nelson's
division, and the men on board of her had perhaps the best view
of all the Fleet. Hercules Robinson wrote: 'How well I remember
the ports of our great ship hauled up, the guns run out, and as
from the sublime to the ridiculous is but a step, the *Pickle*,
schooner, close to our ship with her boarding nets up, her tompions out and her four guns (about as large and formidable as two
pairs of Wellington boots), "their soul alive and eager for the
fray", as imposing as Gulliver waving his hanger [sword] before
the King and Queen of Brobdingnag'.

Although Nelson's division was steering for the enemy in some
semblance of a column, Collingwood's ships, following a signal
from him that they were to form on the larboard line of bearing,
were sailing with each successive ship out on the starboard quarter
of her next ahead. The slower ships were dropping astern and the
Royal Sovereign was drawing ahead. Newly arrived from England,
her coppered bottom was still clean, but many of the others were
foul with months' accumulation of weed and barnacles which,
particularly in the present light winds, slowed them up considerably.

On board Collingwood's flagship young Midshipman Thomas
Aikenhead had just stowed in his sea-chest a letter to his family
living at Portsea, Hampshire, and his will. 'We have just piped to

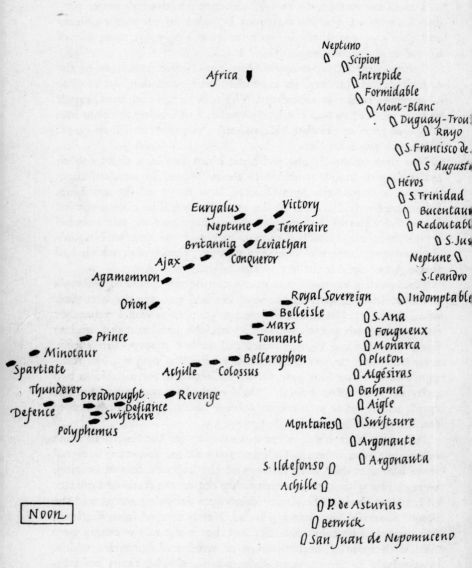

Africa

Neptuno
Scipion
Intrepide
Formidable
Mont-Blanc
Duguay-Trou
Rayo
S. Francisco de
S. August
Héros
S. Trinidad
Bucentaur
Redoutabl
S. Jus
Neptune

Euryalus   Victory
Neptune   Téméraire
Britannia   Leviathan
Ajax   Conqueror
Agamemnon
S. Leandro
Orion   Royal Sovereign   Indomptable
Belleisle
Mars   S. Ana
Tonnant   Fougueux
Prince   Monarca
Minotaur   Bellerophon   Pluton
Spartiate   Achille Colossus   Algésiras
Thunderer Dreadnought. Revenge   Bahama
Defence   Defiance   Aigle
Polyphemus   Swiftsure   Montañes Swiftsure
                                   Argonaute
                        S. Ildefonso   Argonauta
                        Achille
                           P. de Asturias
                           Berwick
                           San Juan de Nepomuceno

NOON

CHART No. 2:

TRAFALGAR: THE OPENING ROUND
The British ships are shown in black. The wind was westerly—i.e.
from the left of the chart

breakfast,' he wrote. 'Thirty-five sail, besides smaller vessels, are now on our beam, about three miles off. Should I, my dear parents, fall in defence of my King, let that thought console you. I feel not the least dread in my spirits. Oh my parents, sisters, brothers, dear grandfather, grandmother and aunt, believe me ever yours!

'Accept, perhaps for the last time, your brother's love; be assured I feel for my friends, should I die in this glorious action —glorious, no doubt, it will be. Every British heart pants for glory. Our old Admiral [Collingwood] is quite young again with the thought of it. If I survive, nothing will give me greater pleasure than embracing my dearest relations. Do not, in case I fall, grieve —it will be to no purpose. Many brave fellows will no doubt fall with me on both sides. Oh! Betsey, with what ardour I shall, if permitted by God's providence, come to England to embrace you all!' And as he had saved another £10 since he had written his will, he added a note to his letter: 'Do not be surprised to find £10 more—it is mine.' Despite his brave words, perhaps he did have a presentiment that he would not survive the battle, for he was one of the two midshipmen killed in the flagship.

Admiral Collingwood had, after breakfast, walked round the various decks, talking to the seamen. Coming across a group of men who had been brought over with him from the *Dreadnought* when he transferred to the *Royal Sovereign*, he paused for a moment. They were all, like Collingwood, from the Newcastle area. 'Today, my lads,' he said, 'we must show those fellows what the "Tars of the Tyne" can do!' To a group of officers he remarked: 'Now, gentlemen, let us do something today which the world may talk of hereafter.'

The *Royal Sovereign* was the nearest ship to the enemy line, but seeing the *Victory* up to the northwards setting studding-sails, Lt Clavell (wearing the silk stockings that Collingwood had earlier advised) asked permission for the *Royal Sovereign* to set hers.[1] Collingwood saw the danger of carrying the unspoken competition with the *Victory* too far, and also was finding himself so far ahead that he would have to fight on his own for longer than was sensible. 'The ships of our line are not sufficiently up for us to do so now,' he said, 'but you may be getting ready.' Clavell gave the necessary orders.

[1] Studding-sails (also known as stunsails or steering sails) were additional sails set on booms which were extensions of the yards. They can be seen clearly in Harold Wyllie's painting on p. 160.

Astern and to starboard of the *Royal Sovereign* was the *Belleisle*, commanded by William Hargood. She was a powerful two-decker, captured from the French ten years earlier, and her band was playing as she bore down towards the enemy. Earlier she had gradually caught up the *Tonnant*, her next ahead which should have been close to the *Royal Sovereign*, but had been unable to keep up. To Hargood's delight he was signalled to change places with her. As the *Belleisle* forged ahead, Hargood ordered the band to play 'Rule, Britannia', and not to be outdone, Captain Tyler ordered the *Tonnant*'s band to reply with 'Britons, Strike Home!' Putting his speaking trumpet to his lips, Tyler called to Hargood from the quarter-deck: 'A glorious day for old England! We shall have one apiece before night!'

Aboard the *Belleisle*, with the band thumping away with more enthusiasm than skill, the young officers were now considerably more cheerful. Their earlier feelings are described by Lt Paul Harris Nicolas. 'The officers now met at breakfast; and though each seemed to exult in the hope of a glorious termination to the contest so near at hand, a fearful presage was experienced that all would not again unite at that festive board. One was particularly impressed with a persuasion that he should not survive the day, nor could he divest himself of this presentiment, but made the necessary disposal of his property in the event of his death. The sound of the drums, however, soon put an end to our meditations, and after a hasty and, alas, a final farewell to some, we repaired to our respective posts.'

Captain George Duff had been trying to give his ship wings. Every stitch of canvas was set: studding-sails hung out over the water at the end of the yards, and Duff tried every trick he knew to add even a fraction of a knot of speed. The reason for this was that Nelson had just signalled direct to Duff, ordering the *Mars* to lead the lee column. The *Prince* should have been ahead, but, as we have seen, she was shifting a topsail and had dropped several miles astern. Now, a plain hint to Collingwood to drop back, Duff was ordered to go ahead and thus be the first to break through the enemy line. But Duff could not manage to overtake the *Royal Sovereign*, and Collingwood was certainly not reducing canvas to slow down—in fact he was just about to let Lt Clavell set the studding-sails.

Duff, sword at his waist, a massive figure on the quarter-deck, was helpless. The descent on the enemy was turning into a race between Nelson and Collingwood. He fingered the ram's horn snuff-box in his pocket and then, clasping his hands behind him, looked up at the sails yet again. They were set perfectly: there was nothing that could be done to improve them. At that moment, a few minutes after Duff had answered Nelson's signal, Lt Clavell on the quarter-deck of the *Royal Sovereign* gave an inquiring look at Collingwood, who nodded. Clavell promptly went over to Captain Rotheram, who was commanding the flagship, and said that the Admiral desired him to make all sail. Rotheram gave the orders to rig out and hoist away the studding-sails, and over on the starboard quarter a disappointed Duff watched the flagship begin to draw ahead. His chance of the honour of leading the British Fleet and being the first to break the enemy's line had now gone for good.

The *Tonnant*, which had been forced to drop back, was one of Nelson's trophies from the Battle of the Nile. As a prize she had been brought back to England, repaired and given a new figure-head (Jupiter hurling a thunderbolt). Now, under Tyler, her band was playing such tunes as 'Britons, Strike Home!' and 'The Down-fall of Paris' as she steered down to assault her erstwhile owners. The *Tonnant*'s third lieutenant has left an amusing picture of some of his fellow officers. The surgeon, Mr Forbes McBean Chevers, who had been with Howe at The Glorious First of June, was clever, dapper and irritable, fond of ethics, etymology and the blue pills which worked remarkable cures with costive seamen; the assistant surgeon was a tall, gangling Scot, his head filled with the *Pharmacopoeia*, bleeding, blistering and gallipots. The sixth lieutenant was fond of gaming and grog, while the seventh, who liked coining new words, was not much of a seaman. The senior of the Marine lieutenants read novels and fancied himself with the ladies, while the Purser was very regular with his accounts and played the flute. The third lieutenant himself, Frederick Hoffman, had fought in eighteen boat actions and one siege, been wounded in the head and deafened in one ear, twice had yellow fever and once been captured by the French. Now the whole of the *Tonnant*'s crew waited patiently for a small portion of cheese and half an allowance of grog to be issued. That, today, was to be their dinner.

The *Bellerophon*—the 'Billy Ruff'n' which led Howe's fleet to victory on The Glorious First of June and single-handed fought the French flagship *L'Orient* at the Nile—was the next in Collingwood's division. In Howe's action a Scotsman had commanded her and fallen wounded; at the Nile an Irishman commanding her had also been badly wounded. Now the Englishman commanding her, John Cooke, was about to be killed and a Welshman was to take over command. Captain Cooke had first gone to sea at the age of eleven. Now happily married with an eight-year-old daughter, and for the past sixteen months—thanks to a recent legacy—owner of a large estate at Lower Donhead, in Wiltshire, he had always had one hope: to serve under Nelson. To be in a general engagement with that admiral would, he declared, crown his military ambition. With his ambition about to be achieved he now stood on the quarter-deck talking to Cumby, his first lieutenant, Edward Overton, the Master, and Captain William James Wemyss, commanding the Marines.

Near them was a young midshipman with a slate in his hand, busy reading off signals from the flagship. He was John Franklin, now aged nineteen, the ninth child and fifth son of a prosperous draper of Spilsby, in Lincolnshire. The boy destined to become world-famous as an Arctic explorer was untidy and round-faced, with a hot, generous temper, and a curiously earnest manner.

With the bandsmen on board the *Bellerophon* thumping at their drums and sawing away with gusto at their fiddles and the fifers getting red in the face, 'one would have thought that the people were preparing for a festival rather than a combat', one of the midshipmen wrote later, 'and no dissatisfaction was expressed, except at the state of the weather, which . . . prevented our quickly nearing the enemy'. One seaman, glancing through the port at the Combined Fleet on the horizon, spat. 'What a fine show them ships will make at Spithead!' And with a piece of chalk several of the men wrote on their guns: '*Bellerophon*—Death or Glory'.

Lt Cumby, describing the day's events aboard the *Bellerophon* up to now wrote later: 'I was aroused from my slumbers by my messmate, Overton, the Master, who called out, "Cumby, my boy, turn out; here they are all ready for you, three and thirty sail of the line close under our lee, and evidently disposed to await our attack."

'You may readily conclude I did not long remain in a recumbent position, but sprang out of bed, hurried on my clothes and, kneeling down by the side of my cot, put up a short but fervent prayer to the great God of Battles for a glorious victory to the

Captain Digby's view from the deck of the *Africa* as he sailed into the battle. *Detail from the painting owned by Lord Digby*

The great storm after the battle: British, French and Spanish ships fight for their lives within sight of Cadiz, which can be seen on the left of the picture. *Detail from the painting owned by Lord Digby*

arms of my country, committing myself individually to His all wise disposal and begging His gracious protection for my dear wife and children, whatever His unerring wisdom might see fit to order for myself.

'This was the substance and, as near as memory will serve me, the actual words of my petition, and I have often since reflected with a feeling of pride how nearly similar they were to what our immortal leader himself committed to paper as his own prayer on that occasion. . . .'

As usual, Cumby had breakfast with the Captain in his cabin under the poop-deck. As soon as they finished eating Cumby prepared to leave, conscious that as first lieutenant he had a lot to do. But Cooke 'begged me to wait a little as he had something to show me, when he produced and requested me to peruse, Lord Nelson's private Memorandum addressed to captains relative to the conduct of the ships in action, which having read he enquired whether I perfectly understood the Admiral's instructions.

'I replied they were so distinct and explicit that it was quite impossible they could be misunderstood; he then expressed his satisfaction, and said he wished me to be made acquainted with it, that in the event of his being "bowl'd out" I might know how to conduct the ship agreeable to the Admiral's wishes. On this I observed that it was very possible that the same shot which disposed of him might have an equally tranquillizing effect upon me, and under that idea I submitted to him the expediency of the Master (as being the only officer who in such case would remain on the quarter-deck) being also apprised. . . .

'To this Captain Cooke immediately assented, and poor Overton, the Master, was desired to read the Memorandum, which he did. And here I may be permitted to remark *en passant* that, of the three officers who carried the knowledge of this private memorandum into action, I was the only one that brought it out [alive]. . . .

'At eleven o'clock, finding we should not be in action for an hour or more, we piped to dinner, which we had ordered to be in readiness for the ship's company at that hour, thinking that Englishmen would fight all the better for having a comfortable meal, and at the same time Captain Cooke joined us in partaking of some cold meat, etc., on the rudder head, all our bulkheads, tables, etc., being necessarily taken down and carried below.'

Away to the westwards were the rest of the ships of the British

H

Fleet. Among them were the *Colossus*, a seventy-four commanded by Captain James Morris; the *Achille*, under Captain Robert King; and the *Revenge*, whose captain, Robert Moorsom, was a gunnery expert. A long gap separated the next ship, the *Defiance*, whose commanding officer, Durham, was thankful he had been bold enough to refuse to go back to England for Calder's court martial. The *Defiance*'s carpenter was making a mental note of the items already thrown overboard—he would have to put them in his report after the battle. One sheep pen, eight wardroom berths, four tables, four hen coops, an arms chest . . . there would be a lot more for his list before the day was out. The three ships following the *Defiance* was almost abreast of each other—the *Swiftsure*, *Dreadnought* and *Polyphemus*. And the last two ships were the *Thunderer* and *Defence*, quite close to the last ships of Nelson's division.

There remained now only the little 64-gun *Africa*, smallest of Nelson's battleships, which had lost the Fleet the night before. She had now appeared to the northward, sailing down towards the British Fleet and passing close to the leading ships of Combined Fleet. (See Chart No. 2 on page 220). Digby had, after losing touch, seen the French Fleet's signals during the night and taken up 'a station of discretion'. It put him in a dangerous position, and a signal from the *Victory* was soon to test him and his ship's company.

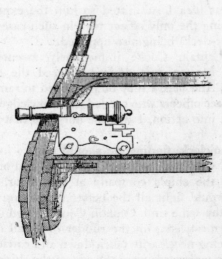

20

PERDIDOS!

*'If the trumpet give an uncertain sound,
who shall prepare himself to the battle?'*
—Romans XIV, 8

SHORTLY after dawn the look-outs in the French frigate *Hermione* had spotted the British Fleet up-wind to the westward. They had counted the number of enemy ships and immediately signalled to Villeneuve: 'The enemy in sight to windward', firing a gun at the same time to summon attention. The French and Spanish ships were sailing southwards, as we have already seen, silhouetted against the rising sun and in some disorder. Villeneuve immediately signalled to the frigates to reconnoitre the enemy, and once again ordered the Fleet to form line of battle.

The four divisions forming the Combined Fleet were the squadron of observation, under the Spanish Admiral Gravina in the *Principe de Asturias*, whose position was supposed to be to windward of the Fleet and thus available to reinforce the line anywhere it was threatened; the van squadron under Vice-Admiral Alava, in the *Santa Ana*, which was to lead the line; the centre squadron under Villeneuve in the *Bucentaure* which would be in the middle, and the rear squadron, under Rear-Admiral Dumanoir in the *Formidable*. Thus the first ship of Alava's van squadron, the *Pluton*, should have been leading the line to the south, while the last ship in Dumanoir's squadron, the *Neptuno*, should have been at the end of it to the north. It was to these positions that, in very light winds and a heavy swell, thirty-three battleships of the Combined Fleet tried to scramble when Villeneuve signalled them to form line of battle on the starboard tack. They had very little chance of succeeding.

As far as manœuvring was concerned the Combined Fleet was worse off than the British because the swell was coming in on their beam, making them roll badly; in addition, with the wind also on the beam they had far more difficulty in keeping their sails filled, because the swaying masts flung the wind out of the canvas. While the three other squadrons tried to get themselves into some semblance of a line, Admiral Gravina ordered his dozen ships of the squadron of observation to take up a position ahead of the main body of the Combined Fleet, instead of staying up to windward, putting the *San Juan Nepomuceno* at the head of the line. This had not been ordered by Villeneuve, and for the moment he did nothing about it, but it was to have a great effect on the battle.

At 7.30 a.m. Villeneuve was in a difficult position. 'The enemy squadron,' he reported, 'which had very soon been discovered to be composed of twenty-seven sail of the line, appeared to me to be standing in a body for my rear, with the double intention of attacking it advantageously and of cutting off the retreat of the Combined Fleet on Cadiz.' To the south-east—on his larboard bow—lay the Strait of Gibraltar. With the wind westerly at least some of his ships would be able to escape after the battle into the Mediterranean and make for Cartagena or Toulon. But there were six other British battleships in that area, he already knew, and there was a chance they might be able to intercept. Cape Trafalgar and its line of dangerous shoals lay twelve miles away to the eastward; Cadiz, his port of refuge, lay astern to the north. Every moment that passed meant he was drawing farther away from it and at the same time Nelson was nearer to cutting off the line of retreat.

Villeneuve finally made up his mind: he would turn about and steer towards Cadiz, 'my sole object being to protect the rear from the projected attack of the entire enemy force.' As we have seen, by wearing together the ships would 'about turn' in the line, so that the *Neptuno* to the north, which had been the last ship in the line, would now be the leader, and the *San Juan Nepomuceno*, which had been the leader, would bring up the rear.

When he saw the signal Commodore Churruca, commanding the *San Juan Nepomuceno* and one of the most capable and brave of the Spanish officers, turned to his second-in-command. '*Está la escuadra perdita*,' he said. 'The Fleet is doomed. The French Admiral does not understand his business. He has compromised us all!'

Churruca had sailed with a heavy heart. Before leaving Cadiz he had told his nephew, who was serving in the *Nepomuceno* as a volunteer: 'Write to your friends that you are going into a battle that will be desperate and bloody. Tell them also that they may be certain of this—that I, for my part, will meet my death there. Let them know that rather than surrender my ship I shall sink her.' Churruca was not a coward: he was a realist, and he had no faith in Villeneuve's ability. Such an evolution as Villeneuve had just ordered, he declared, was bound to throw the Fleet into confusion, and in the light wind it would take them all morning to re-form. In this estimate he was not far wrong. Since the Combined Fleet had not had time to form properly on the starboard tack, it was quite obvious there would be chaos when it was ordered to wear round and head in the opposite direction.

It was like telling a mixed group of new recruits on the parade for the first time, some truculent and some keen, to fall into single file while on the move, and while they were walking to their positions ordering them to about-turn and, still walking, get into line. Some ships sagged off to leeward, unable or unwilling to get into position, while others moved ahead to take their place; more, several places from where they should be, just scrambled into the line wherever they could find a gap. Then, to add to the confusion, a light wind came up from the south-west and, reaching the rear ships first, bunched them up. Thus, like an unruly mob trying to form a queue to go to its own execution, the Combined Fleet formed line of battle.

Desbrière, commenting on Villeneuve's decision to stand in for Cadiz, wrote that he 'seemed to be seeking the possibility of taking refuge in that port. But it was a dangerous temptation to offer to his Fleet and little calculated to inspire all present with the desperate energy requisite. Moreover . . . his order, at the time that it was given, could no longer have the result of assuring the retreat of the whole Fleet in that direction.

'This is certain at any rate, the action was about to be fought off a very dangerous lee shore and in conditions which would render the situation of the disabled ships critical if the lowering weather broke up altogether. Nelson was not to be mistaken, and the order to anchor, which he was to give later, at the very minute when he was breathing his last, shows plainly what peril he foresaw for all those who were to be crippled in the action.'

The order which Villeneuve gave at 8 a.m. for the Fleet to wear was finally completed—inasmuch as his thirty-three ships were steering in roughly a northerly direction—by 10 a.m., but there were large gaps in the line. At about 10.15 a.m. (the time, as usual, varies in the reports of individual ships) Villeneuve signalled to the leading ship, the *Neptuno*, to hug the wind, and the others to

follow in succession. By this, Villeneuve was simply trying to get
his line formed properly—the leading British ship was only some
five miles away on his larboard beam by now, and the Combined
Fleet's line had formed into a huge half moon, the centre sagging
away from the advancing British. But in hugging the wind the
leading ships slowed up, and those astern dropped farther to leeward. In addition Villeneuve now apparently saw from the
Bucentaure that Gravina and his squadron of observation were
sailing down into the wake of what should have been the last ship
in the line, instead of staying up to windward ready to strike
where needed. The French Admiral promptly signalled him to
keep up to windward 'so as to be at hand to cover the centre of the
Fleet, which appeared to be the point on which the enemy was
desirous of concentrating his greatest effort'. But it was too late.
Gravina could never get back into such a position in time.

Churruca, whose ship was now the last in Gravina's squadron
and therefore the most southerly of all, had been standing on his
quarter-deck, telescope to his eyes, watching the *Bucentaure* and
waiting patiently for Villeneuve to make the signal for the move
which Churruca considered would foil Nelson's attack. 'Our van
will be cut away from the main body and our rear will be overwhelmed. Half the line will be compelled to remain inactive,' he
declared. 'The French admiral does not—will not—grasp it. He
has only to act boldly, only to order the van ships to wear round
at once and double on the rear squadron. That will place the
enemy between two fires.' But the signal never came. Churruca
snapped his telescope shut. '*Perdidos!*' he muttered, and stalked
across the quarter-deck. '*Perdidos! Perdidos!*' He then ordered all
available hands to be turned up on deck. Sending for the chaplain
he told him: 'Father, perform your sacred office. Absolve the souls
of these brave fellows, who know not what fate this battle may have
for them!' The chaplain stepped forward. The men bared their
heads, muttering the responses in the short service. Then Churruca walked to the quarter-deck rail and faced them. 'My sons,'
he cried, 'in the name of the God of Battles I promise eternal
happiness to all those who today fall doing their duty.

'On the other hand,' he added ominously, 'if I see any man
shirking I will have him shot on the spot. If the scoundrel escapes
my eye, or that of the gallant officers I have the honour to command, rest assured of this, that bitter remorse will dog the wretch
for the rest of his days, for so long as he crawls through what may

remain of his wretched existence.' He paused for a moment and then called for three cheers for His Catholic Majesty. The men hustled back to their guns and once again the fifes and drums struck up bravely.

The British ships were now drawing very close. With their studding-sails set and hanging out on the ends of the already wide yards, they looked as if they had wings; indeed, with what little breeze there was behind them, they did have wings, by comparison with the Combined Fleet which was trying to hug the wind.

'I made the signal to commence the action as soon as within range,' wrote Villeneuve. The Imperial Eagle, borne by Midshipman Donadieu and Midshipman Arman, who had been ordered to guard it throughout the forthcoming battle, was paraded round the deck by Villeneuve, followed by his flag-captain, Magendie, Major-General Contamine, who was commanding the troops, and the rest of the *Bucentaure*'s officers.

'It is impossible,' wrote Magendie, 'to display greater enthusiasm and eagerness for the fray than was shown and evinced by all the officers, sailors and soldiers of the *Bucentaure*, each one of us putting our hands between the Admiral's and renewing our oath upon the Eagle entrusted to us by the Emperor, to fight to the last gasp; and shouts of *"Vive l'Empereur, vive l'Amiral Villeneuve"* were raised once more.' He adds: 'We returned to the upper-works and each of us resumed our post; the Eagle was displayed at the foot of the mainmast.'

The intrepid little Captain Lucas—he was only four feet four inches tall—in the *Redoutable* was close astern of the *Bucentaure*, so close in fact that a little later someone hailed him several times from the *Bucentaure*'s stern gallery that he was about to run aboard the flagship. 'Actually,' Lucas wrote afterwards, 'the *Redoutable*'s bowsprit did graze her taffrail, but I assured them they had nothing to fear.' Like the crew of the flagship, the men of the *Redoutable* were rousing themselves and being roused to vast heights of patriotic fervour compared with the rather brief speeches being delivered by some of the captains aboard the British ships. Lucas reported: 'I laid the *Redoutable*'s bowsprit against the *Bucentaure*'s stern, fully resolved to sacrifice my ship in defence of the Admiral's flag. I acquainted my officers and crew, who replied to my decision by shouts of *"Vive l'Empereur! Vive l'Amiral! Vive le Commandant!"* repeated a thousand times.

'Preceded by the drums and fifes that I had on board, I paraded at the head of my officers round all the decks; everywhere I found gallant lads burning with impatience to be in the fray; many of them saying to me, "Captain, don't forget to board!"'

For all his rather flamboyant literary style, Lucas almost certainly commanded the best-trained crew in the whole Combined Fleet. His men had cried 'Don't forget to board!' for a good reason: Lucas's ideas 'were always directed towards fighting by boarding'. He said that 'I so counted upon its success that everything had been prepared to undertake it with advantage: I had had canvas pouches to hold two grenades made for all captains of guns, the cross-belts of these pouches carrying a tin tube containing a small match.

'In all our drills, I made them throw a great number of pasteboard grenades and I often landed the grenadiers in order to have them explode iron grenades; they had so acquired the habit of hurling them that on the day of the battle our topmen were throwing two at a time.

'I had a hundred carbines fitted with long bayonets on board; the men to whom these were served out were so well accustomed to their use that they climbed halfway up the shrouds to open a musketry fire.

'All the men armed with swords were instructed in broadsword practice every day and pistols had become familiar arms to them. The grapnels were thrown aboard so skilfully that they succeeded in hooking a ship even though she was not exactly touching us.' Even allowing for Lucas's exaggerations—and they become clearer when he describes how the *Redoutable* engaged the *Victory*—Villeneuve must have regretted not having more captains like him.

The 130-gun *Santissima Trinidad* was an impressive sight. Her huge sides were painted in alternate bands of red and white; her figurehead, as befitted the largest ship in the world, was an imposing white-painted carving of figures representing the Holy Trinity, from whom she took her name. She had a crew of 1,048[1] and one of them, going into action for the first time, wrote later:

'Early in the morning the decks were cleared for action, and

[1] Gravina's ADC was Don Miguel Ricardo de Alava, nephew of Rear-Admiral Alava of the *Santa Ana*. When Spain left Napoleon's side in 1808 he joined the patriot army, later serving as an ADC to the Duke of Wellington. Sent in 1814 as Spanish Minister Plenipotentiary to Holland, he was at Wellington's headquarters for the Battle of Waterloo. He later became the Spanish Ambassador in London.

when all was ready for serving the guns and working the ship, I heard someone say: "The sand—bring the sand". A number of sailors were posted on the ladders from the hatchway to the hold and between decks, and in this way were hauling up sacks of sand . . . they were emptied out on the upper decks, the poop and the fo'c'sle, the sand being spread about so as to cover all the planking. The same thing was done between decks. My curiosity prompted me to ask a lad who stood next to me what this was for. "For the blood," he said very coolly. "For the blood!" I exclaimed, unable to repress a shudder. I looked at the sand—I looked at the men who were busily employed on this task—and for a moment I felt I was a coward.'

So the ships of the Combined Fleet waited. For the moment the drums and fifes were playing; the French Tricolour or the yellow and red flag of Spain was flying. In every Spanish ship a large wooden cross, solemnly blessed by the chaplains, now hung from the boom and over the taffrail. Villeneuve wrote: 'I did not observe a single man daunted at the sight of the formidable enemy column, headed by four three-deckers which bore down on the *Bucentaure*.' Commander Bazin, second-in-command of the 74-gun *Fougueux* (whose crew was owed sixteen months' pay) wrote: 'Captain Baudouin had the colours and the French pendant hoisted and fired the whole broadside at the foremost ship; from that minute the action commenced vigorously on both sides. . . .'

In the *Victory*, after Hardy and Blackwood had witnessed Nelson's will, the Admiral was getting very impatient. Looking at the Combined Fleet spread out ahead of him he remarked to Blackwood: 'They put a good face on it.' But he quickly added: 'I'll give them such a dressing as they never had before!' He then grumbled at the nearness of Cape Trafalgar to leeward. At that moment Blackwood, realizing that the *Victory*, being at the head of the division, would bear the brunt of the enemy's fire, pointed out respectfully to Nelson the value of his life, particularly in the battle about to begin. 'I proposed hoisting his flag in the *Euryalus*, whence he could better see what was going on, as well as what to order in case of necessity,' Blackwood wrote, 'but he would not hear of it, and gave as his reason the force of example; and probably he was right.

'My next object, therefore, was to endeavour to induce his Lordship to allow the *Téméraire*, *Neptune* and *Leviathan* to lead into action before the *Victory* . . . after much conversation, in which I ventured to give it as the joint opinion of Captain Hardy and myself, how advantageous it would be to the Fleet for his Lordship to keep as long as possible out of the Battle, he at last consented to allow the *Téméraire*, which was then sailing abreast of the *Victory*, to go ahead.' Nelson had smiled significantly at Hardy when he said: 'Oh yes, let her go ahead.' Blackwood, how-ever, seems to have missed the implied 'if she can!'

Then, according to Blackwood, the Admiral hailed Captain Harvey in *Téméraire* to tell him to go ahead, but he was too far away to hear. He therefore sent Blackwood over in a boat to pass the order. But if Blackwood thought Nelson was going to stand back and let someone else lead him into battle, he was mistaken. 'On returning to the *Victory*,' the young frigate captain reported, 'I found him doing all he could to increase rather than diminish sail, so that the *Téméraire* could not pass the *Victory*.' Blackwood then managed to get Hardy on his own and tell him that he ought to warn the Admiral that unless he shortened sail the *Victory* would stay ahead, but Hardy had been with Nelson for a long time and he refused as, says the *Victory*'s surgeon, 'he conceived his Lordship's ardour to get into battle would on no account suffer such a measure'.

Nelson, when chatting to Blackwood a little later, asked him what he would regard as a victory. 'Considering the handsome way the enemy are offering battle,' Blackwood replied 'their apparent determination for a fair trial of strength, and the near-ness of the land, I should think that if fourteen ships are captured it would be a glorious result.' Nelson looked up at the burly prince of frigate captains, a gleam in his one remaining eye, 'I shall not, Blackwood, be satisfied with anything short of twenty'.

Nelson, Hardy, Blackwood and Quilliam all trained their telescopes on the row of French and Spanish ships from time to time, trying to discover in which ship was the enemy commander-in-chief—whom Nelson wanted to capture himself. But none of them was then flying an Admiral's flag.

About this time Lt John Yule, commanding on the *Victory*'s fo'c'sle, saw that the starboard lower studding-sail was not set properly. He immediately ordered it to be taken in and reset. Unfortunately for him Nelson saw the sail being lowered with Yule standing by supervising it, and misunderstanding the young lieutenant's motive he scolded him angrily for reducing sail without orders from the captain.

A little earlier Nelson had gone round the various decks, chatting with the men as they stood to their guns, warning them not to waste a single shot. Seaman Brown, part of whose colourful letter we have already seen, described it thus: 'Lord Nelson went round the decks and said My noble lads this will be a glorious day for england who ever lives to see it I Shant be Satisfied with 12 ships this day as I took at the Nile So we piped to dinner and ate a bit of raw pork and half a pint of wine.'

Several of the *Victory*'s officers had been very worried over the fact that the very large stars of the various orders embroidered on Nelson's frock coat would make him—with the one arm and black eye-patch—a most conspicuous and tempting target for sharpshooters. Beatty suggested that the Admiral should be asked to cover up the stars with a handkerchief, but Dr Scott, the chaplain, and John Scott, Nelson's secretary, did not agree. Such a request, they observed, would have no effect: knowing him so well they realized that he would be extremely annoyed with anyone who suggested any change in his dress for this reason. Beatty was not put off by this: he said he would take the opportunity of mentioning it to the Admiral when he made his sick report for the day. 'Take care, Doctor, what you are about,' warned John Scott. 'I would not be the man to mention such a matter to him.' Beatty stayed on deck as long as he could, waiting to take his chance; but Nelson was always occupied.

The wind was falling lighter than ever. According to Midshipman William Rivers, who was on deck, Nelson was afraid that if the wind dropped any more he might have to round up and open fire on the enemy at long range. The guns had been double-shotted and this was effective only at short range. But, Rivers reported, Nelson 'desired me to acquaint the officers to load with *single* shot'. The rolling of the ship had been lifting and slatting the sails when Rivers started off on his mission to the lieutenants on each of the gun decks, but by the time he returned the breeze had become steadier and he 'found the sails asleep'.

A few minutes later Nelson, looking first at the *Royal Sovereign* over on the starboard beam and then at the Combined Fleet, said to Hardy: 'We shall have some warm work, and that pretty close.' He looked round the bulwarks of the *Victory*, seeing the black canvas cloths which covered the hammocks in the nettings. A sudden thought struck him. 'Send young Rivers down with a few hands to get up and spread the white hammock cloths, and let them be well saturated.'

The bustle aboard the flagship was quietening down now: with all preparation made for battle, the main task was to keep the ship sailing as fast as possible. This fell to Thomas Atkinson, the Master. He was a very experienced man, having served at the Nile, commanded a boat at the Siege of Acre, and been Master of the *Elephant* under Nelson at Copenhagen. The Admiral had a high regard for him—back in England Atkinson's young son rejoiced in the Christian names of Horatio Nelson, a tribute to the Admiral who had been only too willing to be the child's godfather.

For Nelson there were still some signals to make. As we have seen, he intended to break through the enemy's line somewhere about the thirteenth or fourteenth ship and then harden in sheets and braces to sail up to attack the van and prevent it coming down to help the rest of the Combined Fleet. By chance the thirteenth ship was the *Bucentaure*, with Villeneuve on board, although Nelson did not know this, and at the moment the *Victory* was heading for the twelfth ship, the *Santissima Trinidad*.

Nelson had already told Collingwood by signal what he proposed doing—'I intend to push through the end of the enemy's line to prevent them from getting into Cadiz.' Now, with the nearest enemy ships less than two miles ahead, the Admiral walked up and down on the quarter-deck with Blackwood. He was completely controlled, but he seemed poised like a coiled spring. Turning to Blackwood he said: 'I'll now amuse the Fleet with a signal. Do you not think there is one yet wanting?' 'I think the whole of the Fleet seem to understand very clearly what they are about,' answered Blackwood.

But Nelson was already walking across to where Pasco and his signalmen were waiting. He ordered a signal to be made to the *Africa*—sailing towards them over on the larboard beam near the head of the enemy's line—to 'Engage the enemy more closely', and another to the Fleet, to 'Prepare to anchor after the close of day'.

Then he said: 'Mr Pasco, I wish to say to the Fleet, "England confides that every man will do his duty".' He added; 'You must be quick, for I have one more to make, which is for Close Action.'

Pasco thought for a moment, mentally searching through Sir Home Popham's telegraphic vocabulary. Then he replied: 'If your Lordship will permit me to substitute "expects" for "confides" the signal will soon be completed, because the word "expects" is in the vocabulary, and "confides " must be spelt.' 'That will do, Pasco, make it directly', Nelson said hurriedly. The signalmen swiftly bent the flags on to the halyards and hoisted them.[1] Nelson then said to Pasco, 'Make the signal for Close Action, and *keep it up.*'

Turning away to Hardy and Blackwood he remarked: 'I can do no more. We must trust to the great Disposer of all events, and the justice of our cause. I thank God for this great opportunity of doing my duty.' As he spoke three flags were being run up—the telegraphic flag and then numbers one and six: 'Engage the enemy more closely'.

Then they looked over on the starboard beam, to where the *Royal Sovereign*, well ahead of the rest of the line, was now within a few hundred yards of what seemed to be a solid wall of enemy ships. Suddenly a row of glowing red dots rippled down their sides. It wanted a few minutes to noon: the *Fougueux* had launched her first broadside at Collingwood's flagship, and the Battle of Trafalgar had begun.

'See how that noble fellow Collingwood carries his ship into action!' exclaimed Nelson. In the *Royal Sovereign* Collingwood turned to Rotheram and remarked quietly: 'What would Nelson give to be here!'

A little earlier some of his officers, appalled at seeing that Rotheram intended to go into action in a gold-laced hat and heavy gold epaulettes, a fine target for enemy sharpshooters, had asked him to change into something less conspicuous. 'Let me alone!' growled Rotheram in reply. 'I've always fought in a cocked hat, and always will!'

Throughout the Fleet the reaction to Nelson's rousing signal was varied. Some ships, however, probably did not receive it. In the *Bellerophon* it was read off by Midshipman Franklin, and immediately reported to Captain Cooke who, realizing what Nelson had meant in making it, promptly went round the decks, where the men were waiting impatiently at the guns, and read it to them. With the sound of their cheers ringing in his ears he

---

[1] The signal is as follows: Telegraphic flag and then— 253 (England) 269 (expects) 863 (that) 261 (every) 471 (man) 958 (will) 220 (do) 370 (his) 4 (D) 21 (U) 19 (T) 24 (Y).

Some confusion has, in the past, been caused because Popham put 'I' and 'J' together, and 'V' before 'U'.

strode back to the poop. Captain Durham of the *Defiance* turned up all hands, read the signal and was answered with cheers. 'Everything then being ready—matches lit—guns double-shotted with grape and rounds, and decks cleared—we piped to dinner and had a good glass of grog.''

The *Neptune*'s crew heard of the signal and gave a cheer, and in the *Britannia* it was 'joyfully welcomed'. In the *Ajax*, Lt Ellis, told to tell the sailors on the main-deck, began with the quarter-master who, without any more ado assembled the men with: 'Avast there, lads, come and hear the Admiral's words.' Ellis repeated Nelson's signal, but at first the men did not appreciate it, 'for there were murmurs from some, whilst others in an audible whisper murmured, "Do our duty? Of course we'll do our duty! I've always done mine, haven't you? Let us come alongside of 'em and we'll soon show whether we'll do our duty." ' Nevertheless, they soon started cheering—'more from love and admiration of the Admiral', says Ellis, 'than from a full appreciation of his signal'. The *Polyphemus*'s men, hearing the signal, gave three cheers and received three in reply from the *Dreadnought* on their starboard beam.

The *Royal Sovereign* opened fire on the enemy, as we shall see later, exactly at noon. Fifteen minutes later the first of the enemy ships opened fire at long range at the *Victory*. But those ships were rolling: the swell waves coming in on the larboard beam gathered them up and rolled them over to starboard. They righted themselves as the crests passed beneath, and then rolled to larboard on the backs of the waves which then moved on to the eastward, to crash along the rocky shore of Cape Trafalgar.

The inexperienced French and Spanish gunners peering down their sights had the same view as a man glancing up at the blue sky and then deliberately lowering his gaze to the sea twenty yards off the ship's side and then looking up skywards again. Their task was similar to a man with a pistol sitting in a rocking chair and trying to shoot a tumbler off the mantelpiece at the far end of the room. For the first few broadsides they were about as successful, but the shooting served a good purpose, because it tended to steady the men—and not only in the enemy ships.

The time had now come for Nelson to send Blackwood back to the *Euryalus* and Prowse to the *Sirius* (the other two frigate cap-tains appear to have left earlier). On their way, said Nelson, they were to tell all the captains of the battleships (i.e. those of Nelson's Division) that he was 'depending on their exertions; and if by the mode of attack prescribed they find it impracticable to get into action immediately, they may adopt whatever they think best, provided it leads them quickly and closely alongside an enemy.'

The three men stood at the forward end of the quarter-deck of the *Victory*. From ahead, like thunder before a summer storm, came the rumble of the French and Spanish guns, and the hiss of shot passing overhead. Prowse said goodbye to his nephew Charles Adair, the *Victory*'s captain of Marines, for the last time.

Blackwood took Nelson's hand. 'I trust, my Lord, that on my return to the *Victory*, which will be as soon as possible, I shall find your Lordship well, and in possession of twenty prizes.' Nelson looked at Blackwood, and his presentiment of death must have been gripping him now. 'God bless you, Blackwood, I shall never speak to you again.'

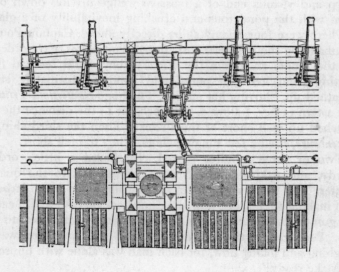

A section of the lower-deck of a seventy-four, showing a gun in the run-in position and the rest run out (tackles and breeching not shown). Between the second and third gun is the pump dale—a long wooden tube taking the water over the ship's side from the pumps, which can be seen behind
the guns

21

NELSON IS SHOT

'When without stratagem
But in plain shock and even play or battle,
Was ever known so great and little loss
On one part and one the other? Take it God,
For it is none but thine.'
                    —Shakespeare (*Henry V*)

THE *Victory* was sailing in the faltering breeze at the speed of a dawdling child. With the *Téméraire, Neptune, Leviathan* and *Conqueror* following close astern, she seemed to the French the sharp and vicious end of a massive wedge driving down on to them with the ponderous and crushing inevitability of a glacier.

There were four enemy ships directly ahead. Captain Poulain, commanding the northernmost, the 74-gun *Héros*, gave orders to try the range, and from the *Victory* they could see red flame spitting from her gun ports, and almost immediately smoke wreathed up, blurring her outline. The huge *Santissima Trinidad*, just astern of her, followed. Like pebbles in the distance the shot splashed up well short of the *Victory*. Then the third ship, the *Bucentaure*, fired a few ranging shots. They too fell short.

Two or three minutes passed. 'Starboard a little', ordered Hardy, and Atkinson, the Master, repeated it to the quarter-master. The *Victory* had for a short while come up to larboard, as if making a feint, but now she came back on course. On each of the gun decks the lieutenants put their speaking trumpets to their lips. Perspiration trickled down naked backs. There was no laughing and joking now, for each man was alone with himself.

'Make ready!'

The second captains at the guns leapt to the flintlocks and a series of metallic clicks showed that they had cocked them. The gun captains, standing six or seven feet behind the guns holding the trigger lines which linked them to the flintlocks, crouched down with right knees bent and left legs flung out a pace to the side. They looked down the glistening barrels but at the moment there was only the sea and an empty horizon in their sight.

Again the *Bucentaure* fired a few rounds. The *Victory* was just over a mile away and they fell short. A few moments elapsed and the other ships again fired. The men on the *Victory*'s upper-deck heard some shots whirr overhead. Then they saw a hole suddenly appear in the main-topgallant sail: a clear indication to the enemy that they were now in range. The desultory firing stopped. There was a minute of awful silence.

Suddenly the fear-sharpened outlines of the French ships blurred and in their place were rolling banks of flame-tinged yellow smoke: nearly two hundred guns, the full broadsides of the *Héros, Santissima Trinidad, Bucentaure* and *Redoutable*, had fired. Before the sound of their discharge reached the *Victory* an invisible hail of death smashed into her: solid shot plunged through the hull, throwing out a hail of great splinters which cut men down like invisible scythes; straining ropes were slashed, whiplashing like elastic; holes pock-marked the sails. Men grunted and sat down abruptly with death inside them; others fell shrieking, stumps of limbs pumping blood on to the scrubbed decks. When the enemy guns stopped—for a moment—vomiting their grotesque mixture of round-shot and grape, livid flame, noise and smoke, it seemed incongruous that the weak sun still shone, that the sails still flapped with lazy majesty, ropes creaked through blocks with easy familiarity, and the sea continued to murmur its quiet song under bow and stern.

Again the enemy guns coughed their vicious death . . . and again, and again. Nelson's secretary, John Scott, was talking to Hardy when suddenly an invisible hand flung him to the deck, dead. Captain Charles Adair, commanding the Royal Marines on the quarter-deck, called a seaman and attempted to carry away the body before Nelson noticed, but the Admiral walked across.

'Is that poor Scott that is gone?' Adair replied that it was. 'Poor fellow!' said Nelson. Then he and Hardy paced up and down the quarter-deck talking with the easy unconcern of two diplomats walking of a summer's morning along Whitehall.

Again the enemy's guns fired. A shot spun into the Marines on the poop and eight collapsed. Seeing this, Nelson called to Adair: 'Disperse your men round the ship.' But for this order they would have dealt with French sharpshooters—and perhaps saved Nelson's life.

Hardy glanced at his heavy gold watch. It was of curious design, with the hours marked in Roman numerals and the minutes in Arabic. Barely 12.20 . . . they had been under fire less than five minutes. A shot cut through four rolled-up hammocks in the nettings, smashed away part of the launch as it lay on the booms, hit the fore-brace bitts on the quarter-deck and whined between the two men. A splinter from the bitts hit Hardy's left foot, tearing away the ornate buckle of the shoe.

Both men stopped instinctively. Nelson glanced up questioningly at the massive Hardy; he in turn looked down at his Admiral. Each feared the other had been wounded. Nelson smiled. 'This is too warm work, Hardy, to last long.'

Again the enemy guns rumbled. A shot smashed the *Victory*'s wheel, and for a moment she was out of control. Quilliam and Atkinson ran down to the gun room to organize emergency steering, using the tackles which had already been hooked on to the tiller when the ship cleared for action. Suddenly there was a crash high above the poop as a shot cut into the mizen-topmast and sent it toppling down. Forward the foresail—it was almost new—began to flap. More than two hundred feet of it had been torn from the yard and it hung down in shreds over the fo'c'sle. Within five minutes each of the studding-sails had been ripped from the booms; every other sail in the ship was pocked with holes. The *Victory* was like a bird with its wings clipped. Thirty men had been carried wounded out of the sunlight and down to the half-darkness of the cockpit for Beatty to attend to them; twenty more were beyond reach of his skill.

Now the *Victory* was only a few hundred yards from the enemy: within a short while she would be able to bring her broadsides to bear.

She was heading for the space between the stern of *Santissima Trinidad* and the bows of *Bucentaure*, but Hardy saw the gap closing as the *Bucentaure* slowly moved ahead. Nor did there seem enough room to pass astern of the *Bucentaure* because Captain Lucas, seeing the French *Neptune* (which should have been just astern of the *Bucentaure*) falling away to leeward, had brought *Redoutable* up close. Hardy, faced with an almost solid wall of ships which were wreathed with smoke and firing as fast as their guns could be loaded, pointed out to Nelson that it would not be possible to break through the line without running aboard one of the enemy ships.

'I cannot help it,' said Nelson above the muffled drumming of the enemy's guns and the cries of the *Victory*'s own wounded. 'Go on

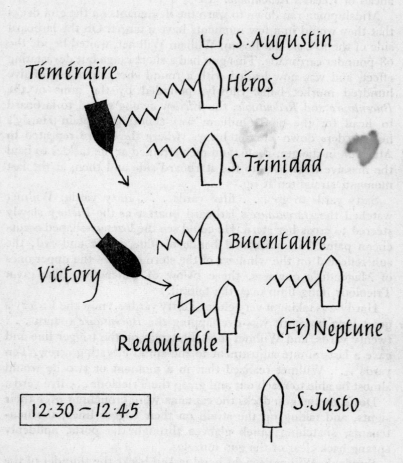

DIAGRAM 1: The *Victory* sailing down to break the line, under fire from *Bucentaure*, *Redoutable* and French *Neptune*. At 12.40 *Téméraire* engages *San Augustin* and *Héros*. It should be noted that this and successive diagrams are not to scale. Zig-zag lines indicate gunfire

board where you please: take your choice.' Hardy chose to try to
break through under the stern of Villeneuve's *Bucentaure* and
ahead of Lucas's *Redoutable*.

Midshipmen ran down to warn the lieutenants on the gun decks
that they would in a few moments have a target. On the larboard
side of the fo'c'sle the Bosun, William Willmet, waited beside the
68-pounder carronade. This gun had a short range but devastating
effect, and was now loaded with a round shot and a keg of five
hundred musket balls. Slowly, pounded by the guns of the
Bucentaure and *Redoutable*, the *Victory* swung round to larboard
to head for the gap. Quilliam was shouting Captain Hardy's
helm orders down the hatchways, where they were repeated to
Atkinson in the gun-room, and men strained at the tackles to haul
the massive tiller over to the starboard side and then, at the last
moment, straighten it up.

Sixty yards to go . . . fifty yards . . . forty yards: Willmet
watched the *Bucentaure*'s larboard quarter as the *Victory* slowly
steered to cross her stern. He could see the lozenge-shaped escut-
cheon painted in horizontal bands of blue, white and red; the
sun reflected on the windows of the stern cabins—the upper ones
of Magendie's quarters, those below of Villeneuve. The great
Tricolour hung limp over the taffrail.

Hardy was taking it very close. Thirty yards . . . now the *Victory*'s
great long bowsprit was overlapping the *Bucentaure*'s stern . . .
twenty yards, and Willmet took the strain on the trigger line and
gave a last-minute adjustment to the spiral elevating screw. Ten
yards . . . Willmet realized that in a moment or two he would
almost be able to reach out and grasp the Tricolour . . . five yards.

Down on the gun decks the captains were crouching over their
sights, and taking up the strain on their trigger lines; the lieutenants, snatching quick glances through the ports, suddenly
sprang back clear of the gun muzzles.

Suddenly Willmet's right hand jerked back: the thunder of the
carronade gave way to the terrible clatter of the shot and five
hundred musket balls smashing through the *Bucentaure*'s flimsy
stern, fanning out to sweep the lines of guns, cutting down in
swathes the mass of Frenchmen working them. But almost before
Willmet's carronade had finished its short recoil the guns on the
decks below were firing into the *Bucentaure*'s stern as, one by one,
they came to bear. From the *Victory*'s decks they could hear the
wild screams of the wounded and dying. The smoke from the

guns blew back into the ports and set the men coughing; up on deck clouds of dust from the shattered woodwork of the French flagship flew across to cover Nelson's and Hardy's uniforms.

As the *Victory* passed through, still rolling in the swell, the end of her main-yardarm caught the vang of the *Bucentaure*'s gaff and ripped it away. But waiting beyond the *Bucentaure* was the French *Neptune*: as soon as the *Victory* was clear she poured a broadside into the British flagship and quickly set a jib to run ahead in case the *Victory* tried to board. Her broadside did much damage to the *Victory*'s foremast and bowsprit; several shot smashed through the bow planking and others damaged her anchors and spritsail-yards.

Hardy, however, had decided to get alongside the *Redoutable*, now on his starboard side, and ordered the helm to be put over. While the men at the larboard guns quickly sponged out and re-loaded with two or three shot to each gun, the starboard gun captains waited for the *Victory* to come round far enough for them to fire their first broadside. In a moment or two they could see Lucas's ship. The captains jerked their trigger-lines and the full starboard broadside smashed into the *Redoutable*. Willmet, who had run across to the starboard carronade, fired it down on to the sailors massed on the enemy's decks. The *Redoutable* shut most of her lower-deck gun ports and then the two ships crunched together, but as they bounced apart again the *Victory*'s topmast-studding-sail boom irons hooked on to the *Redoutable*'s fore-topsail and held the two ships together.

Down below in the *Victory* the lieutenants were yelling them-selves hoarse in the half darkness. Clouds of smoke meant that they could not see farther than a couple of guns away, and the men worked almost instinctively—sponge—in with the cartridge —ram it home—in with the shot—ram—in with a wad and ram— another shot—ram—wad and ram—cock the lock; everyone then jumps well back; there is a jerk on the trigger line and the gun flings back, flame and noise spurting from the muzzle and a little 'huff' of flame coming from the vent-hole to burn the beams overhead.

While all the *Victory*'s starboard guns pounded the *Redout-able*, the larboard guns kept on firing at the *Bucentaure* as she drifted away, and some of them managed to fire into the stern of the *Santissima Trinidad*. The *Bucentaure* had suffered dreadful damage from the *Victory*'s momentary assault. As Nelson's flag-ship approached, Villeneuve had ordered Magendie to prepare to board, but Hardy's sudden turn under his stern had caught him unawares.

'The swell, which made our ships roll, lessened the accuracy of our aim,' Major-General Contamine wrote, 'and a dense cloud of smoke, that the calm prevented from dispersing, often forbade our seeing anything round us.'

Villeneuve, as soon as he had an indication of what Nelson proposed doing with his division, had hoisted a belated signal. It was not the one for which Churruca had earlier waited in vain— for the van to wear round and help the rear. With the line being broken by both British divisions, Villeneuve hoisted a signal which ordered 'all those ships, which by their actual position are not engaging, to take any such as will bring them as speedily as possible into action'. But Dumanoir and his ships ahead, for whom the order was really intended, sailed majestically on to the northward.

Meanwhile Captain Lucas's well-trained sharpshooters perched in the tops of the *Redoutable* kept up a hail of musket fire down on to the *Victory*'s decks. Down below most of the French guns were silent, but the *Victory*'s guns were being constantly run out —their muzzles almost touching the French ship's side—and fired. It seemed likely that the *Redoutable* might be set on fire by the flash of their discharge, and such a blaze would be a danger to the *Victory* as well. So at the *Victory*'s guns men stood by with buckets of water, and as each gun fired they flung the water out of the port to stifle any flames.

While the *Victory* and the *Redoutable* fought it out, locked together, Captain Eliab Harvey brought the *Téméraire* into action. He had been to starboard of the *Victory* and had to cut away his studding-sails to avoid overtaking her. In the great smoke clouds spreading across the line he lost sight of the *Victory* altogether so that 'for a minute or two I ceased my fire fearing I might from the thickness of the smoke be firing into the *Victory*.'

But as he saw her alongside the *Redoutable* he took the *Téméraire* round to break through the enemy line astern of the *Redoutable* (just as Hardy had taken the *Victory* astern of the *Bucentaure*); but ahead of her the French *Neptune* was waiting and, from the same position that she had sent a broadside smashing into the *Victory*, so she launched one at the *Téméraire* as Harvey's ship came slowly through the gap. The French *Neptune*'s gunners fired fast and accurately: in a few moments their shots cut away the

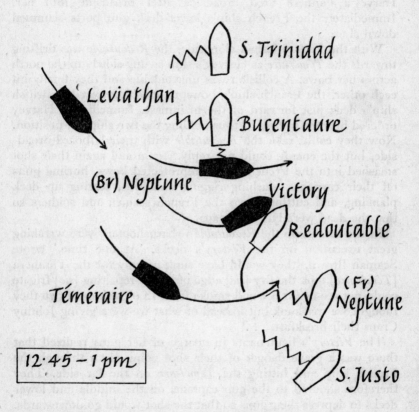

DIAGRAM 2: At 12.45 *Victory* rakes *Bucentaure* and, 12.50, runs aboard *Redoutable*, both ships drifting to leeward. British *Neptune* rakes *Bucentaure*. French *Neptune* and *San Justo* open fire on *Téméraire*

Téméraire's great fore-yard and it crashed down. More shots sliced through the main-topmast which buckled and then collapsed, tumbling down with a mass of rigging. More round-shot punched their way into the foremast and bowsprit. The *Téméraire* was now almost out of control, but as she passed close to the *Redoutable*, Harvey's gunners fired broadside after broadside into her. Immediately the French ship's lower-deck gun ports slammed down shut.

With the *Victory* lashed alongside, the *Redoutable* was drifting towards the *Téméraire* as Harvey's ship swung slowly to the north across her bows. A collision was unavoidable and they finally hit each other, the French ship's bowsprit crashing over the British ship's deck just forward of the mainmast. Immediately Harvey ordered his men to lash it, thus holding the two ships in position. Now they could rake the *Redoutable* with their larboard broadside, but the enemy could not reply. Again and again their shot smashed into the French ship's unprotected bows, hurling guns off their carriages, slashing rigging and sails, tearing up deck planking, and cutting down the French seamen and soldiers so that the dead were lying in heaps.

In the meantime the *Redoutable*'s sharpshooters were wreaking great execution on the *Victory*'s decks. 'At one time,' wrote Seaman Brown, 'they would have sunk us only for the Timmera [*Téméraire*] took the firy [*sic*] edge of us the repaiting [*sic*] frigate could not see us for fire and smoke from 12 o'clock until two they thought we was sunk but instead of what we were giving Johnny Craps their breakfast. . . .'

The *Victory*'s lieutenants in charge of her guns realized that there was a grave danger of their shot going clean through the French ship and hitting the *Téméraire* on the far side. They therefore shouted to the gun captains on the middle and lower decks to depress their guns so that the shot would go downwards.

Down in the cockpit the wounded were being brought down in a never-ending stream. Dr Scott, the chaplain, horrified at the dreadful suffering of many of the men, was almost demented by what he saw in the faint light of the fighting lanterns, but he went round to crouch at the side of each man, doing what he could to comfort him.

Lt William Ram, a twenty-one year old Irishman, was carried down desperately wounded from a shot which had smashed up through the deck at his feet. One of the surgeons tied tourniquets to stop the bleeding, but Ram suddenly realized that he was dying. Impatiently he ripped the tourniquets off so that he bled to death more quickly. The sight of this so upset the frenzied Scott that he ran up the hatchways, now stained with blood, to the upper-deck. But there he found little relief: a pall of smoke and dust hung so thickly that he could only just make out the figures of Nelson and Hardy walking up and down.

But tragedy was about to strike on board the British flagship. Nelson and Hardy were regularly pacing up and down a twenty foot stretch of the quarter-deck between the shattered wheel and the hatchway. They had reached to within two or three feet of the hatch and Nelson turned to the left. Hardy took another pace and also turned—to see Nelson on his knees, trying to support himself with his left hand. Before he could reach him, Nelson's one arm gave way and he collapsed. In a moment Hardy was crouching over him. 'I hope you are not severely wounded, my Lord?' he inquired anxiously.

'They have done for me at last, Hardy,' Nelson gasped.

'I hope not!'

'Yes,' said Nelson, 'my backbone is shot through.'

Hardy called to a Marine sergeant nearby, Sgt Secker, and two seamen. They ran over and knelt down at Nelson's side. 'Take the Admiral down to the cockpit immediately,' ordered Hardy. Gently they lifted the stricken man in their arms, and stepped the few paces to the hatchway leading down to the upper-deck. Somehow Nelson managed to use his one arm to take out a handkerchief and place it over his face, so that no one should recognize him as he was carried below.

Many others had been wounded at about this time by the musket balls of the French sharpshooters and the blast of the grenades, and Secker and the two seamen had to take their turn as they shuffled down to the upper-deck, trying to avoid jolting Nelson. From the upper-deck they gently manœuvred him down to the middle-deck and then to the gun-deck. Each time they reached the bottom of the ladder they had to be careful because on each side of the hatchway there were guns, and they were still being fired as fast as they could be loaded. Finally they left the daylight behind as they scrambled down the last ladder to the orlop-deck, and then slowly made their way past the wounded sitting or lying about on the deck. Several of the wounded men recognized Nelson from the decorations on his jacket.

'Mr Beatty!' they cried. 'Mr Beatty! Lord Nelson is here!'

'Mr Beatty! The Admiral is wounded!'

Beatty, his clothes soaked in the blood of the men he was tending, was already heavy-hearted from the number of wounded all round him and especially from the death of Lt Ram, who had been a great friend. Then above the bedlam of groans and cries punctuated by the rumble of the 32-pounders on the deck above being run out, and the crash of them firing, he heard the agonized call: 'Mr Beatty! Quickly! The Admiral is wounded!'

He turned, and in the gloom and the faint light from the fighting lanterns he saw three men, bent down because of the lack of headroom, stumbling along towards him, carrying a small figure. A handkerchief over the face slipped away, and he saw it was Nelson. His premonition, expressed earlier to the two Scotts, had come true. He ran the last few steps and Burke, the purser, who had also heard the urgent calls, joined him. Quickly they took the Admiral from the arms of the seamen and carried him towards the midshipmen's berth. One of them tripped and stumbled, but managed to avoid falling.

'Who is that carrying me?' asked Nelson.

'Beatty, my Lord, and Burke,' said the surgeon.

'Ah, Mr Beatty! You can do nothing for me. I have but a short time to live: my back is shot through.'

In the near-darkness Beatty could feel the Admiral's blood-soaked coat, but he said: 'I hope the wound is not as dangerous as your Lordship imagines.'

The overwrought Scott, who had been giving lemonade to the wounded in another part of the cockpit after his brief glimpse of the holocaust on the upper-deck, suddenly appeared, grief-stricken at the sight that met his eyes and wringing his hands in anguish. 'Alas, Beatty, how prophetic you were!' he exclaimed.

They bore Nelson to an empty space on the larboard side, just forward of the after hanging magazine, and put him down gently on a rough mattress, his back against one of the massive frames of the ship's side. Swiftly Beatty and Burke slipped off his jacket —an easy task since he had but one arm—shirt and the rest of his clothes, and drew a sheet over him. While they were doing this Nelson said to Dr Scott in a quiet voice: 'Doctor, I told you so. Doctor, I am gone.'

Apparently convinced that he would die within a few minutes he added, after a short pause, 'I have to leave Lady Hamilton, and my adopted daughter Horatia, as a legacy to my country'.

Beatty was by now ready with his surgical instruments. He felt the pulse. Overhead the 32-pounders crashed and rumbled; the frame against which Nelson rested his back shivered and vibrated with the shock of battle as Lucas's *Redoutable* also fought a losing fight for life. A fighting lantern was hung from a beam overhead and Beatty assured Nelson he would not put him to much pain in trying to discover the course of the musket ball. The more Beatty gently probed the more he realized its hopelessness. The ball had plunged deep into the chest and was now probably lodged in the spine. He bent over Nelson and explained this to him.

'I am confident my back is shot through,' said Nelson.

While Burke held him forward, Beatty examined the narrow back; but there was no mark of a wound.

'Tell me all your sensations, my Lord,' requested Beatty.

'I feel a gush of blood every minute within my breast,' said Nelson. 'I have no feeling in the lower part of my body . . . breathing is very difficult and gives me very severe pain about the part of the spine I am sure the ball has struck—for I felt it break my back. . . .'

Beatty heard the Admiral list his symptoms with a sinking heart: they confirmed his suspicions. He wrote later: 'These symptoms, but more particularly the gush of blood which his Lordship complained of, together with the state of his pulse, indicated to the surgeon himself the hopeless situation of the case: but till after the victory was ascertained and announced to his Lordship, the true nature of his wound was concealed by the surgeon from all on board except Captain Hardy, Dr Scott, Mr Burke and Messrs Smith and Westemburg, the Assistant Surgeons.'

Twenty-year-old Midshipman George Westphal was carried down now after being wounded in the head and set down on the deck near Nelson. Someone, wanting to make him a pillow, seized a coat which had been flung down and rolled it up, not noticing the blood-stained orders of knighthood embroidered on its breast. Westphal, born in Lambeth of an old Hanoverian family, little knowing he would survive to be promoted to post captain and receive a knighthood, settled his throbbing head on his Admiral's coat and waited patiently for the surgeon.

The upper decks of the *Victory* now looked like a slaughter-house, thanks mainly to the sharpshooters and grenade-throwers hiding in the *Redoutable*'s tops. Smoke swirled like thick fog on a moor, blinding men and making them cough and splutter. Casualties were so heavy that the crews of the dozen 12-pounders on the quarter-deck had to quit: they were sent below to reinforce the upper, middle and gun-deck guns.

Soon the massive figure of Hardy striding about with his telescope under his arm, Captain Adair, the red-jacketed Marine, and one or two other officers were the only men left alive on deck. The seamen who had escaped were busy carrying their wounded comrades down to the cockpit. At the same time the *Redoutable*'s big guns had almost stopped firing, and this led the *Victory*'s gunners to think she was about to surrender, so they too stopped firing.

This led to an extraordinary misunderstanding because the sharpshooters in the *Redoutable*'s tops shouted down to their officers that the *Victory*'s decks had been swept bare and, coupled with the silence of the guns which had been tearing their ship to pieces, Lucas drew the wrong conclusion. At the same time Hardy and Adair called up Marines and seamen from below to get ready to take possession. Arming themselves with pistols and pikes, muskets and tomahawks, they streamed up the hatchways into the smoke and ran to the bulwarks.

Captain Lucas, describing the *Redoutable*'s point of view, wrote: 'At last the *Victory*'s batteries were not able to reply to us; I perceived that they were preparing to board, the foe thronged up on to their upper-works.

'I ordered the trumpet to sound (it was the recognized signal to summon the boarding parties in our exercises). They came up in such perfect order with the officers and midshipmen at the head of their divisions that one would have said that it was only a sham fight.

'In less than a minute the upper-works were covered with armed men who hurled themselves on to the poop, on the nettings and into the shrouds; it was impossible for me to pick out the most courageous.'

There followed an imaginative touch: 'Then there began a furious musketry fire in which Admiral Nelson was fighting at the head of his crew; our fire became so greatly superior that in less than fifteen minutes we had silenced that of the *Victory*; more than two hundred grenades were thrown aboard her with the most marked success, her upper-works were strewn with the dead and wounded, and Admiral Nelson was killed by the fire of our musketry.' (This in fact refers to the beginning of the battle, but Lucas was preparing to make a very exaggerated claim.)

'Almost immediately the upper-works of the enemy ship were deserted and the Victory ceased absolutely to engage us; but it was difficult to get aboard her owing to the rolling of the two ships and to the superior height afforded by her third deck.

'I gave orders to cut away the slings of the main-yard and to lower it to serve as a bridge. Midshipman Yon and four seamen succeeded in getting on board the Victory by means of the anchor and informed us that there was not a soul on her decks; but at the moment when our brave lads were just hurling themselves after them the three-decker Téméraire—who had doubtless perceived that the Victory had ceased fire and would inevitably be taken— ran foul of us to starboard and overwhelmed us with the point-blank fire of all her guns.'

Once Hardy and Adair had called up men from below, the French attack was quickly beaten off, but nineteen officers and men were killed and twenty-two wounded. Captain Adair was standing on the Victory's gangway encouraging his men when he was killed by a musket ball in the back of the neck.

The arrival of the Téméraire soon changed the picture. 'It would be difficult to describe the horrible carnage caused by the murderous broadside of this ship,' wrote Lucas. 'More than 200 of our brave lads were killed or wounded. I was wounded at the same instant but not so seriously as to prevent me from remaining at my post.

'Not being able to do anything more on the side next the Victory I ordered the rest of the crew to go below promptly and to fire into the Téméraire with those starboard guns which had not been dismounted in the shock of the collision with this ship.'

However, the Redoutable's sharpshooters kept up their fire on the decks of both British ships. In the Victory, the midshipman who had hoisted Nelson's 'England expects' signal, John Pollard, had been the first man on the poop to be wounded, a shot through the bulwarks flinging up a heavy splinter which gashed his right arm. He had tied up the wound and carried on. Later, alongside the Redoutable, a musket ball had knocked the telescope from his hand, and then a bullet hit him in the thigh, smashing a watch in his fob pocket. Some time after Nelson had been shot, Pollard's attention had been drawn to three men in the *Redoutable*'s mizen-top—whence the shot had come. The top was about twenty feet above the *Victory*'s poop, and the men kept bobbing up from behind a strip of canvas, firing their muskets and then crouching to re-load. Pollard picked up a musket from a dead Marine lying nearby and fired back, an old seaman named King bringing him fresh ammunition. While he was having his duel with the sharpshooters, another midshipman, Francis Collingwood, a boy from Greenwich and no relation to the Admiral, arrived and had a shot before going on to carry out another task. Doggedly Pollard waited for the sharpshooters to show themselves again. One stood up, levelling his musket, but Pollard ducked behind the bulwark while King helped him to re-load. He waited and suddenly the second Frenchman appeared. Pollard fired, and he too dropped behind the canvas. The third Frenchman, however, dodged behind the mast, and he fired before Pollard. King dropped dead, shot between the eyes, and the Frenchman tried to scramble down the rigging. But Pollard fired once again and the Frenchman fell to the deck.

By now the *Téméraire*'s broadside had given the *Redoutable* a terrible hammering. 'Our ship was so riddled,' wrote Lucas, 'that she seemed to be no more than a mass of wreckage.

'In this state the *Téméraire* hailed us to strike and not to prolong a useless resistance. I ordered several soldiers who were near me to answer this summons with musket shots, which was performed with great zeal.' But it was a hopeless gesture. Lucas describes the damage to the *Redoutable*. 'All the stern was absolutely stove in, the rudder stock, the tiller, the two tiller sweeps, the stern-post, the helm port and wing transoms, the transom knees, were in general shot to pieces; the decks were all torn open by the fire of the *Victory* and the *Téméraire*; all the guns were shattered or dismounted by the shots or from these two ships having run us aboard.

'An 18-pounder gun on the main deck and a 36-pounder carronade on the fo'c'sle having burst, killed and wounded many of our people; the two sides of the ship, all the lids and bars of the ports were utterly cut to pieces; four of our six pumps were shattered as well as all our ladders in general, in such a [way] that communication between the decks and upper-works was extremely difficult.

'All our decks were covered with dead, buried beneath the debris and the splinters from different parts of the ship. A great number of wounded were killed on the orlop-deck. Out of the ship's company of 643 men we had 522 disabled, 300 being killed and 222 wounded . . . in the midst of this horrible carnage the brave lads who had not yet succumbed and those who were wounded, with whom the orlop-deck was thronged, still cried "Vive l'Emperor! We're not taken yet; is our Captain still alive?" '

There was little point in holding out any longer. 'I only awaited the certain knowledge that the leaks which the ship had sprung were so considerable that it could not be long before she foundered, in order to strike.' [1]

Lucas had no sooner ordered the colours to be hauled down than the mizenmast from which they were flying collapsed across the *Téméraire*'s poop.

Some fires had broken out aboard the *Redoutable* and, without bothering to send a lieutenant from the *Victory* to take possession of her, Captain Hardy ordered Midshipman Collingwood and Midshipman David Ogilvie, with a Marine sergeant-major and eight or ten hands, to go aboard the French ship and put it out. They could not step from one vessel to another because of the tumble-home—the sides of the ships curved in towards the upper decks like a brandy glass—so they went aft and found that one of the two boats which the *Victory* had been towing astern was still there. They hauled in the painter, scrambled down from a stern port, rowed the few yards to the *Redoutable*'s stern and climbed aboard through an open port. To their surprise they were well received by the French.

For the moment it was comparatively quiet in the *Victory*. She had, as already mentioned, lost her mizen-topmast at the beginning of the action. Her fore and mainmasts and their yards, main-topmast, fore and maintops, bowsprit and jib-boom were all badly damaged; her sails were in shreds and the rigging cut to pieces, while the hull was badly damaged. More than fifty officers and men had been killed, and more than a hundred wounded.

Hardy now wanted to get the *Victory* clear of the *Redoutable* and he set men pushing her off with fire booms. A few moments earlier, just after the two midshipmen had left for the French ship, a lieutenant, hearing the *Téméraire*'s guns firing on the

[1] By contrast, the *Téméraire*'s log dismisses the action in two dozen words.

other side, looked out of a gun port aft and saw another French two-decker lying close on the *Téméraire*'s starboard side. A few minutes later he could read the name on the stern. It was the *Fougueux*.

For the moment, however, we must pass on to see the fate of the *Bucentaure*, Villeneuve's flagship.

The dismasted *Belleisle* at 4.15 p.m. The ships, from left to right, are the frigate *Naiad*, *Belleisle*, the Spanish *Santa Ana* (with just her bows showing), *Royal Sovereign* (heeling to port), *Victory* and, with smoke coming from her, the French *Achille*. From an engraving of the painting by *W. Huggins*

'Crippled but Unconquered'—the rescue of the *Belleisle*. *From the painting by W. L. Wyllie, R.A.*

22

THE BROADSIDES

'So much bravery and devotion deserved a better fate, but the moment had not yet arrived when France will have her naval successes to celebrate together with her victories upon land. . .'

—Villeneuve to Decrès

THE *Victory*, by firing her shattering broadside into the *Bucentaure* and then crashing alongside the *Redoutable*, forcing her off to leeward, had prised a big gap in the enemy line. As we have seen, the *Téméraire* could not take advantage of it in time and was forced to go round under the *Redoutable*'s stern, but the third ship in Nelson's division, Thomas Fremantle's *Neptune*, could and did.

The *Neptune*'s band had been playing bravely as the enemy's guns started the overture to their thunderous symphony; Fremantle found the excitement, as he wrote later to Betsey, 'entirely drove away the bile' which had been troubling him, and he was a proud man as he stood on the quarter-deck, the band striking up 'Rule, Britannia' and 'Britons, Strike Home!' and bringing answering cheers from the *Téméraire* ahead and the *Leviathan* on the quarter. 'During the whole of the time we were going down into action and being raked by the enemy,' wrote Midshipman Badcock, 'the whole crew, with the exception of the officers, were made to lie flat on the deck to secure them from the raking shots, some of which came in at the bow and went out at the stern. Had it not been for [this] precaution many lives must have been sacrificed.'

Fremantle watched the *Victory* rake the *Bucentaure* and then run alongside the *Redoutable*, and he immediately decided to go through the gap. (See Diagram 2 on page 247.) 'We put the ship's helm a'starboard and the *Neptune* passed between the *Victory* and the *Bucentaure*, with which ship we were warmly engaged,' noted Lt Andrew Green, Fremantle's signals officer. Villeneuve's flagship was still reeling from the *Victory*'s treble-shotted broadsides—Villeneuve himself described them as 'exceeding deadly and destructive'—when Fremantle took the *Neptune* right across her stern. On the gun decks the lieutenants were shouting themselves hoarse. 'Make ready! . . . Don't fire until your guns bear!'

Through the gun ports the crouching gun captains saw first the horizon and then the *Bucentaure*'s damaged stern apparently rising and falling as the *Neptune* rolled her way along in the swell. One after another the gunners tugged the trigger-lines: in succession the treble-shotted guns belched smoke and flame, and flung back in recoil.

This hail of nearly a hundred and fifty shot pouring in through the *Bucentaure*'s stern flung almost every remaining 24-pounder gun off its carriage, the crews collapsing where they stood, cut down by solid shot or splinters. On the deck below more than half the men serving the 36-pounders were killed. On board the *Neptune* Fremantle ordered the Master to bring the ship round to larboard, and as she swung the whole broadside once again smashed into the French flagship. She appeared a pitiful sight now, and while the *Neptune*'s gunners loaded once again the French ship's captain, Magendie, reeled and fell, wounded by a splinter.

Villeneuve ordered Lt Joseph Daudignon to go aft and take over command, and at the same time he told the men left alive on the upper works to get below to the 24-pounder guns. The *Neptune* fired another broadside and Fremantle peered through the smoke, casting about for another victim.

Just ahead and slightly to starboard of the *Bucentaure* was the great *Santissima Trinidad*, her red and white topsides gleaming through the clouds of smoke, her topsails, topgallants and royals set and, more important, heading away from the *Neptune* so that Fremantle would be able to sail across her unprotected stern and—just as he had done with the *Bucentaure*—give her a devastating raking broadside while being immune from her guns. After a final broadside at the French flagship, the *Neptune* slowly advanced on the *Santissima Trinidad*. Once again the gunners had a good target in their sights as Fremantle steered to within less than a hundred yards to rake her. Leaving the *Neptune* hammering away at the *Santissima Trinidad*, we must again return to the *Bucentaure*, now experiencing the last stages of attacks which were to leave her utterly helpless and a floating tomb.

The fourth ship in Nelson's line, Bayntun's *Leviathan*, followed through the gap in the wake of the *Neptune*. Half-hidden in the smoke he found the *Bucentaure* and, like Fremantle, he took his ship across her stern, fired off a raking broadside, came round

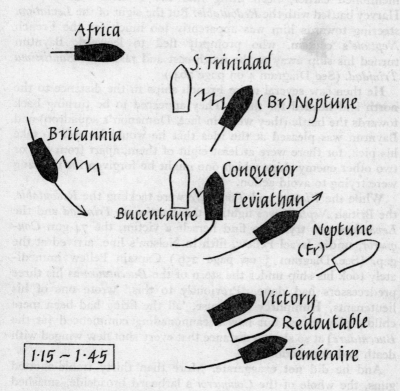

DIAGRAM 3: British *Neptune* luffs up and engages *Santissima Trinidad*.
1.15 *Conqueror* rakes *Bucentaure* and, 1.25, goes alongside. 1.25 *Téméraire*
alongside *Redoutable*; *Britannia* opens fire on *Bucentaure*; *Africa* approaches
Santissima Trinidad

slightly to larboard to get off another broadside, and then looked for another opponent. (See Diagram 3 on page 259.) The *Neptune* was taking care of the *Santissima Trinidad* just to the northwards, and Bayntun spotted a French 80-gun ship to the eastwards on his starboard bow. She too was named the *Neptune* and had, as mentioned earlier, been firing into the *Téméraire* as Captain Harvey battled with the *Redoutable*. But the sight of the *Leviathan* steering towards him was apparently too much for the French *Neptune*'s captain, who promptly fled to leeward. Bayntun turned his ship away to the north-east and raked the *Santissima Trinidad*. (See Diagram 4 on page 264.)

He then saw several more French ships in the distance to the north and headed for them. They appeared to be turning back towards the battle (they were, in fact, Dumanoir's squadron) and Bayntun was pleased at the idea that he would be able to take his pick, for there were at least eight of them, apart from one or two other enemy ships which one might be forgiven for thinking were trying to avoid action.

While the *Victory* and *Téméraire* were tackling the *Redoutable*, the British *Neptune* was fighting the *Santissima Trinidad* and the *Leviathan* was trying to find herself a victim, the 74-gun *Conqueror*, under Israel Pellew, fifth in Nelson's line, arrived at the gap. (See Diagram 3 on page 259.) Captain Pellew immediately took his ship under the stern of the *Bucentaure* as his three predecessors had done. 'Previously to this,' wrote one of his lieutenants, Humphrey Senhouse, 'all the firing had been mere child's play to us, but now a cannonading commenced [at the *Bucentaure*] at so short a distance that every shot flew winged with death and destruction.'

And he did not exaggerate. More than thirty treble-shotted guns, the whole of the *Conqueror*'s larboard broadside, smashed in through the *Bucentaure*'s stern. A few minutes earlier Villeneuve, his ship nearly battered to pieces and, with the hard-pressed *Santissima Trinidad*, cut off from the rest of the Combined Fleet, had ordered one more attempt to be made to get Dumanoir's van squadron into action to try to save the day. Signal number 167 ('The van division to wear together'), which should make Dumanoir turn back, was hoisted. Then the *Conqueror*'s broadside tore into the ship, overturning the remaining guns and trapping more men. Several shot splintered the mizenmast and it began to topple; others cut through the mainmast just above the upper-deck, and that too began to fall, taking Villeneuve's last signal to Dumanoir with it. Slowly, as if reluctant to spoil the symmetry of the flagship's outline, both masts collapsed over the starboard side, wreckage and torn canvas covering many of the gun ports.

Pellew luffed the *Conqueror* round to larboard and brought-to on the *Bucentaure*'s quarter. By this time his guns were again loaded and run out, and the gun captains paused a moment, looking down their sights and waiting until the *Conqueror* rolled to larboard to bring their guns to bear. Aboard the *Bucentaure* the end was very near. Lt Daudignon, who had taken over when Magendie was wounded, was himself hit, and Villeneuve sent down to the lower-deck for Lt Fournier, who was commanding the guns there. Fournier came up on deck to find the foremast crashing over the side. The *Bucentaure*, with the collapse of her foremast, had no colours flying, so Midshipman Donadieu secured the Eagle of the Empire to his body and stood on the upper-deck. Villeneuve, amid the thunder of the *Conqueror*'s broadsides and the thud and crash of the shot biting home, lamented bitterly to Prigny, his Chief-of-Staff, 'that he was spared amidst so many balls, grape and splinters'. His lamentations were cut short by Prigny collapsing at his side, hit in the right leg by a splinter flung up from a shot.

The last minutes of his command are described by Villeneuve: 'I had kept a boat lowered, foreseeing the possibility of being dismasted, with the intention of going aboard another vessel. As soon as the mainmast fell I gave orders for it to be made ready, but whether it had been sunk by shot or crushed by the falling of the masts, it could not be found.

'I had the *Santissima Trinidad*, which was ahead of us, hailed to know if she could send a boat and give us a tow. I had no reply; this ship was herself engaging vigorously with a three-decker [*Neptune*] that was firing into her quarter.

'In the end, surrounded by the enemy ships which had congregated on my quarters, astern and abreast to leeward; being powerless to do them any injury, the upper-works and the 24-pounder gun-deck being deserted and strewn with dead and wounded; the lower-deck guns dismounted or masked by the fallen masts and rigging; the ship isolated in the midst of the enemy, lying motionless, and it being impossible to make any movement, I was obliged to yield to my fate and put an end to a slaughter already vast, which was from henceforward useless.' A white handkerchief was waved at the *Conqueror* in token of surrender. Fournier had the Eagle, which had been broken into pieces by now, flung over the side—'not wishing that the relics should provide a trophy for the enemy'. Both Villeneuve and Magendie (who had come back on deck after having his wound dressed) were mistaken in the number of ships engaging them in the last few minutes, and the only other ships which fired a broadside into the *Bucentaure* just before she surrendered were the *Britannia*, next astern of the *Conqueror*, and the *Agamemnon*. The officers in the *Britannia* saw a white handkerchief being waved from the remains of the larboard gallery and went on to join the attack on the *Santissima Trinidad*.

Pellew was impatient to be on his way. Apparently realizing that there was still some hard fighting ahead, he did not want to weaken his own ship by putting a large prize crew aboard the *Bucentaure*. He sent for Captain James Atcherley, commanding the *Conqueror*'s Marines. Without knowing that it was the French Commander-in-Chief who had just surrendered—for Villeneuve's flag had not been flying for some time—he ordered Atcherley to take a few men and receive the *Bucentaure*'s surrender.

Atcherley hurriedly called up a Marine corporal, two other Marine privates and a couple of seamen. The *Conqueror*'s cutter was lowered and six men climbed in and rowed across to the *Bucentaure*. Atcherley scrambled on board and made his way past groups of wounded and heaps of dead French sailors to the quarter-deck. As soon as they saw his blue hat and bright red coat, with its white sash and gold epaulettes, three French officers slowly walked over towards him. Their leader was a tall, thin-faced man in the uniform of an admiral—a long-tailed coat with a high collar and greenish-coloured corduroy trousers with a wide stripe down each side.

'To whom,' said Villeneuve in good English, proffering his sword, 'have I the honour of surrendering?'

'To Captain Pellew of the *Conqueror*,' replied an over-awed Atcherley.

'It is a satisfaction to me,' Villeneuve said courteously, 'that it is to one so fortunate as Sir Edward Pellew that I have lowered my flag.'

Atcherley looked startled. 'It is his brother, sir.'

'His brother? What, are there two of them? *Hélas!*'

The short and fat, jocund-looking man at Villeneuve's side, who had already been taken to England twice before as a prisoner, shook his head philosophically. '*Fortune de la guerre*,' said the bandaged and bloodstained Magendie. The officer wearing the uniform of a general in the Grand Army, Contamine, kept silent. Atcherley politely suggested that they had better keep their swords and surrender them to an officer of a higher rank than himself, and asked if they would excuse him for a few minutes.

Leaving them waiting on the quarter-deck, he went quickly down to the magazines with the two seamen, picking his way over the bodies (for the *Bucentaure* had suffered more than two hundred and fifty killed and wounded). Suddenly, out of the gloom, a man lunged at them with a sword. One of the two seamen struck back with his cutlass and the man, his head nearly severed from his body, fell to the deck. He had been a Briton, one of eighteen who had deserted from the Royal Navy ships at Gibraltar, crossed into Spain and ended up in Cadiz as welcome reinforcements for the *Bucentaure*'s crew. The men had been kept together and during the battle they had served two of the lower-deck guns. Now, as traitors, the survivors inevitably faced being hanged from the yardarm.

Having locked up the magazines and put the keys in his pocket, Atcherley went back up on to the quarter-deck and asked Villeneuve, Contamine, Magendie and two of Villeneuve's aides to accompany him. The wounded Prigny, who was below, did not go with them: instead he stayed on board—and later helped recapture the ship from the British prize-crew. As he led them down to the cutter waiting alongside, Atcherley saw that Captain Pellew had gone on with the *Conqueror*, so he looked round for the nearest British ship. This was the *Mars*, and he ordered his men to row for it. In a few minutes her surprised commanding officer, Lt William Hennah (for Captain Duff, as will be related later, had been killed), was receiving the sword of Vice-Admiral Pierre Charles Jean Baptiste Sylvestre de Villeneuve, commanding the Combined Fleet of France and Spain.

The *Santissima Trinidad*, putting up a brave and lonely fight ahead of the surrendered *Bucentaure*, was now fighting the *Neptune* on her starboard quarter, and the *Conqueror* which, fresh from her assault on the *Bucentaure*, had just come up on her windward side. Their combined broadsides smashed into the great ship and the effect was almost instantaneous: several shot bit into the massive mizenmast below decks like axes, and slowly it toppled over the side, taking the red and yellow flag of Spain with it. More shot cut into the mainmast, which creaked and

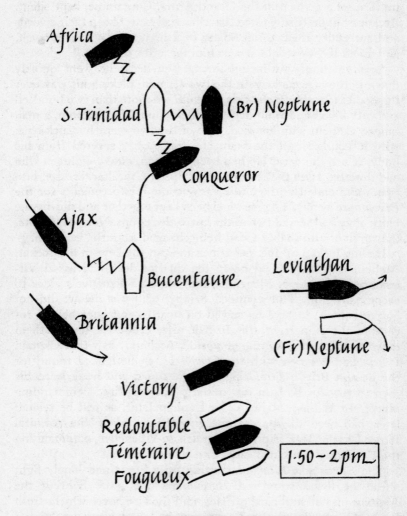

DIAGRAM 4: *Victory* gets clear of *Redoutable*. *Leviathan* engages French *Neptune*, which bears away. *Conqueror* goes ahead to rake *Santissima Trinidad*. *Africa* luffs and opens fire on *Santissima Trinidad*

swayed. Too many shrouds had been cut away to give it much support and the weight of the huge yards slung on it proved too much. Like a great branch-laden tree it crashed down, collapsing over the larboard side. The sails, almost shredded, hung down over the gun ports; the men who had been perched in the tops with muskets were catapulted into the water, where their cries for help went unheard or unheeded.

'Gave three cheers,' noted Lt Green, 'she [*Santissima Trinidad*] then paid off and brought us nearly on her lee beam.'

'Her immense topsails had every reef out,' wrote one of the *Conqueror*'s officers. 'Her royals were sheeted home, but lowered; and the falling of this majestic mass of spars, sails and rigging plunging into the water at the muzzles of our guns, was one of the most magnificent sights I ever beheld.'

By now the little 64-gun *Africa* had joined the fray. As mentioned earlier, she had been coming down from the north to rejoin Nelson. On her way she had passed the eight ships of Dumanoir's van squadron and despite the fact she was the smallest battleship in the action, she exchanged broadsides with them. Finding the largest battleship in the action, the *Santissima Trinidad*, Digby luffed up, brought-to on her weather bow and began firing broadsides into her. (See Diagram 4 opposite.) The *Britannia*, in passing, had also given her a broadside which, wrote Lt Halloran, 'shattered the rich display of sculpture, figures, ornaments and inscriptions with which she was adorned. I never saw so beautiful a ship.'

The *Santissima Trinidad*, flying the flag of Rear-Admiral Cisneros, and commanded by Commodore de Uriarte, had fought bravely. At the beginning of the battle she had been one of the ships which had poured devastating broadsides into the *Victory* as she came to break the line, but the arrival of Fremantle in the *Neptune* had been the beginning of her defeat. The British three-decker's broadsides had soon killed or wounded every man on the upper-deck with the exception of her captain. Rear-Admiral Cisneros was hit and carried below; grapeshot moaned in through gun ports and shot-holes to freeze men for an instant in grotesque poses before they dropped dead. 'Blood ran in streams about the deck, and in spite of the sand, the rolling of the ship carried it hither and thither until it made strange patterns on the deck,' says a Spanish account.

The broadsides of the *Neptune* and the *Conqueror*, helped by the *Africa*, were hitting home in the ship's most vulnerable part —her underwater sections. Shorn of her masts, the *Santissima Trinidad* was rolling considerably in the swell, and first one side and then the other of her weed-stained hull would show above water, and shot would crash in from the British guns. Before the Spanish carpenters' mates could get the shot plugs in position and hammered home, water was flooding across the hold. Men sent to the pumps were cut down by grapeshot and splinters; others who went to take over collapsed at the next broadside.

A splinter hit Commodore Uriarte in the head and knocked him unconscious; the second-in-command, Lt. I. Oleata, was also wounded within a few moments. He managed to drag himself down to the cockpit to report personally to Cisneros that the ship was 'unmanageable, being totally dismasted, a large part of the guns out of action and the rest unable to fire on account of the decks being encumbered with masts, rigging and sails, with many shot holes between wind and water [i.e. on the waterline] and the decks strewn with dead and wounded'.

Cisneros sent his only surviving aide, Don Francisco Basurto, to give fresh orders to the third-in-command; he was to continue the action as long as possible and not to strike before consulting with the surviving officers who were still at their posts. When the third-in-command, who had been below, arrived on the upper-deck he saw that further resistance would be useless. The rest of the officers agreed. But how were they to surrender? There was no mast left, not even a stump, from which a white flag could be flown. Someone discovered a British flag and ran to the gangway waving it.

At last the guns of the *Neptune* and *Conqueror* stopped firing. Lying in heaps, trapped under gun carriages, caught by falling masts and yards, or dragged to one side in the cockpit because the overburdened surgeons reached them too late, were more than two hundred dead Spanish seamen and soldiers; and more than a hundred others were wounded. Fremantle and Pellew then both saw that Dumanoir's van squadron was less than two miles away, coming down southwards, towards them, as if to join in the battle. They could see Bayntun's *Leviathan* boldly steering northwards to meet the enemy, and they too followed.

Digby in the *Africa* had not seen the flag waved from the *Santissima Trinidad*'s gangway, but as she had stopped firing he assumed she had surrendered and ordered Lt John Smith to go across in a boat and take possession. Smith went over, scrambled on board and made his way through the wreckage to the quarter-deck, where a Spanish officer met him. Smith asked him if his ship had struck. Despite the previous flag-waving which had led to the *Neptune* and *Conqueror* ceasing fire, the Spaniard pointed to Dumanoir's squadron, by now drawing closer, and replied, 'No, no!' Smith, who had only a boat's crew with him, left and rowed back to the *Africa*, where Digby was preparing to join the *Neptune* and *Conqueror* and deal with the ships that the Spaniard had used as a reason for changing his mind about surrendering.

In the gloom of the *Victory*'s cockpit Nelson was half-lying, half-sitting on the deck, his back against a thick oak frame. It was the only position that gave him any relief from the gnawing pain in his chest, and Dr Scott and Burke, the purser, squatted down on either side, supporting him. They were soon joined by Chevalier and Gaetano, Nelson's servants, who were anxious to help their master.

The lanterns with their flickering candles swayed, casting eerie shadows which were lengthened and then shortened with the ship's roll. Beatty and his two assistant surgeons hurried from one wounded man to the next, arms scarlet with blood, occasionally ordering someone to be carried to the table to have a limb sawn off. There were groans from some men; screams came from others. More, who had been waiting for the surgeons to reach them, were strangely silent, for death had already stopped their pain.

There were faint cheers from the decks above. 'What is that?' asked Nelson. 'Why are they cheering?' Lt Pasco, lying wounded nearby, raised himself on his elbow. 'Another enemy ship has struck, my Lord.'

Nelson settled back, apparently well satisfied. Occasionally, when particularly bad spasms of pain twisted his emaciated body, he would gasp, 'Fan, fan', and Burke or Scott would wave a cloth in front of him, the cooling air seeming to give him relief. Then he would whisper 'Drink, drink', and they would give him sips of lemonade, or wine and water. Frequently he would ask how the battle was going, his voice revealing his apprehension. Burke and Dr Scott used every argument they could think of to relieve the dying man's anxiety. Burke, trying to comfort him, said: 'The enemy are decisively defeated, and I hope your Lordship will live to be yourself the bearer of the joyful tidings to our country.'

But Nelson, who had seen a man fall and break his back in the *Victory* only a month earlier and had often questioned Beatty in detail about the man's symptoms (for he had taken thirteen days to die) was not to be fooled by such well-meant but clumsy words.

'It is nonsense, Mr Burke,' he gasped, 'to suppose I can live: my sufferings are great, but they will soon be over.' Scott, overwrought and heartbroken, exclaimed: 'Do not despair of living, my Lord,' and added, 'I trust that Divine Providence will restore you once more to your dear country and friends.'

'Ah, doctor!' replied the Admiral. 'It is all over; it is all over.'

For some time Nelson had been very worried about Captain Hardy. Beatty had sent several messengers to fetch him, but the burly Hardy had his hands full dealing with the *Redoutable* alongside, and during the worst of the fighting dare not leave the quarter-deck, although his heart was heavy. Nelson became more and more impatient and anxious about the friend who had served him so faithfully. 'Will no one bring Hardy to me? He must be killed: he is surely destroyed!' A few minutes later Midshipman Richard Bulkley, whose father had served with Nelson twenty-five years earlier in the San Juan Expedition, arrived fresh from the quarter-deck, where he had been acting as aide to the Captain, with a message for Beatty from Hardy.

'Circumstances respecting the Fleet require Captain Hardy's presence on deck,' he said, carefully repeating the message and probably over-conscious of the drama of the occasion, 'but he will avail himself of the first favourable moment to visit his Lordship.'

Nelson overheard the message and asked who had brought it. 'It is Mr Bulkley, my Lord,' said Burke.

'It is his voice,' murmured the Admiral, and raising his voice said to Bulkley: 'Remember me to your father. . . .'

The 'circumstances respecting the Fleet' which now detained Hardy were the ships of Dumanoir's squadron which, as we have seen, had finally turned and were at last sailing down from the north, apparently about to enter the battle. Hardy was carrying Nelson's burden on his shoulders: from the moment the Admiral had fallen wounded, Hardy had in fact been acting as Commander-in-Chief. The *Regulations and Instructions* laid down that if the Commander-in-Chief fell his flag was to be left flying 'till the Battle is ended, and the Enemy is no longer in sight', but the officer next in command was to be told immediately and was to go on board the flagship and take over. This took time and until it happened the responsibility was Hardy's.

By now a new assailant had crashed alongside the *Téméraire*.

Nelson had been wounded about 1.15 p.m. and it will be recalled that the *Victory* and *Redoutable*, lashed together, had the *Téméraire* come alongside, with her mizen and main-topmasts and fore-yard down, at about 1.25 p.m. The fourth ship to join the fray, at about 1.45 p.m., was the *Fougueux* (see Diagram 4 on page 264), commanded by Captain Baudouin. She was a French 74-gun ship and at the beginning of the action she had been immediately astern of Alava's 112-gun *Santa Ana*. As will be related later, it was between these two ships that Collingwood's division had broken the line. In going to the *Santa Ana*'s assistance the *Fougueux* had been raked by the 100-gun *Royal Sovereign* and two seventy-fours, *Belleisle* and *Mars*. With topsail and lower yards shot away she had drifted to the north-west in thick smoke. This cleared in a gentle breeze just in time for Harvey to see her. The *Téméraire*'s powerful starboard broadside had not yet been fired, and Harvey paused, as a spider waiting for the fly to walk into its web, until the *Fougueux* was within one hundred yards.

On all three decks the second captains had cocked the locks and the gun captains were crouching beyond the recoil of the guns, peering over the sights and out into the smoke and daylight beyond the ports. Slowly, like a huge animal lost and blundering about in a yellow fog, the *Fougueux* came into their sights. The lieutenants waited until the *Téméraire*'s starboard side began a downward roll.

'Fire!'

An almost solid wall of round-shot and grape smashed into the *Fougueux* at a range when even grape-shot would go through more than six inches of fir and four inches of oak. The effect on the French ship was devastating: the main and mizzen-masts started to totter; Captain Baudouin collapsed, dying, on the quarter-deck; carriages of many guns were smashed to matchwood; grape-shot and splinters cut down scores of seamen at the guns and soldiers waiting at the bulwarks with muskets. Commander Bazin, the second-in-command, who had been wounded several times earlier, took over command; but the *Fougueux* was out of control, and while the *Téméraire*'s gunners reloaded, the stricken ship glided on towards them through the smoke of the first broadside.

Bazin realized that it would be a matter of seconds before the ships collided, and anticipating the British would try to storm his ship, he ordered all the surviving sailors and soldiers detailed off as boarders to stand by with their muskets, pikes, cutlasses and tomahawks. Again the *Téméraire*'s broadside flung solid shot and grape screaming into the French ship, now almost completely hidden in the swirling, throat-catching smoke. Then, with a rending crash, the *Fougueux* ran into the *Téméraire*, and the impact snapped the wobbling main and mizenmasts and they collapsed over the side. Some of the *Téméraire*'s Marines and sea-men tried to board, but they were beaten back. Captain Harvey then had the carronades, loaded with musket balls, fired across the *Fougeaux*'s decks. (The *Fougeaux*'s earlier moves, against Collingwood's division, are described in the next chapter.)

Bazin, with the captain dead, sent for the third-in-command to help him fight off the boarders and at the same time restore some order on the *Fougueux*'s shattered gun decks. The word soon came back that he too had been killed. Dismayed, Bazin sent for the fourth-in-command—but he was dying. The next in seniority, Lt Peltier, was lying with a musket ball in the leg. Finally Bazin's messenger found one surviving lieutenant, who told him that almost all the lower-deck guns had been silenced and nearly every man who had been serving them was dead. Midshipman Dudrésit, the only surviving officer on the 18-pounder gun-deck, reported every gun out of action and only fifteen of his men left alive. By this time British seamen and Marines, shouting and yelling, were swarming over the bulwarks, lashing out with newly sharpened cutlasses, stabbing with the short-handled boarding pikes, and using their muskets as clubs.

'Seeing the impossibility of repelling boarding, or of defending the ship against the number of the enemies who were getting aboard,' wrote Bazin, 'I gave orders to cease firing and dragged myself, in spite of my wounds, as far as the Captain's cabin to get and throw into the sea the [leaden] box containing the signals and in-structions for the ship, and, reappearing on the quarter-deck, I was taken and conveyed on board the English ship; the enemy hauled down the colours and gradually the slaughter ceased entirely.'

By this time the *Victory* had managed to boom herself off from the *Redoutable* and was moving off to the northwards. Harvey sent his first lieutenant, Kennedy, to the *Fougueux* and another lieutenant to the *Redoutable*, with orders that both ships were 'to be securely lashed to the *Téméraire*'. Then, Captain Harvey wrote in a letter to his wife, 'behold, I was informed some of the enemy's ships were coming up astern of us'.

23

DUFF IS KILLED

'Naval tactics, or the art of war at sea, is limited by the possibilities of navigation; and is therefore much less capable of that variety of stratagem which belongs to the hostility of armies.'

—Steel's *Naval Tactics*, 1797

NELSON had ordered Collingwood with his fifteen ships to attack the last twelve ships in the enemy's line, but Collingwood was free to make his own dispositions and carry out the order as he thought best. We have already seen that very early on he had ordered his ships to form the larboard line of bearing (attacking diagonally, whereas Nelson attacked in column), forming them up diagonally with the *Royal Sovereign* leading to the north. But the line of bearing was never properly formed, because Collingwood would not reduce sail in the *Royal Sovereign* to allow the others to get into position on his quarter: instead he contented himself with signalling his ships to 'Make more sail'. The effect was to put the *Royal Sovereign* well ahead, with seven more ships strung out astern and the rest of the division well behind them.

Although Collingwood later reported that he broke through the enemy line 'about the twelfth from the rear', in fact, as we shall see, he broke through between the fifteenth ship, the *Fougueux*, and the sixteenth, Vice-Admiral Alava's flagship *Santa Ana* (see Diagram 5 on page 273). The result was that the first eight of Collingwood's division attacked sixteen ships of the Combined Fleet: it was nearly an hour after the *Royal Sovereign* opened fire that the first of the other seven managed to get into action.

The weariness wrought by years of responsibility vanished from Collingwood as the *Royal Sovereign*, studding-sails set, bore down on the enemy; gone, for the time being, was his longing for his wife Sarah and the memory of his home and garden. The thought of battle transformed this country-loving Northumbrian to a cold fighting machine, as brave as Nelson but considerably less exuberant. Because his personality was not as colourful, history was destined to pass him by with a nod.

The Plymouth-built *Royal Sovereign*, fresh from the dockyard and her copper bottom still free of weed and barnacles, was belying her nickname of the 'West Country Wagon' and slowly drawing farther ahead of the rest of the division. Rotheram, son of a doctor and like his Admiral a Northumbrian, counted off the enemy ships as they ranged across the *Royal Sovereign*'s bow. Collingwood did the same and, probably not realizing that three more ships were to leeward of the line and masked by the others, numbered off twelve of them. This brought them to the *Fougueux*, which he could see was a 74-gun French ship. Just ahead of her was a Spanish three-decker, quite clearly a flagship. Collingwood pointed her out and told Rotheram to steer between the two ships. At the same time he told him to order the officers to make sure that all the men were lying down on the decks between the guns until they were to fire.

At the bows of the *Royal Sovereign* the figurehead gleamed in the sunshine. It was an appropriate one to adorn the first ship of the British Fleet to go into action in the great battle and was a full-length effigy of George III dressed as a Roman emperor, sword at his side and scarlet cloak on his shoulders. On one side of him was the emblem of Fame, on the other Fortune, and each was blowing a golden trumpet.

Sailing slowly but with easy grace across the swell-waves, the *Royal Sovereign*, the eyes of the fleet upon her, bore down on the *Santa Ana* and *Fougueux*. Slowly the minutes ticked by and the range dropped. From the *Royal Sovereign* sextants measured the angle between the *Santa Ana*'s waterline and the truck of her masts, and reference to a table showed trigonometrically what the eye, because of the slow speed, hardly detected. Three degrees fourteen minutes—she was 1,300 yards away . . . three and a half degrees—1,200 yards . . . three degrees forty-nine minutes— 1,100 yards. The mass of enemy ships ahead would be opening fire any second now. Four degrees ten minutes—that gave a range of 1,000 yards, and the time was 11.58 a.m.

'Open fire!' ordered Captain Baudouin aboard the *Fougueux*, and from the *Royal Sovereign* they could see two lines of gun ports spout red flame and then breathe coils of yellow smoke. As the reverberating rumble of the first broadside reached them, more flashes rippled in a triple tier from the *Santa Ana* ahead of the *Fougueux*, and smoke wreathed the gun ports of the Spanish *Monarca* astern. They were followed by the *San Justo* and *San*

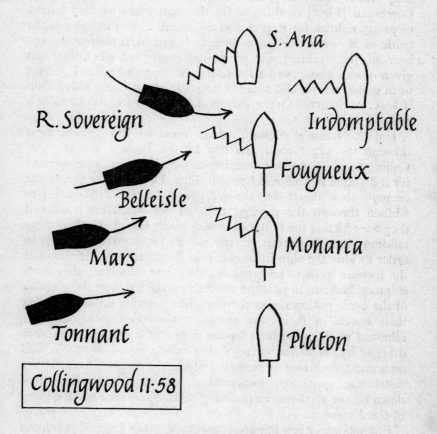

DIAGRAM 5: Approach of Collingwood's division: *Fougueux* opens fire
at 11.58

Leandro, ahead of the *Santa Ana,* and the *Pluton* and *Algésiras* astern of the *Monarca.*

One of the *Royal Sovereign*'s seamen, writing to his father after the battle, said: 'I told brother Tom I should like to see a greadly [*sic*] battle, and I have seen one, and we have peppered the Combined [Fleet] rarely; and for the matter of that they fought us pretty tightish for French and Spanish. . . . But to tell you the truth of it, when the game began, I wished myself at Warnborough [Hampshire] with my plough again; but when they had given us one duster, and I found myself snug and tight, I . . . set to in good earnest, and thought no more about being killed than if I were at Murrell Green Fair, and I was presently as black as a collier.'

Unlike Nelson's column, where most of the vessels went through the gap torn in the line by the *Victory,* the ships of Collingwood's division, advancing on a broad front, were steering for individual French and Spanish ships. For a minute or two the enemy's shot hissed into the sea round the *Royal Sovereign* or whined through the rigging; then an occasional crash showed they were hitting the hull, either with direct hits or ricochets from random shots bouncing off the water. Collingwood, partly in order to hide the ship in smoke, told Rotheram to order some of the forward guns to be fired. Within a few moments, after midshipmen had run to pass the word down the hatches, the muzzles of the guns, poking out of the ports like pointing fingers, erupted their quotas of flame and smoke and recoiled in again, as if ashamed of firing without having a proper target. The minutes dragged by. With the enemy's shot falling round them like hail on a pond, each minute seemed a lifetime; but magnificent in her stateliness, apparently unperturbed, the *Royal Sovereign* bore down for the gap between the stern of the *Santa Ana* and the bows of the *Fougueux.*

She was only a few hundred yards away when Captain Baudouin of the *Fougueux* made a desperate attempt to close the gap: he ordered the main-topgallant sail to be hoisted and sheeted home and the mail-topsail braced around and sheeted in so that it would fill. Gradually the *Fougueux* gathered way, and at the same time the Spanish *Santa Ana*'s mizen-topsail was backed to slow her down. The sharp-eyed Rotheram pointed this out to Collingwood; but the Admiral knew it was too late to try to break through elsewhere.

'Steer for the Frenchman and carry away his bowsprit!' ordered Collingwood. Rotheram quickly passed new helm orders to the Master, and slowly the *Royal Sovereign*'s massive bowsprit began to swing slightly to starboard as Rotheram, allowing for the headway the *Fougueux* was making, selected a spot for the two ships to meet. Baudouin, realizing at the last moment that the British ship intended to smash her way through, quickly ordered the *Fougueux*'s main-topsail to be backed. Almost immediately his ship slowed up, leaving the *Royal Sovereign* just enough room to get past.

As she forged through the gap, the British ship's larboard guns fired a whole broadside into the unprotected stern of the *Santa Ana*. The effect was even more dreadful than in the *Bucentaure* and *Santissima Trinidad*. As successive guns bore and fired their triple-shotted quota, much of the solid planking and rich carvings on the transom was smashed in as if by huge invisible fists, and the shot and splinters spun on down the decks, cutting down men and overturning fourteen guns. Rotheram ordered the helm to be put over and as the men worked swiftly in the choking smoke to reload the larboard guns, the *Royal Sovereign* swung round to larboard to come alongside the Spanish ship. But as she turned, Baudouin fired the *Fougueux*'s full broadside into her starboard quarter, and the 80-gun *Indomptable*, from only five hundred yards away on the British flagship's starboard beam, fired another. (See Diagram 6 on p. 277.)

In the meantime the *Santa Ana*'s captain had guessed that the *Royal Sovereign* would swing round and come alongside to leeward, and had brought all the larboard-side guns' crews over to reinforce those on the starboard side. When the British ship came alongside, their yardarms touching as the two great vessels rolled in the swell, the Spanish gunners fired. According to Collingwood's biographer the *Royal Sovereign* heeled considerably under the impact of the 112-gun *Santa Ana*'s broadside. At the same time two more Spanish ships, the *San Justo* and *San Leandro*, which were well ahead, swung round and started firing into the *Royal Sovereign*, and the French *Neptune*, which was in between them, followed suit. Collingwood's flagship was thus being engaged by three Spanish and three French ships.

Many of the enemy shots cut through the rigging; the studding-sails were slashed to pieces. Collingwood, standing on the poop amid the smoke and noise as unconcerned as if he had been

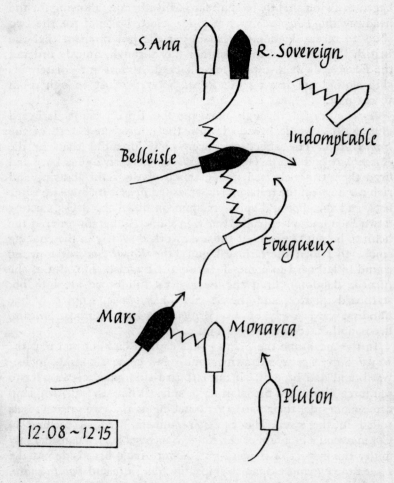

DIAGRAM 6: At 12.08 *Royal Sovereign* rakes *Santa Ana* and then luffs alongside. *Indomptable* opens fire on *R. Sovereign*. 12.11 *Belleisle* rakes *Santa Ana* and opens fire on *Fougueux*. 12.15 *Mars* engages *Monarca*. *Pluton* passes *Monarca* to leeward

standing in the orchard of his home at Morpeth, ordered Captain Vallack to take his Marines off the poop, where they were unnecessarily exposed. Then he walked down to the quarter-deck and talked to the men at the guns, warning them not to waste a shot. Frequently he bent down and looked along a gun-sight before it was fired into one of the *Santa Ana*'s ports. He particularly praised a coloured seaman who, with the Admiral beside him, fired ten rounds at the Spanish ship.

A studding-sail, its halyard shot away, came tumbling down and fell across the hammock nettings at the gangway. This was more than Collingwood's economical nature could stand. He called to Clavell to come and give him a hand to get the studding-sail in, and while the gunners in the *Santa Ana* and the *Royal Sovereign* fired broadside after broadside as fast as they could load, the Admiral and the lieutenant carefully rolled up the canvas and carried it across to a boat resting on the booms.[1]

A few moments later Rotheram came up to the Admiral. It seemed that the *Santa Ana*'s gunners were now shooting less vigorously, and delighted at the thought of capturing a Spanish admiral single-handed in the midst of his own fleet, he seized Collingwood's hand and declared: 'I must congratulate you, sir: she is slackening her fire and must soon strike.' But they were to be disappointed: even though the larboard gunners did their best, the Spanish ship kept pounding away. Collingwood escaped death by what was almost a miracle and was wounded, although he refused to have the fact officially reported. It was five months later that he wrote to his wife, 'Did I not tell you how my leg was hurt? It was by a splinter—a pretty severe blow. I had a good many thumps, one way or the other; one in the back, which I think was the wind of a great shot, for I never saw anything that did it.'

The *Royal Sovereign*'s Master, Mr William Chalmers, was killed at Collingwood's side, and in the same letter the Admiral described it. 'A great shot almost divided his body: he laid his head upon my shoulder, and told me he was slain. I supported him till two men carried him off. He could say nothing to me, but to bless me; but as they carried him down, he wished he could but live to read the account of the action in a newspaper. He lay in

[1] Nearly nine years earlier, in the middle of the Battle of Cape St Vincent, where he had commanded the *Excellent*, Collingwood had looked up and then called out to the bosun, 'Bless me, Mr Peffers, how came we to forget to bend our old topsail? They will quite ruin that new one! It will never be worth a farthing again.'

the cockpit, among the wounded, until the *Santa Ana* struck; and, joining in the cheer which they gave her, expired with it on his lips.'

By now the other ships in Collingwood's division were coming into action. The *Belleisle*, which had been on the *Royal Sovereign*'s starboard quarter, had suffered worse from the enemy broadsides as she approached the line. Captain Hargood, short and stocky, a man of few words, had previously sent for his officers and said: 'Gentlemen, I have only this to say: that I shall pass under the stern of that ship.' He pointed to Vice-Admiral Alava's flagship, whose great figurehead, an effigy of the mother of the Virgin, garbed in red, could now be clearly seen in the sunlight.

'Put in two round shot and then a grape,' he said, 'and give her *that*. Now go to your quarters and mind not to fire until each gun will bear with effect.' With this laconic instruction, reported Lt Nicolas, of the Royal Marines, 'the gallant little man posted himself on the slide of the foremost carronade on the starboard side of the quarterdeck.'

By this time several ships were firing at the *Royal Sovereign* over on the larboard bow and others, says Nicolas, were beginning to shoot at the *Belleisle*, 'and gave us an intimation of what we should in a few minutes undergo. An awful silence prevailed in the ship, only interrupted by the commanding voice of Captain Hargood. "Steady! Starboard a little! Steady so!" echoed by the Master directing the quartermaster at the wheel.

'A shriek soon followed—a cry of agony was produced by the next shot—the loss of a head of a poor recruit was the effect of the succeeding—and, as we advanced, destruction rapidly increased.'

Hargood suddenly fell from where he was standing on the carronade slide, hit in the chest by a flat side of a splinter. He escaped with severe bruising, and refused to be taken below. Within a few minutes he was back on the slide, directing operations. He had given orders that as many people as possible were to lie down, to avoid being wounded. The shot were by now streaming in over the bow, tearing at the heavy timbers, the sails and the rigging, sending up sparks as they crashed into metal, and scooping up scores of splinters as they burrowed into wood.

'Those only who have been in a similar situation to the one I am attempting to describe', declared Lt Nicolas, 'can have a correct idea of such a scene. My eyes were horror-struck at the bloody corpses around me, and my ears rang with the shrieks of the wounded and the moans of the dying.

'At this moment, seeing that almost everyone was lying down, I was half disposed to follow the example, and several times stooped for the purpose, but—and I remember the impression well—a certain monitor seemed to whisper "stand up and do not shrink from your duty."

'Turning round, my much esteemed and gallant senior [Lt John Owen] fixed my attention; the serenity of his countenance and the composure with which he paced the deck, drove more than half my terror away; and joining him, I became somewhat infused with his spirit, which cheered me on to act the part it became me!'

Nicolas goes on: 'It was just twelve o'clock[1] when we reached their line. Our energies became roused and the mind diverted from its appalling condition, by the order "Stand to your guns!"'

By this time the French and Spanish broadsides were beginning to tell against the British seventy-four. 'Although until that moment we had not fired a shot, our sails and rigging bore evident proofs of the manner in which we had been treated: our mizen-topmast was shot away and the ensign had been thrice re-hoisted; numbers lay dead upon the decks, and eleven wounded were already in the surgeon's care. The firing was now tremendous, and at intervals the dispersion of the smoke gave us a sight of the colour of our adversaries.'

There was no need to send men aloft to cut the halyards and bring the studding-sails in with a rush at the last moment, for the enemy's swirling chain shot had torn them down, and before the *Belleisle* could bring her first broadsides to bear, more than fifty of her men had been killed or wounded. Soon she had the *Santa Ana* in the sights of her guns, and the whole larboard broadside crashed out; almost immediately the starboard broadside was fired into the *Fougueux*, and the smoke drifted on ahead of the *Belleisle*, almost hiding the *Indomptable* ahead and the *San Justo* beyond the *Santa Ana*.

Nicolas describes the next few moments: 'At this critical period, while steering for the stern of the *Indomptable* (our masts and yards and sails hanging in utmost confusion over our heads), which continued a galling raking fire upon us, the *Fougueux* being

[1] In fact it was 12.11 p.m.

on our starboard quarter and the Spanish *San Justo* on our larboard bow, the Master earnestly addressed the Captain, 'Shall we go through, sir?'

'"Go through, by ——" was his energetic reply. "There's your ship, sir; place me alongside her!" '

The Master brought the *Belleisle* round to starboard (see Diagram 6 on page 276) to go round the stern of the *Indomptable* and come up on her lee side, but suddenly out of the great banks of smoke, sails hanging from masts like old clothes on a scarecrow, the *Fougueux* loomed up very close on the starboard quarter, and in a few moments her larboard bow crashed against the *Belleisle*'s starboard gangway.

While the after guns on the *Belleisle*'s starboard side fired into the *Fougueux* at the range of a few feet, the crews of those farther forward hastily got their handspikes under the carriages to heave them round to get them to bear. As the two ships drifted together almost covered in smoke, the conditions on the gun decks were appalling. One man wrote: 'At every moment the smoke accumulated more and more thickly, stagnating on board between decks at times so densely as to blur over the nearest objects and often blot out the men at the guns from those close at hand on each side. The guns had to be trained, as it were, mechanically by means of orders passed down from above, and on objects that the men fighting the guns hardly ever got a glimpse of. In these circumstances you frequently heard the order on the main and lower deck to level the guns "two points abaft the beam", "point blank", and so on.

'In fact, the men were as much in the dark as to the external objects as if they had been blindfolded, and the only comfort to be derived from this serious inconvenience was that every man was so isolated from his neighbour that he was not put in mind of his danger by seeing his messmates go down all round.

'All that he knew was that he heard the crash of the shot smashing through the rending timbers, and then followed at once the hoarse bellowings of the captains of the guns, as men were missed at their posts, calling out to the survivors: "Close up there! Close up." '

The *Indomptable*, saved by the *Fougueux*, turned to starboard and fired a broadside into the *Belleisle*. Then, as if she considered her part in the battle fulfilled, she drifted away to leeward into the smoke, like a poacher vanishing in the mist. Locked together, the

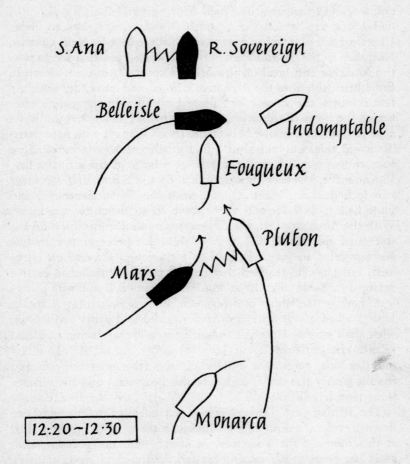

DIAGRAM 7: At 12.20 *Mars* and *Pluton* in close action. 12.30 *Fougueux* collides with *Belleisle*. *Monarca* bears away

Fougueux and *Belleisle* slowly fell away to leeward, hammering away at each other.

By now Captain Duff's 74-gun *Mars* was in action. The *Fougueux*, going ahead to engage the *Royal Sovereign* and then the *Belleisle*, had left a gap which the Spanish *Monarca* was slow to close. Captain Duff planned to pass through there, but Captain Cosmao Kerjulien in the 74-gun *Pluton*, quickly set all possible sail to pass the *Monarca* and head off the *Mars*. Captain Duff came down to fire a broadside into the *Monarca*, who turned away, but within a few minutes the *Pluton* had ranged ahead into the gap, nearly across the bows of the *Mars*, a position from which she would be able to pour in a raking broadside. (See Diagram 7 on page 281.) To avoid this, Captain Duff luffed up the *Mars* to windward on to a course parallel with the *Pluton*, who kept up a heavy fire. But now the *Mars* was fast approaching the *Santa Ana*, who was still locked in a violent struggle with the *Royal Sovereign*, and Duff had to luff up and then heave to in order to avoid her. With the *Mars* stopped, the *Pluton* was in an ideal position on the starboard quarter of the British ship. Desperately the British gunners tried to get their guns to train round far enough aft to bear, but Cosmao realized that he had only to luff and to pour a raking broadside into the *Mars*. (See Diagram 8 opposite.)

A young Banffshire midshipman, Robinson, wrote: 'Captain Duff walked about with steady fortitude, and said: "My God, what shall we do? Here is a Spanish three-decker raking us ahead [*Santa Ana*], a French one [*Pluton*] under our stern!" In a few minutes our poop was totally cleared, the quarter-deck and foc's'le nearly the same, and only the Boatswain and myself and three men left alive.'

The British ship *Tonnant* was now entering the fray and bore down to rake the *Pluton*, who luffed to try to rake her first. But at this moment the *Fougueux*, in action with the *Belleisle*, shot away her antagonist's mizenmast and drifted clear, getting into a perfect position to rake the stricken *Mars*.

Captain Norman, commanding the Marines on board the *Mars*, spotted her through the swirling smoke and ran to the quarter-deck to warn Captain Duff; but the *Mars* was hemmed in, and this combined with the fact that the wind had fallen away, prevented the ship from manœuvring. Norman pointed out the *Fougueux*. 'Do you think our guns will bear on her?' asked Duff.

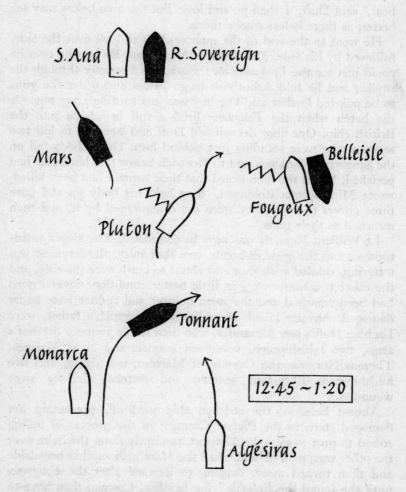

DIAGRAM 8: At 12.15 *Mars* luffs to avoid *Santa Ana*. 1.0 *Pluton* rakes *Mars*. *Tonnant* bears down to rake *Pluton*. 1.10 *Fougueux* drifts clear of *Belleisle*, rakes *Mars* and falls away to leeward, where eventually meets *Téméraire*. *Algésiras* runs aboard *Tonnant*

'I think not,' replied Norman, 'but I cannot see for smoke.'

'Then we must point our guns on the ships on which they will bear,' said Duff. 'I shall go and look, but the men below may see better, as there is less smoke there.'

He went to the end of the quarter-deck to look over the side, followed by his aide, Midshipman Arbuthnot. By leaning over he could just see the *Fougueux* on the starboard quarter through the smoke, and he told Arbuthnot to go below and order the guns to be pointed farther aft. The boy was just turning away towards the hatch when the *Fougueux* fired a full broadside into the British ship. One shot decapitated Duff and went on to kill two seamen who were standing just behind him. Duff's body fell on the gangway. Word was sent to Norwich below that his father had perished. When the men heard that their captain had been killed, wrote Midshipman Robinson, 'they held his body up and gave three cheers to show they were not discouraged by it, and then returned to their guns.'

Lt William Hennah was now in command. The ship's maintopmast and the spanker-boom were shot away; the foremast was tottering, riddled with shot and about to crash over the side, and the other two masts were in little better condition; several guns had been smashed and the stern quarter and rudder were badly damaged. Already killed, in addition to Norwich's father, were Lachlan Duff's son Alexander, who died in his younger brother's arms, two midshipmen, seventeen seamen and eight Marines. Thomas Norman, the Captain of Marines, was dying, and five midshipmen, forty-four seamen and sixteen Marines were wounded.

Almost helpless, the stricken ship paid off, presenting her damaged stern to the *Pluton*. Cosmao, in the process of luffing round to port to rake the *Tonnant*, promptly flung the helm over the other way, paid off and raked the *Mars* with another broadside and then turned away, drifting to leeward after the *Fougueux* until she found the *Belleisle* lying helpless. Cosmao then hove-to the *Pluton* on the British ship's port quarter and opened fire.

The *Tonnant* (which, we have already seen, had fired at the *Pluton* in an attempt to help the *Mars*) had earlier come down to break the line through the gap between the stern of the Spanish 74-gun *Monarca* and the bows of the French *Algésiras*, which was flying the flag of Rear-Admiral Magon. Two of the *Tonnant*'s bandsmen, who had been busy playing 'Britons, Strike Home',

were wounded, along with nine other men during the approach.
Captain Tyler took his ship between the *Monarca* and *Algésiras*
—'so close', according to Lt Hoffman, 'that a biscuit might have
been thrown on either of them.' (See Diagram 8 on page 283.)
He adds: 'Our guns were all double-shotted. The order was given
to fire; being so close, every shot was poured into their hulls, and
down came the Frenchman's [*Algésiras*'s] mizenmast, and after our
second broadside the Spaniard's [*Monarca*'s] fore and crossjack
yards.'

Her third broadside at the *Monarca* thundered out as the
Tonnant came on to a course parallel with the Spanish ship. 'We
gave her such a murdering broadside,' wrote one officer, 'that
she did not return a gun for some minutes.' But even when some
of her guns did get into action the *Monarca* was too badly damaged
to put up a fight, and gradually she dropped astern, hauling down
her colours. The *Tonnant* went ahead, still firing at the *Algésiras*
to starboard. Then the *Monarca*, apparently finding herself safe
for a while, rehoisted her colours.

Seeing the *Pluton* ahead on the starboard bow sending broadside
after broadside into the helpless *Mars*, Tyler brought the *Tonnant*
round to starboard and fired his larboard broadside into Cosmao's
ship. But this was the chance for which Magon, in the *Algésiras*,
was waiting: quickly he had the main and mizen-topsails braced
round and sheeted home so that the ship would forge ahead and
cross under the *Tonnant*'s stern, giving him a chance to cripple her
with a raking broadside. Tyler immediately brought the *Tonnant*
around to starboard and before Magon could do anything the
Algésiras's bow had crashed into the *Tonnant* amidships on the
starboard side, her long bowsprit hooking into the British ship's
main rigging, holding her in position. None of the French guns
could be brought to bear, but almost every one of the *Tonnant*'s
starboard guns were able to rake the *Algésiras*. Her carronades,
loaded with musket balls, and her quarter-deck guns fired and,
reported Commander Laurent Le Tourneur, commanding the
Algésiras, 'totally stripped us of our rigging'.

Magon at once gave orders for the *Tonnant* to be boarded. Lt
Verdreau gathered a boarding party while sharpshooters in the
Algésiras's tops kept up a heavy fire on the *Tonnant*'s upper works
with their muskets. Led by Verdreau, the boarders ran to the
bows, intending to scramble on to the bowsprit and clamber on
board the British ship, but at that moment the British carronades

and quarter-deck guns blasted them with grape-shot and musket balls and most of them, including Verdreau, were killed.

One of the Frenchmen, however, escaped and managed to get aboard the *Tonnant*. He had no sooner set foot on her quarter-deck than a British sailor lunged at him with a half-pike, which went through his right leg. Another was just about to cut him down with a cutlass when Lt Hoffman shouted to him to put up his sword and take the Frenchman down to the cockpit to have his wound dressed.

The battle between the two ships went on for more than an hour. Passing British ships sent their broadsides into the *Algésiras*, which gradually swung round until she was alongside the *Tonnant*, instead of being held by the bowsprit. Hoffman wrote that the sides of the two ships were grinding against each other so much as they pitched and rolled in the swell 'that we were obliged to fire our lower deck guns without running them out'.

Blazing wads from the *Tonnant*'s guns eventually started a fire in the French ship's boatswain's store, killing three men. 'At length,' Hoffman wrote, 'both ships caught fire before the chess-trees, and our firemen, with all the coolness and courage so inherent in British seamen, got the [fire] engine and played it on both ships, and finally extinguished the flames, although two of them were severely wounded in doing so.'

Firing with great coolness, the British gunners gradually got the upper hand. Cdr Le Tourneur reported that on board the *Algésiras*, Magon, 'feeling our position to be critical, went about everywhere encouraging us by his presence and displaying the most heroic coolness and courage'. While he was doing this he was hit in the arm by a musket ball, and later a splinter hit him in the thigh; but the Breton carried on cheering up his men. The *Algésiras*'s foremast crashed over the side and the *Tonnant*'s fire continued clearing the enemy's upper decks.

Le Tourneur was wounded in the shoulder; his second-in-command, Morel, was soon carried down to the cockpit after him. The navigating officer, Lt Leblond-Plassan, was hit in the chest with a bullet. Then Magon, who had refused the pleading of his officers that he should go below to have his wounds dressed because he was bleeding badly, collapsed on to the deck, killed by a bullet in the chest.

'Our 18-pounder battery was at this time deserted and utterly silenced,' says Le Tourneur. 'We collected all our men in the 36-

pounder battery, which continued to be served by them with the utmost activity.'

These guns were doing a considerable amount of damage in the *Tonnant*. Captain Tyler had been carried below wounded and Lt John Bedford had taken over command. Down in the cockpit the surgeon, Forbes Chevers, was busy amputating torn limbs by the dim and flickering light of tallow candles held by two assistants, whom he had told, 'If you look straight into the wound, and see all that I do, I shall see perfectly.' (When later he washed his face he found that the candles had completely burnt his eyebrows.)

Chevers was being helped by the Purser, Mr George Booth, and 'a very powerful and resolute woman', the wife of a petty officer, who had somehow contrived to be on board. She and Booth, who was a small but agile man, 'carried the sailors who had been operated upon to their temporary berths, taking them up in their arms as if they had been children, in a manner which Chevers, himself a tall and very strong young man, always spoke of with expressions of wonder.'

But not all the wounded had gone down to the cockpit. White, one of the captains of the carronades on the poop, had his right toe nearly severed. He took his knife and cut it off, and when Hoffman told him to go below to the cockpit he replied, 'No, sir, I am not the fellow to go below for such a scratch as that. I wish to give the beggars a few more hard pills before I have done with them.' He then untied the handkerchief round his head, used it to bind up his foot, and went back to his carronade.

Another seaman, Fitzgerald, climbed over the side of the *Tonnant* and scrambled up the rigging of the *Algésiras* to where a Tricolour was lashed. After cutting it away he tied it round his waist and began to climb down again, but a French sharpshooter saw him and opened fire. Fitzgerald was hit and fell, plunging between the two ships.

When Captain Tyler sent for Hoffman, the young Lieutenant went down to the cockpit where he saw a Marine he knew standing in a queue, an arm shattered by grape-shot.

'What's the matter, Conolly?'

'Not much,' replied the Marine. 'I am only winged above my elbow, and I'm waiting my turn to be lopped.'

At this time there were fourteen men waiting to have an arm or leg amputated. (Of the sixteen men who were eventually to undergo amputations, only two survived.)

Up on deck again, says Hoffman, they had the satisfaction of seeing the *Algésiras*'s remaining mast 'go by the board, ripping the partners up in their fall, as they had been shot through below the deck, and carrying with them all their sharpshooters to look sharper in the next world, for as all our boats were shot through we could not save one of them in this.'

The French ship was now at the end of her resistance. 'The final broadsides from the enemy so crippled us that they forced us to cease fire,' wrote Commander Le Tourneur. Immediately Lt Bedford ordered the second lieutenant, Charles Bennett, to take the boarding party and capture her. Waving cutlasses, pikes and tomahawks, sixty of the *Tonnant*'s crew, with Bennett leading them, scrambled on board the *Algésiras*. 'They cheered and in a short time carried her,' according to Hoffman. Seventy-seven Frenchmen had been killed and 142 wounded. The boarding party found Magon's body lying at the bottom of the poop ladder.

But the battle, for the *Tonnant*, was not yet over. Commodore Churruca's *San Juan Nepomuceno* had, as will be told later, already been in action with the *Defiance* and the *Dreadnought*. Now badly damaged, she appeared to the south. The *Algésiras* drifted away, and the *Tonnant* was able to use her whole starboard broadside to engage. 'We returned her salute with interest, and her foremast went about four feet above her deck. We cheered and gave her another broadside, and down came her colours.'

The fourth lieutenant, Benjamin Clement, hailed her amid the smoke and noise to make sure she had struck, and when a Spaniard shouted back that they had indeed surrendered, Clement ran aft to tell Lt Bedford. He was then ordered to go aboard the *San Juan Nepomuceno* and take possession of her. 'We had no boat but was shot, but he told me I must try,' says Clement.

With Maclay, a quartermaster, and Macnamara, a coloured seaman, he climbed down into a damaged jolly-boat and they started to row the few score yards to the Spanish ship. They had not covered a quarter of the way when a random shot skimming over the waves smashed in the transom, swamping the boat. Maclay and Macnamara immediately struck out to swim back to the ship, but when they saw that Clement could not swim they turned back and supported him, one on each side. Slowly the trio made their way to the *Tonnant*, bobbing up and down on the swell, until they reached the ship's side, where they found the

The Death of Nelson. The main figures, from left to right, are Lt Yule, Midshipman Collingwood and Nelson's valet, Gaetano, Dr Scott (with his hand on Nelson's chest), Burke (with his arm round the Admiral), Chevalier (in white shirt) and Dr Beatty, who is holding Nelson's hand. *From the painting by Devas*

jolly-boat falls—the tackles used to raise and lower the boat—
still hanging down in the water.

Clement managed to get his leg over one of the falls, and 'as the
ship lifted with the sea,' he wrote, 'so was I, and as she descended
I was ducked; I found myself weak and I thought I was not long
for this world.'

Macnamara managed to scramble on board and found a rope,
which he flung over the side. He jumped back into the water and
secured it under Clement's arms. The bedraggled lieutenant was
then hauled in through a stern port. 'In a short time I felt better
and the anxiety of the time roused me, and I soon returned to my
quarters,' he reported.

K

24

THE SHARPSHOOTERS

'Our God and sailor we adore
In time of danger, not before,
The danger past, both are alike requited,
God is forgotten and the sailor slighted.'
—Old saying quoted by Nelson

THE FIFTH ship in Collingwood's division, Captain John Cooke's 74-gun *Bellerophon*, had come down on to the Combined Fleet's line where there were four seventy-fours—the French *Aigle* and *Swiftsure*, and the Spanish *Montañes* and *Bahama*, which was well up to windward of the others. The *Swiftsure*, although now flying the Tricolour, was a former sister-ship of the *Bellerophon* and was laid down in the same building programme during the American War, later being captured by the French.[1]

Cooke was steering the *Bellerophon*, in the rapidly falling wind, to pass under the stern of the *Bahama* and ahead of the *Aigle*. The latter, although a 74-gun ship like herself, was more powerful, having 40-pounders to the British 32-pounders. About a hundred and fifty of the *Aigle*'s crew of 750 were soldiers; her tops were packed with sharpshooters. Dozens of other men were standing by with grenades, ready to lob them on to the *Bellerophon*'s decks. The *Bellerophon*, her black and yellow sides gleaming, was ready for battle: her guns were double-shotted, the two carronades on the fo'c'sle were each loaded with thirty-two pounds of musket balls, and the six smaller ones on the poop held eighteen pounds.

On the quarter-deck Captain Cooke watched and waited with Cumby, Wemyss and Overton. Nearby was Cooke's thirteen-year-old aide, Midshipman George Pearson, the son of a West Country parson. On the poop the Marines stood with muskets loaded, while the signal lieutenant chatted to Midshipman Franklin. Alexander Whyte, the surgeon, was waiting in the cock-pit with his surgical instruments; Russel Mant, the Bosun, was

[1] The *Bellerophon* was built at Frindsbury, on the Medway, to Sir Thomas Slade's design, dated 1759. She cost £30,232 14s. 3d. and was launched on October 6, 1786.

on the fo'c'sle watching the ships ahead. Altogether nearly six hundred men in the ship waited for their part in the battle to begin.

The *Royal Sovereign* had just broken through the line and the *Belleisle* was about to follow her when, at 12.10 p.m., one of the *Bellerophon*'s midshipmen tripped over a trigger-line. The lock was cocked and the gun went off. The enemy ships ahead apparently thought that this must be some pre-arranged signal, according to one of the *Bellerophon*'s officers, and the *Aigle*, *Bahama*, *Montañes* and *Swiftsure* opened fire on her together. As the enemy shots started whining through the rigging and crashing into the hull, Captain Cooke ordered some of the forward guns to be fired, so that the *Bellerophon* would be partly hidden in her own smoke, which would drift down ahead of her on to the French and Spanish ships.

There was almost a calm now; the *Bellerophon* was down to under two knots—a little faster than a horse dragged a plough across the flat soil of Cooke's native Essex. Slowly she bore down on the enemy line until, at 12.25, seventeen minutes after the *Royal Sovereign* broke through to the northwards, she had the *Bahama* coming into the sights of her larboard guns and *Montañes* into those to starboard.

The tension in the belly of every man on the gun decks, forced to endure the broadsides of four enemy ships without being able to fire back, eased as the lieutenants raised their speaking trumpets. The guns were trained as far forward as possible; and crouched well back, his eyes squinting over the sight, each captain took a firm grip on the trigger-line.

'Fire!'

One after another the larboard guns plunged in a welter of noise and smoke, the crash of the explosions merging into the rumble of the trucks recoiling across the decks.

A few moments later the *Montañes* loomed up in the sights of the starboard guns. There was a brief pause as the gunners waited for the ship's roll, and then, with shattering suddenness the broadside smashed into the Spanish ship. While the guns on both sides were being reloaded, Captain Cooke ordered Overton to bring the *Bellerophon* round to larboard to range up alongside the *Bahama*, but as the ship was swinging they saw in the dirty yellow smoke off to leeward the topgallants of another ship, very close on the starboard side. Cooke bellowed out helm orders and the quarter-masters spun the wheel while sail-trimmers scrambled for the

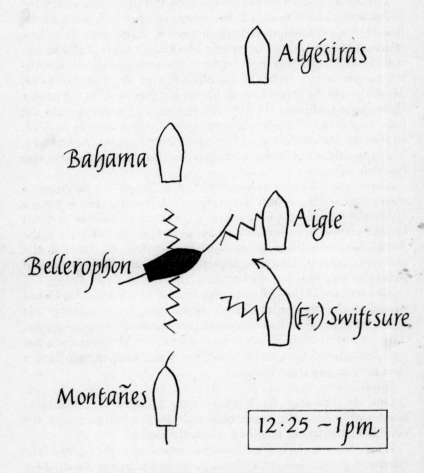

DIAGRAM 9: *Bellerophon* under fire from *Algésiras*, *Bahama*, *Aigle* and *Montañes*; breaks line, raking *Bahama* and *Montañes*. 12.30 *Bellerophon* sees *Aigle* through smoke and *Aigle* tries to avoid collision. French *Swiftsure* luffs to avoid *Aigle* and gets raked by *Bellerophon*, who then goes aboard *Aigle*

braces to haul the yards round and get the sails aback, checking the *Bellerophon*'s way. (See Diagram 9 opposite.)

The seconds sped by with unwanted swiftness and gradually the great ship slowed down, but the smoke thinned and they just had time to read the name *Aigle* carved on the ship's stern before the *Bellerophon*'s starboard bow crashed into the Frenchman's larboard quarter, catching her fore-yard in the enemy's main-yard.

Immediately, reported Lt Asmus Classen, of the *Aigle*, the two ships 'engaged with the utmost fury'. The French *Swiftsure*, coming up astern of the *Aigle* in the smoke, suddenly saw her and the *Bellerophon* locked together and had to luff up quickly, throwing her sails aback. This swung her so that her bows were pointing at the *Bellerophon*'s quarter, and the British ship's after-guns quickly seized the chance of raking her. The *Bellerophon* was now caught between four of the enemy: the *Aigle* alongside on her starboard bow, the *Swiftsure* on the quarter, the *Bahama* away on the larboard bow, and the *Montañes* on the larboard quarter. All kept up a brisk fire on the British ship, which concentrated most of her efforts on the *Aigle*.

While the British Marines, crouching down behind the bulwarks and hammock nettings of the *Bellerophon*'s poop, kept up a heavy fire with their muskets at the men on the *Aigle*'s quarter-decks, the gunners at the carronades sent a rain of musket balls and shot smashing across her decks, cutting down men in swathes. The *Aigle*'s commanding officer, Captain Gourrège, collapsed dying from five wounds, and was carried down to the cockpit, leaving Commander Tempié in charge.

Aboard the *Bellerophon* Captain Cooke, realizing that the battle with the *Aigle* would be a bitter one, ordered Cumby to go round the main and lower decks and order the officers to keep the starboard guns firing at all costs, using the men from the larboard side as reinforcements or replacements if necessary, and at the same time elevating the guns so that the shot would smash upwards through the enemy's decks, causing the maximum amount of damage.

Cumby went down to the main-deck where, amid the thick smoke, he found the lieutenants and gave them their instructions. He then plunged down to the din and darkness of the lower-deck, where the massive 32-pounders were crashing out and recoiling like great berserk animals trying to break free from restraining ropes. Threading his way through scampering powder-monkeys, avoiding trigger lines, coughing as the acrid smoke entered his lungs, he gave his orders and scrambled up the ladder to the main-deck.

As he walked aft, senses reeling from the din and lungs gulping fresh air, he saw a couple of men carrying Overton, the Master. He had one leg hanging down, shattered by a shot, and as blood trailed dripping to the deck and mingled with the sand, his life ebbed away. Before Cumby reached the quarter-deck ladder a quartermaster ran up to him. 'The Captain's been wounded, sir!' he shouted. 'I believe he's dead!'

Cumby found the quarter-deck and poop a bloodstained shambles. Of the fifty-eight men who had been on the *Bellerophon*'s quarter-deck, fifty-four had been cut down by shot, splinters, grenades or musket balls. Captain Cooke had been firing his pistols at Frenchmen on the *Aigle*'s quarter-deck and was just reloading them—standing at the same spot where Captain Paisley, commanding the ship at The Glorious First of June, had his leg shot off—when two musket balls hit him in the chest. He collapsed and a quartermaster ran to his side, asking if he should take him below.

'No,' gasped Cooke, 'let me lie quietly one minute.'

But before the minute had passed he had died. His aide, young Midshipman Pearson, had run across the deck to him but was hit in the thigh with a splinter and fell a few yards away. A burly seaman picked up the boy to carry him down to the cockpit, and at the quarter-deck ladder they met Cumby coming up to take command. Seeing the white-faced lad Cumby paused a moment and above the din said: 'Pearson, my boy, I am sorry you have been hit, but never mind—you and I'll talk over this day's work fifty years hence, depend upon it.'

On the lower-decks the French and British guns' crews were fighting each other through the ports. A midshipman at one group of guns reported that they were battering each other with rammers, slashing out with cutlasses and firing muskets. The French were also hurling grenades through the ports. One of these, wrote another midshipman, burst and killed or wounded more than twenty-five men, 'many of whom were dreadfully scorched. One of the sufferers, in his agony, instead of going down to the surgeon, ran aft and threw himself out of one of the stern-ports.'

The French sailors and soldiers mustered several times on the poop and quarter-deck to attempt to board, and their officers could be heard shouting '*A l'abordage!*' Several Frenchmen, armed with cutlasses, clambered on to the *Bellerophon*'s spritsail-yard and began to work their way along to the bowsprit. A seaman named MacFarlane saw them and ran to the starboard side of the fo'c'sle where the spritsail-brace, supporting the end of the yard, was made up on the cleat. He quickly threw the rope off the cleat and the yard canted sharply, toppling the Frenchmen into the sea.

Midshipman Franklin wrote later to his brother-in-law that with both ships locked together by the yards the space between their sides was not wide enough to prevent the French sailors and soldiers leaping across, grabbing a handhold wherever they could. 'In the attempt their hands received some severe blows from whatever the English could lay their hands on. In this way hundreds of Frenchmen fell between the ships and were drowned.'

The heavy fire from the *Aigle* was slashing the British ship's rigging, and among the ropes cut were those to which the colours were lashed. When they came down for the third time the veteran Yeoman of Signals, Christopher Beatty, one of the few men left unwounded on the poop, growled, 'Well, well, that's too bad. . . . The fellows will say we have struck!' He searched around for the largest ensign he could find, flung it over his shoulder and clambered up the tattered mizen rigging.

Every British seaman who had tried to climb aloft to repair rigging up to that time had been shot down by the French sharpshooters; and as soon as Beatty began his hand-over-hand scramble a hail of musket balls whistled round him. He stopped several feet above the deck and, taking the flag from his shoulders, began to spread it on the shrouds. Almost at once the sharpshooters stopped firing, as if they understood his motives and admired his courage. The ensign lashed, he climbed down to the deck again, unharmed.

Cumby, apparently unworried by the new-found responsibility of command, was standing on the gangway when a French grenade thumped down nearby, its fuse sizzling. He quickly stooped down, picked it up and threw it over the side. Describing the effect of another grenade which had been flung in at a lower-deck port, Cumby wrote: 'Its explosion had blown off the scuttle of the Gunner's store-room, setting fire to the store-room and forcing open the door into the magazine passage. Most providentially this door was so placed with respect to that [door] opening from the passage into the magazine that the same blast which blew open the store-room door shut the door of the magazine, otherwise we must all in both ships inevitably have been blown up together.

'The Gunner [John Stevenson], who was in the store-room at the time, went quietly to Lt Saunders on the lower-deck, and acquainting him the store-room was on fire, requested a few hands with water to extinguish it; these being instantly granted, he returned with them and put the fire out without its having been known to any persons on board except those employed in its extinction.'

The other enemy ships were closing in round the *Bellerophon* by now: the *Bahama* was only a few score yards away to windward, and although her gunners were firing slowly, they were doing considerable damage. Above the deep thunder of the guns and the crackling of the muskets came the sound of wood splintering aloft, and the *Bellerophon*'s main-topmast tumbled down, dragging a tangled mass of rigging with it. The topsail fell on the starboard side, hanging like a curtain over the guns as they pounded the *Aigle*. In a few moments the flash from the muzzles set the canvas ablaze, and the flames threatened to set both ships on fire. Cumby soon had the sail-trimmers cutting it free with axes, and the boarders joined in with their cutlasses. The burning sail soon dropped into the sea. By now, with sails and rigging slashed, main and mizen-topmasts shot away, several feet of deck smashed and the hull riddled with shot-holes, the *Bellerophon* was in a precarious position. Cumby went round the guns' crews 'to stimulate their exertions', telling them that they had nothing else to trust to as the ship aloft 'has become an unmanageable wreck'.

However, the *Aigle*'s fire, like that of the *Bellerophon*, was beginning to ease up appreciably. Each ship's guns were taking a heavy toll: at least half the *Aigle*'s crew had been killed or wounded, while by now more than twenty in the *Bellerophon* had been killed and a hundred wounded. The French sharpshooters were still busy. Midshipman Franklin had seen one, complete with cocked hat, shoot several men from his perch in the *Aigle*'s foretop. Franklin was talking to a great friend of his, Midshipman John Simmonds, when the Frenchman fired again and Simmonds fell dead. A few minutes later Franklin was helping a Marine sergeant to carry a coloured seaman down to the surgeon when the sharpshooter fired once more, hitting the wounded man in the heart and killing him.

'He'll have you next!' Franklin exclaimed.

'Indeed he will not!' declared the sergeant, who swore he would get a musket, find a sheltered spot, and not stop firing until he had finished off the sharpshooter.

A little later, as Franklin walked back to the quarter-deck, he saw the Frenchman lift his musket to his shoulder and take aim. But Franklin, says his biographer, 'with an elasticity very common in his family, bounded behind a mast', the musket ball hitting the deck just behind him. By this time the Marine sergeant had the sharpshooter in his sights and fired. Franklin, stepping warily from behind the mast, saw the Frenchman, 'whose features he vowed he would never forget so long as he lived, fall over head foremost into the sea'.

Seeing the Marine sergeant later, Franklin asked how many times he had fired. 'I killed him,' was the reply, 'at the seventh shot.'

By now the *Aigle* had had enough. Her rate of fire had slackened considerably, and a few minutes later from the *Bellerophon*'s quarter-deck they could see the French seamen hoisting a jib and sheeting it home. Slowly the *Aigle* dragged herself clear and sagged away to leeward. The *Bellerophon*'s gunners fired one more raking broadside. 'Her quarter was entirely beaten in,' wrote an officer. 'I have no doubt she would have struck had we been able to follow and engage her for a quarter of an hour longer.'

However, even though the *Bellerophon* had rid herself of the attentions of the *Aigle*, she was still in grave danger: at 1.50 p.m. Churruca's *San Juan Nepomuceno*—before her encounter with the *Tonnant*—came out of the smoke, manœuvring into position to fire a broadside into the *Bellerophon*'s stern, a broadside which might well have put her out of action altogether. But a huge British three-decker, the 98-gun *Dreadnought*, loomed up alongside her, and in a few seconds the pulsing darts of flame and spurts of smoke rippling along the triple tier of gun ports heralded a devastating broadside. (This action will be described later in the narrative.)

The *Bellerophon* at this time, wrote Cumby, 'was totally unmanageable, the main and mizen-topmasts hanging over the side, the jib-boom, spanker-boom and gaff shot away, and not a a brace or bowline serviceable. We observed that the *Aigle* was engaged by the *Defiance* and soon after two o'clock she struck,' he added.

As the smoke cleared away he could see several enemy ships had struck, including the Spanish *Monarca*, which was lying nearby, a shattered hulk with 101 men lying dead and another 154 wounded. Cumby sent a boarding party to take possession of her. 'We were now without any opponent within reach of our guns, and our fire consequently ceasing, I had a message from the surgeon stating that the cockpit was so crowded with wounded that it was quite impossible for him to attempt some operations that were highly requisite, and begging I would allow him to bring some subjects up into the Captain's cabin for amputations if the fire was not likely to be renewed for a quarter of an hour. I gave the requested permission with an understanding that he must be prepared to go down again if any of the enemy's van who had not been engaged should approach us.'

Cumby then describes how he met the Marine captain, Wemyss, who had been wounded several times but had previously refused to go to the surgeon. Wemyss came up the quarter-deck ladder and Cumby, seeing the darker stains of blood almost covering the scarlet jacket, said: 'Wemyss, my good fellow, I'm sorry you've been wounded, but I trust you will do well.'

Wemyss replied cheerfully, ''Tis but a mere scratch, and I shall have to apologize to you bye and bye for having left the deck on so trifling an occasion.' He was in fact on his way to the Captain's cabin where Whyte, the surgeon, was waiting to amputate his right arm. The *Bellerophon* had lost twenty-seven men killed while 123 had been wounded.

In four days' time Captain James Morris, of the *Colossus*, was due to celebrate the third anniversary of his marriage to Margaretha Cocks, daughter of a Charing Cross banker.[1] But for the moment all thoughts of his wife and home were driven from Morris's mind as he steered his ship, the sixth in Collingwood's division, for the enemy's line. Many of the French and Spanish ships were completely hidden in the smoke which was rolling to leeward in majestic clouds, here opening to reveal a toppling

[1] By a coincidence Margaretha's sister Maria was, in four years' time, to marry William Hargood, now commanding the *Belleisle*, the second in Collingwood's line.

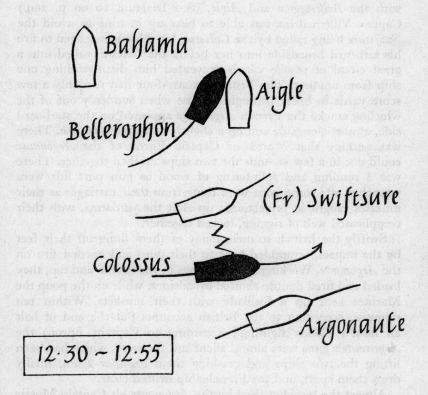

DIAGRAM 10: *Colossus* passes astern of French *Swiftsure* and down starboard side. 12.40 meets *Argonaute* to leeward and falls aboard her

mast, there showing, for a moment, a shattered stem or some
floating wreckage rising and falling on the swell.

The *Colossus* got into close action at about 12.25 p.m., five
minutes after her next ahead, the *Bellerophon*, and seventeen
minutes after the *Royal Sovereign*. The first ship she met was the
French *Swiftsure*, which was falling away after avoiding a collision
with the *Bellerophon* and *Aigle*. (See Diagram 10 on p. 299.)
Captain Villemadrine was able to bear up in time to avoid the
Swiftsure being raked by the *Colossus*, but Morris managed to fire
his larboard broadside into her before the *Colossus* sailed into a
great cloud of smoke which prevented him distinguishing one
ship from another. The British seventy-four had run only a few
score yards to break through the line when suddenly out of the
whirling smoke the French *Argonaute* appeared on the starboard
side, almost alongside and on a slightly converging course. There
was nothing that Morris or Captain Epron of the *Argonaute*
could do: in a few seconds the two ships crashed together. There
was a rending and splintering of wood as gun port lids were
wrenched off; some guns were flung from their carriages as their
muzzles caught in projections; up aloft the yardarms, with their
complicated web of rigging, locked together.

Swiftly the British seamen, many of them flung off their feet
by the impact, scrambled back to their guns and opened fire on
the *Argonaute*. Working like machines in the smoke and din, they
loaded and fired double-shotted broadsides, while on the poop the
Marines kept up a fusillade with their muskets. Within ten
minutes, according to the British accounts ('at the end of half
an hour's bloody fighting', according to Captain Epron) the
Argonaute's guns were almost silent and the swell, which had been
lifting the two ships and crashing them together again, finally
drew them apart, and the French ship drifted clear.

Almost the last shot fired by the *Argonaute* hit Captain Morris
above the knee, wounding him badly, but he refused to be taken
down to the cockpit. Instead he lashed a tourniquet round his
thigh to stop the bleeding and stayed on the poop.

By this time Commodore Galiano, of the Spanish *Bahama*, who
had previously hauled clear of the onslaught of the *Bellerophon*,
had found his former assailant fully occupied with the *Aigle* and
decided to rejoin the fight—a decision which was to cost him his
life. The *Bahama* opened fire from the *Colossus*'s larboard beam,
but a few minutes later the French *Swiftsure* joined in from the

quarter, forging ahead between the two ships to mask the *Bahama*'s fire and get the full force of the *Colossus*'s broadside. The British gunners fired so rapidly and with such accuracy that she soon dropped astern, leaving the *Bahama* once again in the line of fire. The effect on the Spanish ship was devastating.

Commodore Galiano had earlier told his officers, 'Gentlemen, you all know our flag is nailed to the mast,' and turning to Captain Butron, commanding the troops on board, he said, 'I charge you to defend it. No Galiano ever surrenders, and no Butron should either.'

The rapid broadsides from the *Colossus* soon slashed away a lot of the *Bahama*'s rigging; other shot crashed through her hull, several hitting below the waterline as she rolled. One shot flung out a splinter which hit Galiano on the foot, badly bruising him; a few minutes later another gashed his scalp, but he refused to go below to the surgeon. 'Alcala Galiano gave his orders and directed his guns as if the ship had been firing salutes at a review,' says one Spanish account.

It was not long before the constant training which the British gunners had received began to make itself felt: they were firing faster than the Spaniards, and more accurately. The *Bahama*'s mainmast fell.

Galiano was standing on the quarter-deck when a shot passing close spun the telescope out of his hand and made him stagger. His coxswain picked up the telescope and hurried to Galiano's side to see if he was all right, and Galiano gave a reassuring smile. At that moment a cannon ball hit the coxswain, cutting him in two and covering Galiano in blood; a second later another shot from the same broadside hit Galiano in the head, and he fell dead beside the remains of his coxswain. Although a flag was flung over his body so that the men should not know their fearless captain had perished, the news spread rapidly through the whole crew, and the heart went out of them. The surviving officers held a rapidly summoned council of war. Some seventy-five officers and men had been killed and sixty-six wounded—141 casualties out of a crew of 690 sailors and soldiers. The council decided the time had come to take down the nailed-up flag. To emphasize the urgency, the mizenmast crashed down about their ears. Within a few minutes the *Bahama* 'gave signs, by showing an English jack, that she had surrendered.'

However, there was no time to send a prize-crew across from the

Colossus: the French *Swiftsure* had dropped astern and Captain Villemadrin thought he saw a chance of turning suddenly under the stern of the *Colossus* to pour in a raking broadside, but Captain Morris, although faint from loss of blood, was too experienced and too alert to be caught. He gave the order to wear ship: the helm was put up and as sail-trimmers hauled in braces and sheets the *Colossus* swung even faster than the *Swiftsure*. A few of the French ship's larboard guns fired and then, with a succession of deafening crashes the *Colossus* fired her broadside. The French ship's mizenmast slowly toppled over the side as if weary of staying upright, followed by the main-topmast.

Then Codrington's *Orion* came in astern of the *Swiftsure*, half-hidden in the smoke, and luffed up to fire a broadside into her stern. Reloading, she fired a second and then a third broadside. Their effect was disastrous: according to Captain Villemadrin 'they brought down my mainmast, carried away part of the taffrail, the wheel, and dismounted most of the guns on the main-deck and killed many of the people.

'In this painful situation the senior surgeon sent a midshipman from the lower-deck to inform me that he was unable to make room for any more wounded, that the spaces cleared in the hold and the orlop-deck were thronged. I then sent all the men that I had available—both from the main-deck and from the upper-works—to the lower-deck to continue the fire.'

The *Swiftsure*'s foremast then followed the other two over the side. 'Having no longer any hope of being supported—seeing the Fleet at a great distance and having at hand only the *Achille*, who caught fire an instant later,' wrote Villemadrin, 'and [having] five feet of water in the hold—I gave orders to cease fire and I hauled down my colours.'

The *Colossus* hauled up to windward to take possession, and her mizenmast, cut away by several enemy shot, began to creak ominously and sway. Morris, quitting the poop for the first time in the action, hobbled down the ladder to the quarter-deck just in time to avoid being crushed as the mast toppled over the side.

'Sent Lt Huish to bring the two captains on board, who returned with the captain of the French ship *Swiftsure*, and second [-in-command] of the Spaniard, her first being slain,' Captain Morris noted tersely in his Journal.

The seventh ship in Collingwood's division to get into action was

Captain Richard King's 74-gun *Achille*, not to be confused with the French ship of the same name. King, the son of an admiral, brought his ship down to pass through the enemy's line astern of the *Montañes* and ahead of the *San Ildefonso*. He chose the former for his victim, steered boldly under her stern and fired a broadside into her quarter as he passed.

The British ship's broadside was perfectly controlled: the *Montañes*'s senior surviving officer, Lt Alejo de Rubalcava, wrote that the *Achille* 'poured a terrible fire into our larboard quarter, which caused great havoc among the crew, to the hull and to the rigging.' (See Diagram 11 on p. 304.)

Captain Salzedo, commanding the Spanish seventy-four, at first set the topgallants and main-topmast-staysail to get more way on the ship so that he could luff up and bring his larboard broadside to bear on the British *Achille* before she reached him, but King was too quick and the *Achille*, after passing under the Spaniard's stern, came up alongside. Wreathed in thick smoke, the two ships lay close to each other, firing broadsides as boxers might exchange punches. Within half an hour Captain Salzedo was killed and his second-in-command carried wounded to the cockpit. Lt Perez, the only officer left alive on the quarter-deck, sent for the next senior officer, Rubalcava. And when he came to the quarter-deck he found nothing to inspire him. 'I observed in passing the main-deck that the crews of all the guns aft were out of action, many being stretched dead and dying on the deck; the same thing was apparent in the chief guns on the quarter-deck, but it did not detain me from going up on the poop, where I instructed the midshipman entrusted with the charge of the Colours that he should stand by them and on no account should he haul them down.'

While Rubalcava sent orders down to the gun-decks that all available men were to be collected to handle the guns left undamaged, Captain King realized the *Montañes* was beaten and up to the north-east through the smoke he could see the *Belleisle* being savagely attacked. While the *Montañes* sheered off out of the fight he turned away to starboard and a few minutes later, at 1.30 p.m., found another Spanish ship, the *Argonauta* (not to be confused with the French *Argonaute*) in the smoke on his starboard side. He promptly luffed up and hove-to on the *Argonauta*'s larboard bow. For the best part of an hour the British gunners fired broadside after broadside into the Spanish ship.

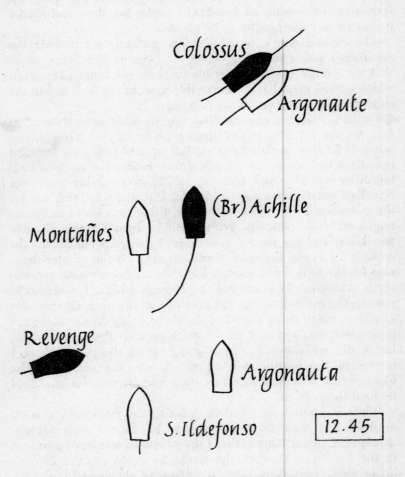

DIAGRAM 11: British *Achille* breaks line, rakes *Montañes* and ranges along-side to engage for forty minutes. *Colossus* passes on as *Argonaute* bears
away

At the end of that time the *Argonauta*, according to her wounded commanding officer, Captain Pareja, 'had all the guns on the quarter-deck and poop dismounted, a great number of guns in the batteries out of action, as much as on account of the pieces [being damaged] as from the want of crews . . . the whole rigging was destroyed, so that there were no shrouds left to the masts—save one to the mainmast—and they were threatening to fall every minute, being shot through.

'In this situation,' he adds, 'it was very evident that the ship could make but slight and feeble resistance. . . . With these inexpressible feelings I was taken below to have my wounds dressed, expecting every minute to find myself brought to the grievous point of having to surrender.'[1] But for the moment the *Argonauta* had won a brief reprieve: the French *Achille* (which, as will be related later, had been in action with the *Revenge*) arrived on the British *Achille*'s larboard side and opened fire.

A short while afterwards the French *Berwick* sailed up on the British *Achille*'s starboard side, between her and the stricken *Argonauta*. For a few minutes the British ship was sandwiched between two of the enemy while the *Argonauta* drifted away to leeward, masts tottering, more like a floating coffin than a ship of war. (See Diagram 12 on p. 306.)

The French *Achille* then went ahead, leaving the British *Achille* and the *Berwick* to fight it out. Although King and his men had already silenced two ships—the *Montañes* and the *Argonauta*—they still had plenty of fight left in them, and within half an hour they forced the *Berwick* to strike. When one of the British *Achille*'s officers went on board to take possession he 'counted upon her decks and in her cockpit and tiers fifty-one dead bodies, including that of her gallant captain, M. Camas'; and the wounded in the *Berwick*, according to the report of her few surviving officers, amounted to nearly 200: her loss in officers was very severe, 'the quarter-deck having thrice been cleared'.

At 12.35 p.m. (at about the same time as the *Victory* and twenty-seven minutes after the *Royal Sovereign*) Captain Robert Moorsom

---

[1] The *Argonauta* was to surrender half an hour later, with 100 men killed and 203 wounded out of a total crew of 780. Lt Owen, of the *Belleisle*, taking possession of her, wrote: 'On getting up the *Argonauta*'s side, I found no living person on her deck; but on making my way, over numerous dead and a confusion of wreck, across the quarter-deck, I was met by the second captain at the cabin door, who gave me his sword.'

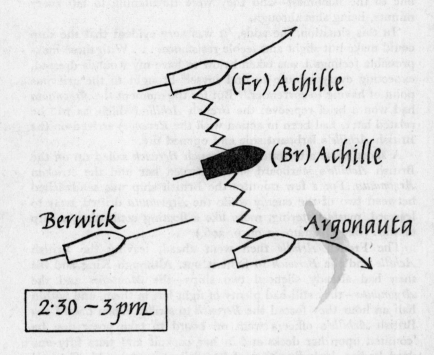

DIAGRAM 12: At 2.30 French *Achille* comes down on British *Achille*'s
larboard side and engages. 3.0 *Berwick* comes between British *Achille* and
Argonauta and engages

brought the 74-gun *Revenge* into action. She was a new ship, built at Chatham and launched only a few months earlier.

'While we were running down to them, of course,' wrote one of the sailors, 'we were favoured with several shots, and some of our men were wounded. Many of the men thought it hard the firing should be all on one side, and became impatient to return the compliment; but our Captain had given orders not to fire until we had got in close with them, so that all our shots would tell.'

'Indeed, these were his words: "We shall want all our shot when we get close in; never mind their firing. When I fire a carronade from the quarter-deck, that will be the signal for you to begin, and I know you will do your duty as Englishmen!"'

The *Revenge* came up to the line obliquely, running almost parallel to the *San Ildefonso* and the French *Achille* (before the latter went north to engage the British *Achille*). Captain Moorsom ordered the *Revenge*'s gunners to open fire on both ships. His men were among the best-trained in the Fleet, for Moorsom was one of the Navy's cleverest gunnery experts. One or more shot from the British ship's opening broadsides bit deep into the *Achille*'s mizenmast five feet above the deck, and as the wood cracked and split, the officers on the poop scrambled to get clear. Slowly it toppled over the side, carrying with it the sharpshooters perched in the top.

The *Achille* had been sailing with her jib-boom very close to the stern of the *San Ildefonso*, but as the mizen went by the board she slowed down, and Moorsom seized the opportunity of taking the *Revenge* close across the *Achille*'s bow to break through the line. He went so close that the French ship's jib-boom, sticking out from the bow like a massive tusk, caught in the *Revenge*'s mizentopsail and ripped it out. According to one of the *Revenge*'s seamen, a number of the *Achille*'s crew were perched on the bowsprit ready to jump on board, 'but they caught a Tartar; for their design was discovered, and our Marines with their small-arms, and the carronades on the poop, loaded with canister shot, swept them off so fast that they were glad to sheer off'. The *Revenge* had by then fired two broadsides into her bows. Moorsom then luffed up and put his ship on the *Achille*'s starboard bow, where he could fire his larboard guns into her and aim his starboard broadside at the stern of the *San Ildefonso*. (See Diagram 13 on p. 308.)

However, Admiral Gravina's flagship, the 112-gun *Principe de*

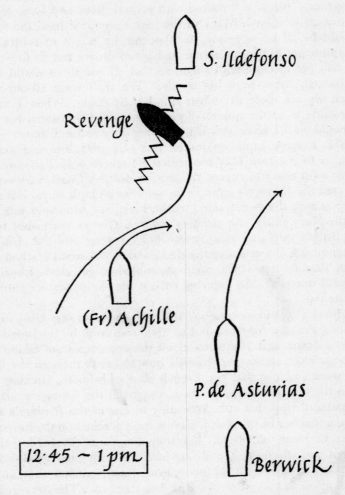

DIAGRAM 13: *Revenge* passes down side of French *Achille*, which loses a mast and falls back; *Revenge* crosses her bow, luffs up and engages her and *San Ildefonso*. *Principe de Asturias* bears away and rakes *Revenge*

Asturias, was just astern of the *Achille*, and she bore away to star-board so that she could rake the British ship. The *Revenge* then found herself in the midst of a triangle of fire from the *San Ildefonso*, *Achille* and *Principe de Asturias*, and she had to endure it for nearly twenty minutes before help arrived. This came in the form of four of the last group of ships in Collingwood's division, led by Captain Durham in the *Defiance*. This gallant Scot—he was born at Largs, in Ayrshire—tried to pass ahead of the *Berwick* (this was before she went on to engage the British *Achille*) and under the stern of the *Principe de Asturias*; but the *Berwick* went ahead to close the gap and ran aboard of the *Defiance*, which tore off the French ship's bowsprit.

Gravina's flagship had, while this was going on, turned away to leeward to pass astern of the *Revenge* and rake her. Durham extricated the *Defiance* from the *Berwick*'s clutches and went off in pursuit of the Spanish flagship. The *Berwick*, apparently un-willing to be left alone (for the *Defiance* was followed by the *Thunderer*, and the *Polyphemus* and British *Swiftsure* were coming up astern) followed the *Principe de Asturias*'s example and turned away to leeward. She was, as we have already seen, to fall into the clutches of the British *Achille*, which forced her to surrender.

Meanwhile Captain Moorsom and his *Revenge* had continued to battle with the French *Achille*. Finally the French ship wore and came round to starboard in an attempt to pass under the *Revenge*'s stern; but Moorsom's gunners raked her and the main-mast—which had already lost its topmast—came tumbling down, leaving her with only a foremast standing.

While the French *Achille* drifted away to leeward, Moorsom took the *Revenge* into action against the *Aigle* which, as already described, had been involved with the *Bellerophon* and *Belleisle*, and raked her. Moorsom's ship had by now suffered badly: her bowsprit, all three lower masts and main-topmast were heavily damaged, nine shot had cut through the copper sheathing of the hull below the water-line and started leaks, and two midshipmen, eighteen seamen and eight Marines had been killed. Captain Moorsom, the Master and a lieutenant, the captain of Marines, thirty-eight seamen and nine Marines had been wounded.

Durham had to break off his chase of the *Principe de Asturias* because of damage to the rigging of the *Defiance*, and shortly after-wards met the *Aigle*, fresh from her encounter with the *Revenge* and, according to Durham's biographer, apparently having been

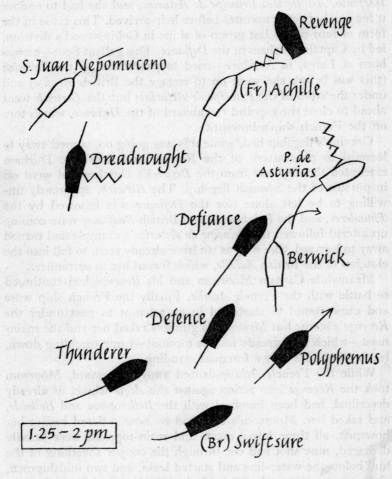

DIAGRAM 14: At 1.25 *Defiance* tries to pass under stern of *Principe de Asturias*; *Berwick* closes gap but runs aboard *Defiance* and loses bowsprit. French *Achille* tries to bear away under *Revenge*'s stern but gets raked and, 1.25, loses mainmast. *Dreadnought* approaches *S. J. Nepomuceno*, opens fire on *Principe de Asturias*

severely handled. 'She was, however, quite ready for action,' he adds, 'and defended herself most gallantly for some time; at length her fire began to slacken, and Captain Durham, thinking she had surrendered, called up his boarders to take possession.' But every one of the *Defiance*'s boats was riddled with shot. There was little or no breeze to get the British ship alongside the *Aigle*, and this situation inspired young Midshipman Jack Spratt, described by Durham's biographer as a 'high-spirited Irishman' and 'one of the handsomest men in the service'.

Spratt volunteered to swim over to the French ship, and Durham agreed. Sticking an axe in his belt, he 'took his cutlass between his teeth, called upon the boarders to follow, leapt overboard and swam to the *Aigle*, followed by a few men.' On reaching the French ship he swam round her stern and scrambled up, by means of the rudder chains, to a gun port. Once on board he quickly discovered that she had not surrendered but—probably having surprise as an ally—he managed to fight through the decks to get up to the poop.

Here, according to one of his shipmates, three French soldiers with bayonets fixed to their muskets charged him. Grabbing a signal halyard, he swung himself up on to an arms chest, 'and before they could repeat the operation, disabled two of them'. Seizing the third soldier, he tried to fling him down the ladder on to the quarter-deck, but the Frenchman grabbed Spratt as he fell. The Frenchman landed on his head, breaking his neck, and Spratt sprawled unhurt on top of him. By this time some other men from the *Defiance* had managed to get aboard and were beginning to fight their way through the ship. Their yells, the clash of cutlasses, the popping of the muskets—sounding like toys against the heavy detonation of the guns of the ships around—echoed across the decks.

Spratt had just saved the life of a French officer who had surrendered when he saw another French soldier, bayonet fixed to his musket, making a lunge. Spratt parried with his cutlass and the Frenchman immediately aimed his musket at the midshipman's chest and squeezed the trigger. Spratt again struck out with his cutlass and managed to knock the musket barrel down as it fired, but the ball hit his right leg just below the knee, breaking both bones. Managing to avoid falling over, Spratt then hopped between two quarter-deck guns to get his back against the bulwarks and thus prevent anyone cutting him down from behind.

The French soldier made repeated jabs with his bayonet, and he was joined by two more. All three attacked Spratt, but fortunately some of the boarding party arrived and saved him. These men had managed to get lines across to the *Defiance* from the *Aigle*, so that Captain Durham could warp the ships together. One of the first people that he saw through the smoke on the French ship's bulwarks was Spratt, who had dragged himself to the side and, holding his bleeding limb over the rail, called out, 'Captain, poor old Jack Spratt is done up at last!' He was brought on board and taken below to the surgeon, William Burnett. [1]

Another British seaman ran aft and hauled down the Tricolour, bent a British flag on to a halyard and ran it up. But the *Aigle* was not yet finished. The boarding party from the *Defiance*, fighting like demons, managed to drive the French seamen and soldiers out of the fo'c'sle and the poop; but sharpshooters in the tops kept firing down, and many more Frenchmen were crouched behind the guns on the lower-deck, firing muskets at the boarding party as they tried to scramble down the ladders. Others were busy throwing grenades through the *Defiance*'s gun ports, killing several men. Captain Durham, rather than lose any more of his men, called the boarding party back on board the *Defiance*. As soon as they had scrambled over, he ordered the lines holding the *Aigle* to be cut. When the two ships had drifted a few yards apart he ordered the guns to open fire. Shot after shot crashed with great precision into the *Aigle*. Lt Asmus Classen, now left in command, was able to get back on his quarter-deck now that the British boarders had quit, but there was little he could do.

'We held out for some time,' he reported, 'but the enemy's flaming sulphur-saturated wads having set the gun-room on fire close to the cable-tier . . . the ship being stripped of her rigging, most of the guns dismounted, the Captain and Commander killed, nearly all the naval officers wounded, and two-thirds of the crew disabled, the ship moreover—by what misfortune I know not— being isolated from the rest of the Fleet, we decided to haul down our colours in order to extinguish the flames and to preserve for

---

[1] A few days later Burnett went to Durham, asking for a written order to amputate Spratt's leg, saying it could not be saved and the Irishman was refusing to have the operation. Durham went below to remonstrate with him. Spratt thereupon held out the other leg and exclaimed, 'Never! If I lose my leg, where shall I find a match for this?' Too crippled to serve at sea again, he was promoted to lieutenant and put in charge of the telegraph station at Dawlish.

the Emperor the scanty number of the gallant defenders who remained.' Classen had not exaggerated: seven officers had been killed and ten wounded, and more than two hundred and fifty of the crew were dead or wounded. 'The slaughter on board of her was horrid,' wrote one of the *Defiance*'s crew, Colin Campbell. 'The decks were covered with dead and wounded. They never heave their dead overboard in time of action as we do.' The *Defiance* had lost seventeen killed, while fifty-three more were wounded. (The disparity in casualties is partly accounted for by the fact that the *Aigle* had been engaged by several other British ships before the *Defiance* arrived.)

The report of the *Defiance*'s carpenter showed that 'stopping the shot holes' in the British ship took one hundredweight and ninety pounds of sheet lead, twenty-one pounds of nails and forty-six pounds of tallow, while 'replacing the bulkheads, cabbins [*sic*] and berths' in different parts of the ship 'took eighty-six pounds of nails, three pounds of brads and a dozen pairs of hinges.'

25

JEANETTE'S RESCUE

'How many ages hence
Shall this our lofty scene be acted o'er
In states unborn, and accents yet unknown?'
— Shakespeare (*Julius Caesar*)

WITH the last ships of Collingwood's division coming into action, Nelson's main purpose had been achieved, although the battle was far from over. The van of the Combined Fleet under Dumanoir had been prevented for more than two hours from taking any effective part in the battle; Villeneuve had been captured, and those battleships round him in the centre which had not surrendered had been driven off to leeward out of the way. The rear ships under Gravina had been savagely handled and the rest of the British ships as they came into action were completing the task.

The 98-gun *Dreadnought*, which had been Collingwood's flagship until the *Royal Sovereign* arrived from England, had come into the battle late because she was a slow ship, but Captain Conn quickly brought her alongside Churruca's *San Juan Nepomuceno*, which was bearing down upon the crippled *Bellerophon*, intending to rake her. (See Diagram 14 on page 310.) The British three-decker's attack was overwhelming: in ten minutes the *San Juan Nepomuceno*, bravely fought, had surrendered. Churruca, according to one Spanish account, had 'directed the battle with gloomy calmness. Knowing that only care and skill could supply the place of strength, he economized our fire, trusting entirely to careful aim, and the consequence was that each ball did terrible havoc on the foe. He saw to everything, settled everything, and the shot flew round him and over his head without his ever once even changing colour. . . .

'It was not the will of God, however, that he should escape alive from that storm of fire. Seeing that no one could hit one of the enemy's ships which was battering us with impunity, he went down himself to judge the line of fire and succeeded in dismasting her.

'He was returning to the quarter-deck when a cannon ball hit

314

his right leg with such violence as almost to take it off, tearing it across the thigh in the most frightful manner. He fell to the ground, but the next moment he made an effort to raise himself, supporting himself on one arm.

'His face was as white as death, but he said, in a voice that was scarcely weaker than his ordinary tones: "It is nothing—go on firing."

'He did all he could to conceal the terrible sufferings of his cruelly-mangled frame. Nothing would induce him, it would seem, to quit the quarter-deck. At last he yielded to our entreaties and then he seemed to understand that he must give up the command. He called for Moyna, his second-in-command, but was told he was dead. Then he called for the officer in command on the main-deck. That officer, though himself seriously wounded, at once came to the quarter-deck and took command.

'It was just before he went below that Churruca, in the midst of his agonies, gave the order that the flag should be nailed to the mast. The ship, he said, must never surrender so long as he breathed.

'The delay, alas, could be but short. He was going fast. He never lost consciousness till the very end, nor did he complain of his sufferings. His sole anxiety was that the crew should not know how dangerous his wound was; that no one should be daunted or fail in his duty. He specially desired that the men should be thanked for their heroic courage.

'Then he spoke a few words to Ruiz de Apodoca, and after sending a farewell message to his poor young wife, whom he had married only a few days before he sailed, he fixed his thoughts on God, Whose name was ever on his lips. So with the calm resignation of a good man and the fortitude of a hero, Churruca passed away.

'After he was gone, it was too quickly known, and the men lost heart. . . . Their courage was really worn out. It was but too plain that they must surrender. . . . A sudden paralysis seemed to seize on the crews; their grief at losing their beloved leader apparently overpowered the disgrace of surrender.

'Quite half of the *San Juan*'s crew were *hors de combat*, dead or wounded.[1] Most of the guns were disabled. All the masts except the mainmast had gone by the board. The rudder was useless. And yet, in this deplorable plight even, they made an attempt to

[1] Actually 103 were killed and 151 wounded out of a crew of 693.

follow the *Principe de Asturias*, which had given the signal to withdraw; but the *San Juan Nepomuceno* had received her death blow. She could neither sail nor steer.'

When the Spanish ship surrendered Captain Conn brought the *Dreadnought* round and joined in the pursuit of the *Principe de Asturias*. The remaining enemy ships in the rear were soon crushed. At 3.15 p.m. the *Defence* attacked the *San Ildefonso* from to leeward, and in fifteen minutes the Spanish ship surrendered; at the same time the *Berwick* struck to the British *Achille*. Thus Gravina's flagship, the *Principe de Asturias*, was the only ship in his squadron which had not surrendered or quit the battle by running to leeward. But she was heavily engaged by several ships, and finally the last three-decker in Collingwood's division, the 98-gun *Prince*, under Captain Grindall, managed to catch up.

'She discharged all her guns at grape-shot range into our stern,' wrote Escaño. '[Admiral Gravina] was wounded in the left leg; he was obliged to go below but while it was being temporarily dressed he gave orders that he should be conveyed back and placed sitting at his post on deck.

'Weakened by loss of blood he fell fainting; but quickly coming to himself and not perceiving the national colours, he ordered them to be hoisted without delay and he resumed command.

'In this critical position we sighted the [French] *Neptune* and the *San Justo* that were coming up to our aid, which was observed by the enemy, who obliged them to sheer off.'

The French *Achille* was lying with her mizenmast and main-topmast down, wheel wrecked and her captain dead, when the three-decker *Prince* arrived close alongside at about 4 p.m. and fired a broadside into her. The shot bit into the French ship's mainmast and a moment or two later it crashed aft, along the centre-line of the ship, smashing boats and leaving her with only the foremast standing. Lt Cauchard, now in command of the *Achille*, was horrified to see flames coming from the foretop. They spread quickly along the dry wood, canvas and ropes. Several officers and midshipmen, with the carpenters and the few men left at the 18-pounder guns and some of those from the 36-pounders, ran forward with axes to chop away the tangle of rigging and then cut the mast over the side before the flames set fire to the whole ship. But even as they started hacking away, the *Prince* was ready with another broadside. This had no sooner been fired than the noise of splintering wood warned the Frenchmen that the foremast was going to collapse, and a few moments later it toppled aft, the whole of the blazing foretop crashing down on to the boats stowed amidships, wrecking the fire engine. The *Prince* immediately sheered off, fearing the *Achille* would explode at any minute, but at the same time Captain Grindall ordered boats to be lowered and manned and sent off to rescue the French crew.

The *Achille*'s boats caught fire and burning debris started falling down the hatches. With the fire engine wrecked, the French crew had no chance of fighting the blaze, which rapidly spread; deck beams and planking smouldered and caught alight, rope burned like fuses, and canvas from the sails dissolved in flames. Lt Cauchard ordered the bilge-cocks to be opened to flood the ship. 'All hands then came up on deck,' reported Lieutenants Lachasse and Clamart, 'and losing all hope of extinguishing the fire, we no longer attended to anything except saving the ship's company, by throwing overboard all the debris that might offer them the means of escaping from almost certain death and awaiting the aid that the neighbouring ships might send them.' With flames crackling up from the whole midship section of the ship, the crew started to leap over the side and swim towards the *Prince*'s boats and to the *Pickle* and *Entreprenante*, which were coming up to their rescue.

But trapped below decks in the *Achille* was a young French-woman, wife of one of the maintopmen. During the battle she had been stationed in the passage to the forward magazine, passing up cartridges for the guns. When the firing had stopped, she later told Captain Moorsom of the *Revenge*, she had climbed up to the lower-deck, anxious to get up to the main-deck and find her husband. To her dismay all the ladders had been taken away or smashed by shot, and she could hear from the shouting that the ship was on fire.

Soon she could hear the crackling of the flames, and pieces of blazing wood fell down the hatches to start new fires on the deck on which she stood. She ran backwards and forwards along the shattered lower-deck, scrambling over wrecked guns and dead and dying men, but could find no way of getting to the upper-deck. . . . Some heavy crashes then startled her, and she saw that the main-deck planking above her was burning and some of the guns were falling through on to the lower-deck. Terrified, she ran aft to the gun-room and climbed through one of the ports whence, with the help of the rudder-chains, she managed to scramble out on to the curved after edge of the rudder itself.

There, trembling with fear, she prayed that the ship would blow up and end her misery. Instead, the flames began to melt the lead lining of the rudder trunk and the molten metal dripped down on to her neck and shoulders. Her only chance now was the sea, and stripping off her clothes, she jumped in and swam to a piece of wreckage to which several Frenchmen were clinging. One of them, however, bit and kicked her until she had to let go. She then swam to another small piece of wreckage and in a few minutes later another survivor from *Achille* swam past and, seeing her, came over with a plank which he put under her arms, as if she was holding on to a rail. She was eventually rescued by one of the *Pickle*'s boats and taken on board the schooner with a hundred and twenty more survivors. Lt Lapenotiere's crew—outnumbered four to one by the French—gave her a pair of trousers and a jacket, and a handkerchief to tie round her head. Then they treated the burns round her neck and shoulders.

Jeanette—for this was the only name by which the British knew her—was eventually transferred with other prisoners from the *Pickle* to the *Revenge*, where one of the officers noticed a youth 'exhibiting a face begrimed with smoke and dirt, without shoes, stockings or shirt, and looking the picture of misery and despair'. Curious, he asked some of the prisoners about this unhappy person and discovered Jeanette. 'It was sufficient to know this, and I lost no time in introducing her to my messmates as a female requiring their compassionate attention.'

'We were not wanting in civility to the lady,' wrote Captain Moorsom. 'I ordered her two purser's shirts to make a petticoat.' A lieutenant gave her his cabin (after the action was over the bulkheads were replaced) and needles and thread, while another came along with some material taken from a Spanish prize. The chaplain helped with a pair of shoes and someone else presented her with a pair of white stockings. Only one thing made Jeanette unhappy: her husband was missing. But four days later she found him on board, unhurt.

There was, according to Lt Halloran of the *Britannia*, another woman rescued from the *Achille*. 'This poor creature', he wrote, 'was brought on board with scarcely any covering and our senior [Marine] subaltern, Lt Jackson, gave her a large cotton dressing-gown for clothing.' He also noted that two Turks, father and son, were brought aboard from one of the ships. The father had both legs amputated, and both men died the same night.

At four o'clock the British ships to the south received a signal from Collingwood—'Come to the wind on the larboard tack.' They had to leave off their pursuit of Gravina because Dumanoir had, at long last, arrived on the scene.

We left Collingwood's flagship engaging the *Santa Ana*, flagship of Admiral Alava, who had just been wounded. The Spanish ship's side, Collingwood wrote later, was 'almost entirely beaten in' by the *Royal Sovereign*'s gunfire. She had just surrendered when a boat from the *Victory* arrived alongside the British ship and Lt Alexander Hills climbed on board, asking to be taken to Admiral Collingwood. The Admiral, his leg swollen and bleeding under its bandage, was told that Nelson had been wounded. 'I asked the officer if his wound was dangerous,' Collingwood later wrote to the Duke of Clarence. 'He hesitated; then said he hoped it was not; but I saw the fate of my friend in his eye; for his look told what his tongue could not utter.'

For the moment the *Royal Sovereign* was helpless. The crippled *Santa Ana* had a few minutes earlier drifted to leeward and then broached to, and the violent motion had brought her tottering masts tumbling over the side. Collingwood's ship was in little better shape, because at about 2.30 p.m. her mainmast, which had been swaying dangerously with only a few remaining shrouds to hold it, finally crashed down, and a few moments later the mizenmast followed. Blackwood's *Euryalus* was signalled to take her in tow. With his ship finally under way again, albeit at the end of the *Euryalus*'s tow-rope, Collingwood hailed Blackwood and told him to go aboard the *Santa Ana* and 'Bring me the Admiral.'

Blackwood lowered a boat and had himself rowed across to find Alava too badly wounded to be moved. He therefore brought Captain Gardoqui back with him. Hercules Robinson later wrote that when he met Alava five years later the Spanish Admiral told him that one broadside from the *Royal Sovereign* had killed three hundred and fifty men, and 'though he fought on afterwards for a couple of hours, like an old hidalgo, like "a man of honour and a cavalier", the first broadside did his business, and there was an end of him. . . .' Despite Alava's compliment to the efficiency of the *Royal Sovereign*'s broadside, according to Spanish official sources five officers and ninety-men were killed, and ten officers and a hundred and twenty-seven wounded in the battle out of a total crew of 1,188.

When Captain Gardoqui got on board the *Royal Sovereign* he asked a sailor the name of the ship. On being told, he patted one of the guns, and said in broken English, 'I think she should be called the "Royal Devil" '.

26

'NOBLE MADNESS'

'Set honour in one eye and death i' the other,
And I will look on both indifferently.'
—Shakespeare (*Julius Caesar*)

WE HAVE SEEN that just before the *Bucentaure*'s main and mizen-masts toppled over the side, Villeneuve had signalled to Dumanoir that the van division—sailing north-westwards away from the battle—was to wear together and come down to the rescue of the rest of the sorely tried Combined Fleet. 'The over-light breeze checked the speed with which I desired to bear down to his assistance,' Dumanoir later said in a report which was aimed at justifying his tardiness. He had ten ships with him—the original seven of his division, plus the *Intrépide*, which had not been able to get into her proper position before the battle, the *Héros* and the *San Augustin*, which had been leading Villeneuve's division. (See Chart 2 and Diagram 1 on pages 220 and 243.) The only way for Dumanoir's *Formidable* to wear was to lower a boat and use it to tow the ship's bow round. The *Scipion* tried to tack and failed, then could not wear because the *Intrépide* was too close, and finally put a boat over the side and was hauled round. The *Intrépide* managed to wear but collided with the *Mont-Blanc*, who smashed her flying jib-boom and split the *Intrépide*'s foresail.

Then, wrote Captain Infernet, of the *Intrépide*, while the rest of the ships wore round or tacked, he 'crowded on canvas and set my course for the ships foul of each other and dismasted, and particularly for the flagship [*Bucentaure*] which was amongst the number. I observed with sorrow', he added, 'that I was followed only by the Spanish *Neptuno*, four French ships keeping to the wind on the larboard tack standing south and south-south-west, which caused them to pass a gun-shot to windward of the enemy fleet, under full sail.' The four ships were Dumanoir's *Formidable*, followed by the *Duguay-Trouin*, *Scipion* and *Mont-Blanc*, followed later by the Spanish *Neptuno*. They were sailing down for a point about half a mile to windward of the *Bucentaure*, towards the British *Spartiate* and *Minotaur*, which were just coming into the

L
321

battle. Dumanoir wrote: 'The Admiral [Villeneuve] was by then totally dismasted; I had still a hope that I might take him in tow and endeavour to get him out of [the line of] fire.'

When Captain Hardy, from the bloodstained and shot-torn decks of the *Victory*, saw Dumanoir's ten ships turn back as though they intended at long last to join in the battle, he hoisted the signal for the British ships to come to the wind on the larboard tack, thus sailing clear of the scattered group of shattered enemy ships and getting into a position to beat off the new threat and at the same time guard the prizes which were to leeward.

However, only seven British captains saw the signal—Bayntun (*Leviathan*), Pellew (*Conqueror*), Bullen (*Britannia*), Digby (*Africa*), Fremantle (*Neptune*), Pilfold (*Ajax*) and Berry (*Agamemnon*). They formed themselves up in that order in a rough line of battle and headed northwards.

Dumanoir's squadron had by now split itself into three distinct groups—Dumanoir's four, followed by the *Neptuno*, keeping up to windward and sailing back parallel with what had been the Combined Fleet's line; the *Intrépide* and *San Augustin*, heading bravely down towards the battle; and the *Héros*, *Rayo*—commanded by the Irishman MacDonell—and the *San Francisco de Asis*, which were to leeward and unashamedly about to steer away for Cadiz. In other words, out of the ten fresh and undamaged French and Spanish ships, only two were attempting to go to Villeneuve's rescue.

Dumanoir, at the head of the five ships to windward, was heavily engaged by the newly-formed British line as he passed them going in the opposite direction, heading down towards the *Spartiate* and *Minotaur*. However, neither Captain Sir Francis Laforey nor Captain Mansfield, both doing their best to get into the battle in the extremely light wind, seemed very concerned at the idea of tackling the five enemy ships now sailing down in line on their larboard side. (See Diagram 15 opposite.)

The two British ships passed just ahead of the *Formidable*. 'The *Minotaur* and *Spartiate* commenced close action with the headmost ships, receiving and returning the fire of the five ships in passing with our topsails to the mast', reported Mr Francis Whitney, Master of the *Spartiate*. 'Observed the sternmost, a Spanish ship's, rigging and sails very much cut up. Lay-to on her quarter with our fore and main-topsails to the mast, all our after-sails set, firing obliquely through her, she returning at times from

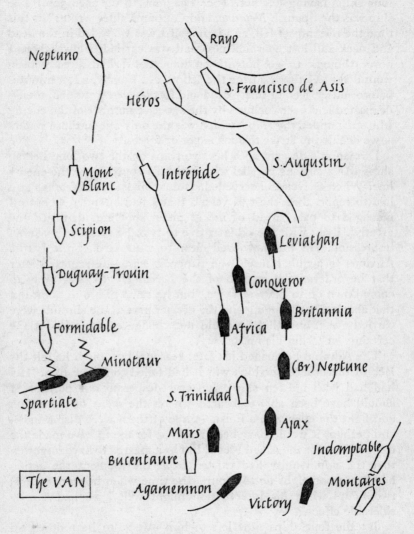

DIAGRAM 15: British ships form line of battle. Dumanoir in *Formidable* sails down and is engaged by *Spartiate* and *Minotaur*. *Intrépide* and *San Augustin* make their brave attacks. *Rayo*, *S.F. de Asis* and *Héros* quit

her stern-chase and quarter guns. . . . Wore, not being able to bring our guns to bear, to engage her on the other tack, the other four ships having left her.' (See Diagram 16 on page 326.) The ship was the Spanish *Neptuno*, and Captain Valdés wrote: 'At this time the mizenmast fell, and in its fall I was wounded in the head and neck and lost consciousness and was carried below, where I never thought to go notwithstanding that I had already been wounded three times during the action. . . . Finally, a few minutes before sunset, having thirty dead and forty-seven wounded, totally dismasted and overwhelmed by the superior number of the enemy who surrounded my ship—which was the only one in those waters —we decided to strike to such superior forces.'

Dumanoir's descent with his five ships on the two lone British ships was a curious parallel with Nelson's approach to the enemy line. Whereas Nelson succeeded, Dumanoir lost the *Neptuno* and had to report that 'the two vessels that I had intended to cut off managed to pass ahead of me at pistol shot and damaged me greatly'. Even with the odds at five to two, he failed to make an impression. He was now well clear to windward of the battle. Anxious to acquit himself—on paper at least—he reported later that he ordered the captain of the *Formidable* to bear away to come down on to the rear ships, 'but he came to me to point out that absolutely all rigging and the greater part of the shrouds were carried away, and that he could not change course without the certainty of losing his masts'.

The Admiral bemoaned his fate: reasonably enough he felt the lack of the other five ships which had failed to follow him. 'If I had had with me ten ships, however desperate our position, I should have been able to bear down on the scene of the action and fight the enemy to a finish—three of them were dismasted— and perhaps it would have been reserved for me to have made the day glorious for the Allied Fleet.' But he appeared to have forgotten that the opportunity had existed from the moment the action began at noon right up to 2 p.m., the time when he wore round; two hours when his intervention might well have had a con- siderable effect.

But the four ships now left to him—well, 'to bear down on the enemy at this moment would have been a desperate stroke which would have only served to increase the number of our losses and augment the advantages to the enemy to whom, on account of the depletion of my division, I could not have done much damage'. Then, in apparent contradiction, he added: 'It was therefore my duty in this painful situation to endeavour to effect the repairs of my Division in the hope of more favourable chances on the morrow.'

On the morrow, of course, the British ships would have carried out repairs, and also taken possession of the enemy ships which had surrendered. However, the quartet sailed on to the south, apparently satisfied. The *Formidable*, despite the damaged masts which kept her out of action, survived the great gales. Dumanoir was to meet Sir Richard Strachan on November 4 (and have his four ships captured), and eventually face two courts martial and a court of inquiry.[1]

Meanwhile the *Intrépide*, with Captain Louis Infernet on the quarter-deck, was steering for the enemy to fight one of the most gallant actions of the whole battle. 'We could hardly make out in the midst of the smoke and confusion of the battle', wrote the Marquis Gicquel des Touches, a young lieutenant on board, 'the situation of our flagship [*Bucentaure*], surrounded as she was by the enemy and having near her only the *Redoutable*, a small seventy-four, crushed by the overpowering mass of the *Victory*. . . .

'It was into the thick of this fray that our Captain Infernet led us. He wanted, he said, to rescue Admiral Villeneuve and take him on board, and then to rally round ourselves the ships that were still in a fit state to fight. It was a reckless and forlorn hope, a mad enterprise; and he himself could not doubt it. It was the pretext Infernet gave for continuing to fight. He would not have it said that the *Intrépide* had quitted the battle while she still could fight a gun or hoist a sail. It was a noble madness, but though we knew it, we all supported him with joyful alacrity—and would that others had imitated his example!'

While Infernet steered the *Intrépide* down towards the new line of British ships, the *San Augustin* went down with him farther to leeward. (See Diagram 15 on page 323.) The *Leviathan*, leading the line, was the first to engage the *San Augustin*, bearing down on the Spanish ship and turning out of the line to run alongside. After firing several broadsides, she attempted to board.

'It was inevitable to surrender to such superior numbers,'

[1] At the first, on his conduct at Trafalgar, he was cleared; at a court of inquiry on his actions on November 4 he was blamed for certain moves and was said to have 'shown too much indecision in all his manœuvres', and in a subsequent court martial he was cleared.

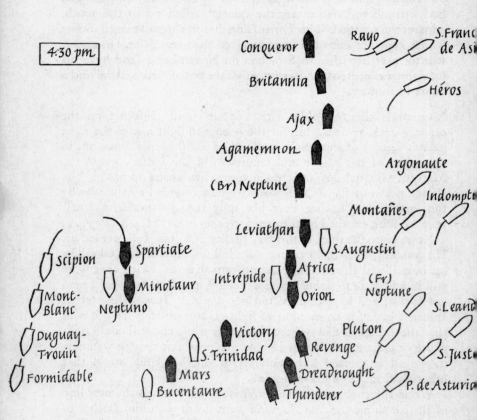

DIAGRAM 16: The probable situation at the end of battle showing the northernmost ships. Dumanoir in the *Formidable* quits to the south-west

wrote Captain Felipe Cajigal, commanding the *San Augustin*, 'and having been boarded twice I had not sufficient men to repel a third boarding, the few who remained being on the gun-decks, continuing to fire into the other ships which were closing round me at pistol range.'

Infernet saw the *Leviathan* engaged with the *San Augustin* and seized the opportunity to pass near the British ship and pour a raking broadside into her bow. The *Conqueror*, the nearest other British ship, was badly damaged aloft—most of her running rigging had been shot away—but opened fire on the *Intrépide* 'at too great a distance to do any material execution', according to Lt Senhouse, one of her officers. The little 64-gun *Africa* was the next nearest ship, and Digby quickly wore her round the *Intrépide*'s stern, luffed up on the starboard tack and opened fire. The *Britannia, Ajax, Agamemnon* and *Neptune* fired into the *Intrépide* as they passed on their way northwards in pursuit of the *Rayo, San Francisco de Asia* and *Héros*, but for forty minutes the *Africa* kept firing her broadsides into the *Intrépide* until finally Codrington brought the *Orion* up and raked the French ship.

The young Marquis in the *Intrépide*, whose post was on the fo'c'sle in charge of the headsails, boarders and sharpshooters, was having a busy time amid the thick smoke and the crash of the guns. 'What took much of my attention', he wrote, 'was to prevent the masts and yards from coming down, and I was able to keep the foremast standing for a considerable time, by means of which we were able to manœuvre the ship to some extent.

'While the fighting was very hot the British *Orion* crossed our bows in order to pour in a raking fire. I got my men ready to board and pointing out to a midshipman her position and what I wanted to do, I sent him to the Captain with a request to have the ship laid on board the *Orion*.

'I saw to the rest, and seeing the ardour of my men, I already imagined myself master of the British seventy-four and taking her into Cadiz with her colours under ours. With keen anxiety I waited; but there was no change in the *Intrépide*'s course.

'Then I dashed off to the quarter-deck myself. On the way I found my midshipman lying flat on the deck, terrified at the sight of the *Britannia*[1], which ship had come abreast of us within pistol

[1] The Marquis actually wrote *Téméraire*, but she was still alongside Lucas's crippled *Redoutable*, and the *Britannia* was the only three-decker near in this position.

shot and was thundering into us from her lofty batteries. I treated my emissary as he deserved—I gave him a hearty kick—and then I hurried aft to explain my project personally to the Captain. It was then, though, too late. The *Orion* swept forward across our bows, letting fly a murderous broadside—and no second chance presented itself.

'At the moment I reached the poop the brave Infernet was brandishing a small curved sabre which struck off one of the pieces of wooden ornamental work by the rail. The sword blade went close to my face, and I said laughingly, "Do you want to cut my head off, Captain?"

' "No, certainly not you, my friend," was the reply, "but that's what I mean to do to the first man who speaks to me of surrender."

'Nearby was a gallant colonel of infantry, who had distinguished himself at Marengo. He was terribly perturbed at the broadside from the *Britannia*. In vain he tried to dodge and shelter behind the stalwart form of the Captain, who at length saw what he was doing.

' "Ah, Colonel," called out the Captain, "do you think I am sheathed in metal then?"

'In spite of the gravity of the moment we could not keep from laughing.

'But by now, indeed, the decks had been almost swept clear, our guns were disabled, and the batteries heaped up with dead and dying. It was impossible to keep up a resistance which meant the doom of what remained of our brave ship's company, and ourselves, without the means of striking back and inflicting harm on the enemy.'

The heavily built Infernet, a Provençal by birth, rough in manner and uneducated, who started off in the French Navy as a cabin boy, wrote a report which gives some idea of the odds he was fighting by now.

'At four o'clock[1] I was dismantled to such a degree that all my rigging was cut to pieces and several guns on deck and in the batteries dismounted. At 4.45 I ordered the few hands remaining on deck to go below to the batteries in order to engage to starboard and larboard; at this minute the mizen-yard where my colours were flying was carried away by a shot; I immediately ordered a

[1] Infernet's times are an hour ahead of those recorded by the British ships.

flag to be flown from the mizen shrouds to starboard and larboard and continued the fight.

'At five o'clock the wheel, the tiller-sweep, the tiller ropes and the tiller were shattered to a thousand pieces; I at once had the spare tiller rigged and steered with it, always fighting desperately. At 5.15 the mizenmast fell; four or five minutes later the mainmast did the same; I still fought—and I am able to say so to the honour of those whom I commanded—undauntedly; I was then surrounded by seven enemy ships, which were all firing into me and I was making all possible resistance; I was firing with the stern-chasers, musketry from the upper-works and from the foretops.

'At 5.53 p.m. the foremast fell; I was then left without masts or sails; seeing myself surrounded by enemies and not being able to escape, having, moreover, no French ships in sight to come to my assistance, the enemy keeping up a terrible fire into me, having about half my crew killed. . . . I was obliged to yield to the seven enemy ships that were engaging me.'

Although the reports of the *Orion* and *Africa* do not bear out Infernet's report that there were seven ships engaging him simultaneously, Senhouse of the *Conqueror* wrote that the French captain surrendered 'after one of the most gallant defences I ever witnessed. The Frenchman's name was Infernet, a member of the Legion of Honour, and it deserves to be recorded in the memory of those who admire true courage.'

It was about 4 p.m. when the *Dreadnought*, *Revenge* and *Thunderer* came up to windward to ward off Dumanoir's apparently impending attack and left Gravina's flagship the *Principe de Asturias* to roll and lurch her way towards Cadiz, with the French *Neptune*, *Pluton* and *San Justo* in company. (See Diagram 16 on page 326.)

At 4.30 p.m. Gravina ordered the remaining French and Spanish ships to rally, and steered towards Cadiz. At 5 p.m. the frigate *Themis* took his ship in tow and on their way they were joined by the *Argonauta*, *Montañes*, *Indomptable*, *Rayo*, *San Francisco de Asis* and *Héros*. Dumanoir was already well clear with his four ships. But the drama off Cape Trafalgar was not yet over.

27

THE BARGAIN

'He that outlives this day and comes safe home,
Will stand a tip-toe when this day is nam'd. . .'
—Shakespeare (*Henry V*)

WHILE brave men and poltroons, silent heroes and noisy brag-garts of many nations were fighting for their lives round the *Victory*, Horatio Nelson lay on a purser's mattress with his back against the ship's side, feeling death within him yet keeping a tenuous but painful grasp on life. Burke had his arm round the emaciated and pain-racked shoulders; Scott knelt beside his chief, fanning him, massaging his chest or offering a drink. The steward, Henry Chevalier, and Gaetano Spedilo, the Admiral's valet, crouched nearby, waiting and anxious to have a task which would ease their feeling of utter helplessness.

Beatty and his assistants hurried to and fro among the men lying and sitting about waiting to have their wounds tended. With bare arms and clothing bloodstained, crouching as they walked because of the lack of headroom, they presented a macabre sight in the fitful glow from the lanterns.

Looking pathetically small and helpless, his face white and his breathing shallow, Nelson waited for Harry to appear: more than an hour had passed since the Admiral had been carried below from the quarter-deck. For the whole of that time he had been without real news of what was happening in this, his last and his greatest battle.

Young Midshipman Westphal, lying next to Nelson with his bleeding head resting on the Admiral's rolled-up coat, waited patiently; on the other side the wounded Pasco tried to comfort Nelson. Finally the huge bulk of Hardy scrambled down the ladder almost opposite where Nelson was lying and, crouching low to avoid banging his head on the beams, he went over to the Admiral and shook hands affectionately.

'Well, Hardy, how goes the battle? How goes the day with us?'

'Very well, my Lord. We have got twelve or fourteen of the enemy's ships in our possession; but five of their van have tacked,' said Hardy, referring to Dumanoir's squadron, 'and show an intention of bearing down upon the *Victory*. I have therefore called two or three of our fresh ships round us, and have no doubt of giving them a drubbing.'

'I hope,' said Nelson, 'none of *our* ships have struck, Hardy.'

'No, my Lord, there is no fear of that.'

Then Nelson, his voice dropping, said, 'I am a dead man, Hardy, I am going fast; it will be all over with me soon. Come nearer to me. . . .'

Sensing that whatever the Admiral was about to say to Hardy would be private, Burke eased his arm from round Nelson's shoulder and made to move away, but he was motioned to stay.

'. . . Pray let my dear Lady Hamilton have my hair, and all other things belonging to me,' whispered Nelson.

Hardy, distressed at this turn in the conversation, said that he hoped that Beatty could yet hold out some prospect of life.

'Oh no,' replied Nelson with what vehemence he could muster, 'It is impossible. My back is shot through. Beatty will tell you so.'

There was little more for Hardy to say, and at this moment his presence was wanted on the quarter-deck. He shook hands with his wounded friend and with a sad heart climbed back up the ladder.

Beatty, who had been attending Midshipman Rivers's shattered leg, came back, but Nelson told him to go back and do what he could for the rest of the wounded, 'for you can do nothing for me.' The surgeon, to whom we are indebted for his description of these last hours, assured him the assistant surgeons were doing everything possible for the men, but Nelson insisted, and Beatty went off to attend to two wounded Marine lieutenants, James Peake and Lewis Reeves. He had not been gone long before Dr Scott called him back.

'Ah, Mr Beatty,' said Nelson, 'I have sent for you to say what I forgot to tell you before, that all power of motion and feeling below my breast are gone; and *you* very well *know* I can live but a short time.' Beatty knew that Nelson had a picture in his mind of James Bush, the seaman who had broken his back in the *Victory* the previous July, and in whose thirteen-day struggle for life, as mentioned earlier, Nelson had taken such a keen interest. The surgeon, confused at the Admiral pronouncing his own death sentence, muttered, 'My Lord, you told me so before,' and knelt down to examine him again. But Nelson knew it was a useless gesture. 'Ah, Beatty! I am too certain of it: Scott and Burke have tried it already. *You know* I am gone.'[1]

By now Beatty realized that it was pointless to argue with his Admiral and unnecessary to comfort him. 'My Lord, unhappily for our country, nothing can be done for you.' As if saying aloud what his thoughts had tried to conceal broke his professional reserve, tears came to his eyes and he turned quickly and walked a few paces so that he could not be seen. Nelson said quite simply, and to no one in particular, as if he had come to terms with death, 'I know it. I feel something rising in my breast'—he put his hand to his left side—'which tells me I am gone.'

By now Dumanoir's ships were passing to windward, and the *Victory*'s larboard guns opened fire, their thundering reverberations once again rolling through the ship, followed by the heavy grinding of their trucks as they were run out and fired again.

'Oh *Victory*, *Victory*, how you distract my poor brain,' groaned Nelson, and then, as an afterthought, 'How dear life is to all men.' Burke and Scott gave him sips of lemonade from time to time, and fanned him, but his brow was cold and he was breathing in short, uneven and painful gasps. Beatty came back and asked if the pain was still very bad. 'It continues so severe,' was the reply, 'that I wish I was dead. Yet,' he said, his voice dropping, as a confiding child might reveal a secret wish, 'one would like to live a little longer, too.'

He was quiet for a few minutes, as if he had gone into a world of his own where there was no pain but only happy memories, but then he came back from wherever he had been and said, 'What would become of poor Lady Hamilton, if she knew my situation!' Once again Beatty left, unable to do anything to ease the pain tormenting the Admiral's body, to attend to Midshipman Robert Smith who, like his Admiral nearby, was dying. From him he went to Lt Bligh and then he came over to Midshipman Westphal, lying next to Nelson and still resting his head on the coat.[2]

Nearly an hour had gone by since Hardy's last visit. During that time Dumanoir had passed and Lt Hills had been sent to tell

---

[1] The italics are Beatty's. He often refers to himself as 'the surgeon'.
[2] 'When the battle was over,' Westphal wrote later, 'and they came to remove the coat, several of the bullions of the epaulettes were found to be so firmly glued into my hair, by the coagulated blood from my wound, that the bullions, four or five of them, were cut off, and left in my hair, one of which I have still in my possession.'

Collingwood that Nelson had been wounded. The Dorset captain now had a few minutes to spare for another visit to the cockpit, which Beatty describes:

'Lord Nelson and Captain Hardy shook hands again, and while the Captain retained his Lordship's hand, he congratulated him, even in the arms of death, on his brilliant victory, "Which," he said, "was complete; though he did not know how many of the enemy were captured, as it was impossible to perceive every ship distinctly. He was certain, however, of fourteen or fifteen having surrendered."'

'That is well, but I bargained for twenty,' said Nelson; then, gripping Hardy's hand tighter, he exclaimed with sudden emphasis, '*Anchor*, Hardy, anchor!'

He had seen the long white streamers of high cloud which had, from early morning, spread like the feathers of a peacock's tail from the westward and, coupled with the heavy swell, he knew this warned that a storm was coming up from the direction of the setting sun, and with the shoals of Cape Trafalgar and the rock-girt coast close under their lee, the British Fleet and the prizes were in great danger. Hardy evidently considered that the time had come for Collingwood to take over command, but it was a difficult suggestion to make to a dying man, and particularly to someone of Nelson's temperament. So he said, with as much tact as he could muster, 'I suppose, my Lord, Admiral Collingwood will now take upon himself the direction of affairs.' The effect on Nelson was startling: he reacted violently, trying to struggle up from the mattress. 'Not while I live, I hope, Hardy!'

'No,' he added, 'do *you* anchor, Hardy.'

'Shall we make the signal, sir?'

'Yes—for if I live, I'll anchor.'

Beatty says that Nelson meant by this order that if he survived until all enemy resistance had ceased, Hardy was then to anchor the ships, 'if it should be found practicable'. He adds that 'the energetic manner in which he uttered these his last orders to Captain Hardy, accompanied by his efforts to raise himself, evinced his determination never to resign the command while he retained the exercise of his transcendent faculties, and that he expected Captain Hardy still to carry into effect the suggestions of his exalted mind, his sense of his duty overcoming the pains of death.'

But, as if this last effort had taken him a few steps nearer to the

end, he said to Hardy: 'I feel that in a few moments I shall be
no more. . . .'

A minute or two later he said in a low voice: 'Don't throw me
overboard, Hardy.'

'Oh no, certainly not.'

'Then,' whispered Nelson, who had often discussed it with
Hardy, 'you know what to do: and take care of my dear Lady
Hamilton, Hardy; take care of poor Lady Hamilton. . . . Kiss me,
Hardy.'

With every beat of his heart the little man's life was ebbing
away fast, and Hardy knelt and kissed his cheek. Nelson looked
up at Hardy's strained face and whispered, 'Now I am satisfied.
Thank God I have done my duty.'

Hardy stood up, looking down at his dying friend, who was
now lying back with his eyes closed, his breath so shallow that the
narrow chest under the coarse, unbleached calico of the sheet
barely moved. Hardy suddenly knelt again and kissed the forehead
which was cold to his lips.

'Who is that?' Nelson whispered.

'It is Hardy. . . .'

'God bless you, Hardy!'

The Captain stood up and walked the few feet to the ladder,
between the mainmast and the hanging magazine, and clambered
up to the quarter-deck.[1]

Nelson now told Chevalier to turn him on to his right side,
apparently hoping that this would ease the pain, and added, 'I
wish I had not left the deck, for I shall soon be gone.' He was
breathing with great difficulty as he drowned in his own blood,
and he said in a faint voice to the Chaplain, Scott, 'Doctor, I
have not been a *great* sinner. . . . *Remember* that I leave Lady
Hamilton and my daughter Horatia as a legacy to my country:
and never forget Horatia.'

Now the pain seemed suddenly to increase to almost more than
he could bear, and with it came a terrible thirst. He had difficulty

---

[1] Beatty says that Nelson frequently told Hardy that if he was killed at
sea he wished his body to be brought back to England, and that 'if his
country should think proper to inter him at the public expense', he wished
to be buried in St Paul's Cathedral. He preferred the Cathedral to
Westminster Abbey because he remembered a tradition that the Abbey
was built where a morass once existed, and he feared the Abbey would
eventually disappear. If there was no public burial he wished to be
buried beside his father at Burnham Thorpe, in Norfolk.

in speaking, and when they came they tumbled over each other in their urgency. 'Fan, fan!' he said. And to Scott, who had previously been massaging his breast with his hand and giving him some relief from the pain, 'Rub, rub!' Then, says Beatty, 'he every now and then, with evident increase of pain, made a great effort with his vocal powers, and pronounced distinctly these last words: "Thank God I have done my duty"; and this great sentiment he continued to repeat as long as he was able to give it utterance.

'His Lordship became speechless in about fifteen minutes after Captain Hardy left him. Dr Scott and Mr Burke, who had all along sustained the bed under his shoulders (which raised him to a semi-recumbent posture, the only one that was supportable to him), forbore to disturb him by speaking to him; and when he had remained speechless about five minutes, his Lordship's steward went to the surgeon, who had been a short time occupied with the wounded in another part of the cockpit, and stated his apprehension that his Lordship was dying.

'The surgeon immediately repaired to him, and found him on the verge of dissolution. He knelt down by his side and took up his hand, which was cold, and the pulse gone from the wrist. On the surgeon's feeling his forehead, which was likewise cold, his Lordship opened his eyes, looked up, and shut them again.

'The surgeon again left him, and returned to the wounded who required his assistance; but was not absent five minutes before the steward announced that "he believed his Lordship had expired". The surgeon returned, and found that the report was but too well founded: his Lordship had breathed his last, at thirty minutes past four o'clock; at which period Dr Scott was in the act of rubbing his Lordship's breast, and Mr Burke supporting the bed under his shoulders.'

The *Victory*'s log recorded: '*Partial firing continued until* 4.30, *when a victory having been reported to the Right Honourable Lord Viscount Nelson, he then died of his wound.*'

28

THE GREAT GALE

EVERY ship set about clearing up the wreckage, tending the wounded and disposing of the dead. Lt Paul Nicolas of the *Belleisle* gives perhaps the best description of the hours immediately following the end of the battle. There were two periods in the life of a sailor which were impressive above all others, he said. One was going to general quarters, when each man hoped to see his friends again; and the other was when the battle was over 'and our kindlier feelings resumed their sway.'

He wrote: 'Eager inquiries were expressed, and earnest congratulations exchanged, at this joyful moment. The officers came to make their report to the Captain, and the fatal results cast a gloom over the scene of our triumph. I have alluded to the impression of our first lieutenant that he should not survive the contest (see page 222).

'This gallant officer was severely wounded in the thigh, and underwent an amputation: but his prediction was realized, for he expired before the action had ceased. The junior lieutenant was likewise mortally wounded on the quarter-deck. These gallant fellows were lying beside each other in the gun-room preparatory to their being committed to the deep; and here many met to take a last look at their departed friends, whose remains soon followed the promiscuous multitude, without distinction of either rank or nation, to their wide ocean grave.

'In the act of launching a poor sailor over the poop he was discovered to breathe; he was, of course, saved. . . .

'The upper-deck presented a confused and dreadful appearance: masts, yards, sails, ropes and fragments of wreck were scattered in every direction; nothing could be more horrible than the scene of blood and mangled remains with which every part was covered, and which, from the quantity of splinters, resembled a shipwright's yard strewed with gore.

'From our extensive loss—thirty-four killed and ninety-six wounded—our cockpit exhibited a scene of suffering which rarely occurs. I visited this abode of suffering with the natural impulse which led many others thither—namely, to ascertain the fate of a friend or companion. So many bodies in such a confined space and under such distressing circumstances would affect the most obdurate heart. My nerves were but little accustomed to such trials but even the dangers of battle did not seem more terrific than the spectacle before me.

'On a long table lay several anxiously looking for their turn to receive the surgeon's care, yet dreading the fate he might pronounce. One subject was undergoing amputation, and every part was heaped with sufferers: their piercing shrieks and expiring groans were echoed through this vault of misery; and even at this distant period the heart-sickening picture is alive in my memory. What a contrast to the hilarity and enthusiastic mirth which reigned in this spot the preceding evening.

'At all other times the cockpit is the region of conviviality and good humour, for here it is that the happy midshipmen reside, at whose board neither discord nor care interrupt the social intercourse. But a few short hours on these benches, which were now covered with mutilated remains, sat these scions of their country's glory, who hailed the coming hour of conflict with cheerful confidence. . . .

'About five o'clock the officers assembled in the Captain's cabin to take some refreshment. The parching effect of the smoke made this a welcome summons, although some of us had been fortunate in relieving our thirst by plundering the Captain's grapes which hung round his cabin; still, four hours' exertion of body with the energies incessantly employed, occasioned a lassitude, both corporeally and mentally, from which the victorious termination so near at hand could not arouse us; moreover there sat a melancholy on the brows of some who mourned a messmate who had shared their perils and their vicissitudes for many years. Then the merits of the departed heroes were repeated with a sigh, but their errors sunk with them into the deep. . . .

'A boat with a lieutenant from the cutter *Entreprenante* shortly after came on board, on his return from the *Victory*, to announce the death of the immortal Nelson. The melancholy tidings spread through the ship in an instant and the paralysing effect was wonderful.

'Our Captain [Hargood] had served under the illustrious chief for years, and had partaken in the anxious pursuit of the enemy across the Atlantic, with the same officers and crew. "Lord Nelson

M

is no more!" was repeated with such despondency and heartfelt sorrow that everyone seemed to mourn a parent. All exertion was suspended: the veteran sailor indulged in silent grief; and some eyes evinced that tenderness of heart is often concealed under the roughest exterior.'

The French *Achille* blew up at 5.30 p.m. and signalled the end of the battle. Midshipman Hercules Robinson wrote later of how boats from the *Euryalus* were engaged 'getting hold of a dozen of her men who were hoisted into the air out of the exploding ship, cursing their fate, *sacré*-ing, tearing their hair, and wiping the gunpowder and the salt water from their faces; and how, in the evening these same fellows, having got their supper and grog and dry clothes, dancing for the amusement of our men under the half-deck'.

Captain Durham left the *Defiance* to visit Admiral Collingwood in his cabin after he had transferred from the *Royal Sovereign* to the *Euryalus*. Going out on deck afterwards he saw a French officer leaning on the capstan. He discovered that it was in fact Admiral Villeneuve, and began talking to him.

'Sir,' said Villeneuve, 'were you in Sir Robert Calder's action?'

Durham replied that he was, and had commanded the ship which had first discovered Villeneuve's fleet, and that he had remained watching them for four or five hours until Calder arrived. Villeneuve sighed and said: 'I wish Sir Robert and I had fought it out that day. He would not be in his present position, or I in mine.'

When the sun went down that evening, its dying rays making a mauve patina on the high clouds, it left behind it a scene of grandeur and of desolation. The Combined Fleet of France and Spain which, a few brief hours earlier had been drawn up in fine array, was now so badly mauled as to be powerless. Seventeen French and Spanish ships had been captured and the eighteenth had blown up—just two short of the twenty for which Nelson had 'bargained'. Dumanoir, with four ships, was sailing off to eventual destruction, and Gravina with the remaining eleven was heading for the safety of Cadiz. Not one of the British Fleet of twenty-seven ships which had gone into action against the thirty-three of the enemy had been sunk, or forced to strike.

But the great swell which had rolled across the scene of battle and the fronds of high cloud which had finally merged into an ominous grey sheet, were no idle portents: by next day there was a gale blowing, and the day after that, October 23, great seas were sweeping in from the west, rolling along before the screaming winds. It was into this that Captain Cosmao, of the *Pluton*, led twelve French and Spanish ships (*Pluton, Indomptable, Neptune, Rayo* and *San Francisco de Asis*, with five frigates and two brigs) out of Cadiz to try to recapture some of the prizes which were now drifting at the mercy of the weather.

The remaining British ships in the area rallied, but the weather was too bad for battle. Cosmao managed to get the *Santa Ana* and French *Neptune* in tow and take them back to Cadiz, but the sally cost him three of his five battleships. The *Indomptable* was wrecked off Rota in the gale and most of her crew, along with about five hundred survivors from the *Bucentaure*, were drowned; the *San Francisco de Asis* went ashore in Cadiz Bay and MacDonell's *Rayo*, forced to anchor off San Lucar, rolled her masts over the side in the heavy seas. She was captured by the British next day, but later went ashore. Of the seventeen prizes left to Collingwood, six went ashore and were wrecked, two were retaken by Cosmao, five were scuttled or burnt because Collingwood thought he could not save them in the gale, and four were taken into Gibraltar. With Dumanoir's four ships captured by Sir Richard Strachan on November 4, the final result was that of the thirty-three French and Spanish ships in the battle of October 21, fifteen were destroyed by sinking or going ashore, eight were taken in as prizes, and ten managed to get into Cadiz, although many of these were very badly damaged and only three were fit for service.

Of the seven French and Spanish admirals who had watched Nelson's coming into action against them, one was now dead and five were wounded. Two of the ten commodores had been killed and four wounded. Approximately 3,370 French officers and men had been killed or drowned and 1,160 wounded; and the Spanish casualties were 1,038 killed or drowned and 1,385 wounded—an approximate total (since French and Spanish reports were not complete) of 4,408 dead and 2,545 wounded. Against this total the British casualties were remarkably small—449 officers and men killed and 1,214 wounded. One admiral and two captains had been killed; one admiral (who failed to report the fact) and four captains wounded.

The *Pickle* was, as described at the beginning of this narrative, sent home with the news of the great battle. In the *Victory* Nelson's body had been put in a large cask—called a leaguer—which had been filled with brandy. The crew of the *Victory* were at first worried because of the rumours that reached them about the *Euryalus* returning home. As Marine James Bagley later wrote home to his sister, 'They have behaved very well to us, for they wanted to take Lord Nelson from us, but we told Captain as we brought him out we would bring him home; so it was so . . .'

But the ship was far from being safe. On the night of the battle Captain Hardy had set the crew to work getting runners and tackles fitted to secure the fore and mainmasts—the mizen had gone by the board. He managed to wear the ship round and, as the Master's log noted, 'stood to the southward under the remnants of the foresail and main-topsail'. At daylight next day, October 22, the men were still busy knotting and splicing, with the carpenter and his mates repairing the foremast. The old mainsail had been shot to pieces, so an old foresail was brought up and set in its place. Next day, the 23rd, as they tried to get the wreck of the mizenmast clear, the cloud and fresh breezes turned into a strong gale, with heavy seas threatening to roll what remained of the masts out of the ship. For the rest of that day and night the *Victory* wallowed; but just before dawn the weather eased up, and after breakfast Hardy mustered the crew to check the casualty list. At 11 a.m. Captain Redmill brought the *Polyphemus* close enough to pass a hawser from the middle-deck bow port of the *Victory* to the wardroom windows of the *Polyphemus*.

The high land of Rota, at the north end of Cadiz Bay, could be seen some fifteen to eighteen miles away to the eastward, and in fresh winds the two ships made their way towards Gibraltar. However, the strong gale returned next day, October 25; by the evening violent winds had carried away the *Victory*'s main-yard and split the mainsail and main-topsail. By the time the wreckage was cleared away they suddenly saw the *Polyphemus* forge ahead —the towing hawser had parted. 'We shipped three heavy seas which filled the deck,' wrote Midshipman Rivers. 'Turned all hands to the pumps. Hoisted the launch lug-sail to a rough spar attached to the cap of the ensign staff [which kept] the ship to and kept her from foundering.'

The former flagship, left drifting almost helpless in the gale, had to be pumped the whole night, and dawn on October 26 brought little encouragement. Across the great grey and swirling waves to the north-east they could see the *Royal Sovereign* flying a distress signal, and the *Africa* near her with all her masts gone. Hardy, disregarding the *Victory*'s danger, sent the *Polyphemus* to the aid of the *Royal Sovereign*.

Later in the afternoon, when the wind had dropped slightly, Thomas Fremantle brought the *Neptune* down to take the *Victory* in tow. On the evening of October 28, Captain Hardy's Journal noted: 'At 7, anchored in Rosia Bay, Gibraltar.'

On November 3, having been partially refitted, the *Victory* sailed for England to take Nelson's body home. On December 4 she anchored at St Helen's, in the Solent, whence, on September 14, Nelson had boarded her to sail for his last battle.

Six days passed before orders arrived to take the ship round to the Thames, and on December 22, after she had weathered the North Foreland and was heading up the Estuary, the *Victory* was met by Commissioner Grey's yacht *Chatham*. The Board of Admiralty had sent her to receive Nelson's body and take it to Greenwich. The body was taken from the coffin in front of 'all the officers in the ship, and several of his Lordship's friends', according to Beatty, and after being dressed in a shirt, stockings and uniform, was placed in the coffin which Captain Hallowell had had made from the *L'Orient*'s mast. This was placed inside a leaden coffin which was sealed and put in a wooden shell.

Commissioner Grey's yacht was brought alongside and the coffin lowered on board. As the yard-tackle lifted it from the deck of the *Victory*, Nelson's flag at the fore was struck for the last time and hoisted, at half-mast, aboard the *Chatham*. On January 9, 1806, Nelson was buried under the great dome of St Paul's Cathedral, and among those who saw the funeral procession were Vice-Admiral Villeneuve and Captain Magendie, who had been given permission to come up from Bishop's Waltham, in Hampshire, where they were living on parole.

The French prisoners—210 officers and 4,589 men—were brought to England. Those landed at Chatham were taken on board four prison hulks (shortly to be reinforced by two Trafalgar prizes, the *Bahama*, and the *Swiftsure*, under her new name of *Irresistible*). Those brought to Plymouth were taken to Millbay Prison or one of the eight hulks in the Hamoaze (some of them were eventually transferred to Dartmoor Jail after it was completed). The rest were landed at Portsmouth and put in prisons or hulks. Most officers were kept on parole at Crediton, Devon, and Wincanton, Somerset. Later, when Villeneuve was given a choice of any town more than thirty miles north or west of London, he chose Reading and was accompanied there by Magendie, Lucas and Infernet. Magendie was soon sent to France to arrange a proper system of exchange for the prisoners, while the other three were allowed to visit English families. Lucas became quite a popular figure in London society.

But in April 1806, having been a prisoner for just over five months, Villeneuve was freed in exchange for four British post captains, and sent back to France. Crossing the Channel in a small boat, he landed at Morlaix, in Brittany. Settling himself in at an hotel, he wrote to Admiral Decrès, reporting his arrival. What were the Minister's instructions? He said he would go on to Rennes, to where the Minister's orders should be sent. Villeneuve then went by coach to Rennes and took a room at the Hotel de la Patrie to await the letter from Decrès. He discovered that Lucas and Infernet, who had already been exchanged and were in Paris, had been promoted rear-admirals.

But no letter came from Decrès; there was no summons from the Emperor bidding him to St Cloud. And all the time, as the days passed, Villeneuve became more agitated. Finally, on the morning of April 22, he was found lying dead in his bed. An ordinary table knife had been driven up to its hilt in his chest, and there were five other stab wounds. The authenticity of a letter alleged to have been left by Villeneuve, addressed to his wife and saying that his life was a disgrace and death a duty, and asking her forgiveness for his suicide, has never been proved. Whether Villeneuve committed suicide or, as rumour had it, he was murdered on Napoleon's orders, will never be known for certain.

EPILOGUE

TRAFALGAR was one of the most decisive naval battles ever fought by the Royal Navy, and its effects are still felt in Britain today. Yet the day before Nelson defeated Napoleon at sea, the Emperor had won an apparently crushing victory on land. As we have already seen (pages 145–6) he had attacked General Mack's 70,000 Austrians at Ulm with 200,000 of his highly-trained, enthusiastic men, and forced him to surrender on October 20. When this news reached England nine days later—seven days before Lapenotiere arrived in a fog-bound London with Collingwood's Trafalgar despatch—the nation despaired: Pitt's masterly plan to bring the power of Russia and Austria to bear against Napoleon had failed even before it was properly launched.

'You have no idea of the consternation here,' Lady Bessborough had written to Lord Granville Leveson-Gower. 'I am so terrified, so shocked with the news, I scarcely know what to wish.' And we have already seen that when the news of Trafalgar eventually arrived in London, the nation mourned the death of Nelson rather than celebrated the victory: they were far too close to the event to see exactly what it achieved.

As far as the war (which was to last another ten years) was concerned, there seemed at the time no hope for Britain. Pitt died less than three months after Nelson. Lord Sheffield spoke for many of the nation when he wrote: 'Unless something extraordinary happens, I shall consider the game as lost.'

Yet the tide *had* turned. After Trafalgar, Napoleon had no fleet to use in the Mediterranean, which was controlled by the Royal Navy. Sicily was in British hands and Napoleon's door to Egypt was shut. With its slamming went his dreams of an Eastern empire.

Trafalgar finally cut Napoleon off from the sea. Forced into a purely continental strategy, he started off on the steps which led him inexorably to defeat on the snow-covered plains of Russia and, eventually, to the decks of the *Bellerophon* and exile. Thus, with the Fleet of France destroyed as a challenger—although Napoleon later partly rebuilt his shattered force—Britain was given more than a hundred years in which to build up and expand an Empire, a century in which the Royal Navy guaranteed that the sea lanes were kept open—not only for Britain but for every other law-abiding nation.

The effect of Trafalgar was still very evident in the Royal Navy's strength at the beginning of the First World War and, despite many sacrifices to political expediency, at the beginning of the Second World War. But the cost of defeating Hitler proved too much for Britain, and the demands of the Welfare State and more political expediency have combined to lose for the nation many of the great material benefits bestowed on it by Nelson's great victory.

Something which in the long run may prove more valuable than the material benefits still remains, and this book may serve to bring it once again into sharper focus: Nelson and Trafalgar established a tradition of bold tactics, a standard of personal bravery, of devotion, and a lesson in dedication to duty which has become a part of the British character. It made Britain stand firm at times of apparent defeat. Yet the victory was in one sense a mixed blessing: Nelson's methods at Trafalgar were so effective that they led to a stagnation in the study and practice of naval tactics which lasted for many decades. It also helped to foster that dangerous legend that Britain 'muddles through': Nelson's victory in the midst of a war for which Britain was singularly ill-equipped to fight has been taken as a justification for lack of political foresight and realism.

The muddlers and their apologists, however, have tended to lose sight of the fact that although Britain was ill-prepared for war in 1805, Nelson, the greatest admiral the world has ever seen, was at the height of his power: natural genius had blended with experience to make him, given reasonable odds, invincible. In a period when naval battles sometimes tended to be indecisive in the long run, it is worth noting that the Nile, Copenhagen and Trafalgar were three of the most decisive naval actions ever fought.

The Battle was not fought exactly in the way that Nelson had laid down in his Memorandum, but as we have seen, subsequent criticism has lost sight of the fact that it was a memorandum and not a rigid set of instructions: it was intended as an *aide-mémoire* after Nelson's discussion with his captains on board the *Victory*. At the last moment Nelson departed from a rigid movement to seize the advantage that speed would give him to smash an enemy making for its home port. He forced battle on an enemy which had a bolt-hole to leeward; he forced them to fight the battle the way he wanted. Villeneuve, as we have seen, guessed the method that Nelson would use, yet such was the brilliance of its conception that Villeneuve could not devise a method of defeating it.

'The risk he took of having the heads of his two columns isolated by a loss of wind or crushed prematurely by the concentration to which he exposed them naked, almost passed the limits of sober leading,' says Corbett. 'Its justification was its success and the known defects of his opponents. Yet it may be permitted to doubt whether if he had realized how much higher was the spirit of his enemy than he expected, he would have dared so greatly.'

The main criticism has been that Nelson with his end-on approach laid his ships open to the risk of being dismasted by the massed broadsides of the enemy before they could break the line and bring their own guns to bear. Yet not one British ship was dismasted before it got into close action with the enemy. Nelson knew from long experience that the enemy gunnery tended to be wild—and it was; he knew the enemy officers and men were for the most part unskilled—and we have seen, from their own accounts, that he was right. Making allowances for the French, Spanish and British ships which came into action too late to affect the issue, twenty-three British ships fought twenty-eight French and Spanish ships and beat them. Yet several French and Spanish ships fought with remarkable bravery—the *Bucentaure*, *Redoutable*, *Intrépide* and *Santissima Trinidad*, to name a few. Although it may seem a harsh judgment, the fact is that when the French and Spanish ships found themselves trapped in the midst of the British ships they fought with skill and fury, but not enough of them found themselves in this situation to prevent victory going to the British. It is quite clear, though, from contemporary accounts already quoted and particularly the council of war held in Cadiz, that many of the French and Spanish captains felt they were defeated even before they cleared Cadiz Roads.

However, Trafalgar was not a victory won cheaply by the British: many long months and years of ceaseless vigilance and blockade had gone into it. Then, as in 1940, Britain fought alone against the most powerful force in the world, holding the ring until other nations could be rallied round. And looking back over the whole campaign, one realizes more fully why Lt Lapenotiere, bursting into the Board Room of the Admiralty at the dead of night, was not being melodramatic when his first words were: 'Sir, we have gained a great victory, but we have lost Lord Nelson.'

It was a woman, Lady Londonderry, stepmother of Lord Castlereagh, the Secretary for War, who wrote perhaps the wisest words about the death of Nelson shortly after his funeral: 'Never was there indeed an event so mournfully and so triumphantly important to England as the Battle of Trafalgar. The sentiment of the lamenting the individual more than rejoicing in the victory, shows the humanity and affection of the people of England; but their good sense and reflection will dwell only on the conquest, because no death, at a future moment, could have been more glorious.'

Then she added, with a mixture of logic and instinct, a few lines which crystallized all that the victory meant for the far distant future. "The public would never have sent him on another expedition; his health was not equal to another effort, and so might have yielded to the natural but less imposing effect of more worldly honours: whereas he now begins his immortal career, having left nothing to achieve on earth, and bequeathing to the English fleet a legacy which they alone are able to improve.

'Had I been his wife, or his mother, I would rather have wept him dead than seen him languish on a less splendid day. In such a death there is no sting, and in such a grave everlasting victory.'

NOTES AND BIBLIOGRAPHY

CHAPTER ONE (pages 15–30)

The Pickle *and* Euryalus*:* log of the *Pickle* (Public Records Office, Admiralty 53/3669, part II) kept by George Almy, Second Master and Pilot; log of *Euryalus*, given in *Logs of the Great Sea Fights*, edited by Rear-Admiral T. Sturges Jackson, vol. 2 (Navy Records Society, 1900); Muster Book of the *Pickle* (PRO, Ady 36/1650). According to this the *Pickle* did not have a Master at this time. The assistant—and apparently sole—surgeon is given as L. G. Britton, although *The Trafalgar Roll*, apparently erroneously, gives him as Simon Gage.

Details of the *Pickle* and the *Entreprenante*, the two smallest ships at Trafalgar, from Progress Books and List of Ships, Admiralty:

	Pickle	*Entreprenante*
Displacement (tons) ..	127	123
Length (on gun deck)..	73 ft	67 ft
Beam	20 ft	21 ft
Complement	40	40
Armament	eight 12-pdr carronades	ten 12-pdr carronades

The *Pickle* was built at Plymouth and originally named the *Sting*. Bought by the Royal Navy in 1800, she was renamed the *Pickle*—the first ever to bear that name—in 1802. She had been under the command of Lapenotiere since December 1804. The *Entreprenante* was captured from the French in 1798.

Collingwood's Dispatches: see *Letters and Dispatches of Lord Nelson*, edited by Sir H. Nicolas, vol. 7 (London, 1846); *London Gazette*, November 6, 1805.

Blackwood: see 'A Memoir of Sir Henry Blackwood', in *Blackwood's Edinburgh Magazine*, No. CCX, vol. 34, July 1833; and Nicolas vol. 7. The two versions of the letter vary slightly.

Lapenotiere: The family originally called itself La Penotiere. John was the son of an RN lieutenant and came from Ilfracombe, joining the Navy in 1780 at the age of ten. See also *The Enemy at Trafalgar*, Edward Fraser (Hodder and Stoughton, 1906).

The Victory's *Crew:* Muster book of the *Victory* (PRO, Ady 36/15900).

The Nautilus*:* She has variously been described as a cutter and a lugger, but the Progress Books and List of Ships, Admiralty, make it quite clear she was a 443-ton, ship-rigged sloop. She was built at

Milford Haven and launched in April 1804. *Movements*—see log of
the *Nautilus* (PRO, Ady 51/15441). Captain Sykes sailed for England
on his own initiative. Some accounts say that he and Lapenotiere
arrived at the Admiralty at the same time, but the logs of both ships
and the direct written evidence of Marsden, Secretary to the Board,
show this to have been impossible.

CHAPTER TWO (pages 31–43)

Lady Bessborough: see *Lord Granville Leveson-Gower, Private
Correspondence 1781–1821,* edited by Castalia, Countess Granville,
vol. 2.

Activities in the Admiralty: Tasks set out by Lord Barham, May
1805 (PRO, Ady 3/256): *A Brief Memoir of the Life and Writings of the
late William Marsden, DCL, FRS* (printed in 1838 for private circu-
lation); *Correspondence of Vice-Admiral Lord Collingwood,* by G. L.
Newnham Collingwood, vol. 2 (published London, 1838); *Naval
Chronicle,* vol. 17; *An Autobiographical Memoir of Sir John Barrow*
(London, 1847); *Diaries and Correspondence of the 1st Earl of Malmes-
bury,* vol. 4; Fraser, *Enemy;* the letters from Colonel Taylor, including
the one naming the battle, are in the possession of Mr Christopher
Marsden; Lord Arden's letter is given in Marsden; *Memoirs of the
Life of Sir Edward Codrington,* by his daughter, Lady Bouchier, vol. 1;
The Wynne Diaries, edited by Anne Fremantle, vol. 3 (OUP, 1940);
Barham's letter to Lady Nelson, British Museum, Add. MSS 28,333.

CHAPTER THREE (pages 44–51)

The Invasion: see *Projets et Tentatives de Débarquement aux Iles
Britanniques,* by Colonel Edouard Desbrière (Paris, 1907); *Napoleon
and the Invasion of England,* by H. F. B. Wheeler and A. M. Broadley,
vol. 2 (Bodley Head, 1908); *Years of Victory,* by Sir Arthur Bryant
(Collins, 1945); *Consulate and Empire,* by Thiers, vol. 3 (English
edition 1893, translated by Forbes Campbell and Stebbing); *Memoirs
of Mme Rémusat,* vol. 1.

CHAPTER FOUR (page 52–58)

The Invasion: see *Wynne Diaries;* Wheeler and Broadley; *The Three
Dorset Captains at Trafalgar,* by Broadley and Bartelot (Murray, 1906);
Bryant; *A Pop-gun Fired by George Cruickshank in Defence of the
British Volunteers of 1803; English Caricature and Satire on Napoleon,*
by John Ashton; 'A Sermon preached in a Country Village previous
to the Enrollment of Volunteers', by the Rev Cornelius Miles, 'Rector
and Captain'; *George Crabbe and His Times 1754–1832,* by Huchon,
translated by Frederick Clarke; *Narrative of Some Passages in the
Great War with France from 1799 to 1810,* by Lieut-General Sir
Henry Bunbury.

CHAPTER FIVE (pages 59–67)

The French Navy: see *The Influence of Sea Power on the French Revolution and Empire,* and *The Influence of Sea Power Upon History,* by Admiral A. T. Mahan; 'The French Navy in 1805', by John Leyland, in *United Services Institute Magazine,* November 1905; Wheeler and Broadley; Fraser, *Enemy.*

The Royal Navy: see *Naval History of Great Britain,* by Captain E. P. Brenton, vol. 1; *The Naval History of Great Britain,* by William James (1902 edition); *Sea Life in Nelson's Time,* by John Masefield (Methuen, 1905); *Naval Chronicle,* vols. 6 and 10; Collingwood; *Buckler's Hard and its Ships,* by the 2nd Lord Montagu of Beaulieu (printed privately, 1909); *History of a Ship,* anonymous.

Nelson Letters: see Nicolas.

CHAPTER SIX (pages 68–79)

The Royal Navy: The wording of Loyagalo's attestation, oath, certificate and receipt was given in *Globe and Laurel,* May 1929; rates of pay in *Naval Regulations and Instructions;* life afloat is taken from a large number of official and private sources and also from Masefield, the novels of Marryat, Chamier and Glascock, *Nautical Economy,* by 'Jack Nasty-Face', court martial reports, ships' logs, and officers' journals.

CHAPTER SEVEN (pages 80–85)

Napoleon's moves: see *Napoleon 1,* by Professor A. Fournier, vol. 1 (second edition, 1904–6, Longmans Green, 1911); *The Campaign of Trafalgar,* by J. S. Corbett (Longmans Green, 1910); *Mémoires de Miot de Melito,* vol. 2, quoted by Fournier, and Corbett; *The Trafalgar Campaign,* by Col E. Desbrière (Paris, 1907). In the present narrative the excellent translation by Miss Constance Eastwick is used (Clarendon Press, 1933).

CHAPTER EIGHT (pages 86–96)

Villeneuve: see Desbrière, *Trafalgar;* Corbett; *The Life of Nelson,* by Admiral A. T. Mahan (Sampson Low, 1897). Corbett says Villeneuve sailed on the 17th, but Desbrière, Mahan and Nelson himself give the 18th—'The French Fleet sailed from Toulon on Friday last, the 18th,' Nelson wrote to Sir John Acton on January 22.

Nelson: see Nicolas; *Nelson and His Captains,* by W. H. Fitchett (Smith, Elder, 1902); Corbett; Mahan, *Nelson; Wynne Diaries; The Life of Nelson,* by Robert Southey (London, 1813); *The Life and Services of Horatio, Viscount Nelson,* by the Rev J. Clarke and J. M'Arthur (London, 1809).

Napoleon: see Fournier; *Relations Secrètes des Agents de Louis XVIII,* by Remacle, quoted by Fournier; *Dispatches and Letters Relating to the Blockade of Brest,* by John Leyland, vol. 2 (Navy Records Society, 1902); Corbett; Desbrière, *Projets* and *Trafalgar.*

CHAPTER NINE (pages 97–107)

Napoleon and Villeneuve: see Desbrière, *Trafalgar*; Leyland, *Blockade*; Corbett.

Fleet movements and Admiralty orders: British Museum, Nelson Papers 34930, folio 74; PRO, Admiralty Secret Orders, 1636; Desbrière, *Trafalgar* and *Projets*; Corbett; Nicolas; Mahan; Leyland, *Blockade: Naval Chronicle*.

Corbett is in error in saying that Lord Mark Kerr sailed from Gibraltar in the *Fisgard* the day *after* Villeneuve passed through the Strait. His letter of April 23, 1805, to Lord Gardner, makes this quite clear as he is using nautical time. Also Nelson's letter to Marsden, dated May 1, says 'As the *Fisgard* sailed from Gibraltar on the 9th, two hours after the enemy's fleet from Toulon passed through the Strait . . .'

CHAPTER TEN (pages 108–112)

Fleet movements: see Desbrière, *Trafalgar*; Leyland, *Blockade*; Corbett; Mahan, *Nelson*; Nicolas; James.

CHAPTER ELEVEN (pages 113–122)

Nelson and Merton: see Nicolas; Fitchett; Clarke and M'Arthur, vol. 3; *Life and Correspondence of H. Addington, Viscount Sidmouth*, by G. Pellew; Leveson-Gower; *Naval Chronicle*. Keats's account of his conversation with Nelson is given in Nicolas, vol. 7.

CHAPTER TWELVE (pages 123–137)

Orders: see PRO, Ady 2/150 (for Berry, and the *Agamemnon, Thunderer, Ajax, Euryalus, Defiance, Superb, Royal Sovereign* and *Victory*, PRO, Admiralty In-Letters (Secret Orders), 1363, September 3; BM, Add MSS. 34931.

Signals: see *Signal Book for Ships of War, 1799*, with corrections; *Nelson's Signals: the Evolution of the Signal Flags*, Admiralty, NID, Historical, 1908; *Trafalgar Signals*, by Cdr Hilary P. Mead (Percival Marshall, 1936); Corbett; Barrow.

According to Corbett, Barrow's memory is at fault in referring to an improved and enlarged version because the third and final part was issued in 1803.

Nelson in London: see *The Croker Papers*, vol. 2 (the Duke of Wellington gave an account of his meeting with Nelson to John Croker, Secretary to the Board of Admiralty, 1809–30, when in retirement at Walmer twenty-nine years later); Nicolas; Southey; Clarke and M'Arthur; *Life and Letters of Sir Gilbert Elliot, 1st Earl of Minto* (London, 1874); Leveson-Gower; *Nelson*, by Carola Oman (Hodder and Stoughton, 1947).

CHAPTER THIRTEEN (pages 138–143)

Napoleon and Villeneuve: see Desbrière, *Trafalgar* and *Projets*; Thiers; Corbett; Fournier.

Writing of Napoleon's decision to attack Austria, Professor Fournier writes: 'Until recent times wide credence was given to General Daru's statement that the idea of a continental war only occurred to Napoleon after receiving Villeneuve's dispatches, and that he then dictated the plan of campaign on a sudden flash of inspiration. But this is only part of the Napoleonic mythology. The struggle had long been foreseen and the time and mode of procedure decided upon after mature deliberation.' (vol. 1, p. 365.)

CHAPTER FOURTEEN (pages 144–150)

Napoleon and the Combined Fleet: see Desbrière, *Trafalgar*; Clarke and M'Arthur; Corbett.

Nelson's comment on General Mack dates from the Admiral's days in Naples, when Mack was sent to command the Neapolitan Army.

The French Navy's habit of firing at their enemy's rigging was probably a hangover from privateering. When chased by a more powerful ship, a privateer often escaped because a lucky shot damaged her opponent's rigging. But in a pitched battle—particularly against the British, whose trained seamen quickly repaired damage to masts and rigging—it was damage to the hull that decided the issue.

CHAPTER FIFTEEN (pages 151–166)

Nelson: see Nicolas; Codrington; Collingwood; *Naval Chronicle*; Leyland, *Blockade*; James.

Nelson's captains: For details of their length of service with Nelson, the author has made use of material supplied by Rear-Admiral A. H. Taylor, to whom he is indebted. The details were also given in Rear-Admiral Taylor's article 'The Battle of Trafalgar', in the journal of the Society for Nautical Research, vol. 36, no. 4, October 1950. See also—Codrington; *Wynne Diaries*; *Naval Chronicle*; *The Book of the Duffs*, by A. and H. Taylor, vol. 2 (Brown, Edinburgh, 1914); *The Naval History of the Patey Family*, by C. Harvey (published privately); *Jane Austen's Sailor Brothers*, by J. H. and E. C. Hubback (Bodley Head, 1906); *Memoirs of the Life and Services of Admiral Sir Philip C. H. C. Durham*, by Captain A. Murray (John Murray, 1846).

For additional information the author is also indebted to the Misses Duff, of Bolton Gardens, South Kensington (descendants of Captain George Duff), who gave him permission to use documents in their possession, and to the Earl of Northesk, who owns many hitherto unpublished documents concerning his forebear, and also Nelson and Trafalgar.

Jane Austen's sailor brothers were Rear-Admiral Charles Austen and Captain Herbert Austen. Francis, to whom we have already referred, eventually became an Admiral of the Fleet and was also knighted.

CHAPTER SIXTEEN (pages 167–179)

Villeneuve and his officers: see Desbrière, *Trafalgar*; Collingwood; Fraser, *Enemy* (which gives a lot of detail unobtainable from any other source); *Sea Drift*, by Vice-Admiral Hercules Robinson.

Fraser says only thirteen officers—seven French and six Spanish—attended the Council of War, but he is in error: fourteen signed the Minute (Desbrière, vol. 2, p. 107)—seven French and seven Spanish. Fraser includes Churruca, who did not sign the Minute, and omits Hore and MacDonell, who did. This is borne out by Villeneuve's letter to Decrès of October 8 which enclosed the signed Minute.

Corbett has apparently misunderstood Escaño's report of the Council's meeting (Desbrière, vol. 2, pp. 107–10) and says it was Prigny who made the speech. He also refers to Galiano as a brigadier commanding some of the Spanish troops, whereas he was a commodore commanding the *Bahama*.

British ship movements: see Desbrière, *Trafalgar*; Corbett; the letter from the midshipman of the *L'Aimable* is used by permission of the Earl of Radnor; Robinson; Broadley and Bartelot; Cumby in a letter printed in the *Nineteenth Century Review*, November 1899.

CHAPTER SEVENTEEN (pages 180–197)

French and Spanish movements: see Desbrière, *Trafalgar*, and *Projets*; Fraser, *Enemy*. The reports of the French and Spanish ships differ considerably over the times that signals were made from October 18 until after the battle. There are discrepancies of up to five hours in the logs.

British movements: see *Logs*; Nicolas; Corbett; Robinson; Codrington; *Report of a Committee Appointed by the Admiralty to Examine and Consider the Evidence Relating to the Tactics used by Nelson at the Battle of Trafalgar* (hereinafter referred to as *Report*), published 1913 (HM Stationery Office); *English Illustrated*, October 1905, in which extracts from Lt Halloran's Journal are given in an article written by his granddaughter; the letter of the Earl of Northesk, previously unpublished, is in the possession of the present Earl.

CHAPTER EIGHTEEN (pages 198–215)

British Fleet: see Robinson; *Five Naval Journals* (Navy Records Society); Collingwood; Captain Duff's letter is in the possession of the Misses Duff; Blackwood (the wording varies slightly from that given in Nicholas, vol. 7); *The Sailors Whom Nelson Led*, by Edward Fraser (Methuen, 1913); Muster List of the *Victory*; *Personal Narrative of Events from 1799 to 1815*, by Vice-Admiral William S. Lovell (Badcock assumed the surname Lovell in 1840); Halloran; Codrington; 'Minutes of the Action of Trafalgar', by W. Thorpe, one of the officers of the *Minotaur*, hitherto unpublished, in National Maritime Museum, MS 9735; *Naval Chronicle; Memoirs of the Life and Services of Admiral Sir William Hargood*, by Joseph Allen; *Bijou* magazine, 1839; *Britain's Sea Soldiers*, by Col C. Field (Lyceum Press, 1924).

'*The Fleet to bear up and sail large*' (see page 202). It is over these two signals that a great deal of controversy has arisen. They naturally had a considerable bearing on the point which was at issue: did the two columns go about 'in succession'—each ship turning when it reached the point that its next ahead turned—to attack in line ahead; or did Nelson want them to manœuvre 'together', so that he could attack in line abreast? Even to outline the controversy would take two long chapters. The present author's views on how the attack was carried out are made clear in successive chapters. The complexity of the subject can be gauged by the fact that the Admiralty in 1912 appointed a special committee to report on it.

British signals: There is considerable variation in the time that individual ships report signals being made and received. Since most of them originated from the *Victory*, her times are used (see *Report*) in preference to the *Euryalus* and other ships (see *Logs*).

CHAPTER NINETEEN (pages 216–226)

British Fleet: As for previous chapter, and *A Sailor of King George, the Journal of Captain Frederick Hoffman, RN, 1793–1814*, edited by A. Beckford Bevan and H. B. Wolryche-Whitmore (John Murray, 1901); Cumby; Report of the *Defiance*'s carpenter, hitherto unpublished, NMM; Mid Aikenhead's letter in *Naval Chronicle; The Life of Sir John Franklin, RN*, by H. D. Traill (John Murray, 1896).

CHAPTER TWENTY (pages 227–239)

French and Spanish movements: see Desbrière, *Trafalgar*; *Trafalgar*, by Perez Galdos, quoted in Fraser, *Enemy*.

British movements: Nicolas; *Narrative of the Death of Lord Nelson*, by Dr Beatty; *Journals*; Midshipman Rivers's account is from his 'Notes on Trafalgar and Naval Affairs', NMM, Wellcome MSS 30; the account of Pasco is in Nicolas; Fraser; Lt Nicolas in *Bijou*, 1929; Blackwood's account in Nicolas.

CHAPTER TWENTY-ONE (pages 240–256)

The Battle: see James; Desbrière, *Trafalgar*; Beatty; Fraser, *Sailors* and *Enemy*; Clarke and M'Arthur; *The Trafalgar Roll*, by Col R. H. Mackenzie.

Some reports say that Lt Ram was wounded after Nelson; but Beatty makes it clear this was not the case.

The *Victory's* official returns listed seventy-five wounded, but Beatty says that a further twenty-seven men reported themselves wounded after the returns were made up.

CHAPTER TWENTY-TWO (pages 257–270)

French and Spanish movements: as for Chapter Twenty.

British movements: see *Wynne Diaries*; Lovell; James; *Logs*; letter of Lt (later Sir) Humphrey Senhouse, printed in *Macmillan's Magazine*, April 1900; Halloran; Fraser, *Sailors*; Robinson; *Regulations and Instructions*.

Certain accounts say that Prigny was taken prisoner, but Prigny's own report (Desbrière, *Trafalgar*, vol. 2, pp. 148–56, dated Cadiz, October 25, 1805) makes it clear that this was not the case.

The exact times at which individual British, French and Spanish ships engaged each other, according to their own reports, are almost impossible to determine accurately. Certain times are taken from Desbrière, James and individual logs; but this narrative relies principally on a detailed time-table worked out by Rear-Admiral Taylor, who kindly placed it at the author's disposal.

CHAPTER TWENTY-THREE (pages 271–289)

British movements: see *Report*; Corbett; James; Taylor; *Logs*; Fraser, *Sailors* (which also gives the letter from the Warnborough sailor, who signs himself 'Sam'); Collingwood; Hargood (which gives Lt Nicolas's account as an appendix); *Duff*; *Naval Chronicle*; Hoffman; *Notes and Queries* (Sixth Series, vol. 4); *Sir Charles Tyler, GCB, Admiral of the White*, by Col Wyndham-Quin (Arthur Humphreys, 1912); Lt Clements, BM Add. MSS 24,813.

French and Spanish movements: Desbrière, *Trafalgar*; Fraser, *Enemy*; *Logs*; *Report*.

CHAPTER TWENTY-FOUR (see pages 290–313)

Movements of both fleets: see Desbrière, *Trafalgar*; Cumby; Franklin; *Logs*; Hargood; *Bellerophon, the Bravest of the Brave*, by Edward Fraser (Wells, Gardner, 1909); Durham; Fraser, *Enemy* and *Sailors*; James; Corbett; Mahan, *Nelson*.

There has been a certain amount of confusion over the *Revenge* and the French *Achille* (see page 309). James refers to her as the *Aigle*—which was busy engaging the *Bellerophon* at that moment. Moorsom does not mention his opponent's name, although other sources make it clear it is the *Achille*. Desbrière says, erroneously (vol. 1, p. 274) that the *Revenge* later passed astern of the *Principe de Asturias*, but Moorsom says he passed ahead.

Gunnery: The words 'fore' and 'aft' were not used when training the guns: the orders were 'left' or 'right'.

CHAPTER TWENTY-FIVE (pages 314–320)

Movements of both fleets: As for Chapter Twenty-four and—logs of the *Pickle* and *Entreprenante*, PRO.

Santa Ana: The Spanish newspaper *Tribuno*, according to Fraser, *Enemy*, reported in April 1882, that Gaspar Vasquez, who had been one of the *Santa Ana*'s crew in the battle, had just died aged 105. The last surviving seaman of the *Victory* in the battle, James Chapman, died in Dundee in 1876, aged ninety-two, while the last surviving officer of the *Victory*, Admiral Sir George Westphal, died a few months earlier. The last two survivors of the battle, both officers, were Admiral Sir George Sartorious (a midshipman in the *Tonnant*), who died in 1885, aged ninety-four; and Lt-Col James Fynmore, RM (of the *Africa*) who died in 1887.

Achille (French): see Desbrière, *Trafalgar*; Moorsom in letter to son; one of the *Revenge*'s lieutenants, quoted in Fraser, *Enemy*; 'Jack Nasty-Face', who gives a slightly different version; Robinson; Durham.

CHAPTER TWENTY-SIX (pages 321–329)

French and Spanish movements: see Desbrière, *Trafalgar*; Fraser, *Enemy*; *Revue des Deux Mondes*, July, 1905.

British movements: see Senhouse; Codrington; *Logs*.

CHAPTER TWENTY-SEVEN (pages 330–335)

Death of Nelson: see Beatty; Nicolas (which also gives a note from Westp hal).

CHAPTER TWENTY-EIGHT (pages 336–342)

Desbrière, *Trafalgar*; Prisoners of War in Britain, 1756–1815, by Francis Abell (OUP, 1914); Fraser, *Enemy*; James; Brenton; *Letters of the English Seamen*, by E. Hallam Moorhouse (Chapman and Hall, 1910); Rivers.

Desbrière says the *Bahama* was sunk, but she was in fact taken to Gibraltar and then to England, where she became a prison hulk at Chatham along with the French *Swiftsure*, which was ironically enough renamed *Irresistible*.

HMS *VICTORY*

Built to the design of Sir Thomas Slade, her keel was laid down at the Old Single Dock, Chatham, on July 23, 1759, and she was launched on May 7, 1765

PARTICULARS

Length on Gun Deck	186′ 0″
Length of Keel	151′ $\frac{5}{8}$″
Moulded Breadth	50′ 6″
Extreme Breadth	51′ 10″
Depth in Hold	21′ 6″
Displacement (Approx.)	3,500 tons
Burthen	2,162 tons

ARMAMENT—1805

Lower Deck	30—32 pounders and 2—12 pounders
Middle Deck	28—24 pounders
Upper Deck	30—12 pounders
Quarter Deck	12—12 pounders
Forecastle	2—68 pounders (Carronades)

KEY TO DRAWING

1. Poop
2. Hammock Nettings
3. Mizenmast
4. Quarter Deck
5. Steering Wheels
6. Here Nelson Fell
7. Pikes
8. Mainmast
9. Gangway
10. Foc's'le
11. Carronades
12. Foremast
13. Captain Hardy's Cabin
14. Upper Deck
15. Nelson's Day Cabin
16. Nelson's Dining Cabin
17. Nelson's Sleeping Cabin with cot
18. Shot Garlands
19. Middle Deck
20. Wardroom
21. Tiller Head
22. Entry Port
23. Capstan Head
24. Galley and Stove
25. Lower Deck
26. Tiller
27. Chain & Elm Tree Pumps
28. Mooring Bitts
29. Manger
30. Orlop
31. Sick Bay
32. Aft Hanging Magazine
33. Lamp Room
34. Midshipman's Berth—here Nelson died
35. Forward Hanging Magazine
36. Powder Store
37. Powder Room
38. Aft Hold
39. Shot Locker
40. Well
41. Main Hold
42. Cable Store
43. Main Magazine
44. Filling Room

APPENDIX I

COMBINED FLEET: Casualties and Damage

Ship	Killed	Wounded	Fate
Bucentaure (F) ..	197	85	Ran ashore, dismasted.
S. Trinidad (Sp) ..	216	116	Dismasted, captured and sunk.
Redoutable (F) ..	490	81	Dismasted, captured and sunk.
Monarca (Sp) ..	101	154	Captured, ran ashore, dismasted.
Argonauta (Sp) ..	100	203	Captured and sunk.
Neptuno (Sp) ..	38	35	Captured, ran ashore, dismasted.
Rayo (Sp) ..	4	14	Went ashore, burnt.*
S. Francisco de Asis (Sp)	5	12	Went ashore.*
San Augustin (Sp)	184	201	Captured and burnt.
Intrépide (F) ..	242	not known	Captured and burnt.
Indomptable ..	Two thirds not known		Went ashore.*
Fougueux (F) ..	546 killed and wounded		Captured, ran ashore, dismasted.
Aigle (F)	Two thirds killed and wounded		Captured, ran ashore, dismasted.
Achille (F) ..	480 killed and wounded		Blew up.
Berwick (F) ..	Nearly all drowned		Captured, ran ashore, dismasted.
Swiftsure (F) ..	68	123	Captured, taken to Gibraltar.
Bahama (Sp) ..	75	66	Captured, taken to Gibraltar.
San Ildefonso (Sp)	36	129	Captured, dismasted, taken to Gibraltar.
S. J. Nepomuceno (Sp)	103	151	Captured, taken to Gibraltar.
Formidable (F) ..	22	45	Captured November 4.
Scipion (F) ..	17	22	Captured November 4.
Duguay-Trouin (F)	12	24	Captured November 4.
Mont-Blanc (F) ..	20	20	Captured November 4.
Santa Ana (Sp) ..	104	137	Recaptured, reached Cadiz, dismasted.
P. de Asturias (Sp)	54	109	Lost main and mizen in gale, reached Cadiz.
Pluton (F) ..	60	132	Again reached Cadiz, sinking.*
Héros (F)	12	24	Reached Cadiz, rigging and rudder damaged.
Neptune (F) ..	15	39	Again reached Cadiz, undamaged.*
Algésiras (F) ..	77	142	Recaptured, dismasted, reached Cadiz.
Argonaute (F) ..	55	132	Masts damaged, rudder lost, reached Cadiz.
San Leandro (Sp)..	8	22	Masts, hulls damaged. Reached Cadiz.
San Justo (Sp) ..	—	7	Masts, hulls damaged. Reached Cadiz.
Montañes (Sp) ..	20	29	Lost foremast, reached Cadiz.

*After sailing on October 23 with Captain Cosmao.

APPENDIX II

BRITISH FLEET; Order of Battle and Sailing, and Casualties

Van Squadron—Starboard Division

Ship	Guns	Killed	Wounded	
Téméraire ..	98	47	76	Captain Eliab Harvey
Victory ..	100	57	102*	V-Ad Lord Nelson; Captain T. M. Hardy
Neptune ..	98	10	34	Captain Thomas Fremantle
Conqueror ..	74	3	9	Captain Israel Pellew
Agamemnon ..	64	2	7	Captain Sir Edward Berry
Leviathan ..	74	4	22	Captain Henry Bayntun
Ajax	74	2	2	Lt John Pilfold
Orion.. ..	74	1	21	Captain Edward Codrington
Minotaur ..	74	3	20	Captain C. J. M. Mansfield
Africa ..	64	18	37	Captain Henry Digby
Spartiate ..	74	3	17	Captain Sir Francis Laforey, Bt

Rear Squadron—Port Division

Ship	Guns	Killed	Wounded	
Prince ..	98	—	—	Captain Richard Grindall
Mars	74	29	69	Captain George Duff
R. Sovereign..	100	47	94	V-Ad C. Collingwood; Captain E. Rotheram
Tonnant ..	80	26	50	Captain Charles Tyler
Belleisle ..	74	33	93	Captain William Hargood
Bellerophon ..	74	27	123	Captain J. Cooke
Colossus ..	74	40	160	Captain James N. Morris
Achille ..	74	13	59	Captain Richard King
Polyphemus ..	64	2	4	Captain Robert Redmill
Revenge ..	74	28	51	Captain Robert Moorsom
Britannia ..	100	10	40	R-Ad the Earl of Northesk; Captain C. Bullen
Swiftsure ..	74	9	8	Captain William Rutherford
Defence ..	74	7	29	Captain George Hope
Thunderer ..	98	4	12	Lt John Stockham
Defiance ..	74	17	53	Captain Philip Durham
Dreadnought ..	98	7	26	Captain John Conn

* Twenty-seven more men reported wounded after the official return of 75 was made up, according to the *Victory*'s surgeon, Beatty.

			Frigates	
Euryalus ..	—	—	—	Captain the Hon Henry Blackwood
Naiad ..	—	—	—	Captain Thomas Dundas
Phoebe ..	—	—	—	Captain the Hon Thomas Bladen Capel
Sirius.. ..	—	—	—	Captain William Prowse
			Schooner	
Pickle.. ..	—	—	—	Lt John Lapenotiere
			Cutter	
Entreprenante	—	—	—	Lt Robert Young

Note: The ships did not eventually go into action in this order. The original Order of Battle and Sailing included several other ships which did not arrive in time for the Battle.

APPENDIX III

NELSON'S MEMORANDUM

NOTE: Subsequent insertions are shown within square brackets and deletions are given in italics.

Victory off Cadiz,

Mem[n.]   9 Octr. 1805.

Thinking it almost impossible to bring a Fleet of forty Sail of the Line into a Line of Battle in variable winds thick weather and other circumstances which must occur, without such a loss of time that the opportunity would probably be lost of bringing the Enemy to Battle in such a manner as to make the business decisive.

I have [therefore] made up my mind to keep the fleet in that position of sailing (with the exception of the first and Second in Command) that the order of Sailing is to be the Order of Battle, placing the fleet in two Lines of Sixteen Ships each with an advanced Squadron of Eight of the fasting [*sic*] sailing Two decked ships [which] will always make if wanted a Line of Twenty four Sail, on which ever Line the Commander in Chief may direct.

The Second in Command will *in fact Command* [his line] *and* after my intentions are made known to him *will* have the entire direction of His Line to make the attack upon the Enemy and to follow up the Blow until they are Capturd or destroy'd.

If the Enemy's fleet should be seen to Windward [in Line of Battle] *but* [and] *in that position that* the Two Lines and the Advanced Squadron can fetch them (I *shall suppose them forty Six Sail* [in] *of the Line of Battle*) they will probably be so extended that their Van could not succour their Rear.

I should therefore probably make *your* the 2nd in Commds signal to Lead through about their Twelfth Ship from their Rear (or wherever *you* [He] could fetch if not able to get so far advanced) My Line would lead through about their Centre and the Advanced Squadron to cut two or three or four Ships Ahead of their Centre, so as to ensure getting at their Commander In Chief on whom every Effort must be made to Capture.

The whole impression of the British [fleet] must be, to overpower from two or three Ships ahead of their Commander In Chief, supposed to be in the centre, to the Rear of their fleet. [I will suppose] twenty Sail of the [Enemys] Line to be untouched, it must be some time before they could perform a Manoeuvre to bring their force compact to attack any part of the British fleet engaged, or to succour their own ships which indeed would be impossible, without mixing with the ships engaged.[1] Something must be left to chance, nothing is sure in a sea fight beyond all others, shot will carry away the masts and yards of friends as well as foes, but I look with confidence to a victory before the van of the Enemy could succour their *friends* [Rear] and then that the British Fleet would most of them be ready to receive their Twenty Sail of the Line or to pursue them should they endeavour to make off.

If the Van of the Enemy tacks the Captured Ships must run to Leeward of the British fleet, if the Enemy wears the British must place themselves between the Enemy and the captured & disabled British Ships and should the Enemy close I have no fear as to the result.

The Second in Command will in all possible things direct the Movements of his Line by keeping them as compact as the nature of the circumstances will admit *and* Captains are to look to their particular Line as their rallying point. But in case signals can neither be seen or perfectly understood no Captain can do very wrong if he places his Ship alongside that of an Enemy.

Of the intended attack from to Windward, the Enemy in Line of Battle ready to receive an attack:

_____

_____   B

_____

_____E_____

The Division of the British fleet will be brought nearly within Gun Shot of the Enemy's Centre. The signal will most probably [then] be made for the Lee Line to bear up together to set all their sails even steering sails[2] in order to get as quickly as possible to the Enemys Line and to Cut through beginning from the 12 ship from the Enemies rear. Some ships may not get through their exact place, but they will always be at hand to assist their friends and if any are thrown round the Rear of the Enemy they will effectually compleat the business of Twelve Sail of the Enemy. Should the Enemy wear together or bear up and sail Large still the Twelve Ships composing in the first position the Enemys rear are to be [the] Object of attack of the Lee Line unless otherwise directed from the Commander In Chief which is scarcely to be expected as the entire management of the Lee Line after the intentions of the Commander In Chief is [are] signified is intended to be left to the Judgement of the Admiral Commanding that Line.

The Remainder of the Enemys fleet 34 Sail are to be left to the Management of the Commander In Chief who will endeavour to take care that the Movements of the Second in Command are as little interrupted as is possible.

[1] The Enemy's Fleet is supposed to consist of 46 Sail of the Line— British Fleet of 40—if either is less only a proportionate number of Enemy's ships are to be cut off; B to be $\frac{1}{4}$ superior to E cut off.

[2] *Vide* instructions for Signal Yellow with Blue fly, page 17, eighth Flag Signal Book, with reference to Appendix.

(This and the above note were both written by Nelson in the margin.)

INDEX

THE
SANE SOCIETY

by

ERICH FROMM

LONDON
ROUTLEDGE & KEGAN PAUL LTD

First published in England 1956
Reprinted 1959 & 1968
Published as a Routledge paperback 1963
by Routledge & Kegan Paul Ltd
Broadway House, 68–74 Carter Lane
London, E.C.4

SBN 7100 3342 7 Cloth Edition
SBN 7100 4642 8 Paper Edition

Printed in Great Britain
by Photolithography
Unwin Brothers Limited
Woking and London

By the same author
THE FEAR OF FREEDOM
MAN FOR HIMSELF: AN ENQUIRY INTO
THE PSYCHOLOGY OF ETHICS

ACKNOWLEDGMENTS

Grateful acknowledgment is made to the following publishers who have so generously granted permission for the use of excerpts from their publications:

FORTUNE, New York, N.Y., for permission to reprint selections from "The Transients," by William H. Whyte, Jr., which appeared in the May, June, July and August 1953 issues of *Fortune*, Copyright 1953 by Time Inc.

HARPER & BROTHERS, New York, N.Y., for permission to reprint selections from *Capitalism, Socialism and Democracy* by Joseph A. Schumpeter, and from *All Things Common* by Claire Huchet Bishop, Copyright, 1950, by Harper & Brothers.

HARPER & BROTHERS, New York, N.Y. and CHATTO & WINDUS LTD., London, England, for permission to reprint Aldous Huxley's Introduction to *Brave New World*, Copyright, 1946, by Aldous Huxley.

THE LINCOLN ELECTRIC COMPANY, Cleveland, Ohio, for permission to reprint selections from *Incentive Management* by J. F. Lincoln.

THE MACMILLAN COMPANY, New York, N.Y. and A. & C. BLACK LTD., London, England, for permission to reprint selections from *The Philosophy of Civilization* by Albert Schweitzer.

FOREWORD

This book is a continuation of *The Fear of Freedom,* written over fifteen years ago. In *The Fear of Freedom* I tried to show that the totalitarian movements appealed to a deep-seated craving to escape from the freedom man had achieved in the modern world; that modern man, free *from* medieval ties, was not free *to* build a meaningful life based on reason and love, hence sought new security in submission to a leader, race or state.

In *The Sane Society* I try to show that life in twentieth-century Democracy constitutes in many ways another escape from freedom, and the analysis of this particular escape, centered around the concept of alienation, constitutes a good part of this book.

In another way too, is *The Sane Society* a continuation of *The Fear of Freedom,* and to some extent, of *Man for Himself* In both books I have treated specific psychological mechanism, as far as it seemed pertinent to the main topic. In *The Fear of Freedom,* I dealt mainly with the problem of the authoritarian character (sadism, masochism, etc.). In *Man for Himself* I developed the idea of various character orientations, substituting for the Freudian scheme of libido development one of the evolution of character in interpersonal terms. In *The Sane Society* I have tried to develop more systematically the basic concepts of what I have called here "humanistic psychoanalysis." Quite nat-

vii

urally, older ideas expressed earlier could not be omitted; but I tried to treat them more briefly and to give more space to those aspects which are the result of my observations and thoughts in the last years.

I hope the reader of my previous books will have no difficulty in seeing the continuity of thought, as well as some changes, leading to the main thesis of humanistic psychoanalysis: that the basic passions of man are not rooted in his instinctive needs, but in the specific conditions of human existence, in the need to find a new relatedness to man and nature after having lost the primary relatedness of the pre-human stage. While in this respect my ideas differ essentially from those of Freud, they are nevertheless based on his fundamental findings, carried further under the influence of ideas and experiences of a generation standing on Freud's shoulders. But just because of the implicit and explicit criticism of Freud contained in these pages, I want to state very clearly that I see great dangers in the development of certain trends in psychoanalysis which, while criticizing certain errors in Freud's system, relinquish with the errors also the most valuable parts of Freud's teaching: his scientific method, his evolutionary concept, his concept of the unconscious as a truly irrational force rather than as a sum total of erroneous ideas. Furthermore, there is danger that psychoanalysis loses another fundamental trait of Freudian thinking, the courage to defy common sense and public opinion.

Eventually, *The Sane Society* proceeds from the purely critical analysis presented in *The Fear of Freedom*, to concrete suggestions for the functioning of a Sane Society. The main point in this last part of the book is not so much the belief that each one of the recommended measures is necessarily "right," but that progress can only occur when changes are made simultaneously in the economic, socio-political and cultural spheres; that any progress restricted to *one* sphere is destructive to progress in *all* spheres. ✗

I am deeply indebted to a number of friends who have been helpful to me by reading the manuscript and expressing constructive suggestions and criticism. Specifically I want to mention only one of them, George Fuchs, who died during the time I was working on this book. Originally we had planned to write the book together, but due to his prolonged illness, this plan could not be carried out. His help, however, was considerable. We had lengthy discussions, and he wrote me many letters and memos, especially with regard to problems of socialist theory, which helped to clarify and sometimes to revise my own ideas. I have mentioned his name in the text a few times, but my obligation to him goes much further than these specific references might indicate.

I want to express my thanks to Dr. G. R. Hargreaves, Chief of the Mental Health Section of the World Health Organization, for his help in securing the data on alcoholism, suicide and homicide.

E. F.

NOTE TO THE THIRD IMPRESSION

I want to use the occasion of this reprint of THE SANE SOCIETY in order to clear up a misunderstanding which I found to occur in a number of readers' minds: I wrote in some detail about the Work Communities in France because I wanted to show that it is possible that people can work together creatively and share responsibility and attain a sense of solidarity in spite of ideological differences – and at the same time be able to be productive economically.

I did not discuss these communities because I thought modern industrial society could be organized along these lines. In this respect I think that the Yugoslav system has shown possibilities for worker-self-management within the framework of a state. I discussed the French work communities because in the first years of their existence they showed such marvellous results of what is possible in the way of humanization of work in industrial society.

E. F.

CONTENTS

xi

Contents

Contents

And he shall judge among many people, and rebuke strong nations afar off; and they shall beat their swords into plowshares, and their spears into pruninghooks: nation shall not lift up a sword against nation, neither shall they learn war any more.

But they shall sit every man under his vine and under his fig tree; and none shall make them afraid: for the mouth of the Lord of hosts hath spoken it.

MICAH

There exists no more difficult art than living. For other arts and sciences, numerous teachers are to be found everywhere. Even young people believe that they have acquired these in such a way, that they can teach them to others: throughout the whole of life, one must continue to learn to live and, what will amaze you even more, throughout life one must learn to die.

SENECA

This world and yonder world are incessantly giving birth: every cause is a mother, its effect the child.

When the effect is born, it too becomes a cause and gives birth to wondrous effects.

These causes are generation on generation, but it needs a very well lighted eye to see the links in their chain.

RUMI

Things are in the saddle and ride mankind.

EMERSON

The human race had the wisdom to create science and art; why should it not be capable to create a world of justice, brotherliness and peace? The human race has produced Plato, Homer, Shakespeare, and Hugo, Michelangelo and Beethoven, Pascal and Newton, all these human heroes whose genius is only the contact with the fundamental truths, with the innermost essence of the universe. Why then should the same race not produce those leaders capable of leading it to those forms of communal life which are closest to the lives and the harmony of the universe?

LEON BLUM

THE SANE SOCIETY

1

ARE WE SANE?

Nothing is more common than the idea that we, the people living in the Western world of the twentieth century, are eminently sane. Even the fact that a great number of individuals in our midst suffer from more or less severe forms of mental illness produces little doubt with respect to the general standard of our mental health. We are sure that by introducing better methods of mental hygiene we shall improve *still further* the state of our mental health, and as far as individual mental disturbances are concerned, we look at them as strictly individual incidents, perhaps with some amazement that so many of these incidents should occur in a culture which is supposedly so sane.

Can we be so sure that we are not deceiving ourselves? Many an inmate of an insane asylum is convinced that everybody else is crazy, except himself. Many a severe neurotic believes that his compulsive rituals or his hysterical outbursts are normal reactions to somewhat abnormal circumstances. What about ourselves?

Let us, in good psychiatric fashion, look at the facts. In the last one hundred years we, in the Western world, have created a greater material wealth than any other society in the history

3

of the human race. Yet we have managed to kill off millions of our population in an arrangement which we call "war." Aside from smaller wars, we had larger ones in 1870, 1914 and 1939. During these wars, every participant firmly believed that he was fighting in his self-defense, for his honor, or that he was backed up by God. The groups with whom one is at war are, often from one day to the next, looked upon as cruel, irrational fiends, whom one must defeat to save the world from evil. But a few years after the mutual slaughter is over, the enemies of yesterday are our friends, the friends of yesterday our enemies, and again in full seriousness we begin to paint them with appropriate colors of black and white. At this moment, in the year 1955, we are prepared for a mass slaughter which would, if it came to pass, surpass any slaughter the human race has arranged so far. One of the greatest discoveries in the field of natural science is prepared for this purpose. Everybody is looking with a mixture of confidence and apprehension to the "statesmen" of the various peoples, ready to heap all praise on them if they "succeed in avoiding a war," and ignoring the fact that it is only these very statesmen who ever cause a war, usually not even through their bad intentions, but by their unreasonable mismanagement of the affairs entrusted to them.

In these outbursts of destructiveness and paranoid suspicion, however, we are not behaving differently from what the civilized part of mankind has done in the last three thousand years of history. According to Victor Cherbulliez, from 1500 B.C. to 1860 A.D. no less than about eight thousand peace treaties were signed, each one supposed to secure permanent peace, and each one lasting on an average two years! [1]

[1] From H. B. Stevens, *The Recovery of Culture*, Harper and Brothers, New York, 1949, p. 221.

4

Our direction of economic affairs is scarcely more encouraging. We live in an economic system in which a particularly good crop is often an economic disaster, and we restrict some of our agricultural productivity in order to "stabilize the market," although there are millions of people who do not have the very things we restrict, and who need them badly. Right now our economic system is functioning very well, because, among other reasons, we spend billions of dollars per year to produce armaments. Economists look with some apprehension to the time when we stop producing armaments, and the idea that the state should produce houses and other useful and needed things instead of weapons, easily provokes accusations of endangering freedom and individual initiative.

We have a literacy above 90 per cent of the population. We have radio, television, movies, a newspaper a day for everybody. But instead of giving us the best of past and present literature and music, these media of communication, supplemented by advertising, fill the minds of men with the cheapest trash, lacking in any sense of reality, with sadistic phantasies which a halfway cultured person would be embarrassed to entertain even once in a while. But while the mind of everybody, young and old, is thus poisoned, we go on blissfully to see to it that no "immorality" occurs on the screen. Any suggestion that the government should finance the production of movies and radio programs which would enlighten and improve the minds of our people would be met again with indignation and accusations in the name of freedom and idealism.

We have reduced the average working hours to about half what they were one hundred years ago. We today have more free time available than our forefathers dared to dream of. But what has happened? We do not know how to use the newly gained free time; we try to kill the time we have saved, and are glad when another day is over.

Why should I continue with a picture which is known to everybody? Certainly, if an individual acted in this fashion, serious doubts would be raised as to his sanity; should he, however, claim that there is nothing wrong, and that he is acting perfectly reasonably, then the diagnosis would not even be doubtful any more.

Yet many psychiatrists and psychologists refuse to entertain the idea that society as a whole may be lacking in sanity. They hold that the problem of mental health in a society is only that of the number of "unadjusted" individuals, and not that of a possible unadjustment of the culture itself. This book deals with the latter problem; not with individual pathology, but with the *pathology of normalcy*, particularly with the pathology of contemporary Western society. But before entering into the intricate discussion of the concept of social pathology, let us look at some data, revealing and suggestive in themselves, which make reference to the incidence of *individual* pathology in Western culture.

What is the incidence of mental illness in the various countries of the Western world? It is a most amazing fact that there are no data which answer this question. While there are exact comparative statistical data on material resources, employment, birth and death rates, there is no adequate information about mental illness. At the most we have some exact data for a number of countries, like the United States and Sweden, but they only refer to admissions of patients to mental institutions, and they are not helpful in making estimates of comparative frequency of mental illness. These figures tell us just as much about improved psychiatric care and institutional facilities as they tell us about increase

6

in incidence of mental illness.[1] The fact that more than half of all hospital beds in the United States are used for mental patients on whom we spend an annual sum of over a billion dollars may not be an indication of any increase in mental illness, but only of an increasing care. Some other figures, however, are more indicative of the occurrence of the more severe mental disturbances. If 17.7 per cent of all rejections of draftees in the last war were for reasons of mental illness, this fact certainly bespeaks a high degree of mental disturbance, even if we have no comparative figures referring to the past, or to other countries.

The only comparative data which can give us a rough indication of mental health, are those for suicide, homicide and alcoholism. No doubt the problem of suicide is a most complex one, and no single factor can be assumed to be *the* cause. But even without entering at this point into a discussion of suicide, I consider it a safe assumption that a high suicide rate in a given population is expressive of a lack of mental stability and mental health. That it is not a consequence of material poverty is clearly evidenced by all figures. The poorest countries have the lowest incidence of suicide, and the increasing material prosperity in Europe was accompanied by an increasing number of suicides.[2] As to alcoholism, there is no doubt that it, too, is a symptom of mental and emotional instability.

The motives for homicide are probably less indicative of pathology than those for suicide. However, though countries with a high homicide rate show a low suicide rate, their combined rates bring us to an interesting conclusion. If we classify both homicide and suicide as "destructive acts," our tables demonstrate that

[1] cf. H. Goldhamer and A. Marshall, *Psychosis and Civilization*, Free Press, Glencoe, 1953.
[2] cf. Maurice Halbwachs, *Les Causes du Suicide*, Félix Alcan, Paris, 1930, pp. 109 and 112.

their combined rate is not constant, but fluctuating between the extremes of 35.76 and 4.24. This contradicts Freud's assumption of the comparative constancy of destructiveness which underlies his theory of the death instinct. It disproves the implication that destructiveness maintains an invariable rate, differing only in directions toward the self or the outside world.

The following tables show the incidence of suicide, homicide and alcoholism for some of the most important European and North American countries.

TABLE I.[1]

COUNTRY	(Per 100,000 of adult population)	
	SUICIDE	HOMICIDE
Denmark	35.09	0.67
Switzerland	33.72	1.42
Finland	23.35	6.45
Sweden	19.74	1.01
United States	15.52	8.50
France	14.83	1.53
Portugal	14.24	2.79
England and Wales	13.43	0.63
Australia	13.03	1.57
Canada	11.40	1.67
Scotland	8.06	0.52
Norway	7.84	0.38
Spain	7.71	2.88
Italy	7.67	7.38
Northern Ireland	4.82	0.13
Ireland (Republic)	3.70	0.54

[1] The information in the first and second tables is derived from 1. World Health Organization (1951) *Annual epidemiological and vital statistics, 1939–46. Part I. Vital statistics and causes of death*, Geneva, pp. 38–71, (the figures from this source have been converted for greater accuracy from total to adult population), and 2. World Health Organization, (1952) *Epidem. vital Statist. Rep.* 5, 377. That of the third table, from the Report on the First Session of the Alcoholism Subcommittee, of the Expert Committee on Mental Health, World Health Organization, Geneva, 1951.

TABLE II.

COUNTRY	DESTRUCTIVE ACTS *Homicide and* *Suicide combined*
Denmark	35.76
Switzerland	35.14
Finland	29.80
United States	24.02
Sweden	20.75
Portugal	17.03
France	16.36
Italy	15.05
Australia	14.60
England and Wales	14.06
Canada	13.07
Spain	10.59
Scotland	8.58
Norway	8.22
Northern Ireland	4.95
Ireland (Republic)	4.24

(Both the above tables show the figures for 1946)

TABLE III.

COUNTRY	ESTIMATED NUMBER OF ALCOHOLICS *With or without* *complications* (Per 100,000 of adult population)	
United States	3,952	(1948)
France	2,850	(1945)
Sweden	2,580	(1946)
Switzerland	2,385	(1947)
Denmark	1,950	(1948)
Norway	1,560	(1947)
Finland	1,430	(1947)
Australia	1,340	(1947)
England and Wales	1,100	(1948)
Italy	500	(1942)

9

A quick glance at these tables shows a remarkable phenomenon: Denmark, Switzerland, Finland, Sweden and the United States are the countries with the highest suicide rate, and the highest combined suicide and homicide rate, while Spain, Italy, Northern Ireland and the Republic of Ireland are those with the lowest suicide and homicide rate. The figures for alcoholism show that the same countries—the United States, Switzerland, Sweden and Denmark—which have the highest suicide rate, have also the highest alcoholism rate, with the main difference that the United States are leading in this group, and that France has the second place, instead of the sixth place it has with regard to suicide.

These figures are startling and challenging indeed. Even if we should doubt whether the high frequency of suicide alone indicates a lack of mental health in a population, the fact that suicide and alcoholism figures largely coincide, seems to make it plain that we deal here with symptoms of mental unbalance.

We find then that the countries in Europe which are among the most democratic, peaceful and prosperous ones, and the United States, the most prosperous country in the world, show the most severe symptoms of mental disturbance. The aim of the whole socio-economic development of the Western world is that of the materially comfortable life, relatively equal distribution of wealth, stable democracy and peace, and the very countries which have come closest to this aim show the most severe signs of mental unbalance! It is true that these figures in themselves do not *prove* anything, but at least they are startling. Even before we enter into a more thorough discussion of the whole problem, these data raise a question as to whether there is not something fundamentally wrong with our way of life and with the aims toward which we are striving.

Could it be that the middle-class life of prosperity, while satisfying our material needs leaves us with a feeling of intense boredom, and that suicide and alcoholism are pathological ways of escape from this boredom? Could it be that these figures are a drastic illustration for the truth of the statement that "man lives not by bread alone," and that they show that modern civilization fails to satisfy profound needs in man? If so, what are these needs?

The following chapters are an attempt to answer this question, and to arrive at a critical evaluation of the effect contemporary Western culture has on the mental health and sanity of the people living under our system. However, before we enter into the specific discussion of these questions, it seems that we should take up the general problem of the pathology of normalcy, which is the premise underlying the whole trend of thought expressed in this book.

2

CAN A SOCIETY BE SICK?—
THE PATHOLOGY OF NORMALCY [1]

To speak of a whole society as lacking in mental health implies a controversial assumption contrary to the position of *sociological relativism* held by most social scientists today. They postulate that ← each society is normal inasmuch as it functions, and that pathology can be defined only in terms of the individual's lack of adjustment to the ways of life in his society. ←

To speak of a "sane society" implies a premise different from sociological relativism. It makes sense only if we assume that there can be a society which is *not* sane, and this assumption, in turn, implies that there are universal criteria for mental health which are valid for the human race as such, and according to which the state of health of each society can be judged. This position of *normative humanism* is based on a few fundamental premises.

The species "man," can be defined not only in anatomical and physiological terms; its members share basic *psychic* qualities, the laws which govern their mental and emotional functioning, and the aims for a satisfactory solution of the problem of human

---

[1] In this chapter I have drawn on my paper, "Individual and Social Origins of Neurosis," *Am. Soc. Rev.* IX, 4, 1944, p. 380 ff.

existence. It is true that our knowledge of man is still so incomplete that we cannot yet give a satisfactory definition of man in a psychological sense. It is the task of the "science of man" to arrive eventually at a correct description of what deserves to be called human nature. What has often been called "human nature" is but one of its many manifestations—and often a pathological one—and the function of such mistaken definition usually has been to defend a particular type of society as being the necessary outcome of man's mental constitution.

Against such reactionary use of the concept of human nature, the Liberals, since the eighteenth century, have stressed the malleability of human nature and the decisive influence of environmental factors. True and important as such emphasis is, it has led many social scientists to an assumption that man's mental constitution is a blank piece of paper, on which society and culture write their text, and which has no intrinsic quality of its own. This assumption is just as untenable and just as destructive of social progress as the opposite view was. The real problem is to infer the *core* common to the whole human race from the innumberable *manifestations* of human nature, the normal as well as the pathological ones, as we can observe them in different individuals and cultures. The task is furthermore to recognize the laws inherent in human nature and the inherent goals for its development and unfolding.

This concept of human nature is different from the way the term "human nature" is used conventionally. Just as man transforms the world around him, so he transforms himself in the process of history. He is his own creation, as it were. But just as he can only transform and modify the natural materials around him according to their nature, so he can only transform and modify himself according to his own nature. What man *does* in the process of history is to develop this potential, and to transform it according to its own possibilities. The point of view taken here is neither a "biological" nor a "sociological" one if that would mean separating these two aspects from each other. It is rather one transcending such dichotomy by the assumption that the main passions and drives in man result from the *total exist-ence* of man, that they are definite and ascertainable, some of them conducive to health and happiness, others to sickness and unhappiness. Any given social order does not *create* these funda-mental strivings but it determines which of the limited number of potential passions are to become manifest or dominant. Man as he appears in any given culture is always a manifestation of hu-man nature, a manifestation, however, which in its specific out-come is determined by the social arrangements under which he lives. Just as the infant is born with all human potentialities which are to develop under favorable social and cultural condi-tions, so the human race, in the process of history, develops into what it potentially is.

The approach of *normative humanism* is based on the assump-tion that, as in any other problem, there are right and wrong, satisfactory and unsatisfactory solutions to the problem of human existence. Mental health is achieved if man develops into full maturity according to the characteristics and laws of human nature. Mental illness consists in the failure of such development. From this premise the criterion of mental health is not one of individual adjustment to a given social order, but a universal one, valid for all men, of giving a satisfactory answer to the problem of human existence.

What is so deceptive about the state of mind of the members of a society is the "consensual validation" of their concepts. It is naïvely assumed that the fact that the majority of people share certain ideas or feelings proves the validity of these ideas and feelings. Nothing is further from the truth. Consensual validation as such has no bearing whatsoever on reason or mental health. Just as there is a *"folie à deux"* there is a *"folie à millions."* The fact that millions of people share the same vices does not make these vices virtues, the fact that they share so many errors does not make the errors to be truths, and the fact that millions of people share the same forms of mental pathology does not make these people sane.

There is, however, an important difference between individual and social mental illness, which suggests a differentiation between two concepts: that of *defect,* and that of *neurosis.* If a person fails to attain freedom, spontaneity, a genuine expression of self, he may be considered to have a severe defect, provided we assume that freedom and spontaneity are the objective goals to be attained by every human being. If such a goal is not attained by the majority of members of any given society, we deal with the phenomenon of *socially patterned* defect. The individual shares it with many others; he is not aware of it as a defect, and his security is not threatened by the experience of being different, of being an outcast, as it were. What he may have lost in richness and in a genuine feeling of happiness, is made up by the security of fitting in with the rest of mankind—*as he knows them.* As a matter of fact, his very defect may have been raised to a virtue by his culture, and thus may give him an enhanced feeling of achievement.

An illustration is the feeling of guilt and anxiety which Calvin's doctrines aroused in men. It may be said that the person who is overwhelmed by a feeling of his own powerlessness and unworthiness, by unceasing doubt as to whether he is saved or condemned to eternal punishment, who is hardly capable of genuine joy, suffers from a severe defect. Yet this very defect was culturally patterned; it was looked upon as particularly valuable, and the individual was thus protected from the neurosis which he would have acquired in a culture where the same defect gave him a feeling of profound inadequacy and isolation.

Spinoza formulated the problem of the socially patterned defect very clearly. He says: "Many people are seized by one and the same affect with great consistency. All his senses are so strongly affected by one object that he believes this object to be present even if it is not. If this happens while the person is awake, the person is believed to be insane. . . . But if the *greedy* person thinks only of money and possessions, the *ambitious* one only of fame, one does not think of them as being insane, but only as annoying; generally one has contempt for them. But *factually* greediness, ambition, and so forth are forms of insanity, although usually one does not think of them as 'illness.' " [1]

These words were written a few hundred years ago; they still hold true, although the defects have been culturally patterned to *such* an extent now that they are not even generally thought any more to be annoying or contemptible. Today we come across a person who acts and feels like an automaton; who never experiences anything which is really his; who experiences himself entirely as the person he thinks he is supposed to be; whose artificial smile has replaced genuine laughter; whose meaningless chatter has replaced communicative speech; whose dulled despair has taken the place of genuine pain. Two statements can be made about this person. One is that he suffers from a defect of spontaneity and individuality which may seem incurable. At the same time, it may be said that he does not differ essentially from millions of others who are in the same position. For most of them, the culture provides patterns which enable them *to live with a defect without becoming ill*. It is as if each culture provided the remedy against the outbreak of manifest neurotic symptoms which would result from the defect produced by it.

[1] cf. Spinoza, *Ethics*, IV Prop. 44 Schol.

Suppose that in our Western culture movies, radios, television, sports events and newspapers ceased to function for only four weeks. With these main avenues of escape closed, what would be the consequences for people thrown back upon their own resources? I have no doubt that even in this short time thousands of nervous breakdowns would occur, and many more thousands of people would be thrown into a state of acute anxiety, not different from the picture which is diagnosed clinically as "neurosis." [1] If the opiate against the socially patterned defect were withdrawn, the manifest illness would make its appearance.

For a minority, the pattern provided by the culture does not work. They are often those whose individual defect is more severe than that of the average person, so that the culturally offered remedies are not sufficient to prevent the outbreak of manifest illness. (A case in point is the person whose aim in life is to attain power and fame. While this aim is, in itself, a pathological one, there is nevertheless a difference between the person who uses his powers to attain this aim realistically, and the more severely sick one who has so little emerged from his infantile grandiosity that he does not do anything toward the attainment of his goal but waits for a miracle to happen and, thus feeling more and more powerless, ends up in a feeling of futility and bitterness.) But there are also those whose character structure, and hence whose conflicts, differ from those of the majority, so that the remedies which are effective for most of their fellow men are of no help to them. Among this group we sometimes find

[1] I have made the following experiment with various classes of undergraduate college students: they were told to imagine that they were to stay for three days alone in their rooms, without a radio, or escapist literature, although provided with "good" literature, normal food and all other physical comforts. They were asked to imagine what their reaction to this experience would be. The response of about 90 per cent in each group ranged from a feeling of acute panic, to that of an exceedingly trying experience, which they might overcome by sleeping long, doing all kinds of little chores, eagerly awaiting the end of this period. Only a small minority felt that they would be at ease and enjoy the time when they were with themselves.

people of greater integrity and sensitivity than the majority, who for this very reason are incapable of accepting the cultural opiate, while at the same time they are not strong and healthy enough to live soundly "against the stream."

The foregoing discussion on the difference between neurosis and the socially patterned defect may give the impression that if society only provides the remedies against the outbreak of manifest symptoms, all goes well, and it can continue to function smoothly, however great the defects created by it. History shows us, however, that this is not the case.

It is true indeed, that man, in contrast to the animal, shows an almost infinite malleability; just as he can eat almost anything, live under practically any kind of climate and adjust himself to it, there is hardly any psychic condition which he cannot endure, and under which he cannot carry on. He can live free, and as a slave. Rich and in luxury, and under conditions of half-starvation. He can live as a warrior, and peaceably; as an exploiter and robber, and as a member of a co-operating and loving fellowship. There is hardly a psychic state in which man cannot live, and hardly anything which cannot be done with him, and for which he cannot be used. All these considerations seem to justify the assumption that there is no such thing as a nature common to all men, and that would mean in fact that there is no such thing as a species "man," except in a physiological and anatomical sense.

Yet, in spite of all this evidence, the history of man shows that we have omitted one fact. Despots and ruling cliques can succeed in dominating and exploiting their fellow man, but they cannot prevent *reactions* to this inhuman treatment. Their subjects become frightened, suspicious, lonely and, if not due to external reasons, their systems collapse at some point because fears, suspicions and loneliness eventually incapacitate the majority to function effectively and intelligently. Whole nations, or social groups within them, can be subjugated and exploited for a long time, but *they react*. They react with apathy or such impairment of intelligence, initiative and skills that they gradually fail to perform the functions which should serve their rulers. Or they react by the accumulation of such hate and destructiveness as to bring about an end to themselves, their rulers and their system. Again their reaction may create such independence and longing for freedom that a better society is built upon their creative impulses. Which reaction occurs, depends on many factors: on economic and political ones, and on the spiritual climate in which people live. But whatever the reactions are, the statement that man can live under almost any condition is only half true; it must be supplemented by the other statement, that if he lives under conditions which are contrary to his nature and to the basic requirements for human growth and sanity, he cannot help reacting; he must either deteriorate and perish, or bring about conditions which are more in accordance with his needs.

That human nature and society can have conflicting demands, and hence that a whole society can be sick, is an assumption which was made very explicitly by Freud, most extensively in his *Civilization and Its Discontent*.

He starts out with the premise of a human nature common to the human race, throughout all cultures and ages, and of certain ascertainable needs and strivings inherent in that nature. He believes that culture and civilization develop in an ever-increasing contrast to the needs of man, and thus he arrives at the concept of the "social neurosis." "If the evolution of civilization," he writes, "has such a far-reaching similarity with the development of an individual, and if the same methods are employed in both, would not the diagnosis be justified that many systems of civilization—or epochs of it—possibly even the whole of humanity—have become 'neurotic' under the pressure of the civilizing trends?

To analytic dissection of these neuroses, therapeutic recommendations might follow which could claim a great practical interest. I would not say that such an attempt to apply psychoanalysis to civilized society would be fanciful or doomed to fruitlessness. But it behooves us to be very careful, not to forget that after all we are dealing only with analogies, and that it is dangerous, not only with men but also with concepts, to drag them out of the region where they originated and have matured. The diagnosis of *collective neuroses*, moreover, will be confronted by a special difficulty. In the neurosis of an individual we can use as a starting point the contrast presented to us between the patient and his environment which we assume to be 'normal.' No such background as this would be available for any society similarly affected; it would have to be supplied in some other way. And with regard to any therapeutic application of our knowledge, what would be the use of the most acute analysis of social neuroses, since no one possesses the power to compel the community to adopt the therapy? In spite of all these difficulties, we may expect that one day someone will venture upon this *research into the pathology of civilized communities.*" [1]

This book *does* venture upon this research. It is based on the idea that a sane society is that which corresponds to the needs of man—not necessarily to what he *feels* to be his needs, because even the most pathological aims can be felt subjectively as that which the person wants most; but to what his needs are *objectively*, as they can be ascertained by the study of man. It is our first task then, to ascertain what is the nature of man, and what are the needs which stem from this nature. We then must proceed to examine the role of society in the evolution of man and to study

---

[1] S. Freud, *Civilization and Its Discontents*, translated from the German by J. Riviere, The Hogarth Press, Ltd., London, 1953, pp. 141–142. (Italics mine.)

its furthering role for the development of men as well as the recurrent *conflicts between human nature and society*—and the consequences of these conflicts, particularly as far as modern society is concerned.

3

THE HUMAN SITUATION—
THE KEY TO HUMANISTIC
PSYCHOANALYSIS

The Human Situation

Man, in respect to his body and his physiological functions, belongs to the animal kingdom. The functioning of the animal is determined by instincts, by specific action patterns which are in turn determined by inherited neurological structures. The higher an animal is in the scale of development, the more flexibility of action pattern and the less completeness of structural adjustment do we find at birth. In the higher primates we even find considerable intelligence; that is, use of thought for the accomplishment of desired goals, thus enabling the animal to go far beyond the instinctively prescribed action pattern. But great as the development within the animal kingdom is, certain basic elements of existence remain the same.

The animal "is lived" through biological laws of nature; it is part of nature and never transcends it. It has no conscience of a moral nature, and no awareness of itself and of its existence; it has no reason, if by reason we mean the ability to penetrate the surface grasped by the senses and to understand the essence behind that surface; therefore the animal has no concept of the truth, even though it may have an idea of what is useful.

Animal existence is one of harmony between the animal and nature; not, of course, in the sense that the natural conditions do not often threaten the animal and force it to a bitter fight for survival, but in the sense that the animal is equipped by nature to cope with the very conditions it is to meet, just as the seed of a plant is equipped by nature to make use of the conditions of soil, climate, etcetera, to which it has become adapted in the evolutionary process.

At a certain point of animal evolution, there occurred a unique break, comparable to the first emergence of matter, to the first emergence of life, and to the first emergence of animal existence. This new event happens when in the evolutionary process, action ceases to be essentially determined by instinct; when the adaptation of nature loses its coercive character; when action is no longer fixed by hereditarily given mechanisms. When the animal transcends nature, when it transcends the purely passive role of the creature, when it becomes, biologically speaking, the most helpless animal, *man is born*. At this point, the animal has emancipated itself from nature by erect posture, the brain has grown far beyond what it was in the highest animal. This birth of man may have lasted for hundreds of thousands of years, but what matters is that a new species arose, transcending nature, that *life became aware of itself*.

Self-awareness, reason and imagination disrupt the "harmony" which characterizes animal existence. Their emergence has made man into an anomaly, into the freak of the universe. He is part of nature, subject to her physical laws and unable to change them, yet he transcends the rest of nature. He is set apart while being a part; he is homeless, yet chained to the home he shares with all creatures. Cast into this world at an accidental place and time, he is forced out of it, again accidentally. Being aware of himself, he realizes his powerlessness and the limitations of his existence. He visualizes his own end: death. Never is he free from the dichotomy of his existence: he cannot rid himself of his mind, even if he should want to; he cannot rid himself of his body as long as he is alive—and his body makes him want to be alive.

Reason, man's blessing, is also his curse; it forces him to cope everlastingly with the task of solving an insoluble dichotomy. Human existence is different in this respect from that of all other organisms; it is in a state of constant and unavoidable disequilibrium. Man's life cannot "be lived" by repeating the pattern of his species; *he* must live. Man is the only animal that can be *bored,* that can feel evicted from paradise. Man is the only animal who finds his own existence a problem which he has to solve and from which he cannot escape. He cannot go back to the prehuman state of harmony with nature; he must proceed to develop his reason until he becomes the master of nature, and of himself.

But man's birth ontogenetically as well as phylogenetically is essentially a *negative* event. He lacks the instinctive adaptation to nature, he lacks physical strength, he is the most helpless of all animals at birth, and in need of protection for a much longer period of time than any of them. While he has lost the unity with nature, he has not been given the means to lead a new existence outside of nature. His reason is most rudimentary, he has no knowledge of nature's processes, nor tools to replace the lost instincts; he lives divided into small groups, with no knowledge of himself or of others; indeed, the biblical Paradise myth expresses the situation with perfect clarity. Man, who lives in the Garden of Eden, in complete harmony with nature but without awareness of himself, begins his history by the first act of freedom, disobedience to a command. Concomitantly, he becomes aware of himself, of his separateness, of his helplessness; he is expelled from Paradise, and two angels with fiery swords prevent his return.

Man's evolution is based on the fact that he has lost his original home, nature—and that he can never return to it, can never become an animal again. There is only one way he can take: to emerge fully from his natural home, to find a new home—one which he creates, by making the world a human one and by becoming truly human himself.

When man is born, the human race as well as the individual, he is thrown out of a situation which was definite, as definite as the instincts, into a situation which is indefinite, uncertain and open. There is certainty only about the past, and about the future as far as it is death—which actually is return to the past, the inorganic state of matter.

The problem of man's existence, then, is unique in the whole of nature; he has fallen out of nature, as it were, and is still in it; he is partly divine, partly animal; partly infinite, partly finite. *The necessity to find ever-new solutions for the contradictions in his existence, to find ever-higher forms of unity with nature, his fellowmen and himself, is the source of all psychic forces which motivate man, of all his passions, affects and anxieties.*

The animal is content if its physiological needs—its hunger, its thirst and its sexual needs—are satisfied. Inasmuch as man is *also* animal, these needs are likewise imperative and must be satisfied. *But inasmuch as man is human, the satisfaction of these instinctual needs is not sufficient to make him happy; they are not even sufficient to make him sane. The archimedic point of the specifically human dynamism lies in this uniqueness of the human situation; the understanding of man's psyche must be based on the analysis of man's needs stemming from the conditions of his existence.*

The problem, then, which the human race as well as each individual has to solve is that of being born. Physical birth, if we think of the individual, is by no means as decisive and singular an act as it appears to be. It is, indeed, an important change from intrauterine into extrauterine life; but in many respects the infant after birth is not different from the infant before birth; it cannot perceive things outside, cannot feed itself; it is completely dependent on the mother, and would perish without her help. Actually, the process of birth continues. The child begins to recognize outside objects, to react affectively, to grasp things and to co-ordinate his movements, to walk. But birth continues. The child learns to speak, it learns to know the use and function of things, it learns to relate itself to others, to avoid punishment and gain praise and liking. Slowly, the growing person learns to love, to develop reason, to look at the world objectively. He begins to develop his powers; to acquire a sense of identity, to overcome the seduction of his senses for the sake of an integrated life. Birth then, in the conventional meaning of the word, is only the beginning of birth in the broader sense. The whole life of the individual is nothing but the process of giving birth to himself; indeed, we should be fully born, when we die—although it is the tragic fate of most individuals to die before they are born.

From all we know about the evolution of the human race, the birth of man is to be understood in the same sense as the birth of the individual. When man had transcended a certain threshold of minimum instinctive adaptation, he ceased to be an animal; but he was as helpless and unequipped for human existence as the individual infant is at birth. The birth of man began with the first members of the species homo sapiens, and human history is nothing but the whole process of this birth. It has taken man hundreds of thousands of years to take the first steps into human life; he went through a narcissistic phase of magic omnipotent orientation, through totemism, nature worship, until he arrived at the beginnings of the formation of conscience, objectivity, brotherly love. In the last four thousand years of his history, he has developed visions of the fully born and fully awakened man, visions expressed in not too different ways by the great teachers of man in Egypt, China, India, Palestine, Greece and Mexico.

The fact that man's birth is primarily a negative act, that of being thrown out of the original oneness with nature, that he cannot return to where he came from, implies that the process of birth is by no means an easy one. Each step into his new human existence is frightening. It always means to give up a secure state, which was relatively known, for one which is new, which one has not yet mastered. Undoubtedly, if the infant could think at the moment of the severance of the umbilical cord, he would experience the fear of dying. A loving fate protects us from this first panic. But at any new step, at any new stage of our birth, we are afraid again. We are never free from two conflicting tendencies: one to emerge from the womb, from the animal form of existence into a more human existence, from bondage to freedom; another, to return to the womb, to nature, to certainty and security. In the history of the individual, and of the race, the progressive tendency has proven to be stronger, yet the phenomena of mental illness and the regression of the human race to positions apparently relinquished generations ago, show the intense struggle which accompanies each new act of birth.[1]

MAN'S NEEDS—AS THEY STEM FROM THE CONDITIONS OF HIS EXISTENCE

Man's life is determined by the inescapable alternative between regression and progression, between return to animal exist-

---

[1] It is in this polarity that I see the true kernel in Freud's hypothesis of the existence of a life and death instinct; the difference to Freud's theory is, that the forward-going and the retrogressive impulse have not the same biologically determined strength, but that normally, the forward-going life instinct is stronger and increases in relative strength the more it grows.

ence and arrival at human existence. Any attempt to return is painful, it inevitably leads to suffering and mental sickness, to death either physiologically or mentally (insanity). Every step forward is frightening and painful too, until a certain point has been reached where fear and doubt have only minor proportions. Aside from the physiologically nourished cravings (hunger, thirst, sex), all essential human cravings are determined by this polarity. Man has to solve a problem, he can never rest in the given situation of a passive adaptation to nature. Even the most complete satisfaction of all his instinctive needs does not solve his *human* problem; his most intensive passions and needs are not those rooted in his body, but those rooted in the very peculiarity of his existence.

There lies also the key to humanistic psychoanalysis. Freud, searching for the basic force which motivates human passions and desires believed he had found it in the libido. But powerful as the sexual drive and all its derivations are, they are by no means the most powerful forces within man and their frustration is not the cause of mental disturbance. The most powerful forces motivating man's behavior stem from the condition of his existence, the "human situation."

Man cannot live statically because his inner contradictions drive him to seek for an equilibrium, for a new harmony instead of the lost animal harmony with nature. After he has satisfied his animal needs, he is driven by his human needs. While his body tells him what to eat and what to avoid—his conscience ought to tell him which needs to cultivate and satisfy, and which needs to let wither and starve out. But hunger and appetite are functions of the body with which man is born—conscience, while potentially present, requires the guidance of men and principles which develop only during the growth of culture.

All passions and strivings of man are attempts to find an answer to his existence or, as we may also say, they are an attempt to avoid insanity. (It may be said in passing that the real problem of mental life is not why some people become insane, but rather why most avoid insanity.) Both the mentally healthy and the neurotic are driven by the need to find an answer, the only difference being that one answer corresponds more to the total needs of man, and hence is more conducive to the unfolding of his powers and to his happiness than the other. All cultures provide for a patterned system in which certain solutions are predominant, hence certain strivings and satisfactions. Whether we deal with primitive religions, with theistic or non-theistic religions, they are all attempts to give an answer to man's existential problem. The finest, as well as the most barbaric cultures have the same function—the difference is only whether the answer given is better or worse. The deviate from the cultural pattern is just as much in search of an answer as his more well-adjusted brother. His answer may be better or worse than the one given by his culture—it is always another answer to the same fundamental question raised by human existence. In this sense all cultures are religious and every neurosis is a private form of religion, provided we mean by religion an attempt to answer the problem of human existence. Indeed, the tremendous energy in the forces producing mental illness, as well as those behind art and religion could never be understood as an outcome of frustrated or sublimated physiological needs; they are attempts to solve the problem of being born human. All men are idealists and cannot help being idealists, provided we mean by idealism the striving for the satisfaction of needs which are specifically human and transcend the physiological needs of the organism. The difference is only that one idealism is a good and adequate solution, the other a bad and destructive one. The decision as to what is good and bad has to be made on the basis of our knowledge of man's nature and the laws which govern its growth.

What are these needs and passions stemming from the existence of man?

A.   RELATEDNESS VS. NARCISSISM

vanity

Man is torn away from the primary union with nature, which characterizes animal existence. Having at the same time reason and imagination, he is aware of his aloneness and separateness; of his powerlessness and ignorance; of the accidentalness of his birth and of his death. He could not face this state of being for a second if he could not find new ties with his fellow man which replace the old ones, regulated by instincts. Even if all his physiological needs were satisfied, he would experience his state of aloneness and individuation as a prison from which he had to break out in order to retain his sanity. In fact, the insane person is the one who has completely failed to establish any kind of union, and is imprisoned, even if he is not behind barred windows. The necessity to unite with other living beings, to be related to them, is an imperative need on the fulfillment of which man's sanity depends. This need is behind all phenomena which constitute the whole gamut of intimate human relations, of all passions which are called love in the broadest sense of the word.

There are several ways in which this union can be sought and achieved. Man can attempt to become one with the world by *submission* to a person, to a group, to an institution, to God. In this way he transcends the separateness of his individual existence by becoming part of somebody or something bigger than himself, and experiences his identity in connection with the power to which he has submitted. Another possibility of overcoming separateness lies in the opposite direction: man can try to unite himself with the world by having *power* over it, by making others a part of himself, and thus transcending his individual existence by domination. The common element in both submission and domination is the symbiotic nature of relatedness. Both persons involved have lost their integrity and freedom; they live on each other and from each other, satisfying their craving for closeness, yet suffering from the lack of inner strength and self-reliance which would require freedom and independence, and furthermore constantly threatened by the conscious or unconscious hostility which is bound to arise from the symbiotic relationship.[1] The realization of the submissive (masochistic) or the domineering (sadistic) passion never leads to satisfaction. They have a self-propelling dynamism, and because no amount of submission, or domination (or possession, or fame) is enough to give a sense of identity and union, more and more of it is sought. The ultimate result of these passions is defeat. It cannot be otherwise; while these passions aim at the establishment of a sense of union, they destroy the sense of integrity. The person driven by any one of these passions actually becomes dependent on others; instead of developing his own individual being, he is dependent on those to whom he submits, or whom he dominates.

There is only one passion which satisfies man's need to unite himself with the world, and to acquire at the same time a sense of integrity and individuality, and this is *love*. *Love is union* with somebody, or something, outside oneself, *under the condition of retaining the separateness and integrity of one's own self*. It is an experience of sharing, of communion, which permits the full unfolding of one's own inner activity. The experience of love does away with the necessity of illusions. There is no need to inflate the image of the other person, or of myself, since the reality of

---

[1] cf. the more detailed analysis of the symbiotic relatedness in E. Fromm, *The Fear of Freedom*, Kegan Paul, London, 1942, p. 136 ff.

active sharing and loving permits me to transcend my individualized existence, and at the same time to experience myself as the bearer of the active powers which constitute the act of loving. What matters is the particular *quality* of loving, not the object. Love is in the experience of human solidarity with our fellow creatures, it is in the erotic love of man and woman, in the love of the mother for the child, and also in the love for oneself, as a human being; it is in the mystical experience of union. In the act of loving, I am one with All, and yet I am myself, a unique, separate, limited, mortal human being. Indeed out of the very polarity between separateness and union, love is born and reborn.

Love is one aspect of what I have called the productive orientation: the active and creative relatedness of man to his fellow man, to himself and to nature. In the realm of *thought*, this productive orientation is expressed in the proper grasp of the world by reason. In the realm of *action*, the productive orientation is expressed in productive work, the prototype of which is art and craftsmanship. In the realm of *feeling*, the productive orientation is expressed in love, which is the experience of union with another person, with all men, and with nature, under the condition of retaining one's sense of integrity and independence. In the experience of love the paradox happens that two people become one, and remain two at the same time. Love in this sense is never restricted to one person. If I can love only one person, and nobody else, if my love for one person makes me more alienated and distant from my fellow man, I may be attached to this person in any number of ways, yet I do not love. If I can say, "I love you," I say, "I love in you all of humanity, all that is alive; I love in you also myself." Self-love, in this sense, is the opposite of selfishness. The latter is actually a greedy concern with oneself which springs from and compensates for the lack of genuine love for oneself.

Love, paradoxically, makes me more independent because it makes me stronger and happier—yet it makes me one with the loved person to the extent that individuality seems to be extinguished for the moment. In loving I experience "I am you," you—the loved person, you—the stranger, you—everything alive. In the experience of love lies the only answer to being human, lies sanity.

Productive love always implies a syndrome of attitudes; that of *care, responsibility, respect* and *knowledge*.[1] If I love, I care—that is, I am actively concerned with the other person's growth and happiness; I am not a spectator. I am responsible, that is, I respond to his needs, to those he can express and more so to those he cannot or does not express. I respect him, that is (according to the original meaning of *re-spicere*) I look at him as he is, objectively and not distorted by my wishes and fears. I know him, I have penetrated through his surface to the core of his being and related myself to him from my core, from the center, as against the periphery, of my being.[2]

Productive love when directed toward equals may be called *brotherly love*. In *motherly love* (Hebrew: *rachamim*, from *rechem* = womb) the relationship between the two persons involved is one of inequality; the child is helpless and dependent on the mother. In order to grow, it must become more and more independent, until he does not need mother any more. Thus the mother-child relationship is paradoxical and, in a sense, tragic. It requires the most intense love on the mother's side, and yet this very love must help the child to grow away from the mother, and to become fully independent. It is easy for any mother to

---

[1] cf. for a more detailed discussion of these concepts my *Man for Himself*, Rinehart & Company, Inc., New York, 1947, p. 96 ff.

[2] The identity between "to love" and "to know" is contained in the Hebrew *jadoa* and in the German *meinen* and *minnen*.

love her child before this process of separation has begun—but it is the task in which most fail, to love the child and at the same time to let it go—and to *want* to let it go.

In *erotic love* (Gr. *eros;* Hebrew: *ahawa,* from the root "to glow"), another drive is involved: that for fusion and union with another person. While brotherly love refers to all men and motherly love to the child and all those who are in need of our help, erotic love is directed to one person, normally of the opposite sex, with whom fusion and oneness is desired. Erotic love begins with separateness, and ends in oneness. Motherly love begins with oneness, and leads to separateness. If the need for fusion were realized in motherly love, it would mean destruction of the child as an independent being, since the child needs to emerge from his mother, rather than to remain tied to her. If erotic love lacks brotherly love and is *only* motivated by the wish for fusion, it is sexual desire without love, or the perversion of love as we find it in the sadistic and masochistic forms of "love."

One understands fully man's need to be related only if one considers the outcome of the failure of any kind of relatedness, if one appreciates the meaning of *narcissism.* The only reality the infant can experience is his own body and his needs, physiological needs and the need for warmth and affection. He has not yet the experience of "I" as separate from "thou." He is still in a state of oneness with the world, but a oneness before the awakening of his sense of individuality and reality. The world outside exists only as so much food, or so much warmth to be used for the satisfaction of his own needs, but not as something or somebody who is recognized realistically and objectively. This orientation has been named by Freud that of "primary narcissism." In normal development, this state of narcissism is slowly overcome by a growing awareness of reality outside, and by a correspondingly growing sense of "I" as differentiated from "thou." This change occurs at first on the level of sensory perception, when things and people are perceived as different and specific entities, a recognition which lays the foundation for the possibility of speech; to name things pre-supposes recognizing them as individual and separate entities.[1] It takes much longer until the narcissistic state is overcome emotionally; for the child up to the age of seven or eight years, other people still exist mainly as means for the satisfaction of his needs. They are exchangeable inasmuch as they fulfill the function of satisfying these needs, and it is only around the ages of between eight and nine years that another person is experienced in such a way that the child can begin to love, that is to say, in H. S. Sullivan's formulation, to feel that the needs of another person are as important as his own.[2] [3]

Primary narcissism is a normal phenomenon, conforming with the normal physiological and mental development of the child. But narcissism exists also in later stages of life ("secondary narcissism," according to Freud), if the growing child fails to develop the capacity for love, or loses it again. Narcissism is the essence of all severe psychic pathology. For the narcissistically involved person, there is only one reality, that of his own thought

[1] cf. Jean Piaget's discussion of this point in *The Child's Conception of the World*, Harcourt, Brace & Company, Inc., New York, p. 151.

[2] cf. H. S. Sullivan, *The Interpersonal Theory of Psychiatry*, Norton Co., New York, 1953, p. 49 ff.

[3] This love is usually felt at first toward the child's contemporaries, and not toward the parents. The pleasing idea that children "love" their parents before they love anybody else must be considered as one of the many illusions which stem from wishful thinking. For the child, at this age, father and mother are more objects of dependency or fear than of love, which by its very nature is based on equality and independence. Love for parents, if we differentiate it from affectionate but passive attachment, incestuous fixation, conventional or fearful submission, develops—if at all—at a later age rather than in childhood, although its beginnings can be found—under fortunate circumstances—at an earlier age. (The same point has been made, somewhat more sharply, by H. S. Sullivan in his *Interpersonal Theory of Psychiatry*.) Many parents, however, are not willing to accept this reality and react to it by resenting the child's first real love attachments either overtly or in the even more effective form of making fun of them. Their conscious or unconscious jealousy is one of the most powerful obstacles to the child's development of the capacity to love.

processes, feelings and needs. The world outside is not experienced or perceived *objectively, i.e.,* as existing in its own terms, conditions and needs. The most extreme form of narcissism is to be seen in all forms of insanity. The insane person has lost contact with the world; he has withdrawn into himself; he cannot experience reality, either physical or human reality *as it is,* but only as formed and determined by his own inner processes. He either does *not* react to the world outside, or if he does, reacts not in terms of *its* reality, but only in terms of his own processes of thought and feeling. Narcissism is the opposite pole to objectivity, reason and love.

The fact that utter failure to relate oneself to the world is insanity, points to the other fact: that some form of relatedness is the condition for any kind of sane living. But among the various forms of relatedness, only the productive one, love, fulfills the condition of allowing one to retain one's freedom and integrity while being, at the same time, united with one's fellow man.

B. TRANSCENDENCE—CREATIVENESS VS. DESTRUCTIVENESS

Another aspect of the human situation, closely connected with the need for relatedness, is man's situation as a *creature,* and his need to transcend this very state of the passive creature. Man is thrown into this world without his knowledge, consent or will, and he is removed from it again without his consent or will. In this respect he is not different from the animal, from the plants, or from inorganic matter. But being endowed with reason and imagination, he cannot be content with the passive role of the creature, with the role of dice cast out of a cup. He is driven by the urge to transcend the role of the creature, the accidentalness and passivity of his existence, by becoming a "creator."

Man can create life. This is the miraculous quality which he indeed shares with all living beings, but with the difference that he alone is aware of being created and of being a creator. Man can create life, or rather, woman can create life, by giving birth to a child, and by caring for the child until it is sufficiently grown to take care of his own needs. Man—man and woman—can create by planting seeds, by producing material objects, by creating art, by creating ideas, by loving one another. In the act of creation man transcends himself as a creature, raises himself beyond the passivity and accidentalness of his existence into the realm of purposefulness and freedom. In man's need for transcendence lies one of the roots for love, as well as for art, religion and material production.

To create presupposes activity and care. It presupposes love for that which one creates. How then does man solve the problem of transcending himself, if he is not capable of creating, if he cannot love? *There is another answer to this need for transcendence: if I cannot create life, I can destroy it. To destroy life makes me also transcend it.* Indeed, that man can destroy life is just as miraculous a feat as that he can create it, for life is *the* miracle, the inexplicable. In the act of destruction, man sets himself above life; he transcends himself as a creature. Thus, the ultimate choice for man, inasmuch as he is driven to transcend himself, is to create or to destroy, to love or to hate. The enormous power of the will for destruction which we see in the history of man, and which we have witnessed so frightfully in our own time, is rooted in the nature of man, just as the drive to create is rooted in it. To say that man is capable of developing his primary potentiality for love and reason does not imply the naïve belief in man's goodness. Destructiveness is a secondary potentiality, rooted in the very existence of man, and having the same intensity and power as any passion can have.[1] But—and this is the essential point of my argument—it is only the *alternative* to creativeness. Creation and destruction, love and hate, are not two instincts which exist independently. They are both answers to the same need for transcendence, and the will to destroy must rise when the will to create cannot be satisfied. However, the satisfaction of the need to create leads to happiness; destructiveness to suffering, most of all, for the destroyer himself.

C. ROOTEDNESS—BROTHERLINESS VS. INCEST

Man's birth as man means the beginning of his emergence from his natural home, the beginning of the severance of his natural ties. Yet, this very severance is frightening; if man loses his natural roots, where is he and who is he? He would stand alone, without a home; without roots; he could not bear the isolation and helplessness of this position. He would become insane. He can dispense with the *natural* roots only insofar as he finds new *human* roots and only after he has found them can he feel at home again in this world. Is it surprising, then, to find a deep craving in man not to sever the natural ties, to fight against being torn away from nature, from mother, blood and soil?

The most elementary of the natural ties is the tie of the child to the mother. The child begins life in the mother's womb, and exists there for a much longer time than is the case with most animals; even after birth, the child remains physically helpless, and completely dependent on the mother; this period of helplessness and dependence again is much more protracted than with any animal. In the first years of life no full separation between child and mother has occurred. The satisfaction of all his physio-

[1] The formulation given here does not contradict the one given in *Man for Himself*, loc. cit., where I wrote that: "destructiveness is the outcome of unlived life." In the concept of transcendence presented here, I try to show more specifically what aspect of unlived life leads to destructiveness.

logical needs, of his vital need for warmth and affection depend on her; she has not only given birth to him, but she continues to give life to him. Her care is not dependent on anything the child does for her, on any obligation which the child has to fulfill; it is unconditional. She cares because the new creature is her child. The child, in these decisive first years of his life, has the experience of his mother as the fountain of life, as an all-enveloping, protective, nourishing power. Mother is food; she is love; she is warmth; she is earth. To be loved by her means to be alive, to be rooted, to be at home.

Just as birth means to leave the enveloping protection of the womb, growing up means to leave the protective orbit of the mother. Yet even in the mature adult, the longing for this situation as it once existed never ceases completely, in spite of the fact that there is, indeed, a great difference between the adult and the child. The adult has the means to stand on his own feet, to take care of himself, to be responsible for himself and even for others, while the child is not yet capable of doing all this. But considering the increased perplexities of life, the fragmentary nature of our knowledge, the accidentalness of adult existence, the unavoidable errors we make, the situation of the adult is by no means as different from that of the child as it is generally assumed. Every adult is in need of help, of warmth, of protection, in many ways differing and yet in many ways similar to the needs of the child. Is it surprising to find in the average adult a deep longing for the security and rootedness which the relationship to his mother once gave him? Is it not to be expected that he cannot give up this intense longing unless he finds other ways of being rooted?

In psychopathology we find ample evidence for this phenomenon of the refusal to leave the all-enveloping orbit of the mother. In the most extreme form we find the craving to return to the mother's womb. A person completely obsessed by this desire may offer the picture of schizophrenia. He feels and acts like the foetus in the mother's womb, incapable of assuming even the most elementary functions of a small child. In many of the more severe neuroses we find the same craving, but as a repressed desire, manifested only in dreams, symptoms and neurotic behavior, which results from the conflict between the deep desire to stay in the mother's womb and the adult part of the personality which tends to live a normal life. In dreams this craving appears in symbols like being in a dark cave, in a one-man submarine, diving into deep water, etc. In the behavior of such a person, we find a fear of life, and a deep fascination for death (death, in phantasy, being the return to the womb, to mother earth).

The less severe form of the fixation to mother is to be found in those cases where a person has permitted himself to be born, as it were, but where he is afraid to take the next step of birth, to be weaned from mother's breasts. People who have become stuck at this stage of birth, have a deep craving to be mothered, nursed, protected by a motherly figure; they are the eternally dependent ones, who are frightened and insecure when motherly protection is withdrawn, but optimistic and active when a loving mother or mother-substitute is provided, either realistically or in phantasy.

These pathological phenomena in individual life have their parallel in the evolution of the human race. The clearest expression of this lies in the fact of the universality of the incest tabu, which we find even in the most primitive societies. The incest tabu is the necessary condition for all human development, not because of its sexual, but because of its affective aspect. Man, in order to be born, in order to progress, has to sever the umbilical cord; he has to overcome the deep craving to remain tied to mother. The incestuous desire has its strength not from the sexual attraction to mother, but from the deep-seated craving to remain in, or to return to the all-enveloping womb, or to the all-nourishing breasts. The incest tabu is nothing else but the two cherubim with fiery swords, guarding the entrance to paradise and preventing man from returning to the pre-individual existence of oneness with nature.

The problem of incest, however, is not restricted to fixation to the mother. The tie to her is only the most elementary form of all natural ties of blood which give man a sense of rootedness and belonging. The ties of blood are extended to those who are blood relatives, whatever the system is according to which such relationships are established. The *family* and the *clan*, and later on the state, nation or church, assume the same function which the individual mother had originally for the child. The individual leans on them, feels rooted in them, has his sense of identity as a part of them, and not as an individual apart from them. The person who does not belong to the same clan is considered as alien and dangerous—as not sharing in the same human qualities which only the own clan possesses.

The fixation to the mother was recognized by Freud as the crucial problem of human development, both of the race and of the individual. In accordance with his system, he explained the intensity of the fixation to the mother as derived from the little boy's *sexual* attraction to her, as the expression of the incestuous striving inherent in man's nature. He assumed that the fixation's perpetuation in later life resulted from the continuing sexual desire. By relating this assumption to his observations of the son's opposition to the father, he reconciled assumption and observation into a most ingenious explanation, that of the "Oedipus complex." He explained hostility to the father as a result of sexual rivalry with him.

But while Freud saw the tremendous importance of the fixation to the mother, he emasculated his discovery by the peculiar interpretation he gave to it. He projects into the little boy the sexual feeling of the adult man; the little boy having, as Freud recognized, sexual desires, was supposed to be sexually attracted to the woman closest to him, and only by the superior power of the rival in this triangle, is he forced to give up his desire, without ever recovering fully from this frustration. Freud's theory is a curiously rationalistic interpretation of the observable facts. In putting the emphasis on the *sexual* aspect of the incestuous desire, Freud explains the boy's desire as something rational in itself and evades the real problem: the depth and intensity of the *irrational affective* tie to the mother, the wish to return into her orbit, to remain a part of her, the fear of emerging fully from her. In Freud's explanation the incestuous wish cannot be fulfilled because of the presence of the father-rival, while in reality the incestuous wish is in contrast to all requirements of adult life.

Thus, the theory of the Oedipus complex is at the same time the acknowledgment *and* the denial of the crucial phenomenon: man's longing for mother's love. In giving the incestuous striving paramount significance, the importance of the tie with mother is recognized; by explaining it as sexual the emotional—and true —meaning of the tie is denied.

Whenever fixation to the mother is also sexual—and this undoubtedly happens—it is because the affective fixation is so strong that it also influences the sexual desire, but not because the sexual desire is at the root of the fixation. On the contrary, sexual desire as such is notoriously fickle with regard to its objects, and generally sexual desire is precisely the force which helps the adolescent in his *separation* from mother, and not the one which binds him to her. Where we find that the intense attachment to mother has changed this normal function of the sexual drive, two possibilities must be considered. One is that the sexual desire for mother is a defense against the desire to return to the womb; the latter leads to insanity or death, while the sexual desire is at least compatible with life. One is saved from the fear of the threatening womb by the nearer-to-life phantasy of entering the vagina with the appropriate organ.[1] The other possibility to be considered is that the phantasy of sexual intercourse with the mother does not have the quality of adult male sexuality, that of voluntary, pleasurable activity, but that of passivity, of being conquered and possessed by the mother, even in the sexual sphere. Aside from these two possibilities which are indicative of more severe pathology, we find instances of sexual incestuous wishes which are stimulated by a seductive mother and, although expressive of mother fixation, less indicative of severe pathology.

That Freud himself distorted his great discovery may have been due to an unsolved problem in the relationship to his own mother, but it was certainly largely influenced by the strictly patriarchal attitude which was so characteristic of Freud's time, and which he shared so completely. The mother was dethroned from her paramount place as the object of love—and her place was given to the father, who was believed to be the most important figure in the child's affections. It sounds almost unbelievable today, when the patriarchal bias has lost much of its strength, to read the following statement written by Freud: "I could not point to any need in childhood as strong as that for a *father's protection.*" [2] Similarly, he wrote in 1908, referring to the death of his father, that the father's death is "the most important event, the most poignant loss, in a man's life." [3] Thus Freud gives the father the place which in reality is that of the mother, and degrades the mother into the

---

[1] This sequence is expressed, for instance, in dreams in which the dreamer finds himself in a cave, with the fear of being suffocated, then having intercourse with his mother with a feeling of relief.

[2] S. Freud, *Civilization and Its Discontent*, translated by J. Riviere, The Hogarth Press Ltd., London, 1953, p. 21. (My italics, E. F.)

[3] Quoted from E. Jones, *The Life and Work of Sigmund Freud*, Basic Books, Inc., New York, 1953, Vol. I, p. 324.

object of sexual lust. The goddess is transformed into the prostitute, the father elevated to the central figure of the universe.[1]

There was another genius, living a generation before Freud, who saw the central role of the tie to the mother in the development of man: Johann Jacob Bachofen.[2] Because he was not narrowed down by the rationalistic, sexual interpretation of the fixation to the mother, he could see the facts more profoundly and more objectively. In his theory of the matriarchal society he assumed that mankind went through a stage, preceding that of the patriarchate, where the ties to the mother, as well as those to blood and soil, were the paramount form of relatedness, both individually and socially. In this form of social organization, as was pointed out above, the mother was the central figure in the family, in social life and in religion. Even though many of Bachofen's historical constructions are not tenable, there can be no doubt that he uncovered a form of social organization and a psychological structure which had been ignored by psychologists and anthropologists because, from their patriarchal orientation, the idea of a society ruled by women rather than by men was just absurd. Yet, there is a great deal of evidence that Greece and India, before the invasion from the north, had cultures of a matriarchal structure. The great number and the significance of mother goddesses points in the same direction. (Venus of Willendorf, Mother Goddess at Mohengo-Daro, Isis, Istar, Rhea, Cybele, Hathor, the Serpent Goddess at Nippur, the Akkadian Water Goddess Ai, Demeter and the Indian Goddess Kali, the giver and destroyer of life, are only a few examples.) Even in many contemporary primitive societies, we can see remnants of the matriarchal structure in matrilineal forms of consanguinity, or matrilocal forms of mar-

[1] In this elimination of the mother figure, Freud does for psychology what Luther did for religion. Properly speaking, Freud is the psychologist of Protestantism.

[2] cf. J. J. Bachofen, *Mutterrecht und Ur Religion*, ed. R. Marx, A. Kroener Verl. Stuttgart, 1954.

riage; more significantly we can find many examples of the matriarchal kind of relatedness to mother, blood and soil, even where the social forms are not matriarchal any more.

While Freud saw in the incestuous fixation only a negative, pathogenic element, Bachofen saw clearly both the negative and the positive aspects of the attachment to the mother figure. *The positive aspect is a sense of affirmation of life, freedom, and equality which pervades the matriarchal structure.* Inasmuch as men are childen of nature, and children of mothers, they are all equal, have the same rights and claims, and the only value that counts is that of life. To put it differently, the mother loves her children not because one is better than the other, not because one fulfills her expectations more than the other, but because they are her children, and in that quality they are all alike and have the same right to love and care. The *negative* aspect of the matriarchal structure was also clearly seen by Bachofen: *by being bound to nature, to blood and soil, man is blocked from developing his individuality and his reason.* He remains a child and incapable of progress.[1]

Bachofen gave an equally broad and profound interpretation of the role of the father, again pointing out both the positive and negative aspects of the fatherly function. Paraphrasing Bachofen's ideas and somewhat enlarging on them, I would say that man, not equipped to create children (I am speaking here, of course, of the *experience* of pregnancy and birth, and not of the purely rational knowledge that the male sperm is necessary for

[1] It is interesting to note how these two aspects of the matriarchal structure have been seized upon by two opposite philosophies in the last hundred years. The Marxist school embraced Bachofen's theories with great enthusiasm because of the element of equality and freedom inherent in the matriarchal structure (cf. Friedrich Engels *The Origin of the Family, Private Property and the State*). After many years in which Bachofen's theories had hardly found any attention, the Nazi philosophers seized upon them and showed equal enthusiasm, but for the opposite reasons. They were attracted by the very irrationality of the bonds of blood and soil which is the other aspect of the matriarchal structure as presented by Bachofen.

the creation of a child), not charged with the task of nursing and taking care of them, is more remote from nature than woman. Because he is less rooted in nature, he is forced to develop his reason, to build up a man-made world of ideas, principles and man-made things which replace nature as a ground of existence and security. The relationship of the child to the father does not have the same intensity as that to the mother, because the father never has the all-enveloping, all-protective, all-loving role which the mother has for the first years of the child's life. On the contrary, in all patriarchal societies, the relationship of the son to the father is one of submission on the one hand, but of rebellion on the other, and this contains in itself a permanent element of dissolution. The submission to the father is different from the fixation to the mother. The latter is a continuation of the natural tie, of the fixation to nature. The former is man-made, artificial, based on power and law, and therefore less compelling and forceful than the tie to the mother. While the mother represents nature and unconditioned love, the father represents abstraction, conscience, duty, law and hierarchy. The father's love for the son is not like the unconditioned love of the mother for her children *because they are her children,* but it is the love for the son whom he likes best because he lives up most to his expectations, and is best equipped to become the heir to the father's property and worldly functions.

From this follows an important difference between motherly and fatherly love; in the relationship to mother, there is little the child can do to regulate or control it. Motherly love is like an act of grace; if it is there, it is a blessing—if it is not there it cannot be created. Here lies the reason why individuals who have not overcome the fixation to mother often try to procure motherly love in a neurotic, magical way by making themselves helpless, sick or by regressing emotionally to the stage of an infant. The magic idea is: if I make myself into a helpless child, mother is bound to appear and to take care of me. The relationship to father, on the other hand, can be controlled. He wants the son to grow up, to take responsibility, to think, to build; or/and to be obedient, to serve father, to be like him. Whether father's expectations are more on development or on obedience, the son has a chance to acquire father's love, to produce father's affection by doing the desired things. To sum up: *the positive aspects of the patriarchal complex are reason, discipline, conscience and individualism; the negative aspects are hierarchy, oppression, inequality, submission.*[1]

It is of special significance to note the close connection between the fatherly and motherly figures and *moral* principles. Freud, in his concept of the super-ego, relates only the father figure to the development of conscience. He assumed that the little boy, frightened by the castration threat of the rival father, incorporates the male parent—or rather his commands and prohibitions—into the formation of a conscience.[2] But there is not only a *fatherly* but also a *motherly conscience;* there is a voice which tells us to do our duty, and a voice which tells us to love and to forgive— others as well as ourselves. It is true that both types of conscience are originally influenced by the fatherly and motherly figures, but in the process of maturing, the conscience becomes more and more independent from these original father and mother figures; *we become,* as it were, *our own father and our own mother,* and we become *also our own child.* The father within ourselves tells us "this you ought to do" and "that you ought not to do." If we have

---

[1] These negative aspects are nowhere more clearly expressed than in the figure of Kreon in Aeschylus' *Antigone.*

[2] In *Man for Himself* I have discussed the relativistic character of Freud's Super-Ego concept, and differentiated between an authoritarian conscience, and humanistic conscience, which is the voice recalling us to ourselves. cf. *Man for Himself, loc. cit.,* Ch. IV, 2.

done the wrong thing, he scolds us, and if we have done the right thing, he praises us. But while the father in us speaks in this manner, the mother in us speaks in a very different language. It is as if she were saying "your father is quite right in scolding you, but do not take him too seriously; whatever you have done, you are my child, I love you, and I forgive you; nothing you have done can interfere with your claim to life and happiness." Father's and mother's voices speak a different language; in fact, they seem to say opposite things. Yet the contradiction between the principle of duty and the principle of love, of fatherly and motherly conscience is a contradiction inherent in human existence, and both sides of the contradiction must be accepted. The conscience which follows only the commands of duty is as distorted as a conscience which follows only the commands of love. The inner father's and the inner mother's voices speak not only with regard to man's attitude toward himself, but also toward all his fellow men. He may judge his fellow man with his fatherly conscience, but he must at the same time hear in himself the voice of the mother, who feels love for all fellow creatures, for all that is alive, and who forgives all transgressions.[1]

Before I continue the discussion of man's basic needs, I want to give a brief description of the various phases of rootedness as they can be observed in the history of mankind, even though this exposition interrupts somewhat the main line of thought of this chapter.

While the infant is rooted in mother, man in his historical in-

---

[1] It is interesting to study the respective weight of the fatherly and motherly principle in the concept of God in the Jewish and Christian religions. The God who sends the flood because everybody is wicked except Noah, represents the fatherly conscience. The God who speaks to Jonah, feeling compassion "with that great city wherein are more than six score thousand persons that cannot discern between their right hand and their left hand and also much cattle" speaks with the voice of the all-forgiving mother. The same polarity between the fatherly and motherly function of God can be clearly seen in the further development of the Jewish, as well as of the Christian religions, especially in mysticism.

fancy (which is still by far the largest part of history in terms of time) remains rooted in nature. Though having emerged from nature the natural world remains his home; here are still his roots. He tries to find security regressing to and identifying himself with nature, the world of plants and animals. This attempt to hold on to nature can be clearly seen in many primitive myths and religious rituals. When man worships trees and animals as his idols, he worships particularizations of nature; they are the protecting, powerful forces whose worship is the worship of nature itself. In relating himself to them, the individual finds his sense of identity and belonging, as part of nature. The same holds true for the relationship to the *soil* on which one lives. The tribe often is not only unified by the common blood, but also by the common soil, and this very combination of blood and soil gives it its strength as the real home and frame of orientation for the individual.

In this phase of human evolution man still feels himself as part of the natural world, that of animals and plants. Only when he has taken the decisive step to emerge fully from nature does he try to create a definite demarcation line between himself and the animal world. An illustration of this idea can be found in the belief of the Winnebago Indians, that in the beginning the creatures did not yet have any permanent form. All were a kind of neutral being which could transform itself into either man or animal. At a certain period they decided to evolve definitely into animal or into man. Since that time, animals have remained animals, and man has remained man.[1] The same idea is expressed in the Aztec belief that the world, before the era in which we live now, was only populated by animals, until with Quetzalcoatl the era of human beings emerged; the same feeling is expressed in the

---

[1] This example is taken from Paul Radin, *Gott und Mensch in der Primitiven Welt*, Rhein Verlag, Zürich, 1953, p. 30.

belief still to be found among some Mexican Indians that a certain animal corresponds to one particular person; or in the belief of the Maoris that a certain tree (planted at birth) corresponds to one individual. It is expressed in the many rituals in which man identifies himself with an animal by garbing himself as one or in the selection of an animal totem.

This passive relationship to nature corresponded to man's economic activities. He started out as a food gatherer and hunter, and were it not for primitive tools and the use of fire he could be said to differ but little from the animal. In the process of history his skills grew, and his relationship to nature is transformed from a passive into an active one. He develops animal husbandry, learns to cultivate the land, achieves an ever-increasing skill in art and craftsmanship, exchanges his products for those of foreign countries and thus becomes a traveller and trader.

His gods change correspondingly. As long as he feels largely identified with nature, his gods are part of nature. When his skills as an artisan grow, he builds idols out of stone or wood, or gold. When he has evolved still further, and gained a greater feeling of his own strength, his gods have the shape of human beings. At first—and this seems to correspond to an agricultural stage— God appears to him in the form of the all-protecting and all-nourishing "Great Mother." Eventually he begins to worship fatherly gods, representing reason, principles, laws. This last and decisive turn away from rootedness in nature and from dependence on a loving mother seems to have begun with the emergence of the great rational and patriarchal religions. In Egypt, with the religious revolution of Ikhnaton in the fourteenth century B.C.; in Palestine with the formation of the Mosaic religion around the same time; in India and Greece with the arrival of the Northern invaders not much later. Many rituals expressed this new idea. In the sacrifice of animals, the animal in man is sacrificed to God. In the biblical food taboo, which forbids eating the blood of the animal (because "the blood is its life"), a strict demarcation line is put between man and animal. In the concept of God—who represents the unifying principle of all life, who is invisible and unlimited—the opposite pole to the natural, finite, diversified world, to the world of things, has been established. Man, created in God's likeness, shares God's qualities; he emerges from nature and strives to be fully born, to be fully awake.[1] This process reached a further stage in the middle of the first millennium in China, with Confucius and Lao-tse; in India with Buddha; in Greece with the philosophers of the Greek enlightenment and in Palestine with the biblical prophets, and then a new peak with Christianity and Stoicism within the Roman Empire, with Quetzalcoatl in Mexico [2] and another half millennium later with Mohammed in Africa.

Our Western culture is built on two foundations: the Jewish and the Greek cultures. Considering the Jewish tradition, the foundations of which are laid down in the Old Testament, we find that it constitutes a relatively pure form of patriarchal culture, built upon the power of the father in the family, of the priest and king in society, and of a fatherly God in Heaven. However, in spite of this extreme form of patriarchalism, one can still recognize the older matriarchal elements as they existed in the earth and nature-bound (telluric) religions, which were defeated by the rational, patriarchal religions during the second millennium B.C.

In the story of Creation we find man still in a primitive unity with the soil, without the necessity to work, and without con-

---

[1] While revising this manuscript, I find in Alfred Weber's *Der Dritte oder der Vierte Mensch*, R. Piper Co., München, 1953, pp. 9 ff., a scheme of historical development which has some similarities to the one in my text. He assumes a "chthonic period" from 4000 to 1200 B.C. which was characterized by the fixation to earth in agricultural peoples.

[2] I follow in this unorthodox dating the writings and personal communications of Laurette Séjourné, cf. her "El Mensaje de Quetzalcoatl," *Cuadernos Americanos*, V, 1954.

sciousness of himself. The woman is the more intelligent, active and daring of the two, and only after the "fall" the patriarchal God announces the principle that man shall rule over woman. The entire Old Testament is an elaboration of the patriarchal principle in various ways, by the establishment of a hierarchical pattern of a theocratic state, and a strictly patriarchal family organization. In the family structure as described by the Old Testament, we find always the figure of the *favorite* son: Abel as against Cain; Jacob as against Esau; Joseph against his brothers; and in a broader sense, the people of Israel as the favorite son of God. Instead of the equality of all children in the eyes of the mother, we find the favorite, who is most like the father, and most liked by the father as his successor and as the heir to his property. In the fight for the position of the favorite son, and thus for the inheritance, the brothers turn into enemies, equality gives way to hierarchy.

The Old Testament postulates not only a strict tabu of incest, but also a prohibition of the fixation to the soil. *Human history* is described as beginning with the expulsion of man from paradise, from the soil in which he was rooted, and with which he felt one. *Jewish* history is described as beginning with the command to Abraham to leave the country in which he was born, and to go "to a country which thou knowest not." From Palestine, the tribe wanders to Egypt; from there, again it returns to Palestine. But the new settlement is not final either. The teachings of the prophets are directed against the new incestuous involvement with the soil and nature as it was manifest in Canaanitic idolatry. They proclaimed the principle that a people who has regressed from the principles of reason and justice to those of the incestuous tie to the soil, will be driven away from its soil and will wander in the world homeless and soilless until it has fully developed the principles of reason, until it has overcome the incestuous tie to the soil and nature; only then can the people return to their homeland, only then will the soil be a blessing, a *human* home freed from the curse of incest. The concept of the Messianic time is that of the complete victory over the incestuous ties, and the full establishment of the spiritual reality of moral and intellectual conscience, not only among the Jews, but among all peoples of the earth.

The crowning and central concept of the patriarchal development of the Old Testament lies, of course, in the concept of God. He represents the unifying principle behind the manifoldness of phenomena. Man is created in the likeness of God; hence all men are equal—equal in their common spiritual qualities, in their common reason, and in their capacity for brotherly love.

Early Christianity is a further development of this spirit, not so much in the emphasis on the idea of love which we find expressed in many parts of the Old Testament, but by its emphasis on the supernational character of religion. As the prophets challenged the validity of the existence of their own state, because it did not live up to the demands of conscience, so the early Christians challenged the moral legitimacy of the Roman Empire, because it violated the principles of love and justice.

While the Jewish-Christian tradition emphasized the *moral* aspect, Greek thought found its most creative expression in the *intellectual* aspect of the patriarchal spirit. In Greece, as in Palestine, we find a patriarchal world which, in both its social and religious aspects, had victoriously emerged from an earlier matriarchal structure. Just as Eve was not born from a woman but made from Adam's rib, so Athene was not a child of a woman, but came from Zeus's head. The remainder of an older matriarchal world can still be seen, as Bachofen has shown, in the figures of goddesses which are subordinate to the patriarchal Olympic world. The Greeks laid the foundation for the intellectual development of the Western world. They laid down the "first principles" of scientific thought, were the first to build "theory" as a foundation of science, to develop a systematic philosophy as it had not existed in any culture before. They created a theory of the state and of society based on their experience of the Greek polis, to be continued in Rome, on the social basis of a vast unified empire.

On account of the incapacity of the Roman Empire to continue a progressive social and political evolution, the development came to a standstill around the fourth century, but not before a new powerful institution had been built, the Catholic Church. While earlier Christianity had been a spiritually revolutionary movement of the poor and disinherited, who questioned the moral legitimacy of the existing state, the faith of a minority which accepted persecution and death as God's witnesses, it was to change in an incredibly short time into the official religion of the Roman State. While the Roman Empire's social structure was slowly freezing into a feudal order that was to survive in Europe for a thousand years, the Catholic religion's social structure began to change, too. The prophetic attitude that encouraged the questioning and criticizing of secular power's violation of the principles of love and justice receded in importance. The new attitude called for indiscriminating support of the Church's power as an institution. Such psychological satisfaction was given to the masses, that they accepted their dependency and poverty with resignation, making little effort to improve their social condition.[1]

[1] The change in the social role and function of Christianity was connected with profound changes in its spirit; the church became a hierarchical organization. The emphasis shifted increasingly from expectation of Christ's second coming and the establishment of a new order of love and justice, to the fact of the original coming—and the apostolic message of man's salvation from his inherent sinfulness. Connected with this was another change. The original concept of Christ was contained in the adoptionist dogma which said that God had adopted the man Jesus as

The most important change from the standpoint of this discussion is that of a shifting of emphasis from a purely patriarchal to a blending between matriarchal and patriarchal elements. The Jewish God of the Old Testament had been a strictly patriarchal god; in the Catholic development, the idea of the all-loving and all-forgiving mother is re-introduced. The Catholic Church herself—the all-embracing mother—and the Virgin Mother, symbolize the maternal spirit of forgiveness and love, while God, the father, represented in the hierarchichal principle the authority to which man had to submit without complaining or rebelling. No doubt this blending of fatherly and motherly elements was one of the main factors to which the church owed its tremendous attraction and influence over the minds of the people. The masses, oppressed by patriarchal authorities, could turn to the loving mother who would comfort them and intercede for them.

The historical function of the church was by no means only that of helping to establish a feudal order. Its most important achievement, greatly helped by the Arabs and Jews, was to transmit the essential elements of Jewish and Greek thought to the primitive culture of Europe. It is as if Western history had stood still for about a thousand years to wait for the moment when Northern Europe had been brought to the point of development at which the Mediterranean world had arrived at the beginning of the dark ages. When the spiritual heritage of Athens and Jerusalem had been transmitted to, and had saturated the Northern European peoples, the frozen social structure began to

---

his son, that is to say, that a man, a suffering and poor one, had become a god. In this dogma the revolutionary hopes and longings of the poor and downtrodden had found a religious expression. One year after Christianity was declared the official religion of the Roman Empire, the dogma was officially accepted that God and Jesus were identical, of the same essence, and that God had only manifested himself in the flesh of a man. In this new view, the revolutionary idea of the elevation of man to God had been substituted by God's act of love to come down to man, as it were, and thus save him from his corruption. (cf. E. Fromm, *Die Entwicklung des Christus Dogmas,* Psychoanalytischer Verlag, Vienna, 1931.)

thaw and an explosive social and spiritual development began again.

The Catholic theology in the thirteenth and fourteenth centuries, the ideas of the Italian Renaissance, "discovering the individual and nature," the concepts of humanism and of natural law and the Reformation are the foundations of the new development. The most drastic and most far-reaching effect on European and world development was that of the Reformation. Protestantism and Calvinism went back to the purely patriarchal spirit of the Old Testament and eliminated the mother element from the religious concept. Man was not any more enveloped by the motherly love of the church and the Virgin; he was alone, facing a severe and strict God whose mercy he could obtain only by an act of complete surrender. The princes and the state became all-powerful, sanctioned by the demands of God. The emancipation from feudal bonds led to the increased feeling of isolation and powerlessness, but at the same time the positive aspect of the paternal principle asserted itself in the renaissance of rational thought and individualism.[1]

The renaissance of the patriarchal spirit since the sixteenth century, especially in Protestant countries, shows both the *positive* and *negative* aspect of patriarchism. The negative aspect manifested itself in a new submission to the state and temporal power, to the ever-increasing importance of man-made laws and secular hierarchies. The positive aspect showed itself in the increasing spirit of rationality and objectivity and in the growth of individual and social conscience. The flowering of science in our day is one of the most impressive manifestations of rational thought the human race has ever produced. But the *matriarchal complex,* in both its positive and negative aspects, has by no means

[1] cf. the thorough and brilliant analysis of these problems in M. N. Roy, *Reason, Romanticism and Revolution,* Renaissance Publishing Co., Calcutta, 1952.

disappeared from the modern Western scene. Its positive aspect, the idea of human equality, of the sacredness of life, of all men's right to share in the fruits of nature, found expression in the ideas of natural law, humanism, enlightenment philosophy and the objectives of democratic socialism. Common to all these ideas is the concept that all men are children of Mother Earth and have a right to be nourished by her, and to enjoy happiness without having to prove this right by the achievement of any particular status. The brotherhood of all men implies that they are all the sons of the same mother, who have an inalienable right to love and happiness. In this concept, the incestuous tie to the mother is eliminated. By the mastery over nature as it manifests itself in industrial production, man frees himself from his fixation to the bonds of blood and soil, he humanizes nature and naturalizes himself.

But side by side with the development of the positive aspects of the matriarchal complex we find, in the European development, the persistence of, or even further, regression to its negative aspects—the fixation to blood and soil. Man—freed from the traditional bonds of the medieval community, afraid of the new freedom which transformed him into an isolated atom—escaped into a new idolatry of blood and soil, of which nationalism and racism are the two most evident expressions. Along with the progressive development, which is a blending of the positive aspect of both patriarchal and matriarchal spirit, went the development of the negative aspects of both principles: the worship of the state, blended with the idolatry of the race or nation. Fascism, Nazism and Stalinism, are the most drastic manifestations of this blend of state and clan worship, both principles embodied in the figure of a "Fuehrer."

But the new totalitarianisms are by no means the only manifestations of incestuous fixation in our time. The breakdown of the Catholic supernational world of the Middle Ages would have led to a higher form of "catholicism," that is, of human universalism overcoming clan worship, had the development followed the intentions of the spiritual leaders of humanist thought since the Renaissance. But while science and technique created the conditions for such development, the Western world fell back into new forms of clan idolatry, that very orientation which the prophets of the Old Testament and early Christianity tried to uproot. Nationalism, originally a progressive movement, replaced the bonds of feudalism and absolutism. The average man today obtains his sense of identity from his belonging to a nation, rather than from his being a "son of man." His objectivity, that is, his reason, is warped by this fixation. He judges the "stranger" with different criteria than the members of his own clan. His feelings toward the stranger are equally warped. Those who are not "familiar" by bonds of blood and soil (expressed by common language, customs, food, songs, etc.) are looked upon with suspicion, and paranoid delusions about them can spring up at the slightest provocation. This incestuous fixation not only poisons the relationship of the individual to the stranger, but to the members of his own clan and to himself. The person who has not freed himself from the ties to blood and soil is not yet fully born as a human being; his capacity for love and reason are crippled; he does not experience himself nor his fellow man in their—and his own—human reality.

Nationalism is our form of incest, is our idolatry, is our insanity. "Patriotism" is its cult. It should hardly be necessary to say, that by "patriotism" I mean that attitude which puts the own nation above humanity, above the principles of truth and justice; not the loving interest in one's own nation, which is the concern with the nation's spiritual as much as with its material welfare—never with its power over other nations. Just as love for one individual which excludes the love for others is not love, love for one's country which is not part of one's love for humanity is not love, but idolatrous worship.[1]

The idolatrous character of national feeling can be seen in the reaction to the violations of clan symbols, a reaction which is very different from that to the violation of religious or moral symbols. Let us picture a man who takes the flag of his country to a street of one of the cities of the Western world, and tramples on it in view of other people. He would be lucky not to be lynched. Almost everybody would feel a sense of furious indignation, which hardly permits of any objective thought. The man who desecrated the flag would have done something unspeakable; he would have committed a crime which is not *one* crime among others, but *the* crime, the one unforgivable and unpardonable. Not quite as drastic, but nevertheless qualitatively the same would be the reaction to a man who says, "I do not love my country," or, in the case of war, "I do not care for my country's victory." Such a sentence is a real sacrilege, and a man saying it becomes a monster, an outlaw in the feelings of his fellow men.

In order to understand the particular quality of the feeling aroused, we may compare this reaction to one which would occur if a man got up and said, "I am in favor of killing all Negroes, or all Jews; I am in favor of starting a war in order to conquer new territory." Indeed, most people would feel that this was an unethical, inhuman opinion. But the crucial point is that the particular feeling of an uncontrollable deep-seated indignation and rage would not occur. Such an opinion is just "bad," but it is not a sacrilege, it is not an attack against "the sacred." Even if a man should speak disparagingly of God, he would hardly arouse the same feeling of indignation as against *the* crime, against the

[1] cf. to the problem of nationalism the comprehensive and profound study by R. Rocker, "Nationalism and Culture," *Rocker Publ. Comm.*, Los Angeles, 1937.

sacrilege which is the violation of the symbols of the country. It is easy to rationalize the reaction to a violation of the national symbols by saying that a man who does not respect his country shows a lack of human solidarity and of social feeling; but is this not true also of the man who advocates war, or the killing of innocent people, or who exploits others for his own advantage? Undoubtedly, lack of concern for one's own country is an expression of a lack of social responsibility and of human solidarity, as are the other acts mentioned here, but the reaction to the violation of the flag is fundamentally different from the reaction to the denial of social responsibility in all other aspects. The one object is "sacred," a symbol of clan worship; the others are not.

After the great European Revolutions of the seventeenth and eighteenth centuries failed to transform "freedom from" into "freedom to," nationalism and state worship became the symptoms of a regression to incestuous fixation. Only when man succeeds in developing his reason and love further than he has done so far, only when he can build a world based on human solidarity and justice, only when he can feel rooted in the experience of universal brotherliness, will he have found a new, human form of rootedness, will he have transformed his world into a truly human home.

D.   SENSE OF IDENTITY—INDIVIDUALITY VS.
     HERD CONFORMITY

Man may be defined as the animal that can say "I," that can be aware of himself as a separate entity. The animal being within nature, and not transcending it, has no awareness of himself, has no need for a sense of identity. Man, being torn away from nature, being endowed with reason and imagination, needs to form a concept of himself, needs to say and to feel: "I am I." Because he is not *lived*, but *lives*, because he has lost the original unity with nature, has to make decisions, is aware of himself and of his neighbor as different persons, he must be able to sense himself as the subject of his actions. As with the need for related-ness, rootedness, and transcendence, this need for a sense of identity is so vital and imperative that man could not remain sane if he did not find some way of satisfying it. Man's sense of identity de-velops in the process of emerging from the "primary bonds" which tie him to mother and nature. The infant, still feeling one with mother, cannot yet say "I," nor has he any need for it. Only after he has conceived of the outer world as being separate and different from himself does he come to the awareness of him-self as a distinct being, and one of the last words he learns to use is "I," in reference to himself.

In the development of *the human race* the degree to which man is aware of himself as a separate self depends on the extent to which he has emerged from the clan and the extent to which the process of individuation has developed. The member of a primitive clan might express his sense of identity in the formula "I am we"; he cannot yet conceive of himself as an "individual," existing apart from his group. In the medieval world, the in-dividual was identified with his social role in the feudal hierarchy. The peasant was not a man who happened to be a peasant, the feudal lord not a man who happened to be a feudal lord. *He was* a peasant or a lord, and this sense of his unalterable station was an essential part of his sense of identity. When the feudal system broke down, this sense of identity was shaken and the acute question "who am I?" arose—or more precisely, "How do I know that I am I?" This is the question which was raised, in a philo-sophical form, by Descartes. He answered the quest for identity by saying, "I doubt—hence I think, I think—hence I am." This answer put all the emphasis on the experience of "I" as the subject of any *thinking* activity, and failed to see that the "I" is experienced also in the process of feeling and creative action.

The development of Western culture went in the direction of creating the basis for the full experience of individuality. By making the individual free politically and economically, by teaching him to think for himself and freeing him from an authoritarian pressure, one hoped to enable him to feel "I" in the sense that he was the center and active subject of his powers and experienced himself as such. But only a minority achieved the new experience of "I." For the majority, individualism was not much more than a façade behind which was hidden the failure to acquire an individual sense of identity.

Many substitutes for a truly individual sense of identity were sought for, and found. Nation, religion, class and occupation serve to furnish a sense of identity. "I am an American," "I am a Protestant," "I am a businessman," are the formulae which help a man experience a sense of identity after the original clan identity has disappeared and before a truly individual sense of identity has been acquired. These different identifications are, in contemporary society, usually employed together. They are in a broad sense status identifications, and they are more efficient if blended with older feudal remnants, as in European countries. In the United States, in which so little is left of feudal relics, and in which there is so much social mobility, these status identifications are naturally less efficient, and the sense of identity is shifted more and more to the experience of conformity.

Inasmuch as I am not different, inasmuch as I am like the others, and recognized by them as "a regular fellow," I can sense myself as "I." I am—"as you desire me"—as Pirandello put it in the title of one of his plays. Instead of the pre-individualistic clan identity, a new herd identity develops, in which the sense of identity rests on the sense of an unquestionable belonging to the crowd. That this uniformity and conformity are often not recognized as such, and are covered by the illusion of individuality, does not alter the facts.

The problem of the sense of identity is not, as it is usually understood, merely a philosophical problem, or a problem only concerning our mind and thought. The need to feel a sense of identity stems from the very condition of human existence, and it is the source of the most intense strivings. Since I cannot remain sane without the sense of "I," I am driven to do almost anything to acquire this sense. Behind the intense passion for status and conformity is this very need, and it is sometimes even stronger than the need for physical survival. What could be more obvious than the fact that people are willing to risk their lives, to give up their love, to surrender their freedom, to sacrifice their own thoughts, for the sake of being one of the herd, of conforming, and thus of acquiring a sense of identity, even though it is an illusory one.

E. THE NEED FOR A FRAME OF ORIENTATION AND
DEVOTION—REASON VS. IRRATIONALITY

The fact that man has reason and imagination leads not only to the necessity for having a sense of his own identity, but also for orienting himself in the world intellectually. This need can be compared with the process of physical orientation which develops in the first years of life, and which is completed when the child can walk by himself, touch and handle things, knowing what they are. But when the ability to walk and to speak has been acquired, only the first step in the direction of orientation has been taken. Man finds himself surrounded by many puzzling phenomena and, having reason, he has to make sense of them, has to put them in some context which he can understand and which permits him to deal with them in his thoughts. The further his reason develops, the more adequate becomes his system of orientation, that is, the more it approximates reality. But even if man's frame of orientation is utterly illusory, it satisfies his need for some picture which is meaningful to him. Whether he believes in the power of a totem animal, in a rain god, or in the superiority and destiny of his race, his need for some frame of orientation is satisfied. Quite obviously, the picture of the world which he has depends on the development of his reason and of his knowledge. Although biologically the brain capacity of the human race has remained the same for thousands of generations, it takes a long evolutionary process to arrive at *objectivity*, that is, to acquire the faculty to see the world, nature, other persons and oneself as they are, and not distorted by desires and fears. The more man develops this objectivity, the more he is in touch with reality, the more he matures, the better can he create a human world in which he is at home. Reason is man's faculty for *grasping* the world by thought, in contradiction to intelligence, which is man's ability to *manipulate* the world with the help of thought. Reason is man's instrument for arriving at the truth, intelligence is man's instrument for manipulating the world more successfully; the former is essentially human, the latter belongs to the animal part of man.

Reason is a faculty which must be practiced, in order to develop, and it is indivisible. By this I mean that the faculty for objectivity refers to the knowledge of nature as well as to the knowledge of man, of society and of oneself. If one lives in illusions about one sector of life, one's capacity for reason is restricted or damaged, and thus the use of reason is inhibited with regard to all other sectors. Reason in this respect is like love. Just as love is an orientation which refers to all objects and is incompatible with the restriction to one object, so is reason a human faculty which must embrace the whole of the world with which man is confronted.

The need for a frame of orientation exists on two levels; the first and the more fundamental need is to have *some* frame of orientation, regardless of whether it is true or false. Unless man has such a subjectively satisfactory frame of orientation, he cannot live sanely. On the second level the need is to be in touch with reality by reason, to grasp the world objectively. But the necessity to develop his reason is not as immediate as that to develop some frame of orientation, since what is at stake for man in the latter case is his happiness and serenity, and not his sanity. This becomes very clear if we study the function of *rationalization*. However unreasonable or immoral an action may be, man has an insuperable urge to rationalize it, that is, to prove to himself and to others that his action is determined by reason, common sense, or at least conventional morality. He has little difficulty in acting irrationally, but it is almost impossible for him not to give his action the appearance of reasonable motivation.

If man were only a disembodied intellect, his aim would be achieved by a comprehensive thought system. But since he is an entity endowed with a body as well as a mind, he has to react to the dichotomy of his existence not only in thinking but in the total process of living, in his feelings and actions. Hence any satisfying system of orientation contains not only intellectual elements but elements of feeling and sensing which are expressed in the relationship to an object of devotion.

The answers given to man's need for a system of orientation and an object of devotion differ widely both in content and in form. There are primitive systems such an animism and totemism in which natural objects or ancestors represent answers to man's quest for meaning. There are non-theistic systems like Buddhism, which are usually called religions although in their original form there is no concept of God. There are purely philosophical systems, like Stoicism, and there are the monotheistic religious systems which give an answer to man's quest for meaning in reference to the concept of God.

But whatever their contents, they all respond to man's need to have not only some thought system, but also an object of devotion which gives meaning to his existence and to his position in the world. Only the analysis of the various forms of religion can show which answers are better and which are worse solutions to man's quest for meaning and devotion, "better" or "worse" always considered from the standpoint of man's nature and his development.[1]

[1] cf. for a more extensive discussion of this problem, my *Psychoanalysis and Religion,* Yale University Press, 1950. The discussion of the need for an object of devotion and for rituals is continued in Chapter VIII, 4, of this book.

4

MENTAL HEALTH AND SOCIETY

The concept of mental health depends on our concept of the nature of man. In the previous chapter the attempt was made to show that the needs and passions of man stem from the peculiar condition of his existence. Those needs which he shares with the animal—hunger, thirst, need for sleep and sexual satisfaction—are important, being rooted in the inner chemistry of the body, and they can become all powerful when they remain unsatisfied. (This holds true, of course, more of the need for food and sleep than of sex, which if not satisfied never assumes the power of the other needs, at least not for physiological reasons.) But even their complete satisfaction is not a sufficient condition for sanity and mental health. These depend on the satisfaction of those needs and passions which are specifically human, and which stem from the conditions of the human situation: the need for relatedness, transcendence, rootedness, the need for a sense of identity and the need for a frame of orientation and devotion. The great passions of man, his lust for power, his vanity, his search for truth, his passion for love and brotherliness, his destructiveness as well as his creativeness, every powerful desire which motivates man's actions, is rooted in this specific human source, not in the various stages of his libido as Freud's construction postulated.

Man's solution to his physiological needs is, psychologically speaking, utterly simple; the difficulty here is a purely sociological and economic one. Man's solution to his human needs is exceedingly complex, it depends on many factors and last, not least, on the way his society is organized and how this organization determines the human relations within it.

The basic psychic needs stemming from the peculiarities of human existence must be satisfied in one form or other, unless man is to become insane, just as his physiological needs must be satisfied lest he die. But *the way* in which the psychic needs can be satisfied are manifold, and the difference between various ways of satisfaction is tantamount to the difference between various degrees of mental health. If one of the basic necessities has found no fulfillment, insanity is the result; if it is satisfied but in an unsatisfactory way—considering the nature of human existence—neurosis (either manifest or in the form of a socially patterned defect) is the consequence. Man has to relate himself to others; but if he does it in a symbiotic or alienated way, he loses his independence and integrity; he is weak, suffers, becomes hostile, or apathetic; only if he can relate himself to others in a loving way does he feel one with them and at the same time preserve his integrity. Only by productive work does he relate himself to nature, becoming one with her, and yet not submerging in her. As long as man remains rooted incestuously in nature, mother, clan, he is blocked from developing his individuality, his reason; he remains the helpless prey of nature, and yet he can never feel one with her. Only if he develops his reason and his love, if he can experience the natural and the social world in a human way, can he feel at home, secure in himself, and the master of his life. It is hardly necessary to point out that of two possible forms of transcendence, destructiveness is conducive to suffering, creativeness to happiness. It is also easy to see that only a sense of identity based on the experience of his own powers can give strength, while all forms of identity experience based on the group, leave man dependent, hence weak. Eventually, only to the extent to which he grasps reality, can he make this world *his;* if he lives in illusions, he never changes the conditions which necessitate these illusions.

Summing up, it can be said that the concept of mental health follows from the very conditions of human existence, and it is the same for man in all ages and all cultures. *Mental health is characterized by the ability to love and to create, by the emergence from incestuous ties to clan and soil, by a sense of identity based on one's experience of self as the subject and agent of one's powers, by the grasp of reality inside and outside of ourselves, that is, by the development of objectivity and reason.*

This concept of mental health coincides essentially with the norms postulated by the great spiritual teachers of the human race. This coincidence appears to some modern psychologists to be a proof that our psychological premises are not "scientific" but philosophic or religious "ideals." They find it difficult, apparently, to draw the conclusion that the great teachings of all cultures were based on rational insight into the nature of man, on the conditions for his full development. This latter conclusion seems also to be more in line with the fact that in the most diverse places of this globe, at different periods of history, the "awakened ones" have preached the same norms, with none, or with little influence from one upon the other. Ikhnaton, Moses, Kung Futse, Lao-tse, Buddha, Jesaja, Socrates, Jesus have postulated the same norms for human life, with only small and insignificant differences.

There is one particular difficulty which many psychiatrists and psychologists have to overcome in order to accept the ideas of *humanistic psychoanalysis*. They still think in the philosophic premises of the nineteenth-century materialism which assumed that all important psychic phenomena must be rooted in (and caused by) corresponding *physiological*, somatic processes. Thus Freud, whose basic philosophical orientation was molded by this type of materialism, believed that he had found this physiological substratum of human passion in the "libido." In the theory presented here, there are no corresponding *physiological* substrata to the needs for relatedness, transcendence, etc. The substratum is not a physical one, but the total human personality in its interaction with the world, nature and man; *it is the human practice of life as it results from the conditions of human existence*. Our philosophic premise is not that of the nineteenth-century materialism, but one which takes the action of man and his interaction with his fellow man and with nature as the basic empirical datum for the study of man.

Our concept of mental health leads into a theoretical difficulty if we consider the concept of human evolution. There is reason to assume that the history of man, hundreds of thousands of years ago, starts out with a truly "primitive" culture, where man's reason has not developed beyond the most rudimentary beginnings, where his frame of orientation has little relation to reality and truth. Should we speak of this primitive man as lacking in mental health, when he is simply lacking in qualities which only further evolution could give him? Indeed, one answer could be given to this question which would open up an easy solution; this answer lies in the obvious analogy between the evolution of the human race, and the evolution of the individual. If an adult had the attitude and orientation of a one-month-old child, we certainly would classify him as severely sick, probably as schizophrenic. For the one-month-old baby, however, the same attitude is normal and healthy, because it corresponds to the stage of his psychic development. The mental sickness of the adult, then, can be characterized, as Freud has shown, as a fixation or regression to an orientation which belongs to a former evolutionary state, and which is not adequate any more, considering the state of development the person should have reached. In the same way one could say that the human race, like the infant, starts out with a primitive orientation, and one would call healthy all forms of human orientation, which correspond to the adequate state of human evolution; while one would call "sick" those "fixations" or "regressions" which represent earlier states of development after the human race has already passed through them. Attractive as such a solution is, it does not take into account one fact. The one-month-old child has not yet the organic basis for a mature attitude. He could under no circumstances think, feel or act like a mature adult. Man, on the contrary, for hundreds of thousands of years, has had all the organic equipment for maturity; his brain, bodily co-ordination, physical strength have not changed in all that time. His evolution depended entirely on his ability to transmit knowledge to future generations, and thus to accumulate it. Human evolution is the result of cultural development, and not of an organic change. The infant of the most primitive culture, put into a highly developed culture, would develop like all other children in this culture, because the only factor determining his development is the cultural factor. In other words, while the one-month-old child could never have the spiritual maturity of an adult—whatever the cultural conditions are—any man from the primitive stage on, could have the perfection of man at the peak of his evolution provided he were given the cultural conditions for such maturity. It follows that to speak of primitive, incestuous, unreasonable man, as being in a normal evolutionary phase is different from making the same statement about the infant. Yet, on the other hand, the development of culture is a necessary condition for human development. Thus, there does not seem to be a completely satisfactory answer to the problem; from one standpoint we may speak of a lack in mental health; from another standpoint we may speak of an early phase in development. But the difficulty is great only if we deal with the problem in its most general form; as soon as we come to the more concrete problems of our time, we find the problem much less complicated. We have reached a state of individuation in which only the fully developed mature personality can make fruitful use of freedom; if the individual has not developed his reason and his capacity for love, he is incapable of bearing the burden of freedom and individuality, and tries to escape into artificial ties which give him a sense of belonging and rootedness. Any regression today from freedom into artificial rootedness in state or race is a sign of mental illness, since such regression does not correspond to the state of evolution already reached and results in unquestionably pathological phenomena.

Regardless of whether we speak of "mental health" or of the "mature development" of the human race, the concept of mental health or of maturity is an objective one, arrived at by the examination of the "human situation" and the human necessities and needs stemming from it. It follows, as I pointed out in Chapter II, that mental health cannot be defined in terms of the "adjustment" of the individual to his society, but, on the contrary, *that it must be defined in terms of the adjustment of society to the needs of man,* of its role in furthering or hindering the development of mental health. Whether or not the individual is healthy, is primarily not an individual matter, but depends on the structure of his society. A healthy society furthers man's capacity to love his fellow men, to work creatively, to develop his reason and objectivity, to have a sense of self which is based on the experience of his own productive powers. An unhealthy society is one which creates mutual hostility, distrust, which transforms man into an instrument of use and exploitation for others, which deprives him of a sense of self, except inasmuch as he submits to others or becomes an automaton. [Society can have both functions; it can further man's healthy development, and it can hinder it; in fact most societies do both, and the question is only to what degree and in what directions their positive and negative influence is exercised.]

This view that mental health is to be determined *objectively* and that society has both a furthering *and* a distorting influence on man, contradicts not only the relativistic view, discussed above, but two other views which I want to discuss now. One, decidedly the most popular one today, wants to make us believe that contemporary Western society and more especially, the "American way of life" corresponds to the deepest needs of human nature and that adjustment to this way of life means mental health and maturity. Social psychology, instead of being a tool for the criticism of society, thus becomes the apologist for the status quo. The concept of "maturity" and "mental health" in this view, corresponds to the desirable attitude of a worker or employee in industry or business. To give one example for this adjustment concept, I take a definition by Dr. Strecker, on emotional maturity. "I define maturity," he says, "as the ability to stick to a job, the capacity to give more on any job than is asked for, reliability, persistence to carry out a plan regardless of the difficulties, the ability to work with other people under organization and authority, the ability to make decisions, a will to life, flexibility, independence, and tolerance." [1] It is quite clear that what Strecker here describes as maturity are the virtues of a good worker, employee or soldier in the big social organizations of our time; they are the qualities

[1] E. A. Strecker, *Their Mothers' Sons*, J. B. Lippincott Company, Philadelphia and New York, 1951, p. 211.

73

which are usually mentioned in advertisements for a junior executive. To him, and many others who think like him, maturity is the same as adjustment to our society, without ever raising the question whether this adjustment is to a healthy or a pathological way of conducting one's life.

In contrast to this view is the one which runs from Hobbes to Freud, and which assumes a basic and unalterable *contradiction between human nature and society*, a contradiction which follows from the alleged asocial nature of man. For Freud, man is driven by two biologically rooted impulses: the craving for sexual pleasure, and for destruction. The aim of his sexual desire is complete sexual freedom, that is, unlimited sexual access to all women he might find desirable. "Man discovered by experience that sexual (genital) love afforded him his greatest gratification, so that it became in effect the prototype of all happiness to him." He thus must have been impelled "to seek his happiness further along the path of sexual relations, to make genital erotism the central point of his life." [1]

The other aim of the natural sexual desire is the incestuous desire for the mother which, by its very nature, creates conflict with and hostility against the father. Freud expressed the importance of this aspect of sexuality by stating that the prohibition against incest is "perhaps the most maiming wound ever inflicted throughout the ages on the erotic life of man." [2]

Quite in line with the ideas of Rousseau, Freud maintains that primitive man has yet to cope with no, or exceedingly few restrictions to the satisfaction of those basic desires. He can give vent to his aggression, and there are few limitations to the satisfaction of his sexual impulses. "In actual fact, primitive man . . . knew nothing of any restrictions on his instincts. . . .

[1] *Civilization and Its Discontent, loc. cit.*, p. 69.
[2] *Ibid.*, p. 74.

Civilized man has exchanged some part of his chances of happiness for a measure of 'security.' " [1]

While Freud follows Rousseau in the idea of the "happy savage," he follows Hobbes in his assumption of the basic hostility between men. *"Homo homini lupus;* who has the courage to dispute it in the face of all the evidence in his own life and in history?" [2] Freud asks. Man's aggressiveness, Freud thinks, has two sources: one, the innate striving for destruction (death instinct) and the other the frustration of his instinctual desires, imposed upon him by civilization. While man may channel part of his aggression against himself, through the Super-Ego, and while a minority can sublimate their sexual desire into brotherly love, aggressiveness remains ineradicable. Men will always compete with, and attack each other, if not for material things, then for the "prerogatives in sexual relationships, which must arouse the strongest rancour and most violent enmity among men and women who are otherwise equal. Let us suppose this were also to be removed by instituting complete liberty in sexual life, so that the family, the germ-cell of culture, ceased to exist; one could not, it is true, foresee the new paths on which cultural development might then proceed, but one thing one would be bound to expect, and that is that the ineffaceable feature of human nature would follow wherever it led." [3] Since for Freud love is in its essence sexual desire, he is compelled to assume a contradiction between love and social cohesion. Love, according to him, is by its very nature egotistical and antisocial, and the sense of solidarity and brotherly love are not primary feelings rooted in man's nature, but aim-inhibited sexual desires.

On the basis of his concept of man, that of his inherent wish

[1] *Ibid.,* pp. 91, 92.
[2] *Ibid.,* p. 85.
[3] *Ibid.,* p. 89.

for unlimited sexual satisfaction, and of his destructiveness, Freud must arrive at a picture of the necessary *conflict* between civilization and mental health and happiness. Primitive man is healthy and happy because he is not frustrated in his basic instincts, but he lacks the blessings of culture. Civilized man is more secure, enjoys art and science, but he is bound to be neurotic because of the continued frustration of his instincts, enforced by civilization.

For Freud, social life and civilization are essentially in contrast to the needs of human nature as he sees it, and man is confronted with the tragic alternative between happiness based on the unrestricted satisfaction of his instincts, and security and cultural achievements based on instinctual frustration, hence conducive to neurosis and all other forms of mental sickness. Civilization, to Freud, is the product of instinctual frustration and thus the cause of mental illness.

Freud's concept of human nature as being essentially competitive (and asocial) is the same as we find it in most authors who believe that the characteristics of man in modern Capitalism are his natural characteristics. Freud's theory of the Oedipus complex is based on the assumption of the "natural" antagonism and competitiveness between father and sons for the love of the mother. This competition is said to be unavoidable because of the natural incestuous strivings in the sons. Freud only follows the same trend of thought in his assumption that the instincts of each man make him desire to have the prerogative in sexual relationships, and thus create violent enmity among themselves. We cannot fail to see that Freud's whole theory of sex is conceived on the anthropological premise that competition and mutual hostility are inherent in human nature.

Darwin gave expression to this principle in the sphere of *biology* with his theory of a competitive "struggle for survival." Economists like Ricardo and the Manchester school translated it into the sphere of *economy*. Later, Freud, under the influence of the same anthropological premises, was to claim it for the sphere of *sexual desires*. His basic concept is that of a "homo sexualis" as that of the economists was that of the "homo economicus." Both the "economic" man and the "sexual" man are convenient fabrications whose alleged nature—isolated, asocial, greedy and competitive—makes Capitalism appear as the system which corresponds perfectly to human nature, and places it beyond the reach of criticism.

Both positions, the "adjustment view" and the Hobbes-Freudian view of the necessary conflict between human nature and society, imply the defense of contemporary society and they both are one-sided distortions. Furthermore, they both ignore the fact that society is not only in conflict with the *asocial* aspects of man, partly produced by itself, but often also with his most valuable human qualities, which it suppresses rather than furthers.

An objective examination of the relation between society and human nature must consider both the furthering and the inhibiting impact of society on man, taking into account the nature of man and the needs stemming from it. Since most authors have emphasized the positive influence of modern society on man, I shall in this book pay less attention to this aspect and more to the somewhat neglected pathogenic function of modern society.

5

MAN IN CAPITALISTIC SOCIETY

THE SOCIAL CHARACTER

Mental health cannot be discussed meaningfully as an abstract quality of abstract people. If we are to discuss now the state of mental health in contemporary Western man, and if we are to consider what factors in his mode of life make for in-sanity and what others are conducive to sanity, we have to study the influence of the specific conditions of our mode of production and of our social and political organization on the nature of man; we have to arrive at a picture of the personality of the average man living and working under these conditions. Only if we can arrive at such a picture of the *"social character,"* tentative and incomplete as it may be, do we have a basis on which to judge the mental health and sanity of modern man.

What is meant by social character? I refer in this concept to *the nucleus of the character structure which is shared by most members of the same culture* in contradistinction to the *individual character in which people belonging to the same culture differ from each other.* The concept of social character is not a statistical concept in the sense that it is simply the sum total of character traits to be found in the majority of people in a given culture.

It can be understood only in reference to the *function* of the social character which we shall now proceed to discuss.[1]

Each society is structuralized and operates in certain ways which are necessitated by a number of objective conditions. These conditions include methods of production and distribution which in turn depend on raw materials, industrial techniques, climate, size of population, and political and geographical factors, cultural traditions and influences to which society is exposed. There is no "society" in general, but only specific social structures which operate in different and ascertainable ways. Although these social structures do change in the course of historical development, they are relatively fixed at any given historical period, and society can exist only by operating within the framework of its particular structure. The members of the society and/or the various classes or status groups within it have to behave in such a way as to be able to function in the sense required by the social system. It is the function of the social character to shape the energies of the members of society in such a way that their behavior is not a matter of conscious decision as to whether or not to follow the social pattern, but one of *wanting to act as they have to act* and at the same time finding gratification in acting according to the requirements of the culture. In other words, it is the social character's function *to mold and channel human energy within a given society for the purpose of the continued functioning of this society.*

Modern, industrial society, for instance, could not have attained its ends had it not harnessed the energy of free men for work in an

[1] In the following pages I have drawn on my paper, "Psychoanalytic Characterology and Its Application to the Understanding of Culture," in *Culture and Personality*, ed. by G. S. Sargent and M. Smith, Viking Fund, 1949, pp. 1–12. The concept of the social character was developed originally in my "Die psychoanalytische Charakterologie in ihrer Anwendurg für die Soziologie" in *Zeitschrift für Sozialforschung*, I, Hirschfeld, Leipzig, 1931.

unprecedented degree. Man had to be molded into a person who was eager to spend most of his energy for the purpose of work, who acquired discipline, particularly orderliness and punctuality, to a degree unknown in most other cultures. It would not have sufficed if each individual had to make up his mind consciously every day that he wanted to work, to be on time, etcetera, since any such conscious deliberation would lead to many more exceptions than the smooth functioning of society can afford. Nor would threat and force have sufficed as a motive, since the highly differentiated tasks in modern industrial society can in the long run only be the work of free men and not of forced labor. The *necessity* for work, for punctuality and orderliness had to be transformed into an inner *drive* for these aims. This means that society had to produce a social character in which these strivings were inherent.

The *genesis* of the social character cannot be understood by referring to one single cause but by understanding the interaction of sociological and ideological factors. Inasmuch as economic factors are less easily changeable, they have a certain predominance in this interplay. This does not mean that the drive for material gain is the only or even the most powerful motivating force in man. It does mean that the individual and society are primarily concerned with the task of survival, and that only when survival is secured can they proceed to the satisfaction of other imperative human needs. The task of survival implies that man has to produce, that is, he has to secure the minimum of food and shelter necessary for survival, and the tools needed for even the most rudimentary processes of production. The method of production in turn determines the social relations existing in a given society. It determines the mode and practice of life. However, religious, political and philosophical ideas are not purely secondary projective systems. While they are rooted in the social character, they in turn also determine, systematize and stabilize the social character.

Let me state again, in speaking of the socio-economic structure of society as molding man's character, we speak only of one pole in the interconnection between social organization and man. The other pole to be considered is man's nature, molding in turn the social conditions in which he lives. The social process can be understood only if we start out with the knowledge of the reality of man, his psychic properties as well as his physiological ones, and if we examine the interaction between the nature of man and the nature of the external conditions under which he lives and which he has to master if he is to survive.

While it is true that man can adapt himself to almost any conditions, he is not a blank sheet of paper on which culture writes its text. Needs like the striving for happiness, harmony, love and freedom are inherent in his nature. They are also dynamic factors in the historical process which, if frustrated, tend to arouse psychic reactions, ultimately creating the very conditions suited to the original strivings. As long as the objective conditions of the society and the culture remain stable, the social character has a predominantly stabilizing function. If the external conditions change in such a way that they do not fit any more with the traditional social character, a *lag* arises which often changes the function of character into an element of disintegration instead of stabilization, into dynamite instead of a social mortar, as it were.

Provided this concept of the genesis and function of the social character is correct, we are confronted with a puzzling problem. Is not the assumption that the character structure is molded by the role which the individual has to play in his culture contradicted by the assumption that a person's character is molded in his childhood? Can both views pretend to be true in view of the fact that the child in his early years of life has comparatively little contact with society as such? This question is not as difficult to answer as it may seem at first glance. We must differentiate between the factors which are responsible for the particular *contents* of the social character and the *methods* by which the social character is produced. The structure of society and the function of the individual in the social structure may be considered to determine the content of the social character. The family on the other hand may be considered to be the *psychic agency of society,* the institution which has the function of transmitting the requirements of society to the growing child. The family fulfills this function in two ways. First, and this is the most important factor, by the influence the character of the parents has on the character formation of the growing child. Since the character of most parents is an expression of the social character, they transmit in this way the essential features of the socially desirable character structure to the child. The parents' love and happiness are communicated to the child as well as their anxiety or hostility. In addition to the character of the parents, the methods of childhood training which are customary in a culture also have the function of molding the character of the child in a socially desirable direction. There are various methods and techniques of child training which can fulfill the same end, and on the other hand there can be methods which seem identical but which nevertheless are different because of the character structure of those who practice these methods. By focusing on methods of child training, we can never explain the social character. Methods of child training are significant only as a mechanism of *transmission,* and they can be understood correctly only if we understand first what kinds of personalities are desirable and necessary in any given culture.[1]

[1] In the assumption that methods of child training in themselves are the cause for the particular formation of a culture lies the weakness of the approach by Kardiner,

The problem, then, of the socio-economic conditions in modern industrial society which create the personality of modern Western man and are responsible for the disturbances in his mental health require an understanding of those elements specific to the capitalistic mode of production, of an "acquisitive society" in an industrial age. Sketchy and elementary as such a description by a noneconomist must necessarily be, I hope it is neverthless sufficient to form the basis for the following analysis of the social character of man in present-day Western society.

THE STRUCTURE OF CAPITALISM AND THE CHARACTER OF MAN

A. SEVENTEENTH- AND EIGHTEENTH-CENTURY CAPITALISM

The economic system which has become dominant in the West since the seventeenth and eighteenth centuries is Capitalism. In spite of great changes which have occurred within this system, there are certain features which have endured throughout its history and, with reference to these common features, it is legitimate to use the concept of Capitalism for the economic system existing throughout this whole period.

Briefly, these common features are: 1—the existence of politically and legally free men; 2—the fact that free men (workers and employees) sell their labor to the owner of capital on the labor market, by contract; 3—the existence of the commodity market as a mechanism by which prices are determined and the exchange of the social product is regulated; 4—the principle that each individual acts with the aim of seeking a profit for himself, and

---

Gorer and others, whose work is based in this respect on the orthodox Freudian premises.

yet that, by the competitive action of many, the greatest advantage is supposed to accrue for all.

While these features are common to Capitalism throughout the last few centuries, the changes within this period are as important as are the similarities. While we are most concerned in our analysis with the impact of the contemporary socio-economic structure on man, we shall at least briefly discuss the features of seventeenth- and eighteenth-century Capitalism, and those of nineteenth-century Capitalism which are different from the development of society and man in the twentieth century.

Speaking of the seventeenth and eighteenth centuries, two aspects must be mentioned which characterize this early period of Capitalism. First, that technique and industry were in the beginning compared with the development in the nineteenth and twentieth centuries, and second that at the same time the practices and ideas of medieval culture still had a considerable influence on the economic practices of this period. Thus it was supposed to be un-Christian and unethical for one merchant to try to lure customers from another by force of lower prices or any other inducements. In the fifth edition of the *Complete English Tradesman* (1745), it is stated that since the death of the author, Defoe, in 1731, "this underselling practice is grown to such a shameful height, that particular persons publicly advertise that they undersell the rest of the trade." [1] The *Complete English Tradesman*, fifth edition, cites a concrete case in which an "overgrown tradesman" who had more money than his competitors, and thus was not forced to use credit, bought his wares directly from the producer, transported them himself, instead of through a middleman, and sold them directly to the retailer, thus enabling the latter to sell the material for one penny cheaper per yard. The

[1] I follow here the description and quote illustrations given by W. Sombart, *Der Bourgeois,* München and Leipzig, 1923, p. 201 ff.

comment of the Complete Tradesman is that the result of this whole method is only to enrich this "covetous man," and to enable another man to buy his cloth a little cheaper, "a very small advantage" which is in no relation to the damage done the other businessmen.[1] We find similar prohibitions against underselling in ordinances in Germany and France throughout the whole eighteenth century.

It is well known how skeptical people were in that period toward new machines, inasmuch as they threatened to take away work from man. Colbert called them "the enemy of labour," and Montesquieu says, "Esprit de Loi" (XXIII, 15,) that machines which diminish the numbers of workers are "pernicious." The various attitudes just mentioned are based on principles which had determined the life of man for many centuries. Most important of all was the principle that society and economy exist for man, and not man for them. No economic progress was supposed to be healthy if it hurt any group within the society; needless to say this concept was closely related to traditionalist thoughts in so much as the traditional social balance was to be preserved, and any disturbance was believed to be harmful.

B.   NINETEENTH-CENTURY CAPITALISM

In the nineteenth century the traditionalistic attitude of the eighteenth changes, first slowly and then rapidly. The living human being, with his desires and woes, loses more and more his central place in the system, and this place is occupied by business and production. Man ceases to be "the measure of all things" in the economic sphere. The most characteristic element of nineteenth-century Capitalism was first of all, ruthless exploitation of the worker; it was believed to be a natural or a social law that hundreds of thousands of workers were living at the point of

[1] *Ibid.*, p. 206.

starvation. The owner of capital was supposed to be morally right if, in the pursuit of profit, he exploited to the maximum the labor he hired. There was hardly any sense of human solidarity between the owner of capital and his workers. The law of the economic jungle was supreme. All the restrictive ideas of previous centuries were left behind. One seeks out the customer, tries to undersell one's competitor, and the competitive fight against equals is as ruthless and unrestricted as the exploitation of the worker. With the use of the steam engine, division of labor grows, and so does the size of enterprises. The capitalistic principle that each one seeks his own profit and thus contributes to the happiness of all becomes the guiding principle of human behavior.

The market as the prime regulator is freed from all traditional restrictive elements and comes fully into its own in the nineteenth century. While everybody believes himself to act according to his own interest, he is actually determined by the anonymous laws of the market and of the economic machine. The individual capitalist expands his enterprise not primarily because he *wants* to, but because he *has* to, because—as Carnegie said in his autobiography—postponement of further expansion would mean regression. Actually as a business grows, one has to continue making it bigger, whether one wants to or not. In this function of the economic law which operates behind the back of man and forces him to do things without giving him the freedom to decide, we see the beginning of a constellation which comes to its fruition only in the twentieth century.

In our time it is not only the law of the market which has its own life and rules over man, but also the development of science and technique. For a number of reasons, the problems and organization of science today are such that a scientist does not choose his problems; the problems force themselves upon the scientist. He solves one problem, and the result is not that he is more secure or certain, but that ten other new problems open up in place of the single solved one. They force him to solve them; he has to go ahead at an ever-quickening pace. The same holds true for industrial techniques. The pace of science forces the pace of technique. Theoretical physics forces atomic energy on us; the successful production of the fission bomb forces upon us the manufacture of the hydrogen bomb. *We* do not choose our problems, we do not choose our products; we are pushed, we are forced —by what? By a system which has no purpose and goal transcending it, and which makes man its appendix.

We shall say a great deal more about this aspect of man's powerlessness in the analysis of contemporary Capitalism. At this point, however, we ought to dwell a little longer on the importance of the modern market as the central mechanism of distributing the social product, since the market is the basis for the formation of human relations in capitalistic society.

If the wealth of society corresponded to the actual needs of all its members, there would be no problem of distributing it; each member could take from the social product as much as he likes, or needs, and there would be no need of regulation, except in the purely *technical* sense of distribution. But aside from primitive societies, this condition has never existed up to now in human history. The needs were always greater than the sum total of the social product, and therefore a regulation had to be made on how to distribute it, how many and who should have the optimal satisfaction of their needs, and which classes had to be satisfied with less than they wanted. In most highly developed societies of the past, this decision was made essentially by force. Certain classes had the power to appropriate the best of the social product for themselves, and to assign to other classes the heavier and dirtier work and a smaller share of the product. Force was often implemented by social and religious tradition, which constituted such a strong psychic force within people that it often made the threat of physical force unnecessary.

The modern market is a self-regulating mechanism of distribution, which makes it unnecessary to divide the social product according to an intended or traditional plan, and thus does away with the necessity of the use of force within society. Of course, the absence of force is more apparent than real. The worker who has to accept the wage rate offered him on the labor market is forced to accept the market condition because he could not survive otherwise. Thus the "freedom" of the individual is largely illusory. He is aware of the fact that there is no *outer* force which compels him to enter into certain contracts; he is less aware of the laws of the market which operate behind his back, as it were; hence he believes that he is free, when he actually is not. But while this is so, the capitalist method of distribution by the market mechanism is better than any other method devised so far in a class society, because it is a basis for the relative political freedom of the individual, which characterizes capitalistic democracy.

The economic functioning of the market rests upon *competition* of many individuals who want to sell their commodities on the commodity market, as they want to sell their labor or services on the labor and personality market. This economic necessity for competition led, especially in the second half of the nineteenth century, to an increasingly competitive attitude, characterologically speaking. Man was driven by the desire to surpass his competitor, thus reversing completely the attitude characteristic of the feudal age—that each one had in the social order his traditional place with which he should be satisfied. As opposed to the social stability in the medieval system, an unheard of social mobility developed, in which everybody was struggling for the best places, even though only a few were chosen to attain them. In this scramble for success, the social and moral rules of human solidarity broke down; the importance of life was in being first in a competitive race.

Another factor which constitutes the capitalistic mode of production is that in this system the aim of all economic activity is *profit*. Now around this "profit motive" of Capitalism, a great deal of calculated and uncalculated confusion has been created. We have been told—and rightly so—that all economic activity is meaningful only if it results in a profit, that is to say, if we gain more than we have spent in the act of production. To make a living, even the pre-capitalist artisan had to spend on raw material and his apprentice's wage less than the price he charged for his product. In any society that supports industry, simple or complex, the value of the salable product must exceed the cost of production in order to provide capital needed for the replacement of machinery or other instruments for the development and increase of production. But the question of the profitableness of production is not the issue. Our problem is that our motive for production is not social usefulness, not satisfaction in the work process, but the profit derived from investment. The usefulness of his product to the consumer need not interest the individual capitalist at all. This does not mean that the capitalist, psychologically speaking, is driven by an insatiable greed for money. This may or may not be so, but it is not essential for the capitalistic mode of production. In fact, greed was much more frequently the capitalist's motive in an earlier phase than it is now, when ownership and management are largely separated, and when the aim of obtaining higher profits is subordinate to the wish for the ever-growing expansion and smooth running of an enterprise.

Income can, under the present system, be quite apart from personal effort or service. The owner of capital can earn without working. The essential human function of exchange of effort for income can become the abstracted manipulation of money for more money. This is most obvious in the case of the absentee owner of an industrial enterprise. It does not make any difference whether he owns the whole enterprise, or only a share of it. In each case he makes a profit from his capital and from the work of others without having to make any effort himself. There have been many pious justifications for this state of affairs. It has been said that the profits were a payment for the risk he takes in his investment, or for his self-depriving effort to save, which enabled him to accumulate the capital he can invest. But it is hardly necessary to prove that these marginal factors do not alter the elementary fact that Capitalism permits the making of profits without personal effort and productive function. But even as far as those who do work and perform services, their income is not in any reasonable correlation to the effort they make. A school-teacher's earnings are but a fraction of those of a physician, in spite of the fact that her social function is of equal importance and her personal effort hardly less. The miner earns a fraction of the income of the manager of the mine, though his personal effort is greater if we consider the dangers and discomforts connected with his work.

What characterizes income distribution in Capitalism is the lack of balanced proportion between an individual's effort and work and the social recognition accorded them—financial compensation. This disproportion would, in a poorer society than ours, result in greater extremes of luxury and poverty than our standards of morals would tolerate. I am not stressing, however, the material effects of this disproportion, but its moral and psychological effects. One lies in the underevaluation of work, of human effort and skill. The other lies in the fact that as long as my gain is limited by the effort I make, my desire is limited. If, on the other hand, my income is not in proportion to my effort, there are no limitations to my desires, since their fulfillment is a matter of opportunities offered by certain market situations, and not dependent on my own capacities.[1]

Nineteenth-century Capitalism was truly *private* Capitalism. Individuals saw and seized new opportunities, acted economically, sensed new methods, acquired property, both for production and consumption—and enjoyed their property. This pleasure in property, aside from competitiveness and profit seeking, is one of the fundamental aspects of the character of the middle and upper classes of the ninteenth century. It is all the more important to note this trait because with regard to the pleasure in property and in saving, man today is so markedly different from his grandfathers. The mania for saving and for possession, in fact, has become the characteristic feature of the most backward class, the lower middle class, and is much more readily found in Europe than in America. We have here one of the examples where a trait of the social character which was once that of the most advanced class became, in the process of economic development, obsolete as it were, and is retained by the very groups which have developed the least.

Characterologically, the pleasure in possession and property has been described by Freud as an important aspect of the "anal character." From a different theoretical premise, I have described the same clinical picture in terms of the "hoarding orientation." Like all other character orientations, the hoarding one has positive and negative aspects, and whether the positive or the negative aspects are dominant depends on the relative strength of the productive

[1] We find here the same difference that exists with regard to physical desires in contrast to those which are not rooted in bodily needs; my desire to eat, for instance, is self-regulated by my physiological organization, and only in pathological cases is this desire not regulated by a physiological saturation point. Ambition, lust for power, and so on, which are not rooted in physiological needs of the organism have no such self-regulating mechanisms, and that is the reason why they are ever increasing and so dangerous.

orientation within the individual or social character. The positive aspects of this orientation, as I have described them in "Man for Himself" are: to be practical, economical, careful, reserved, cautious, tenacious, imperturbable, orderly, methodical and loyal. The corresponding negative aspects are, to be unimaginative, stingy, suspicious, cold, anxious, stubborn, indolent, pedantic, obsessional and possessive.[1] It can be easily seen that in the eighteenth and nineteenth centuries, when the hoarding orientation was geared to the necessities of economic progress, the positive characteristics were predominant, while in the twentieth century when these traits are the obsolete feature of an obsolete class, the negative aspects are almost exclusively present.

The breakdown of the traditional principle of human solidarity led to new forms of exploitation. In feudal society the lord was supposed to have the divine right to demand services and things from those subject to his domination, but at the same time he was bound by custom and was obligated to be responsible for his subjects, to protect them, and to provide them with at least the minimum—the traditional standard of living. Feudal exploitation took place in a system of mutual human obligations, and thus was governed by certain restrictions. Exploitation as it developed in the nineteenth century was essentially different. The worker, or rather his labor, was a commodity to be bought by the owner of capital, not essentially different from any other commodity on the market, and it was used to its fullest capacity by the buyer. Since it had been bought for its proper price on the labor market, there was no sense of reciprocity, or of any obligation on the part of the owner of capital, beyond that of paying the wages. If hundreds of thousands of workers were without work and on the point of starvation, that was their bad luck, the result of their inferior talents, or simply a social and natural law, which could not be

[1] cf. *Man for Himself,* p. 114.

changed. Exploitation was not personal any more, but it had become anonymous, as it were. It was the law of the market that condemned a man to work for starvation wages, rather than the intention or greed of any one individual. Nobody was responsible or guilty, nobody could change conditions either. One was dealing with the iron laws of society, or so it seemed.

In the twentieth century, such capitalistic exploitation as was customary in the nineteenth century has largely disappeared. This must not, however, becloud the insight into the fact that twentieth-century as well as nineteenth-century Capitalism is based on the principle that is to be found in all class societies: *the use of man by man.*

Since the modern capitalist "employs" labor, the social and political form of this exploitation has changed; what has not changed is that the owner of capital uses other men for the purpose of his own profit. The basic concept of *use* has nothing to do with cruel, or not cruel, ways of human treatment, but with the fundamental fact that one man serves another for purposes which are not his own but those of the employer. The concept of use of man by man has nothing to do even with the question whether one man uses another, or uses himself. The fact remains the same, that a man, a living human being, ceases to be an end in himself, and becomes the means for the economic interests of another man, or himself, or of an impersonal giant, the economic machine.

There are two obvious objections to the foregoing statements. One is that modern man is free to accept or to decline a contract, and therefore he is a voluntary participant in his social relation to the employer, and not a "thing." But this objection ignores the fact that in the first place he has no choice but to accept the existing conditions, and secondly, that even if he were not forced to accept these conditions, he would still be "employed," that is, made use of for purposes not his own, but of the capital whose profit he serves.

The other objection is that all social life, even in its most primitive form, requires a certain amount of social co-operation, and even discipline, and that certainly in the more complex form of industrial production, a person has to fulfill certain necessary and specialized functions. While this statement is quite true, it ignores the basic difference: in a society where no person has power over another, each person fulfills his functions on the basis of co-operation and mutuality. No one can command another person, except insofar as a relationship is based on mutual co-operation, on love, friendship or natural ties. Actually we find this present in many situations in our society today: the normal co-operation of husband and wife in their family life is to a large extent not any more determined by the power of the husband to command his wife, as it existed in older forms of patriarchal society, but on the principle of co-operation and mutuality. The same holds true for the relationship of friends, inasmuch as they perform certain services for each other and co-operate with each other. In these relationships no one would dare to think of *commanding* the other person; the only reason for expecting his help lies in the mutual feeling of love, friendship or simply human solidarity. The help of another person is secured by my active effort, as a human being, to elicit his love, friendship and sympathy. In the relationship of the employer to the employee, this is not the case. The employer has bought the services of the worker, and however human his treatment may be, he still commands him, not on a basis of mutuality, but on the basis of having bought his working time for so many hours a day.

The use of man by man is expressive of the *system of values* underlying the capitalistic system. *Capital, the dead past, employs*

labor—the living vitality and power of the present. In the capitalistic hierarchy of values, capital stands higher than labor,
amassed things higher than the manifestations of life. Capital
employs labor, and not labor capital. The person who owns
capital commands the person who "only" owns his life, human
skill, vitality and creative productivity. "Things" are higher than
man. The conflict between capital and labor is much more than
the conflict between two classes, more than their fight for a
greater share of the social product. It is the conflict between two
principles of value: *that between the world of things, and their
amassment, and the world of life and its productivity.*[1]

Closely related to the problem of exploitation and use, although
even more complicated, is the problem of *authority* in nineteenth-
century man. Any social system in which one group of the population is commanded by another, especially if the latter is a minority,
must be based on a strong sense of *authority,* a sense which is
increased in a strongly patriarchal society where the male sex is
supposed to be superior to and in control of the female sex. Since
the problem of authority is so crucial for our understanding of
human relations in any kind of society, and since the attitude of
authority has changed fundamentally from the nineteenth to
the twentieth century, I want to begin the discussion of this problem by referring to a differentiation of authority which I made in
"Escape from Freedom," and which still seems to me valid enough
to be quoted as a basis for the following discussion: Authority
is not a quality one person 'has,' in the sense that he has property
or physical qualities. Authority refers to an interpersonal relation
in which one person looks upon another as somebody superior to
him. But there is a fundamental difference between a kind of

[1] cf. R. M. Tawney's discussion of the same point in *The Acquisitive Society,* Harcourt Brace & Company, New York, 1920, p. 99.

superiority-inferiority relation which can be called *rational* authority and one which may be described as *inhibiting,* or irrational authority.

An example will show what I have in mind. The relationship between teacher and student and that between slave owner and slave are both based on the superiority of the one over the other. The interests of teacher and pupil lie in the same direction. The teacher is satisfied if he succeeds in furthering the pupil; if he has failed to do so, the failure is his and the pupil's. The slave owner, on the other hand, wants to exploit the slave as much as possible; the more he gets out of him, the more he is satisfied. At the same time, the slave seeks to defend as best he can his claims for a minimum of happiness. These interests are definitely antagonistic, as what is of advantage to the one is detrimental to the other. The superiority has a different function in both cases: in the first, it is the condition for helping of the person subjected to the authority; in the second, it is the condition for his exploitation.

The dynamics of authority in these two types are different too: the more the student learns, the less wide is the gap between him and the teacher. He becomes more and more like the teacher himself. In other words, *the rational authority relationship tends to dissolve itself.* But when the superiority serves as a basis for exploitation, the distance becomes intensified through its long duration.

The psychological situation is different in each of these authority situations. In the first, elements of love, admiration, or gratitude are prevalent. The authority is at the same time an example with which one wants to identify one's self partially or totally. In the second situation, resentment or hostility will arise against the exploiter, subordination to whom is against one's own interests. But often, as in the case of a slave, his hatred would only lead to conflicts which would subject the slave to suffering without a chance of winning. Therefore, the tendency will usually be to repress the feeling of hatred and sometimes even to replace it by a feeling of blind admiration. This has two functions: (1) to remove the painful and dangerous feeling of hatred, and (2) to soften the feeling of humiliation. If the person who rules over me is so wonderful or perfect, then I should not be ashamed of obeying him. I cannot be his equal because he is so much stronger, wiser, better, and so on, than I am. As a result, in the inhibiting kind of authority, the element either of hatred or of irrational overestimation and admiration of the authority will tend to *increase*. In the rational kind of authority, the strength of the emotional ties will tend to *decrease* in direct proportion to the degree in which the person subjected to the authority becomes stronger and thereby more similar to the authority.

The difference between rational and inhibiting authority is only a relative one. Even in the relationship between slave and master there are elements of advantage for the slave. He gets a minimum of food and protection which at least enables him to work for his master. On the other hand, it is only in an ideal relationship between teacher and student that we find a complete lack of antagonism of interests. There are many gradations between these two extreme cases, as in the relationship of a factory worker with his boss, or a farmer's son with his father, or a 'hausfrau' with her husband. Nevertheless, although in reality the two types of authority are blended, they are essentially different, and an analysis of a concrete authority situation must always determine the specific weight of each kind of authority.

The nineteenth-century social character is a good example of a mixture between rational and irrational authority. The character of society was essentially a hierarchical one, though no longer like the hierarchical character of feudal society based on divine law and tradition, but rather on the ownership of capital; those who owned it could buy, and thus command the labor of those who did not, and the latter had to obey, under penalty of starvation. There was a certain blending between the new and the old hierarchical pattern. The state, especially in the monarchial form, cultivated the old virtues of obedience and submission, to apply them to new contents and values. Obedience, in the nineteenth-century middle class, was still one of the fundamental virtues and disobedience one of the elementary vices.

At the same time, however, rational authority had developed side by side with irrational authority. Since the Reformation and the Renaissance man had begun to rely on his own reason as a guide to action and value judgment. He felt proud to have convictions which were his, and he respected the authority of scientists, philosophers, historians, who helped him to form his own judgments and to be sure of his own convictions. The decision between true and false, right and wrong, was of the utmost importance and, indeed, both the moral and the intellectual conscience assumed a paramount place in the character structure of nineteenth-century man. He may not have applied the rules of his conscience to men of a different color or even of a different social class, yet to some extent he was determined by his sense of right and wrong, and at least by the repression of the awareness of wrongdoing, if he did not succeed in avoiding wrong action.

Closely related to this sense of intellectual and moral conscience is another trait characteristic of the nineteenth century: the sense of pride and mastery. If we look today at the pictures of nineteenth-century life, the man with the beard, the tall silk hat and walking cane, we are easily struck by the ridiculous and negative aspect of nineteenth-century male pride—a man's vanity and naïve belief in himself as the highest accomplishment of nature and of history; but, especially if we consider the absence of this trait in our own time, we can see the positive aspects of this pride. Man had the feeling of having put himself into the saddle, so to speak, of having freed himself from domination by natural forces, and for the first time in history having become their master. He had freed himself from the shackles of medieval superstition, had even succeeded in the hundred years between 1814 and 1914 in creating one of the most peaceful periods history has ever known. He felt himself to be an individual, subject only to the laws of reason, following only his own decisions.

Summing up then, we may say that the social character of the nineteenth century was essentially competitive, hoarding, exploitative, authoritarian, aggressive, individualistic. Anticipating our later discussion, we may already emphasize here the great difference between nineteenth- and twentieth-century Capitalism. Instead of the exploitative and hoarding orientation we find the receptive and marketing orientation. Instead of competitiveness we find an increasing tendency toward "teamwork"; instead of a striving for ever-increasing profit, a wish for a steady and secure income; instead of exploitation, a tendency to share and spread wealth, and to manipulate others—and oneself; instead of rational and irrational but *overt* authority, we find *anonymous* authority —the authority of public opinion and the market; [1] instead of the individual conscience, the need to adjust and be approved of; instead of the sense of pride and mastery, an ever-increasing though mainly unconscious sense of powerlessness. [2]

If we look back at the pathological problems of nineteenth-

[1] However, as Russia and Germany show, the escape from freedom can also in the twentieth century take the form of complete submission to overt, irrational authority.

[2] It must be added that the foregoing description holds true mainly for the nineteenth-century middle class. The worker and farmer were different in many essential aspects. It is one of the elements in the development of the twentieth century that the character differences between the various social classes, especially those living in cities, have almost completely disappeared.

century man, they are, of course, closely related to the peculiarities of his social character. The exploitative and hoarding attitude caused human suffering and lack of respect for the dignity of man; it caused Europe to exploit Africa and Asia and her own working class ruthlessly and without regard for human values. The other pathogenic phenomenon of the nineteenth century, the role of irrational authority and the need to submit to it, led to the repression of thoughts and feelings which were tabooed by society. The most obvious symptom was the repression of sex and all that was natural in the body, movements, dress, architectural style, and so on. This repression resulted, as Freud thought, in various forms of neurotic pathology.

The reform movements of the nineteenth century and the beginning of the twentieth, which tried to cure social pathology, started from these main symptoms. All forms of Socialism from Anarchism to Marxism emphasized the necessity for abolishing exploitation and transforming the workingman into an independent, free and respected human being; they believed that if economic suffering were abolished, and if the workingman were free from the domination of the capitalist, all the positive achievements of the nineteenth century would come to their full fruition, while the vices would disappear. In the very same way Freud believed that if sexual repression were considerably diminished, neuroses and all forms of mental sickness would be diminished in consequence (even though in his later life his original optimism became more and more reduced). The liberals believed that complete freedom from irrational authorities would usher in a new millenium. The prescriptions for the care of human ills given by the liberals, the socialists and the psychoanalysts, different as they were from each other, nevertheless fit into the pathology and symptomatology characteristic of the nineteenth century. What was more natural than to expect that by abolishing exploitation and economic suffering, or by doing away with sexual repression and irrational authority, man would enter into an era of greater freedom, happiness, and progress than he had had in the nineteenth century?

Half a century has passed, and the main demands of the nine-teenth-century reformers have been fulfilled. Speaking of the economically most progressive country, the United States, the economic exploitation of the masses has disappeared to a degree which would have sounded fantastic in Marx's time. The working class, instead of falling behind in the economic development of the whole society, has an increasing share in the national wealth, and it is a perfectly valid assumption that provided no major catastrophe occurs, there will, in about one or two generations, be no more marked poverty in the United States. Closely related to the increasing abolishment of economic suffering is the fact that the human and political situation of the worker has changed dras-tically. Largely through his unions, he has become a social "part-ner" of management. He cannot be ordered around, fired, abused, as he was even thirty years ago. He certainly does not look up any more to the "boss" as if he were a higher and superior being. He neither worships him nor hates him, although he might envy him for the greater advances he has made in the attainment of the socially desirable aims. As far as submission to irrational authority goes, the picture has changed drastically since the nineteenth century, as far as parent-child relations are concerned. Children are no longer afraid of their parents. They are companions, and if anybody feels slightly uneasy, it is not the child but the parents who fear not being up-to-date. In industry as well as in the army, there is a spirit of "team work" and equality which would have seemed unbelievable fifty years ago. In addition to all that, sexual repression has diminished to a remarkable degree; after the First World War, a sexual revolution took place in which old inhibitions and principles were thrown overboard. The idea of not satisfying a sexual wish was supposed to be old-fashioned or unhealthy. Even though there was a certain reaction against this attitude, on the whole the nineteenth-century system of tabus and repressions has almost disappeared.

Looked upon from the standards of the nineteenth century, we have achieved almost everything which seemed to be necessary for a saner society, and indeed, many people who still think in terms of the past century are convinced that we continue to progress. Consequently they also believe that the only threat to further progress lies in authoritarian societies, like the Soviet Union which, with its ruthless economic exploitation of workers for the sake of quicker accumulation of capital and the ruthless political authority necessary for the continuation of exploitation, resembles in many ways the earlier phase of Capitalism. For those, however, who do not look at our present society with the eyes of the nineteenth century, it is obvious that the fulfillment of the nineteenth-century hopes has by no means led to the expected results. In fact, it seems that in spite of material prosperity, political and sexual freedom, the world in the middle of the twentieth century is mentally sicker than it was in the nineteenth century. Indeed, "we are not in danger of becoming slaves any more, but of becoming robots," as Adlai Stevenson said so succinctly.[1] There is no overt authority which intimidates us, but we are governed by the fear of the anonymous authority of conformity. We do not submit to anyone personally; we do not go through conflicts with authority, but we have also no convictions of our own, almost no individuality, almost no sense of self. Quite obviously, the diagnosis of our pathology cannot follow the lines of the nineteenth century. We have to recognize the specific pathological problems of our time in order to arrive at a vision of that which

[1] In his speech at Columbia University, 1954.

is necessary to save the Western world from an increasing insanity. This diagnosis will be attempted in the following section, dealing with the social character of Western man in the twentieth century.

C. TWENTIETH-CENTURY SOCIETY

1. *Social and Economic Changes*

Drastic changes in industrial technique, economy and social structure have occurred in Capitalism between the nineteenth and the middle of the twentieth centuries. The changes in the character of man are not less drastic and fundamental. While we have already mentioned certain changes from nineteenth- to twentieth-century Capitalism—changes in the form of exploitation, in the form of authority, in the role of possessiveness—the following discussion will deal with those economic and characterological features of contemporary Capitalism which are the most fundamental ones in our time, even though they may have their origins in the nineteenth century or even earlier.

To begin with a negative statement, in contemporary Western society, the feudal traits are disappearing more and more, and the pure form of capitalistic society thus becomes further apparent. However, the absence of feudal remnants is still much more marked in the United States than in Western Europe. Capitalism in the United States is not only more powerful and more advanced than in Europe, it is also the model toward which European Capitalism is developing. It is such a model not because Europe is trying to imitate it, but because it is the most progressive form of Capitalism, freed from feudal remnants and shackles. The feudal heritage has, aside from its obvious negative qualities, many human traits which, compared with the attitude produced by pure Capitalism, are exceedingly attractive. European criticism of the United States is based essentially on the older human values of feudalism, inasmuch as they are still alive in Europe. It is a criticism of the present in the name of a past which is rapidly disappearing in Europe itself. The difference between Europe and the United States in this respect is only the difference between an older and a newer phase of Capitalism, between a Capitalism still blended with feudal remnants and a pure form of it.

The most obvious change from the nineteenth to the twentieth century is the technical change, the increased use of the steam engine, of the combustion motor, of electricity and the beginning of the use of atomic energy. The development is characterized by the increasing replacement of manual work by machine work, and beyond that, of human intelligence by machine intelligence. While in 1850 men supplied 15 per cent of the energy for work, animals 79 per cent and machines 6 per cent, the ratio in 1960 will be 3 per cent, 1 per cent and 96 per cent respectively.[1] In the middle of the twentieth century we find an increasing tendency to employ automatically regulated machines which have their own "brains," and which bring about a fundamental change in the whole process of production.

The technical change in the mode of production is caused by, and in its turn necessitates, an increasing concentration of capital. The decrease in number and importance of smaller firms is in direct proportion to the increase of big economic colossi. A few figures may help to make concrete the picture which, in its general outline, is very well known. Of 573 independent American corporations covering most stocks traded on the New York Stock Exchange in 1930, 130 companies controlled more than 80 per cent of the assets of all the companies represented. The 200 largest nonbanking corporations controlled "nearly half of all non-

[1] cf. Th. Carskadom and R. Modley, *U.S.A., Measure of a Nation*, The Macmillan Company, New York, 1949, p. 3.

banking corporate wealth, while the remaining half was owned
by the more than 300,000 smaller companies." [1] It must further
be remembered that the influence of one of these huge companies
extends far beyond the assets under its direct control. "Smaller companies which sell to or buy from the larger companies are likely
to be influenced by them to a vastly greater extent than by other
smaller companies with which they might deal. In many cases the
continued prosperity of the smaller company depends on the
favor of the larger and almost inevitably the interests of the latter
become the interests of the former. The influence of the larger
company on prices is often greatly increased by its mere size,
even though it does not begin to approach a monopoly. Its political
influence may be tremendous. Therefore, if roughly half of the
corporate wealth is controlled by two hundred large corporations
and half by smaller companies it is fair to assume that very much
more than half of industry is dominated by these great units.
This concentration is made even more significant when it is recalled that as a result of it, approximately 2,000 individuals out
of a population of one hundred and twenty-five million are in a
position to control and direct half of industry." [2] This concentration of power has been growing since 1933, and has yet not
come to a stop.

The number of self-employed entrepreneurs has decreased considerably. While in the beginning of the nineteenth century approximately four fifths of the occupied population were self-
employed entrepreneurs, around 1870 only one third belonged to
this group, and by 1940 this old middle class comprised only one
fifth of the occupied population, that is to say, only 25 per cent
of its relative strength a hundred years earlier. Twenty-seven

---

[1] cf. A. A. Berle, Jr., and G. C. Means, *The Modern Corporation and Private Property*, The Macmillan Company, New York, 1940, pp. 27, 28.
[2] *Ibid.*, pp. 32, 33.

thousand giant firms, constituting only 1 per cent of all the firms in the United States, employ over 50 per cent of all people engaged in business today, while on the other hand 1,500,000 one-man enterprises (nonfarming) employ only 6 per cent of all people employed in business.[1]

As these figures already indicate, with the concentration of enterprises goes an enormous increase of employees in these big enterprises. While the old middle class, composed of farmers, independent businessmen and professionals, formerly constituted 85 per cent of the middle class, it is now only 44 per cent; the new middle classes have increased from 15 per cent to 56 per cent in the same period. This new middle class is composed of managers, who have risen from 2 per cent to 6 per cent; salaried professionals, from 4 per cent to 14 per cent; sales people from 7 per cent to 14 per cent, and office workers from 2 per cent to 22 per cent. Altogether the new middle class has risen from 6 per cent to 25 per cent of the total labor force between 1870 and 1940, while the wage workers have declined from 61 per cent to 55 per cent of the labor force within the same period. As Mills puts it very succinctly *". . . fewer individuals manipulate things; more handle people and symbols."* [2]

With the increase in the importance of the giant enterprises, another development of utmost importance has occurred: the increasing separation of management from ownership. This point is illustrated by revealing figures in the classic work of Berle and Means. Of 144 companies for which information could be obtained among the 200 largest companies (in 1930) only 20 had under 5,000 stockholders, while 71 had between 20,000 and 500,000 stockholders.[3] Only in small companies did the manage-

---

[1] These figures are quoted from C. W. Mills, *White Collar,* Oxford University Press, New York, 1951, p. 63 ff.

[2] *Loc. cit.,* p. 63.

[3] These and the following figures are quoted from Berle and Means.

ment appear to hold an important stock interest, while in the large, and that is to say, the most important companies, there is an almost complete separation between stock ownership and management. In some of the largest railroad and utility companies, in 1929, the size of the largest holding by any one stockholder did not exceed 2.74 per cent, and this condition, according to Berle and Means, exists also in the industrial field. "When the industries are arranged in order of the average size of the management's holdings of stock . . . the proportion held by the officers and directors is seen to vary in almost exactly inverse ratio to the average size of the companies under consideration. With only two major exceptions, the larger the size of the company, the smaller was the proportion of the stock held by the management. In the railroads, with common stock averaging $52,000,000 per company, the holdings of the management amounted to 1.4% and in . . . miscellaneous mining and quarrying it amounted to 1.8%. Only where the companies are small did the management appear to hold important stock interest. The holdings of the latter amounted to less than 20%, except in industries with companies having an average capital under $1,000,-000, while but three industrial groups, each composed of companies averaging less than $200,000 showed directors and officers owning more than half the stock." [1] Taking the two tendencies, that of the relative increase of big enterprise and of the smallness of management holdings of big enterprises together, it is quite evident that the general trend is increasingly one in which the owner of capital is separate from the management. How the management controls the enterprise in spite of the fact that it does not own a considerable part, is a sociological and psychological problem which will be taken up later on.

Another fundamental change from nineteenth-century to con-

[1] Berle and Means, *loc. cit.*, p. 52.

temporary Capitalism is the increase in significance of the domestic market. Our whole economic machine rests upon the principle of mass production and mass consumption. While in the nineteenth century the general tendency was to save, and not to indulge in expenses which could not be paid for immediately, the contemporary system is exactly the opposite. Everybody is coaxed into buying as much as he can, and before he has saved enough to pay for his purchases. The need for more consumption is strongly stimulated by advertising and all other methods of psychological pressure. This development goes hand in hand with the rise of the economic and social status of the working class. Especially in the United States, but also all over Europe, the working class has participated in the increased production of the whole economic system. The salary of the worker, and his social benefits, permit him a level of consumption which would have seemed fantastic one hundred years ago. His social and economic power has increased to the same degree and this not only with regard to salary and social benefits, but also to his human and social role in the factory.

Let us take another look at the most important elements in twentieth-century Capitalism: the disappearance of feudal traits, the revolutionary increase in industrial production, the increasing concentration of capital and bigness of business and government, the increasing number of people who manipulate figures and people, the separation of ownership from management, the rise of the working class economically and politically, the new methods of work in factory and office—and let us describe these changes from a slightly different aspect. The disappearance of feudal factors means the disappearance of irrational authority. Nobody is supposed to be higher than his neighbor by birth, God's will, natural law. Everybody is equal and free. Nobody may be exploited or commanded by virtue of a natural right. If one person is commanded by another, it is because the commanding one bought the labor or the services of the commanded one, on the labor market; he commands because they are both free and equal and thus could enter into a contractual relationship. However, with irrational authority—rational authority became obsolete, too. If the market and the contract regulates relationships, there is no need to know what is right and what is wrong and good and evil. All that is necessary is to know that things are *fair*—that the exchange is fair, and that things "work"—that they function.

Another decisive fact which the twentieth-century man experiences is the miracle of production. He commands forces thousands of times stronger than the ones nature had given him before; steam, oil, electricity, have become his servants and beasts of burden. He crosses the oceans, the continents—first in weeks, then in days, now in hours. He seemingly overcomes the law of gravity, and flies through the air; he converts deserts into fertile land, makes rain instead of praying for it. The miracle of production leads to the miracle of consumption. No more traditional barriers keep anyone from buying anything he takes a fancy to. He only needs to have the money. But more and more people have the money—not for the genuine pearls perhaps, but for the synthetic ones; for Fords which look like Cadillacs, for the cheap dresses which look like the expensive ones, for cigarettes which are the same for millionaires and for the workingman. Everything is within reach, can be bought, can be consumed. Where was there ever a society where this miracle happened?

Men work together. Thousands stream into the industrial plants and the offices—they come in cars, in subways, in buses, in trains —they work together, according to a rhythm measured by the experts, with methods worked out by the experts, not too fast, not too slow, but together; each a part of the whole. The evening stream flows back: they read the same newspaper, they listen to the radio, they see the movies, the same for those on the top and for those at the bottom of the ladder, for the intelligent and the stupid, for the educated and the uneducated. Produce, consume, enjoy together, in step, without asking questions. That is the rhythm of their lives.

What kind of men, then, does our society need? What is the "social character" suited to twentieth-century Capitalism?

It needs men who co-operate smoothly in large groups; who want to consume more and more, and whose tastes are standardized and can be easily influenced and anticipated.

It needs men who feel free and independent, not subject to any authority, or principle, or conscience—yet willing to be commanded, to do what is expected, to fit into the social machine without friction. How can man be guided without force, led without leaders, be prompted without any aim—except the one to be on the move, to function, to go ahead . . . ?

2. *Characterological Changes*

a. Quantification, Abstractification

In analyzing and describing the social character of contemporary man, one can choose any number of approaches, just as one does in describing the character structure of an individual. These approaches can differ either in the depth to which the analysis penetrates, or they can be centered around different aspects which are equally "deep," yet chosen according to the particular interest of the investigator.

In the following analysis I have chosen the concept of *alienation* as the central point from which I am going to develop the analysis of the contemporary social character. For one reason, because this concept seems to me to touch upon the deepest level of the modern personality; for another, because it is the most appropriate if one is concerned with the interaction between the contemporary socio-economic structure and the character structure of the average individual.[1]

We must introduce the discussion of alienation by speaking of one of the fundamental economic features of Capitalism, the process of *quantification* and *abstractification*.

The medieval artisan produced goods for a relatively small and known group of customers. His prices were determined by the need to make a profit which permitted him to live in a style traditionally commensurate with his social status. He knew from experience the costs of production, and even if he employed a few journeymen and apprentices, no elaborate system of bookkeeping or balance sheets was required for the operation of his business. The same held true for the production of the peasant, which required even less quantifying abstract methods. In contrast, the modern business enterprise rests upon its balance sheet. It cannot rest upon such concrete and direct observation as the artisan used to figure out his profits. Raw material, machinery, labor costs, as well as the product can be expressed in the same money value, and thus made comparable and fit to appear in the balance equation. All economic occurrences have to be strictly quantifiable, and only the balance sheets, the exact comparison of economic processes quantified in figures, tell the manager whether and to what degree he is engaged in a profitable, that is to say, a meaningful business activity.

This transformation of the concrete into the abstract has developed far beyond the balance sheet and the quantification of the economic occurrences in the sphere of production. The modern businessman not only deals with millions of dollars, but also with millions of customers, thousands of stockholders, and thousands

[1] As the reader familiar with the concept of the marketing orientation developed in *Man for Himself* will see, the phenomenon of alienation is the more general and underlies the more specific concept of the "marketing orientation."

of workers and employees; all these people become so many pieces in a gigantic machine which must be controlled, whose effects must be calculated; each man eventually can be expressed as an abstract entity, as a figure, and on this basis economic occurrences are calculated, trends are predicted, decisions are made.

Today, when only about 20 per cent of our working population is self-employed, the rest work for somebody else, and a man's life is dependent on someone who pays him a wage or a salary. But we should say "something," instead of "someone," because a worker is hired and fired by an institution, the managers of which are impersonal parts of the enterprise, rather than people in personal contact with the men they employ. Let us not forget another fact: in precapitalistic society, exchange was to a large extent one of goods and services; today, all work is rewarded with money. The close fabric of economic relations is regulated by money, the abstract expression of work—that is to say, we receive different quantities of the same for different qualities; and we give money for what we receive—again exchanging only different quantities for different qualities. Practically nobody, with the exception of the farm population, could live for even a few days without receiving and spending money, which stands for the abstract quality of concrete work.

Another aspect of capitalist production which results in increasing abstractification is the increasing division of labor. Division of labor as a whole exists in most known economic systems, and, even in most primitive communities, in the form of division of labor between the sexes. What is characteristic of capitalistic production is the degree to which this division has developed. While in the medieval economy there was a division of labor let us say between agricultural production and the work of the artisan, there was little such division within each sphere of production itself. The carpenter making a chair or table made the whole chair or the whole table, and even if some preparatory work was done by his apprentices, he was in control of the production, overseeing it in its entirety. In the modern industrial enterprise, the worker is not in touch with the whole product at any point. He is engaged in the performance of one specialized function, and while he might shift in the course of time from one function to another, he is still not related to the concrete product *as a whole*. He develops a specialized function, and the tendency is such, that the function of the modern industrial worker can be defined as working in a machinelike fashion in activities for which machine work has not yet been devised or which would be costlier than human work. The only person who is in touch with the whole product is the manager, but to him the product is an abstraction, whose essence is exchange value, while the worker, for whom it is concrete, never works on it as a whole.

Undoubtedly without quantification and abstractification modern mass production would be unthinkable. But in a society in which economic activities have become the main preoccupation of man, this process of quantification and abstractification has transcended the realm of economic production, and spread to the attitude of man to things, to people, and to himself.

In order to understand the abstractification process in modern man, we must first consider the ambiguous function of abstraction in general. It is obvious that abstractions in themselves are not a modern phenomenon. In fact, an increasing ability to form abstractions is characteristic of the cultural development of the human race. If I speak of "a table," I am using an abstraction; I am referring, not to a specific table in its full concreteness, but to the genus "table" which comprises all possible concrete tables. If I speak of "a man" I am not speaking of this or that person, in his concreteness and uniqueness, but of the genus "man," which comprises all individual persons. In other words, I make an abstraction. The development of philosophical or scientific thought is based on an increasing ability for such abstractification, and to give it up would mean to fall back into the most primitive way of thinking.

However, there are *two* ways of relating oneself to an object: one can relate oneself to it in its full concreteness; then the object appears with all its specific qualities, and there is no other object which is identical with it. And one can relate oneself to the object in an abstract way, that is, emphasizing only those qualities which it has in common with all other objects of the same genus, and thus accentuating some and ignoring other qualities. The full and productive relatedness to an object comprises this polarity of perceiving it in its uniqueness, and at the same time in its generality; in its concreteness, and at the same time in its abstractness.

In contemporary Western culture this polarity has given way to an almost exclusive reference to the abstract qualities of things and people, and to a neglect of relating oneself to their concreteness and uniqueness. Instead of forming abstract concepts where it is necessary and useful, everything, including ourselves, is being abstractified; the concrete reality of people and things to which we can relate with the reality of our own person, is replaced by abstractions, by ghosts that embody different quantities, but not different qualities.

It is quite customary to talk about a "three-million-dollar bridge," a "twenty-cent cigar," a "five-dollar watch," and this not only from the standpoint of the manufacturer or the consumer in the process of buying it, but as the essential point in the description. When one speaks of the "three-million-dollar bridge," one is not primarily concerned with its usefulness or beauty, that is, with its concrete qualities, but one speaks of it as of a commodity, the main quality of which is its exchange value, expressed in a quantity, that of money. This does not mean, of course, that one is not concerned also with the usefulness or beauty of the bridge, but it does mean that its concrete (use) value is *secondary* to its abstract (exchange) value in the way the object is experienced. The famous line by Gertrude Stein "a rose is a rose is a rose," is a protest against this abstract form of experience; for most people a rose is just *not* a rose, but a flower in a certain price range, to be bought on certain social occasions; even the most beautiful flower, provided it is a wild one, costing nothing, is not experienced in its beauty, compared to that of the rose, because it has no exchange value.

In other words, things are experienced as commodities, as embodiments of exchange value, not only while we are buying or selling, but in our attitude toward them when the economic transaction is finished. A thing, even after it has been bought, never quite loses its quality as a commodity in this sense; it is expendable, always retaining its exchange-value quality. A good illustration of this attitude is to be found in a report of the Executive Secretary of an important scientific organization as to how he spent a day in his office. The organization had just bought and moved into a building of their own. The Executive Secretary reports that during one of the first days after they had moved into the building, he got a call from a real estate agent, saying that some people were interested in buying the building and wanted to look at it. Although he knew that it was most unlikely that the organization would want to sell the building a few days after they had moved in, he could not resist the temptation to know whether the value of the building had risen since they had bought it, and spent one or two valuable hours in showing the real estate agent around. He writes: "very interested in fact we can get an offer for more than we have put in building. Nice coincidence that offer comes while treasurer is in the office. All agree it will be good for Board's morale to learn that the building will sell for a good deal more than it cost. Let's see what happens." In spite of all the pride and pleasure in the new building, it had still retained its quality as a commodity, as something expendable, and to which no full sense of possession or use is attached. The same attitude is obvious in the relationship of people to the cars they buy; the car never becomes fully a thing to which one is attached, but retains its quality as a commodity to be exchanged in a successful bargain; thus, cars are sold after a year or two, long before their use value is exhausted or even considerably diminished.

This abstractification takes place even with regard to phenomena which are not commodities sold on the market, like a flood disaster; the newspapers will headline a flood, speaking of a "million-dollar catastrophe," emphasizing the abstract quantitative element rather than the concrete aspects of human suffering.

But the abstractifying and quantifying attitude goes far beyond the realm of things. People are also experienced as the embodiment of a quantitative exchange value. To speak of a man as being "worth one million dollars," is to speak of him not any more as a concrete human person, but as an abstraction, whose essence can be expressed in a figure. It is an expression of the same attitude when a newspaper headlines an obituary with the words "Shoe Manufacturer Dies." Actually a *man* has died, a man with certain human qualities, with hopes and frustrations, with a wife and children. It is true that he manufactured shoes, or rather, that he owned and managed a factory in which workers served machines manufacturing shoes; but if it is said that a "Shoe Manufacturer Dies," the richness and concreteness of a human life is expressed in the abstract formula of economic function.

The same abstractifying approach can be seen in expressions like "Mr. Ford produced so many automobiles," or this or that general "conquered a fortress"; or if a man has a house built for himself, he says, "I built a house." Concretely speaking, Mr.

Ford did not manufacture the automobiles; he directed automobile production which was executed by thousands of workers. The general never conquered the fortress; he was sitting in his headquarters, issuing orders, and his soldiers did the conquering. The man did not build a house; he paid the money to an architect who made the plans and to workers who did the building. All this is not said to minimize the significance of the managing and directing operations, but in order to indicate that in this way of experiencing things, sight of what goes on concretely is lost, and an abstract view is taken in which one function, that of making plans, giving orders, or financing an activity, is identified with the whole concrete process of production, or of fighting, or of building, as the case may be.

The same process of abstractification takes place in all other spheres. The New York *Times* recently printed a news item under the heading: "B.Sc. + PhD = $40,000." The information under this somewhat baffling heading was that statistical data showed that a student of engineering who has acquired his Doctor's degree will earn, in a lifetime, $40,000 more than a man who has only the degree of Bachelor of Sciences. As far as this is a fact it is an interesting socio-economic datum, worth while reporting. It is mentioned here because the way of expressing the fact as an equation between a scientific degree and a certain amount of dollars is indicative of the abstractifying and quantifying thinking in which knowledge is experienced as the embodiment of a certain exchange value on the personality market. It is to the same point when a political report in a news magazine states that the Eisenhower administration feels it has so much "capital of confidence" that it can risk some unpopular measures, because it can "afford" to lose some of that confidence capital. Here again, a human quality like confidence is expressed in its abstract form, as if it were a money investment to be dealt with in terms of a market speculation. How drastically commercial categories have entered even religious thinking is shown in the following passage by Bishop Sheen, in an article on the birth of Christ. "Our reason tells us," so writes the author, "that if anyone of the claimants (for the role of God's son) came from God, the least that God could do to support His Representative's claim would be to preannounce His coming. Automobile manufacturers tell us when to expect a new model." [1] Or, even more drastically, Billy Graham, the evangelist, says: "I am selling the greatest product in the world; why shouldn't it be promoted as well as soap?" [2]

The process of abstractification, however, has still deeper roots and manifestations than the ones described so far, roots which go back to the very beginning of the modern era; to the *dissolution* of any *concrete frame of reference* in the process of life.

In a primitive society, the "world" is identical with the tribe. The tribe is in the center of the Universe, as it were; everything outside is shadowy and has no independent existence. In the medieval world, the Universe was much wider; it comprised this globe, the sky and the stars above it; but it was seen with the earth as the center and man as the purpose of Creation. Everything had its fixed place, just as everybody had his fixed position in feudal society. With the fifteenth and sixteenth centuries, new vistas opened up. The earth lost its central place, and became one of the satellites of the sun; new continents were found, new sea lanes discovered; the static social system was more and more loosened up; everything and everybody was moving. Yet, until the end of the twentieth century, nature and society had not lost their concreteness and definiteness. Man's natural and social world was still manageable, still had definite contours. But with the progress

[1] From *Colliers'* magazine, 1953.
[2] *Time* magazine, October 25, 1954.

in scientific thought, technical discoveries and the dissolution of all traditional bonds, this definiteness and concreteness is in the process of being lost. Whether we think of our new cosmological picture, or of theoretical physics, or of atonal music, or abstract art—the concreteness and definiteness of our frame of reference is disappearing. We are not any more in the center of the Universe, we are not any more the purpose of Creation, we are not any more the masters of a manageable and recognizable world—we are a speck of dust, we are a nothing, somewhere in space—without any kind of concrete relatedness to anything. We speak of millions of people being killed, of one third or more of our population being wiped out if a third World War should occur; we speak of billions of dollars piling up as a national debt, of thousands of light years as interplanetary distances, of interspace travel, of artificial satellites. Tens of thousands work in one enterprise, hundreds of thousands live in hundreds of cities.

The dimensions with which we deal are figures and abstractions; they are far beyond the boundaries which would permit of any kind of concrete experience. There is no frame of reference left which is manageable, observable, which is adapted to *human dimensions*. While our eyes and ears receive impressions only in humanly manageable proportions, our concept of the world has lost just that quality; it does not any longer correspond to our human dimensions.

This is especially significant in connection with the development of modern means of destruction. In modern war, one individual can cause the destruction of hundreds of thousands of men, women and children. He could do so by pushing a button; he may not feel the emotional impact of what he is doing, since he does not see, does not know the people whom he kills; it is almost as if his act of pushing the button and their death had no real connection. The same man would probably be incapable of even slapping, not to speak of killing, a helpless person. In the latter case, the concrete situation arouses in him a conscience reaction common to all normal men; in the former, there is no such reaction, because the act and his object are alienated from the doer, his act is not *his* any more, but has, so to speak, a life and a responsibility of its own.

Science, business, politics, have lost all foundations and proportions which make sense humanly. We live in figures and abstractions; since nothing is concrete, nothing is real. Everything is possible, factually and morally. Science fiction is not different from science fact, nightmares and dreams from the events of next year. Man has been thrown out from any definite place whence he can overlook and manage his life and the life of society. He is driven faster and faster by the forces which originally were created by him. In this wild whirl he thinks, figures, busy with abstractions, more and more remote from concrete life.

b. Alienation

The foregoing discussion of the process of abstractification leads to the central issue of the effects of Capitalism on personality: the phenomenon of alienation.

By alienation is meant a mode of experience in which the person experiences himself as an alien. He has become, one might say, estranged from himself. He does not experience himself as the center of his world, as the creator of his own acts—but his acts and their consequences have become his masters, whom he obeys, or whom he may even worship. The alienated person is out of touch with himself as he is out of touch with any other person. He, like the others, are experienced as things are experienced; with the senses and with common sense, but at the same time without being related to oneself and to the world outside productively.

The older meaning in which "alienation" was used was to denote an insane person; *aliéné* in French, *alienado* in Spanish are older words for the psychotic, the thoroughly and absolutely alienated person. ("Alienist," in English, is still used for the doctor who cares for the insane.)

In the last century the word "alienation" was used by Hegel and Marx, referring not to a state of insanity, but to a less drastic form of self-estrangement, which permits the person to act reasonably in practical matters, yet which constitutes one of the most severe socially patterned defects. In Marx's system alienation is called that condition of man where his "own act becomes to him an alien power, standing over and against him, instead of being ruled by him." [1]

But while the use of the word "alienation" in this general sense is a recent one, the concept is a much older one; it is the same to which the prophets of the Old Testament referred as *idolatry*. It will help us to a better understanding of "alienation" if we begin by considering the meaning of "idolatry."

The prophets of monotheism did not denounce heathen religions as idolatrous primarily because they worshiped several gods instead of one. The essential difference between monotheism and polytheism is not one of the *number* of gods, but lies in the fact of self-alienation. Man spends his energy, his artistic capacities on building an idol, and then he worships this idol, which is nothing but the result of his own human effort. His life forces have flown into a "thing," and this thing, having become an idol,

---

[1] K. Marx, *Capital.* cf. also Marx-Engels, *Die Deutsche Ideologie* (1845/6), in K. Marx, *Der Historische Materialismus, Die Frühschriften,* S. Landshut and D. P. Mayer, Leipzig, 1932, II, p. 25.

is not experienced as a result of his own productive effort, but as something apart from himself, over and against him, which he worships and to which he submits. As the prophet Hosea says (XIV, 8) : "Assur shall not save us; we will not ride upon horses; *neither will we say any more to the work of our hands, you are our gods;* for in thee the fatherless finds love." Idolatrous man bows down to the work of his own hands. *The idol represents his own life-forces in an alienated form.*

The principle of monotheism, in contrast, is that man is infinite, that there is no partial quality in him which can be hypostatized into the whole. God, in the monotheistic concept, is unrecognizable and indefinable; God is not a "thing." If man is created in the likeness of God, he is created as the bearer of infinite qualities. In idolatry man bows down and submits to the projection of one partial quality in himself. He does not experience himself as the center from which living acts of love and reason radiate. He becomes a thing, his neighbor becomes a thing, just as his gods are things. "The idols of the heathen are silver and gold, the work of men's hands. They have mouths but they speak not; eyes have they, but they see not; they have ears but they hear not; neither is there any breath in their mouths. They that make them are like them; so is everyone that trusts in them." (Psalm 135).

Monotheistic religions themselves have, to a large extent, regressed into idolatry. Man projects his power of love and of reason unto God; he does not feel them any more as his own powers, and then he prays to God to give him back some of what he, man, has projected unto God. In early Protestantism and Calvinism, the required religious attitude is that man *should* feel himself empty and impoverished, and put his trust in the grace of God, that is, into the hope that God may return to him part of his own qualities, which he has put into God.

Every act of submissive worship is an act of alienation and idolatry in this sense. What is frequently called "love" is often nothing but this idolatrous phenomenon of alienation; only that not God or an idol, but another person is worshiped in this way. The "loving" person in this type of submissive relationship, projects all his or her love, strength, thought, into the other person, and experiences the loved person as a superior being, finding satisfaction in complete submission and worship. This does not only mean that he fails to experience the loved person as a human being in his or her reality, but that he does not experience *himself* in his full reality, as the bearer of productive human powers. Just as in the case of religious idolatry, he has projected all his richness into the other person, and experiences this richness not any more as something which is his, but as something alien from himself, deposited in somebody else, with which he can get in touch only by submission to, or submergence in the other person. The same phenomenon exists in the worshiping submission to a political leader, or to the state. The leader and the state actually are what they are by the consent of the governed. But they become idols when the individual projects all his powers into them and worships them, hoping to regain some of his powers by submission and worship.

In Rousseau's theory of the state, as in contemporary totalitarianism, the individual is supposed to abdicate his own rights and to project them unto the state as the only arbiter. In Fascism and Stalinism the absolutely alienated individual worships at the altar of an idol, and it makes little difference by what names this idol is known: state, class, collective, or what else.

We can speak of idolatry or alienation not only in relationship to other people, but also in relationship to oneself, when the person is subject to irrational passions. The person who is mainly motivated by his lust for power, does not experience himself any more in the richness and limitlessness of a human being, but he becomes a slave to one partial striving in him, which is projected into external aims, by which he is "possessed." The person who is given to the exclusive pursuit of his passion for money is possessed by his striving for it; money is the idol which he worships as the projection of one isolated power in himself, his greed for it. In this sense, the neurotic person is an alienated person. His actions are not his own; while he is under the illusion of doing what *he* wants, he is driven by forces which are separated from his self, which work behind his back; he is a stranger to himself, just as his fellow man is a stranger to him. He experiences the other and himself not as what they really are, but distorted by the unconscious forces which operate in them. The insane person is the *absolutely alienated* person; he has completely lost himself as the center of his own experience; he has lost the sense of self.

What is common to all these phenomena—the worship of idols, the idolatrous worship of God, the idolatrous love for a person, the worship of a political leader or the state, and the idolatrous worship of the externalizations of irrational passions—is the process of alienation. It is the fact that *man does not experience himself as the active bearer of his own powers and richness, but as an impoverished "thing," dependent on powers outside of himself, unto whom he has projected his living substance.*

As the reference to idolatry indicates, alienation is by no means a modern phenomenon. It would go far beyond the scope of this book to attempt a sketch on the history of alienation. Suffice it to say that it seems alienation differs from culture to culture, both in the specific spheres which are alienated, and in the thoroughness and completeness of the process.

Alienation as we find it in modern society is almost total; it pervades the relationship of man to his work, to the things he consumes, to the state, to his fellow man, and to himself. Man has created a world of man-made things as it never existed before. He has constructed a complicated social machine to administer the technical machine he built. Yet this whole creation of his stands over and above him. He does not feel himself as a creator and center, but as the servant of a Golem, which his hands have built. The more powerful and gigantic the forces are which he unleashes, the more powerless he feels himself as a human being. He confronts himself with his own forces embodied in things he has created, alienated from himself. He is owned by his own creation, and has lost ownership of himself. He has built a golden calf, and says "these are your gods who have brought you out of Egypt."

What happens to the *worker?* To put it in the words of a thoughtful and thorough observer of the industrial scene: "In industry the person becomes an economic atom that dances to the tune of atomistic management. Your place is just here, you will sit in this fashion, your arms will move x inches in a course of y radius and the time of movement will be .ooo minutes.

"Work is becoming more repetitive and thoughtless as the planners, the micromotionists, and the scientific managers further strip the worker of his right to think and move freely. Life is being denied; need to control, creativeness, curiosity, and independent thought are being baulked, and the result, the inevitable result, is flight or fight on the part of the worker, apathy or destructiveness, psychic regression." [1]

The role of the *manager* is also one of alienation. It is true, he manages the whole and not a part, but he too is alienated from his product as something concrete and useful. His aim is to employ profitably the capital invested by others, although in comparison with the older type of owner-manager, modern management is much less interested in the amount of profit to be paid

[1] J. J. Gillespie, *Free Expression in Industry*, The Pilot Press Ltd., London, 1948.

out as dividend to the stockholder than it is in the efficient operation and expansion of the enterprise. Characteristically, within management those in charge of labor relations and of sales—that is, of human manipulation—gain, relatively speaking, an increasing importance in comparison with those in charge of the technical aspects of production.

The manager, like the worker, like everybody, deals with impersonal giants: with the giant competitive enterprise; with the giant national and world market; with the giant consumer, who has to be coaxed and manipulated; with the giant unions, and the giant government. All these giants have their own lives, as it were. They determine the activity of the manager and they direct the activity of the worker and clerk.

The problem of the manager opens up one of the most significant phenomena in an alienated culture, that of *bureaucratization*. Both big business and government administrations are conducted by a bureaucracy. Bureaucrats are specialists in the administration of things *and of men*. Due to the bigness of the apparatus to be administered, and the resulting abstractification, the bureaucrats' relationship to the people is one of complete alienation. They, the people to be administered, are objects whom the bureaucrats consider neither with love nor with hate, but completely impersonally; the manager-bureaucrat must not feel, as far as his professional activity is concerned; he must manipulate people as though they were figures, or things. Since the vastness of the organization and the extreme division of labor prevents any single individual from seeing the whole, since there is no organic, spontaneous co-operation between the various individuals or groups within the industry, the managing bureaucrats are necessary; without them the enterprise would collapse in a short time, since nobody would know the secret which makes it function. Bureaucrats are as indispensable as the tons of paper consumed under their leadership. Just because everybody senses, with a feeling of powerlessness, the vital role of the bureaucrats, they are given an almost godlike respect. If it were not for the bureaucrats, people feel, everything would go to pieces, and we would starve. Whereas, in the medieval world, the leaders were considered representatives of a god-intended order, in modern Capitalism the role of the bureaucrat is hardly less sacred—since he is necessary for the survival of the whole.

Marx gave a profound definition of the bureaucrat saying: "The bureaucrat relates himself to the world as a *mere object* of his activity." It is interesting to note that the spirit of bureaucracy has entered not only business and government administration, but also trade unions and the great democratic socialist parties in England, Germany and France. In Russia, too, the bureaucratic managers and their alienated spirit have conquered the country. Russia could perhaps exist without terror—if certain conditions were given—but it could not exist without the system of total bureaucratization—that is, alienation.[1]

What is the attitude of the *owner* of the enterprise, the capitalist? The small businessman seems to be in the same position as his predecessor a hundred years ago. He owns and directs his small enterprise, he is in touch with the whole commercial or industrial activity, and in personal contact with his employees and workers. But living in an alienated world in all other economic and social aspects, and furthermore being more under the constant pressure of bigger competitors, he is by no means as free as his grandfather was in the same business.

But what matters more and more in contemporary economy is big business, the large corporation. As Drucker puts it very succinctly: "In fine, it is the large corporation—the specific form in

---

[1] cf. the interesting article by W. Huhn, "Der Bolschevismus als Manager Ideologie" in Funken, Frankfurt V, 8/1954.

which Big Business is organized in a free-enterprise economy—
which has emerged as the representative and determining socio-
economic institution which sets the pattern and determines the
behavior even of the owner of the corner cigar store who never
owned a share of stock, and of his errand boy who never set foot
in a mill. And thus the character of our society is determined
and patterned by the structural organization of Big Business, the
technology of the mass-production plant, and the degree to which
our social beliefs and promises are realized in and by the large
corporations." [1]

What then is the attitude of the "owner" of the big corporation
to "his" property? It is one of almost complete alienation. His
ownership consists in a piece of paper, representing a certain
fluctuating amount of money; he has no responsibility for the
enterprise and no concrete relationship to it in any way. This
attitude of alienation has been most clearly expressed in Berle's
and Means' description of the attitude of the stockholder to the
enterprise which follows here: "(1) The position of ownership
has changed from that of an active to that of a passive agent.
In place of actual physical properties over which the owner could
exercise direction and for which he was responsible, the owner
now holds a piece of paper representing a set of rights and expectations with respect to an enterprise. But over the enterprise and
over the physical property—the instruments of production—in
which he has an interest, the owner has little control. At the same
time he bears no responsibility with respect to the enterprise or
its physical property. It has often been said that the owner of a
horse is responsible. If the horse lives he must feed it. If the horse
dies he must bury it. No such responsibility attaches to a share

[1] cf. Peter F. Drucker, *Concept of the Corporation*, The John Day Company, New
York, 1946, pp. 8, 9.

of stock. The owner is practically powerless through his own efforts to affect the underlying property.

"(2) The spiritual values that formerly went with ownership have been separated from it. Physical property capable of being shaped by its owner could bring to him direct satisfaction apart from the income it yielded in more concrete form. It represented an extension of his own personality. With the corporate revolution, this quality has been lost to the property owner much as it has been lost to the worker through the industrial revolution.

"(3) The value of an individual's wealth is coming to depend on forces entirely outside himself and his own efforts. Instead, its value is determined on the one hand by the actions of the individuals in command of the enterprise—individuals over whom the typical owner has no control, and on the other hand, by the actions of others in a sensitive and often capricious market. The value is thus subject to the vagaries and manipulations characteristic of the market place. It is further subject to the great swings in society's appraisal of its own immediate future as reflected in the general level of values in the organized market.

"(4) The value of the individual's wealth not only fluctuates constantly—the same may be said of most wealth—but it is subject to a constant appraisal. The individual can see the change in the appraised value of his estate from moment to moment, a fact which may markedly affect both the expenditure of his income and his enjoyment of that income.

"(5) Individual wealth has become extremely liquid through the organized markets. The individual owner can convert it into other forms of wealth at a moment's notice and, provided the market machinery is in working order, he may do so without serious loss due to forced sales.

"(6) Wealth is less and less in a form which can be employed directly by its owner. When wealth is in the form of land, for instance, it is capable of being used by the owner even though the value of land in the market is negligible. The physical quality of such wealth makes possible a subjective value to the owner quite apart from any market value it may have. The newer form of wealth is quite incapable of this direct use. Only through sale in the market can the owner obtain its direct use. He is thus tied to the market as never before.

" (7) Finally, in the corporate system, the 'owner' of industrial wealth is left with a mere symbol of ownership while the power, the responsibility and the substance which have been an integral part of ownership in the past are being transferred to a separate group in whose hands lies control." [1]

Another important aspect of the alienated position of the stockholder is his control over his enterprise. Legally, the stockholders control the enterprise, that is, they elect the management much as the people in a democracy elect their representatives. Factually, however, they exercise very little control, due to the fact that each individual's share is so exceedingly small, that he is not interested in coming to the meetings and participating actively. Berle and Means differentiate among five major types of control: "These include (1) control through almost complete ownership, (2) majority control, (3) control through a legal device without majority ownership, (4) minority control, and (5) management control." [2] Among the five types of control the first two—private ownership or majority ownership—exercise control in only 6 per cent (according to wealth) of the two hundred largest companies (around 1930), while in the remaining 94 per cent control is exercised either by the management, or by a legal device in col-

---

[1] cf. A. A. Berle and G. C. Means, *The Modern Corporation and Private Property,* The Macmillan Company, New York, 1940, pp. 66–68.
[2] *Ibid.*, p. 70.

laring a small proportion of the ownership or by a minority of the stockholders.[1] How this miracle is accomplished without force, deception or any violation of the law is most interestingly described in Berle's and Means' classic work.

The process of *consumption* is as alienated as the process of production. In the first place, we acquire things with money; we are accustomed to this and take it for granted. But actually, this is a most peculiar way of acquiring things. Money represents labor and effort in an abstract form; not necessarily *my* labor and *my* effort, since I can have acquired it by inheritance, by fraud, by luck, or any number of ways. But even if I have acquired it by *my* effort (forgetting for the moment that *my* effort might not have brought me the money were it not for the fact that I employed men), I have acquired it in a specific way, by a specific kind of effort, corresponding to my skills and capacities, while, in spending, the money is transformed into an abstract form of labor and can be exchanged against anything else. Provided I am in the possession of money, no effort or interest of mine is necessary to acquire something. If I have the money, I can acquire an exquisite painting, even though I may not have any appreciation for art; I can buy the best phonograph, even though I have no musical taste; I can buy a library, although I use it only for the purpose of ostentation. I can buy an education, even though I have no use for it except as an additional social asset. I can even destroy the painting or the books I bought, and aside from a loss of money, I suffer no damage. Mere possession of money gives me the right to acquire and to do with my acquisition whatever I like. The *human* way of acquiring would be to make an effort qualitatively commensurate with what I acquire. The acquisition of bread and clothing would depend on no other premise than that of being alive; the acquisition of books and paintings, on my effort

[1] *Ibid.*, pp. 94 and 114–117.

to understand them and my ability to use them. How this principle could be applied practically is not the point to be discussed here. What matters is that the way we acquire things is separated from the way in which we use them.

The alienating function of money in the process of acquisition and consumption has been beautifully described by Marx in the following words: "Money . . . transforms the real human and natural powers into merely abstract ideas, and hence imperfections, and on the other hand it transforms the real imperfections and imaginings, the powers which only exist in the imagination of the individual into real powers. . . . It transforms loyalty into vice, vices into virtue, the slave into the master, the master into the slave, ignorance into reason, and reason into ignorance. . . . He who can buy valour is valiant although he be cowardly. . . . Assume *man* as *man*, and his relation to the world as a human one, and you can exchange love only for love, confidence for confidence, etc. If you wish to enjoy art, you must be an artistically trained person; if you wish to have influence on other people, you must be a person who has a really stimulating and furthering influence on other people. Every one of your relationships to man and to nature must be a definite expression of your *real, individual* life corresponding to the object of your will. If you love without calling forth love, that is, if your love as such does not produce love, if by means of an *expression of life* as a loving person you do not make of yourself a *loved person,* then your love is impotent, a misfortune." [1]

But beyond the method of acquisition, how do we use things, once we have acquired them? With regard to many things, there is not even the pretense of use. We acquire them to *have* them. We are satisfied with useless possession. The expensive dining set or

[1] "Nationalökonomie und Philosophie," 1844, published in Karl Marx' *Die Frühschriften,* Alfred Kröner Verlag, Stuttgart, 1953, pp. 300, 301. (My translation, E.F.)

crystal vase which we never use for fear they might break, the mansion with many unused rooms, the unnecessary cars and servants, like the ugly bric-à-brac of the lower-middle-class family, are so many examples of pleasure in possession instead of in use. However, this satisfaction in possessing per se was more prominent in the nineteenth century; today most of the satisfaction is derived from possession of things-to-be-used rather than of things-to-be-kept. This does not alter the fact, however, that even in the pleasure of things-to-be-used the satisfaction of prestige is a paramount factor. The car, the refrigerator, the television set are for real, but also for conspicuous use. They confer status on the owner.

How do we use the things we acquire? Let us begin with food and drink. We eat a bread which is tasteless and not nourishing because it appeals to our phantasy of wealth and distinction—being so white and "fresh." Actually, we "eat" a phantasy and have lost contact with the real thing we eat. Our palate, our body, are excluded from an act of consumption which primarily concerns them. We drink labels. With a bottle of Coca-Cola we drink the picture of the pretty boy and girl who drink it in the advertisement, we drink the slogan of "the pause that refreshes," we drink the great American habit; least of all do we drink with our palate. All this is even worse when it comes to the consumption of things whose whole reality is mainly the fiction the advertising campaign has created, like the "healthy" soap or dental paste.

I could go on giving examples ad infinitum. But it is unnecessary to belabor the point, since everybody can think of as many illustrations as I could give. I only want to stress the principle involved: the act of consumption should be a concrete human act, in which our senses, bodily needs, our aesthetic taste—that is to say, in which *we* as concrete, sensing, feeling, judging human beings—are involved; the act of consumption should be a meaningful, human, productive experience. In our culture, there is little of that. Consuming is essentially the satisfaction of artificially stimulated phantasies, a phantasy performance alienated from our concrete, real selves.

There is another aspect of alienation from the things we consume which needs to be mentioned. We are surrounded by things of whose nature and origin we know nothing. The telephone, radio, phonograph, and all other complicated machines are almost as mysterious to us as they would be to a man from a primitive culture; we know how to use them, that is, we know which button to turn, but we do not know on what principle they function, except in the vaguest terms of something we once learned at school. And things which do not rest upon difficult scientific principles are almost equally alien to us. We do not know how bread is made, how cloth is woven, how a table is manufactured, how glass is made. We consume, as we produce, without any concrete relatedness to the objects with which we deal; we live in a world of things, and our only connection with them is that we know how to manipulate or to consume them.

Our way of consumption necessarily results in the fact that we are never satisfied, since it is not our real concrete person which consumes a real and concrete thing. We thus develop an ever-increasing need for more things, for more consumption. It is true that as long as the living standard of the population is below a dignified level of subsistence, there is a natural need for more consumption. It is also true that there is a legitimate need for more consumption as man develops culturally and has more refined needs for better food, objects of artistic pleasure, books, etc. But our craving for consumption has lost all connection with the real needs of man. Originally, the idea of consuming more and better things was meant to give man a happier, more satisfied life. Consumption was a means to an end, that of happiness. It now has become an aim in itself. The constant increase of needs forces us to an ever-increasing effort, it makes us dependent on these needs and on the people and institutions by whose help we attain them. "Each person speculates to create a new need in the other person, in order to force him into a new dependency, to a new form of pleasure, hence to his economic ruin. . . . With a multitude of commodities grows the realm of alien things which enslave man." [1]

Man today is fascinated by the possibility of buying more, better, and especially, new things. He is consumption-hungry. The act of buying and consuming has become a compulsive, irrational aim, because it is an end in itself, with little relation to the use of, or pleasure in the things bought and consumed. To buy the latest gadget, the latest model of anything that is on the market, is the dream of everybody, in comparison to which the real pleasure in use is quite secondary. Modern man, if he dared to be articulate about his concept of heaven, would describe a vision which would look like the biggest department store in the world, showing new things and gadgets, and himself having plenty of money with which to buy them. He would wander around open-mouthed in this heaven of gadgets and commodities, provided only that there were ever more and newer things to buy, and perhaps that his neighbors were just a little less privileged than he.

Significantly enough, one of the older traits of middle-class society, the attachment to possessions and property, has undergone a profound change. In the older attitude, a certain sense of loving possession existed between a man and his property. It grew on him. He was proud of it. He took good care of it, and it was painful when eventually he had to part from it because it could not be used any more. There is very little left of this sense of property today. One loves the newness of the thing bought, and is ready to betray it when something newer has appeared.

[1] K. Marx, *ibid.*, p. 254.

Expressing the same change in characterological terms, I can refer to what has been stated above with regard to the *hoarding* orientation as dominant in the picture of the nineteenth century. In the middle of the twentieth century the hoarding orientation has given way to the *receptive* orientation, in which the aim is to receive, to "drink in," to have something new all the time, to live with a continuously open mouth, as it were. This receptive orientation is blended with the marketing orientation, while in the nineteenth century the hoarding was blended with the exploitative orientation.

The alienated attitude toward consumption not only exists in our acquisition and consumption of commodities, but it determines far beyond this the employment of leisure time. What are we to expect? If a man works without genuine relatedness to what he is doing, if he buys and consumes commodities in an abstractified and alienated way, how can he make use of his leisure time in an active and meaningful way? He always remains the passive and alienated consumer. He "consumes" ball games, moving pictures, newspapers and magazines, books, lectures, natural scenery, social gatherings, in the same alienated and abstractified way in which he consumes the commodities he has bought. He does not participate actively, he wants to "take in" all there is to be had, and to have as much as possible of pleasure, culture and what not. Actually, he is not free to enjoy "his" leisure; his leisure-time consumption is determined by industry, as are the commodities he buys; his taste is manipulated, he wants to see and to hear what he is conditioned to want to see and to hear; entertainment is an industry like any other, the customer is made to buy fun as he is made to buy dresses and shoes. The value of the fun is determined by its success on the market, not by anything which could be measured in human terms.

In any productive and spontaneous activity, something happens within myself while I am reading, looking at scenery, talking to friends, etcetera. I am not the same after the experience as I was before. In the alienated form of pleasure nothing happens within me; I have consumed this or that; nothing is changed within myself, and all that is left are memories of what I have done. One of the most striking examples for this kind of pleasure consumption is the taking of snapshots, which has become one of the most significant leisure activities. The Kodak slogan, "You press the button, we do the rest," which since 1889 has helped so much to popularize photography all over the world, is symbolic. It is one of the earliest appeals to push-button power-feeling; you do nothing, you do not have to know anything, everything is done for you; all you have to do is to press the button. Indeed, the taking of snapshots has become one of the most significant expressions of alienated visual perception, of sheer consumption. The "tourist" with his camera is an outstanding symbol of an alienated relationship to the world. Being constantly occupied with taking pictures, actually *he* does not see anything at all, except through the intermediary of the camera. The camera sees for him, and the outcome of his "pleasure" trip is a collection of snapshots, which are the substitute for an experience which he could have had, but did not have.

Man is not only alienated from the work he does, and the things and pleasures he consumes, but also from the *social forces* which determine our society and the life of everybody living in it.

Our actual helplessness before the forces which govern us appears more drastically in those social catastrophes which, even though they are denounced as regrettable accidents each time, so far have never failed to happen: economic depressions and wars. These social phenomena appear as if they were natural catastrophes, rather than what they really are, occurrences made by man, but without intention and awareness.

This anonymity of the social forces is inherent in the structure of the capitalist mode of production.

In contrast to most other societies in which social laws are explicit and fixed on the basis of political power or tradition—Capitalism does not have such explicit laws. It is based on the principle that if only everybody strives for himself on the market, the common good will come of it, order and not anarchy will be the result. There are, of course, economic laws which govern the market, but these laws operate behind the back of the acting individual, who is concerned only with his private interests. You try to guess these laws of the market as a Calvinist in Geneva tried to guess whether God had predestined him for salvation or not. But the laws of the market, like God's will, are beyond the reach of your will and influence.

To a large extent the development of Capitalism has proven that this principle works; and it is indeed a miracle that the antagonistic co-operation of self-contained economic entities should result in a blossoming and ever-expanding society. It is true that the capitalistic mode of production is conducive to political freedom, while any centrally planned social order is in danger of leading to political regimentation and eventually to dictatorship. While this is not the place to discuss the question of whether there are other alternatives than the choice between "free enterprise" and political regimentation, it needs to be said in this context that the very fact that we are governed by laws which we do not control, and do not even want to control, is one of the most outstanding manifestations of alienation. *We* are the producers of our economic and social arrangements, and at the same time we decline responsibility, intentionally and enthusiastically, and await hopefully or anxiously—as the case may be—what "the future" will bring. Our own actions are embodied in the laws which govern us, but these laws are above us, and we are their slaves.

The giant state and economic system are not any more controlled by man. They run wild, and their leaders are like a person on a runaway horse, who is proud of managing to keep in the saddle, even though he is powerless to direct the horse.

What is modern man's *relationship to his fellow man?* It is one between two abstractions, two living machines, who use each other. The employer uses the ones whom he employs; the salesman uses his customers. Everybody is to everybody else a commodity, always to be treated with certain friendliness, because even if he is not of use now, he may be later. There is not much love or hate to be found in human relations of our day. There is, rather, a superficial friendliness, and a more than superficial fairness, but behind that surface is distance and indifference. There is also a good deal of subtle distrust. When one man says to another, "You speak to John Smith; he is all right," it is an expression of reassurance against a general distrust. Even love and the relationship between sexes have assumed this character. The great sexual emancipation, as it occurred after the First World War, was a desperate attempt to substitute mutual sexual pleasure for a deeper feeling of love. When this turned out to be a disappointment the erotic polarity between the sexes was reduced to a minimum and replaced by a friendly partnership, a small combine which has amalgamated its forces to hold out better in the daily battle of life, and to relieve the feeling of isolation and aloneness which everybody has.

The alienation between man and man results in the loss of those general and social bonds which characterize medieval as well as most other precapitalist societies.[1] Modern society consists of "atoms" (if we use the Greek equivalent of "individual"), little particles estranged from each other but held together by selfish

[1] cf. the concept of "Gemeinschaft" (community) as against "Gesellschaft" (society) in Toennies' usage.

interests and by the necessity to make use of each other. Yet man is a social being with a deep need to share, to help, to feel as a member of a group. What has happened to these social strivings in man? They manifest themselves in the special sphere of the *public* realm, which is strictly separated from the private realm. Our private dealings with our fellow men are governed by the principle of egotism, "each for himself, God for us all," in flagrant contradiction to Christian teaching. The individual is motivated by egotistical interest, and not by solidarity with and love for his fellow man. The latter feelings may assert themselves secondarily as private acts of philanthropy or kindness, but they are not part of the basic structure of our social relations. Separated from our private life as individuals is the realm of our social life as "citizens." In this realm the state is the embodiment of our social existence; as citizens we are supposed to, and in fact usually do, exhibit a sense of social obligation and duty. We pay taxes, we vote, we respect the laws, and in the case of war we are willing to sacrifice our lives. What clearer example could there be of the separation between private and public existence than the fact that the same man who would not think of spending one hundred dollars to relieve the need of a stranger does not hesitate to risk his life to save this same stranger when in war they both happen to be soldiers in uniform? The uniform is the embodiment of our social nature—civilian garb, of our egotistic nature.

An interesting illustration of this thesis is to be found in S. A. Stouffer's newest work.[1] In answer to a question directed to a cross section of the American public "what kinds of things do you worry about most," the vast majority answers by mentioning personal, economic, health or other problems; only 8 per cent are worried about world problems including war—and one

---

[1] *Communism, Conformity and Civil Liberties,* Doubleday & Co., Inc. Garden City, New York, 1955.

per cent about the danger of Communism or the threat to civil liberties. But, on the other hand, almost half of the population of the sample thinks that Communism is a serious danger, and that war is likely to occur within two years. These social concerns, however, are not felt to be a personal reality, hence are no cause for worry, although for a good deal of intolerance. It is also interesting to note that in spite of the fact that almost the whole population believes in God, there seems to be hardly anyone who is worried about his soul, salvation, his spiritual development. God is as alienated as the world as a whole. What causes concern and worry is the private, separate sector of life, not the social, universal one which connects us with our fellow men.

The division between the community and the political state has led to the projection of all social feelings into the state, which thus becomes an idol, a power standing over and above man. Man submits to the state as to the embodiment of his own social feelings, which he worships as powers alienated from himself; in his private life as an individual he suffers from the isolation and aloneness which are the necessary result of this separation. The worship of the state can only disappear if man takes back the social powers into himself, and builds a community in which his social feelings are not something *added* to his private existence, but in which his private and social existence are one and the same.

What is the relationship of *man toward himself?* I have described elsewhere this relationship as "marketing orientation." [1] In this orientation, man experiences himself as a thing to be em-

---

[1] cf. my description of the marketing orientation in *Man for Himself*, p. 67 ff. The concept of alienation is not the same as one of the character orientations in terms of the receptive, exploitative, hoarding, marketing and productive orientations. Alienation can be found in any of these non-productive orientations, but it has a particular affinity to the marketing orientation. To the same extent it is also related to Riesman's "other-directed" personality which, however, though "developed from the marketing orientation," is a different concept in essential points. Cf. D. Riesman, *The Lonely Crowd*, Yale University Press, New Haven, 1950, p. 23.

ployed successfully on the market. He does not experience himself as an active agent, as the bearer of human powers. He is alienated from these powers. His aim is to sell himself successfully on the market. His sense of self does not stem from his activity as a loving and thinking individual, but from his socio-economic role. If things could speak, a typewriter would answer the question "Who are you?" by saying "I am a typewriter," and an automobile, by saying "I am an automobile," or more specifically by saying, "I am a Ford," or "a Buick," or "a Cadillac." If you ask a man "Who are you?", he answers "I am a manufacturer," "I am a clerk," "I am a doctor"—or "I am a married man," "I am the father of two kids," and his answer has pretty much the same meaning as that of the speaking *thing* would have. That is the way he experiences himself, not as a man, with love, fear, convictions, doubts, but as that abstraction, alienated from his real nature, which fulfills a certain function in the social system. His sense of value depends on his success: on whether he can sell himself favorably, whether he can make more of himself than he started out with, whether he is a success. His body, his mind and his soul are his capital, and his task in life is to invest it favorably, to make a profit of himself. Human qualities like friendliness, courtesy, kindness, are transformed into commodities, into assets of the "personality package," conducive to a higher price on the personality market. If the individual fails in a profitable investment of himself, he feels that *he* is a failure; if he succeeds, *he* is a success. Clearly, his sense of his own value always depends on factors extraneous to himself, on the fickle judgment of the market, which decides about his value as it decides about the value of commodities. He, like all commodities that cannot be sold profitably on the market, is worthless as far as his exchange value is concerned, even though his use value may be considerable.

The alienated personality who is for sale must lose a good deal of the sense of dignity which is so characteristic of man even in most primitive cultures. He must lose almost all sense of self, of himself as a unique and induplicable entity. The sense of self stems from the experience of myself as the subject of *my* experiences, *my* thought, *my* feeling, *my* decision, *my* judgment, *my* action. It presupposes that my experience is my own, and not an alienated one. *Things* have no self and men who have become things can have no self.

This selflessness of modern man has appeared to one of the most gifted and original contemporary psychiatrists, the late H. S. Sullivan, as being a natural phenomenon. He spoke of those psychologists who, like myself, assume that the lack of the sense of self is a pathological phenomenon, as of people who suffer from a "delusion." The self for him is nothing but the many roles we play in relations to others, roles which have the function of eliciting approval and avoiding the anxiety which is produced by disapproval. What a remarkably fast deterioration of the concept of self since the nineteenth century, when Ibsen made the loss of self the main theme of his criticism of modern man in his Peer Gynt! Peer Gynt is described as a man who, chasing after material gain, discovers eventually that he has lost his self, that he is like an onion with layer after layer, and without a kernel. Ibsen describes the dread of nothingness by which Peer Gynt is seized when he makes this discovery, a panic which makes him desire to land in hell, rather than to be thrown back into the "casting ladle" of nothingness. Indeed, with the experience of self disappears the experience of identity—and when this happens, man could become insane if he did not save himself by acquiring a *secondary sense of self*; he does that by experiencing himself as being approved of, worth while, successful, useful—briefly, as a salable commodity which is *he* because he is looked upon by others as an entity, not unique but fitting into one of the current patterns.

One cannot fully appreciate the nature of alienation without considering one specific aspect of modern life: its *routinization*, and the *repression of the awareness of the basic problems of human existence*. We touch here upon a universal problem of life. Man has to earn his daily bread, and this is always a more or less absorbing task. He has to take care of the many time- and energy-consuming tasks of daily life, and he is enmeshed in a certain routine necessary for the fulfillment of these tasks. He builds a social order, conventions, habits and ideas, which help him to perform what is necessary, and to live with his fellow man with a minimum of friction. It is characteristic of all culture that it builds a man-made, artificial world, superimposed on the natural world in which man lives. But man can fulfill himself only if he remains in touch with the fundamental facts of his existence, if he can experience the exaltation of love and solidarity, as well as the tragic fact of his aloneness and of the fragmentary character of his existence. If he is completely enmeshed in the routine and in the artefacts of life, if he cannot see anything but the man-made, common-sense appearance of the world, he loses his touch with and the grasp of himself and the world. We find in every culture the conflict between routine and the attempt to get back to the fundamental realities of existence. To help·in this attempt has been one of the functions of art and of religion, even though religion itself has eventually become a new form of routine.

Even the most primitive history of man shows us an attempt to get in touch with the essence of reality by artistic creation. Primitive man is not satisfied with the practical function of his tools and weapons, but strives to adorn and beautify them, transcending their utilitarian function. Aside from art, the most significant way of breaking through the surface of routine and of getting in touch with the ultimate realities of life is to be found in what may be called by the general term of "ritual." I am referring here to ritual in the broad sense of the word, as we find it in the performance of a Greek drama, for instance, and not only to rituals in the narrower religious sense. What was the function of the Greek drama? Fundamental problems of human existence were presented in an artistic and dramatic form, and participating in the dramatic performance, the spectator—though not as a spectator in our modern sense of the consumer—was carried away from the sphere of daily routine and brought in touch with himself as a human being, with the roots of his existence. He touched the ground with his feet, and in this process gained strength by which he was brought back to himself. Whether we think of the Greek drama, the medieval passion play, or an Indian dance, whether we think of Hindu, Jewish or Christian religious rituals, we are dealing with various forms of dramatization of the fundamental problems of human existence, with an *acting out* of the very same problems which are *thought out* in philosophy and theology.

What is left of such dramatization of life in modern culture? Almost nothing. Man hardly ever gets out of the realm of man-made conventions and things, and hardly ever breaks through the surface of his routine, aside from grotesque attempts to satisfy the need for a ritual as we see it practiced in lodges and fraternities. The only phenomenon approaching the meaning of a ritual, is the participation of the spectator in competitive sports; here at least, one fundamental problem of human existence is dealt with: the fight between men and the vicarious experience of victory and defeat. But what a primitive and restricted aspect of human existence, reducing the richness of human life to one partial aspect!

If there is a fire, or a car collision in a big city, scores of people will gather and watch. Millions of people are fascinated daily by reportings of crimes and by detective stories. They religiously go to movies in which crime and passion are the two central themes.

All this interest and fascination is not simply an expression of bad taste and sensationalism, but of a deep longing for a dramatization of ultimate phenomena of human existence, life and death, crime and punishment, the battle between man and nature. But while Greek drama dealt with these problems on a high artistic and metaphysical level, our modern "drama" and "ritual" are crude and do not produce any cathartic effect. All this fascination with competitive sports, crime and passion, shows the need for breaking through the routine surface, but the way of its satisfaction shows the extreme poverty of our solution.

The marketing orientation is closely related to the fact that the *need to exchange* has become a paramount drive in modern man. It is, of course, true that even in a primitive economy based on a rudimentary form of division of labor, men exchange goods with each other within the tribe or among neighboring tribes. The man who produces cloth exchanges it for grain which his neighbor may have produced, or for sickles or knives made by the blacksmith. With increasing division of labor, there is increasing exchange of goods, but normally the exchange of goods is nothing but a means to an economic end. In capitalistic society *exchanging has become an end in itself.*

None other than Adam Smith saw the fundamental role of the need to exchange, and explained it as a basic drive in man. "This division of labour," he says, "from which so many advantages are derived, is not originally the effect of any human wisdom, which foresees and intends that general opulence to which it gives occasion. It is the necessary, though very slow and gradual, consequence of a certain *propensity in human nature* which has in view no such extensive utility; the propensity to truck, barter, and exchange one thing for another. Whether this propensity be one of those original principles in human nature, of which no further account can be given; or whether, as seems more probable, it be

146

the necessary consequence of the faculties of reason and speech, it belongs not to our present subject to enquire. *It is common to all men, and to be found in no other race of animals,* which seem to know neither this nor any other species of contracts. . . . Nobody ever saw a dog make a fair and deliberate exchange of one bone for another with another dog." [1]

The principle of exchange on an ever-increasing scale on the national and world market is indeed one of the fundamental economic principles on which the capitalistic system rests, but Adam Smith foresaw here that this principle was also to become one of the deepest psychic needs of the modern, alienated personality. Exchanging has lost its rational function as a mere means for economic purposes, and has become an end in itself, extended to the noneconomic realms. Quite unwittingly, Adam Smith himself indicates the irrational nature of this need to exchange in his example of the exchange between the two dogs. There could be no possible realistic purpose in this exchange; either the two bones are alike, and then there is no reason to exchange them, or the one is better than the other, and then the dog who has the better one would not voluntarily exchange it. The example makes sense only if we assume that to exchange is a need in itself, even if it does not serve any practical purpose—and this is indeed what Adam Smith does assume.

As I have already mentioned in another context, the love of exchange has replaced the love of possession. One buys a car, or a house, intending to sell it at the first opportunity. But more important is the fact that the drive for exchange operates in the realm of interpersonal relations. Love is often nothing but a favorable exchange between two people who get the most of what they can expect, considering their value on the personality market.

[1] Adam Smith, *An Enquiry into the Nature and Causes of the Wealth of Nations,* The Modern Library, New York, 1937, p. 13. (Italics mine, E.F.)

Each person is a "package" in which several aspects of his exchange value are blended into one: his "personality," by which is meant those qualities which make him a good salesman of himself; his looks, education, income, and chance for success—each person strives to exchange this package for the best value obtainable. Even the function of going to a party, and of social intercourse in general, is to a large extent that of exchange. One is eager to meet the slightly higher-priced packages, in order to make contact and possibly a profitable exchange. One wishes to exchange one's social position, and that is, one's own self, for a higher one, and in this process one exchanges one's old set of friends, set of habits and feelings for the new ones, just as one exchanges one's Ford for a Buick. While Adam Smith believed this need for exchange to be an inherent part of human nature, it is actually a symptom of the abstractification and alienation inherent in the social character of modern man.

The whole process of living is experienced analogously to the profitable investment of capital, my life and my person being the capital which is invested. If a man buys a cake of soap or a pound of meat, he has the legitimate expectation that the money he pays corresponds to the value of the soap or the meat he buys. He is concerned that the equation "so much soap = so much money" makes sense in terms of the existing price structure. But this expectation has become extended to all other forms of activity. If a man goes to a concert or to the theater, he asks himself more or less explicitly whether the show is "worth the money" he paid. While this question makes some marginal sense, fundamentally the question does not make any sense, because two incommensurable things are brought together in the equation; the pleasure of listening to a concert cannot possibly be expressed in terms of money; the concert is not a commodity, nor is the experience of listening to it. The same holds true when a man makes a pleasure trip, goes to a lecture, gives a party, or any of the many activities which involve the expenditure of money. The activity in itself is a productive act of living, and incommensurable with the amount of money spent for it. The need to measure living acts in terms of something quantifiable appears also in the tendency to ask whether something was "worth the time." A young man's evening with a girl, a visit with friends, and the many other actions in which expenditure of money may or may not be involved, raise the question of whether the activity was worth the money or the time.[1] In each case one needs to justify the activity in terms of an equation which shows that it was a profitable investment of energy. Even hygiene and health have to serve for the same purpose; a man taking a walk every morning tends to look on it as a good investment for his health, rather than a pleasurable activity which does not need any justification. This attitude found its closest and most drastic expression in Bentham's concept of pleasure and pain. Starting on the assumption that the aim of life was to have pleasure, Bentham suggested a kind of bookkeeping which would show for each action whether the pleasure was greater than the pain, and if the pleasure was greater, the action was worth while doing. Thus the whole of life to him was something analogous to a business in which at any given point the favorable balance would show that it was profitable.

While Bentham's views are not very much in the minds of people any more, the attitude which they express has become ever more firmly established.[2] A new question has arisen in modern man's mind, the question, namely, whether "life is worth living," and

---

[1] cf. Marx' critical description of man in capitalist society: "Time is everything; man is nothing; he is no more than the carcass of time." (*The Poverty of Philosophy*, p. 57.)

[2] In Freud's concept of the pleasure principle and in his pessimistic views concerning the prevalence of suffering over pleasure in civilized society, one can detect the influence of Benthamian calculation.

correspondingly, the feeling that one's life "is a failure," or is "a success." This idea is based on the concept of life as an enterprise which should show a profit. The failure is like the bankruptcy of a business in which the losses are greater than the gains. This concept is nonsensical. We may be happy or unhappy, achieve some aims, and not achieve others; yet there is no sensible balance which could show whether life is worth while living. Maybe from the standpoint of a balance life is never worth while living. It ends necessarily with death; many of our hopes are disappointed; it involves suffering and effort; from a standpoint of the balance, it would seem to make more sense not to have been born at all, or to die in infancy. On the other hand, who will tell whether one happy moment of love, or the joy of breathing or walking on a bright morning and smelling the fresh air, is not worth all the suffering and effort which life implies? Life is a unique gift and challenge, not to be measured in terms of anything else, and no sensible answer can be given to the question whether it is "worth while" living, because the question does not make any sense.

This interpretation of life as an enterprise seems to be the basis for a typical modern phenomenon, about which a great deal of speculation exists: the *increase of suicide* in modern Western society. Between 1836 and 1890 suicide increased 140 per cent in Prussia, 355 per cent in France. England had 62 cases of suicide per million inhabitants in 1836 to 1845, and 110 between 1906 and 1910. Sweden 66, as against 150 respectively.[1] How can we explain this increase in suicide, accompanying the increasing prosperity in the nineteenth century?

No doubt that the motives for suicide are highly complex, and that there is not a single motivation which we can assume to be

[1] Quoted from *Les Causes du Suicide* by Maurice Halbwachs, Felix Alcan, Paris, 1930, pp. 92 and 481.

the cause. We find "revenge suicide" as a pattern in China; we find suicide caused by melancholia all over the world; but neither of these motivations play much of a role in the increase of suicide rates in the nineteenth century. Durkheim, in his classic work on suicide, assumed that the cause is to be found in a phenomenon which he called "anomie." He referred by that term to the destruction of all the traditional social bonds, to the fact that all truly collective organization has become secondary to the state, and that all genuine social life has been annihilated.[1] He believed that the people living in the modern political state are "a disorganized dust of individuals."[2] Durkheim's explanation lies in the direction of assumptions made in this book, and I shall return to discuss them later on. I believe also that the boredom and monotony of life which is engendered by the alienated way of living is an additional factor. The suicide figures for the Scandinavian countries, Switzerland and the United States, together with the figures on alcoholism seem to support this hypothesis.[3] But there is another reason which has been ignored by Durkheim and other students of suicide. It has to do with the whole "balance" concept of life as an enterprise which can fail. Many cases of suicide are caused by the feeling that "life has been a failure," that "it is not worth while living any more"; one commits suicide just as a businessman declares his bankruptcy when losses exceed gains, and when there is no more hope of recuperating the losses.

[1] cf. Emil Durkheim, *Le Suicide*, Felix Alcan, Paris, 1897, p. 446.

[2] *loc. cit.*, p. 448.

[3] All figures show also that Protestant countries have a much higher suicide rate than Catholic countries. This may be due to a number of factors inherent in the differences between the Catholic and Protestant religions, such as the greater influence which the Catholic religion has on the life of its adherents, the more adequate means to deal with a sense of guilt employed by the Catholic Church, etc. But it must also be taken into account that the Protestant countries are the ones in which the capitalistic mode of production is developed further, and has molded the character of the population more completely than in the Catholic countries, so that the difference between Protestant and Catholic countries is also largely the difference between various stages in the development of modern Capitalism.

c. Various Other Aspects

Thus far I have tried to give a general picture of the alienation of modern man from himself and his fellow man in the process of producing, consuming and leisure activities. I want now to deal with some specific aspects of the contemporary social character which are closely related to the phenomenon of alienation, the treatment of which, however, is facilitated by dealing with them separately rather than as subheadings of alienation.

i. *Anonymous Authority—Conformity*

The first such aspect to be dealt with is modern man's attitude toward *authority*.

We have discussed the difference between rational and irrational, furthering and inhibiting authority, and stated that Western society in the eighteenth and nineteenth centuries was characterized by the mixture of both kinds of authority. What is common to both rational and irrational authority is that it is *overt authority*. You know who orders and forbids: the father, the teacher, the boss, the king, the officer, the priest, God, the law, the moral conscience. The demands or prohibitions may be reasonable or not, strict or lenient, I may obey or rebel; I always know that there is an authority, who it is, what it wants, and what results from my compliance or my rebellion.

Authority in the middle of the twentieth century has changed its character; it is not overt authority, but *anonymous, invisible, alienated authority*. Nobody makes a demand, neither a person, nor an idea, nor a moral law. Yet we all conform as much or more than people in an intensely authoritarian society would. Indeed, nobody is an authority except "*It*." What is *It?* Profit, economic necessities, the market, common sense, public opinion, what "*one*" does, thinks, feels. The laws of anonymous authority are as invisible as the laws of the market—and just as unassailable. Who can attack the invisible? Who can rebel against Nobody?

The disappearance of overt authority is clearly visible in all spheres of life. Parents do not give commands any more; they suggest that the child "will want to do this." Since they have no principles or convictions themselves, they try to guide the children do what the law of conformity expects, and often, being older and hence less in touch with "the latest," they learn from the children what attitude is required. The same holds true in business and in industry; you do not give orders, you "suggest"; you do not command, you coax and manipulate. Even the American army has accepted much of the new form of authority. The army is propagandized as if it were an attractive business enterprise; the soldier should feel like a member of a "team," even though the hard fact remains that he must be trained to kill and be killed.

As long as there was overt authority, there was conflict, and there was rebellion—against irrational authority. In the conflict with the commands of one's conscience, in the fight against irrational authority, the personality developed—specifically the sense of self developed. I experience myself as "I" because I doubt, I protest, I rebel. Even if I submit and sense defeat, I experience myself as "I"—I, the defeated one. But if I am not aware of submitting or rebelling, if I am ruled by an anonymous authority, I lose the sense of self, I become a "one," a part of the "It."

The mechanism through which the anonymous authority operates is *conformity*. I ought to do what everybody does, hence, I must conform, not be different, not "stick out"; I must be ready and willing to change according to the changes in the pattern; I must not ask whether I am right or wrong, but whether I am adjusted, whether I am not "peculiar," not different. The only thing which is permanent in me is just this readiness for change. Nobody has power over me, except the herd of which I am a part, yet to which I am subjected.

It is hardly necessary to demonstrate to the reader the degree which this submission to anonymous authority by conformity has reached. However, I want to give a few illustrations taken from the very interesting and illuminating report on a settlement in Park Forest, Illinois, which seems to justify a formulation which the author puts at the head of one of his chapters, "The Future, c/o Park Forest." [1] This development near Chicago was made to house 30,000 people, partly in clusters of rental garden apartments (rent for two-bedroom duplex, $92), partly in ranch-type houses for sale ($11,995). The inhabitants are mostly junior executives, with a sprinkling of chemists and engineers, with an average income of $6,000 to $7,000, between 25 and 35 years of age, married, and with one or two children.

What are the social relations, and the "adjustment" in this package community? While people move there mainly out of "a simple economic necessity and not because of any yen for a womb image," the author notes "that after exposure to such an environment some people find a warmth and support in it that makes other environments seem unduly cold—it is somewhat unsettling, for example, to hear the way residents of the new suburbs occasionally refer to 'the outside.'" This feeling of warmth is more or less the same as the feeling of being accepted: "I could afford a better place than the development we are going to" says one of the people, "and I must say it isn't the kind of place where you have the boss or a customer to dinner. But you get real acceptance in a community like that." This craving for acceptance is indeed a very characteristic feeling in the alienated person. Why should

[1] The following quotations are taken from the article by William H. Whyte, Jr., "The Transients," *Fortune*, May, June, July and August 1953. Copyright 1953 Time Inc.

anyone be so grateful for acceptance unless he doubts that he is acceptable, and why should a young, educated, successful couple have such doubts, if not due to the fact that they cannot accept themselves—because they *are not* themselves. The only haven for having a sense of identity is conformity. Being acceptable really means not being different from anybody else. Feeling inferior stems from feeling different, and no question is asked whether the difference is for the better or the worse.

Adjustment begins early. One parent expresses the concept of anonymous authority quite succinctly: "The adjustment to the group does not seem to involve so many problems for them [the children]. I have noticed that they seem to get the feeling that nobody is the boss—there is a feeling of complete co-operation. Partly this comes from early exposure to court play." The ideological concept in which this phenomenon is expressed here is that of absence of authority, a positive value in terms of eighteenth- and nineteenth-century freedom. The reality behind this concept of freedom is the presence of anonymous authority and the absence of individuality. What could be clearer for this concept of conformity than the statement made by one mother: "Johnny has not been doing so well at school. The teacher told me he was doing fine in some respects but *that his social adjustment was not as good as it might be. He would pick one or two friends to play with—and sometimes he was happy to remain by himself.*" (Italics mine.) Indeed, the alienated person finds it almost impossible to remain by himself, because he is seized by the panic of experiencing nothingness. That it should be formulated so frankly is nevertheless surprising, and shows that we have even ceased to be ashamed of our herdlike inclinations.

The parents sometimes complain that the school might be a bit too "permissive," and that the children lack discipline, but "whatever the faults of Park Forest parents may be, harshness and authoritarianism are not among them." Indeed not, but why would you need authoritarianism in its overt forms if the anonymous authority of conformism makes your children submit completely to the It, even if they do not submit to their individual parents? The complaint of the parents, however, about lack of discipline is not meant too seriously, for "What we have in Park Forest, it is becoming evident, is the apotheosis of pragmatism. It would be an exaggeration, perhaps, to say that the transients have come to deify society—and the job of adjusting to it—but certainly they have remarkably little yen to quarrel with society. They are, as one puts it, the practical generation."

Another aspect of alienated conformity is the leveling-out process of taste and judgment which the author describes under the heading "The Melting Pot." " 'When I first came here I was pretty rarefied,' a self-styled 'egghead' explained to a recent visitor. 'I remember how shocked I was one day when I told the girls in the court how much I had enjoyed listening to 'The Magic Flute' the night before. They didn't know what I was talking about. I began to learn that diaper talk is a lot more important to them. I still listen to 'The Magic Flute' but now I realize that for most people other things in life seem as important.' " Another woman reports that she was discovered reading Plato when one of the girls made a surprise visit. The visitor " 'almost fell over from surprise. Now all of them are sure I'm strange.' " Actually, the author tells us, the poor woman overestimates the damage. The others do not think her overly odd, "for her deviance is accompanied by enough tact, enough observance of the little customs that oil court life, so that equilibrium is maintained." What matters is to transform value judgment into matters of opinion, whether it is listening to "The Magic Flute" as against diaper talk, or whether it is being a Republican as against being a Democrat. All that matters is that nothing is too serious, that one exchanges views, and that one is ready to accept any opinion or conviction (if there is such a thing) as being as good as the other. On the market of opinions everybody is supposed to have a commodity of the same value, and it is indecent and not fair to doubt it.

The word which is used for alienated conformity and sociability is of course one which expresses the phenomenon in terms of a very positive value. Indiscriminating sociability and lack of individuality is called being *outgoing*. The language here becomes psychiatrically tinged with the philosophy of Dewey thrown in for good measure. " 'You can really help make a lot of people happy here,' says one social activist. 'I've brought out two couples myself; I saw potentialities in them they didn't realize they had. Whenever we see someone who is shy and withdrawn, we make a special effort with them.' "

Another aspect of social "adjustment" is the complete lack of privacy, and the indiscriminate talking about one's "problems." Here again, one sees the influence of modern psychiatry and psychoanalysis. Even the thin walls are greeted as a help from feeling alone. " 'I never feel lonely, even when Jim's away,' goes a typical comment. 'You know friends are nearby, because at night you hear the neighbors through the walls.' " Marriages which might break up otherwise are saved, depressed moods are kept from becoming worse, by talking, talking, talking. " 'It's wonderful,' says one young wife. 'You find yourself discussing all your problems with your neighbors—things that back in South Dakota we would have kept to ourselves.' As time goes on, this capacity for self-revelation grows; and on the most intimate details of family life, court people become amazingly frank with each other. No one, they point out, ever need face a problem alone." We may add that it would be more correct to say that never do they face a problem.

Even the architecture becomes functional in the battle against loneliness. "Just as doors inside houses—which are sometimes said to have marked the birth of the middle class—are disappearing, so are the barriers against neighbors. The picture in the picture window, for example, is what is going on *inside*—or, what is going on inside other people's picture windows."

The conformity pattern develops a new morality, a new kind of super-ego. But the new morality is not the conscience of the humanistic tradition nor is the new super-ego made in the image of an authoritarian father. Virtue is to be adjusted and to be like the rest. Vice, to be different. Often this is expressed in psychiatric terms, where "virtuous" means being healthy, and "evil," being neurotic. "From the eye of the court there is no escape." Love affairs are rare for that reason, rather than for moral reasons or the fact that the marriages are so satisfactory. There are feeble attempts at privacy. While the rule is that you walk into the house without knocking, or making any other sign, some people gain a little privacy by moving the chair to the front, rather than the court side of the apartment, to show that they do not want to be disturbed. "But there is an important corollary of such efforts at privacy—*people feel a little guilty about making them*. Except very occasionally, to shut oneself off from others like this is regarded as either a childish prank or, more likely, an indication of some inner neurosis. The individual, not the group has erred. So, at any rate, many errants seem to feel, and they are often penitent about what elsewhere would be regarded as one's own business, and rather normal business at that. 'I've promised myself to make it up to them,' one court resident recently told a confidant. 'I was feeling bad and just plain didn't make the effort to ask the others in later. I don't blame them, really, for reacting the way they did. I'll make it up to them somehow.' "

Indeed, "privacy has become clandestine." Again the terms which are used are taken from the progressive political and philosophic tradition; what could sound finer than the sentence "Not in solitary and selfish contemplation but in doing things with other people does one fulfill oneself." What it really means, however, is giving up oneself, becoming part and parcel of the herd, and liking it. This state is often called by another pleasant word, "togetherness." The favorite way of expressing the same state of mind is that of putting it in psychiatric terms: " 'We have learned not to be so introverted,' one junior executive, and a very thoughtful and successful one, describes the lesson. 'Before we came here we used to live pretty much to ourselves. On Sundays, for instance, we used to stay in bed until around maybe two o'clock, reading the paper and listening to the symphony on the radio. Now we stop around and visit with people, or they visit with us. I really think Park Forest has broadened us.' "

Lack of conformity is not only punished by disapproving words like "neurotic," but sometimes by cruel sanctions. " 'Estelle is a case,' says one resident of a highly active block. 'She was dying to get in with the gang when she moved in. She is a very warm-hearted gal and is always trying to help people, but she's well—sort of elaborate about it. One day she decided to win over everybody by giving an afternoon party for the gals. Poor thing, she did it all wrong. The girls turned up in their bathing suits and slacks, as usual, and here she had little doilies and silver and everything spread around. Ever since then it's been almost like a planned campaign to keep her out of things. It's really pitiful. She sits there in her beach chair out front just dying for someone to come and kaffeeklatsch with her, and right across the street four or five of the girls will be yakking away. Every time they suddenly all laugh at some jokes she thinks they are laughing at her. She came over here yesterday and cried all afternoon. She told me she and her husband are thinking about moving somewhere else so they can make a fresh start.' " Other cultures have punished deviants from the prescribed political or religious creed by prison or the stake. Here the punishment is only ostracism which drives a poor woman into despair and an intense feeling of guilt. What is the crime? One act of error, one single sin toward the god of conformity.

It is only another aspect of the alienated kind of interpersonal relationship that friendships are not formed on the basis of individual liking or attraction, but that they are determined by the location of one's own house or apartment in relation to the others. This is the way it works. "It begins with the children. The new suburbs are matriarchies, yet the children are in effect so dictatorial that a term like *filiarchy* would not be entirely facetious. It is the children who set the basic design; their friendships are translated into the mother's friendships, and these, in turn, to the family's. Fathers just tag along.

"It is the flow of wheeled juvenile traffic, . . . that determines which is to be the functional door; i.e., in the homes, the front door; in the courts, the back door. It determines, further, the route one takes from the functional door; for when wives go visiting with neighbors they gravitate toward the houses within sight and hearing of their children and the telephone. This crystallizes into the court 'checkerboard movement' (i.e., the regular kaffeeklatsch route) and this forms the basis of adult friendships." Actually, this determination of friendship goes so far that the reader of the article is invited by the author to pick out the clusters of friendship in one sector of the settlement, just from the picture of the location of the houses, their entrance and exit doors in this sector.

What is important in this picture is not only the fact of alienated friendships, and automaton conformity, but the reaction of people to this fact. Consciously it seems people fully accept the new form of adjustment. "Once people hated to concede that their behavior was determined by anything except their own free will. Not so with the new suburbanites; they are fully aware of the all-pervading power of the environment over them. As a matter of fact, there are few subjects they like so much to talk about; and with the increasing lay curiosity about psychology, psychiatry, and sociology, they discuss their social life in surprisingly clinical terms. But they have no sense of plight; this, they seem to say, is the way things are, and the trick is not to fight it but to understand it."

This young generation has also its philosophy to explain their way of life. "Not merely as an instinctive wish, but as an articulate set of values to be passed on to one's children, the next generation of leaders are coming to deify social utility. *Does it work*, not why, has become the key question. With society having become so complex, the individual can have meaning only as he contributes to the harmony of the group, transients explain—and for them, constantly on the move, ever exposed to new groups, the adapting to groups has become particularly necessary. They are all, as they themselves so often put it, in the same boat." On the other hand, the author tells us: "The value of solitary thought, the fact that conflict is sometimes necessary, and other such disturbing thoughts rarely intrude." The most important, or really the only important thing children as well as adults have to learn, is to get along with other people which, if taught in school is called "citizenship," the equivalent for "outgoingness" and "togetherness" as the adults call it.

Are people really happy, are they as satisfied, unconsciously, as they believe themselves to be? Considering the nature of man, and the conditions for happiness, this can hardly be so. But they even have some doubts consciously. While they feel that conformity and merging with the group is their duty, many of them sense that they are "frustrating other urges." They feel that "responding to the group mores is akin to a moral duty—and so they continue, hesitant and unsure, *imprisoned in brotherhood.* (My italics) 'Every once in a while I wonder,' says one transient in an almost furtive moment of contemplation. 'I don't want to do anything to offend the people here: they're kind and decent, and I'm proud we've been able to get along with each other—with all our differences—so well. But then, once in a while, I *think of myself and my husband and what we are not doing, and I get depressed. Is is just enough not to be bad?'*" (Italics mine.) Indeed, this life of compromise, this "outgoing" life, is the life of imprisonment, selflessness and depression. They *are* all "in the same boat," but, as the author says very pointedly, *"where is the boat going? No one seems to have the faintest idea;* nor, for that matter, do they see much point in even raising the question."

The picture of conformity as we have illustrated it with the "outgoing" inhabitants of Park Forest is certainly not the same all over America. The reasons are obvious. These people are young, they are middle class and they move upwards, they are mostly people who in their work career manipulate symbols and men, and whose advancement depends on whether they permit themselves to be manipulated. There are undoubtedly many older people of the same occupational group, and many equally young people of different occupational groups who are less "advanced," as for instance those engineers, chemists and physicists, more interested in their work than in the hope of jumping into an executive career as soon as possible; furthermore, there are millions of farmers and farm-hands, whose style of life has only been changed partly by the conditions of the twentieth century; eventually the industrial workers, whose income is not too different from the white-collar workers, but whose work situation is. Although this is not the place to discuss the meaning of work for the industrial worker today, this much can be said here: there is undoubtedly a difference between people who manipulate other people and people who create things, even though their role in the process of production is a partial and in many ways an alienated one. The worker in a big steel mill co-operates with others, and has to do so if he is to protect his life; he faces dangers, and shares them with others; his colleagues as well as the foreman can judge and appreciate his skill rather than his smile and "pleasant personality"; he has a considerable amount of freedom outside of work; he has paid vacations, he may be busy in his garden, with a hobby, with local and union politics.[1] However, even taking into account all these factors which differentiate the industrial worker from the white-collar worker and the higher strata of the middle classes, there seems little chance that eventually the industrial worker will escape being molded by the dominant conformity pattern. In the first place, even the most positive aspects of his work situation, like the ones just mentioned, do not alter the fact that his work is alienated and only to a limited extent a meaningful expression of his energy and reason; secondly, the trend for increasing automatization of industrial work diminishes this latter factor rapidly. Eventually, he is under the influence of our whole cultural apparatus, the advertisements, movies, television, newspapers, just as everybody else, and can hardly escape being driven into conformity, although perhaps more slowly than other sectors of the population.[2] What holds true for the industrial worker holds true also for the farmer.

[1] Cf. Warner Bloomberg Jr.'s article "The Monstrous Machine and the Worried Workers," in *The Reporter,* September 28, 1953, and his lectures at the University of Chicago, "Modern Times in the Factory," 1934, a transcript of which he was kind enough to let me have.

[2] A detailed analysis of modern industrial work follows later.

ii. *The Principle of Nonfrustration*

As I have pointed out before, anonymous authority and automaton conformity are largely the result of our mode of production, which requires quick adaptation to the machine, disciplined mass behavior, common taste and obedience without the use of force. Another facet of our economic system, the need for mass consumption, has been instrumental in creating a feature in the social character of modern man which constitutes one of the most striking contrasts to the social character of the nineteenth century. I am referring to *the principle that every desire must be satisfied immediately, no wish must be frustrated*. The most obvious illustration of this principle is to be found in our system of buying on the installment plan. In the nineteenth century you bought what you needed, when you had saved the money for it; today you buy what you need, or do not need, on credit, and the function of advertising is largely to coax you into buying and to whet your appetite for things, so that you can be coaxed. You live in a circle. You buy on the installment plan, and about the time you have finished paying, you sell and you buy again —the latest model.

The principle that desires must be satisfied without much delay has also determined sexual behavior, especially since the end of the First World War. A crude form of misunderstood Freudianism used to furnish the appropriate rationalizations; the idea being that neuroses result from "repressed" sexual strivings, that frustrations were "traumatic," and the less you repressed the healthier you were. Even parents anxious to give their children everything they wanted lest they be frustrated, acquired a "complex." Unfortunately, many of these children as well as their parents landed on the analyst's couch, provided they could afford it.

The greed for things and the inability to postpone the satisfaction of wishes as characteristic of modern man has been stressed by thoughtful observers, such as Max Scheler and Bergson. It has been given its most poignant expression by Aldous Huxley in the *Brave New World*. Among the slogans by which the adolescents in the Brave New World are conditioned, one of the most important ones is *"Never put off till tomorrow the fun you can have today."* It is hammered into them, "two hundred repetitions, twice a week from fourteen to sixteen and a half." This instant realization of wishes is felt as happiness. "Everybody's happy nowadays" is another of the Brave New World slogans; people "get what they want and they never want what they can't get." This need for the immediate consumption of commodities and the immediate consummation of sexual desires is coupled in the Brave New World, as in our own. It is considered immoral to keep one "love" partner beyond a relatively short time. "Love" is short-lived sexual desire, which must be satisfied immediately. "The greatest care is taken to prevent you from loving anyone too much. There's no such thing as a divided allegiance; you're so conditioned that you can't help doing what you ought to do. And what you ought to do is on the whole so pleasant, so many of the natural impulses are allowed free play, that there really aren't any temptations to resist." [1]

This lack of inhibition of desires leads to the same result as the lack of overt authority—the paralysis and eventually the destruction of the self. If I do not postpone the satisfaction of my wish (and am conditioned only to wish for what I can get), I have no conflicts, no doubts; no decision has to be made; I am never alone with myself, because I am always busy—either working, or having fun. I have no need to be aware of myself as myself because I am constantly absorbed having pleasure. *I am—a system*

[1] cf. Aldous Huxley, *Brave New World,* The Vanguard Library, p. 196.

of desires and satisfactions; I have to work in order to fulfill my desires—and these very desires are constantly stimulated and directed by the economic machine. Most of these appetites are synthetic; even sexual appetite is by far not as "natural" as it is made out to be. It is to some extent stimulated artificially. And it needs to be if we want to have people as the contemporary system needs them—people who feel "happy," who have no doubts, who have no conflicts, who are guided without the use of force.

Having fun consists mainly in the satisfaction of consuming and "taking in"; commodities, sights, food, drinks, cigarettes, people, lectures, books, movies—all are consumed, swallowed. The world is one great object for our appetite, a big apple, a big bottle, a big breast; we are the sucklers, the eternally expectant ones, the hopeful ones—and the eternally disappointed ones. How can we help being disappointed if our birth stops at the breast of the mother, if we are never weaned, if we remain over-grown babes, if we never go beyond the receptive orientation?

So people do worry, feel inferior, inadequate, guilty. They sense that they live without living, that life runs through their hands like sand. How do they deal with their troubles, which stem from the passivity of constant taking in? By another form of passivity, a constant spilling out, as it were: by *talking*. Here, as in the case of authority and consumption, an idea which once was productive has been turned into its opposite.

iii. *Free Association and Free Talk*

Freud had discovered the principle of *free association*. By giving up the control of your thoughts in the presence of a skilled listener, you can discover your unconscious feelings and thoughts without being asleep, or crazy, or drunk, or hypnotized. The psycholanalyst reads between your lines, he is capable of

understanding you better than you understand yourself because
you have freed your thinking from the limitations of conventional thought control. But free association soon deteriorated,
like freedom and happiness. First it deteriorated in the orthodox
psychoanalytic procedure itself. Not always, but often. Instead
of giving rise to a meaningful expression of imprisoned thoughts,
it became meaningless chatter. Other therapeutic schools reduced
the role of the analyst to that of a sympathetic listener, who re-
peats in a slightly different version the words of the patient,
without trying to interpret or to explain. All this is done with the
idea that the patient's freedom must not be interfered with. The
Freudian idea of free association has become the instrument of
many psychologists who call themselves counselors, although
the only thing they do not do is to counsel. These counselors
play an increasingly large role as private practitioners and as
advisers in industry.[1] What is the effect of the procedure? Obviously not a cure which Freud had in mind when he devised
free association as a basis for understanding the unconscious.
Rather a release of tension which results from talking things out
in the presence of a sympathetic listener. Your thoughts, as long
as you keep them within yourself, may disturb you—but something fruitful may come out of this disturbance; you mull them
over, you think, you feel, you may arrive at a new thought born
out of this travail. But when you talk right away, when you do
not let your thoughts and feelings build up pressure, as it were,
they do not become fruitful. It is exactly the same as with un-
obstructed consumption. You are a system in which things go
in and out continuously—and within it is nothing, no tension,
no digestion, no self. Freud's discovery of free association had

[1] cf. W. J. Dickson, *The New Industrial Relations*, Cornell University Press, 1948,
and G. Friedmann's discussion in *Où va le Travail Humain?*, Gallimard, Paris, 1950,
p. 142 ff. Also H. W. Harrell, *Industrial Psychology*, Rinehart & Company, Inc.,
New York, 1949, p. 372 ff.

the aim of finding out what went on in you underneath the
surface, of *discovering who you* really were; the modern talking
to the sympathetic listener has the opposite, although unavowed
aim; its function is to make a man *forget* who he is (provided
he has still some memory), to lose all tension, and with it all
sense of self. Just as one oils machines, one oils people and especially those in the mass organizations of work. One oils them
with pleasant slogans, material advantages, and with the sympathetic understanding of the psychologists.

The talking and listening to eventually has become the indoor
sport of those who cannot afford a professional listener, or prefer
the layman for one reason or another. It has become fashionable,
sophisticated, to "talk things out." There is no inhibition, no
sense of shame, no holding back. One speaks about the tragic
occurrences of one's own life with the same ease as one would
talk about another person of no particular interest, or as one
would speak about the various troubles one has had with one's
car.

Indeed, psychology and psychiatry are in the process of changing their function fundamentally. From the Delphic Oracle's
"Know thyself!" to Freud's psychoanalytic therapy, the function
of psychology was to discover the self, to understand the individual, to find the "truth that makes you free." Today the
function of psychiatry, psychology and psychoanalysis threatens
to become the tool in the manipulation of men. The specialists
in this field tell you what the "normal" person is, and, correspondingly, what is wrong with you; they devise the methods to
help you adjust, be happy, be normal. In the Brave New World
this conditioning is done from the first month of fertilization
(by chemical means), until after puberty. With us, it begins a
little later. Constant repetition by newspaper, radio, television,
does most of the conditioning. But the crowning achievement

of manipulation is modern psychology. What Taylor did for industrial work, the psychologists do for the whole personality —all in the name of understanding and freedom. There are many exceptions to this among psychiatrists, psychologists and psycho-analysts, but it becomes increasingly clear that these professions are in the process of becoming a serious danger to the develop-ment of man, that their practitioners are evolving into the priests of the new religion of fun, consumption and self-lessness, into the specialists of manipulation, into the spokesmen for the alienated personality.

iv. *Reason, Conscience, Religion*

What becomes of *reason, conscience* and *religion* in an alienated world? Superficially seen, they prosper. There is hardly any illiteracy to speak of in the Western countries; more and more people go to college in the United States; everybody reads the newspapers and talks reasonably about world affairs. As to conscience, most people act quite decently in their narrow per-sonal sphere, in fact surprisingly so, considering their general confusion. As far as religion is concerned, it is well known that church affiliation is higher than ever, and the vast majority of Americans believe in God—or so they say in public-opinion polls. However, one does not need to dig too deeply to arrive at less pleasant findings.

If we talk about reason, we must first decide what human capacity we are referring to. As I have suggested before, we must differentiate between intelligence and reason. By intelli-gence I mean the ability to manipulate concepts for the purpose of achieving some practical end. The chimpanzee—who puts the two sticks together in order to get at the banana because no one of the two is long enough to do the job—uses intelligence. So do we all when we go about our business, "figuring out" how to do things. *Intelligence*, in this sense, is taking things for granted as they are, making combinations which have the purpose of facilitating their manipulation; intelligence is thought in the service of biological survival. *Reason*, on the other hand, aims at understanding; it tries to find out what is behind the surface, to recognize the kernel, the essence of the reality which surrounds us. Reason is not without a function, but its function is not to further physical as much as mental and spiritual existence. However, often in individual and social life, reason is required in order to predict (considering that prediction often depends on recognition of forces which operate underneath the surface), and prediction sometimes is necessary even for physical survival.

Reason requires relatedness and a sense of self. If I am only the passive receptor of impressions, thoughts, opinions, I can compare them, manipulate them—but I cannot penetrate them. Descartes deduced the existence of myself as an individual from the fact that I think. I doubt, so he argued, hence I think; I think, hence I am. The reverse is true, too. Only if I am I, if I have not lost my individuality in the It, can I think, that is, can I make use of my reason.

Closely related to this is the lacking sense of reality which is characteristic of the alienated personality. To speak of the "lacking sense of reality" in modern man is contrary to the widely held idea that we are distinguished from most periods of history by our greater realism. But to speak of our realism is almost like a paranoid distortion. What realists, who are playing with weapons which may lead to the destruction of all modern civilization, if not of our earth itself! If an individual were found doing just that, he would be locked up immediately, and if he prided himself on his realism, the psychiatrists would consider this an additional and rather serious symptom of a diseased mind. But quite aside from this—the fact is that modern man exhibits an amazing lack of realism for all that matters. For the meaning of life and death, for happiness and suffering, for feeling and serious thought. He has covered up the whole reality of human existence and replaced it with his artificial, prettified picture of a pseudo-reality, not too different from the savages who lost their land and freedom for glittering glass beads. Indeed, he is so far away from human reality, that he can say with the inhabitants of the Brave New World: "When the individual feels, the community reels."

Another factor in contemporary society already mentioned is destructive to reason. Since nobody ever does the whole job, but only a fraction of it, since the dimension of things and of the organization of people is too vast to be understood as a whole, nothing can be seen in its totality. Hence the laws underlying the phenomena cannot be observed. Intelligence is sufficient to manipulate properly one sector of a larger unit, whether it is a machine or a state. But reason can develop only if it is geared to the whole, if it deals with observable and manageable entities. Just as our ears and eyes function only within certain quantitative limits of wave length, our reason too is bound by what is observable as a whole and in its total functioning. To put it differently, beyond a certain order of bigness, concreteness is necessarily lost and abstractification takes place; with it, the sense for reality fades out. The first one to see this problem was Aristotle, who thought that a city which transcended in number what we would call today a small town was not livable.

In observing the quality of thinking in alienated man, it is striking to see how his intelligence has developed and how his reason has deteriorated. He takes his reality for granted; he wants to eat it, consume it, touch it, manipulate it. He does not even ask what is behind it, why things are as they are, and where they are going. You cannot eat the meaning, you cannot consume the sense, and as far as the future is concerned—*après nous le déluge!* Even from the nineteenth century to our day, there seems to have occurred an observable increase in stupidity, if by this we mean the opposite to reason, rather than to intelligence. In spite of the fact that everybody reads the daily paper religiously, there is an absence of understanding of the meaning of political events which is truly frightening, because our intelligence helps us to produce weapons which our reason is not capable of controlling. Indeed, we have the know-how, but we do not have the know-why, nor the know-what-for. We have many persons with good and high intelligence quotients, but our intelligence tests measure the ability to memorize, to manipulate thoughts quickly—but not to reason. All this is true notwithstanding the fact that there are men of outstanding reason in our midst, whose thinking is as profound and vigorous as ever existed in the history of the human race. But they think apart from the general herd thought, and they are looked upon with suspicion—even if they are needed for their extraordinary achievements in the natural sciences.

The new automatic brains are indeed a good illustration of what is meant here by intelligence. They manipulate data which are fed into them; they compare, select, and eventually come out with results more quickly or more error-proof than human intelligence could. However, the condition of all this is that the basic data are fed into them beforehand. What the electric brain cannot do is think creatively, to arrive at an insight into the essence of the observed facts, to go beyond the data with which it has been fed. The machine can duplicate or even improve on intelligence, but it cannot simulate reason.

Ethics, at least in the meaning of the Greco-Judaeo-Christian tradition, is inseparable from reason. Ethical behavior is based on the faculty of making value judgments on the basis of reason; it means deciding between good and evil, and to act upon the decision. Use of reason presupposes the presence of self; so does ethical judgment and action. Furthermore, ethics, whether it is that of monotheistic religion or that of secular humanism, is based on the principle that no institution and no thing is higher than any human individual; that the aim of life is to unfold man's love and reason and that every other human activity has to be subordinated to this aim. How then can ethics be a significant part of a life in which the individual becomes an automaton, in which he serves the big It? Furthermore, how can conscience develop when the principle of life is conformity? Conscience, by its very nature is nonconforming; it must be able to say no, when everybody else says yes; in order to say this "no" it must be certain in the rightness of the judgment on which the no is based. To the degree to which a person conforms he cannot hear the voice of his conscience, much less act upon it. Conscience exists only when man experiences himself as man, not as a thing, as a commodity. Concerning *things* which are exchanged on the market there exists another quasi ethical code, that of *fairness*. The question is, whether they are exchanged at a fair price, no tricks and no force interfering with the fairness of the bargain; this fairness, not good and evil, is the ethical principle of the market and it is the ethical principle governing the life of the marketing personality.

This principle of fairness, no doubt, makes for a certain type of ethical behavior. You do not lie, cheat or use force—you even give the other person a chance—if you act according to the code of fairness. But to love your neighbor, to feel one with him, to devote your life to the aim of developing your spiritual powers, is not part of the fairness ethics. We live in a paradoxical situation: we practice fairness ethics, and profess Christian ethics. Must we not stumble over this obvious contradiction? Obviously, we do not stumble. What is the reason? Partly, it is to be found in the fact that the heritage of four thousand years of the development of conscience is by no means completely lost. On the contrary, in many ways the liberation of man from the powers of the feudal state and the Church, made it possible for this heritage to be brought to fruition and in the period between the eighteenth century and now it blossomed as perhaps never before. We still are part of this process—but given our own twentieth-century condition of life, it seems that there is no new bud which will blossom when this flower has wilted.

Another reason why we do not stumble over the contradiction between humanistic ethics and fairness ethics lies in the fact that we reinterpret religious and humanistic ethics in the light of fairness ethics. A good illustration of this interpretation is the Golden Rule. In its original Jewish and Christian meaning, it was a popular phrasing of the Biblical maxim to "love thy neighbor as thyself." In the system of fairness ethics, it means simply "Be fair when you exchange. Give what you expect to get. Don't cheat!" No wonder the Golden Rule is the most popular religious phrase of today. It combines two opposite systems of ethics and helps us to forget the contradiction.

While we still live from the Christian-humanistic heritage it is not surprising that the younger generation exhibits less and less of the traditional ethics and that we come across a moral barbarism among our youth which is in complete contrast to the economic and educational level society has reached. Today, while revising this manuscript, I read two items. One in the *New York Times,* regarding the fact of the murder of a man, cruelly trampled to death by four teen-agers of average middle-class families. The other in *Time* magazine, a description of the new Guatemalan chief of police, who as former chief of police under the Ubico dictatorship had "perfected a head-shrinking steel skull cap to pry loose secrets and crush improper political thoughts." [1] His picture is published with the caption "For improper thought, a crusher." Could anything be more insanely insensitive to extremes of sadism than this flippant line? Is it surprising when in a culture in which the most popular news magazine can write this, teen-agers have no scruples about beating a man to death? Is the fact that we show brutality and cruelty in comic books and movies, because money is made with these commodities, not enough of an explanation for the growing barbarism and vandalism in our youth? Our movie censors watch that no sexual scenes are shown, since this could suggest illicit sexual desires. How innocent would this result be in comparison with the dehumanizing effect of what the censors permit and the churches seem to object to less than to the traditional sins. Yes, we still have an ethical heritage, but it will soon be spent and will be replaced by the ethics of the Brave New World, or "1984," unless it ceases to be a heritage and is re-created in our whole mode of life. At the moment, it seems that ethical behavior is still to be found in the concrete situation of many individuals, while society is marching toward barbarism. [2]

Much of what has been said about ethics is to be said about *religion*. Of course, speaking of the role of religion among alienated men, everything depends on what we call religion. If we are referring to religion in its widest sense, as a system of orientation and an object of devotion, then, indeed, every human being is religious, since nobody can live without such a system and remain sane. Then, our culture is as religious as any. Our gods are the machine, and the idea of efficiency; the meaning of our life is to move, to forge ahead, to arrive as near to the top as possible. But if by religion we mean monotheism, then, indeed,

---

[1] *Time,* August 23, 1954.

[2] cf. the similar point of view made by A. Gehlen in his very thoughtful and profound *Sozialpsychologische Probleme in der Industriellen Gesellschaft.* I. C. B. Mohr, 1949.

our religion is not more than one of the commodities in our show windows. Monotheism is incompatible with alienation and with our ethics of fairness. It makes man's unfolding, his salvation, the supreme aim of life, an aim which never can be subordinated to any other. Inasmuch as God is unrecognizable, indefinable, and inasmuch as man is made in the likeness of God, *man* is indefinable—which means he is not and can never be considered a *thing*. The fight between monotheism and idolatry is exactly the fight between the productive and the alienated way of life. Our culture is perhaps the first completely secularized culture in human history. We have shoved away awareness of and concern with the fundamental problems of human existence. We are not concerned with the meaning of life, with the solution to it; we start out with the conviction that there is no purpose except to invest life successfully and to get it over with without major mishaps. The majority of us believe in God, take it for granted that God exists. The rest, who do not believe, take it for granted that God does not exist. Either way, God is taken for granted. Neither belief nor disbelief cause any sleepless nights, nor any serious concern. In fact, whether a man in our culture believes in God or not makes hardly any difference either from a psychological or from a truly religious standpoint. In both instances he does not care—either about God or about the answer to the problem of his own existence. Just as brotherly love has been replaced by impersonal fairness, God has been transformed into a remote General Director of Universe, Inc.; you know that He is there, He runs the show, (although it probably would run without Him too), you never see Him, but you acknowledge His leadership while you are "doing your part."

The religious 'renaissance' which we witness in these days is perhaps the worst blow monotheism has yet received. Is there any greater sacrilege than to speak of "the Man upstairs," to teach to pray in order to make God your partner in business, to "sell" religion with the methods and appeals used to sell soap?

In view of the fact that the alienation of modern man is incompatible with monotheism, one might expect that ministers, priests and rabbis would form the spearhead of criticism of modern Capitalism. While it is true that from high Catholic quarters and from a number of less highly placed ministers and rabbis such criticism has been voiced, all churches belong essentially to the conservative forces in modern society and use religion to keep man going and satisfied with a profoundly irreligious system. The majority of them do not seem to recognize that this type of religion will eventually degenerate into overt idolatry, unless they begin to define and then to fight against modern idolatry, rather than to make pronouncements about God and thus to use His name in vain—in more than one sense.

v. *Work*

What becomes the meaning of *work* in an alienated society?

We have already made some brief comments about this question in the general discussion of alienation. But since this problem is of utmost importance, not only for the understanding of present-day society, but also for any attempt to create a saner society, I want to deal with the nature of work separately and more extensively in the following pages.

Unless man exploits others, he has to work in order to live. However primitive and simple his method of work may be, by the very fact of production, he has risen above the animal kingdom; rightly has he been defined as "the animal that produces." But work is not only an inescapable necessity for man. Work is also his liberator from nature, his creator as a social and independent being. *In the process of work, that is, the molding and changing of nature outside of himself, man molds and changes himself.* He emerges from nature by mastering her; he develops his powers of co-operation, of reason, his sense of beauty. He separates himself from nature, from the original unity with her, but at the same time unites himself with her again as her master and builder. The more his work develops, the more his individuality develops. In molding nature and re-creating her, he learns to make use of his powers, increasing his skill and creativeness. Whether we think of the beautiful paintings in the caves of Southern France, the ornaments on weapons among primitive people, the statues and temples of Greece, the cathedrals of the Middle Ages, the chairs and tables made by skilled craftsmen, or the cultivation of flowers, trees or corn by peasants —all are expressions of the creative transformation of nature by man's reason and skill.

In Western history, craftsmanship, especially as it developed in the thirteenth and fourteenth centuries, constitutes one of the peaks in the evolution of creative work. Work was not only a useful activity, but one which carried with it a profound satisfaction. The main features of craftsmanship have been very lucidly expressed by C. W. Mills. "There is no ulterior motive in work other than the product being made and the processes of its creation. The details of daily work are meaningful because they are not detached in the worker's mind from the product of the work. The worker is free to control his own working action. The craftsman is thus able to learn from his work; and to use and develop his capacities and skills in its prosecution. There is no split of work and play, or work and culture. The craftsman's way of livelihood determines and infuses his entire mode of living." [1]

With the collapse of the medieval structure, and the begin-

---

[1] C. W. Mills, *White Collar*, Oxford University Press, New York, 1951, p. 220.

ning of the modern mode of production, the meaning and function of work changed fundamentally, especially in the Protestant countries. Man, being afraid of his newly won freedom, was obsessed by the need to subdue his doubts and fears by developing a feverish activity. The outcome of this activity, success or failure, decided his salvation, indicating whether he was among the saved or the lost souls. *Work, instead of being an activity satisfying in itself and pleasureable, became a duty and an obsession.* The more it was possible to gain riches by work, the more it became a pure means to the aim of wealth and success. Work became, in Max Weber's terms, the chief factor in a system of "inner-worldly asceticism," an answer to man's sense of aloneness and isolation.

However, work in this sense existed only for the upper and middle classes, those who could amass some capital and employ the work of others. For the vast majority of those who had only their physical energy to sell, work became nothing but forced labor. The worker in the eighteenth or nineteenth century who had to work sixteen hours if he did not want to starve was not doing it because he served the Lord in this way, nor because his success would show that he was among the "chosen" ones, but because he was forced to sell his energy to those who had the means of exploiting it. The first centuries of the modern era find the meaning of work divided into that of *duty* among the middle class, and that of *forced labor* among those without property.

The religious attitude toward work as a duty, which was still so prevalent in the nineteenth century, has been changing considerably in the last decades. Modern man does not know what to do with himself, how to spend his lifetime meaningfully, and he is driven to work in order to avoid an unbearable boredom. But work has ceased to be a moral and religious obligation in the sense of the middle-class attitude of the eighteenth and nineteenth centuries. Something new has emerged. Ever-increasing production, the drive to make bigger and better things, have become aims in themselves, new ideals. Work has become alienated from the working person.

What happens to the industrial worker? He spends his best energy for seven or eight hours a day in producing "something." He needs his work in order to make a living, but his role is essentially a passive one. He fulfills a small isolated function in a complicated and highly organized process of production, and is never confronted with "his" product as a whole, at least not as a producer, but only as a consumer, provided he has the money to buy "his" product in a store. He is concerned neither with the whole product in its physical aspects nor with its wider economic and social aspects. He is put in a certain place, has to carry out a certain task, but does not participate in the organization or management of the work. He is not interested, nor does he know why one produces this, instead of another commodity—what relation it has to the needs of society as a whole. The shoes, the cars, the electric bulbs, are produced by "the enterprise," using the machines. He is a part of the machine, rather than its master as an active agent. The machine, instead of being in his service to do work for him which once had to be performed by sheer physical energy, has become his master. Instead of the machine being the substitute for human energy, man has become a substitute for the machine. *His work can be defined as the performance of acts which cannot yet be performed by machines.*

Work is a means of getting money, not in itself a meaningful human activity. P. Drucker, observing workers in the automobile industry, expresses this idea very succinctly: "For the great majority of automobile workers, the only meaning of the job is in the pay check, not in anything connected with the work or the product. Work appears as something unnatural, a disagreeable, meaningless and stultifying condition of getting the pay check, devoid of dignity as well as of importance. No wonder that this puts a premium on slovenly work, on slow-downs, and on other tricks to get the same pay check with less work. No wonder that this results in an unhappy and discontented worker—because a pay check is not enough to base one's self-respect on." [1]

This relationship of the worker to his work is an outcome of the whole social organization of which he is a part. Being "employed," [2] he is not an active agent, has no responsibility except the proper performance of the isolated piece of work he is doing, and has little interest except the one of bringing home enough money to support himself and his family. Nothing more is expected of him, or wanted from him. He is part of the equipment hired by capital, and his role and function are determined by this quality of being a piece of equipment. In recent decades, increasing attention has been paid to the psychology of the worker, and to his attitude toward his work, to the "human problem of industry"; but this very formulation is indicative of the underlying attitude; there is a human being spending most of his life-time at work, and what should be discussed is the *"industrial problem of human beings," rather than "the human problem of industry."*

Most investigations in the field of industrial psychology are concerned with the question of how the productivity of the individual worker can be increased, and how he can be made to work with less friction; psychology has lent its services to "hu-

[1] cf. Peter F. Drucker, *Concept of the Corporation*, The John Day Company, New York, 1946, p. 179.
[2] The English "employed" like the German *angestellt* are terms which refer to things rather than to human beings.

man engineering," an attempt to treat the worker and employee like a machine which runs better when it is well oiled. While Taylor was primarily concerned with a better organization of the technical use of the worker's physical powers, most industrial psychologists are mainly concerned with the manipulation of the worker's psyche. The underlying idea can be formulated like this: if he works better when he is happy, then let us make him happy, secure, satisfied, or anything else, provided it raises his output and diminishes friction. In the name of "human relations," the worker is treated with all devices which suit a completely alienated person; even happiness and human values are recommended in the interest of better relations with the public. Thus, for instance, according to *Time* magazine, one of the best-known American psychiatrists said to a group of fifteen hundred Supermarket executives: "It's going to be an increased satisfaction to our customers if we are happy. . . . It is going to pay off in cold dollars and cents to management, if we could put some of these general principles of values, human relationships, really into practice." One speaks of "human relations" and one means the most in-human relations, those between alienated automatons; one speaks of happiness and means the perfect routinization which has driven out the last doubt and all spontaneity.[1]

The alienated and profoundly unsatisfactory character of work results in two reactions: one, the ideal of complete *laziness;* the other a deep-seated, though often unconscious *hostility* toward work and everything and everybody connected with it.

It is not difficult to recognize the widespread longing for the state of complete laziness and passivity. Our advertising appeals to it even more than to sex. There are, of course, many useful and labor saving gadgets. But this usefulness often serves only as a

[1] The problem of work will be dealt with further in Chapter VIII.

rationalization for the appeal to complete passivity and receptivity. A package of breakfast cereal is being advertised as *"new—easier to eat."* An electric toaster is advertised with these words: ". . . the most distinctly different toaster in the world! Everything is done *for* you with this new toaster. You need not even bother to lower the bread. Power-action, though a unique electric motor, *gently takes the bread right out of your fingers!"* How many courses in languages, or other subjects are announced with the slogan "effortless learning, no more of the old drudgery." Everybody knows the picture of the elderly couple in the advertisement of a life-insurance company, who have retired at the age of sixty, and spend their life in the complete bliss of having nothing to do except just travel.

Radio and television exhibit another element of this yearning for laziness: the idea of "push-button power"; by pushing a button, or turning a knob on my machine, I have the power to produce music, speeches, ball games, and on the television set, to command events of the world to appear before my eyes. The pleasure of driving cars certainly rests partly upon this same satisfaction of the wish for push-button power. By the effortless pushing of a button, a powerful machine is set in motion; little skill and effort is needed to make the driver feel that he is the ruler of space.

But there is far more serious and deep-seated reaction to the meaninglessness and boredom of work. It is a hostility toward work which is much less conscious than our craving for laziness and inactivity. Many a businessman feels himself the prisoner of his business and the commodities he sells; he has a feeling of fraudulency about his product and a secret contempt for it. He hates his customers, who force him to put up a show in order to sell. He hates his competitors because they are a threat; his employees as well as his superiors, because he is in a constant competitive fight with them. Most important of all, he hates himself, because he sees his life passing by, without making any sense beyond the momentary intoxication of success. Of course, this hate and contempt for others and for oneself, and for the very things one produces, is mainly unconscious, and only occasionally comes up to awareness in a fleeting thought, which is sufficiently disturbing to be set aside as quickly as possible.

vi. *Democracy*

Just as work has become alienated, the expression of the will of the voter in modern democracy is an alienated expression. The principle of *democracy* is the idea that not a ruler or a small group, but the people as a whole, determine their own fate and make their decisions pertaining to matters of common concern. By electing his own representatives, who in a parliament decide on the laws of the land, each citizen is supposed to exercise the function of responsible participation in the affairs of the community. By the principle of the division of powers, an ingenious system was created that served to retain the integrity and independence of the judiciary system, and to balance the respective functions of the legislature and executive. Ideally, every citizen is equally responsible for and influential in making decisions.

In reality, the emerging democratic system was beset by one important contradiction. Operating in states with tremendous inequalities of opportunity and income, the privileged classes naturally did not want to lose the privileges which the status quo gave them, and which they could easily have lost if the will of the majority, who were without property, had found its full expression. To avoid such a danger, many among the property-less population were excluded from the franchise, and only very slowly was the principle accepted that every citizen, without restrictions and qualifications, had the right to vote.

In the nineteenth century it seemed as if universal franchise would solve all problems of democracy. O'Connor, one of the Chartist leaders, said in 1838: "Universal suffrage would at once change the whole character of society from a state of watchfulness, doubt and suspicion to that of brotherly love, reciprocal interest and universal confidence," and in 1842 he said: ". . . six months after the Charter is passed, every man, woman and child in the country will be well fed, well housed and well clothed." [1] Since then, all great democracies have established general suffrage for men, and with the exception of Switzerland, for women, but even in the richest country in the world, one third of the population was still "ill fed, ill housed, and ill clothed," to quote Franklin D. Roosevelt.

The introduction of universal suffrage not only disappointed the hopes of the Chartists, it disappointed all those who believed that universal suffrage would help to transform the citizenry into responsible, active, independent personalities. It became clear that the *problem of democracy today is not any more the restriction of franchise but the manner in which the franchise is exercised.*

How can people express "their" will if they do not have any will or conviction of their own, if they are alienated automatons, whose tastes, opinions and preferences are manipulated by the big conditioning machines? Under these circumstances universal suffrage becomes a fetish. If a government can prove that everybody has a right to vote, and that the votes are counted honestly, it is democratic. If everybody votes, but the votes are not counted honestly, or if the voter is afraid of voting against the governing party, the country is undemocratic. It is true indeed that there is a considerable and important difference between free and ma-

---

[1] Quoted from J. R. M. Butler, *History of England*, Oxford University Press, London, 1928, p. 86.

nipulated elections, but noting this difference must not lead us to forget the fact that even free elections do not necessarily express "the will of the people." If a highly advertised brand of toothpaste is used by the majority of people because of some fantastic claims it makes in its propaganda, nobody with any sense would say that the people have "made a decision" in favor of the toothpaste. All that could be claimed is that the propaganda was sufficiently effective to coax millions of people into believing its claims.

In an alienated society the mode in which people express their will is not very different from that of their choice in buying commodities. They are listening to the drums of propaganda and facts mean little in comparison with the suggestive noise which hammers at them. In recent years we see more and more how the wisdom of public relations' counsels determines political propaganda. Accustomed to make the public buy anything for the build-up of which there is enough money, they think of political ideas and political leaders in the same terms. They use television to build up political personalities as they use it to build up a soap; what matters is the effect, in sales or votes, not the rationality or usefulness of what is presented. This phenomenon found a remarkably frank expression in recent statements about the future of the Republican Party. They are to the effect that since one cannot hope the majority of voters will vote for the Republican Party, one must find a personality who wants to represent the Party—then *he* will get the votes. In principle this is not different from the endorsement of a cigarette by a famous sportsman or movie actor.

Actually, the functioning of the political machinery in a democratic country is not essentially different from the procedure on the commodity market. The political parties are not too different from big commercial enterprises, and the professional politicians try to sell their wares to the public. Their method is more and more like that of high-pressure advertising. A particularly clear formulation of this process has been given by a keen observer of the political and economic scene, J. A. Schumpeter. He starts out with the formulation of the classical eighteenth-century concept of democracy. "The democratic method is that institutional arrangement for arriving at political decisions which realizes the common good by making the people itself decide issues through the election of individuals who are to assemble in order to carry out its will." [1] Schumpeter then analyzes modern man's attitudes toward the problem of public welfare, and arrives at a result not too different from the ones outlined above. "However, when we move still farther away from the private concerns of the family and the business office into those regions of national and international affairs that lack a direct and unmistakable link with those private concerns, individual volition, command of facts and method of inference soon cease to fulfill the requirements of the classical doctrine. What strikes me most of all and seems to me to be the core of the trouble is the fact that the sense of reality is so completely lost. Normally, the great political questions take their place in the psychic economy of the typical citizen with those leisure-hour interests that have not attained the rank of hobbies, and with the subjects of irresponsible conversation. These things seem so far off; they are not at all like a business proposition; dangers may not materialize at all and if they should they may not prove so very serious; one feels oneself to be moving in a fictitious world.

"This reduced sense of reality accounts not only for a reduced sense of responsibility but also for the absence of effective volition. One has one's phrases, of course, and one's wishes and daydreams

[1] Joseph A. Schumpeter, *Capitalism, Socialism, and Democracy,* Harper and Brothers New York and London, 1947, p. 250.

and grumbles; especially, one has one's likes and dislikes. But ordinarily they do not amount to what we call a will—the psychic counterpart of purposeful responsible action. In fact, for the private citizen musing over national affairs there is no scope for such a will and no task at which it could develop. He is a member of an unworkable committee, the committee of the whole nation, and this is why he expends less disciplined effort on mastering a political problem than he expends on a game of bridge.

"The reduced sense of responsibility and the absence of effective volition in turn explain the ordinary citizen's ignorance and lack of judgment in matters of domestic and foreign policy which are if anything more shocking in the case of educated people and of people who are successfully active in non-political walks of life than it is with uneducated people in humble situations. Information is plentiful and readily available. But this does not seem to make any difference. Nor should we wonder at it. We need only compare a lawyer's attitude to his brief and the same lawyer's attitude to the statements of political fact presented in his newspaper in order to see what is the matter. In the one case the lawyer has qualified for appreciating the relevance of his facts by years of purposeful labor done under the definite stimulus of interest in his professional competence; and under a stimulus that is no less powerful he then bends his acquirements, his intellect, his will to the contents of the brief. In the other case, he has not taken the trouble to qualify; he does not care to absorb the information or to apply to it the canons of criticism he knows so well how to handle; and he is impatient of long or complicated argument. All of this goes to show that without the initiative that comes from immediate responsibility, ignorance will persist in the face of masses of information however complete and correct. It persists even in the face of the meritorious efforts that are being made to go beyond presenting information and to teach the use of it by means of lectures, classes, discussion groups. Results are not zero. But they are small. People cannot be carried up the ladder.

"Thus the typical citizen drops down to a lower level of mental performance as soon as he enters the political field. He argues and analyzes in a way which he would readily recognize as infantile within the sphere of his real interests. He becomes a primitive again." [1]

Schumpeter too points to the similarity between the manufacturing of the popular will in political issues and that in commercial advertising. "The ways," he says, "in which issues and the popular will on any issue are being manufactured is exactly analogous to the ways of commercial advertising. We find the same attempts to contact the subconscious. We find the same technique of creating favorable and unfavorable associations which are the more effective the less rational they are. We find the same evasions and reticences and the same trick of producing opinion by reiterated assertion that is successful precisely to the extent to which it avoids rational argument and the danger of awakening the critical faculties of the people. And so on. Only, all these arts have infinitely more scope in the sphere of public affairs than they have in the sphere of private and professional life. The picture of the prettiest girl that ever lived will in the long run prove powerless to maintain the sales of a bad cigarette. There is no equally effective safeguard in the case of political decisions. Many decisions of fateful importance are of a nature that makes it impossible for the public to experiment with them at its leisure and at moderate cost. Even if that is possible, however, judgment is as a rule not so easy to arrive at as it is in the case of the cigarette, because effects are less easy to interpret." [2]

[1] *Ibid.*, pp. 261, 262.
[2] *Ibid.*, p. 263.

On the basis of his analysis, Schumpeter arrives at a definition of democracy which, while less lofty than the first one, is undoubtedly more realistic. "The democratic method is that institutional arrangement for arriving at political decisions *in which individuals acquire the power to decide by means of a competitive struggle for the people's vote*." [1] (My italics.)

The comparison between the process of opinion formation in politics with that in the commodity market can be supplemented with another one dealing not so much with the formation of opinion, but rather with its expression. I am referring to the role of the stockholder in America's big corporations, and of the influence of his will on the management.

As has been pointed out above, ownership in the big corporations rests today in the hands of hundreds of thousands of individuals, each of whom owns an exceedingly small fraction of the total stocks. Legally speaking, the stockholders own the enterprise and hence have the right to determine its policy and to appoint the management. Practically speaking, they feel little responsibility for their ownership, and acquiesce in what the management does, satisfied to have a regular income. The vast majority of the stockholders do not bother to go to the meetings and are willing to send the required proxies to the management. As has been pointed out above, only in 6 per cent of the big corporations (in 1930) is control exercised by total or majority ownership.

The situation of control in a modern democracy is not too different from the control in a big corporation. It is true, over 50 per cent of the voters cast their votes personally. They make the decision between two party machines competing for their votes. Once one of the machines is voted into office, the relationship to the voter becomes remote. The real decisions often do not lie any more with individual members of the parliament, representing the

[1] *Ibid.*, p. 269.

190

interests and wishes of their constituency, but with the party.[1] But even there decisions are made by influential key personalities, often little known to the public. The fact is that while the individual citizen believes that he directs the decisions of his country, he does it only a little more than the average stockholder participates in the controlling of "his" company. Between the act of voting and the most momentous high-level political decisions is a connection which is mysterious. One cannot say that there is none at all, nor can one say that the final decision is an outcome of the voter's will. This is exactly the situation of an alienated expression of the citizen's will. He does something, voting, and is under the illusion that he is the creator of decisions which he accepts as if they were his own, while in reality they are largely determined by forces beyond his control and knowledge. No wonder this situation gives the average citizen a deep sense of powerlessness in political matters (though not necessarily consciously so) and hence that his political intelligence is reduced more and more. For while it is true that one must think *before* one acts, it is also true that if one has no chance to act, the thinking becomes impoverished; in other words, if one cannot act effectively—one cannot think productively either.

3. *Alienation and Mental Health*

What is the effect of alienation on mental health? The answer depends of course on what is meant by health; if it means that man can fulfill his social function, carry on with production, and reproduce himself, alienated man can quite obviously be healthy. After all, we have created the most powerful production machine which has existed so far on earth—even though we have also created the most powerful destruction machine, accessible to the

---

[1] cf. R. H. S. Crossman's article "The Party Oligarchies," in *The New Statesman and Nation*, London, August 21, 1954.

grasp of the madman. If we look into the current psychiatric definition of mental health, then one should think too that we are healthy. Quite naturally the concepts of health and illness are the products of those men who formulate them—hence of the culture in which these men live. Alienated psychiatrists will define mental health in terms of the alienated personality, and therefore consider healthy what might be considered sick from the standpoint of normative humanism. In this respect what H. G. Wells has described so beautifully for the psychiatrists and surgeons in the "Country of the Blind," also holds true for many psychiatrists in our culture. The young man who has found an abode in an isolated tribe of congenitally blind people, is examined by their doctors.

"Then afterwards one of the elders, who thought deeply, had an idea. He was the great doctor among these people, their medicine-man, and he had a very philosophical and inventive mind, and the idea of curing Nunez of his peculiarities appealed to him. One day when Yacob was present he returned to the topic of Nunez.

" 'I have examined Bogota,' he said, 'and the case is clearer to me. I think very probably he might be cured.'

" 'That is what I have always hoped,' said old Yacob.

" 'His brain is affected,' said the blind doctor.

"The elders murmured assent.

" 'Now, *what* affects it?'

" 'Ah!' said old Yacob.

" '*This*,' said the doctor, answering his own question. 'Those queer things that are called the eyes, and which exist to make an agreeable soft depression in the face, are diseased, in the case of Bogota, in such a way as to affect his brain. They are greatly distended, he has eyelashes, and his eyelids move, and consequently his brain is in a state of constant irritation and distraction.'

" 'Yes?' said old Yacob. 'Yes?'

" 'And I think I may say with reasonable certainty that, in order to cure him completely, all that we need do is a simple and easy surgical operation—namely, to remove these irritant bodies.'

" 'And then he will be sane?'

" 'Then he will be perfectly sane, and a quite admirable citizen.'

" 'Thank Heaven for science!' said old Yacob, and went forth at once to tell Nunez of his happy hopes." [1]

Our current psychiatric definitions of mental health stress those qualities which are part of the alienated social character of our time: adjustment, co-operativeness, aggressiveness, tolerance, ambition, etc. I quoted above Strecker's definition of "maturity," as an illustration for the naïve translation of an ad for a junior executive into psychiatric parlance. But as was already briefly mentioned in another context, even one of the most profound and brilliant psychoanalysts of our period, H. S. Sullivan, was influenced in his theoretical concepts by the all pervasive alienation. Just because of his eminence and the important contribution he made to psychiatry, it will be enlightening to dwell somewhat on this point. Sullivan took the fact that the alienated person lacks a feeling of selfhood and experiences himself in terms of a response to the expectation of others, as part of human nature, just as Freud had taken the competitiveness characteristic of the beginning of the century as a natural phenomenon. Sullivan thus called the view that there exists a unique individual self the "delusion of unique individuality." [2] Equally clear is the influence of alienated thinking on his formulation of the basic needs of man. They are, according to him, "the need for personal

[1] H. G. Wells, *In the Days of the Comet and Seventeen Short Stories*, New York, Charles Scribner's Sons, 1925.

[2] H. S. Sullivan, *The Interpersonal Theory of Psychiatry*, W. W. Norton & Company, Inc., New York, 1953, p. 140.

security—that is for freedom from anxiety; the need for intimacy—that is, for collaboration with at least one other person; and the need for lustful satisfaction, which is concerned with genital activity in pursuit of the orgasm." [1] The three criteria for mental health which Sullivan postulates here are quite generally accepted. At first glance, nobody will have any quarrel with the idea that love, security and sexual satisfaction are perfectly normal goals of mental health. A critical examination of these concepts, however, shows that they mean something different in an alienated world than what they might have meant in other cultures.

Perhaps the most popular modern concept in the arsenal of psychiatric formulae is that of *security*. In recent years there is an increasing emphasis on the concept of security as the paramount aim of life, and as the essence of mental health. One reason for this attitude lies, perhaps, in the fact that the threat of war hanging over the world for many years has increased the longing for security. Another, more important reason, lies in the fact that people feel increasingly more insecure as the result of an increasing automatization and overconformity.

The problem becomes more complicated by the confusion between *psychic* and *economic* security. It is one of the fundamental changes of the last fifty years that in all Western countries the principle has been adopted that every citizen must have a minimum material security in case of unemployment, sickness and old age. Yet, while this principle has been adopted, there is still, among many businessmen, intense hostility against it, and especially its widening application; they speak contemptuously of the "welfare state" as killing private initiative and the spirit of adventure, and in fighting social security measures, they pretend to fight for the freedom and initiative of the worker. That these

[1] *Ibid.* p. 264.

arguments are sheer rationalizations is evidenced by the fact that the same people have no qualms about praising economic security as one of the chief aims of life. One needs only to read the advertisements of insurance companies, with their promises to free their customers from insecurity which could be caused by accidents, death, sickness, old age, etc., to be aware of the important role which the ideal of economic security plays for the moneyed class, and what else is the idea of saving, but practicing the aim of economic security? This contradiction between the denunciation of the striving for security among the working class, and the praise of the same aim for those in the higher income brackets is another example of man's unlimited capacity for thinking contradictory thoughts, without even making a feeble attempt to become aware of the contradiction.

Yet the propaganda against the "welfare state" and the principle of economic security is more effective than it would otherwise be, because of the widespread confusion between *economic* and *emotional* security.

Increasingly people feel that they should have no doubts, no problems, that they should have to take no risks, and that they should always feel "secure." Psychiatry and psychoanalysis have lent considerable support to this aim. Many writers in this field postulate security as the main aim of psychic development and consider a sense of security more or less equivalent with mental health. (Sullivan is the most profound and the most searching among these.) Thus parents, especially those who follow this literature, get worried that their little son or daughter may, at an early age, acquire a sense of "insecurity." They try to help them avoid conflicts, to make everything easy, to do away with as many obstacles as they can, in order to make the child feel "secure." Just as they try to inoculate the child against all illnesses, and to prevent it from getting in touch with any germ, they think they can banish insecurity by preventing any contact with it. The result is often as unfortunate as exaggerated hygiene sometimes is: once an infection occurs, the person becomes more vulnerable and helpless before it.

How can a sensitive and alive person ever feel secure? Because of the very conditions of our existence, we cannot feel secure about anything. Our thoughts and insights are at best partial truths, mixed with a great deal of error, not to speak of the unnecessary misinformation about life and society to which we are exposed almost from the day of birth. Our life and health are subject to accidents beyond our control. If we make a decision, we can never be certain of the outcome; any decision implies a risk of failure, and if it does not imply it, it has not been a decision in the true sense of the word. We can never be certain of the outcome of our best efforts. The result always depends on many factors which transcend our capacity of control. Just as a sensitive and alive person cannot avoid being sad, he cannot avoid feeling insecure. The psychic task which a person can and must set for himself, *is not to feel secure, but to be able to tolerate insecurity, without panic and undue fear.*

Life, in its mental and spiritual aspects, is by necessity insecure and uncertain. There is certainty only about the fact that we are born and that we shall die; there is complete security only in an equally complete submission to powers which are supposed to be strong and enduring, and which relieve man from the necessity of making decisions, taking risks, and having responsibilities. *Free man is by necessity insecure; thinking man by necessity uncertain.*

How, then, can man tolerate this insecurity inherent in human existence? One way is to be rooted in the group in such a way that the feeling of identity is guaranteed by the membership to the group, be it family, clan, nation, class. As long as the process of individualism has not reached a stage where the individual emerges from these primary bonds, he is still "we," and as long as the group functions he is certain of his own identity by his membership in it. The development of modern society has led to the dissolution of these primary bonds. Modern man is essentially alone, he is put on his own feet, expected to stand all by himself. He can achieve a sense of identity only by developing the unique and particular entity which is "he" to a point where he can truly sense "I am I." This accomplishment is possible only if he develops his active powers to such an extent that he can be related to the world without having to submerge in it; if he can achieve a productive orientation. The alienated person, however, tries to solve the problem in a different way, namely by conforming. He feels secure in being as similar as possible to his fellow man. His paramount aim is to be approved of by others; his central fear, that he may not be approved of. To be different, to find himself in a minority, are the dangers which threaten his sense of security; hence a craving for limitless conformity. It is obvious that this craving for conformity produces in turn a continuously operating, though hidden, sense of insecurity. Any deviation from the pattern, any criticism, arouses fear and insecurity; one is always dependent on the approval of others, just as a drug addict is dependent on his drug, and similarly, one's own sense of self and "self"-reliance becomes ever increasingly weaker. The sense of guilt, which some generations ago pervaded the life of man with reference to sin, has been replaced by a sense of uneasiness and inadequacy with regard to being different.

Another goal of mental health, *love*, like that of security, has assumed a new meaning in the alienated situation. For Freud, according to the spirit of his time, love was basically a sexual phenomenon. "Man having found by experience that sexual (genital) love afforded him his greatest gratification, so that it became in fact a prototype of all happiness to him, must have been thereby impelled to seek his happiness further along the path of sexual relations, to make genital eroticism the central point of his life. . . . In doing so he becomes to a very dangerous degree dependent on a part of the outer world, namely, on his chosen love object, and this exposes him to most painful suffering if he is rejected by it, or loses it by death or defection." [1] In order to protect himself from the danger of suffering by love, man, but only a "small minority," can transform the erotic functions of love by transferring "the main value from the fact of being loved to their own act of loving," and "by attaching their love not to individual objects, but to all men equally." Thus "they avoid the uncertainties and disappointments of genital love by turning away from its sexual aim and modifying the instinct into an impulse with an *inhibited aim*. . . . Love with an inhibited aim was indeed originally full sensual love, and in men's unconscious minds is so still." [2] The feeling of oneness and fusion with the world (the "oceanic feeling") which is the essence of religious experience and specifically of mystical experience, and the experience of oneness and union with the beloved person is interpreted by Freud as a regression to a state of an early "limitless narcissism." [3]

In accordance with his basic concepts, mental health for Freud is the full achievement of the capacity for love, which is attained if the libido development has reached the genital stage.

In H. S. Sullivan's psychoanalytic system we find, in contrast to Freud, a strict division between sexuality and love. What is the meaning of love and intimacy in Sullivan's concept? "In-

---

[1] S. Freud, *Civilization and Its Discontents, loc. cit.,* p. 69.
[2] *Ibid.,* p. 69 ff.
[3] *Ibid.,* p. 21.

timacy is that type of situation involving two people which permits validation of all components of personal worth. Validation of personal worth requires a type of relationship which I call collaboration, by which I mean clearly formulated adjustments of one's behavior to the expressed needs of the other person in the pursuit of increasingly identical—that is, more and more nearly mutual satisfactions, and in the maintenance of increasingly similar security operations." [1] Sullivan, putting it more simply, defined the essence of love as a situation of collaboration, in which two people feel: 'we play according to the rules of the game to preserve our prestige and feeling of superiority and merit.' [2]

Just as Freud's concept of love is a description of the experience of the patriarchal male in terms of nineteenth-century materialism, Sullivan's description refers to the experience of the alienated, marketing personality of the twentieth century. It is a description of an *"egotism à deux,"* of two people pooling their common interests, and standing together against a hostile and alienated world. Actually his definition of intimacy is in principle valid for the feeling of any co-operating team, in which everybody "adjusts his behavior to the expressed needs of the other person in the pursuit of common aims." (It is remarkable that Sullivan speaks here of *expressed* needs, when the least one could say about love is that it implies a reaction to *unexpressed* needs between two people.)

In more popular terms one can discover the marketing connotation of love in discussions on marital love and on the need for children for love and affection. In numerous articles, in counseling, in lectures, marital love is described as a state of

[1] *Ibid.*, p. 246.
[2] *Ibid.*, p. 246. Another definition of love by Sullivan, that love begins when a person feels another person's needs to be as important as his own, is less colored by the marketing aspect than the above mentioned formulation.

mutual fairness and mutual manipulation, called "understanding each other." The wife is supposed to consider the needs and sensibilities of the husband, and vice versa. If he comes home tired and disgruntled, she should not ask him questions—or should ask him questions—according to what the authors think is best for "oiling" him. And he should say appreciative words about her cooking or her new dress—and all this in the name of love. Every day now one can hear that a child must "get affection" in order to feel secure, or that another child "did not get enough love from his parents," and that is why he became a criminal or schizophrenic. Love and affection have assumed the same meaning as that of the formula for the baby, or the college education one should get, or the latest film one should "take in." You feed love, as you feed security, knowledge and everything else—and you have a happy person!

Happiness is another, and one of the more popular concepts by which mental health is defined today. As the formula runs in the *Brave New World*: "everybody is happy nowadays."

What is meant by happiness? Most people today would probably answer the question by saying that to be happy is to have "fun," or "to have a good time." The answer to the question, "What is fun?" depends somewhat on the economic situation of the individual, and more, on his education and personality structure. Economic differences, however, are not as important as they may seem. The "good time" of society's upper strata is the fun model for those not yet able to pay for it while earnestly hoping for that happy eventuality—and the "good time" of society's lower strata is increasingly a cheaper imitation of the upper strata's, differing in cost, but not so much in quality.

What does this fun consist in? Going to the movies, parties, ball games, listening to the radio and watching television, taking a ride in the car on Sundays, making love, sleeping late on Sunday mornings, and traveling, for those who can afford it. If we use a more respectable term, instead of the word "fun," and "having a good time," we might say that the concept of happiness is, at best, identified with that of pleasure. Taking into consideration our discussion of the problem of consumption, we can define the concept somewhat more accurately as the pleasure of unrestricted consumption, push-button power and laziness.

From this standpoint, happiness could be defined as the opposite of sadness or sorrow, and indeed, the average person defines happiness as a state of mind which is free from sadness or sorrow. This definition, however, shows that there is something profoundly wrong in this concept of happiness. A person who is alive and sensitive cannot fail to be sad, and to feel sorrow many times in his life. This is so, not only because of the amount of unnecessary suffering produced by the imperfection of our social arrangements, but because of the nature of human existence, which makes it impossible not to react to life with a good deal of pain and sorrow. Since we are living beings, we must be sadly aware of the necessary gap between our aspirations and what can be achieved in our short and troubled life. Since death confronts us with the inevitable fact that either we shall die before our loved ones or they before us—since we see suffering, the unavoidable as well as the unnecessary and wasteful, around us every day, how can we avoid the experience of pain and sorrow? The effort to avoid it is only possible if we reduce our sensitivity, responsiveness and love, if we harden our hearts and withdraw our attention and our feeling from others, as well as from ourselves.

If we want to define happiness by its opposite, we must define it not in contrast to *sadness,* but in contrast to *depression.*

What is depression? It is the inability to feel, it is the sense of being dead, while our body is alive. It is the inability to experience joy, as well as the inability to experience sadness. A depressed person would be greatly relieved if he could feel sad. A state of depression is so unbearable because one is incapable of feeling anything, either joy or sadness. If we try to define happiness in contrast to depression, we approach Spinoza's definition of joy and happiness as that state of intensified vitality that fuses into one whole our effort both to understand our fellow men and be one with them. Happiness results from the experience of productive living, and the use of the powers of love and reason which unite us with the world. Happiness consists in our touching the rock bottom of reality, in the discovery of our self and our oneness with others as well as our difference from them. Happiness is a state of intense inner activity and the experience of the increasing vital energy which occurs in productive relatedness to the world and to ourselves.

It follows that happiness cannot be found in the state of inner passivity, and in the consumer attitude which pervades the life of alienated man. Happiness is to experience fullness, not emptiness which needs to be filled. The average man today may have a good deal of fun and pleasure, but in spite of this, he is fundamentally depressed. Perhaps it clarifies the issue if instead of using the word "depressed" we use the word "bored." Actually there is very little difference between the two, except a difference in degree, because boredom is nothing but the experience of a paralysis of our productive powers and the sense of un-aliveness. Among the evils of life, there are few which are as painful as boredom, and consequently every attempt is made to avoid it.

It can be avoided in two ways; either fundamentally, by being productive, and in this manner experiencing happiness, or by trying to avoid its manifestations. The latter attempt seems to characterize the chasing after fun and pleasure in the average person today. He senses his depression and boredom, which becomes manifest when he is alone with himself or with those closest to him. All our amusements serve the purpose of making it easy for him to run away from himself and from the threatening boredom by taking refuge in the many ways of escape which our culture offers him; yet covering up a symptom does not do away with the conditions which produce it. Aside from the fear of physical illness, or of being humiliated by the loss of status and prestige, the fear of boredom plays a paramount role among the fears of modern man. In a world of fun and amusement, he is afraid of boredom, and glad when another day has passed without mishap, another hour has been killed without his having become aware of the lurking boredom.

From the standpoint of normative humanism we must arrive at a different concept of mental health; the very person who is considered healthy in the categories of an alienated world, from the humanistic standpoint appears as the sickest one—although not in terms of individual sickness, but of the socially patterned defect. Mental health, in the humanistic sense, is characterized by the ability to love and to create, by the emergence from the incestuous ties to family and nature, by a sense of identity based on one's experience of self as the subject and agent of one's powers, by the grasp of reality inside and outside of ourselves, that is, by the development of objectivity and reason. The aim of life is to live it intensely, to be fully born, to be fully awake. To emerge from the ideas of infantile grandiosity into the conviction of one's real though limited strength; to be able to accept the paradox that every one of us is the most important thing there is in the universe—and at the same time not more important than a fly or a blade of grass. To be able to love life, and yet to accept death without terror; to tolerate uncertainty about the most important questions with which life confronts us— and yet to have faith in our thought and feeling, inasmuch as they are truly ours. To be able to be alone, and at the same time one with a loved person, with every brother on this earth, with all that is alive; to follow the voice of our conscience, the voice that calls us to ourselves, yet not to indulge in self hate when the voice of conscience was not loud enough to be heard and followed. The mentally healthy person is the person who lives by love, reason and faith, who respects life, his own and that of his fellow man.

The alienated person, as we have tried to describe him in this chapter, cannot be healthy. Since he experiences himself as a thing, an investment, to be manipulated by himself and by others, he is lacking in a sense of self. This lack of self creates deep anxiety. The anxiety engendered by confronting him with the abyss of nothingness is more terrifying than even the tortures of hell. In the vision of hell, *I* am punished and tortured—in the vision of nothingness I am driven to the border of madness—because I cannot say "I" any more. If the modern age has been rightly called the age of anxiety, it is primarily because of this anxiety engendered by the lack of self. Inasmuch as "I am as you desire me"—*I* am *not*; I am anxious, dependent on approval of others, constantly trying to please. The alienated person feels inferior whenever he suspects himself of not being in line. Since his sense of worth is based on approval as the reward for con-. formity, he feels naturally threatened in his sense of self and in his self-esteem by any feeling, thought or action which could be suspected of being a deviation. Yet, inasmuch as he *is* human and not an automaton, he cannot help deviating, hence he must feel afraid of disapproval all the time. As a result he has to try all the harder to conform, to be approved of, to be successful. Not the voice of his conscience gives him strength and security but the feeling of not having lost the close touch with the herd.

Another result of alienation is the prevalence of a feeling of guilt. It is, indeed, amazing that in as fundamentally irreligious a culture as ours, the sense of guilt should be so widespread and deep-rooted as it is. The main difference from, let us say, a Calvinistic community, is the fact that the feeling of guilt is neither very conscious, nor does it refer to a religiously patterned concept of sin. But if we scratch the surface, we find that people feel guilty about hundreds of things; for not having worked hard enough, for having been too protective—or not protective enough—toward their children, for not having done enough for Mother, or for having been too kindhearted to a debtor; people feel guilty for having done good things, as well as for having done bad things; it is almost as if they had to find something to feel guilty about.

What could be the cause of so much guilt feeling? It seems that there are two main sources which, though entirely different in themselves, lead to the same result. The one source is the same as that from which the feelings of inferiority spring. Not to be like the rest, not to be totally adjusted, makes one feel guilty toward the commands of the great It. The other source of guilt feeling is man's one conscience; he senses his gifts or talents, his ability to love, to think, to laugh, to cry, to wonder and to create, he senses that his life is the one chance he is given, and that if he loses this chance he has lost everything. He lives in a world with more comfort and ease than his ancestors ever knew—yet he senses that, chasing after more comfort, his life runs through his fingers like sand. He cannot help feeling guilty for the waste, for the lost chance. This feeling of guilt is much less conscious than the first one, but one reinforces the other, the one often serving as a rationalization for the other. Thus, alienated man feels guilty for being himself, and for not being himself, for being alive and for being an automaton, for being a person and for being a thing.

Alienated man is unhappy. Consumption of fun serves to repress the awareness of his unhappiness. He tries to save time, and yet he is eager to kill the time he has saved. He is glad to have finished another day without failure or humiliation, rather than to greet the new day with the enthusiasm which only the "I am I" experience can give. He is lacking the constant flow of energy which stems from productive relatedness to the world.

Having no faith, being deaf to the voice of conscience, and having a manipulating intelligence but little reason, he is bewildered, disquieted and willing to appoint to the position of a leader anyone who offers him a total solution.

Can the picture of alienation be connected with any of the established pictures of mental illness? In answering this question we must remember that man has two ways of relating himself to the world. One in which he sees the world as he needs to see it in order to manipulate or use it. Essentially this is sense experience and common-sense experience. Our eye sees that which we have to see, our ear hears what we have to hear in order to live; our common sense perceives things in a manner which enables us to act; both senses and common sense work in the service of survival. In the matter of sense and common sense and for the logic built upon them, things are the same for all people because the laws of their use are the same.

The other faculty of man is to see things from within, as it were; subjectively, formed by *my* inner experience, feeling, mood.[1] Ten painters paint the same tree in one sense, yet they paint ten different trees in another. Each tree is an expression of their individuality while also being the same tree. In the dream we see the world entirely from within; it loses its objective meaning and is transformed into a symbol of our own purely individual experience. The person who dreams while

[1] See a more detailed discussion of this point in E. Fromm, *The Forgotten Language,* Rinehart & Company, Inc., New York, 1952.

awake, that is, the person who is in touch only with his inner world and who is incapable of perceiving the outer world in its objective-action context, is insane. The person who can only experience the outer world photographically, but is out of touch with his inner world, with himself, is the alienated person. Schizophrenia and alienation are complementary. In both forms of sickness one pole of human experience is lacking. If both poles are present, we can speak of the productive person, whose very productiveness results from the polarity between an inner and an outer form of perception.

Our description of the alienated character of contemporary man is somewhat one-sided; there are a number of positive factors which I have failed to mention. There is in the first place still a humanistic tradition alive, which has not been destroyed by the in-human process of alienation. But beyond that, there are signs that people are increasingly dissatisfied and disappointed with their way of life and trying to regain some of their lost selfhood and productivity. Millions of people listen to good music in concert halls or over the radio, an ever-increasing number of people paint, do gardening, build their own boats or houses, indulge in any number of "do it yourself" activities. Adult education is spreading, and even in business the awareness is growing that an executive should have reason and not only intelligence.[1]

But promising and real as all these trends are, they are not enough to justify an attitude which is to be found among a number of very sophisticated writers who claim that criticisms of our society, such as the one which has been offered here, are dated and old-fashioned; that we have already passed the peak of alienation and are now on our way to a better world. Appeal-

---

[1] An impressive example of this new trend is the course in literature and philosophy for junior executives of the Bell Telephone Co., under the directorship of Professors Morse Peckham and Rex Crawford at the University of Pennsylvania.

ing as this type of optimism is, it is nevertheless only a more sophisticated form of the defense of the status quo, a translation of the praise of the American Way of Life into the concepts of a cultural anthropology which, enriched by Marx and Freud, has "gone beyond" them and is reassuring man that there is no reason for serious worry..

VARIOUS OTHER DIAGNOSES

NINETEENTH CENTURY

The diagnosis of the illness of present-day Western culture, as we tried to give it in the previous chapter, is by no means new; its only claim toward furthering the understanding of the problem is the attempt to apply the concept of alienation more empirically to various observable phenomena, and to establish the connection between the illnesses of alienation and the humanistic concept of human nature and mental health. In fact, it is most remarkable that a critical view of twentieth-century society was already held by a number of thinkers living in the nineteenth century, long before the symptomatology which seems so apparent today had become fully manifest. It is also remarkable that their critical diagnosis and prognosis should have so much in common among themselves and with the critics of the twentieth century.

The prognosis of the decay and barbarism into which the twentieth century will sink was made by people of the most varied philosophical and political views. The Swiss conservative, Burckhardt; the Russian religious radical, Tolstoy; the French anarchist, Proudhon, as well as his conservative compatriot, Baudelaire; the American anarchist, Thoreau, and later his more politically minded compatriot, Jack London; the German revolutionary, Karl Marx—they all agreed in the most severe criticism of the modern culture and most of the them visualized the possibility of the advent of an age of barbarism. Marx's predictions were mitigated by his assumption that Socialism was a possible and even probable alternative to it. Burckhardt, from his conservative perspective, colored by the Swiss capacity for a stubborn refusal to be impressed by words and glamour, stated in a letter written in 1876, that perhaps Europe might still enjoy a few peaceful decades before it transformed itself by a number of terrible wars and revolutions into a new kind of Imperium Romanum, into a military and economic despotism: "The 20th century is chosen for everything else but for a true democracy." In 1872, Burckhardt writes to a friend: "I have a premonition which still sounds like folly, and yet it will not leave me alone: the military state must become a big industrialist. Those concentrations of people in the big workshops must not forever be left to their greed and want; the logical consequence would be a predetermined and supervised amount of misery with advancement and in uniform, begun and completed daily with the accompaniment of drums. . . . There is the prospect of long and voluntary submission to single leaders and usurpers. The people no longer believe in principles, but will probably periodically believe in saviours. Because of this reason, authority will again raise its head in the delightful 20th century and a frightful head it will be." [1]

In his prediction of systems like Fascism and Stalinism for the twentieth century, Burckhardt differs little from the predictions of the revolutionary Proudhon. The threat for the future

---

[1] J. Burckhardt's *Briefe*, ed. F. Kaplan, Leipzig, 1935, letters of April 26th, 1872; April 13, 1882; July 24, 1899. (My translation, E.F.)

is, Proudhon writes, ". . . a compact democracy having the appearance of being founded on the dictatorship of the masses, but in which the masses have no more power than is necessary to ensure a general serfdom in accordance with the following precepts and principles borrowed from the old absolutism: indivisibility of public power, all-consuming centralization, systematic destruction of all individual, corporative and regional thought (regarded as disruptive), inquisitorial police. . . ." "We should no longer deceive ourselves," he wrote. "Europe is sick of thought and order; it is entering into an era of brute force and contempt of principles." And later on: "Then the great war of the six great powers will begin. . . . Carnage will come and the enfeeblement that will follow these bloodbaths will be terrible. We shall not live to see the work of the new age, we shall fight in the darkness; we must prepare ourselves to endure this life without too much sadness, by doing our duty. Let us help one another, call to one another in the gloom, and practice justice wherever opportunity offers." And finally: "To-day civilization is in the grip of a crisis for which one can only find a single analogy in history—that is the crisis which brought the coming of Christianity. All the traditions are worn out, all the creeds abolished; but the new programme is not yet *ready,* by which I mean that it has not yet entered the consciousness of the masses. Hence what I call *the dissolution.* This is the cruellest moment in the life of societies. . . . I am under no illusions and do not expect to wake up one morning to see the resurrection of freedom in our country, as if by a stroke of magic. . . . No, no; decay, and decay for a period whose end I cannot fix and which will last for not less than one or two generations—is our lot. . . . I shall witness the evil only, I shall die in the midst of the darkness." [1]

[1] Quoted from E. Dolleans' *Proudhon,* Gallimard, Paris, 1948, p. 96 ff. (My translation, E.F.)

While Burckhardt and Proudhon visualized Fascism and Stalinism as the outcome of nineteenth-century culture (a prophecy repeated more specifically in 1907 by Jack London in his *Iron Heel*), others centered their diagnosis on the spiritual poverty and alienation of contemporary society, which, according to them must lead to an increasing dehumanization and decay of culture.

How similar are two statements made by two authors as different from each other as Baudelaire and Tolstoy. Baudelaire writes in 1851 in some fragments entitled "Fusées": "The world is drawing to a close. Only for one reason can it last longer: just because it happens to exist. But how weak a reason is this compared with all that forebodes the contrary, particularly with the question: What is left to the world of man in the future? Supposing it should continue materially, would that be an existence worthy of its name and of the historical dictionary? I do not say the world would fall back into a spectral condition and the odd disorder of South American republics; nor do I say that we should return to primitive savagery and, with a rifle in our arms, hunt for food through the grass-covered ruins of our civilization. No, such adventures would still call for a certain vital energy, an echo from primordial times. We shall furnish a new example of the inexorability of the spiritual and moral laws and shall be their new victims: *we shall perish by the very thing by which we fancy that we live.* Technocracy will Americanize us, progress will starve our spirituality so far that nothing of the bloodthirsty, frivolous or unnatural dreams of the utopist will be comparable to those positive facts. I invite any thinking person to show me what is left of life. Religion! It is useless to talk about it, or to look for its remnants; it is a scandal that one takes the trouble even of denying God. Private property! It was —strictly speaking—abolished with the suppression of the right of primogeniture; yet the time will come when mankind like a revengeful cannibal will snatch the last piece from those who rightfully deemed themselves the heirs of revolutions. And even this will not be the worst. . . . Universal ruin will manifest itself not solely or particularly in political institutions or general progress or whatever else might be a proper name for it; it will be seen, above all, in the baseness of hearts. Shall I add that that little left-over of sociability will hardly resist the sweeping brutality, and that the rulers, in order to hold their own and to produce a sham order, will ruthlessly resort to measures which will make us, who already are callous, shudder?" [1]

Tolstoy wrote some years later: "The medieval theology, or the Roman corruption of morals, poisoned only their own people, a small part of mankind; today, electricity, railways and telegraphs spoil the whole world. Everyone makes these things his own. He simply cannot help making them his own. Everyone suffers in the same way, is forced to the same extent to change his way of life. All are under the necessity of betraying what is most important for their lives, the understanding of life itself, religion. Machines—to produce what? The telegraph—to despatch what? Books, papers—to spread what kind of news? Railways—to go to whom and to what place? Millions of people herded together and subject to a supreme power—to accomplish what? Hospitals, physicians, dispensaries in order to prolong life—for what? How easily do individuals as well as whole nations take their own so-called civilization as the true civilization: finishing one's studies, keeping one's nails clean, using the tailor's and the barber's services, travelling abroad, and the most civilized man is complete. And with regard to nations: as many railways as possible, academies, industrial works, battleships, forts, newspapers, books, parties, parliaments. Thus the most civilized nation is complete.

[1] Quoted from K. Löwith, *Meaning in History*, The University of Chicago Press, Chicago, 1949, pp. 97, 98.

Enough individuals therefore, as well as nations, can be interested in civilization but not in true enlightenment. The former is easy and meets with approval; the latter requires rigorous efforts and therefore, from the great majority, always meets with nothing but contempt and hatred, for it exposes the lie of civilization." [1]

Less drastic, yet just as clear as the foregoing writer's, is Thoreau's criticism of modern culture. In his "Life without Principle" (1861) [2] he says: "Let us consider the way in which we spend our lives. This world is a place of business. What an infinite bustle! I am awaked almost every night by the panting of the locomotive. It interrupts my dreams. There is no sabbath. It would be glorious to see mankind at leisure for once. It is nothing but work, work, work. I cannot easily buy a blankbook to write thoughts in; they are commonly ruled for dollars and cents. An Irishman, seeing me making a minute in the fields, took it for granted that I was calculating my wages. If a man was tossed out of a window when an infant, and so made a cripple for life, or scared out of his wits by the Indians, it is regretted chiefly because he was thus incapacitated for—business! I think that there is nothing, not even crime, more opposed to poetry, to philosophy, ay, to life itself, than this incessant business. . . .

"If a man walk in the woods for love of them half of each day, he is in danger of being regarded as a loafer; but if he spends his whole day as a speculator, shearing off those woods and making earth bald before her time, he is esteemed an industrious and enterprising citizen. As if a town had no interest in its forests but to cut them down! . . .

"The ways by which you may get money almost without exception lead downward. To have done anything by which you

---

[1] Quoted from Löwith, *loc. cit.*, p. 99. From *Tolstois Flucht und Tod,* ed. by R. Fülöp-Miller and F. Eckstein, Berlin, 1925, p. 103.

[2] Published in *The Portable Thoreau,* ed. by Carl Bode, The Viking Press, New York, 1947, pp. 631–655.

earned money *merely* is to have been truly idle or worse. If the laborer gets no more than the wages which his employer pays him, he is cheated, he cheats himself. If you would get money as a writer or lecturer, you must be popular, which is to go down perpendicularly. . . .

"The aim of the laborer should be, not to get his living, to get 'a good job,' but to perform well a certain work; and, even in a pecuniary sense, it would be economy for a town to pay its laborers so well that they would not feel that they were working for low ends, as for a livelihood merely, but for scientific, or even moral ends. Do not hire a man who does your work for money, but him who does it for love of it. . . . The ways in which most men get their living, that is, live, are mere makeshifts, and a shirking of the real business of life—chiefly because they do not know, but partly because they do not mean, any better. . . ."

In summing up his views he says: "America is said to be the arena on which the battle of freedom is to be fought; but surely it cannot be freedom in a merely political sense that is meant. Even if we grant that the American has freed himself from a political tyrant, he is still the slave of an economical and moral tyrant. Now that the republic—*the res-publica*—has been settled, it is time to look after the *res-privata*—the private state—to see, as the Roman senate charged its consuls, '*ne quid res-privata detrimenti caperet*,' that the *private* state receive no detriment.

"Do we call this the land of the free? What is it to be free from King George and continue the slaves of King Prejudice? What is it to be born free and not to live free? What is the value of any political freedom, but as a means to moral freedom? Is it a freedom to be slaves, or a freedom to be free, of which we boast? We are a nation of politicians, concerned about the outmost defenses only of freedom. It is our children's children who may perchance be really free. We tax ourselves unjustly. There is a part of us which is not represented. It is taxation without representation. We quarter troops, we quarter fools and cattle of all sorts upon ourselves. We quarter our gross bodies on our poor souls, till the former eat up all the latter's substance. . . .

"Those things which now most engage the attention of men, as politics and the daily routine, are, it is true, vital functions of human society, but should be unconsciously performed, like the corresponding functions of the physical body. They are *infra*-human, a kind of vegetation. I sometimes awake to a half-consciousness of them going on about me, as a man may become conscious of some of the processes of digestion in a morbid state, and so have the dyspepsia, as it is called. It is as if a thinker submitted himself to be rasped by the great gizzard of creation. Politics is, as it were, the gizzard of society, full of grit and gravel, and the two political parties are its two opposite halves— sometimes split into quarters, it may be, which grind on each other. Not only individuals, but states, have thus a confirmed dyspepsia, which expresses itself, you can imagine by what sort of eloquence. Thus our life is not altogether a forgetting, but also, alas! to a great extent, a remembering, of that which we should never have been conscious of, certainly not in our waking hours. Why should we not meet, not always as dyspeptics, to tell our bad dreams, but sometimes as *eu*peptics, to congratulate each other on the ever-glorious morning? I do not make an exorbitant demand, surely."

One of the most penetrating diagnoses of the capitalist culture in the nineteenth century was made by a sociologist, E. Durkheim, who was neither a political nor a religious radical. He states that in modern industrial society the individual and the group have ceased to function satisfactorily; that they live in a condition of "anomie," that is, a lack of meaningful and structuralized social life; that the individual follows more and more "a restless movement, a planless self-development, an aim of living which has no criterion of value and in which happiness lies always in the future, and never in any present achievement." The ambition of man, having the whole world for his customer, becomes unlimited, and he is filled with disgust, with the "futility of endless pursuit." Durkheim points out that only the *political state* survived the French Revolution as a solitary factor of collective organization. As a result, a genuine social order has disappeared, the state emerging as the only collective organizing activity of a social character. The individual, free from all genuine social bonds, finds himself abandoned, isolated, and demoralized.[1] Society becomes *"a disorganized dust of individuals."* [2]

TWENTIETH CENTURY

Turning now to the twentieth century there is also a remarkable similarity in the criticisms and diagnosis of the mental ill health of contemporary society, just as in the nineteenth century, remarkable particularly in view of the fact that it comes from people with different philosophical and political views. Although I leave out from this survey most of the socialist critics of the nineteenth and twentieth centuries, because I shall deal with them separately in the next chapter, I shall begin here with the views of the British socialist, R. H. Tawney, because they are in many ways related to the views expressed in this book. In his classic work, *The Acquisitive Society* [3] (originally published under the title *The Sickness of an Acquisitive Society*), he points to the fact that the principle on which capitalistic society is based, is the domination of man by things. In our society, he

[1] Emil Durkheim, *Le Suicide*, Felix Alcan, Paris, 1897, p. 449.
[2] *Ibid.*, p. 448. (My italics, E.F.)
[3] R. H. Tawney, *The Acquisitive Society*, Harcourt, Brace & Company, Inc., New York, 1920.

says, ". . . even sensible men are persuaded that capital 'employs' labour, such as our pagan ancestors imagined that the other pieces of wood and iron, which they deified in their day, sent their crops, and won their battles. When men have gone so far as to talk as though their idols have come to life, it is time that someone broke them. Labour consists of persons, capital of things. The only use of things is to be applied to the service of persons."[1] He points out that the worker in modern industry does not give his best energies because he lacks in interest in his work, owing to his nonparticipation in control.[2] He postulates, as the only way out of the crisis of modern society, a change in moral values. It is necessary to assign ". . . to economic activity itself its proper place as the servant, not a master, of society. The burden of our civilization is not merely, as many suppose, that the product of industry is ill-distributed, or its conduct tyrannical, or its operation interrupted by embittered disagreements. It is that industry itself has come to hold a position of exclusive predominance among human interests, which no single interest, and least of all the provision of the material means of existence, is fit to occupy. Like a hypochondriac who is so absorbed in the processes of his own digestion that he goes to his grave before he has begun to live, industrialized communities neglect the very objects for which it is worth while to acquire riches in their feverish preoccupation with the means by which riches can be acquired.

"That obsession by economic issues is as local and transitory as it is repulsive and disturbing. To future generations it will appear as pitiable as the obsession of the seventeenth century by religious quarrels appears to-day; indeed, it is less rational, since the object with which it is concerned is less important. And it is a poison which inflames every wound and turns each trivial

[1] *Ibid.*, p. 99.
[2] *Ibid.*, pp. 106, 107.

scratch into a malignant ulcer. Society will not solve the particular problems of industry which afflict it, until that poison is expelled, and it has learned to see industry itself in the right perspective. If it is to do that, it must rearrange its scale of values. It must regard economic interests as one element in life, not as the whole of life. It must persuade its members to renounce the opportunity of gains which accrue without any corresponding service, because the struggle for them keeps the whole community in a fever. It must so organize industry that the instrumental character of economic activity is emphasized by its subordination to the social purpose for which it is carried on." [1]

One of the most outstanding contemporary students of the industrial civilization in the United States, Elton Mayo, shared, although somewhat more cautiously, Durkheim's viewpoint. "It is true," he said, "that the problem of social disorganization, with its consequent *anomie*, probably exists in a more acute form in Chicago than in other parts of the United States. It is probable that it is a more immediate issue in the United States than in Europe. But it is a problem of order in social development with which the whole world is concerned." [2] Discussing the modern preoccupation with economic activities, Mayo says: "Just as our political and economic studies have for 200 years tended to take account only of the economic functions involved in living, so also in our actual living we have inadvertently allowed pursuit of economic development to lead us in a condition of extensive social disintegration. . . . It is probable that the work a man does represents his most important function in the society; but unless there is some sort of integral social background to his life, he cannot even assign a value to his work. Durkheim's findings in

[1] *Ibid.*, pp. 183, 184.
[2] E. Mayo, *The Human Problems of an Industrial Civilization*, The Macmillan Company, New York, 1933, p. 125.

19th century France would seem to apply to 20th century America." [1] Referring to his comprehensive study of the attitude of the Hawthorne workers toward their work, he comes to the following conclusion: "The failure of workers and supervisors to understand their work and working conditions, the wide-spread sense of personal futility is general to the civilized world, and not merely characteristic of Chicago. The belief of the individual in his social function and solidarity with the group—his capacity for collaboration in work—these are disappearing, destroyed in part by rapid scientific and technical advance. With this belief, his sense of security and of well-being also vanishes, and he begins to manifest those exaggerated demands of life which Durkheim has described." [2] Mayo not only agrees with Durkheim in the essential point of his diagnosis, but he also comes to the critical conclusion that in the half century of scientific effort after Durkheim, very little progress has been made in the understanding of the problem. "Whereas" he writes, "in the material and scientific spheres we have been careful to develop knowledge and technique, in the human and socio-political, we have contented ourselves with haphazard guess and opportunist fumbling." [3] And further, ". . . we are faced with the fact, then, that in the important domain of human understanding and control we are ignorant of the facts and their nature; our opportunism in administration and social enquiry has left us incapable of anything but impotent inspection of a cumulative disaster. . . . So we are compelled to wait for the social organism to recover or perish, without adequate medical aid." [4] Speaking more specifically of the backwardness of our political theory, he states: "Political theory has tended to relate itself for the most part to its historic origins;

[1] *Ibid.*, p. 131.
[2] *Ibid.*, p. 159.
[3] *Ibid.*, p. 132.
[4] *Ibid.*, pp. 169, 170.

it has failed to originate and sustain a vigorous enquiry into the changing structure of society. In the meantime the social context, the actual condition of civilized peoples has undergone so great a variety of changes that any mere announcement of the ancient formulae rings hollow and carries no conviction to anyone." [1]

Another thoughtful student of the contemporary social scene, F. Tannenbaum, arrives at conclusions which are not unrelated to those of Tawney, in spite of the fact that Tannenbaum emphasizes the central role of the trade union, in contrast to Tawney's socialist insistence on the direct participation of the workers. Concluding his "Philosophy of Labor," Tannenbaum writes: "The major error of the last century has been the assumption that a total society can be organized upon an economic motive, upon profit. The trade-union has proved that notion to be false. It has demonstrated once again that men do not live by bread alone. Because the corporation can offer only bread or cake, it has proved incompetent to meet the demands for the good life. The union, with all its faults, may yet save the corporation and its great efficiencies by incorporating it into its own natural 'society,' its own cohesive labor force, and by endowing it with the meanings that all real societies possess, meanings that give some substance of idealism to man in his journey between the cradle and the grave. Those meanings cannot be embraced by expanding the economic motive. If the corporation is to survive, it will have to be endowed with a moral role in the world, not merely an economic one. From this point of view, the challenge to management by the trade-union is salutary and hopeful. It is a route, perhaps the only available one, for saving the values of our democratic society, and the contemporary industrial system as well. In some way the corporation and its labor

[1] *Ibid.*, p. 138.

force must become one corporate group and cease to be a house divided and seemingly at war." [1]

Lewis Mumford, with whose writings my own ideas have many points in common, says this about our contemporary civilization: "The most deadly criticism one could make of modern civilization is that apart from its man-made crises and catastrophes, it is not humanly *interesting*. . . .

"In the end, such a civilization can produce only a mass man: incapable of choice, incapable of spontaneous, self-directed activities: at best patient, docile, disciplined to monotonous work to an almost pathetic degree, but increasingly irresponsible as his choices become fewer and fewer: finally, a creature governed mainly by his conditioned reflexes—the ideal type desired, if never quite achieved, by the advertising agency and the sales organizations of modern business, or by the propaganda office and the planning bureaus of totalitarian and quasi-totalitarian governments. The handsomest encomium for such creatures is: 'They do not make trouble'. Their highest virtue is: 'They do not stick their necks out'. Ultimately, such a society produces only two groups of men: the conditioners and the conditioned; the active and the passive barbarians. The exposure of this web of falsehood, self-deception, and emptiness is perhaps what made *Death of a Salesman* so poignant to the metropolitan American audiences that witnessed it.

"Now this mechanical chaos is plainly not self-perpetuating, for it affronts and humiliates the human spirit; and the tighter and more efficient it becomes as a mechanical system, the more stubborn will be the human reaction against it. Eventually, it must drive modern man to blind rebellion, to suicide, or to renewal: and so far it has worked in the first two ways. On this

[1] Frank Tannenbaum, *A Philosophy of Labor*, Alfred A. Knopf, Inc., New York, 1952, p. 168.

analysis, the crisis we now face would be inherent in our culture even if it had not, by some miracle, also unleashed the more active disintegrations that have taken place in recent history." [1]

A. R. Heron, a convinced supporter of Capitalism and a writer with a much more conservative bent than the ones quoted so far, nevertheless comes to critical conclusions which are essentially very close to those of Durkheim and Mayo. In his *Why Men Work,* a 1948 selection of the Executive Book Club of New York, he writes: "It is fantastic to picture a great multitude of workers committing mass suicide because of boredom, a sense of futility, and frustration. But the fantastic nature of the picture disappears when we broaden our concept of suicide beyond the killing of the physical life of the body. The human being who has resigned himself to a life devoid of thinking, ambition, pride, and personal achievement, has resigned himself to the death of attributes which are distinctive elements of human life. Filling a space in the factory or office with his physical body, making motions designed by the minds of others, applying physical strength, or releasing the power of steam or electricity, are not in themselves contributions of the essential abilities of human beings.

"This inadequate demand upon human abilities can be no more forcibly indicated than by reference to modern techniques for the placement of workers. Experience has shown that there are jobs, a startling number of them, which cannot be satisfactorily filled by persons of average or superior intelligence. It is no answer to say that large numbers of persons with inferior intelligence need the jobs. Management shares responsibility with statesmen, ministers, and educators for the improvement of the intelligence of all of us. We shall always be governed in a democ-

---

[1] L. Mumford, *The Conduct of Life,* Harcourt, Brace & Company, New York, 1951, pp. 14 and 16.

racy by the votes of people as people, including those whose native intelligence is low or whose potential mental and spiritual development have been cramped.

"We must never abandon the material benefits we have gained from technology and mass production and specialization of tasks. But we shall never achieve the ideals of America if we create a class of workers denied the satisfactions of significant work. We shall not be able to maintain those ideals if we do not apply every tool of government, education, and industry to the improvement of the human abilities of those who are our rulers —the tens of millions of ordinary men and women. The part of this task assigned to management is the provision of working conditions which will release the creative instinct of every worker, and which will give play to his divine-human ability to think." [1]

After having heard the voices of various social scientists, let us conclude this chapter by listening to three men outside of the field of social science: A. Huxley, A. Schweitzer, and A. Einstein. Huxley's indictment of twentieth-century Capitalism is contained in his *Brave New World*. In this novel (1931), he describes a picture of an automatized world which is clearly insane and yet which only in details and somewhat in degree is different from the reality of 1954. The only alternative he sees is the life of the savage with a religion which is half fertility cult and half penitente ferocity. In a foreword written for the new edition of the *Brave New World* (1946) he writes: "Assuming, then, that we are capable of learning as much from Hiroshima as our forefathers learned from Magdeburg, we may look forward to a period, not indeed of peace, but of limited and only partially ruinous warfare. During that period it may

[1] A. R. Heron, *Why Men Work*, Stanford University Press, Stanford, 1948, pp. 121, 122.

be assumed that nuclear energy will be harnessed to industrial uses. The result, pretty obviously, will be a series of economic and social changes unprecedented in rapidity and completeness. All the existing patterns of human life will be disrupted and new patterns will have to be improvised to conform with the non-human fact of atomic power. Procrustes in modern dress, the nuclear scientist will prepare the bed on which mankind must lie; and if mankind doesn't fit—well, that will be just too bad for mankind. There will have to be some stretching and a bit of amputation—the same sort of stretching and amputation as have been going on ever since applied science really got into its stride, only this time they will be a good deal more drastic than in the past. These far from painless operations will be directed by highly centralized totalitarian governments. Inevitably so; for the immediate future is likely to resemble the immediate past, and in the immediate past rapid technological changes, taking place in a mass-producing economy and among a population predominantly propertyless, have always tended to produce economic and social confusion. To deal with confusion, power has been centralized and government control increased. It is probable that all the world's governments will be more or less completely totalitarian even before the harnessing of atomic energy; that they will be totalitarian during and after the harnessing seems almost certain. *Only a large-scale popular movement toward decentralization and self-help can arrest the present tendency toward statism.*[1] At present there is no sign that such a movement will take place.

"There is, of course, no reason why the new totalitarianisms should resemble the old. Government by clubs and firing squads, by artificial famine, mass imprisonment and mass deportation, is not merely inhumane (nobody cares much about that nowa-

[1] My italics. E.F.

days) ; it is demonstrably inefficient—and in an age of advanced technology, inefficiency is the sin against the Holy Ghost. A really efficient totalitarian state would be one in which the all-powerful executive of political bosses and their army of managers control a population of slaves who do not have to be coerced, because they love their servitude. To make them love it is the task assigned, in present-day totalitarian states, to ministries of propaganda, newspaper editors and schoolteachers. But their methods are still crude and unscientific. The old Jesuits' boast that, if they were given the schooling of the child, they could answer for the man's religious opinions, was a product of wishful thinking. And the modern pedagogue is probably rather less efficient at conditioning his pupils' reflexes than were the reverend fathers who educated Voltaire. The greatest triumphs of propaganda have been accomplished, not by doing something, but by refraining from doing. Great is the truth, but still greater, from a practical point of view, is silence about truth. By simply not mentioning certain subjects, by lowering what Mr. Churchill calls an 'iron curtain' between the masses and such facts or arguments as the local political bosses regard as undesirable, totalitarian propagandists have influenced opinion much more effectively than they could have done by the most eloquent denunciations, the most compelling of logical rebuttals. But silence is not enough. If persecution, liquidation and other symptoms of social friction are to be avoided, the positive sides of propaganda must be made as effective as the negative. The most important Manhattan Projects of the future will be vast government-sponsored enquiries into what the politicians and the participating scientists will call "the problem of happiness"—in other words, the problem of making people love their servitude. Without economic security, the love of servitude cannot possibly come into existence; for the sake of brevity, I assume that the all-powerful executive and its managers will succeed in solving the problem of permanent security. But security tends very quickly to be taken for granted. Its achievement is merely a superficial, external revolution. The love of servitude cannot be established except as the result of a deep, personal revolution in human minds and bodies. To bring about that revolution we require, among others, the following discoveries and inventions. First, a greatly improved technique of suggestion—through infant conditioning and, later, with the aid of drugs, such as scopolamine. Second, a fully developed science of human differences, enabling government managers to assign any given individual to his or her proper place in the social and economic hierarchy. (Round pegs in square holes tend to have dangerous thoughts about the social system and to infect others with their discontents.) Third (since reality, however utopian, is something from which people feel the need of taking pretty frequent holidays), a substitute for alcohol and the other narcotics, something at once less harmful and more pleasure-giving than gin or heroin. And fourth (but this would be a long-term project, which would take generations of totalitarian control to bring to a successful conclusion), a foolproof system of eugenics, designed to standardize the human product and so to facilitate the task of the managers. In *Brave New World* this standardization of the human product has been pushed to fantastic, though not perhaps impossible, extremes. Technically and ideologically we are still a long way from bottled babies and Bokanovsky groups of semi-morons. But by A.F. 600, who knows what may not be happening? Meanwhile the other characteristic features of that happier and more stable world—the equivalents of soma and hypnopaedia and the scientific caste system—are probably not more than three or four generations away. Nor does the sexual promiscuity of *Brave New World* seem so very distant. There are already certain American cities in which the number of divorces is equal to the number of marriages. In a few years, no doubt, marriage licenses will be sold like dog licenses, good for a period of twelve months, with no law against changing dogs or keeping more than one animal at a time. As political and economic freedom diminishes, sexual freedom tends compensatingly to increase. And the dictator (unless he needs cannon fodder and families with which to colonize empty or conquered territory) will do well to encourage that freedom. In conjunction with the freedom to daydream under the influence of dope and movies and the radio, it will help to reconcile his subjects to the servitude which is their fate.

"All things considered, it looks as though Utopia were far closer to us than anyone, only fifteen years ago, could have imagined. Then, I projected it six hundred years into the future. To-day, it seems quite possible that the horror may be upon us within a single century. That is, if we refrain from blowing ourselves to smithereens in the interval. Indeed, unless we choose to decentralize and to use applied science, not as the end to which human beings are to be made the means, but as the means to producing a race of free individuals, we have only two alternatives to choose from: either a number of national, militarized totalitarianisms, having as their root the terror of the atomic bomb and as their consequence the destruction of civilization (or, if the warfare is limited, the perpetuation of militarism); or else one supra-national totalitarianism, called into existence by the social chaos resulting from rapid technological progress in general and the atom revolution in particular, and developing, under the need for efficiency and stability, into the welfare-tyranny of Utopia. You pays your money and you takes your choice." [1]

[1] A. Huxley, *Brave New World*, The Vanguard Library, London, 1952, pp. 11–15.

Albert Schweitzer and Albert Einstein, who perhaps more than any living person manifest the highest development of the intellectual and moral traditions of Western culture have this to say on present-day culture.

Albert Schweitzer writes: "A new public opinion must be created privately and unobtrusively. The existing one is maintained by the press, by propaganda, by organization, and by financial and other influences which are at its disposal. This unnatural way of spreading ideas must be opposed by the natural one, which goes from man to man and relies solely on the truth of our thoughts and the hearer's receptiveness for new truth. Unarmed, and following the human spirit's primitive and natural fighting method, it must attack the other, which faces it, as Goliath faced David, in the mighty armour of the age.

"About the struggle which must needs ensue no historical analogy can tell us much. The past has, no doubt, seen the struggle of the free-thinking individual against the fettered spirit of a whole society, but the problem has never presented itself on the scale on which it does to-day, because the fettering of the collective spirit as it is fettered to-day by modern organizations, modern unreflectiveness, and modern popular passions, is a phenomenon without precedent in history.

"Will the man of to-day have strength to carry out what the spirit demands from him, and what the age would like to make impossible?

"In the over-organized societies which in a hundred ways have him in their power, he must somehow become once more an independent personality and so exert influence back upon them. They will use every means to keep him in that condition of impersonality which suits them. They fear personality because the spirit and the truth, which they would like to muzzle, find in it a means of expressing themselves. And their power is, unfortunately, as great as their fear.

"There is a tragic alliance between society as a whole and its economic conditions. With a grim relentlessness those conditions tend to bring up the man of to-day as a being without freedom, without self-collectedness, without independence, in short as a human being so full of deficiencies that he lacks the qualities of humanity. And they are the last things that we can change. Even if it should be granted us that the spirit should begin its work, we shall only slowly and incompletely gain power over these forces. There is, in fact, being demanded from the will that which our conditions of life refuse to allow.

"And how heavy the tasks that the spirit has to take in hand! It has to create the power of understanding the truth that is really true where at present nothing is current but propagandist truth. It has to depose ignoble patriotism, and enthrone the noble kind of patriotism which aims at ends that are worthy of the whole of mankind, in circles where the hopeless issues of past and present political activities keep nationalist passions aglow even among those who in their hearts would fain be free from them. It has to get the fact that civilization is an interest of all men and of humanity as a whole recognized again in places where national civilization is to-day worshipped as an idol, and the notion of a humanity with a common civilization lies broken to fragments. It has to maintain our faith in the civilized State, even though our modern States, spiritually and economically ruined by the war, have no time to think about the tasks of civilization, and dare not devote their attention to anything but how to use every possible means, even those which undermine the conception of justice, to collect money with which to prolong their own existence. It has to unite us by giving us a single ideal of civilized men, and this in a world where one nation has robbed its neighbour of all faith in humanity, idealism, righteousness, reasonableness, and truthfulness, and all alike have come under the domination of powers which are plunging us ever deeper into barbarism. It has to get attention concentrated on civilization while the growing difficulty of making a living absorbs the masses more and more in material cares, and makes all other things seem to them to be mere shadows. It has to give us faith in the possibility of progress while the reaction of the economic on the spiritual becomes more pernicious every day and contributes to an ever growing demoralization. It has to provide us with reasons for hope at a time when not only secular and religious institutions and associations, but the men, too, who are looked upon as leaders, continually fail us, when artists and men of learning show themselves as supporters of barbarism, and notabilities who pass for thinkers, and behave outwardly as such, are revealed, when crises come, as being nothing more than writers and members of academies.

"All these hindrances stand in the path of the will to civilization. A dull despair hovers about us. How well we now understand the men of the Greco-Roman decadence, who stood before events incapable of resistance, and, leaving the world to its fate, withdrew upon their inner selves! Like them, we are bewildered by our experience of life. Like them, we hear enticing voices which say to us that the one thing which can still make life tolerable is to live for the day. We must, we are told, renounce every wish to think or hope about anything beyond our own fate. We must find rest in resignation.

"The recognition that civilization is founded on some sort of theory of the universe, can be restored only through a spiritual awakening, and a will for ethical good in the mass of mankind, compels us to make clear to ourselves those difficulties in the way of a rebirth of civilization which ordinary reflection would overlook. But at the same time it raises us above all considerations of possibility or impossibility. If the ethical spirit provides a sufficient standing ground in the sphere of events for making civilization a reality, then we shall get back to civilization, if we return to a suitable theory of the universe and the convictions to which this properly gives birth." [1]

In a short article, "Why Socialism," Einstein writes: "I have now reached the point where I may indicate briefly what to me constitutes the essence of the crisis of our time. It concerns the relationship of the individual to society. The individual has become more conscious than ever of his dependence upon society. But he does not experience this dependence as a positive asset, as an organic tie, as a protective force, but rather as a threat to his natural rights, or even to his economic existence. Moreover, his position in society is such that the egotistical drives of his make-up are constantly being accentuated, while his social drives, which are by nature weaker, progressively deteriorate. All human beings, whatever their position in society, are suffering from this process of deterioration. Unknowingly prisoners of their own egotism, they feel insecure, lonely, and deprived of the naïve, simple, and unsophisticated enjoyment of life. Man can find meaning in life, short and perilous as it is, only through devoting himself to society." [2]

[1] Quoted from *Man and God*, by V. Gollancz, Houghton Mifflin Company, Boston, 1951, p. 216 ff.

[2] A. Einstein, "Why Socialism," in *Monthly Review*, Vol. I, i 1949, pp. 9–15.

7

VARIOUS ANSWERS

In the nineteenth century men with vision saw the process of decay and dehumanization behind the glamour and wealth and political power of Western society. Some of them were resigned to the necessity of such a turn toward barbarism, others stated an alternative. But whether they took the one or the other position, their criticism was based on a religious-humanistic concept of man and history. By criticizing their own society they transcended it. They were not relativists who said, as long as the society functions it is a sane and good society—and as long as the individual is adjusted to his society he is a sane and healthy individual. Whether we think of Burckhardt or Proudhon, of Tolstoy or Baudelaire, of Marx or Kropotkin, they had a concept of man which was essentially a religious and moral one. Man is the end, and must never be used as a means; material production is for man, not man for material production; the aim of life is the unfolding of man's creative powers; the aim of history is a transformation of society into one governed by justice and truth—these are the principles on which explicitly and implicitly, all criticism of modern Capitalism was based.

These religious-humanistic principles were also the basis for the proposals for a better society. In fact, the main expression of religious enthusiasm in the last two hundred years is to be found exactly in those movements which had broken with traditional religion. Religion as an organization and a profession of dogma was carried on in the churches; religion in the sense of religious fervor and living faith was largely carried on by the anti-religionists.

In order to give more substance to the statements just made, it is necessary to consider some salient features in the development of Christian Western culture. While for the Greeks history had no aim, purpose or end, the Judaeo-Christian concept of history was characterized by the idea that its inherent meaning was the salvation of man. The symbol for this final salvation was the Messiah; the time itself, the Messianic time. There are, however, two different concepts of what constitutes the *eschaton,* the "end of days," the aim of history. One connects the biblical myth of Adam and Eve with the concept of salvation. Briefly stated, the essence of this idea is that originally man was one with nature. There was no conflict between him and nature, or between man and woman. But man also lacked the most essential human trait: that of knowledge of good and evil. Hence he was incapable of free decision and responsibility. The first act of disobedience became also the first act of freedom, thus the beginning of human history. Man is expelled from paradise, he has lost his harmony with nature, he is put on his own feet. But he is weak, his reason is still undeveloped, his power to resist temptation is still small. He has to develop his reason, to grow into full humanity in order to achieve a new harmony with nature, with himself and with his fellow men. The aim of history is the full birth of man, his full humanization. Then "the earth shall be full of the knowledge of the Lord, as the waters cover the sea." All nations will form a single community and swords will be transformed into ploughs. In this concept, God does not perform an act of grace. Man has to go through many errors, he has to sin and to take the consequences. God does not solve his problems for him except by revealing to him the aims of life. Man has to achieve his own salvation, he has to give birth to himself, and at the end of the days, the new harmony, the new peace [1] will be established, the curse pronounced against Adam and Eve will be repealed, as it were, by man's own unfolding in the historical process.

The other Messianic concept of salvation, which became predominant in the Christian Church, is that man can never absolve himself from the corruption he underwent as a consequence of Adam's disobedience. Only God, by an act of grace, can save man, and He saved him by becoming human in the person of Christ, who died the sacrificial death of the Saviour. Man, through the sacraments of the church, becomes a participant in this salvation—and thus obtains the gift of God's grace. The end of history is the second coming of Christ—which is a supernatural and not a historical event.

This tradition continued in that part of the Western world in which the Catholic Church remained dominant. But for the rest of Europe and America in the eighteenth and nineteenth centuries, theological thinking lost more and more in vitality. The age of enlightenment was characterized by its fight against the Church, and clericalism, and the further development by a growing doubt and eventually the negation of all religious concepts. But this negation of religion was only a new form of thought expressing the old religious enthusiasm, especially as far as the meaning and purpose of history was concerned. In the name of reason and happiness, of human dignity and freedom, the Messianic idea found a new expression.

[1] In Hebrew "Schalom" means both harmony (completeness) and peace.

In France, Condorcet, in his *Esquisse d'un Tableau Historique des Progrès de l'Esprit Humain* (1793), laid the foundation for the faith in the eventual perfection of the human race, which would bring about a new era of reason and happiness, and to which there were no limitations. The coming of the Messianic realm was Condorcet's message, which was to influence St. Simon, Comte and Proudhon. Indeed, the fervor of the French Revolution was Messianic fervor in secular language.

In German enlightenment philosophy the same translation from the theological concept of salvation into secular language occurred. Lessing's *Die Erziehung des Menschengeschlechts* became most influential on German, but also on French thinking. To Lessing the future was to be the age of reason and self-realization, brought about by the education of mankind, thus realizing the promise of Christian revelation. Fichte believed in the coming of a spiritual millenium, Hegel in the realization of God's realm in history, thus translating Christian theology into this-worldly philosophy. Hegel's philosophy found its most significant historical continuation in Marx. More clearly perhaps than that of many other enlightenment philosophers, Marx' thought is Messianic-religious, in secular language. All past history is only "prehistory," it is the history of self-alienation; with Socialism the realm of *human* history, of human freedom will be ushered in. The classless society of justice, brotherliness and reason will be the beginning of a new world, toward the formation of which all previous history was moving.[1]

While it is the main purpose of this chapter to present the ideas of Socialism as the most important attempt to find an answer to the ills of Capitalism, I shall first discuss briefly the Totalitarian answers, and one which may be properly called Super-Capitalism.

[1] Cf. K. Löwith, *loc. cit.*, p. 191 ff.

AUTHORITARIAN IDOLATRY

Fascism, Nazism and Stalinism have in common that they offered the atomized individual a new refuge and security. These systems are the culmination of alienation. The individual is made to feel powerless and insignificant, but taught to project all his human powers into the figure of the leader, the state, the "fatherland," to whom he has to submit and whom he has to worship. He escapes from freedom into a new idolatry. All the achievements of individuality and reason, from the late Middle Ages to the nineteenth century are sacrificed on the altars of the new idols. The new systems were built on the most flagrant lies, both with regard to their programs and to their leaders. In their program they claimed to fulfill some sort of Socialism, when what they were doing was the negation of everything that was meant by this word in the socialist tradition. The figures of their leaders only emphasize the great deception. Mussolini, a cowardly braggart, became a symbol for manliness and courage. Hitler, a maniac of destruction, was praised as the builder of a new Germany. Stalin, a cold-blooded, ambitious schemer, was painted as the loving father of his people.

Nevertheless, in spite of the common element, one must not ignore certain important differences between the three forms of dictatorship. Italy, industrially the weakest of the great *Western* European powers, remained relatively weak and powerless in spite of her victory in the First World War. Her upper classes were unwilling to undertake any of the necessary reforms, especially in the agricultural sphere, and her population was seized by a deep dissatisfaction with the status quo. Fascism was to cure the hurt national vanity by its bragging slogans and to channel the resentment of the masses away from its original objectives; at the same time, it wanted to convert Italy into a more advanced industrial power. It failed in all its realistic aims, because Fascism never made a serious attempt to solve the pressing economic and social problems of Italy.

Germany, on the contrary, was the most developed and progressive industrial country in Europe. While Fascism could have had at least an economic function, Nazism had none. It was the insurrection of the lower middle class, and jobless officers and students, based on the demoralization brought about by military defeat and inflation, and more specifically by the mass unemployment during the depression after 1929. But it could not have been victorious without the active support of important sectors of financial and industrial capital, who felt threatened by an ever-increasing dissatisfaction of the masses with the capitalist system. The German Reichstag in the early 1930's had a majority of those parties which partly sincerely, and partly insincerely, had a program of some kind of anti-Capitalism. This threat led important sectors of German Capitalism to support Hitler.

Russia was the exact opposite of Germany. She was industrially the most backward of all the European great powers, just emerging from a semifeudal state, even though her industrial sector in itself was highly developed and centralized. The sudden collapse of the Czarist system had created a vacuum, so that Lenin, disbanding the only other force which could have filled this vacuum, the Constituent Assembly, hoped to be able to jump directly from the semifeudal phase into that of an industrialized socialist system. However, Lenin's policy was not a product of the moment, it was the logical consequence of his political thinking, conceived many years before the outbreak of the Russian revolution. He, like Marx, believed in the historic mission of the working class to emancipate society, but he had little faith in the will and ability of the working class to achieve this aim spontaneously. Only if the working class was led, so he thought, by a small well-disciplined group of professional revolutionaries, only if it was forced by this group to execute the laws of history, as Lenin saw them, could the revolution succeed and be prevented from ending up in a new version of a class society. The crucial point in Lenin's position was the fact that he had no faith in the spontaneous action of the workers and peasants—and he had no faith in them *because he had no faith in man*. It is this lack of faith in man which antiliberal and clerical ideas have in common with Lenin's concept; on the other hand faith in man is the basis for all genuinely progressive movements throughout history; it is the most essential condition of Democracy and of Socialism. Faith in *mankind* without faith in *man* is either insincere or, if sincere, it leads to the very results which we see in the tragic history of the Inquisition, Robespierre's terror and Lenin's dictatorship. Many democratic socialist and socialist revolutionaries saw the dangers in Lenin's concept; nobody saw it more clearly than Rosa Luxemburg. She warned that the choice to be made was between *democratism* and *bureaucratism*, and the development in Russia proved the correctness of her prediction. While an ardent and uncompromising critic of Capitalism, she was a person with an unshakable and profound faith in man. When she and Gustav Landauer were murdered by the soldiers of the German counter-revolution, the humanistic tradition of faith in man was meant to be killed with them. It was this lack of faith in man which made it possible for the authoritarian systems to conquer man, leading him on to have faith in an idol rather than in himself.

Between the exploitation in early Capitalism and that of Stalinism, there is not a small difference; the brutal exploitation of the worker in early Capitalism, even though it was backed by the political power of the state apparatus, did not prevent the

239

rise of new and progressive ideas; in fact, all great socialist ideas had their birth in this very period, a period in which Owenism could flourish and in which the Chartist movement was destroyed by force only after ten years. Indeed, the most reactionary government in Europe, that of the Czar, did not use methods of repression which could be compared with those of Stalinism. Since the brutal destruction of the Kronstadt rebellion, Russia offered no chance for any progressive development, such as even the darkest periods of early Capitalism did. Under Stalin, the Soviet system lost the last remnants of its original socialist intentions; the killing of the Old Guard of Bolsheviks in the thirties was only the final dramatic expression of this fact. In many respects the Stalinist system shows similarities with the earlier phase of European Capitalism, characterized by a quick accumulation of capital and by a ruthless exploitation of the workers, with the difference, however, that political terror is used in place of the economic laws which forced the nineteenth-century worker to accept the economic conditions to which he was exposed.

SUPER-CAPITALISM

Exactly the opposite pole is represented by certain ideas proposed by a group of industrialists in the United States (and also in France), seeking for a solution of the industrial problem. The philosophy of this group, which is united into a "Council of Profit Sharing Industries" is clearly and lucidly expressed in *Incentive Management,* by James F. Lincoln, for the past thirty-eight years the executive head of the Lincoln Electric Company. The thinking of this group starts out on premises which, in some ways, are reminiscent of the above-quoted critics of Capitalism. "The industrialist," writes Lincoln, "*concentrates on machines and neg-*

lects man, who is the producer and developer of the machine and, obviously, has far greater potentialities. He will not consider the fact that undeveloped geniuses are doing manual jobs in his plant where they have neither the opportunity nor are given the incentive to develop themselves to genius *or even to normal intelligence and skill.*" [1] The author feels that the lack of interest of the worker in his work creates dissatisfaction which either leads to a decrease in the productiveness of the worker, or to industrial strife and class struggle. He considers his solution not as an embellishment for our industrial system, but as a matter vital to the survival of Capitalism. "America," he writes, "is at the crossroads in this matter. A decision must be made, and soon. There is much lack of understanding by the people generally, yet they must choose. On their decision rests the future of the United States, and of the individual." [2] He criticizes, quite in contrast to most defenders of the capitalist system, the prevalence of the profit motive in the industrial system. "In industry," he writes, "the goal of the company's operation that is stated in the by-laws is to make a 'profit,' and profit only. There is no one outside of the stockholders, who gets that profit, and few stockholders generally are workers for the company. As long as that is true, the goal of profit will engender no enthusiasm in the workers. That goal will not do; in fact, most workers feel that too much profit is already given to the stockholder." [3]

"He, the worker, resents being fooled by economic theories about paying for the tools of production, when he often sees these costs being frittered away by incompetence and selfishness in high places." [4] These criticisms are very much the same as

---

[1] J. F. Lincoln, *Incentive Management,* published by the Lincoln Electric Co., Cleveland, 1951, pp. 113, 114. (Italics mine, E.F.)

[2] *Ibid.,* p. 117.

[3] *Ibid.,* pp. 106, 107.

[4] *Ibid.,* p. 108.

they have been made by many socialist critics of Capitalism, and they show a sober and realistic appreciation of the economic and human facts. The philosophy behind it, however, is quite the contrary of socialist ideas. Lincoln is convinced "that development of the individual can only take place in the fiercely competitive game of life." [1] *"Selfishness is the driving force that makes the human race what it is,* for good or evil. Hence, it is the force that we must depend on, and properly guide, if the human race is to progress." [2] He then goes on to differentiate between "stupid" and "intelligent" selfishness, the former being the selfishness that permits man to steal, the latter that causes a man to struggle toward perfection, so that he becomes more prosperous.[3] Discussing the incentives for work, Lincoln states that just as with the amateur athlete the incentive is not money, we can conclude that money is not necessarily an incentive for the industrial workers, nor are short hours, safety, seniority, security and bargaining power an incentive for work.[4] The only potent incentive, according to him, is "recognition of our abilities by our contemporaries and ourselves." [5] As a practical consequence of these ideas, Lincoln suggests a method of industrial organization in which the worker is "rewarded for all the things he does that are of help, and penalized if he does not do as well as others in all these same ways. He is a member of the team, and is rewarded or penalized, depending on what he can do and does do in all opportunities to win the game." [6] In applying this system, ". . . the man is rated by all those who have accurate knowledge of some phase of his work. On this rating, he is rewarded or penalized. This program runs parallel to the write-ups following the playing of a

[1] *Ibid.*, p. 72.
[2] *Ibid.*, p. 89.
[3] *Ibid.*, p. 91.
[4] *Ibid.*, p. 99.
[5] *Ibid.*, p. 101.
[6] *Ibid.*, p. 109.

game, or the selecting of an All-American team. The best man gets the praise and the standing he warrants and craves. In the bonus plan described here, man is rewarded in direct proportion to his contribution to the success of the company. The parallel is obvious. Each man is advanced or retarded in his standing by his current record. He is rated three times per year. The sum of these ratings determines his share in the bonus and advancement. At the time of giving each man his rating, any question that he may want to ask as to why the rating is as it is and how it can be improved is answered in complete detail by the executives responsible." [1] The size of the bonus is determined in this way: 6 per cent of the profit is paid to the stockholders as a dividend. "After the dividend is provided for, we set aside 'seed money' for the future of the company. The amount of this 'seed money' is determined by the directors, based on current operations." [2] The "seed money" is used for expansion and replacement. After these deductions from the profits, all the balance is divided as a bonus among the workers and management. The bonus has represented a total amount of from 20 per cent of wages and salaries per year as a minimum, to a maximum of 28 per cent a year, over the last 16 years. The average total bonus for each employee was around $40,000 in 16 years, that is, $2,500 per year. All workers have, aside from the bonus, the same basic wage rates as those usual for comparable operations. The average employment costs for the employee at the Lincoln factory for 1950 was $7,701, as compared with $3,705 at the General Electric Co.[3] Under this system the Lincoln company, which employs

[1] *Ibid.*, p. 109, 110.

[2] *Ibid.*, p. 111.

[3] Since the bonus is divided among the workers and managers, one would want to know how much of this average figure refers to wages, and how much to the sums paid to higher employees and managers, and also whether the figure for the General Electric Co. refers only to workers, or also to employees in the higher strata of the company bureaucracy.

around 1,000 workers and employees has been very prosperous, and the sales value of products per employee has been about twice as high as that of the rest of the electrical machinery industry. The number of work stoppages in the Lincoln factory between 1934 and 1945 was zero, as against a minimum of 11 to a maximum of 96 in the rest of the electrical machinery industry. The labor turnover rates were more or less only 25 per cent of those of all other manufacturing industries.[1]

The principle involved in incentive management is in one respect drastically different from that of traditional Capitalism. The worker's wages, instead of being independent from the efforts and results of his work, are related to it. He participates in increasing profits, while the stockholder gets a regular income which is not quite as directly related to the earnings of the company.[2] The company records show clearly that this system led to increased productivity of the worker, low labor turnover, and absence of strikes. But while this system differs in one important respect from the concept and practice of traditional Capitalism, it is, at the same time, the expression of some of its most important principles, especially as far as the human aspect is concerned. It is based on the principle of selfishness and competition, of monetary reward as the expression of social recognition, and it does not change essentially the position of the worker in the process of work, as far as the meaningfulness of the work for him is concerned. As Lincoln points out again and again, the model for this system is the football team, a group of men fiercely competing with all others outside of the group, competing with each other within the group, and producing results in this spirit of competitive co-operation. Actually, the

---

[1] cf. Lincoln, *loc. cit.*, p. 254 ff.

[2] It is, however, not unrelated either, since dividends paid per share increased from $2.00 in 1933 to $8.00 in 1941, going back to an average of $6.00 since then.

system of incentive management is the most logical consequence of the capitalistic system. It tends to make every man, the worker and employee as well as the manager, into a small capitalist; it tends to encourage the spirit of competition and selfishness in everybody, to transform Capitalism in such a way that it comprises the whole of the nation.[1]

The profit-sharing system is not as different from traditional capitalistic practices as it pretends to be. It is a glorified form of the piece-work system, combined with a certain disregard for

[1] There are quite a number of enterprises organized in the Council of Profit Sharing Industries, which have a more or less radical plan of profit sharing in their business. Their principles are expressed in the following paragraphs:

"1. The Council defines profit sharing as any procedure under which an employer pays to all employees, in addition to good rates of regular pay, special current or deferred sums, based not only upon individual or group performance, but on the prosperity of the business as a whole.

"2. The Council considers as the essential factor of economic life the human person. A free company must be based on freedom of opportunity for each to achieve his maximum personal development.

"3. The Council holds that profit sharing affords a most significant means of granting workers freedom of opportunity to participate in the rewards of their co-operation with capital and management.

"4. While the Council feels that profit sharing is entirely justified as a principle in its own right, the Council considers well-planned profit sharing to be the best means of developing group cooperation and efficiency.

"5. The Council holds that widespread profit sharing should assist in stabilizing the economy. Flexibility in compensations as well as in prices and profits affords the best insurance of ready adjustment to changing conditions, either upward or downward.

"6. The Council maintains that stabilized prosperity can be maintained only under a fair relationship between prices, pay and profits. It believes that if our free economy is to survive, management must accept the responsibility of trusteeship to see that this relationship prevails.

"7. The Council holds of paramount importance the true spirit of partnership which sound profit sharing engenders. The only solution to industrial strife is the spreading of this spirit. The council is convinced, through the experience of its members, that this approach will be reciprocated by a large body of labor.

"8. The Council is dedicated to the purpose of extending profit sharing in every practical way. At the same time it does not offer profit sharing as a panacea. No policy or plan in the industrial relation field can succeed unless it is well adapted and unless it has behind it the sincere desire of management to be fair and the faith of management in the importance, dignity and response of the human individual."

the importance of the rates of profit paid to the stockholders. In spite of the talk about the "human person," everything, the rating of the work as well as the amount of the worker's bonus and of the dividends, is determined by the management in an autocratic fashion. The essential principle is 'sharing of profits,' not 'sharing of work.' However, even if the principles are not new, the profit-sharing concept is interesting because it is the most logical aim for a super-Capitalism in which the dissatisfaction of the worker is overcome by making him feel that he too is a capitalist, and an active participant in the system.

SOCIALISM

Aside from Fascist or Stalinist authoritarianism and super-Capitalism of the "incentive management" type, the third great reaction to and criticism of Capitalism is the socialist theory. It is essentially a theoretical vision, in contrast to Fascism and Stalinism, which became political and social realities. This is so in spite of the fact that socialist governments were in power for a shorter or longer time in England and in Scandinavian countries, since the majority upon which their power rested was so small that they could not transform society beyond the most tentative beginnings of the realization of their program.

Unfortunately, at the time of this writing the words "Socialism" and "Marxism" have been charged with such an emotional impact that it is difficult to discuss these problems in a calm atmosphere. The association which these words evoke today in many people are those of "materialism," "godlessness," "bloodshed," or the like—briefly, of the bad and evil. One can understand such a reaction only if one appreciates the degree to which words can assume a magical function, and if one takes into account the decrease in reasonable thought, that is to say, in objectivity, which is so characteristic of our age.

The irrational response which is evoked by the words Socialism and Marxism is furthered by an astounding ignorance on the part of most of those who become hysterical when they hear these words. In spite of the fact that all of Marx's and other socialist's writings are available to be read by everybody, most of those who feel most violently about Socialism and Marxism have never read a word by Marx, and many others have only a very superficial knowledge. If this were not so, it would seem impossible that men with some degree of insight and reason could have distorted the idea of Socialism and Marxism to the degree which is current today. Even many Liberals, and those who are relatively free from hysterical reactions, believe that "Marxism" is a system based on the idea that the interest in material gain is the most active power in man, and that it aims at furthering material greed and its satisfaction. If we only remind ourselves that the main argument in favor of Capitalism is the idea that interest in material gain is the main incentive for work, it can easily be seen that the very materialism which is ascribed to Socialism is the most characteristic feature of Capitalism, and if anyone takes the trouble to study the socialist writers with a modicum of objectivity, he will find that their orientation is exactly the opposite, that they criticize Capitalism for its materialism, for its crippling effect on the genuinely human powers in man. Indeed, Socialism in all its various schools can be understood only as one of the most significant, idealistic and moral movements of our age.

Aside from everything else, one cannot help deploring the political stupidity of this misrepresentation of Socialism on the part of the Western democracies. Stalinism won its victories in Russia and Asia by the very appeal which the idea of Socialism has on vast masses of the population of the world. The appeal lies in the very idealism of the socialist concept, in the spiritual and moral encouragement which it gives. Just as Hitler used the word "Socialism" to give added appeal to his racial and nationalistic ideas, Stalin misappropriated the concept of Socialism and of Marxism for the purpose of his propaganda. His claim is false in the essential points. He separated the purely economic aspect of Socialism, that of the socialization of the means of production, from the whole concept of Socialism, and perverted its human and social aims into their opposite. The Stalinist system today, in spite of its state ownership of the means of production, is perhaps closer to the early and purely exploitative forms of Western Capitalism than to any conceivable idea of a socialist society. An obsessional striving for industrial advance, ruthless disregard for the individual and greed for personal power are its mainsprings. By accepting the thesis that Socialism and Marxism are more or less identical with Stalinism, we do the greatest service in the field of propaganda which the Stalinists could wish to obtain. Instead of showing the falsity of their claims, we confirm them. This may not be an important problem in the United States, where socialist concepts have no strong hold on the minds of the people, but it is a very serious problem for Europe and especially for Asia, where the opposite is true. To combat the appeal of Stalinism in those parts of the world, we must uncover this deception, and not confirm it.

There are considerable differences between the various schools of socialist thought, as they have developed since the end of the eighteenth century, and these differences are significant. However, as happens so often in the history of human thought, the arguments between the representatives of the various schools obscure the fact that the common element among the various socialist thinkers is by far greater and more decisive than are the differences.

Socialism as a political movement, and at the same time as a theory dealing with the laws of society and a diagnosis of its ills, may be said to have been started in the French Revolution, by Babeuf. He speaks in favor of the abolition of private ownership of the soil, and demands the common consumption of the fruits of the earth, the abolition of the difference between rich and poor, ruler and ruled. He believes that the time has come for a Republic of the Equals (*égalitaires*), "the great hospitable house (*hospice*) open for all."

In contrast to the relatively simple and primitive theory of Babeuf, Charles Fourier, whose first publication, "Théorie de Quatre Movements," appeared in 1808, offers a most complex and elaborate theory and diagnosis of society. He makes man and his passions a basis of all understanding of society, and believes that a healthy society must serve, not so much the aim of increasing material wealth, as a realization of our basic passion, brotherly love. Among the human passions, he emphasizes particularly the "butterfly passion," man's need for change, which corresponds to the many and diverse potentialities present in every human being. Work should be a pleasure (*"travail attrayant"*) and two daily hours of work should be sufficient. Against the universal organization of great monopolies in all branches of industry, he postulates communal associations in the field of production and consumption, free and voluntary associations in which individualism will combine spontaneously with collectivism. Only in this way can the third historical phase, that of harmony, supersede the two previous ones: that of societies based on relations between slave and master, and that between wage-earners and entrepreneurs.[1]

While Fourier was a theoretician with a somewhat obsessional mind, Robert Owen was a man of practice, manager and owner of one of the best-managed textile mills in Scotland. For Owen,

[1] cf. Charles Fourier, *The Passions of the Human Soul,* with a general introduction by H. Doherty, translated by J. R. Morell, H. Bailliere, London, 1851.

too, the aim of a new society was not primarily that of increasing production, but the improvement of the most precious thing there is, man. Like Fourier's, his thinking is based on psychological considerations of man's character. While men are born with certain characteristic traits, their character is definitely determined only by the circumstances under which they live. If the social conditions of life are satisfactory, man's character will develop its inherent virtues. He believed that men were trained in all previous history only to defend themselves or to destroy others. A new social order must be created, in which men are trained in principles that would permit them to act in union, and to create real and genuine bonds between individuals. Federal groups of three hundred and up to two thousand persons will cover the earth and be organized according to the principle of collective help, within each other, and among each other. In each community, the local government will work in closest harmony with each individual.

An even more drastic condemnation of the principle of authority and hierarchy is to be found in Proudhon's writings. For him the central problem is not the substitution of one political regime for another, but the building of a political order which is expressive of society itself. He sees as the prime cause of all disorders and ills of society the single and hierarchical organization of authority, and he believes: "The limitations of the State's task is a matter of life and death for freedom, both collective and individual."

"Through monopoly," he says, "mankind has taken possession of the globe, and through association it will become its real master." His vision of a new social order is based on the idea of ". . . reciprocity, where all workers instead of working for an entrepreneur who pays them and keeps the products, work for one another and thus collaborate in the making of a common product whose profits they share amongst themselves." What is essential for him is that these associations are free and spontaneous, and not state imposed, like the state-financed social workshops demanded by Louis Blanc. Such a state-controlled system, he says, would mean a number of large associations "in which labour would be regimented and ultimately enslaved through a state policy of Capitalism. What would freedom, universal happiness, civilization, have gained? Nothing. We would merely have exchanged our chains and the social idea would have made no step forward; we would still be under the same arbitrary power, not to say under the same economic fatalism." Nobody has seen the danger which has come to pass under Stalinism more clearly than Proudhon, in the middle of the nineteenth century, as the passage already quoted clearly indicates. He was also aware of the danger of dogmatism, which should prove so disastrous in the development of the Marxist theory, and he expressed it clearly in a letter to Marx. "Let us," he writes, "if you wish, search together for the laws of society, the manner in which they are realized, the method according to which we can discover them, but, for God's sake, after having demolished all dogmas, let us not think of indoctrinating the people ourselves; let us not fall into the contradiction of your compatriot Luther, who began with excommunications and anathemas to found the Protestant theology, after having over-thrown the Catholic theology." [1] Proudhon's thinking is based on an ethical concept in which self-respect is the first maxim of ethics. From self-respect follows respect of one's neighbor as the second maxim of morality. This concern with the inner change in man as the basis of a new social order was expressed by Proudhon in a letter, saying, "The Old World is in a

[1] Quoted from E. Dolleans *Proudhon*, Gallimard, Paris, 1948, p. 96. (My translation, E.F.)

process of dissolution . . . one can change it only by the *integral revolution in the ideas and in the hearts. . . .*" [1]

The same awareness of the dangers of centralization, and the same belief in the productive powers of man, although mixed with a romantic glorification of destruction, is to be found in the writings of Michael Bakunin; in a letter of 1868 he says: "The great teacher of us all, Proudhon, said that the unhappiest combination which might occur, could be that Socialism should unite itself to Absolutism; the striving of the people for economic freedom, and material well-being, through dictatorship and the concentration of all political and social powers in the State. May the future protect us from the favours of despotism; but may it preserve us from the unhappy consequences and stultifications of indoctrinated, or State Socialism. . . . Nothing living and human can prosper without freedom, and a form of Socialism which would do away with freedom, or which would not recognize it as the sole creative principle and basis, would lead us directly into slavery and bestiality."

Fifty years after Proudhon's letter to Marx, Peter Kropotkin summed up his idea of Socialism in the statement that the fullest development of individuality "will combine with the highest development of voluntary association in all its aspects, in all possible degrees, and for all possible purposes; an association that is always changing, that bears in itself the elements of its own duration, that takes on the forms which best correspond at any given moment to the manifold strivings of all." Kropotkin, like many of his socialist predecessors stressed the inherent tendencies for co-operation and mutual help present in man and in the animal kingdom.

Following the humanistic and ethical thought of Kropotkin was one of the last great representatives of anarchist thought, Gustav

[1] Letter to Jules Michelet, (January 1860) quoted in E. Dolleans, *loc. cit.*, p. 7. (Italics mine, E.F.)

Landauer. Referring to Proudhon, he said that social revolution bears no resemblance at all to political revolution; that "although it cannot come alive and remain living without a good deal of the latter, it is nevertheless a peaceful structure, an organizing of new spirit *for* new spirit, and nothing else." He defined as the task of the socialists and their movement: "to loosen the hardening of hearts so that what lies buried may rise to the surface: so that what truly lives yet now seems dead may emerge and grow light." [1] [2]

The discussion of the theories of Marx and Engels requires more space than that of the other socialist thinkers mentioned above: partly because their theories are more complex, covering a wider range, and are not without contradictions, partly because the Marxian school of Socialism has become the dominant form which socialist thought has assumed in the world.

As with all other socialists, Marx's basic concern is man. "To be radical," he once wrote, "means to go to the root, and the root —is man himself." [3] The history of the world is nothing but the creation of man, is the history of the birth of man.[3] But all history is also the history of man's alienation from himself, from his own human powers; "the consolidation of our own product to an objective force above us, outgrowing our control, defeating our expectations, annihilating our calculations is one of the main factors in all previous historical development." Man has been the *object* of circumstances, he must become the *subject*, so that "man be-

---

[1] Quoted from M. Buber, *Paths in Utopia*, The Macmillan Company, New York, 1950, p. 48.

[2] The Socialist Revolutionary party in Russia adhered to a concept of Socialism which contained many elements to be found in the aforementioned socialist schools, rather than in those of Marxism. cf. I. N. Steinberg, *In the Workshop of the Revolution*, Rinehart & Company, Inc., New York, 1953.

[3] cf. "Nationalökonomie und Philosophie," published by S. Landshut, A. Kröner Verlag, Stuttgart, 1953, in Karl Marx, *Die Frühschriften*, p. 247. (My translation, E.F.)

comes the highest being for man." Freedom, for Marx, is not only freedom from political oppressors, but the freedom from the domination of man by things and circumstances. The free man is the rich man, but not the man rich in an economic sense, but rich in the human sense. The wealthy man, for Marx, is the man who *is* much, and not the one who *has* much.[1]

The analysis of society and of the historical process must begin with man, not with an abstraction, but with the real, concrete man, in his physiological and psychological qualities. It must begin with a concept of the essence of man, and the study of economics and of society serves only the purpose of understanding how circumstances have crippled man, how he has become alienated from himself and his powers. The nature of man cannot be deduced from the specific manifestation of human nature as it is engendered by the capitalist system. Our aim must be to know what is good for man. But, says Marx, "to know what is useful for a dog one must study dog nature. This nature itself is not to be deduced from the principle of utility. Applying this to man, he that would criticise all human acts, movements, relations, etc., by the principle of utility, must first deal with human nature in general, and then with human nature as modified in each historical epoch. Bentham makes short work of it. With the direst naïveté, he takes the modern shopkeeper, especially the English shopkeeper, as the normal man." [2]

The aim of the development of man, for Marx, is a new harmony between man and man, and between man and nature, a development in which man's relatedness to his fellow man will correspond to his most important human need. Socialism, for him, is "an association in which the free development of each is the condition

[1] *loc. cit., Die Frühschriften*, p. 243 ff.
[2] Karl Marx, *Capital*, translated from the third German edition, by S. Moore and E. Aveling, The Modern Library, Random House, Inc., New York, I, p. 688, footnote.

for the free development of all," a society in which "the full and free development of each individual becomes the ruling principle." This aim he calls the realization of naturalism, and of humanism, and states that it is different "from idealism as well as from materialism, and yet combines the truth in both of them." [1]

How does Marx think this "emancipation of man" can be attained? His solution is based on the idea that in the capitalistic mode of production the process of self-alienation has reached its peak, because man's physical energy has become a commodity, hence man has become a thing. The working class, he says, is the most alienated class of the population, and for this very reason the one which will lead the fight for human emancipation. In the socialization of the means of production he sees the condition for the transformation of man into an active and responsible participant in the social and economic process, and for the overcoming of the split between the individual and the social nature of man. "Only when man has recognized and organized his 'forces propres' as social forces (it is therefore not necessary, as Rousseau thinks, to change man's nature, to deprive him of his 'forces propres,' and give him new ones of a social character) and, consequently, no longer cuts off his social power from himself in the form of political power (*i.e.*, no longer establishes the state as the sphere of organized rule), only then will the emancipation of mankind be achieved." [2]

Marx assumes that if the worker is not "employed" any more, the nature and character of his work process will change. Work will become a meaningful expression of human powers, rather than meaningless drudgery. How important this new concept of work was for Marx, becomes clear when we consider that he went so far as to criticize the proposal for complete abolishment of child

[1] *Ibid.*, p. 273.
[2] Karl Marx, *On the Jewish Question.*

labor in the Gotha Program of the German Socialist Party.[1]
While he was, of course, against the exploitation of children, he
opposed the principle that children should not work at all, but
demanded that education should be combined with manual labor.
"From the factory system budded," he writes, "as Robert Owen
has shown us in detail, the germ of the education of the future, an
education that will, in the education of every child over a given
age, combine productive labour with instruction and humanistics,
not only as one of the methods of adding to the efficiency of
production, but as the only method of producing fully developed
human beings." [2] To Marx, as to Fourier, work must become
attractive and correspond to the needs and desires of man. For
this reason, he suggests, as Fourier and others did, that nobody
should become specialized in one particular kind of work, but
should work in different occupations, corresponding to his different interests and potentialities.

Marx saw in the economic transformation of society from Capitalism to Socialism the decisive means for the liberation and
emancipation of men, for a "true democracy." While in his later
writings the discussion of economics plays a greater role than that
of man and his human needs, the economic sphere became at no
point an end in itself, and never ceased to be a *means* for satisfying
human needs. This becomes particularly clear in his discussion of
what he calls "vulgar Communism," by which he means a Communism in which the exclusive emphasis is on the abolition of
private property in the means of production. "Physical, immediate property remains for it [vulgar Communism] the only purpose of life and existence; the quality of the work is not changed,
but only extended to all human beings; . . . This Communism

---

[1] On this point, I am much indebted to G. Fuchs for his comments and suggestions.
[2] Karl Marx, *Capital*, translated from the third German edition by S. Moore and E.
Aveling, New York, 1889, p. 489.

by negating the personality of man throughout is only the consequent expression of private property which is, exactly, the negation of man. . . . The vulgar communist is only the perfection
of envy, and of the levelling process on the basis of an imagined
minimum. . . . How little this abolition of private property is a
real appropriation [of human powers] is proven by the abstract
negation of the whole world of education and civilization; the
return to the unnatural simplicity of the poor man is not a step
beyond private property, but a stage which has not even arrived at
private property." [1]

Much more complex, and in many ways contradictory, are the
views of Marx and Engels on the question of the State. There
is no doubt that Marx and Engels were of the opinion that the
aim of Socialism was not only a classless society, but a stateless
society, stateless at least in the sense, as Engels put it, that the
State would have the function of the "administration of things,"
and not that of the "government of people." Engels said, in 1874,
quite in line with the formulation Marx gave in the report of the
commission to examine the activities of the Bakuninists in 1872
"that all socialists were agreed that the State would wither away
as a result of victorious Socialism." These anti-state views of Marx
and Engels, and their opposition to a centralized form of political
authority found a particularly clear expression in Marx's statements on the Paris Commune. In his address to the General Council
of the International on the civil war in France, Marx stressed the
necessity of decentralization, in place of a centralized State power,
the origins of which lie in the principle of the absolute monarchy.
There would be a largely decentralized community. "The few,
but important, functions still left over for a Central Government
were to be transferred to communal, *i.e.*, strictly answerable officials. . . . The communal constitution would have rendered up

[1] *Ibid.*, p. 233, 234.

to the body social all the powers which have hitherto been devoured by the parasitic excrescence of the 'State,' which fattens on society and inhibits its free movement." He sees in the Commune "the finally discovered political form, in whose sign the economic liberation of labour can march forward." The Commune wanted "to make individual property a truth, by converting the means of production, land and capital into the mere tools of free and associated labour, and labour amalgamated in Producer Co-operatives at that." [1]

Eduard Bernstein pointed out the similarity between these concepts of Marx with the antistatist, and anticentralistic views of Proudhon, while Lenin claimed that Marx's comments in no way indicate his favoring of decentralization. It seems that both Bernstein and Lenin were right in their interpretation of the Marx-Engels position, and that the solution of the contradiction lies in the fact that Marx was for decentralization and the withering of the state as the aim for which Socialism should strive, and at which it would eventually arrive, but he thought that this could happen only *after* and not *before* the working class had seized political power and transformed the state. The seizure of the state was, for Marx, the means which was necessary to arrive at the end, its abolition.

Nevertheless, if one considers Marx's activities in the First International, his dogmatic and intolerant attitude to everybody who disagreed with him in the slightest, there can be little doubt that Lenin's centralist interpretation of Marx did no injustice to Marx, even though Marx's decentralist agreement with Proudhon was also a genuine part of his views and doctrines. In this very centralism of Marx lies the basis for the tragic development of the socialist idea in Russia. While Lenin may have at least hoped for the

[1] Quoted from M. Buber, *Paths in Utopia*, The Macmillan Company, New York, 1950, pp. 86, 87.

eventual achievement of decentralization, an idea which in fact was manifest in the concept of the Soviets, where the decision making was rooted in the smallest and most concrete level of decentralized groups, Stalinism developed one side of the contradiction, the principle of centralization, into the practice of the most ruthless State organization the modern world has known, surpassing even the centralization principle which Fascism and Nazism followed.

The contradiction in Marx goes deeper than is apparent in the contradiction between the principles of centralization and decentralization. On the one hand Marx, like all other socialists, was convinced that the emancipation of man was not primarily a political, but an economic and social question; that the answer to freedom was not to be found in the change of the political form of the state, but in the economic and social transformation of society. On the other hand, and in spite of their own theories, Marx and Engels were in many ways caught in the traditional concept of the dominance of the political over the socio-economic spheres. They could not free themselves from the traditional view of the importance of the state and political power, from the idea of the primary significance of mere political change, an idea which had been the guiding principle of the great middle-class revolutions of the seventeenth and eighteenth centuries. In this respect Marx and Engels were much more "bourgeois" thinkers than were men like Proudhon, Bakunin, Kropotkin and Landauer. Paradoxical as it sounds, the Leninist development of Socialism represents a regression to the bourgeois concepts of the state and of political power, rather than the new socialist concept as it was expressed so much more clearly by Owen, Proudhon and others. This paradox in Marx's thinking has been clearly expressed by Buber: "Marx," he writes, "accepted these essential components of the commune-idea but without weighing them up against his own centralism and deciding between them. That he apparently did not see the profound problem that this opens up is due to the hegemony of the political point of view; a hegemony which persisted everywhere for him as far as it concerned the revolution, its preparation and its effects. Of the three modes of thinking in public matters—the economic, the social and the political—Marx exercised the first with methodical mastery, devoted himself with passion to the third, but—absurd as it may sound in the ears of the unqualified Marxist—only very seldom did he come into more intimate contact with the second, and it never became a deciding factor for him." [1]

Closely related to Marx's centralism is his attitude toward revolutionary action. While it is true that Marx and Engels admitted that socialist control of the state must not be necessarily acquired by force and revolution (as for instance, in England and the United States), it is equally true that on the whole they believed that the working class, in order to obtain their aims, had to seize power by a revolution. In fact, they were in favor of universal military service, and sometimes of international wars, as means which would facilitate the revolutionary seizure of power. Our generation has witnessed the tragic results of force and dictatorship in Russia; we have seen that the application of force within society is as destructive of human welfare as its application in international relations in the form of war. But when today Marx is accused primarily for his advocation of force and revolution, this is a twisting of facts. The idea of political revolution is not a specifically Marxist, or socialist idea, but it is the traditional idea of the middle class, bourgeois society in the last three hundred years. Because of the fact that the middle class believed that abolition of the political power vested in a monarchy, and the seizure of political power by the people was the solution

[1] Buber, *loc. cit.,* pp. 95, 96.

of the social problem, political revolution was seen as a means to the achievement of freedom. Our modern democracy is a result of force and revolution, the Kerensky revolution of 1917 and the German revolution of 1918 were warmly greeted in the Western democratic countries. It is the tragic mistake of Marx, a mistake which contributed to the development of Stalinism, that he had not freed himself from the traditional overevaluation of political power and force; but these ideas were part of the previous heritage, and not of the new socialist concept.

Even a brief discussion of Marx would be incomplete without a reference to his theory of historical materialism. In the history of thought this theory is probably the most lasting and important contribution of Marx to the understanding of the laws governing society. His premise is that before man can engage in any kind of cultural activity, he must produce the means for his physical subsistence. The ways in which he produces and consumes are determined by a number of objective conditions: his own physiological constitution, the productive powers which he has at his disposal and which, in turn, are conditioned by the fertility of the soil, natural resources, communications and the techniques which he develops. Marx postulated that the material conditions of man determine his mode of production and consumption, and that these in turn, determine his socio-political organization, his practice of life, and eventually his mode of thought and feeling. The widespread misunderstanding of this theory was to interpret it as if Marx had meant that the *striving for gain* was the main motive in man. Actually, this is the dominant view expressed in capitalistic thinking, a view which has stressed again and again that the main incentive for man's work is his interest in monetary rewards. Marx's concept of the significance of the economic factor was not a *psychological* one, namely, an economic motivation in a *subjective* sense; it was a *sociological* one, in which the economic development was the *objective* condition for the cultural development.[1] His main criticism of Capitalism was exactly that it had crippled man by the preponderance of economic interests, and Socialism for him was a society in which man would be freed from this domination by a more rational and hence productive form of economic organization. Marx's materialism was essentially different from the materialism which was prevalent in the nineteenth century. In the latter type of materialism one understood spiritual phenomena as being *caused* by material phenomena. Thus, for instance, the extreme representatives of this kind of materialism believed that thought was a product of brain activity, just "as urine is a product of kidney activity." Marx's view, on the other hand was, that the mental and spiritual phenomenon must be understood as an outcome of the whole practice of life, as the result of the kind of relatedness of the individual to his fellow men and to nature. Marx, in his dialectic method, overcame the materialism of the nineteenth century and developed a truly dynamic and holistic theory based on man's *activity*, rather than on his *physiology*.

The theory of historical materialism offers important scientific concepts for the understanding of the laws of history; it would have become more fruitful had the followers of Marx developed it further rather than permitting it to become bogged down in a sterile dogmatism. The point of development would have been to recognize that Marx and Engels had only made a first step, that of seeing the correlation between the development of economy and culture. Marx had underestimated the complexity of human passions. He had not sufficiently recognized that human nature has itself needs and laws which are in constant interaction with the

[1] cf. to this point my discussion in *Zur Aufgabe einer Analytischen Sozialpsychologie* in Ztsch. f. Sozialforschung, Leipzig, 1932, and J. A. Schumpeter's discussion of Marxism in *Capitalism, Socialism and Democracy*, Harper and Brothers, New York, 1947, pp. 11, 12.

economic conditions which shape historical development; [1] lacking in satisfactory psychological insights, he did not have a sufficient concept of human character, and was not aware of the fact that while man was shaped by the form of social and economic organization, he in turn also molded it. He did not sufficiently see the passions and strivings which are rooted in man's nature, and in the conditions of his existence, and which are in themselves the most powerful driving force for human development. But these deficiencies are limitations of one-sidedness, as we find them in every productive scientific concept, and Marx and Engels themselves were aware of these limitations. Engels expressed this awareness in a well-known letter, in which he said that because of the newness of their discovery, Marx and he had not paid sufficient attention to the fact that history was not only determined by economic conditions, but that cultural factors in turn also influenced the economic basis of society.

Marx's own preoccupation became more and more that with the purely economic analysis of Capitalism. The significance of his economic theory is not altered by the fact that his basic assumptions and predictions were only partly right and to a considerable extent mistaken, the latter especially as far as his assumption of the necessity of the (relative) deterioration of the working class is concerned. He was also wrong in his romantic idealization of the working class, which was a result of a purely theoretical scheme rather than of an observation of the human reality of the working class. But whatever its defects, his economic theory and penetrating analysis of the economic structure of Capitalism constitutes a definite progress over all other socialist theories from a scientific viewpoint.

However, this strength was at the same time its weakness. While

---

[1] cf. my analysis of this interaction in *The Fear of Freedom*, Kegan Paul, London, 1942.

Marx started his economic analysis with the intention of discovering the conditions for the alienation of man, and while he believed that this would require only a relatively short study, he spent the greater part of his scientific work almost exclusively with economic analysis, and while he never lost sight of the aim —the emancipation of man—both the criticism of Capitalism and the socialist aim in *human terms* became more and more overgrown by economic considerations. He did not recognize the irrational forces in man which make him afraid of freedom, and which produce his lust for power and his destructiveness. On the contrary, underlying his concept of man was the implicit assumption of man's natural goodness, which would assert itself as soon as the crippling economic shackles were released. The famous statement at the end of the Communist Manifesto that the workers "have nothing to lose but their chains," contains a profound psychological error. With their chains they have also to lose all those irrational needs and satisfactions which were originated while they were wearing the chains. In this respect, Marx and Engels never transcended the naïve optimism of the eighteenth century.

This underestimation of the complexity of human passions led to the three most dangerous errors in Marx's thinking. First of all, to his neglect of the *moral* factor in man. Just because he assumed that the goodness of man would assert itself automatically when the economic changes had been achieved, he did not see that a better society could not be brought into life by people who had not undergone a moral change within themselves. He paid no attention, at least not explicitly, to the necessity of a new moral orientation, without which all political and economic changes are futile.

The second error, stemming from the same source, was Marx's grotesque misjudgment of the chances for the realization of Socialism. In contrast to men like Proudhon and Bakunin (and later on, Jack London in his "Iron Heel"), who foresaw the darkness which would envelop the Western world before new light would shine, Marx and Engels believed in the immediate advent of the "good society," and were only dimly aware of the possibility of a new barbarism in the form of communist and fascist authoritarianism and wars of unheard of destructiveness. This unrealistic misapprehension was responsible for many of the theoretical and political errors in Marx's and Engels's thinking, and it was the basis for the destruction of Socialism which began with Lenin.

The third error was Marx's concept that the socialization of the means of production was not only the *necessary,* but also the *sufficient* condition for the transformation of the capitalist into a socialist co-operative society. At the bottom of this error is again his oversimplified, overoptimistic, rationalistic picture of man. Just as Freud believed that freeing man from unnatural and overstrict sexual taboos would lead to mental health, Marx believed that the emancipation from exploitation would automatically produce free and co-operative beings. He was as optimistic about the immediate effect of changes in environmental factors as the encyclopedists of the eighteenth century had been, and had little appreciation for the power of irrational and destructive passions which were not transformed from one day to another by economic changes. Freud, after the experience of the First World War, came to see this strength of destructiveness, and changed his whole system drastically by accepting the drive for destruction as being equally strong and as ineradicable as Eros. Marx never came to such an awareness, and never changed his simple formula of socialization of the means of production as a straight way to the socialist aim.

The other source for this error was his overevaluation of political and economic arrangements to which I have pointed above. He was curiously unrealistic in ignoring the fact that it makes very little difference to the personality of the worker whether the enterprise is owned by the "people"—the State—a Government bureaucracy, or by the private bureaucracy hired by the stockholders. He did not see, quite in contrast to his own theoretical thought, that the only things that matter are the actual and realistic conditions of work, the relation of the worker to his work, to his fellow workers, and to those directing the enterprise.

In the later years of his life, Marx seems to have been ready to make certain changes in his theory. The most important one probably under the influence of Bachofen's and Morgan's work, led him to believe that the primitive agrarian community based on co-operation and common property in the land was a potent form of social organization, which could lead directly into higher forms of socialization without having to go through the phase of capitalistic production. He expressed this belief in his answer to Vera Zazulich, who asked him about his attitude toward the "mir," the old forms of agricultural community in Russia. G. Fuchs has pointed out [1] the great significance of this change in Marx's theory, and also the fact that Marx, in the last eight years of his life, was disappointed and discouraged, sensing the failure of his revolutionary hopes. Engels recognized, as I have mentioned above, the failure to pay enough attention to the power of ideas in their theory of historical materialism, but it was not given to Marx or to Engels to make the necessary drastic revisions in their system.

For us in the middle of the twentieth century, it is very easy to recognize Marx's fallacy. We have seen the tragic illustration of this fallacy occurring in Russia. While Stalinism proved that a socialist economy can operate successfully from an economic viewpoint, it also proved that it is in itself by no means bound to create a spirit of equality and co-operation; it showed that the owner-

[1] In personal communications.

ship of the means of production by "the people" can become the ideological cloak for the exploitation of the people by an industrial, military and political bureaucracy. The socialization of certain industries in England, undertaken by the Labour Government tends to show that to the British miner or worker in the steel or chemical industries it makes very little difference who appoints the managers of his enterprise, since the actual and realistic conditions of his work remain the same.

Summing up, it can be said that the ultimate aims of Marxist Socialism were essentially the same as those of the other socialist schools: emancipating man from domination and exploitation by man, freeing him from the preponderance of the economic realm, restoring him as the supreme aim of social life, creating a new unity between man and man, and man and nature. The errors of Marx and Engels, their overestimation of political and legal factors, their naïve optimism, their centralistic orientation, were due to the fact that they were much more rooted in the middle-class tradition of the eighteenth and nineteenth centuries, both psychologically and intellectually than men like Fourier, Owen, Proudhon and Kropotkin.

Marx's errors were to become important historically because the Marxist concept of Socialism became victorious in the European Continental labor movement. The successors of Marx and Engels in the European Labour Movement were so much under the influence of Marx's authority, that they did not develop the theory further, but largely repeated the old formulae with an ever-increasing sterility.

After the first World War, the Marxist labor movement became strictly divided into hostile camps. Its Social Democratic wing, after the moral collapse during the first World War, became more and more a party representing the purely economic interests of the working class, together with the trade unions from whom it, in turn, depended. It carried on the Marxist formula of "the socialization of the means of production," like a ritual to be pronounced by the party priests on the proper occasions. The Communist wing took a jump of despair, trying to build a socialist society on nothing except seizure of power, and socialization of the means of production; the results of this jump led to more frightful results than did the loss of faith in the Social Democratic parties.

Contradictory as the development of these two wings of Marxist Socialism is, they have certain elements in common. First, the deep disillusionment and despondency with regard to the over-optimistic hopes which were inherent in the earlier phase of Marxism. In the Right Wing, this disillusionment often led to the acceptance of nationalism, to the abandonment of a genuine socialist vision, and of any radical criticism of capitalistic society. The same disillusionment led the Communist Wing, under Lenin, to an act of despair, to a concentration of all efforts into political and purely economic realms, an emphasis which by its neglect of the social sphere was the complete contradiction of the very essence of socialist theory.

The other point which both wings of the Marxist movement have in common is their (in the case of Russia) complete neglect of man. The criticism of Capitalism became entirely a criticism from an economic standpoint. In the nineteenth century, when the working class suffered from ruthless exploitation and lived below the standard of dignified existence, this criticism was justified. With the development of Capitalism in the twentieth century, it became more and more obsolete, yet it is only a logical consequence of this attitude that the Stalinist bureaucracy in Russia is still feeding the population with the nonsense that workers in capitalistic countries are terribly impoverished and lacking any decent basis for subsistence. The concept of Socialism deteriorated more and more; in Russia, into the formula that Socialism meant state ownership of the means of production. In the Western countries, Socialism tended more and more to mean higher wages for the workers, and to lose its messianic pathos, its appeal to the deepest longings and needs of man. I say intentionally that it "tended" to because Socialism has by no means completely lost its humanistic and religious pathos. It has, even after 1914, been the rallying moral idea for millions of European workers and intellectuals, an expression of their hope for the liberation of man, for the establishment of new moral values, for the realization of human solidarity. The sharp criticism voiced in the foregoing pages was meant primarily to accentuate the necessity that Democratic Socialism must return to, and concentrate on the *human* aspects of the social problem; must criticize Capitalism from the standpoint of what it does to the human qualities of man, to his soul and his spirit, and must consider any vision of Socialism in human terms, asking in what way a socialist society will contribute toward ending the alienation of man, the idolatry of economy and of the state.

8

ROADS TO SANITY

General Considerations

In the various critical analyses of Capitalism we find remarkable agreement. While it is true that the Capitalism of the nineteenth century was criticized for its neglect of the material welfare of the workers, this was never the main criticism. What Owen and Proudhon, Tolstoy and Bakunin, Durkheim and Marx, Einstein and Schweitzer talk about is *man*, and what happens to him in our industrial system. Although they express it in different concepts, they all find that man has lost his central place, that he has been made an instrument for the purposes of economic aims, that he has been estranged from, and has lost the concrete relatedness to, his fellow men and to nature, that he has ceased to have a meaningful life. I have tried to express the same idea by elaborating on the concept of alienation and by showing psychologically what the psychological results of alienation are; that man regresses to a receptive and marketing orientation and ceases to be productive; that he loses his sense of self, becomes dependent on approval, hence tends to conform and yet to feel insecure; he is dissatisfied, bored, and anxious, and spends most of his energy in the attempt to compensate for or just to cover up this anxiety. His intelligence is excellent, his reason deteriorates and in view of his technical powers he is seriously endangering the existence of civilization, and even of the human race.

If we turn to views about the *causes* for this development, we find less agreement than in the diagnosis of the illness itself. While the early nineteenth century was still prone to see the causes of all evil in the lack of *political* freedom, and especially of universal suffrage, the socialists, and especially the Marxists stressed the significance of economic factors. They believed that the alienation of man resulted from his role as an object of exploitation and use. Thinkers like Tolstoy and Burckhardt on the other hand, stressed the spiritual and moral impoverishment as the cause of Western man's decay; Freud believed that modern man's trouble was the over-repression of his instinctual drives and the resulting neurotic manifestations. But any explanation which analyzes one sector to the exclusion of others is unbalanced, and thus wrong. The socio-economic, spiritual and psychological explanations look at the same phenomenon from different aspects, and the very task of a theoretical analysis is to see how these different aspects are inter-related, and how they interact.

What holds true for the causes holds, of course, true for the remedies by which modern man's defect can be cured. If I be-lieve that "the" cause of the illness is economic, *or* spiritual, *or* psychological, I necessarily believe that remedying "the" cause leads to sanity. On the other hand, if I see how the various aspects are interrelated, I shall arrive at the conclusion that sanity and mental health can be attained only by simultaneous changes in the sphere of industrial and political organization, of spiritual and philosophical orientation, of character structure, and of cultural activities. The concentration of effort in any of these spheres, to the exclusion or neglect of others, is destructive of *all* change. In fact, here seems to lie one of the most important obstacles to the progress of mankind. Christianity has preached spiritual renewal, neglecting the changes in the social order without which spiritual renewal must remain ineffective for the majority of people. The age of enlightenment has postulated as the highest norms independent judgment and reason; it preached political equality without seeing that political equality could not lead to the realization of the brotherhood of man if it was not accompanied by a fundamental change in the social-economic organization. Socialism, and especially Marxism, has stressed the necessity for social and economic changes, and neglected the necessity of the inner change in human beings, without which economic change can never lead to the "good society." Each of these great reform movements of the last two thousand years has emphasized one sector of life to the exclusion of the others; their proposals for reform and renewal were radical—but their results were almost complete failure. The preaching of the Gospel led to the establishment of the Catholic Church; the teachings of the rationalists of the eighteenth century to Robespierre and Napoleon; the doctrines of Marx to Stalin. The results could hardly have been different. Man is a unit; his thinking, feeling, and his practice of life are inseparably connected. He cannot be free in his thought when he is not free emotionally; and he cannot be free emotionally if he is dependent and unfree in his practice of life, in his economic and social relations. Trying to advance radically in one sector to the exclusion of others must necessarily lead to the result to which it did lead, namely, that the radical demands in one sphere are fulfilled only by a few individuals, while for the majority they become formulae and rituals, serving to cover up the fact that in other spheres nothing has changed. Undoubtedly *one* step of integrated progress in all spheres of life will have more far-reaching and more lasting results for the progress of the human race than a hundred steps preached —and even for a short while lived—in only one isolated sphere.

Several thousands of years of failure in "isolated progress" should be a rather convincing lesson.

Closely related to this problem is that of *radicalism* and *reform*, which seems to form such a dividing line between various political solutions. Yet, a closer analysis can show that this differentiation as it is usually conceived of is deceptive. There is reform and reform; reform can be *radical*, that is, going to the roots, or it can be superficial, trying to patch up symptoms without touching the causes. Reform which is not radical, in this sense, never accomplishes its ends and eventually ends up in the opposite direction. So-called "radicalism" on the other hand, which believes that we can solve problems by force, when observation, patience and continuous activity is required, is as unrealistic and fictitious as reform. Historically speaking, they both often lead to the same result. The revolution of the Bolsheviks led to Stalinism, the reform of the right wing Social Democrats in Germany, led to Hitler. The true criterion of reform is not its tempo but its realism, its true "radicalism"; it is the question whether it goes to the roots and attempts to change causes—or whether it remains on the surface and attempts to deal only with symptoms.

If this chapter is to discuss roads to sanity, that is, methods of cure, we had better pause here for a moment and ask ourselves what we know about the nature of cure in cases of individual mental diseases. The cure of social pathology must follow the same principle, since it is the pathology of so many human beings, and not of an entity beyond or apart from individuals.

The conditions for the cure of individual pathology are mainly the following:

1.) A development must have occurred which is contrary to the proper functioning of the psyche. In Freud's theory this means that the libido has failed to develop normally and that as a result, symptoms are produced. In the frame of reference of humanistic psychoanalysis, the causes of pathology lie in the failure to develop a productive orientation, a failure which results in the development of irrational passions, especially of incestuous, destructive and exploitative strivings. The *fact* of suffering, whether it is conscious or unconscious, resulting from the failure of normal development, produces a dynamic *striving to overcome the suffering, that is, for change in the direction of health.* This striving for health in our physical as well as in our mental organism is the basis for any cure of sickness, and it is absent only in the most severe pathology.

2.) The first step necessary to permit this tendency for health to operate is the *awareness* of the suffering and of that which is shut out and disassociated from our conscious personality. In Freud's doctrine, repression refers mainly to *sexual* strivings. In our frame of reference, it refers to the repressed irrational passions, to the repressed feeling of aloneness and futility, and to the longing for love and productivity, which is also repressed.

3.) Increasing self-awareness can become fully effective only if a next step is taken, that of changing a practice of life which was built on the basis of the neurotic structure, and which reproduces it constantly. A patient, for instance, whose neurotic character makes him want to submit to parental authorities has usually constructed a life where he has chosen dominating or sadistic father images as bosses, teachers, and so on. He will be cured only if he changes his realistic life situation in such a way that it does not constantly reproduce the submissive tendencies he wants to give up. Furthermore, he must change his systems of values, norms and ideals, so that they further rather than block his striving for health and maturity.

The same conditions—*conflict* with the requirements of human nature and resulting suffering, *awareness* of what is shut out, and *change* of the realistic situation and of values and norms— are also necessary for a cure of *social* pathology.

To show the conflict between human needs and our social structure, and to further the awareness of our conflicts and of that which is dissociated, was the purpose of the previous chapter of this book. To discuss the various possibilities of practical changes in our economic, political and cultural organization is the intention of this chapter.

However, before we start discussing the practical questions, let us consider once more what, on the basis of the premises developed in the beginning of this book, constitutes mental sanity, and what type of culture could be assumed to be conducive to mental health.

The mentally healthy person is the productive and unalienated person; the person who relates himself to the world lovingly, and who uses his reason to grasp reality objectively; who experiences himself as a unique individual entity, and at the same time feels one with his fellow man; who is not subject to irrational authority, and accepts willingly the rational authority of conscience and reason; who is in the process of being born as long as he is alive, and considers the gift of life the most precious chance he has.

Let us also remember that these goals of mental health are not ideals which have to be forced upon the person, or which man can attain only if he overcomes his "nature," and sacrifices his "innate selfishness." On the contrary, the striving for mental health, for happiness, harmony, love, productiveness, is inherent in every human being who is not born as a mental or moral idiot. Given a chance, these strivings assert themselves forcefully, as can be seen in countless situations. It takes powerful constellations and circumstances to pervert and stifle this innate striving for sanity; and indeed, throughout the greater part of known history, the use of man by man has produced such perversion. To believe that this perversion is inherent in man is like throwing seeds in the soil of the desert and claiming they were not meant to grow.

What society corresponds to this aim of mental health, and what would be the structure of a sane society? First of all, a society in which no man is a means toward another's ends, but always and without exception an end in himself; hence, where nobody is used, nor uses himself, for purposes which are not those of the unfolding of his own human powers; where man is the center, and where all economic and political activities are subordinated to the aim of his growth. A sane society is one in which qualities like greed, exploitativeness, possessiveness, narcissism, have no chance to be used for greater material gain or for the enhancement of one's personal prestige. Where acting according to one's conscience is looked upon as a fundamental and necessary quality and where opportunism and lack of principles is deemed to be asocial; where the individual is concerned with social matters so that they become personal matters, where his relation to his fellow man is not separated from his relationship in the private sphere. A sane society, furthermore, is one which permits man to operate within manageable and observable dimensions, and to be an active and responsible participant in the life of society, as well as the master of his own life. It is one which furthers human solidarity and not only permits, but stimulates, its members to relate themselves to each other lovingly; a sane society furthers the productive activity of everybody in his work, stimulates the unfolding of reason and enables man to give expression to his inner needs in collective art and rituals.

Economic Transformation

A. socialism as a problem

We have discussed in the previous chapter the three answers to the problem of present-day insanity, those of Totalitarianism, Super-Capitalism and Socialism. The totalitarian solution, be it of the Fascist or Stalinist type, quite obviously leads only to increased insanity and dehumanization; the solution of Super-Capitalism only deepens the pathology which is inherent in Capitalism; it increases man's alienation, his automatization, and completes the process of making him a servant to the idol of production. The only constructive solution is that of Socialism, which aims at a fundamental reorganization of our economic and social system in the direction of freeing man from being used as a means for purposes outside of himself, of creating a social order in which human solidarity, reason and productiveness are furthered rather than hobbled. Yet there can be no doubt that the results of Socialism, where it has been practiced so far, have been at least disappointing. What are the reasons for this failure? What are the aims and goals of social and economic reconstruction which can avoid this failure and lead to a sane society?

According to Marxist Socialism, a socialist society was built on two premises: the socialization of the means of production and distribution, and a centralized and planned economy. Marx and the early socialists had no doubt that if these aims could be accomplished, the human emancipation of all men from alienation, and a classless society of brotherliness and justice, would follow almost automatically. All that was necessary for the human transformation was, as they saw it, that the working class gained political control, either by force or by ballot, socialized industry, and instituted a planned economy. The question whether they were right in their assumption is not an academic question any more; Russia has done what the Marxist socialists thought was necessary to do in the economic sphere. While the Russian system showed that economically a socialized and planned economy can work efficiently, it proved that it is in no way a sufficient condition to create a free, brotherly and unalienated society. On the contrary, it showed that centralized planning can even create a greater degree of regimentation and authoritarianism than is to be found in Capitalism or in Fascism. The fact, however, that a socialized and planned economy has been realized in Russia does not mean that the Russian system is the realization of Socialism as Marx and Engels understood it. It means that Marx and Engels were mistaken in thinking that legal change in ownership and a planned economy were sufficient to bring about the social and human changes desired by them.

While socialization of the means of production in combination with a planned economy were the most central demands of Marxist Socialism, there were some others which have completely failed to materialize in Russia. Marx did not postulate complete equality of income, but nevertheless had in mind a sharp reduction of inequality as it exists in Capitalism. The fact is that inequality of income is much greater in Russia than in the United States or Britain. Another Marxist idea was that Socialism would lead to the withering of the state, and to the gradual disappearance of social classes. The fact is that the power of the state, and the distinction between social classes are greater in Russia than in any capitalist country. Eventually, the center of Marx's concept of Socialism was the idea that man, his emotional and intellectual powers, are the aim and goal of culture, that things (= capital) must serve life (labor) and that life must not be subordinated to that which is dead. Here again, the disregard for the individual and his human qualities is greater in Russia than in any of the capitalist countries.

But Russia was not the only country which tried to apply the economic concepts of Marxist Socialism. The other country was Great Britain. Paradoxically enough, the Labour Party, which is not based on Marxist theory, in its practical measures followed exactly the path of Marxist doctrine, that the realization of Socialism is based on the socialization of industry. The difference to Russia is clear enough. The British Labour Party always relied on peaceful means for the realization of its aims; its policy was not based on an all-or-nothing demand, but made it possible to socialize medicine, banking, steel, mining, railroads and the chemical industry, without nationalizing the rest of British industry. But while it introduced an economy in which socialist elements were blended with Capitalism, nevertheless the main idea for attaining Socialism was that of socialization of the means of production.

However, the British experiment, while less drastic in its failures, was also discouraging. On the one hand it created a good deal of regimentation and bureaucratization which did not endear it to anyone concerned with increase in human freedom and independence. On the other hand, it did not accomplish any of the basic expectations of Socialism. It became quite clear that it made very little or no difference to a worker in the British mining or steel industry whether the owner of the industry were a few thousand, or even hundred thousand individuals as in a public corporation, or the state. His wages, rights, and most important of all, his conditions of work, his role in the process of work remained essentially the same. There are few advantages brought about by nationalization which the worker could not have attained through his unions in a purely capitalist economy. On the other hand, while the main aim of Socialism has not been fulfilled by the measures of the Labour government, it would be shortsighted to ignore the fact that British Socialism has brought about favorable changes of the utmost importance in the life of the British people. One is the extension of the social security system to health. That no person in Great Britain has to be afraid of illness as of a catastrophe which may completely disorganize his life (not to speak of the possibility of losing it for lack of proper medical care), may sound little to a member of the middle or upper classes in the United States, who has no trouble paying the doctor's bill and hospitalization. But it is indeed a fundamental improvement to be compared to the progress made by the introduction of public education. It is furthermore true that the nationalization of industry, even to the limited degree that it was introduced in Britain (about ⅕ of the whole industry), permitted the state to regulate the total economy to a certain extent, a regulation from which the whole of the British economy profited.

But with all respect and appreciation for the achievements of the Labour government, their measures were not conducive to the realization of Socialism, if we take it in a human rather than in a purely economic sense. And if one were to argue that the Labour Party only began with the realization of its program, and that it would have introduced Socialism if it had been in power long enough to complete its work, such argument is not very convincing. Even visualizing the socialization of the whole of British heavy industry, one can see greater security, greater prosperity, and one need not be afraid that the new bureaucracy would be more dangerous to freedom than the bureaucracy of General Motors or General Electric. But in spite of all that could be said about its advantages, such socialization and planning would not be Socialism, if we mean by it a new form of life, a society of solidarity and faith, in which the individual has found himself and has emerged from the alienation inherent in the capitalistic system.

The terrifying result of Soviet Communism on the one hand, the disappointing results of Labour Party Socialism on the other, has led to a mood of resignation and hopelessness among many democratic socialists. Some still go on believing in Socialism, but more out of pride or stubbornness than out of real conviction. Others, busy with smaller or bigger tasks in one of the socialist parties, do not reflect too much and find themselves satisfied with the practical activities at hand; still others, who have lost faith in a renewal of society, consider it their main task to lead the crusade against Russian Communism; while they reiterate the charges against Communism, well-known and accepted by anybody who is not a Stalinist, they refrain from any radical criticism of Capitalism, and from any new proposals for the functioning of Democratic Socialism. They give the impression that everything is all right with the world, if only it can be saved from the Communist threat; they act like disappointed lovers who have lost all faith in love.

As one symptomatic expression of the general discouragement among democratic socialists, I quote from an article by R. H. S. Crossman, one of the most thoughtful and active leaders of the left wing of the Labour Party. "Living in an age not of steady progress towards a world welfare capitalism," Crossman writes, "but of world revolution, it is folly for us to assume that the socialist's task is to assist in the gradual improvement of the material lot of the human race and the gradual enlargement of the area of human freedom. The forces of history are all pressing toward totalitarianism: in the Russian bloc, owing to the conscious policy of the Kremlin; in the free world, owing to the growth of the managerial society, the effects of total rearmament, and the repression of colonial aspirations. The task of socialism is neither to accelerate this Political Revolution, nor to oppose it (this would be as futile as opposition to the Industrial revolution a hundred years ago), but to civilise it." [1]

It appears to me that Crossman's pessimism leads to two errors. One is the assumption that managerial or Stalinist totalitarianism can be "civilized." If by civilized is meant a less cruel system than that of Stalinist dictatorship, Crossman may be right. But the version of the Brave New World which rests entirely on suggestion and conditioning is as inhuman and as insane as Orwell's version

---

[1] *New Fabian Essays, ed.* by R. H. S. Crossman, Turnstile Press, London, 1953, p. 31.

of "1984." Neither version of a completely alienated society can be humanized. The other error lies in Crossman's pessimism itself. Socialism, in its genuine human and moral aspirations is still a potent aim of many millions all over the world, and the objective conditions for humanistic democratic socialism are more given today than in the nineteenth century. The reasons for this assumption are implicit in the following attempt to outline some of the proposals for a socialist transformation in the economic, political and cultural spheres. Before I go on, however, I should like to state, although it is hardly necessary, that my proposals are neither new nor are they meant to be exhaustive, or necessarily correct in detail. They are made in the belief that it is necessary to turn from a general discussion of principles to practical problems of how these principles can be realized. Long before political democracy was realized, the thinkers of the eighteenth century discussed blueprints of constitutional principles which were to show that—and how—the democratic organization of the state was possible. The problem in the twentieth century is to discuss ways and means to implement political democracy and to transform it into a truly human society. The objections which are made are largely based on pessimism and on a profound lack of faith. It is claimed that the advance of managerial society and the implied manipulation of man cannot be checked unless we regress to the spinning wheel, because modern industry needs managers and automatons. Other objections are due to a lack of imagination. Still others, to the deep-seated fear of being freed from commands and given full freedom to live. Yet it is quite beyond doubt that the problems of social transformation are not as difficult to solve —theoretically and practically—as the technical problems our chemists and physicists have solved. And it can also not be doubted that we are more in need of a human renaissance than we are in need of airplanes and television. Even a fraction of the reason and practical sense used in the natural sciences, applied to human problems, will permit the continuation of the task our ancestors of the eighteenth century were so proud of.

B. THE PRINCIPLE OF COMMUNITARIAN SOCIALISM

The Marxist emphasis on socialization of the means of production was influenced in itself by nineteenth-century Capitalism. Ownership and property rights were the central categories of capitalist economy, and Marx remained within this frame of reference when he defined Socialism by reversing the capitalist property system, demanding the "expropriation of the expropriators." Here, as in his orientation of political versus social factors, Marx and Engels were more influenced by the bourgeois spirit than other socialist schools of thought, which were concerned with the function of the worker in the work process, with his social relatedness to others in the factory, with the effect of the method of work on the character of the worker.

The failure—as perhaps also the popularity—of Marxist Socialism lies precisely in this bourgeois overestimation of property rights and purely economic factors. But other socialist schools of thought have been much more aware of the pitfalls inherent in Marxism, and have formulated the aim of Socialism much more adequately. Owenists, syndicalists, anarchists and guild socialists agreed in their main concern, which was the social and human situation of the worker in his work and the kind of relatedness to his fellow workers. (By "worker" I mean here and in the following pages everybody who lives from his own work, without additional profits from the employment of others.) The aim of all these various forms of Socialism, which we may call "communitarian Socialism," was an industrial organization in which *every working person would be an active and responsible participant, where work would be attractive and meaningful, where*

capital would not employ labor, but labor would employ capital.
They stressed the organization of work and the social relations
between men, not primarily the question of ownership. As I shall
show later, there is a remarkable return to this attitude by socialists
all over the world, who some decades ago considered the pure form
of Marxist doctrine to be *the* solution of all problems. In order to
give the reader a general idea of the principles of this type of
communitarian socialist thought, which in spite of considerable
differences is common to syndicalists, anarchists, guild socialists,
and increasingly so to Marxist Socialists, I quote the following
formulations by Cole:

He writes: "Fundamentally the old insistence on liberty is right;
it was swept away because it thought of liberty in terms of political
self-government alone. The new conception of liberty must be
wider. It must include the idea of man not only as a citizen in a
free state, but as a partner in an industrial commonwealth. The
bureaucratic reformer, by laying all the stress upon the purely
material side of life, has come to believe in a society made up of
well-fed, well-housed, well-clothed machines, working for a
greater machine, the state; the individualist has offered to men
the alternative of starvation and slavery under the guise of liberty
of action. The real liberty, which is the goal of the new Socialism,
will assure freedom of action and immunity from economic stress
by treating man as a human being, and not as a problem or a god.

"Political liberty by itself is, in fact, always illusory. A man
who lives in economic subjection six days, if not seven, a week,
does not become free merely by making a cross on a ballot-paper
once in five years. If freedom is to mean anything to the average
man it must include industrial freedom. Until men at their work
can know themselves members of a self-governing community of
workers, they will remain essentially servile, whatever the political
system under which they live. It is not enough to sweep away the

284

degrading relation in which the wage-slave stands to an individual employer. State Socialism, too, leaves the worker in bondage to a tyranny that is no less galling because it is impersonal. Self-government in industry is not merely the supplement, but the precursor of political liberty.

"Man is everywhere in chains, and his chains will not be broken till he feels that it is degrading to be a bondsman, whether to an individual or to a State. The disease of civilization is not so much the material poverty of the many as the decay of the spirit of freedom and self-confidence. The revolt that will change the world will spring, not from the benevolence that breeds "reform," but from the will to be free. Men will act together in the full con-sciousness of their mutual dependence; but they will act for them-selves. Their liberty will not be given them from above; they will take it on their own behalf.

"Socialists, then, must put their appeal to the workers not in the question, 'Is it not unpleasant to be poor, and will you not help to raise the poor?' but in this form: 'Poverty is but the sign of man's enslavement: to cure it *you* must cease to labour for others and must believe in yourself.' Wage-slavery will exist as long as there is a man or an institution that is the master of men: it will be ended when the workers learn to set freedom before comfort. The average man will become a socialist not in order to secure a 'minimum standard of civilized life,' but because he feels ashamed of the slavery that blinds him and his fellows, and because he is resolved to end the industrial system that makes them slaves." [1]

"First, then, what is the nature of the ideal at which Labour must aim? What is meant by that 'control of industry' which the workers are to demand? It can be summed up in two words—

[1] G. D. H. Cole and W. Mellor, *The Meaning of Industrial Freedom,* Geo. Allen and Unwin, Ltd., London, 1918, pp. 3, 4.

direct management. The task of actually conducting the business must be handed over to the workers engaged in it. To them it must belong to order production, distribution, and exchange. They must win industrial self-government, with the right to elect their own officers; they must understand and control all the complicated mechanism of industry and trade; they must become the accredited agents of the community in the economic sphere." [1]

C.   SOCIO-PSYCHOLOGICAL OBJECTIONS

Before discussing practical suggestions for the realization of communitarian Socialism in an industrial society, we had better stop and discuss some of the main objections to such possibilities; the first type of objection being based on the idea of the nature of industrial work, the other on the nature of man and the psychological motivations for work.

It is precisely with regard to any change in the work situation itself, that the most drastic objections to the ideas of communitarian Socialism are made by many thoughtful and well-meaning observers. Modern industrial work, so the argument runs, is by its very nature mechanical, uninteresting and alienated. It is based on an extreme degree of division of labor, and it can never occupy the interest and attention of the whole man. All ideas to make work interesting and meaningful again are really romantic dreams —and followed up with more consequence and realism they would logically result in the demand to give up our system of industrial production and to return to the pre-industrial mode of handicraft production. On the contrary, so the argument goes on, the aim must be to make work *more* meaningless and *more* mechanized. We have witnessed a tremendous reduction of working hours within the last hundred years, and a working day of four, or even two hours does not seem to be a fantastic expectation for the

[1] *Ibid.,* p. 22.

286

future. We are witnessing right now a drastic change in work methods. The work process is divided into so many small components, that each worker's task becomes automatic and does not require his active attention; thus, he can indulge in daydreams and reveries. Besides, we are using increasingly automatized machines, working with their own "brains" in clean, well-lit, healthy factories, and the "worker" does nothing but watch some instrument and pull some lever from time to time. Indeed, say the adherents of this point of view, *the complete automatization of work is what we hope for;* man will work a few hours; it will not be uncomfortable, nor require much attention; it will be an almost unconscious routine like brushing one's teeth, and the center of gravity will be the leisure hours in everybody's life.

This argument sounds convincing and who can say that the completely automatized factory and the disappearance of all dirty and uncomfortable work is not the goal which our industrial evolution is approaching? But there are several considerations to prevent us from making the automatization of work our main hope for a sane society.

First of all it is, at the least, doubtful whether the mechanization of work will have the results which are assumed in the foregoing argument. There is a good deal of evidence pointing to the contrary. Thus, for instance, a very thoughtful recent study among automobile workers shows that they disliked the job to the degree to which it embodied mass-production characteristics like repetitiveness, mechanical pacing, or related characteristics. While the vast majority liked the job for economic reasons (147 to 7), an even greater majority (96 to 1) disliked it for reasons of the immediate job content.[1] The same reaction was also expressed in the behavior of the workers. "Workers whose jobs had 'high mass

[1] Ch. R. Walker and R. H. Guest, *The Man on the Assembly Line,* Harvard University Press, Cambridge, Mass., 1952, pp. 142, 143.

production scores'—that is, exhibited mass production characteristics in an extreme form—were absent more often from their jobs than workers on jobs with low mass production scores. More workers quit jobs with high mass production scores than quit jobs with low ones." [1] It must also be questioned whether the freedom for daydreaming and reverie which mechanized work gives is as positive and healthy a factor as most industrial psychologists assume. Actually, daydreaming is a symptom of lacking relatedness to reality. It is not refreshing or relaxing—it is essentially an escape with all the negative results that go with escape. What the industrial psychologists describe in such bright colors is essentially the same lack of concentration which is so characteristic of modern man in general. You do three things at once because you do not do anything in a concentrated fashion. It is a great mistake to believe that doing something in a nonconcentrated form is refreshing. On the contrary, any concentrated activity, whether it is work, play or rest (rest, too, is an activity), is invigorating—any nonconcentrated activity is tiring. Anybody can find out the truth of this statement by a few simple self-observations.

But aside from all this, it will still be many generations before such a point of automatization and reduction of working time is reached, especially if we think not only of Europe and America but of Asia and Africa, which still have hardly started their industrial revolution. Is man, during the next few hundred years, to continue spending most of his energy on meaningless work, waiting for the time when work will hardly require any expenditure of energy? What will become of him in the meantime?

---

[1] *Ibid.*, p. 144. The experiences with job enlargement made by I.B.M. point to similar considerations. When one worker performed several operations which were subdivided before among several workers, so that the worker could have a sense of accomplishment and be related to the product of work, production rose and fatigue decreased.

Will he not become more and more alienated and this just as much in his leisure hours as in his working time? Is the hope for effortless work not a daydream based on the fantasy of laziness and push-button power, and a rather unhealthy fantasy at that? Is not work such a fundamental part of man's existence that it cannot and should never be reduced to almost complete insignificance? Is not the mode of work in itself an essential element in forming a person's character? Does completely automatized work not lead to a completely automatized life?

While all these questions are so many doubts concerning the idealization of completely automatized work, we must now deal with those views which deny the possibility that work could be attractive and meaningful, hence that it could be truly humanized. The argument runs like this: modern factory work is by its very nature not conducive to interest and satisfaction; furthermore, there is necessary work to be done, which is positively unpleasant or repelling. Active participation of the worker in management is incompatible with the requirements of modern industry, and would lead to chaos. In order to function properly in this system, man must obey, adjust himself to a routinized organization. By nature man is lazy, and not prone to be responsible; he therefore must be conditioned to function smoothly and without too much initiative and spontaneity.

To deal with these arguments properly we must indulge in some speculations on the problem of *laziness* and on that of the various *motivations for work*.

It is surprising that the view of man's natural laziness can still be held by psychologists and laymen alike, when so many observable facts contradict it. *Laziness, far from being normal, is a symptom of mental pathology*. In fact, one of the worst forms of mental suffering is boredom, not knowing what to do with oneself and one's life. Even if man had no monetary, or any other reward, he would be eager to spend his energy in some meaningful way because he could not stand the boredom which inactivity produces.

Let us look at children: they are never lazy; given the slightest encouragement, or even without it, they are busy playing, asking questions, inventing stories, without any incentive except the pleasure in the activity itself. In the field of psycho-pathology we find that the person who has no interest in doing anything is seriously sick and is far from exhibiting the normal state of human nature. There is plenty of material about workers during periods of unemployment, who suffer as much, or more, from the enforced "rest," as from the material deprivations. There is just as much material to show that for many people over sixty-five the necessity to stop working leads to profound unhappiness, and in many instances to physical deterioration and illness.

Nevertheless, there are good reasons for the widespread belief in man's innate laziness. The main reason lies in the fact that alienated work is boring and unsatisfactory; that a great deal of tension and hostility is engendered, which leads to an aversion against the work one is doing and everything connected with it. As a result, we find a longing for laziness and for "doing nothing" to be the ideal of many people. Thus, people feel that their laziness is the "natural" state of mind, rather than the symptom of a pathological condition of life, the result of meaningless and alienated work. Examining the current views on work motivation, it becomes evident that they are based on the concept of alienated work and hence that their conclusions do not apply to non-alienated, attractive work.

The conventional and most common theory is that *money* is the main incentive for work. This answer can have two different meanings: first, that fear of starvation is the main incentive for work; in this case the argument is undoubtedly true. Many types of work would never be accepted on the basis of wages or other work conditions were the worker not confronted with the alternative of accepting these conditions or of starvation. The unpleasant, lowly work in our society is done not voluntarily, but because the need to make a living forces so many people to do it.

More often the concept of money incentive refers to the wish to earn *more* money as the motivation to greater effort in working. If man were not lured by the hope of greater monetary reward, this argument says, he would not work at all, or at least, would work without interest.

This conviction still exists among the majority of industrialists, as well as among many union leaders. Thus, for instance, fifty manufacturing executives replied to the question as to what is of importance in increasing worker's productivity as follows:

"Money alone is the answer" 44%

"Money is by far the chief thing but some importance is to be attached to less tangible things" 28%

"Money is important but beyond a certain point it will not produce results" 28%

100% [1]

Actually, employers throughout the world are in favor of wage-incentive plans as the only means which would lead to higher productivity of the individual worker, to higher earnings for the workers and employers and thus, indirectly, to reduced absenteeism, easier supervision, and so on. Reports and surveys from industry and government bureaus "generally attest to the effectiveness of wage-incentive plans in increasing productivity and achieving other objectives." [2] It seems that workers also believe

[1] cf. Survey reported in the Public Opinion Index for Industry in 1947, quoted from M. S. Viteles, *Motivation and Morale in Industry*, W. W. Norton & Company, New York, 1953.
[2] *Ibid.*, p. 27.

that incentive pay gets the most output per man. In a survey conducted by the Opinion Research Corporation in 1949, involving 1,021 manual workers comprising a national sample of employees of manufacturing companies, 65 per cent said that incentive pay increases output, and only 22 per cent that hourly pay makes for higher production. However, as to the question of which method of pay *they prefer*, 65 per cent answered hourly pay, and only 29 per cent were in favor of incentive pay. (The ratio of preference for hourly pay was 74 to 20 in the case of hourly workers, but even in the case of workers already on incentive pay, 59 per cent were in favor of hourly pay as against 36 per cent in favor of incentive pay.)

The latter findings are interpreted by Viteles as showing that "as useful as incentive pay is in raising output, it does not in itself solve the problem of obtaining workers' cooperation. In some circumstances it may intensify that problem." [1] This opinion is shared increasingly by industrial psychologists and even some industrialists.

However, the discussion about money incentives would be incomplete if we did not consider the fact that the wish for more money is constantly fostered by the same industry which relies on money as the main incentive for work. By advertising, installment plan systems, and many other devices, the individual's greed to buy more and newer things is stimulated to the point that he can rarely have enough money to satisfy these *"needs."* Thus, being artificially stimulated by industry, the monetary incentive plays a greater role than it otherwise would. Furthermore, it goes without saying that the monetary incentive must play a paramount role as long as it is the *only* incentive because the work process in itself is unsatisfactory and boring. There are many examples of

[1] *Ibid.*, pp. 49, 50.

cases in which people choose work with less monetary reward if the work itself is more interesting.

Aside from money, *prestige, status* and the *power* that goes with it are assumed to be the main incentives for work. There is no need to prove that the craving for prestige and power constitutes the most powerful incentive for work today among the middle and upper classes; in fact, the importance of money is largely that of representing prestige, at least as much as security and comfort. But the role which the need for prestige plays also among workers, clerks and the lower echelons of the industrial and business bureaucracy is often ignored. The name-plate of the Pullman porter, the bank teller, etcetera, are significant psychological boosts to his sense of importance; as are the personal telephone, larger office space for the higher ranks. These prestige factors play a role also among industrial workers.[1]

Money, prestige and power are the main incentives today for the largest sector of our population—that which is employed. But there are other motivations: the satisfaction in building an *independent economic existence,* and the performance of *skilled work,* both of which made work much more meaningful and attractive than it is under the motivation of money and power. But while economic independence and skill were important satisfactions for the independent businessman, artisan, and the highly skilled worker in the nineteenth, and beginning of the twentieth century, the role of these motivations is now rapidly decreasing.

As to the increase of employed, in contrast to independents, we note that in the beginning of the nineteenth century more or less four fifths of the occupied population were self-employed entrepreneurs; around 1870 only one third belonged to this group,

---

[1] cf. W. Williams, *Mainsprings of Men,* Charles Scribner's Sons, New York, 1925, p. 56, quoted in M. S. Viteles, *loc. cit.,* p. 65 ff.

and by 1940 this old middle class comprises only one fifth of the occupied population.

This shift from independents to employees is in itself conducive to decreasing work satisfaction for the reasons which have already been discussed. The employed person, more than the independent one, works in an alienated position. Whether he is paid a lower or a higher salary, he is an accessory to the organization rather than a human being doing something for himself.

There is one factor, however, which could mitigate the alienation of work, and that is the skill required in its performance. But here too, development moves in the direction of decreasing skill requirements, and hence increasing alienation.

Among the office workers there is a certain amount of skill required, but the factor of a "pleasant personality," able to sell himself, becomes of ever-increasing importance. Among industrial workers the old type of all-around skilled worker loses ever more in importance compared with the semi-skilled worker. At Ford, at the end of 1948, the number of workers who could be trained in less than two weeks was 75 to 80 per cent of the whole working personnel of the plant. From a professional school with an apprentice program at Ford, only three hundred men graduated each year, of which half entered other factories. In a factory making batteries in Chicago, there are, among one hundred mechanics who are considered as highly qualified, only fifteen who have a thorough all-round technical knowledge; forty-five others are "skilled" only in the use of one particular machine. At one of the Western Electric plants in Chicago, the average training of the workers takes from three to four weeks, and up to six months for the most delicate and difficult tasks. The total personnel of 6,400 employees was composed in 1948 of about 1,000 white collar workers, 5,000 industrial workers, and only 400 workers who could be considered skilled. In other words, less than 10 per cent of the total personnel is technically qualified. In a big candy factory in Chicago, 90 per cent of the workers require a training "on the job" which is not longer than 48 hours.[1]

Even an industry like the Swiss-watch industry, which was based on the work of highly qualified and skilled men, has changed drastically in this respect. While there are still a number of factories producing according to the traditional principle of craftsmanship, the great watch factories established in the Canton of Solothurn have only a small percentage of genuinely skilled workers.[2]

To sum up, the vast majority of the population work as employees with little skill required, and with almost no chance to develop any particular talents, or to show any outstanding achievements. While the managerial or professional groups have at least considerable interest in achieving something more or less personal, the vast majority sell their physical, or an exceedingly small part of their intellectual capacity to an employer to be used for purposes of profit in which they have no share, for things in which they have no interest, with the only purpose of making a living, and for some chance to satisfy their consumer's greed.

Dissatisfaction, apathy, boredom, lack of joy and happiness, a sense of futility and a vague feeling that life is meaningless, are the unavoidable results of this situation. This socially patterned syndrome of pathology may not be in the awareness of people; it may be covered by a frantic flight into escape activities, or by a craving for more money, power, prestige. But the weight of the latter motivations is so great only because the alienated person cannot help seeking for such compensations for his inner vacuity, not because these desires are the "natural" or most important incentives for work.

[1] These figures are quoted from G. Friedmann, *loc. cit.*, p. 152 ff.
[2] cf. G. Friedmann, *loc. cit.*, pp. 319, 320.

Is there any empirical evidence that most people today are not satisfied with their work?

In an attempt to answer this question we must differentiate between what people *consciously think* about their satisfaction, and what they *feel unconsciously*. It is evident from psychoanalytic experience that the sense of unhappiness and dissatisfaction can be deeply repressed; a person may consciously feel satisfied and only his dreams, psychosomatic illness, insomnia, and many other symptoms may be expressive of the underlying unhappiness. The tendency to repress dissatisfaction and unhappiness is strongly supported by the widespread feeling that not to be satisfied means to be "a failure," queer, unsuccessful, etcetera. (Thus, for instance, the number of people who consciously think they are happily married, and express this belief sincerely in answer to a questionnaire is by far greater than the number of those who are really happy in their marriage.)

But even the data on *conscious* job satisfaction are rather telling.

In a study about job satisfaction on a national scale, satisfaction with and enjoyment of their job was expressed by 85 per cent of the professionals and executives, by 64 per cent of white-collar people, and by 41 per cent of the factory workers. In another study, we find a similar picture: 86 per cent of the professionals, 74 per cent of the managerial, 42 per cent of the commercial employees, 56 per cent of the skilled, and 48 per cent of the semi-skilled workers expressed satisfaction.[1]

We find in these figures a significant discrepancy between professionals and executives on the one hand, workers and clerks on the other. Among the former only a minority is dissatisfied— among the latter, more than half. Regarding the total population, this means, roughly, that over half of the total employed population is consciously dissatisfied with their work, and do not enjoy

[1] cf. C. W. Mills, *White Collar*, Oxford University Press, New York, 1951, p. 229.

it. If we consider the unconscious dissatisfaction, the percentage would be considerably higher. Taking the 85 per cent of "satisfied" professionals and executives, we would have to examine how many of them suffer from psychologically determined high blood pressure, ulcers, insomnia, nervous tension and fatigue. Although there are no exact data on this, there can be no doubt that, considering these symptoms, the number of really satisfied persons who enjoy their work would be much smaller than the above figures indicate.

As far as factory workers and office clerks are concerned, even the percentage of *consciously* dissatisfied people is remarkably high. Undoubtedly the number of unconsciously dissatisfied workers and clerks is much higher. This is indicated by several studies which show that neurosis and psychogenic illnesses are the main reasons for absenteeism (the estimates for the presence of neurotic symptoms among factory workers go up to about 50 per cent). Fatigue and high labor turnover are other symptoms of dissatisfaction and resentment.

The most important symptom from the economic standpoint, hence the best studied one, is the widespread tendency of factory workers, not to give their best to the work, or "work restriction" as it is often called. In a poll conducted by the Opinion Research Corporation in 1945, 49 per cent of all the manual workers questioned answered that "when a man takes a job in a factory he should turn out *as much as he can*," but 41 per cent answered that he should *not do his best*, but only "turn out the average amount." [1] [2]

[1] M. S. Viteles, *loc. cit.*, p. 61.

[2] Under the heading "The Decline of 'Economic' Man," Viteles comes to this conclusion: "In general, studies of the type cited above give continuing support to the conclusions reached by Mathewson, as a result of plant observations and interviews with management representatives, that

"1. Restrictions is a widespread institution, deeply intrenched in the working habits of American laboring people.

"2. Scientific management has failed to develop that spirit of confidence between

We see that there is a great deal of conscious, and even more unconscious dissatisfaction with the kind of work which our industrial society offers most of its members. One tries to counteract their dissatisfaction by a mixture of monetary and prestige incentives, and undoubtedly these incentives produce considerable eagerness to work, especially in the middle and higher echelons of the business hierarchy. But it is one thing that these incentives make people work, and it is quite another thing whether the mode of this work is conducive to mental health and happiness. The discussion on motivation of work usually considers only the first problem, namely whether this or that incentive increases the *economic* productivity of the worker, but not the second, that of his *human* productivity. One ignores the fact that there are many incentives which can make a person do something, but which at the same time are detrimental to his personality. A person can work hard out of fear, or out of an inner sense of guilt; psychopathology gives us many examples of neurotic motives leading to overactivity as well as to inactivity.

Most of us assume that the kind of work current in our society, namely, alienated work, is the only kind there is, hence that aversion to work is natural, hence that money and prestige and power are the only incentives for work. If we would use our imagination

---

the parties to labor contracts which has been so potent in developing good-will between the parties to a sales contract.

"3. Underwork and restriction are greater problems than over-speeding and over-work. The efforts of managers to speed up working people have been offset by the ingenuity of the workers in developing restrictive practices.

"4. Managers have been so content with the over-all results of man-hour output that only superficial attention has been given to the workers' contribution or lack of contribution to the increased yield. Attempts to secure increased output have been marked by traditional and unscientific methods, while the workers have held to the time-honored practices of self-protection which antedate time study, bonus plans, and other devices to encourage capacity production.

"5. Regardless of how much the individual may or may not desire to contribute a full day's work, his actual experiences often turn him away from good working habits." (M. S. Viteles, *loc. cit.*, pp. 58, 59).

just a little bit, we could collect a good deal of evidence from our own lives, from observing children, from a number of situations which we can hardly fail to encounter, to convince us that we long to spend our energy on something meaningful, that we feel refreshed if we can do so, and that we are quite willing to accept rational authority if what we are doing makes sense.

But even if this is true, most people object, what help is this truth to us? Industrial, mechanized work cannot, by its very nature, be meaningful; it cannot give any pleasure or satisfaction —there are no ways of changing these facts, unless we want to give up our technical achievements. In order to answer this objection and proceed to discuss some ideas on how modern work could be meaningful, I want to point out two different aspects of work which it is very important to discern for our problem: the difference *between the technical and the social aspects of work.*

D.   INTEREST AND PARTICIPATION AS MOTIVATION

If we consider separately the technical and the social aspects of the work situation, we find that many types of work would be attractive as far as the technical aspect is concerned, provided the social aspect were satisfactory; on the other hand, there are types of work where the technical aspect can by its very nature not be interesting, and yet where the social aspect of the work situation could make it meaningful and attractive.

Starting with the discussion of the first instance, we find that there are many men who would, for example, take keen pleasure in being railroad engineers. But although railroad engineering is one of the highest paid and most respected positions in the working class, it is, nevertheless, not the fulfillment of the ambition of those who could "do better." No doubt, many a business executive would find more pleasure in being a railroad engineer than in his own work if the social context of the job were different.

Let us take another example: that of a waiter in a restaurant. This job could be an exceedingly attractive one for many people, provided its social prestige were different. It permits of constant interpersonal intercourse, and to people who like food, it gives pleasure to advise others about it, to serve it pleasantly, and so on. Many a man would find much more pleasure in working as a waiter than in sitting in his office over meaningless figures were it not for the low social rating and low income of this job. Again, many others would love the job of a cab driver were it not for its negative social and economic aspects.

It is often said that there are certain types of work which nobody would want to perform unless forced to do so by economic necessity; the work of a miner is often given as an example. But considering the diversity of people, and of their conscious and unconscious fantasies, it seems that there would be a considerable number of people for whom working within the earth, and extracting its riches would have a great attraction were it not for the social and financial disadvantages of this type of work. There is hardly any kind of work which would not attract certain types of personalities, provided it were freed from the negative aspects, socially and economically.

But even granted that the foregoing considerations are correct, it is undoubtedly true that much of the highly routinized work which is required by mechanized industry cannot in itself be a source of pleasure or satisfaction. Here again the differentiation between the technical and the social aspect of the work proves to be important. While the technical aspect may indeed be uninteresting, the total work situation may offer a good deal of satisfaction.

Here are some examples which serve to illustrate this point. Let us compare a housewife who takes care of the house and does the cooking, with a maid who is paid for doing exactly the same work. Both for the housewife and the maid, the work in its technical aspects is the same, and it is not particularly interesting. Yet it will have an entirely different meaning and satisfaction for the two, provided we think of a woman with a happy relationship to husband and children, and of an average maid, who has no sentimental attachment to her employer. To the former, the work will not be drudgery, while to the latter it will be exactly 'that, and the only reason for doing it is that she needs the money paid for it. The reason for this difference is obvious: while the work is the same in its technical aspects, the work situation is entirely different. For the housewife it is part of her total relationship to her husband and children, and in this sense her work is meaningful. The maid does not participate in the satisfaction of this social aspect of the work.

Let us take another example: a Mexican Indian selling his goods on the market. The technical aspect of the work, that of waiting the whole day for customers and performing from time to time the transaction of answering questions as to price, etcetera, would be as boring and disagreeable as is the work of a salesgirl in a five-and-ten-cent store. There is, however, one essential difference. For the Mexican Indian the market situation is one of a rich and stimulating human intercourse. He responds with pleasure to his customers, is interested in talking with them, and would feel very frustrated if he had sold all his wares in the early morning and had no further occasion for this satisfaction in human relations. For the salesgirl in the five-and-ten-cent store the situation is radically different. While she does not have to smile as much as a higher-paid salesgirl at a more fashionable store, her alienation from the customer is exactly the same. There is no genuine human intercourse. She operates as part of the sales' machine, is afraid of being fired, and eager to make good. The work situation as a social situation is inhuman, empty and deprived of any kind of satisfaction. It is true, of course that the Indian sells his own product, and reaps his own profit, but even a small independent shopkeeper will also be bored unless he transforms the social aspect of the work situation into a human one.

Turning now to recent studies in the field of industrial psychology, we find a good deal of evidence for the significance of the differentiation between the technical and the social aspect of the work situation, and furthermore for the enlivening and stimulat-' ing effect of the active and responsible participation of the worker in his job.

One of the most striking examples of the fact that technically monotonous work can be interesting, if the work situation as a whole permits of interest and active participation, is the by now classic experiment carried out by Elton Mayo [1] at the Chicago Hawthorne Works of the Western Electric Company. The operation selected was that of assembling telephone coils, work which ranks as a repetitive performance, and is usually performed by women. A standard assembly bench with the appropriate equipment, and with places for five women workers was put into a room, which was separated by a partition from the main assembly room; altogether six operatives worked in this room, five working at the bench, and one distributing parts to those engaged in the assembly. All of the women were experienced workers. Two of them dropped out within the first year, and their places were taken by two other workers of equal skill. Altogether, the experiment lasted for five years, and was divided into various experimental periods, in which certain changes were made in the conditions of work. Without going into the details of these changes, it suffices to state that rest pauses were adopted in the morning

[1] cf. Elton Mayo, *The Human Problems of an Industrial Civilization*, The Macmillan Company, 2nd ed., New York, 1946. cf. also F. J. Roethlisberger and W. J. Dickson, *Management and the Worker*, Harvard University Press, Cambridge, 10th ed. 1950.

and afternoon, refreshments offered during these rest pauses, and the hours of work cut by half an hour. Throughout these changes, the output of each worker rose considerably. So far, so good; nothing was more plausible than the assumption that increased rest periods and some attempt to make the worker "feel better" were the cause for an increased efficiency. But a new arrangement in the twelfth experimental period disappointed this expectation and showed rather dramatic results: by arrangement with the workers, the group returned to the conditions of work as they had existed in the beginning of the experiment. Rest periods, special refreshments, and other improvements were all abolished for approximately three months. To everybody's amazement this did not result in a *decrease* of output but, on the contrary, the daily and weekly output rose to a higher point than at any time before. In the next period, the old concessions were introduced again, with the only exception that the girls provided their own food, while the company continued to supply coffee for the midmorning lunch. The output still continued to rise. And not only the output. What is equally important is the fact that the rate of sickness among the workers in this experiment fell by about 80 per cent in comparison with the general rate, and that a new social friendly intercourse developed among the working women participating in the experiment.

How can we explain the surprising result that "the steady increase seemed to ignore the experimental changes in its upward development"? [1] If it was not the rest pauses, the tea, the shortened working time, what was it that made the workers produce more, be more healthy and more friendly among themselves? The answer is obvious: while the *technical* aspect of monotonous, uninteresting work remained the same, and while even certain improvements like rest pauses were not decisive, the *social* aspect of the total

[1] E. Mayo, *loc. cit.*, p. 63.

work situation had changed, and caused a change in the attitude of the workers. They were informed of the experiment, and of the several steps in it; their suggestions were listened to and often followed, and what is perhaps the most important point, they were aware of participating in a meaningful and interesting experiment, which was important not only to themselves, but to the workers of the whole factory. While they were at first "shy and uneasy, silent and perhaps somewhat suspicious of the company's intentions," later their attitude was marked "by confidence and candour." The group developed a sense of participation in the work, because they knew what they were doing, they had an aim and purpose, and they could influence the whole procedure by their suggestions.

The startling results of Mayo's experiment show that sickness, fatigue and a resulting low output are not caused primarily by the monotonous *technical* aspect of the work, but by the alienation of the worker from the total work situation in its social aspects. As soon as this alienation was decreased to a certain extent by having the worker participate in something that was meaningful to him, and in which he had a voice, his whole psychological reaction to the work changed, although technically he was still doing the same kind of work.

Mayo's Hawthorne experiment was followed by a number of research projects which tend to prove that the social aspect of the work situation has a decisive influence on the attitude of the worker, even though the work process in its technical aspect remains the same. Thus, for instance, Wyatt and his associates ". . . provided clues as to other characteristics of the work situation which affect the *will to work*. These showed that variation in the rate of work in different individuals was dependent upon the prevailing group or *social atmosphere*, *i.e.*, on a collective influence which formed an intangible background and determined the general nature of the reactions to the conditions of work." [1] It is to the same point that in a smaller-sized working group, subjective satisfaction and output are higher than in larger working groups, although in the factories compared, the nature of the work process was almost identical, and physical conditions and welfare amenities were of a high order and much alike.[2] The relationship between group size and morale have also been noted in a study by Hewitt and Parfit, conducted in a British textile plant.[3] Here, the nonsickness "absence rate" was found to be significantly greater among workers in large-sized rooms than among those in smaller rooms accommodating fewer employees." [4] An earlier study in the aircraft industry, conducted during World War II by Mayo and Lombard,[5] arrives at very similar results.

The social aspect of the work situation as against the purely technical one has been given special emphasis by G. Friedmann. As one example of the difference between these two aspects, he describes the "Psychological climate" which often develops among the men working together on a conveyor belt. Personal bonds and interests develop among the working team, and the work situation in its total aspect is much less monotonous than it would appear to the outsider who takes into account only the technical aspect.[6]

[1] Survey reported in the Public Opinion Index for Industry in 1947, quoted from M. S. Viteles, *Motivation and Morale in Industry*, W. W. Norton & Company, New York, 1953, p. 134.

[2] M. S. Viteles, *loc. cit.*, p. 138.

[3] D. Hewitt and J. Parfit on *Working Morale and Size of Group Occupational Psychology*, 1953.

[4] M. S. Viteles, *loc. cit.*, p. 139.

[5] E. Mayo and G. F. F. Lombard, "Team Work and Labour Turnover in the Aircraft Industry of Southern California," Harvard Graduate School of Business, *Business Research Series No. 32*, 1944.

[6] G. Friedmann, *Où va le Travail Humain?*, Gallimard, Paris, 1950, p. 139. cf. also his *Machine et Humanisme*, Gallimard, Paris, 1946, pp. 329, 330 and 370 ff.

While the previous examples from research in industrial psychology [1] show us the results of even a small degree of active participation within the framework of modern industrial organization, we arrive at insights which are much more convincing from the standpoint of the possibilities of the transformation of our industrial organization by turning to the reports on the *communitarian movement,* one of the most significant and interesting movements in Europe today.

There are around one hundred Communities of Work in Europe, mainly in France, but also some in Belgium, Switzerland and Holland. Some of them are industrial, and some of them are agricultural. They differ among themselves in various aspects; nevertheless the basic principles are sufficiently similar so that the description of one gives an adequate picture of the essential features of all.[2]

Boimondau is a watch-case factory. In fact, it has become one of the seven largest such factories in France. It was founded by Marcel Barbu. He had to work hard in order to save enough to

[1] In the same direction are the experiments with "job enlargement" made by I.B.M. the main point of which is to show that the worker feels more satisfied if the extreme division of labor and the ensuing senselessness of his work is changed for an operation which combines several thus far separated operations in one more meaningful one. Furthermore, the experience reported by Walker and Guest, who found that automobile workers preferred a method of work in which they could at least *see* the parts they had finished ("banking"). In an experiment conducted in a Harwood Manufacturing Co. plant, democratic methods and decision making by the workers in an experimental group, led to an increase of output of 14 per cent within this group. (cf. Viteles, *loc. cit.*, pp. 164–167.) A study by P. French Jr. on sewing machine operators reports a rise of output of 18 per cent as a result of increased participation of workers in planning of the work and decision making. (J. R. P. French, "Field Experiments," in J. G. Miller, [ed.] *Experiments in Social Process,* The McGraw-Hill Book Co., New York, 1950, pp. 83–88). The same principle was applied in England during the war, when pilots came to visit factories to explain to the workers how their products were actually used in combat.

[2] I follow here a description of the Work Communities given in *All Things Common,* by Claire Huchet Bishop, Harper and Brothers, New York, 1950. I consider this penetrating and thoughtful work one of the most enlightening ones dealing with the psychological problems of industrial organization and the possibilities for the future.

have a factory of his own, where he introduced a factory council and a wage rating approved by all, including sharing in the profits. But this enlightened paternalism was not what Barbu was aiming at. After the French defeat in 1940, Barbu wanted to make a real start toward the liberation he had in mind. Since he could not find mechanics in Valence, he went out into the streets, and found a barber, a sausagemaker, a waiter—practically anyone except specialized industrial workers. "The men were all under thirty. He offered to teach them watch-case making, provided they would agree to *search* with him for a setup in which the 'distinction between employer and employee would be abolished.' The point was the search." . . . "The first and epoch-making discovery was that each worker should be free to tell the other off. . . . At once, this complete freedom of speech between themselves and their employer created a buoyant atmosphere of confidence.

"It soon became evident, however, that 'telling each other off' led to discussions and a waste of time on the job. So they unanimously set apart a time every week for an informal meeting to iron out differences and conflicts.

"But as they were not out just for a better economic setup but a new way of living together, discussions were bound to lead to the disclosure of basic attitudes. 'Very soon,' says Barbu, 'we saw the necessity of a common basis, or what we called, from then on, our common ethics.'

"Unless there was a common ethical basis, there was no point to start from together and therefore no possibility of building anything. To find a common ethical basis was not easy, because the two dozen workers now engaged were all different: Catholics, Protestants, materialists, Humanists, atheists, Communists. They all examined their own individual ethics, that is, not what they had been taught by rote, or what was conventionally accepted, but what they, out of their own experiences and thoughts, found necessary.

"They discovered that their individual ethics had certain points in common. They took those points and made them the common minimum on which they agreed unanimously. It was not a theoretical, vague declaration. In their foreword they declared:

" 'There is no danger that our common ethical minimum should be an arbitrary convention, for, in order to determine the points we rely on life experiences. All our moral principles have been tried in real life, everyday life, everybody's life. . . .'

"What they had rediscovered, all by themselves and step by step, was natural ethics, the Decalogue,[1] which they expressed in their own words as follows:

"Thou wilt love thy neighbor.
"Thou shalt not kill.
"Thou shalt not take thy neighbor's good.
"Thou shalt not lie.
"Thou wilt be faithful to thy promise.
"Thou shalt earn thy bread by the sweat of thy brow.
"Thou shalt respect thy neighbor, his person, his liberty.
"Thou shalt respect thyself.
"Thou shalt fight first against thyself, all vices which debase man, all the passions which hold man in slavery and are detrimental to social life: pride, avarice, lust, covetousness, gluttony, anger, laziness.
"Thou shalt hold that there are goods higher than life itself: liberty, human dignity, truth, justice. . . ."

"The men pledged themselves to do their best to practice their common ethical minimum in their everyday life. They pledged themselves to each other. Those who had more exacting private ethics pledged themselves to try to live what they believed, but recognized that they had absolutely no right to infringe on the

[1] Minus the first commandment, which bears on man's destiny and not on ethics.

liberties of others. In fact, they all agreed to respect fully the others' convictions or absence of convictions to the extent of never laughing at them or making jokes about it." [1]

The second discovery the group made was that they craved to educate themselves. They figured out that the time they saved on production could be used for education. Within three months, the productivity of their work grew so much, that they could save nine hours on a forty-eight-hour week. What did they do? They used these nine hours for education and were paid for it as for regular work hours. First they wanted to sing well together, then to polish their French grammar, then to learn how to read business accounts. From there, other courses developed, all given at the factory by the best instructors they could find. The instructors were paid the regular rates. There were courses in engineering, physics, literature, Marxism, Christianity, dancing, singing and basket ball.

Their principle is: "We do not start from the plant, from the technical activity of man, but from man himself. . . . In a Community of Work accent is not on *acquiring* together, but on *working together* for a collective and personal fulfillment." [2] The aim is not increased productivity, or higher wages, but a new style of life which "far from relinquishing the advantages of the industrial revolution, is adapted to them." [3] These are the principles on which this and other Communities of Work are built:

"1. In order to live a man's life one has to enjoy the whole fruit of one's labor.

"2. One has to be able to educate oneself.

[1] C. H. Bishop, *loc. cit.*, pp. 5, 6, 7.
[2] *Ibid.*, p. 12. (Italics mine, E.F.)
[3] *Ibid.*, p. 13.

"3. One has to pursue a common endeavor within a professional group proportioned to the stature of man (100
families maximum).

"4. One has to be actively related to the whole world.

"When these requisites are examined one discovers that they
amount to a shifting of the center of the problem of living—
from making and acquiring 'things,' to discovering, fostering
and developing human relationships. From a civilization of objects to a civilization of persons; better even—a civilization of
movement between persons." [1]

As to payment, it corresponds to the achievement of the single worker, but it takes into account not only professional work,
but also "any human activity which had value for the group:
A first-class mechanic who can play the violin, who is jolly and
a good mixer, etc., has more value to the Community than another mechanic, equally capable professionally, but who is a
sourpuss, a bachelor, etc." [2] On an average all workers earn between 10 and 20 per cent more than they would with union
wages, not counting all the special advantages.

The Community of Work acquired a farm of 235 acres, on
which everybody, including the wives, work three periods of
ten days each year. As everybody has a month's vacation, it
means that people work only ten months a year at the factory.
The idea behind it is not only the characteristic love of the
Frenchman for the country, but also the conviction that no man
should be entirely divorced from the soil.

Most interesting is the solution they have found for a blend
between centralization and decentralization which avoids the
danger of chaos, and at the same time makes every member of
the community an active and responsible participant in the life

[1] *Ibid.*, p. 13.
[2] *Ibid.*, p. 14.

of the factory and of the community. We see here how the same kind of thought and observation which led to the formulation of the theories underlying the modern democratic state in the eighteenth and nineteenth centuries, (division of powers, system of checks and balances, etcetera) was applied to the organization of an industrial enterprise.

"Ultimate power rests on the *General Assembly,* which meets twice a year. Only unanimous decisions bind the Companions (members).

"The General Assembly elects a *Chief of Community.* Unanimous vote only. The Chief is not only the most qualified technically, as a manager should be, he is also 'the man who is an example, who educates, who loves, who is selfless, who serves. To obey a so-called Chief without those qualities would be cowardice.'

"The Chief has all executive power for three years. At the end of this period he may find himself back at the machines.

"The Chief has the right of veto against the General Assembly. If the General Assembly does not want to yield, a vote of confidence has to be taken. If confidence is not granted unanimously, the Chief has the choice either to rally to the General Assembly's opinion or to resign.

"The General Assembly elects the members of the *General Council.* The General Council's task is to counsel the Chief of Community. Members are elected for one year. The General Council meets at least every four months. There are seven members plus the Heads of Departments. All decisions have to be taken unanimously.

"Within the General Council, section managers and eight members (including two wives) and the Chief of Community form the *Council of Direction,* which meets weekly.

"All responsible positions in the Community, including section managers and foremen, are secured only through 'double trust' appointment, that is, the person is proposed by one level and unanimously accepted by the other level. Usually, but not always, candidates are proposed by the higher level and accepted or rejected by the lower. This, say the members, prevents both demagogy and authoritarianism.

"All members meet once a week in an *Assembly of Contact,* which, as the name indicates, aims at keeping everybody abreast of what is happening in the Community and also of keeping in touch with each other." [1]

A particularly important feature of the whole Community are the *Neighbor Groups,* which meet periodically. "A Neighbor Group is the smallest organism of the Community. Five or six families which do not live too far from each other get together in the evening after supper under the guidance of a Chief of Neighbor Groups chosen according to the principle mentioned above.

"In a sense, the Neighbor Group is the most important unit in the Community. It is 'leaven' and 'lever.' It is required to meet at one of the families' home and at no other place. There, while drinking coffee, all the issues are thrashed out together. Minutes of the meeting are taken down and sent to the Chief of Community, who sums up the minutes of all the Neighbor Groups. Answers to their questions are then given by those who are in charge of the different departments. In that way Neighbor Groups not only ask questions but voice discontent or make suggestions. It is also of course in the Neighbor Groups that people come to know each other best and help each other." [2]

Another feature of the Community is the *Court.* It is elected

[1] *Ibid.*, pp. 17, 18.
[2] *Ibid.*, pp. 18, 19.

by the General Assembly, and its function is to decide on conflicts which arise between two departments, or between a department and a member; if the Chief of the Community cannot iron it out, the eight members of the Court (unanimous votes, as usual), do so. There is no set of laws, and the verdict is based on, and directed by the constitution of the Community, the common ethic minimum and common sense.

At Boimondau there are two main sectors: the social and the industrial sector. The latter has the following structure:

"Men—maximum 10—form technical teams.

"Several teams form a section, a shop.

"Several sections form a service.

"Members of teams are responsible all together toward the section, several sections toward the service." [1]

The social department deals with all activities other than technical ones. "All members, including wives, are expected to carry on their spiritual, intellectual, artistic and physical development. In that respect reading the monthly review of Boimondau, *Le Lien*, is enlightening. Reports and commentaries on everything: football matches (competing with outside teams), photographic displays, visits to art exhibits, cooking recipes, ecumenical gatherings, reviews of musical performances such as Loewenguth Quartet, appreciation of films, lectures on Marxism, basketball scores, discussion on conscientious objectors, accounts of days at the farm, reports on what America has to teach, passages from St. Thomas of Aquinas regarding money, reviews of books such as Louis Bromfield's *Pleasant Valley* and Sartre's *Dirty Hands*, etcetera. A resilient spirit of good will permeates it all. *Le Lien* is a candid picture of people who have said 'yes' to life, and this with a maximum of consciousness.

[1] *Ibid.*, p. 23.

"There are 28 social sections, but new ones are constantly added:

"(Teams listed according to numerical importance).

"1. Spiritual Section:
Catholic team
Humanist team
Materialist team
Protestant team

"2. Intellectual Section:
General Knowledge team
Civic Instruction team
Library team

"3. Artistic Section:
Theater team
Singing team
Interior Decorating team
Photo team

"4. Communitarian Life Section:
Cooperative team
Festivals and Gatherings team
Movie team
Countereffort team

"5. Mutual Aid Section:
Solidarity team
Household Maintenance team
Bookbinding team

"6. Family Section:
Child Care team
Education team
Social Life team

"7. Health Section:
2 registered nurses

1 practical nurse for general information
3 visiting nurses
"8. Sports Section:
Basketball team (men)
Basketball team (women)
Cross-country team
Football team
Volleyball team
Physical Culture team (men)
Physical Culture team (women)
"9. Newspaper Team" [1]

Perhaps better than any definition, some statements of members of the Community can give an idea of the spirit and practice of the Community of Work:

"A union member writes:

"I was shop delegate in 1936, arrested in 1940 and sent to Buchenwald. For twenty years I have known many capitalist firms. . . . In the Community of Work production is not the aim for living, but the means. . . . I did not dare hope such large and complete results during my generation.

"A Communist writes:

"As a member of the French Communist Party, and in order to avoid misunderstanding, I declare that I am entirely satisfied with my work and my communitarian life; my political opinions are respected, my complete liberty and my previous life ideal have become a reality.

"A materialist writes:

"As an atheist and a materialist, I consider that one of the most beautiful human values is tolerance and the respect of religious and philosophical opinions. For that reason I feel particularly at home in our Community of Work. Not only is my

[1] *Ibid.*, p. 35.

315

freedom of thought and expression left intact, but I find in the Community the material means and the time necessary to a deeper study of my philosophical conviction.

"A Catholic writes:

"I have been in the Community for four years. I belong to the Catholic group. Like all Christians I am trying to build a society in which the liberty and the dignity of the human being will be respected. . . . I declare, in the name of the whole Catholic group, that the Community of Work is the type of society that a Christian can wish for. There, every man is free, respected, and everything inclines him to do better and to search for Truth. If outwardly that society cannot be called Christian, it is Christian in fact. Christ gave us the sign through which it is possible to recognize his own: And we do love one another.

"A Protestant writes:

"We, Protestants in the Community, declare that this revolution of society is the solution that enables every man, freely to find his fulfillment in the way he has chosen. This without any conflict with his materialist or Catholic companions. . . . The Community composed of men who love one another fulfills our wishes to see men living in harmony together and knowing why they want to live.

"A Humanist writes:

"I was 15 years old when I left school, I left the church at 11, after my first communion. I had gone a little ahead in my schooling, but the spiritual problem was gone out of my mind. I was like the great majority: 'I did not give a d——' At 22 I entered the Community. At once I found there an atmosphere of study and work like in no other place. First I was attracted by the social side of the Community, and it was only later that I understood what the human value could be. Then I rediscovered that spiritual and moral side which is in man and which I had lost at the age of 11. . . . I belong to the humanist group, because I do not see the problem like the Christians or the materialists do. I love our Community because through it all the deep aspirations which are in each of us can be awakened, met and developed, so that we may be transformed from individuals into men." [1]

The principles of other communities whether they are agricultural or industrial, resemble those of Boimondau. Here are some statements from the Rule of the R. G. Workshops, a Community of Work which manufactures picture frames, quoted by the author of *All Things Common*:

"Our Community of Work is not a new form of enterprise nor a reform in order to harmonize the relation capital-labor.

"It is a new mode of living in which man should find his fulfillment, and in which all problems are solved in relation to the whole man. Thereby it is in opposition to present-day society, where solutions for the one or for the few are the usual concern.

". . . the consequence of bourgeois morality and capitalist system is a specialization of the activities of man to such a degree that man lives in moral misery, physical misery, intellectual misery or material misery.

"Often, in the working class, men suffer these four kinds of misery all together, and, under such conditions, it is a lie to speak of liberty, equality, fraternity.

"The aim of the Community of Work is to make possible the full development of man.

"Companions of R. G. declare that this is possible only within an atmosphere of liberty, equality, fraternity.

"But it should be acknowledged that, very often, those three words bring nothing to our mind except the picture on currency or the inscriptions on front doors of public buildings.

[1] *Ibid.*, pp. 35–37.

"LIBERTY

"A Man is really free only under three conditions:

"Economic freedom

"Intellectual freedom

"Moral freedom

"*Economic Freedom.* Man has an inalienable right to work. He has to have absolute right to the fruit of his work from which he should not part except freely.

"This conception is opposed to private property of collective means of production and to the reproducing of money by money which makes possible the exploitation of man by man.

"We also declare that by 'Work' should be understood everything of value man brings to society.

"*Intellectual Freedom.* A man is free only if he can choose. He can choose only if he knows enough to compare.

"*Moral Freedom.* A man cannot be really free if he is enslaved by his passions. He can be free only if he has an ideal and a philosophical attitude which makes it possible for him to have a coherent activity in life.

"He cannot, under pretext of hastening his economic or intellectual liberation, use means contrary to the ethics of the Community.

"Last, moral freedom does not mean license. It would be easy to demonstrate that moral freedom is to be found only within strict observance of the group ethics freely accepted.

"FRATERNITY

"Man can blossom only in society. Selfishness is a dangerous and non-lasting way of helping oneself. Man cannot separate his true interests from those of society. He can help himself only by helping society.

"He should become conscious that his own inclination makes him find an increase of joy with others.

"Solidarity is not only a task, it is a satisfaction and the best guarantee of security.

"Fraternity leads to mutual tolerance and to the determination never to separate. This makes it possible to take all decisions unanimously on a common minimum.

"EQUALITY

"We condemn those who declare demagogically that all men are equal. We can see that men are not equal in value.

"For us equality of rights means to put at the disposal of everyone the means to fulfill oneself completely.

Thereby we substitute a hierarchy of personal value for the conventional or hereditary hierarchy." [1]

Summing up the most remarkable points in the principles of these Communities, I want to mention the following:

1. The Communities of Work do make use of all modern industrial techniques, and avoid the tendency of going back to handicraft production.

2. They have devised a scheme in which active participation of everyone does not contradict a sufficiently centralized leadership; irrational authority has been replaced by rational authority.

3. The emphasis on the practice of life as against ideological differences. This emphasis enables men of the most varied and contradictory convictions to live together in brotherliness and tolerance without any danger of having to follow the "right opinion" proclaimed by the community.

4. The integration of work, social and cultural activities. Inasmuch as the work is not attractive technically, it is meaningful and attractive in its social aspect. Activity in the arts and sciences is an integral part of the total situation.

5. The situation of alienation is overcome, work has become a

[1] *Ibid.*, pp. 134–137.

meaningful expression of human energy, human solidarity is established without restriction of freedom—or the danger of conformity.

While many of the arrangements and principles of the Communities can be questioned and argued about, it seems nevertheless that we have here one of the most convincing empirical examples of a productive life, and of possibilities which are generally looked upon as fantastic from the standpoint of our present-day life in Capitalism.[1]

The communities described so far are, of course not the only examples for the possibility of communitarian life. Whether we take Owen's communities, or those of the Mennonites or Hutterites,[2] or the agricultural settlements in the State of Israel, they all contribute to our knowledge of the possibilities of a new style of life. They also show that most of these communitarian experiments are executed by men with a shrewd intelligence, and an immensely practical sense. They are by no means the dreamers our so-called realists believe them to be; on the contrary, they are mostly more realistic and imaginative than our conventional business leaders appear to be. Undoubtedly there have been many shortcomings in the principles and practice of these experiments,

[1] Mention must be made of the efforts of A. Olivetti in Italy to create a communitarian movement there. As head of the greatest typewriter factory in Italy, he has not only organized his factory in terms of the most enlightened practices to be found anywhere, but he has also worked out a whole scheme for an organization of society in a federation of communities based on principles which have Christian and socialist concerns (cf. his *L'Ordine Politico delle Communitá*, Roma, 1946). Olivetti has also made a certain beginning by founding community centers in various Italian cities; nevertheless the main difference from the communities mentioned so far is that on the one hand his own factory has not been transformed into a Community of Work, and apparently cannot be because Olivetti is not the sole owner, and also the fact that Olivetti has made specific plans for the organization of the whole society, thus giving more emphasis to a specific picture of the social and political structure than the communities in the communitarian movement have done.

[2] Cf. the article by C. Kratu, J. W. Fretz, R. Kreider, "Altruism in Mennonite Life" in *Form and Techniques of Altruistic and Spiritual Growth*, ed. by P. A. Sorokin, The Beacon Press, Boston, 1954.

which must be recognized in order to be avoided. Undoubtedly also, the nineteenth century with its unshakable belief in the wholesome effect of industrial competitiveness was less conducive to the success of these colonies than the second half of the twentieth century will be. But the glib condescension implying the futility and lack of realism of all these experiments is not any more reasonable than was the first popular reaction to the possibilities of railroad and later of aeroplane travel. It is essentially a symptom of the laziness of the mind and the inherent conviction that what has not been cannot be and will not be.

E. PRACTICAL SUGGESTIONS

The question is whether conditions similar to those created by the communitarians can be created for the whole of our society. The aim then would be to create a work situation in which man gives his lifetime and energy to something which has meaning for him, in which he knows what he is doing, has an influence on what is being done, and feels united with, rather than separated from, his fellow man. This implies that the work situation is made concrete again; that the workers are organized into sufficiently small groups to enable the individual to relate himself to the group as real, concrete human beings, even though the factory as a whole may have many thousands of workers. It means that methods of blending centralization and decentralization are found which permit active participation and responsibility for everybody, and at the same time create a unified leadership as far as it is necessary.

How can this be done?

The first condition for an active participation of the worker is that he is well informed not only about his own work, but about the performance of the whole enterprise. Such knowledge is, for one thing, technical knowledge of the work process.

A worker may have to make only a specific move on the conveyor belt, and it may be sufficient for his performance if he is trained on the job for two days, or two weeks, but his whole attitude toward his work would be different if he had a wider knowledge of all the technical problems involved in the production of the whole product. Such technical knowledge can be acquired in the first place by attendance at an industrial school, simultaneously with his first years of work in a factory. Furthermore, they can be acquired continuously by participating in technical and scientific courses given to all the workers of the factory, even at the expense of time taken from the job.[1] If the technical process employed in the factory is an object of interest and knowledge to the worker, if his own thinking process is stimulated by such knowledge, even the otherwise monotonous technical work he has to perform will assume a different aspect. Aside from technical knowledge about the industrial process, another knowledge is necessary: that of the economic function of the enterprise he is working for, and its relationship to the economic needs and problems of the community as a whole. Again, by schooling during the first years of his work, and by constant information given to him about the economic processes involved in his enterprise, the worker can acquire real knowledge of its function within the national and world economy.

However important, technically and economically, this knowledge of the work process and the functioning of the whole enterprise is, it is not enough. Theoretical knowledge and interest stagnate if there is no way of translating them into action. The worker can become an active, interested and responsible partici-

[1] This is already being done as a first step in this direction by some of the great industrial enterprises. The Communitarians have shown that not only technical, but also many other kinds of instruction can be given during working time.

pant only if he can have influence on the decisions which bear upon his individual work situation and the whole enterprise. His alienation from work can be overcome only if he is not employed by capital, if he is not the object of command, but if he becomes a responsible *subject who employs capital.* The principal point here is not *ownership of the means of production,* but *participation in management and decision making.* As in the political sphere, the problem here is to avoid the danger of an anarchic state of affairs in which central planning and leadership would be lacking; but the alternative between centralized authoritarian management and planless, unco-ordinated workers' management is not a necessary one. The answer lies in a blending of centralization and decentralization, in a synthesis between decision making flowing from above to below, and from below to above.

The principle of co-management and workers' participation [1] can be worked out in such a way that the responsibility for management is divided between the central leadership and the rank and file. Well-informed small groups discuss matters of their own work situation and of the whole enterprise; their decisions would be channelled to the management and form the basis for a real co-management. As a third participant, the consumer would have to participate in the decision making and planning in some form. Once we accept the principle that the primary purpose of any work is to serve people, and not to make a profit, those who are served must have a say in the operation of those

[1] cf. the ideas expressed by G. G. Friedmann in his wise and stimulating study *Machine et Humanisme,* Gallimard, Paris, 1946, especially p. 371 ff. One of the great masters of sociology, and one of the great personalities of our time, Alfred Weber, in his profound *Der Drittee oder der Vierte Mensch,* Piper Co., München, 1953, arrives at conclusions similar to the ones expressed here. He emphasizes the need for co-management of workers and employees, and the reduction of big enterprises into smaller units of optimal size coupled with the abolition of the profit motive, and introduction of a socialist form of competition. However, no external change will suffice; "we need a new human cristallization." (*loc. cit.,* p. 91 ff.)

who serve them. Again, as in the case of political decentralization, it is not easy to find such forms, but certainly it is not an
unsurmountable problem, provided the general principle of co-
management is accepted. In constitutional law we have solved
similar problems with regard to the respective rights of various
branches of government, and in the laws concerning corporations
we have solved the same problem with regard to the right of
various types of stockholders, management, etc.

The principle of co-management and co-determination means
a serious restriction of property rights. The owner or owners of
an enterprise would be entitled to a reasonable rate of interest
on their capital investment, but not to the unrestricted command
over men whom this capital can hire. They would have at least
to share this right with those who work in the enterprise. In
fact, as far as the big corporations are concerned, the stockholders
do not really exercise their property rights by making decisions;
if the workers shared the right to make decisions with the management, the factual role of the stockholders would not be fundamentally different. A law introducing co-management would be
a restriction of property rights, but by no means any revolutionary change in such rights. Even an industrialist as conservative as the protagonist of profit sharing in industry, J. F. Lincoln, proposes, as we have seen, that the dividends should not
exceed a relatively fixed and constant amount, and that the profit
exceeding this amount should be divided among the workers.
There are possibilities for workers co-management and control
even on the basis of present-day conditions. B. F. Fairless, for
instance, the chairman of the Board of the United States Steel
Corporation said in a recent address, (published in a condensed
form in the *Reader's Digest*, November 15, 1953, p. 17) that
the three hundred thousand employees of United States Steel
could buy all the common stock of the corporation by purchasing

87 shares apiece, at a total cost of $3,500. "By investing $10 (per week) apiece—which is about what our steel workers gained in the recent wage increase—the employees of U.S. Steel could buy all of the outstanding common stock in less than seven years." Actually, they would not even have to purchase that much, but only part of it in order to have enough of the stock to give them a voting majority.

Another proposal has been made by F. Tannenbaum in his *A Philosophy of Labor*. He suggests that the unions could buy sufficient shares of the enterprises whose workers they represent to control the management of these enterprises.[1] Whatever the method employed is, it is an evolutionary one, only continuing trends in property relations which already exist, and they are means to an end—and only means—to make it possible that men work for a meaningful aim in a meaningful way, and are not bearers of a commodity—physical energy and skill—which is bought and sold like any other commodity.

In discussing workers' participation one important point must be stressed, the danger namely, that such participation could develop in the direction of the profit sharing concepts of the super-capitalist type. If the workers and employees of an enterprise were exclusively concerned with *their* enterprise, the alienation between man and his social forces would remain unchanged. The egotistical, alienated attitude would only have been extended from one individual to the "team." It is therefore not an incidental but an essential part of workers' participation that they look beyond their own enterprise, that they be interested in and connected with consumers as well as with other workers in the same industry, and with the working population as a whole. The development of a kind of local patriotism for the firm, of an "esprit de corps" similar to that of college and uni-

[1] F. Tannenbaum, *A Philosophy of Labor*, *loc. cit.*

versity students, as recommended by Wyatt and other British social psychologists, would only reinforce the asocial and egotistical attitude which is the essence of alienation. All such suggestions in favor of "team" enthusiasm ignore the fact that there is only one truly social orientation, namely the one of solidarity with mankind. Social cohesion within the group, combined with antagonism to the outsider, is not social feeling but extended egotism.

Concluding these remarks on workers' participation, I want to stress again, even at the risk of being repetitious, that all suggestions in the direction of the humanization of work do not have the aim of increasing economic output nor is their goal a greater satisfaction with work *per se*. They make sense only in a totally different social structure, in which economic activity is a part—and a subordinate part—of social life. One cannot separate work activity from political activity, from the use of leisure time and from personal life. If work were to become interesting without the other spheres of life becoming human, no real change would occur. In fact, it could not become interesting. It is the very evil of present-day culture that it separates and compartmentalizes the various spheres of living. The way to sanity lies in overcoming this split and in arriving at a new unification and integration within society and within the individual human being.

I have spoken before of the discouragement among many socialists with the results of applied Socialism. But there is a growing awareness that the fault was not with the basic aim of Socialism, an unalienated society in which every working person participates actively and responsibly in industry and in politics, but with the wrong emphasis on private versus communal property and the neglect of the human and properly social factors. There is, correspondingly, a growing insight into the necessity for a socialist vision which is centered around the idea of workers' participation and co-management, on decentralization, and on the concrete function of man in the working process, rather than on the abstract concept of property. The ideas of Owen, Fourier, Kropotkin, Landauer, of religious and secular communitarians, become fused with those of Marx and Engels; one becomes skeptical of purely ideological formulations of the "final aims," and more concerned with the concrete person, with the here and now. There is hope that there may be also growing awareness among democratic and humanist socialists that Socialism begins at home, that is to say, with the *socialization of the socialist parties*. Socialism is meant here, of course, not in terms of property rights, but in terms of responsible participation of each member. As long as the socialist parties do not realize the principle of Socialism within their own ranks, they cannot expect to convince others; their representatives would, if they had political power, execute their ideas in the spirit of Capitalism, regardless of the socialist labels they used. The same holds true for trade unions; inasmuch as their aim is industrial democracy, they must introduce the principle of democracy in their own organizations, rather than run them as any other big business is run in Capitalism—or sometimes even worse.

The influence of this communitarian emphasis on the concrete situation of the worker in his work process was quite powerful in the past among Spanish and French anarchists and syndicalists, and among the Russian Social Revolutionaries. Although the importance of these ideas had been receding in most countries for some time, it seems that they are slowly gaining ground again in less ideological and dogmatic and hence more real and concrete forms.

In one of the most interesting recent publications on the problems of Socialism, the *New Fabian Essays,* one can detect this

growing emphasis on the functional and human aspect of Socialism. C. A. R. Crosland writes in his essay on "The Transition
from Capitalism": "Socialism requires that this hostility in industry should give way to a feeling of participation in a joint endeavour. How is this to be achieved? The most direct and easily
exploitable line of advance is in the direction of joint consultation. Much fruitful work has been done in this sphere, and it is
now clear that something more is needed than joint production
committees on the present model—some more radical effort to
give the worker a sense of participation in the making of decisions. A few progressive firms have already made bold advances,
and the results are encouraging." [1] He suggests three measures:
large-scale extension of nationalization, statutory dividend limi-
tation or: "A third possibility is so to alter the legal structure of
company ownership as to substitute for shareholders' sole control
a constitution which explicitly defines the responsibilities of the
firm to worker, consumer and community; workers would become members of the company, and have their representatives
on the board of directors." [2]

R. Jenkins in his paper on "Equality" sees as the issue of the
future, ". . . in the first place, whether the capitalists, having
surrendered or had taken from them so much of their power, and
therefore of their functions, should be allowed to retain the quite
substantial portion of their privileges which still remain to them;
and, in the second place, whether the society which is growing
out of capitalism is to be a participant, democratic socialist
society, or whether it is to be a managerial society, controlled by
a privileged elite enjoying a standard of living substantially
different from that of the mass of the population." [3] Jenkins

[1] cf. C. A. R. Crosland, "The Transition from Capitalism," in the *New Fabian
Essays,* ed. by R. H. S. Crossman, Turnstile Press, Ltd., London, 1953, p. 66.
[2] *loc. cit.,* p. 67.
[3] *Ibid.,* p. 72.

came to the conclusion that "a participant, democratic socialist society" requires that the "ownership of enterprises, when it passes from wealthy individuals, should go, not to the state, but to less remote public bodies," and should permit greater diffusion of power and "encourage people of all sorts to play a more active part in the work and control of public and voluntary organizations."

A. Albu in "The Organisation of Industry" states: "However successful the nationalisation of basic industries has been in technical and economic terms, it has not satisfied the desire for a wider and more democratic distribution of authority nor built up any real measure of participation, by those engaged in them, in managerial decisions and their execution. This has been a disappointment to many socialists who never wished for a great concentration of state power, but who had none but the most hazy and Utopian ideas of any alternatives. The lessons of totalitarianism abroad and the growth of the managerial revolution at home have underlined their anxiety; all the more so as full employment in a society which remains democratic is seen to create problems which need for their solution the widest possible popular sanction based on information and consultation. Consultation is the less successful the further it recedes from face-to-face discussion on the job; and the size and structure of industrial units and the degree to which they can exercise independent initiative are therefore seen as matters of supreme importance." [1] "What is finally required," says Albu, "is a consultative system which will provide sanction for policy decisions and for an executive authority willingly accepted by all the members of an industry. How to reconcile this conception of industrial democracy with the more primitive desire for self-government which activated the syndicalists, and which underlies so much current discussion

[1] *New Fabian Essays*, p. 121, 122.

329

on joint consultation, is a matter on which much research needs still to be done. It would seem, however, that there must exist some process by which all those employed in an industry are enabled to participate in policy decisions; either through directly elected representatives on the board or through a hierarchical system of joint consultation with considerable powers. In either case there must also be an increasing participation in the process of interpreting policy and of making decisions at subordinate levels.

"The creation of a feeling of common purpose in the activities of industry still remains, therefore, one of the outstanding un-attained objectives of socialist industrial policy." [1]

John Strachey, who is the most optimistic and perhaps the most satisfied with the result of the Labour government among the writers in the *New Fabian Essays,* agrees with Albu's emphasis on the necessity of workers participation. "After all," Strachey writes in *Tasks and Achievement of British Labour,* "what is the matter with the joint stock company is the irresponsible dictatorship exercised over it, nominally by its shareholders, actually in many cases by one or two self-appointing and self-perpetuating directors. Make public companies directly responsible both to the community and to the whole body of those engaged in their activities, and they would become institutions of a very different kind." [2]

I have quoted the voices of some of the British Labour leaders because their views are the result of a good deal of practical experience with the socialization measures of the Labour Government, and of a thoughtful criticism of these accomplishments. But also Continental socialists have paid more and more attention to workers' participation in industry than ever before. In France and Germany after the war, laws were adopted which

[1] *Ibid.,* p. 129, 130.
[2] *Ibid.,* p. 198.

provided for workers' participation in the management of enterprises. Even though the results of these new provisions were far from satisfactory (the reasons being the halfheartedness of the measures and the fact that in Germany union representatives were transformed into "managers" rather than that the workers of the factory themselves participated), it is nevertheless clear that there is a growing insight among socialists into the fact that the transfer of property rights from the private capitalist to society or the state has, in itself, only a negligible effect on the situation of the worker, and that the central problem of Socialism lies in the change of the work situation. Even in the rather weak and confused declarations of the newly formed Socialist International in Frankfurt (1951) emphasis is put on the necessity of decentralizing economic power, wherever this is compatible with the aims of planning.[1] Among scientific observers of the industrial scene, it is especially Friedmann, and to some extent Gillespie, who arrive at conclusions similar to my own, concerning the transformation of work.

Emphasizing the necessity for co-management rather than centering plans for communitarian transformation on the change of property rights does not mean that a certain degree of direct state intervention and socialization are not necessary. The most important problem, aside from co-management, lies in the fact that our whole industry is built upon the existence of an ever-widening inner market. Each enterprise wants to sell more and more in order to conquer an ever-widening share of the market. The result of this economic situation is that industry uses all means within its power to whet the buying appetite of the population, to create and reinforce the receptive orientation which is so detrimental to mental sanity. As we have seen, this means

[1] cf. A. Albu "The Organization of Industry," in the *New Fabian Essays, loc. cit.*, p. 121, and also A. Sturmthal "Nationalization and Workers Control in Britain and France," *The Journal of Pol. Economy*, Vol. 61, I, 1953.

that there is a craving for new but unnecessary things, a constant wish to buy more, even though from the standpoint of human, unalienated use, there is no need for the new product. (The automobile industry, for instance, spent some billion dollars on the changes for the new 1955 models, Chevrolet alone some hundred million dollars to compete with Ford. Without doubt, the older Chevrolet was a good car, and the fight between Ford and General Motors has not primarily the effect of giving the public a better car, but of making them buy a new car when the old one would have done for another few years.)[1] Another aspect of the same phenomenon is the tendency to waste, which is furthered by the economic need for increasing mass production. Aside from the economic loss implied in this waste, it has also an important psychological effect: it makes the consumer lose respect for work and human effort; it makes him forget the needs of people within his own and in poorer lands, for whom the product he wastes could be a most valuable possession; in short, our habits of waste show a childish disregard for the realities of human life, for the economic struggle for existence which nobody can evade.

It is quite obvious that in the long run no amount of spiritual influence can be successful if our economic system is organized in such a way that a crisis threatens when people do not want to buy more and more newer and better things. Hence if our aim is to change alienated into human consumption, changes are necessary in those economic processes which produce alienated consumption.[2] It is the task of economists to devise such measures.

[1] R. Moley expressed the point very lucidly: when writing in *Newsweek* on the expenses for the new 1955 car models, he stated that Capitalism wants to make people feel unhappy with what they have, so that they want to buy something new, while Socialism would want to do the opposite.

[2] cf. Clark's statement in *Condition of Economic Progress*: "The same amount of income comparatively equally distributed will create a greater relative demand for manufacture than if it is unequally distributed" (quoted from N. N. Foote and

Generally speaking, it means to direct production into fields where existing real needs have not yet been satisfied, rather than where needs must be created artificially. This can be done by means of credits through state-owned banks, by the socialization of certain enterprises, and by drastic laws which accomplish a transformation of advertising.

Closely related to this problem is that of economic help from the industrialized societies to the economically less developed part of the world. It is quite clear that the time of colonial exploitation is over, that the various parts of the world have been brought together as closely as one continent was a hundred years ago, and that peace for the wealthier part of the world is dependent on the economic advancement of the poorer part. Peace and liberty in the Western World cannot, in the long run, coexist with hunger and sickness in Africa and China. Reduction of unnecessary consumption in the industrialized countries is a must if they want to help the nonindustrialized countries, and they must want to help them, if they want peace. Let us consider a few facts: according to H. Brown, a world development program covering fifty years would increase agricultural production to the point where all persons would receive adequate nutrition and would lead to an industrialization of the now undeveloped areas similar to the prewar level of Japan.[1] The yearly outlay for the United States for such a program would be between four and five billion dollars each year for the first thirty years, and afterwards less. "When we compare this to our national income," says the author, "to our present federal budget, to the

---

P. K. Hatt, "Social Mobility and Economic Advancement," *The American Econ. Rev.,* XLII, May, 1953).

[1] cf. Harrison Brown, *The Challenge of Man's Future,* The Viking Press, New York, 1954, pp. 245 ff. I know few books which present so clearly the alternative between sanity and insanity, progress and destruction for modern society, based on compelling reasoning and indisputable facts.

funds required for armament, and to the cost of waging war, the amount required does not appear to be excessive. When we compare it to the potential gains that can result from a successful program, it appears even smaller. And when we compare the cost with that of inaction and to the consequences of maintaining the status quo, it is indeed insignificant." [1]

The foregoing problem is only part of the more general problem as to what extent the interests of profitable capital investment may be permitted to manipulate the public needs in a detrimental and unhealthy way. The most obvious examples are our movie industry, the comic-book industry and the crime pages of our newspapers. In order to make the highest profit, the lowest instincts are artificially stimulated and the mind of the public is poisoned. The Food and Drug Act has regulated the unrestricted production and advertising of harmful food and drugs; the same can be done with regard to all other vital necessities. If such laws should prove to be ineffective, certain industries, such as the film industry, must be socialized, or at least competing industries must be created, financed with public funds. In a society in which the only aim is the development of man, and in which material needs are subordinated to spiritual needs, it will not be difficult to find legal and economic means to insure the necessary changes.

As far as the economic situation of the individual citizen is concerned, the idea of equality of income has never been a socialist demand and is for many reasons neither practical nor even desirable. What is necessary is an income which will be the basis for a dignified human existence. As far as inequalities of income are concerned, it seems that they must not transcend the point where differences in income lead to differences in the experience

[1] *Ibid.*, p. 247, 248.

of life. The man with an income of millions, who can satisfy any whim without even thinking about it, experiences life in a different way from the man who to satisfy one costly wish has to sacrifice another. The man who can never travel beyond his town, who can never afford any luxury (that is to say, something that is not necessary), again has a different life experience from his neighbor who can do so. But even within certain differences of income the basic experience of life can remain the same, provided the income difference does not exceed a certain margin. What matters is not so much the greater or lesser income as such, but the point where quantitative differences of income are transformed into a qualitative difference of life experience.

Needless to say, the system of social security, as it exists now in Great Britain for instance, must be retained. But this is not enough. The existing social-security system must be extended to a *universal subsistence guarantee.*

Each individual can act as a free and responsible agent only if one of the main reasons for present-day un-freedom is abolished: the economic threat of starvation which forces people to accept working conditions which they would otherwise not accept. There will be no freedom as long as the owner of capital can enforce his will on the man who owns "only" his life, because the latter, being without capital, has no work except what the capitalist offers him.

A hundred years ago it was a widely accepted belief that no one had the responsibility for his neighbor. It was assumed—and scientifically "proved" by economists—that the laws of society made it necessary to have a vast army of poor and jobless people in order to keep the economy going. Today, hardly anybody would dare to voice this principle any longer. It is generally accepted that nobody should be excluded from the wealth of the nation, either by the laws of nature, or by those of society. The rationalizations which were current a hundred years ago, that the poor owed their condition to their ignorance, lack of responsibility —briefly, to their "sins"—are outdated. In all Western industrialized countries a system of insurance has been introduced which guarantees everyone a minimum for subsistence in case of unemployment, sickness and old age. It is only one step further to postulate that, even if these conditions are not present, everyone has a right to receive the means to subsist. Practically speaking, that would mean that every citizen can claim a sum, enough for the minimum of subsistence even though he is not unemployed, sick, or aged. He can demand this sum if he has quit his job voluntarily, if he wants to prepare himself for another type of work, or for any personal reason which prevents him from earning money, without falling under one of the categories of the existing insurance benefits; shortly, he can claim this subsistence minimum without having to have any "reason." It should be limited to a definite time period, let us say two years, so as to avoid the fostering of a neurotic attitude which refuses any kind of social obligation.

This may sound like a fantastic proposal,[1] but so would our insurance system have sounded to people a hundred years ago. The main objection to such a scheme would be that if each person were entitled to receive minimum support, people would not work. This assumption rests upon the fallacy of the inherent laziness in human nature; actually, aside from neurotically lazy people, there would be very few who would not want to earn more than the minimum, and who would prefer to do nothing rather than to work.

[1] Dr. Meyer Shapiro called my attention to the fact that Bertrand Russell made the same suggestion in *Proposed Roads to Freedom*, Blue Ribbon Books, New York, p. 86 ff.

However, the suspicions against a system of guaranteed subsistence minimum are not unfounded from the standpoint of those who want to use ownership of capital for the purpose of forcing others to accept the work conditions they offer. If nobody were forced any more to accept work in order not to starve, work would have to be sufficiently interesting and attractive to induce one to accept it. Freedom of contract is possible only if both parties are free to accept and reject it; in the present capitalist system this is not the case.

But such a system would be not only the beginning of real freedom of contract between employers and employees; it would also enhance tremendously the sphere of freedom in interpersonal relationships between person and person in daily life.

Let us look at some examples. A person who is employed today, and dislikes his job, is often forced to continue in it because he does not have the means to risk unemployment even for one or two months, and naturally if he quits the job, he has no right to unemployment benefits. But actually the psychological effects of this situation go much deeper; the very fact that he cannot risk being fired, tends to make him afraid of his boss or whomever he is dependent on. He will be inhibited in answering back; he will try to please and to submit, because of the constantly present fear that the boss could fire him if he asserted himself. Or let us take the man who at the age of forty decides that he wants an entirely different kind of job, for which it will take one or two years to prepare himself. Since under the conditions of a guaranteed existence minimum this decision would imply having to live with a minimum of comfort, it would require great enthusiasm for and interest in his newly chosen field, and thus only those who were gifted and really interested would make the choice. Or let us take a woman living in an unhappy marriage, whose only reason for not leaving her husband is the inability to support herself even for the time necessary to be trained for a job. Or let us think of an adolescent living in severe conflicts with a neurotic or destructive father, whose mental health would be saved if he were free to leave his family. Briefly, the most fundamental coercion on economic grounds in business and private relations would be removed and the freedom to act would be restored to everybody.

What about costs? Since we already have adopted the principle for the unemployed, the sick and the aged, there would only be a marginal group of additional people who would make use of this privilege, the ones who are particularly gifted, those who find themselves in a temporary conflict, and the neurotic ones who have no sense of responsibility, or interest in work. Considering all factors involved, it would seem that the number of people using this privilege would not be extraordinarily high, and by careful research an approximate estimate could even be made today. But it must be emphasized that this proposal is to be taken together with the other social changes suggested here, and that in a society in which the individual citizen actively participates in his work, the number of people not interested in work would only be a fraction of what it is under present-day conditions. Whatever their number, it seems that the cost for such a scheme would hardly be more than what big states have spent for the maintenance of armies in the last decades, not taking into consideration the cost of armaments. It should also not be forgotten that in a system which restores interest in life and in work to everybody, the productivity of the individual worker would be far above that reported today as a result of even a few favorable changes in the work situation; in addition, our expenses due to criminality, neurotic or psychosomatic illness would be considerably less.

POLITICAL TRANSFORMATION

I have tried to show in a previous chapter that democracy cannot work in an alienated society, and that the way our democracy is organized contributes to the general process of alienation. If democracy means that the individual expresses his conviction and asserts his will, the premise is that he has a conviction, and that he has a will. The facts, however, are that the modern, alienated individual has opinions and prejudices but no convictions, has likes and dislikes, but no will. His opinions and prejudices, likes and dislikes, are manipulated in the same way as his taste is, by powerful propaganda machines—which might not be effective were he not already conditioned to such influences by advertising and by his whole alienated way of life.

The average voter is poorly informed too. While he reads his newspaper regularly, the whole world is so alienated from him that nothing makes real sense or carries real meaning. He reads of billions of dollars being spent, of millions of people being killed; figures, abstractions, which are in no way interpreted in a concrete, meaningful picture of the world. The science fiction he reads is little different from the science news. Everything is unreal, unlimited, impersonal. Facts are so many lists of memory items, like puzzles in a game, not elements on which his life and that of his children depends. It is indeed a sign of resilience and basic sanity of the average human being, that in spite of these conditions, political choices today are not entirely irrational, but that to some extent sober judgment finds expression in the process of voting.

In addition to all this, one must not forget that the very idea of majority vote lends itself to the process of abstractification and alienation. Originally, majority rule was an alternative to minority rule, the rule by the king or feudal lords. It did not mean that the majority was *right*; it meant that it is better for the majority to be wrong than for a minority to impose its will on the majority. But in our age of conformity the democratic method has more and more assumed the meaning that a majority decision is necessarily right, and morally superior to that of the minority, and hence has the moral right to impose *its* will on the minority. Just as a nationally advertised product claims, "Ten million Americans can't be wrong," so the majority decision is taken as an argument for its rightness. This is obviously an error; in fact, historically speaking, all "right" ideas in politics as well as in philosophy, religion or science, were originally the ideas of minorities. If one had decided the value of an idea on the basis of numbers, we would still be dwelling in caves.

As Schumpeter has pointed out, the voter simply expresses preferences between two candidates competing for his vote. He is confronted with various political machines, with a political bureaucracy which is torn between good will for the best for the country, and the professional interest of keeping in office, or getting back into it. This political bureaucracy, needing votes is, of course, forced to pay attention to the will of the voter to some extent. Any signs of great dissatisfaction force the political parties to change their course in order to obtain votes, and any sign of a very popular course of action will induce them to continue it. In this respect even the nondemocratic authoritarian regime is to some extent dependent on the popular will, except that by its coercive methods it can afford for a much longer time to pursue an unpopular course. But aside from the restricting or furthering influence which the electorate has on the decisions of the political bureaucracy, and which is more an indirect than a direct influence, there is little the individual citizen can do to participate in the decision making. Once he has cast his vote, he has abdicated his political will to his representative, who exercises it according to the mixture of responsibility and egotistical professional interest which is characteristic of him, and the individual citizen can do little except vote at the next election, which gives him a chance to continue his representative in office or "to throw the rascals out." The voting process in the great democracies has more and more the character of a plebiscite, in which the voter cannot do much more than register agreement or disagreement with powerful political machines, to one of which he surrenders his political will.

The progress of the democratic process from the middle of the nineteenth to the middle of the twentieth centuries is one of the enlargement of franchise, which has by now led to the general acceptance of unrestricted and universal suffrage. But even the fullest franchise is not enough. The further progress of the democratic system must take a new step. In the first place, it must be recognized that true decisions cannot be made in an atmosphere of mass voting, but only in the relatively small groups corresponding perhaps to the old Town Meeting, and comprising not more than let us say five hundred people. In such small groups the issues at stake can be discussed thoroughly, each member can express his ideas, can listen to, and discuss reasonably other arguments. People have personal contact with each other, which makes it more difficult for demagogic and irrational influences to work on their minds. Secondly, the individual citizen must be in the possession of vital facts which enables him to make a reasonable decision. Thirdly, whatever he, as a member of such a small and face-to-face group decides, must have a direct influence on the decision making exercised by a centrally elected parliamentary executive. If this were not so, the citizen would remain as politically stupid as he is today.

The question arises whether such a system of combining a centralized form of democracy, as it exists today, with a high degree of decentralization is possible; whether we can reintroduce the principle of the Town Meeting into modern industrialized society.

I do not see any insoluble difficulty in this. One possibility is to organize the whole population into small groups of say five hundred people, according to local residence, or place of work, and as far as possible these groups should have a certain diversification in their social composition. These groups would meet regularly, let us say once a month, and choose their officials and committees, which would have to change every year. Their program would be the discussion of the main political issues, both of local and of national concern. According to the principle mentioned above, any such discussion, if it is to be reasonable, will require a certain amount of factual information. How can this be given? It seems perfectly feasible that a cultural agency, which is politically independent, can exercise the function of preparing and publishing factual data to be used as material in these discussions. This is only what we do in our school system, where our children are given information which is relatively objective and free from the influence of fluctuating governments. One could imagine arrangements, for instance, by which personalities from the fields of art, sciences, religion, business, politics, whose outstanding achievements and moral integrity are beyond doubt, could be chosen to form a nonpolitical cultural agency. They would differ in their political views, but it can be assumed that they could agree reasonably on what is to be considered objective information about facts. In the case of disagreement, different sets of facts could be presented to the citizens, explaining the basis for the difference. After the small face-to-face groups have received information and have discussed matters, they will vote; with the help of the technical devices we have today, it would be very easy to register the over-all result of these votes in a short time, and then the problem would be how decisions arrived at in this way could be channeled into the level of the central government and made effective in the field of decision making. There is no reason why forms for this process could not be found. In the parliamentary tradition we have usually two parliamentary houses, both participating in the decision making, but elected according to different principles. The decision of the face-to-face groups would constitute the true "House of Commons," which would share power with the house of universally elected representatives and a universally elected executive. In this way, decision making would constantly flow, not only from above to below, but from below to above, and it would be based on an active and responsible thinking of the individual citizen. Through the discussion and voting in small face-to-face groups, a good deal of the irrational and abstract character of decision making would disappear, and political problems would become in reality a concern for the citizen. The process of alienation in which the individual citizen surrenders his political will by the ritual of voting to powers beyond him would be reversed, and each individual would take back into himself his role as a participant in the life of the community.[1]

CULTURAL TRANSFORMATION

No social or political arrangement can do more than further or hinder the realization of certain values and ideals. The ideals of the Judaeo-Christian tradition cannot possibly become realities in a materialistic civilization whose structure is centered around production, consumption and success on the market. On the other hand, no socialist society could fulfill the goal of brotherliness, justice and individualism unless its ideas are capable of filling the hearts of man with a new spirit.

We do not need new ideals or new spiritual goals. The great

[1] cf. to the problem of face-to-face groups, Robert A. Nisbet, *The Quest for Community*, Oxford University Press, New York, 1953.

teachers of the human race have postulated the norms for sane living. To be sure, they have spoken in different languages, have emphasized different aspects and have had different views on certain subjects. But, altogether, these differences were small; the fact that the great religions and ethical systems have so often fought against each other, and emphasized their mutual differences rather than their basic similarities, was due to the influence of those who built churches, hierarchies, political organizations upon the simple foundations of truth laid down by the men of the spirit. Since the human race made the decisive turn away from rootedness in nature and animal existence, to find a new home in conscience and brotherly solidarity, since it conceived first the idea of the unity of the human race and its destiny to become fully born—the ideas and ideals have been the same. In every center of culture, and largely without any mutual influence, the same insights were discovered, the same ideals were preached. We, to-day, who have easy access to all these ideas, who are still the immediate heirs to the great humanistic teachings, we are not in need of new knowledge of how to live sanely—but in bitter need of taking seriously what we believe, what we preach and teach. The revolution of our hearts does not require new wisdom—but new seriousness and dedication.

The task of impressing on people the guiding ideals and norms of our civilization is, first of all, that of education. But how woefully inadequate is our educational system for this task. Its aim is primarily to give the individual the knowledge he needs in order to function in an industrialized civilization, and to form his character into the mold which is needed: ambitious and competitive, yet co-operative within certain limits; respectful of authority, yet "desirably independent," as some report cards have it; friendly, yet not deeply attached to anybody or anything. Our high schools and colleges continue with the task of providing their students with the knowledge they must have to fulfill their practical tasks in life, and with the character traits wanted on the personality market. Very little, indeed, do they succeed in imbuing them with the faculty of critical thought, or with character traits which correspond to the professed ideals of our civilization. Surely there is no need to elaborate on this point, and to repeat a criticism which has been made so competently by Robert Hutchins and others. There is only one point which I want to emphasize here: the necessity of doing away with the harmful separation between theoretical and practical knowledge. This very separation is part of the alienation of work and thought. It tends to separate theory from practice, and to make it more difficult, rather than easier, for the individual to participate meaningfully in the work he is doing. If work is to become an activity based on his knowledge and on the understanding of what he is doing, then indeed there must be a drastic change in our method of education, in the sense that from the very beginning theoretical instruction and practical work are combined; for the young people, practical work should be secondary to theoretical instruction; for the people beyond school age, it should be the reverse; but at no age of development would the two spheres be separated from each other. No youngster should graduate from school unless he had learned some kind of handicraft in a satisfactory and meaningful manner; no primary education would be considered finished before the student has a grasp of the fundamental technical processes of our industry. Certainly high school ought to combine practical work of a handicraft and of modern industrial technique with theoretical instruction.

The fact that we aim primarily at the usefulness of our citizens for the purposes of the social machine, and not at their human development is apparent in the fact that we consider education necessary only up to the age of fourteen, eighteen, or at most, the early twenties. Why should society feel responsible only for the education of children, and not for the education of all adults of every age? Actually, as Alvin Johnson has pointed out so convincingly, the age between six and eighteen is not by far as suitable for learning as is generally assumed. It is, of course, the best age to learn the three R's, and languages, but undoubtedly the understanding of history, philosophy, religion, literature, psychology, etcetera, is limited at this early age, and in fact, even around twenty, at which age these subjects are taught in college, is not ideal. In many instances to really understand the problems in these fields, a person must have had a great deal more experience in living than he has had at college age. For many people the age of thirty or forty is much more appropriate for learning—in the sense of understanding rather than of memorizing—than school or college age, and in many instances the general interest is also greater at the later age than at the stormy period of youth. It is around this age also at which a person should be free to change his occupation completely, and hence to have a chance to study again, the same chance which today we permit only our youngsters.

A sane society must provide possibilities for adult education, much as it provides today for the schooling of children. This principle finds expression today in the increasing number of adult-education courses, but all these private arrangements encompass only a small segment of the population, and the principle needs to be applied to the population as a whole.

Schooling, be it transmission of knowledge or formation of character, is only one part, and perhaps not the most important part of education; using "education" here in its literal and most fundamental sense of "e-ducere" = "to bring out," that which is within man. Even if man has knowledge, even if he performs his work well, if he is decent, honest, and has no worries with regard to his material needs—he is not and cannot be satisfied.

Man, in order to feel at home in the world, must grasp it not only with his head, but with all his senses, his eyes, his ears, with all his body. He must act out with his body what he thinks out with his brain. Body and mind cannot be separated in this, or in any other aspect. If man grasps the world and thus unites himself with it by thought, he creates philosophy, theology, myth and science. If man expresses his grasp of the world by his senses, he creates art and ritual, he creates song, dance, drama, painting, sculpture. Using the word "art," we are influenced by its usage in the modern sense, as a separate area of life. We have, on the one hand, the artist, a specialized profession—and on the other hand the admirer and consumer of art. But this separation is a modern phenomenon. Not that there were not "artists" in all great civilizations. The creation of the great Egyptian, Greek or Italian sculptures were the work of extraordinarily gifted artists who specialized in their art; so were the creators of Greek drama or of music since the seventeenth century.

But what about a Gothic cathedral, a Catholic ritual, an Indian rain dance, a Japanese flower arrangement, a folk dance, community singing? Are they art? Popular art? We have no word for it, because art in a wide and general sense, as a part of everybody's life, has lost its place in our world. What word can we use then? In the discussion of alienation I used the term "ritual." The difficulty here is, of course, that it carries a religious meaning, which puts it again in a special and separate sphere. For lack of a better word, I shall use "collective art," meaning the same as ritual; it means *to respond to the world with our senses in a meaningful, skilled, productive, active, shared way.* In this description the "shared" is important, and differentiates the concept of "collective art" from that of art in the modern sense. The latter is individualistic, both in its production, and in its consumption.

"Collective art," is shared; it permits man to feel one with others in a meaningful, rich, productive way. It is not an individual "leisure time" occupation, *added* to life, it is an integral part of life. It corresponds to a basic human need, and if this need is not fulfilled, man remains as insecure and anxious as if the need for a meaningful thought picture of the world were unrealized. In order to grow out of the receptive into the productive orientation, he must relate himself to the world artistically and not only philosophically or scientifically. If a culture does not offer such a realization, the average person does not develop beyond his receptive or marketing orientation.

Where are *we*? Religious rituals have little importance any more, except for the Catholics. Secular rituals hardly exist. Aside from the attempts to imitate rituals in lodges, fraternities, etc., we have a few patriotic and sport rituals, appealing only to a most limited extent to the needs of the total personality. We are a culture of consumers. We "drink in" the movies, the crime reports, the liquor, the fun. There is no active productive participation, no common unifying experience, no meaningful acting out of significant answers to life. What do we expect from our young generation? What are they to do when they have no opportunity for meaningful, shared artistic activities? What else are they to do but to escape into drinking, movie-daydreaming, crime, neurosis and insanity? What help is it to have almost no illiteracy, and the most widespread higher education which has existed at any time—if we have no collective expression of our total personalities, no common art and ritual? Undoubtedly a relatively primitive village in which there are still real feasts, common artistic shared expressions, and no literacy at all—is more advanced culturally and more healthy mentally than our educated, newspaper-reading, radio-listening culture.

No sane society can be built upon the mixture of purely intellectual knowledge and almost complete absence of shared artistic experience, college plus football, crime stories plus Fourth of July celebrations, with Mothers' and Fathers' day and Christmas thrown in for good measure. In considering how we can build a sane society, we must recognize that the need for the creation of collective art and ritual on a nonclerical basis is at least as important as literacy and higher education. The transformation of an atomistic into a communitarian society depends on creating again the opportunity for people to sing together, walk together, dance together, admire together—together, and not, to use Riesman's succinct expression, as a member of a "lonely crowd."

A number of attempts have been made to revive collective art and ritual. The "Religion of Reason" with its new feast days and rituals, was the form created by the French Revolution. National feelings created some new rituals, but they never gained the importance which the lost religious ritual once had. Socialism created its ritual in the First of May celebration, in the use of the fraternal "comrade," etcetera, but the significance was never greater than that of the patriotic ritual. Perhaps the most original and profound expression of collective art and ritual was to be found in the German Youth movement, which flourished in the years before and after the first World War. But this movement remained rather esoteric and was drowned in the rising flood of Nationalism and Racism.

On the whole, our modern ritual is impoverished and does not fulfill man's need for collective art and ritual, even in the remotest sense, either as to quality or its quantitive significance in life.

What are we to do? Can we invent rituals? Can one artificially create collective art? Of course not! But once one recognizes the need for them, once one begins to cultivate them, seeds will grow, and gifted people will come forth who will add new forms to old ones, and new talents will appear which would have gone unnoticed without such new orientation.

Collective art will begin with the children's games in kindergarten, be continued in school, then in later life. We shall have common dances, choirs, plays, music, bands, not entirely replacing modern sport, but subordinating it to the role of one of the many nonprofit and nonpurpose activities.

Here again, as in industrial and political organization, the decisive factor is decentralization; concrete face-to-face groups, active responsible participation. In the factory, in the school, in the small political discussion groups, in the village, various forms of common artistic activities can be created; they can be stimulated as much as is necessary by the help and suggestion from central artistic bodies, but not "fed" by them. At the same time, modern radio and television techniques give marvelous possibilities to bring the best of music and literature to large audiences. Needless to say it cannot be left to business to provide for these opportunities, but that they must rank with our educational facilities which do not make a profit for anybody.

It might be argued that the idea of a large-scale revival of ritual and collective art is romantic; that it suits an age of handicrafts, and not an age of machine production. If this objection were true, we might as well resign ourselves to the fact that our way of life would destroy itself soon, because of its lack of balance, and sanity. But actually, the objection is not any more compelling than the objections made to the "possibility" of railroads and heavier-than-air flying machines. There is only one valid point in this objection. The way we *are*, atomized, alienated, without any genuine sense of community, we shall not be able to create new forms of collective art and ritual.

But this is just what I have been emphasizing all along. One cannot separate the change in our industrial and political organization from that of the structure of our educational and cultural life. No serious attempt for change and reconstruction will succeed if it is not undertaken in all those spheres simultaneously.

Can one speak of a spiritual transformation of society without mentioning *religion?* Undoubtedly, the teachings of the great monotheistic religions stress the humanistic aims which are the same as those which underlie the "productive orientation." The aims of Christianity and Judaism are those of the dignity of man as an aim and an end in himself, of brotherly love, of reason and of the supremacy of spiritual over material values. These ethical aims are related to certain concepts of God in which the believers of the various religions differ among themselves, and which are unacceptable to millions of others. However, it was an error of the nonbelievers to focus on attacking the idea of God; their real aim ought to be to challenge religionists to take their religion, and especially the concept of God, seriously; that would mean to practice the spirit of brotherly love, truth and justice, hence to become the most radical critics of present-day society.

On the other hand, even from a strictly monotheistic standpoint, discussions about God mean to use God's name in vain. But while we cannot say what God *is,* we can state what God is *not*. Is it not time to cease to argue about God, and instead to unite in the unmasking of contemporary forms of idolatry? Today it is not Baal and Astarte but the deification of the state and of power in authoritarian countries and the deification of the machine and of success in our own culture; it is the all-pervading alienation which threatens the spiritual qualities of man. Whether we are religionists or not, whether we believe in the necessity for a new religion or in the continuation of the Judaeo-Christian tradition, inasmuch as we are concerned with the essence and not with the shell, with the experience and not with the word, with man and not with the institution, we can unite in firm negation of idolatry and find perhaps more of a common faith in this negation than in any affirmative statements about God. Certainly we shall find more of humility and of brotherly love.

This statement remains true even if one believes, as I do, that the theistic concepts are bound to disappear in the future development of humanity. In fact, for those who see in the monotheistic religions only one of the stations in the evolution of the human race, it is not too far-fetched to believe that a new religion will develop within the next few hundred years, a religion which corresponds to the development of the human race; the most important feature of such a religion would be its universalistic character, corresponding to the unification of mankind which is taking place in this epoch; it would embrace the humanistic teachings common to all great religions of the East and of the West; its doctrines would not contradict the rational insight of mankind today, and its emphasis would be on the practice of life, rather than on doctrinal beliefs. Such a religion would create new rituals and artistic forms of expression, conducive to the spirit of reverence toward life and the solidarity of man. Religion can, of course, not be invented. It will come into existence with the appearance of a new great teacher, just as they have appeared in previous centuries when the time was ripe. In the meantime, those who believe in God should express their faith by *living* it; those who do not believe, by living the precepts of love and justice and—waiting.[1]

[1] The same suggestion for a new humanistic religion has been made by Julian Huxley in "Evolutionary Humanism," *The Humanist*, Vol. XII, 5, 1953, p. 201 ff.

9

SUMMARY—CONCLUSION

Man first emerged from the animal world as a freak of nature. Having lost most of the instinctive equipment which regulates the animal's activities, he was more helpless, less well equipped for the fight for survival, than most animals. Yet he had developed a capacity for thought, imagination and self-awareness, which was the basis for transforming nature and himself. For many thousands of generations man lived by food gathering and hunting. He was still tied to nature, and afraid of being cast out from her. He identified himself with animals and worshiped these representatives of nature as his gods. After a long period of slow development, man began to cultivate the soil, to create a new social and religious order based on agriculture and animal husbandry. During this period he worshiped goddesses as the bearers of natural fertility, experienced himself as the child dependent on the fertility of the earth, on the life-giving breast of Mother. At a time some four thousand years ago, a decisive turn in man's history took place. He took a new step in the long-drawn-out process of his emergence from nature. He severed the ties with nature and with Mother, and set himself a new goal, that of being fully born, of being fully awake, of being fully human; of being free.

Reason and conscience became the principles which were to guide him; his aim was a society bound by the bonds of brotherly love, justice and truth, a new and truly human home to take the place of the irretrievably lost home in nature.

And then again about five hundred years before Christ in the great religious systems of India, Greece, Palestine, Persia and China, the idea of the unity of mankind and of a unifying spiritual principle underlying all reality assumed new and more developed expressions. Lao-tse, Buddha, Isajah, Heraclitus and Socrates, and later, on Palestinian soil, Jesus and the Apostles, on American soil, Quetzalcoatl, and later again, on Arabian soil, Mohammed, taught the ideas of the unity of man, of reason, love and justice as the goals man must strive for.

Northern Europe seemed to sleep for a long time. Greek and Christian ideas were transmitted to its soil, and it took a thousand years before Europe was saturated with them. Around 1500 A.D. a new period began. Man discovered nature and the individual, he laid the foundations for the natural sciences, which began to transform the face of the earth. The closed world of the Middle Ages collapsed, the unifying heaven broke up, man found a new unifying principle in science, and was searching for a new unity in the social and political unification of the earth and in the domination of nature. Moral conscience, the heritage of the Judaeo-Christian tradition, and intellectual conscience, the heritage of the Greek tradition, fused and brought about a flowering of human creation as man had hardly ever known it before.

Europe, the youngest child of humanity, culturally speaking, developed such wealth and such weapons that it became the master of the rest of the world for several hundred years. But again, in the middle of the twentieth century, a drastic change is occurring, a change as great as ever occurred in the past. The new techniques replace the use of the physical energy of animals and men by that of steam, oil and electricity; they create means of communication which transform the earth into the size of one continent, and the human race into one society where the fate of one group is the fate of all; they create marvels of devices which permit the best of art, literature and music to be brought to every member of society; they create productive forces which will permit everybody to have a dignified material existence, and reduces work to such dimensions that it will fill only a fraction of man's day.

Yet today, when man seems to have reached the beginning of a new, richer, happier human era, his existence and that of the generations to follow is more threatened than ever. How is this possible?

Man had won his freedom from clerical and secular authorities, he stood alone with his reason and his conscience as his only judges, but he was afraid of the newly won freedom; he had achieved "freedom from"—without yet having achieved "freedom to"— to be himself, to be productive, to be fully awake. Thus he tried to escape from freedom. His very achievement, the mastery over nature, opened up the avenues for his escape.

In building the new industrial machine, man became so absorbed in the new task that it became the paramount goal of his life. His energies, which once were devoted to the search for God and salvation, were now directed toward the domination of nature and ever-increasing material comfort. He ceased to use production as a means for a better life, but hypostatized it instead to an end in itself, an end to which life was subordinated. In the process of an ever-increasing division of labor, ever-increasing mechanization of work, and an ever-increasing size of social agglomerations, man himself became a part of the machine, rather than its master. He experienced himself as a commodity, as an investment; his aim became to be a success, that is, to sell himself as profitably as possible on the market. His value as a person lies in his salability, not in his human qualities of love, reason, or in his artistic capacities. Happiness becomes identical with consumption of newer and better commodities, the drinking in of music, screen plays, fun, sex, liquor and cigarettes. Not having a sense of self except the one which conformity with the majority can give, he is insecure, anxious, depending on approval. He is alienated from himself, worships the product of his own hands, the leaders of his own making, as if they were above him, rather than made by him. He is in a sense back where he was before the great human evolution began in the second millenium B.C.

He is incapable to love and to use his reason, to make decisions, in fact incapable to appreciate life and thus ready and even willing to destroy everything. The world is again fragmentalized, has lost its unity; he is again worshiping diversified things, with the only exception that now they are man-made, rather than part of nature.

The new era started with the idea of individual initiative. Indeed, the discoverers of new worlds and sea lanes in the sixteenth and seventeenth centuries, the pioneers of science, and the founders of new philosophies, the statesmen and philosophers of the great English, French and American revolutions, and eventually, the industrial pioneers, and even the robber barons showed marvelous individual initiative. But with the bureaucratization and managerialization of Capitalism, it is exactly the individual initiative that is disappearing. Bureaucracy has little initiative, that is its nature; nor have automatons. The cry for individual initiative as an argument for Capitalism is at best a nostalgic yearning, and at worst a deceitful slogan used against those plans for reform which are based on the idea of truly human individual initiative. Modern society has started out with the vision of creating a culture which would fulfil man's needs; it has as its ideal the harmony between the individual and social needs, the end of the conflict between human nature and the social order. One believed one would arrive at this goal in two ways; by the increased productive technique which permitted feeding everybody satisfactorily, and by a rational, objective picture of man and of his real needs. Putting it differently, the aim of the efforts of modern man was to create a sane society. More specifically, this meant a society whose members have developed their reason to that point of objectivity which permits them to see themselves, others, nature, in their true reality, and not distorted by infantile omniscience or paranoid hate. It meant a society, whose members have developed to a point of independence when they know the difference between good and evil, where they make their own choices, where they have convictions rather than opinions, faith rather than superstitions or nebulous hopes. It meant a society whose members have developed the capacity to love their children, their neighbors, all men, themselves, all of nature; who can feel one with all, yet retain their sense of individuality and integrity; who transcend nature by creating, not by destroying.

So far, we have failed. We have not bridged the gap between a minority which realized these goals and tried to live according to them, and the majority whose mentality is far back, in the Stone Age, in totemism, in idol worship, in feudalism. Will the majority be converted to sanity—or will it use the greatest discoveries of human reason for its own purposes of unreason and insanity? Will we be able to create a vision of the good, sane life, which will stir the life forces of those afraid of marching forward? This time, mankind is at one crossroad where the wrong step could be the last step.

In the middle of the twentieth century, two great social collosi have developed which, being afraid of each other, seek security in ever-increasing military rearmament. The United States and her allies are wealthier; their standard of living is higher, their interest in comfort and pleasure is greater than that of their rivals, the Soviet Union and her satellites, and China. Both rivals claim that their system promises final salvation for man, guarantees the paradise of the future. Both claim that the opponent represents the exact opposite to himself, and that his system must be eradicated—in the short or long run—if mankind is to be saved. Both rivals speak in terms of nineteenth-century ideals. The West in the name of the ideas of the French Revolution, of liberty, reason, individualism. The East in the name of the socialist ideas of solidarity, equality. They both succeed in capturing the imagination and the fanatical allegiance of hundreds of millions of people.

There is today a decisive difference between the two systems. In the Western world there is freedom to express ideas critical of the existing system. In the Soviet world criticism and expression of different ideas is suppressed by brutal force. Hence, the Western world carries within itself the possibility for peaceful progressive transformation, while in the Soviet world such possibilities are almost non-existent; in the Western world the life of the individual is free from the terror of imprisonment, torture or death, which confront any member of the Soviet society who has not become a well-functioning automaton. Indeed, life in the Western world has been, and is even now sometimes as rich and joyous as it has ever been anywhere in human history; life in the Soviet system can never be joyous, as indeed it can never be where the executioner watches behind the door.

But without ignoring the tremendous differences between free Capitalism and authoritarian Communism today, it is short-sighted not to see the similarities, especially as they will develop in the future. Both systems are based on industrialization, their goal is ever-increasing economic efficiency and wealth. They are societies run by a managerial class, and by professional politicians. They both are thoroughly materialistic in their outlook, regardless of Christian ideology in the West and secular messianism in the East. They organize man in a centralized system, in large factories, political mass parties. Everybody is a cog in the machine, and has to function smoothly. In the West, this is achieved by a method of psychological conditioning, mass suggestion, monetary rewards. In the East by all this, plus the use of terror. It is to be assumed that the more the Soviet system develops economically, the less severely will it have to exploit the majority of the population, hence the more can terror be replaced by methods of psychological manipulation. The West develops rapidly in the direction of Huxley's *Brave New World*, the East *is* today Orwell's "1984." But both systems tend to converge.

What, then, are the prospects for the future? The first, and perhaps most likely possibility, is that of atomic war. The most likely outcome of such a war is the destruction of industrial civilization, and the regression of the world to a primitive agrarian level. Or, if the destruction should not prove to be as thorough as many specialists in the field believe, the result will be the necessity for the victor to organize and dominate the whole world. This could only happen in a centralized state based on force—and it would make little difference whether Moscow or Washington were the seat of government. But, unfortunately, even the avoidance of war alone does not promise a bright future. In the development of both Capitalism and of Communism as we can visualize them in the next fifty or a hundred years, the process of automatization and alienation will proceed. Both systems are developing into managerial societies, their inhabitants well fed, well clad, having their wishes satisfied, and not having wishes which cannot be satisfied; automatons, who follow without force, who are guided without leaders, who make machines which act like men and produce men who act like machines; men, whose reason deteriorates while their intelligence rises, thus creating the dangerous situation of equipping man with the greatest material power without the wisdom to use it.

This alienation and automatization leads to an ever-increasing insanity. Life has no meaning, there is no joy, no faith, no reality. Everybody is "happy"—except that he does not feel, does not reason, does not love.

In the nineteenth century the problem was that *God is dead;* in the twentieth century the problem is that *man is dead.* In the nineteenth century inhumanity meant cruelty; in the twentieth century it means schizoid self-alienation. The danger of the past was that men became slaves. The danger of the future is that men may become robots. True enough, robots do not rebel. But given man's nature, robots cannot live and remain sane, they become "Golems," they will destroy their world and themselves because they cannot stand any longer the boredom of a meaningless life.

Our dangers are war and robotism. What is the alternative? To get out of the rut in which we are moving, and to take the next step in the birth and self-realization of humanity. The first condition is the abolishment of the war threat hanging over all of us now and paralyzing faith and initiative. We must take the responsibility for the life of all men, and develop on an international scale what all great countries have developed internally, a relative sharing of wealth and a new and more just division of economic resources. This must lead eventually to forms of international economic co-operation and planning, to forms of world government and to complete disarmament. We must retain the industrial method. But we must decentralize work and state so as to give it *human proportions*, and permit centralization only to an optimal point which is necessary because of the requirements of industry. In the economic sphere we need co-management of all who work in an enterprise, to permit their active and responsible participation. The new forms for such participation can be found. In the political sphere, return to the town meetings, by creating thousands of small face-to-face groups, which are well informed, which discuss, and whose decisions are integrated in a new "lower house." A cultural renaissance must combine work education for the young, adult education and a new system of popular art and secular ritual throughout the whole nation.

Our only alternative to the danger of robotism is humanistic communitarianism. The problem is not primarily the legal problem of property ownership, nor that of sharing *profits;* it is that of sharing *work,* sharing *experience.* Changes in ownership must be made to the extent to which they are necessary to create a community of work, and to prevent the profit motive from directing production into socially harmful directions. Income must be equalized to the extent of giving everybody the material basis for a dignified life, and thus preventing the economic differences from creating a fundamentally different experience of life for various social classes. Man must be restituted to his supreme place in society, never being a means, never a thing to be used by others or by himself. Man's use by man must end, and economy must become the servant for the development of man. Capital must serve labor, things must serve life. Instead of the exploitative and hoarding orientation, dominant in the nineteenth century, and the receptive and marketing orientation dominant today, the *productive orientation* must be the end which all social arrangements serve.

No change must be brought about by force, it must be a simultaneous one in the economic, political and cultural spheres. Changes restricted to *one* sphere are destructive of every change.

Just as primitive man was helpless before natural forces, modern man is helpless before the social and economic forces created by himself. He worships the works of his own hands, bowing to the new idols, yet swearing by the name of the God who commanded him to destroy all idols. Man can protect himself from the consequences of his own madness only by creating a sane society which conforms with the needs of man, needs which are rooted in the very conditions of his existence. A society in which man relates to man lovingly, in which he is rooted in bonds of brotherliness and solidarity, rather than in the ties of blood and soil; a society which gives him the possibility of transcending nature by creating rather than by destroying, in which everyone gains a sense of self by experiencing himself as the subject of his powers rather than by conformity, in which a system of orientation and devotion exists without man's needing to distort reality and to worship idols.

Building such a society means taking the next step; it means the end of "humanoid" history, the phase in which man had not become fully human. It does not mean the "end of days," the "completion," the state of perfect harmony in which no conflicts or problems confront men. On the contrary, it is man's fate that his existence is beset by contradictions, which he has to solve without ever solving them. When he has overcome the primitive state of human sacrifice, be it in the ritualistic form of the Aztecs or in the secular form of war, when he has been able to regulate his relationship with nature reasonably instead of blindly, when things have truly become his servants rather than his idols, he will be confronted with the truly human conflicts and problems; he will have to be adventuresome, courageous, imaginative, capable of suffering and of joy, but his powers will be in the service of life, and not in the service of death. The new phase of human history, if it comes to pass, will be a new beginning, not an end.

Man today is confronted with the most fundamental choice; not that between Capitalism or Communism, but that between *robotism* (of both the capitalist and the communist variety), or Humanistic Communitarian Socialism. Most facts seem to indicate that he is choosing robotism, and that means, in the long run, insanity and destruction. But all these facts are not strong enough to destroy faith in man's reason, good will and sanity. As long as we can think of other alternatives, we are not lost; as long as we can consult together and plan together, we can hope. But, indeed, the shadows are lengthening; the voices of insanity are becoming louder. We are in reach of achieving a state of humanity which corresponds to the vision of our great teachers; yet we are in danger of the destruction of all civilization, or of robotization. A small tribe was told thousands of years ago: "I put before you life and death, blessing and curse—and you chose life." This is our choice too.

INDEX